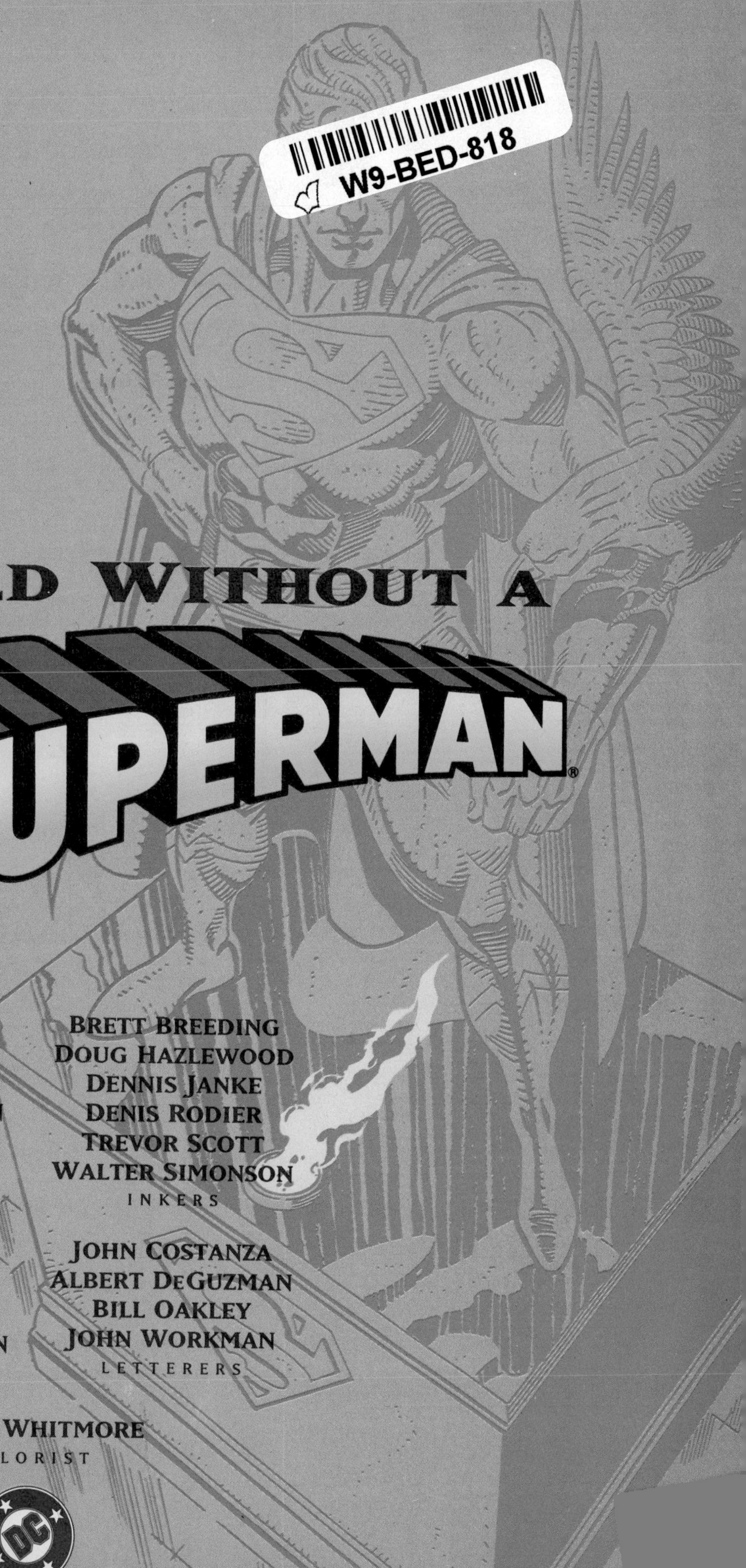

WORLD WITHOUT A SUPERMAN®

DAN JURGENS
KARL KESEL
JERRY ORDWAY
LOUISE SIMONSON
ROGER STERN
WRITERS

BRETT BREEDING
DOUG HAZLEWOOD
DENNIS JANKE
DENIS RODIER
TREVOR SCOTT
WALTER SIMONSON
INKERS

JON BOGDANOVE
TOM GRUMMETT
JACKSON GUICE
DAN JURGENS
WALTER SIMONSON
PENCILLERS

JOHN COSTANZA
ALBERT DEGUZMAN
BILL OAKLEY
JOHN WORKMAN
LETTERERS

GLENN WHITMORE
COLORIST

DC®

"I was there...
and all I could do
was report on
the fight...and
watch him die.
I couldn't do
anything but
watch him die."

LOIS LANE

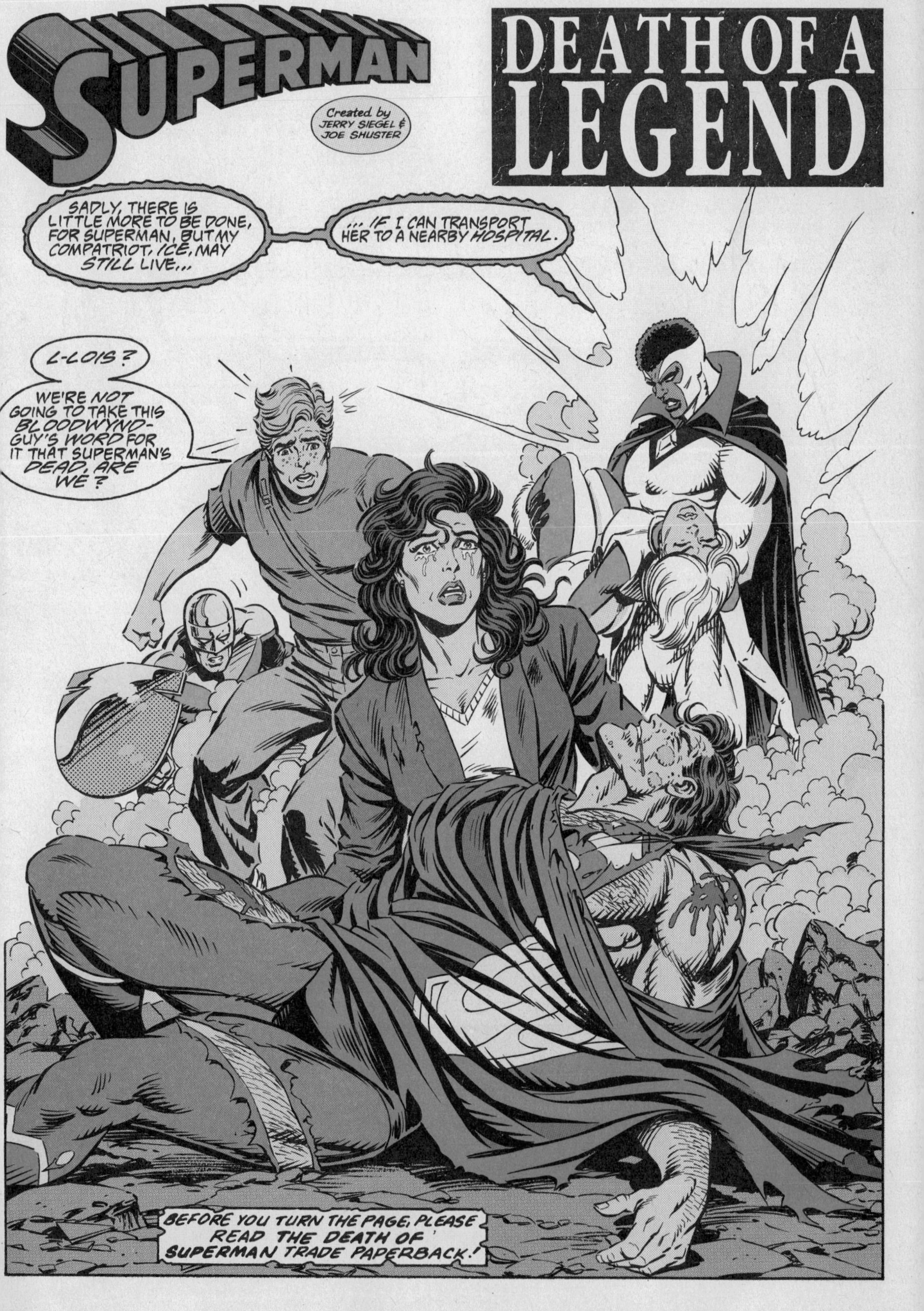

SUPERMAN
Created by JERRY SIEGEL & JOE SHUSTER
DEATH OF A LEGEND
SADLY, THERE IS LITTLE MORE TO BE DONE, FOR SUPERMAN, BUT MY COMPATRIOT, ICE, MAY STILL LIVE...
...IF I CAN TRANSPORT HER TO A NEARBY HOSPITAL.
L-LOIS?
WE'RE NOT GOING TO TAKE THIS BLOODWYND-GUY'S WORD FOR IT THAT SUPERMAN'S DEAD, ARE WE?
BEFORE YOU TURN THE PAGE, PLEASE READ THE DEATH OF SUPERMAN TRADE PAPERBACK!

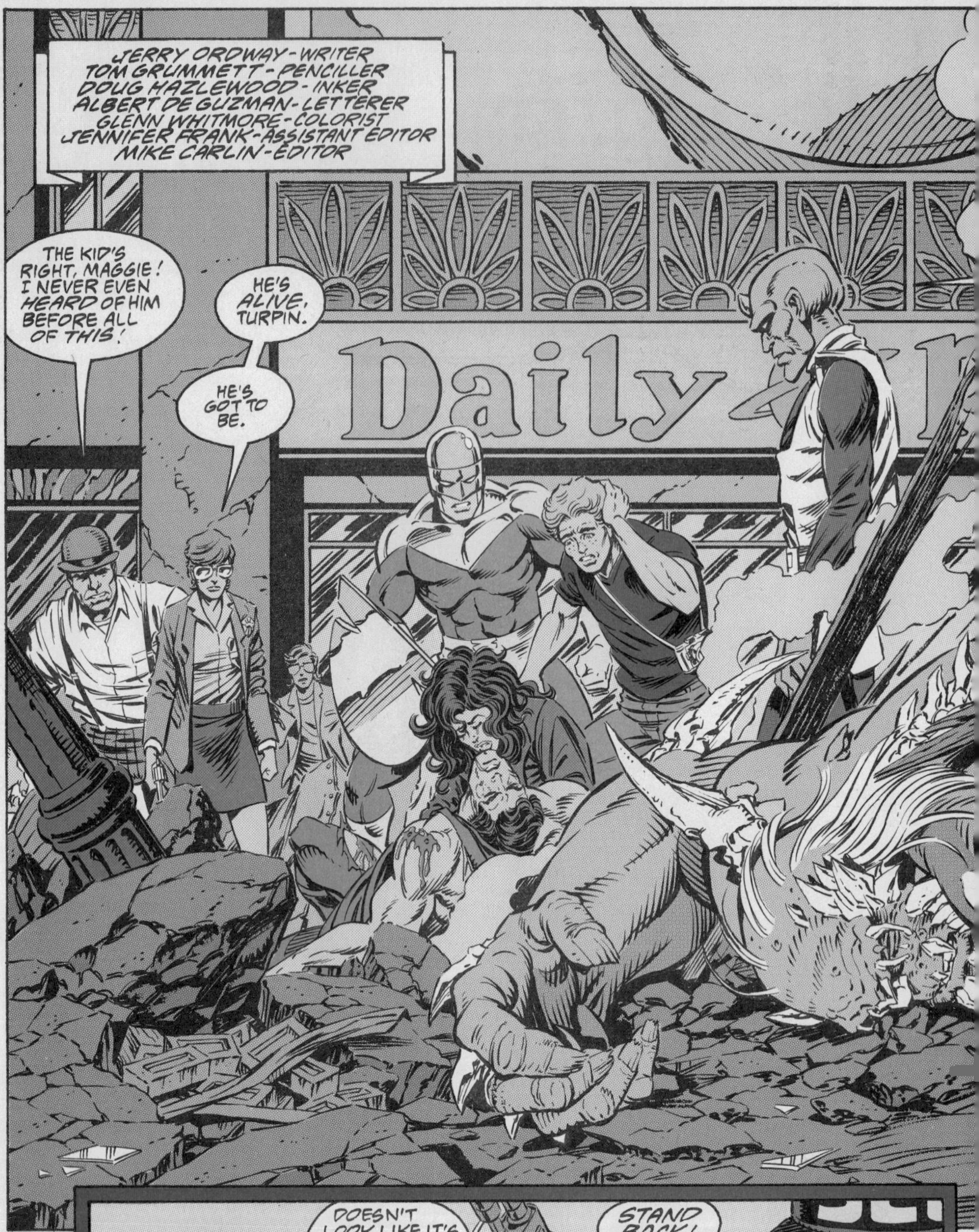
JERRY ORDWAY - WRITER
TOM GRUMMETT - PENCILLER
DOUG HAZLEWOOD - INKER
ALBERT DE GUZMAN - LETTERER
GLENN WHITMORE - COLORIST
JENNIFER FRANK - ASSISTANT EDITOR
MIKE CARLIN - EDITOR
THE KID'S RIGHT, MAGGIE! I NEVER EVEN HEARD OF HIM BEFORE ALL OF THIS!
HE'S ALIVE, TURPIN.
HE'S GOT TO BE.
Daily

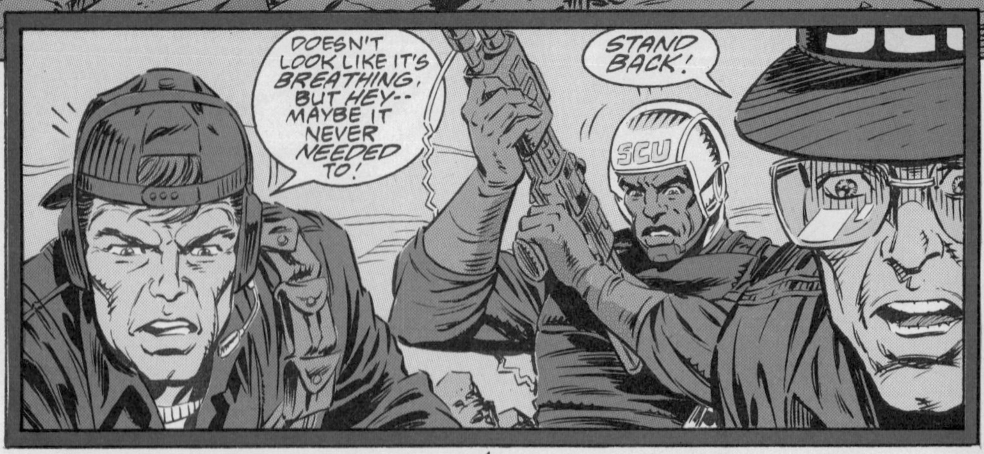
DOESN'T LOOK LIKE IT'S BREATHING, BUT HEY-- MAYBE IT NEVER NEEDED TO!
STAND BACK!
SCU

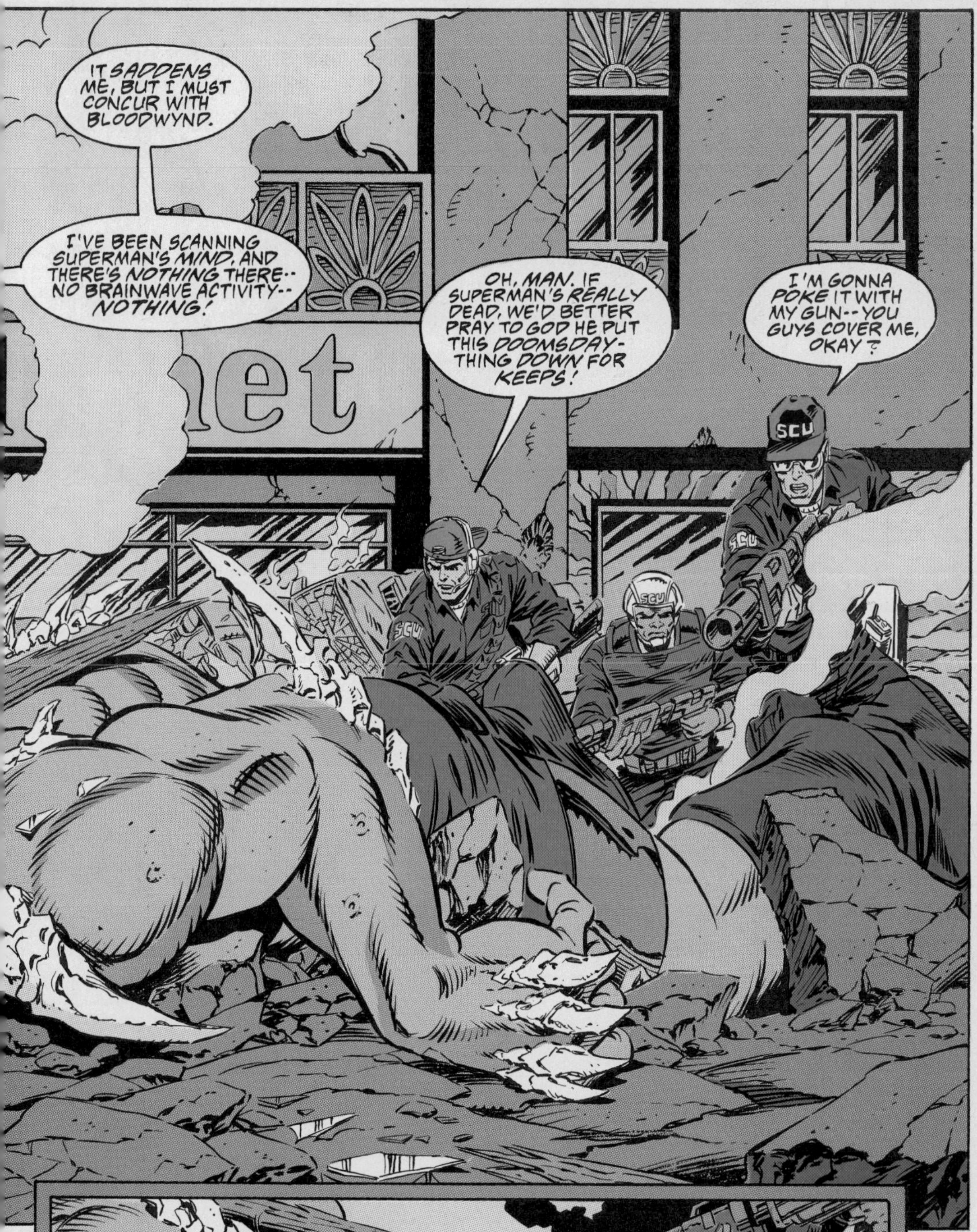
IT SADDENS ME, BUT I MUST CONCUR WITH BLOODWYND.
I'VE BEEN SCANNING SUPERMAN'S MIND, AND THERE'S NOTHING THERE-- NO BRAINWAVE ACTIVITY-- NOTHING!
OH, MAN. IF SUPERMAN'S REALLY DEAD, WE'D BETTER PRAY TO GOD HE PUT THIS DOOMSDAY-THING DOWN FOR KEEPS!
I'M GONNA POKE IT WITH MY GUN--YOU GUYS COVER ME, OKAY?

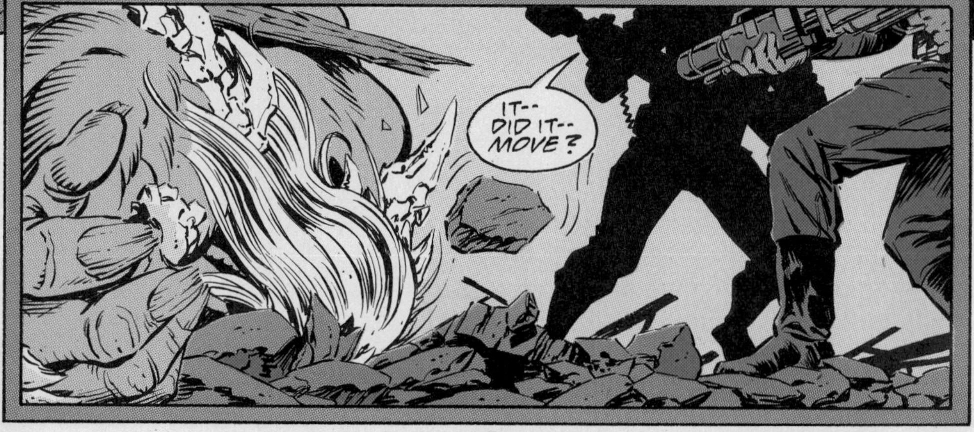
IT-- DID IT-- MOVE?

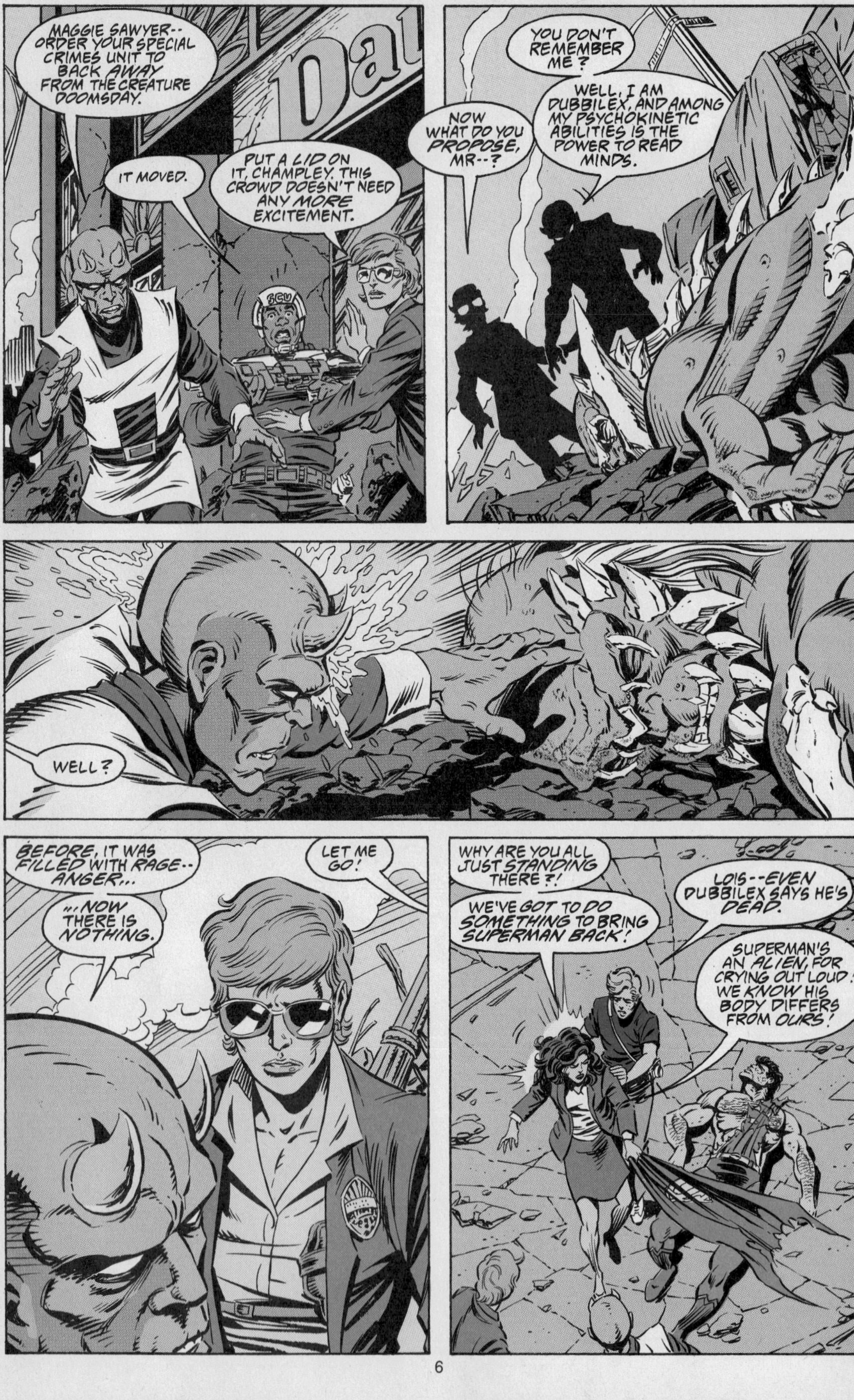
MAGGIE SAWYER-- ORDER YOUR SPECIAL CRIMES UNIT TO BACK AWAY FROM THE CREATURE DOOMSDAY.
IT MOVED.
PUT A LID ON IT, CHAMPLEY. THIS CROWD DOESN'T NEED ANY MORE EXCITEMENT.
NOW WHAT DO YOU PROPOSE, MR--?
YOU DON'T REMEMBER ME?
WELL, I AM DUBBILEX, AND AMONG MY PSYCHOKINETIC ABILITIES IS THE POWER TO READ MINDS.
WELL?
BEFORE, IT WAS FILLED WITH RAGE-- ANGER...
...NOW THERE IS NOTHING.
LET ME GO!
WHY ARE YOU ALL JUST STANDING THERE?!
WE'VE GOT TO DO SOMETHING TO BRING SUPERMAN BACK!
LOIS--EVEN DUBBILEX SAYS HE'S DEAD.
SUPERMAN'S AN ALIEN, FOR CRYING OUT LOUD! WE KNOW HIS BODY DIFFERS FROM OURS!

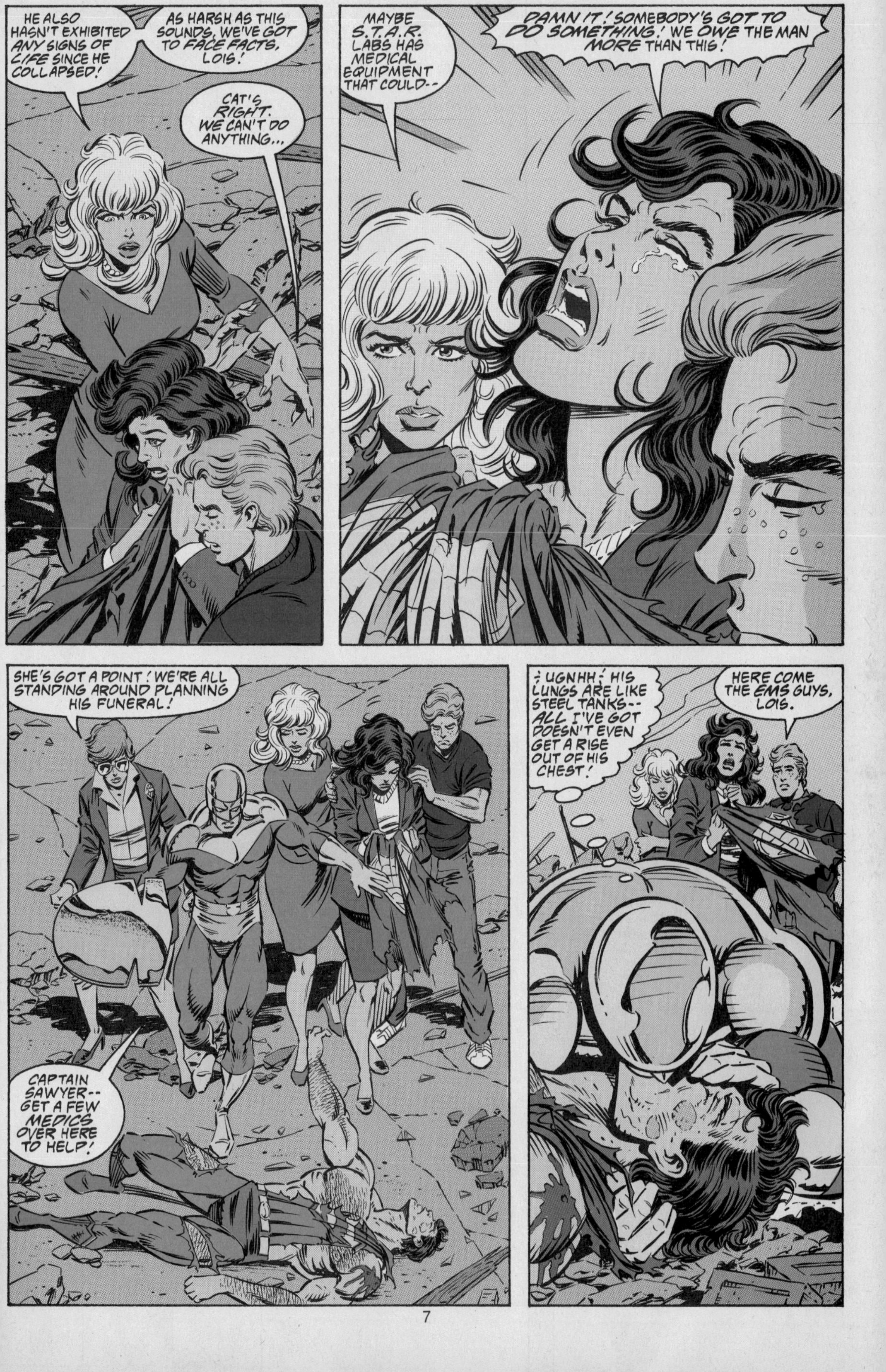
HE ALSO HASN'T EXHIBITED ANY SIGNS OF LIFE SINCE HE COLLAPSED!
AS HARSH AS THIS SOUNDS, WE'VE GOT TO FACE FACTS, LOIS!
CAT'S RIGHT. WE CAN'T DO ANYTHING...
MAYBE S.T.A.R. LABS HAS MEDICAL EQUIPMENT THAT COULD--
DAMN IT! SOMEBODY'S GOT TO DO SOMETHING! WE OWE THE MAN MORE THAN THIS!
SHE'S GOT A POINT! WE'RE ALL STANDING AROUND PLANNING HIS FUNERAL!
CAPTAIN SAWYER-- GET A FEW MEDICS OVER HERE TO HELP!
UGNHH! HIS LUNGS ARE LIKE STEEL TANKS-- ALL I'VE GOT DOESN'T EVEN GET A RISE OUT OF HIS CHEST!
HERE COME THE EMS GUYS, LOIS.

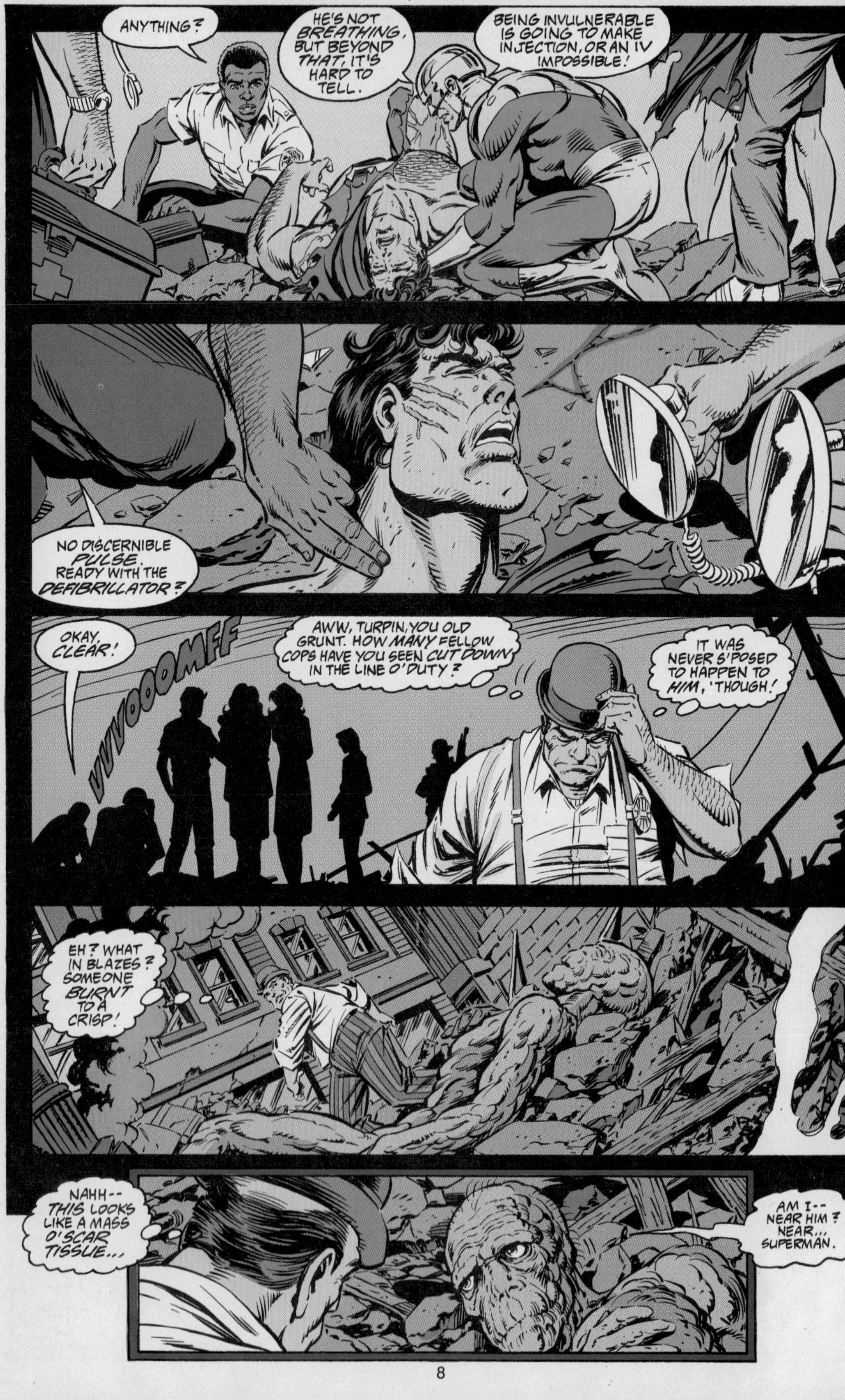
ANYTHING?
HE'S NOT BREATHING, BUT BEYOND THAT, IT'S HARD TO TELL.
BEING INVULNERABLE IS GOING TO MAKE INJECTION, OR AN IV IMPOSSIBLE!
NO DISCERNIBLE PULSE. READY WITH THE DEFIBRILLATOR?
OKAY, CLEAR!
VVVOOOMFF
AWW, TURPIN, YOU OLD GRUNT. HOW MANY FELLOW COPS HAVE YOU SEEN CUT DOWN IN THE LINE O'DUTY?
IT WAS NEVER S'POSED TO HAPPEN TO HIM, 'THOUGH!
EH? WHAT IN BLAZES? SOMEONE BURNT TO A CRISP!
NAHH-- THIS LOOKS LIKE A MASS O'SCAR TISSUE...
AM I-- NEAR HIM? NEAR... SUPERMAN.

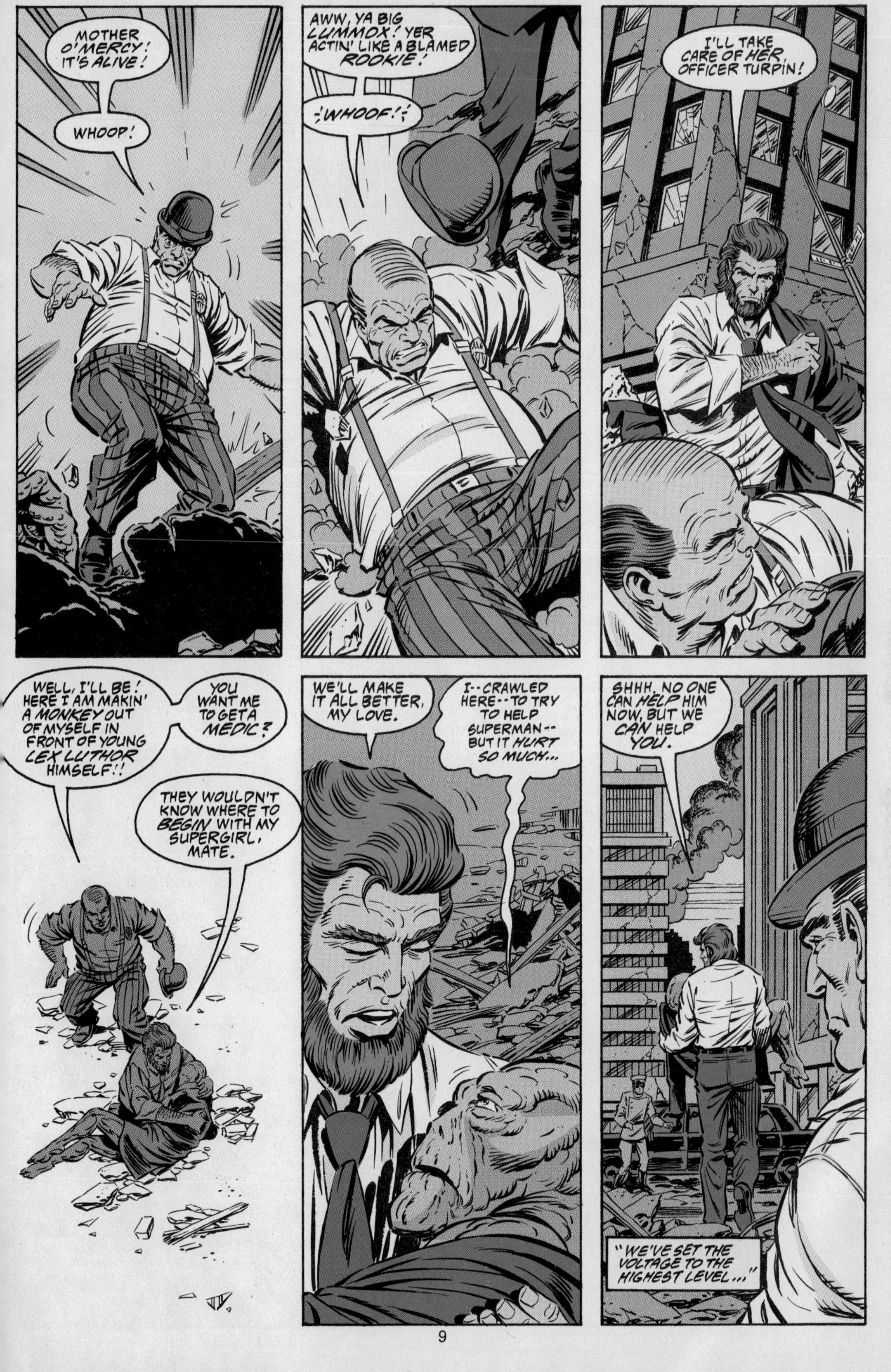
MOTHER O'MERCY! IT'S ALIVE!
WHOOP!
AWW, YA BIG LUMMOX! YER ACTIN' LIKE A BLAMED ROOKIE!
WHOOF!
I'LL TAKE CARE OF HER, OFFICER TURPIN!
WELL, I'LL BE! HERE I AM MAKIN' A MONKEY OUT OF MYSELF IN FRONT OF YOUNG LEX LUTHOR HIMSELF!!
YOU WANT ME TO GET A MEDIC?
THEY WOULDN'T KNOW WHERE TO BEGIN WITH MY SUPERGIRL, MATE.
WE'LL MAKE IT ALL BETTER, MY LOVE.
I--CRAWLED HERE--TO TRY TO HELP SUPERMAN--BUT IT HURT SO MUCH...
SHHH. NO ONE CAN HELP HIM NOW, BUT WE CAN HELP YOU.
"WE'VE SET THE VOLTAGE TO THE HIGHEST LEVEL..."

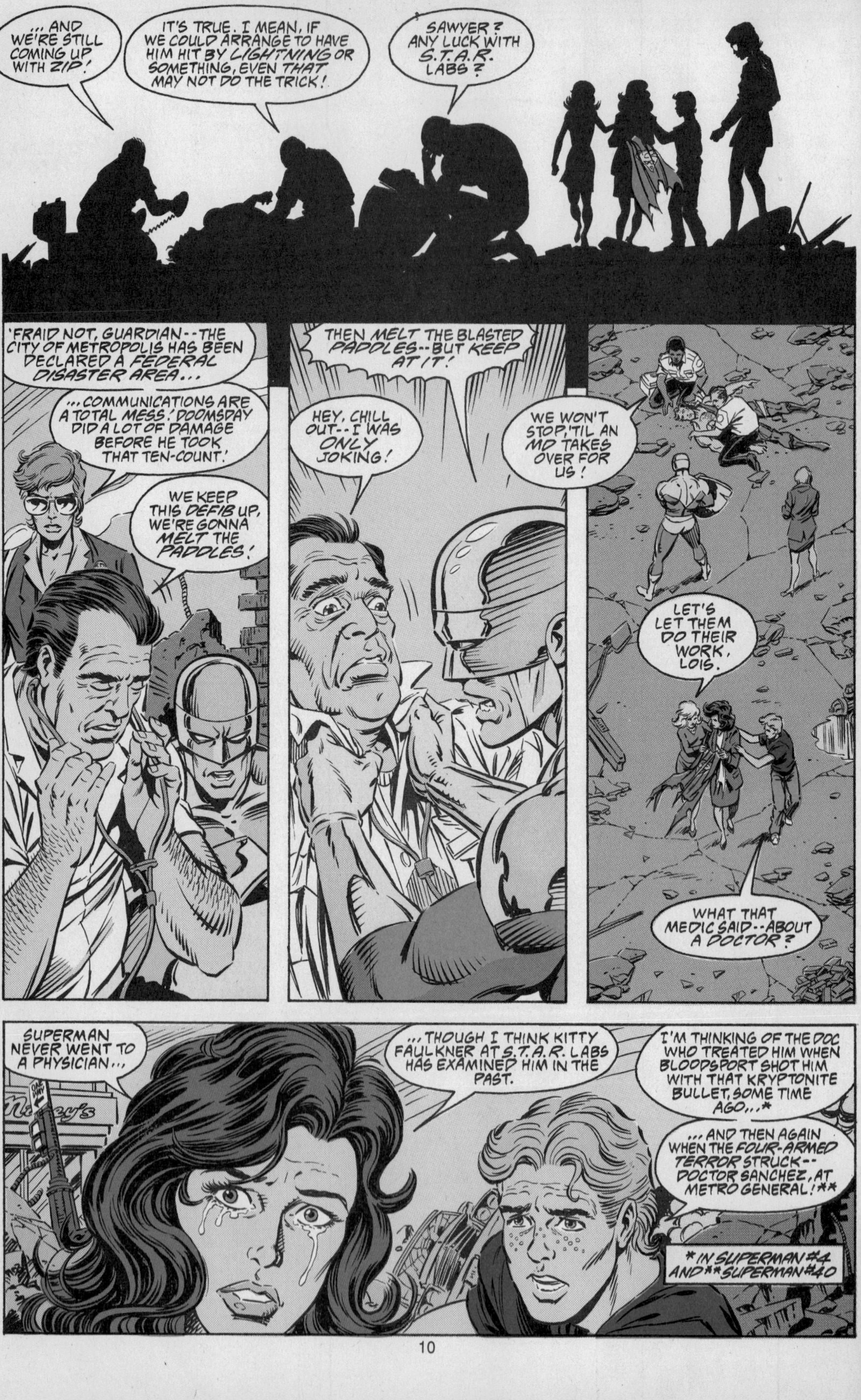
...AND WE'RE STILL COMING UP WITH ZIP!
IT'S TRUE. I MEAN, IF WE COULD ARRANGE TO HAVE HIM HIT BY LIGHTNING OR SOMETHING, EVEN THAT MAY NOT DO THE TRICK!
SAWYER? ANY LUCK WITH S.T.A.R. LABS?
'FRAID NOT, GUARDIAN--THE CITY OF METROPOLIS HAS BEEN DECLARED A FEDERAL DISASTER AREA...
...COMMUNICATIONS ARE A TOTAL MESS! DOOMSDAY DID A LOT OF DAMAGE BEFORE HE TOOK THAT TEN-COUNT!
WE KEEP THIS DEFIB UP, WE'RE GONNA MELT THE PADDLES!
THEN MELT THE BLASTED PADDLES--BUT KEEP AT IT!
HEY, CHILL OUT--I WAS ONLY JOKING!
WE WON'T STOP 'TIL AN MD TAKES OVER FOR US!
LET'S LET THEM DO THEIR WORK, LOIS.
WHAT THAT MEDIC SAID--ABOUT A DOCTOR?
SUPERMAN NEVER WENT TO A PHYSICIAN...
...THOUGH I THINK KITTY FAULKNER AT S.T.A.R. LABS HAS EXAMINED HIM IN THE PAST.
I'M THINKING OF THE DOC WHO TREATED HIM WHEN BLOODSPORT SHOT HIM WITH THAT KRYPTONITE BULLET, SOME TIME AGO...*
...AND THEN AGAIN WHEN THE FOUR-ARMED TERROR STRUCK--DOCTOR SANCHEZ, AT METRO GENERAL!**
*IN SUPERMAN #4 AND **SUPERMAN #40

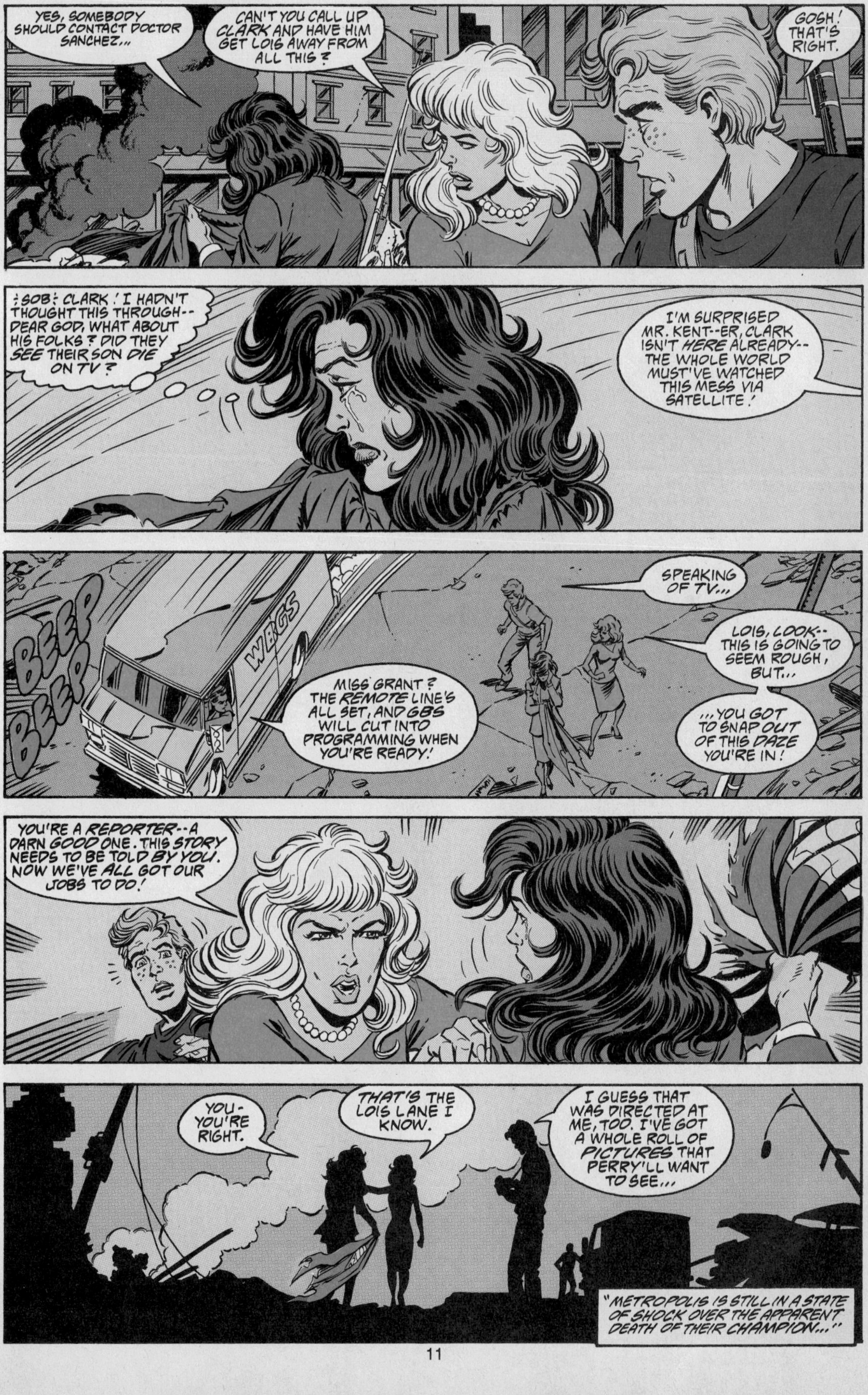
YES, SOMEBODY SHOULD CONTACT DOCTOR SANCHEZ...
CAN'T YOU CALL UP CLARK AND HAVE HIM GET LOIS AWAY FROM ALL THIS?
GOSH! THAT'S RIGHT.
:SOB: CLARK! I HADN'T THOUGHT THIS THROUGH-- DEAR GOD, WHAT ABOUT HIS FOLKS? DID THEY SEE THEIR SON DIE ON TV?
I'M SURPRISED MR. KENT--ER, CLARK ISN'T HERE ALREADY-- THE WHOLE WORLD MUST'VE WATCHED THIS MESS VIA SATELLITE!
BEEP BEEP
WBGS
MISS GRANT? THE REMOTE LINE'S ALL SET, AND GBS WILL CUT INTO PROGRAMMING WHEN YOU'RE READY!
SPEAKING OF TV...
LOIS, LOOK-- THIS IS GOING TO SEEM ROUGH, BUT...
...YOU GOT TO SNAP OUT OF THIS DAZE YOU'RE IN!
YOU'RE A REPORTER--A DARN GOOD ONE. THIS STORY NEEDS TO BE TOLD BY YOU. NOW WE'VE ALL GOT OUR JOBS TO DO!
YOU-- YOU'RE RIGHT.
THAT'S THE LOIS LANE I KNOW.
I GUESS THAT WAS DIRECTED AT ME, TOO. I'VE GOT A WHOLE ROLL OF PICTURES THAT PERRY'LL WANT TO SEE...
"METROPOLIS IS STILL IN A STATE OF SHOCK OVER THE APPARENT DEATH OF THEIR CHAMPION..."

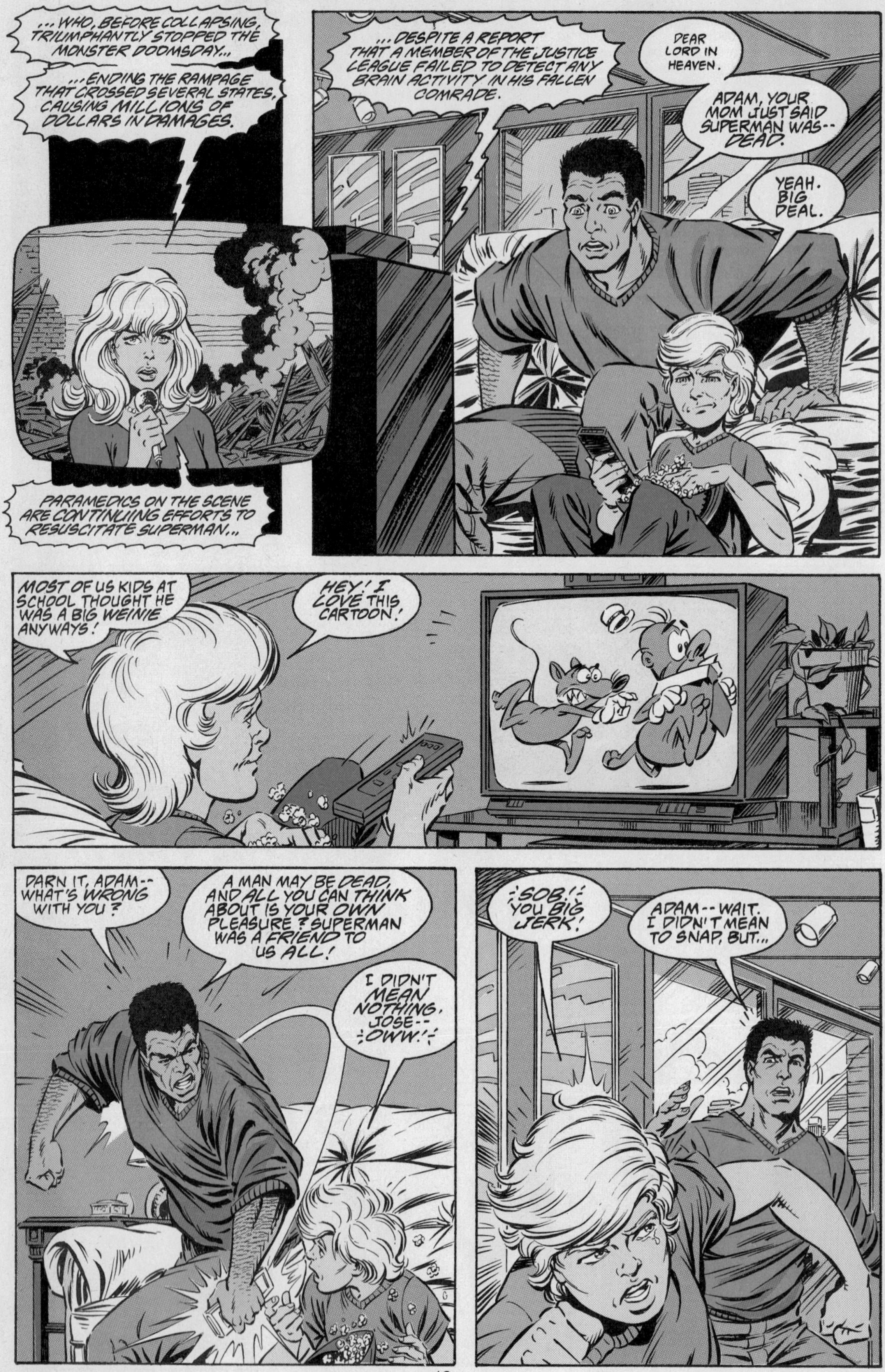
...WHO, BEFORE COLLAPSING, TRIUMPHANTLY STOPPED THE MONSTER DOOMSDAY...
...ENDING THE RAMPAGE THAT CROSSED SEVERAL STATES, CAUSING MILLIONS OF DOLLARS IN DAMAGES.
PARAMEDICS ON THE SCENE ARE CONTINUING EFFORTS TO RESUSCITATE SUPERMAN...
...DESPITE A REPORT THAT A MEMBER OF THE JUSTICE LEAGUE FAILED TO DETECT ANY BRAIN ACTIVITY IN HIS FALLEN COMRADE.
DEAR LORD IN HEAVEN.
ADAM, YOUR MOM JUST SAID SUPERMAN WAS-- DEAD.
YEAH. BIG DEAL.
MOST OF US KIDS AT SCHOOL THOUGHT HE WAS A BIG WEINIE ANYWAYS!
HEY! I LOVE THIS CARTOON!
DARN IT, ADAM-- WHAT'S WRONG WITH YOU?
A MAN MAY BE DEAD, AND ALL YOU CAN THINK ABOUT IS YOUR OWN PLEASURE? SUPERMAN WAS A FRIEND TO US ALL!
I DIDN'T MEAN NOTHING, JOSE-- -OWW!-
-SOB!- YOU BIG JERK!
ADAM-- WAIT. I DIDN'T MEAN TO SNAP, BUT...

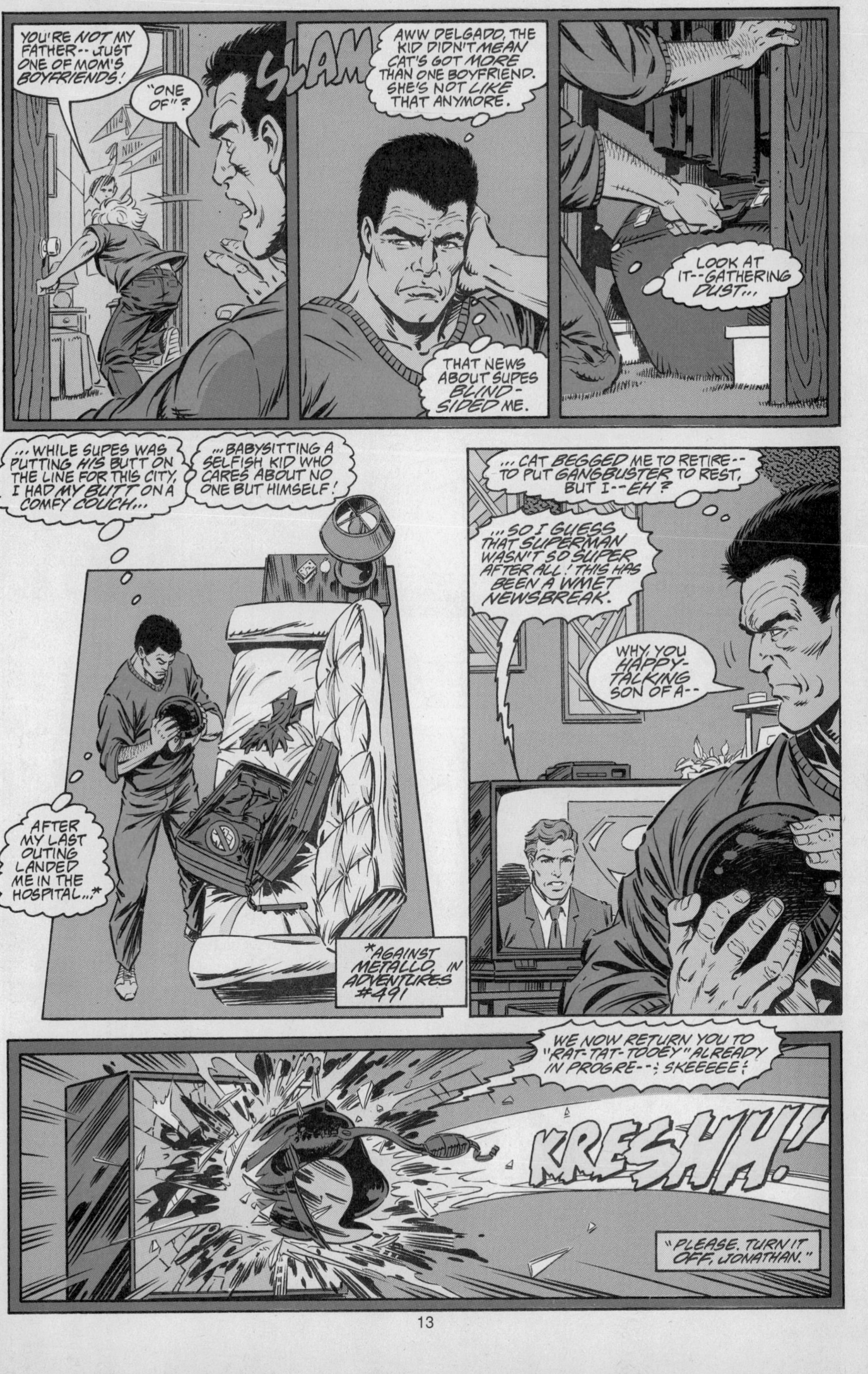

YOU'RE NOT MY FATHER-- JUST ONE OF MOM'S BOYFRIENDS!
"ONE OF"?
SLAM
AWW DELGADO, THE KID DIDN'T MEAN CAT'S GOT MORE THAN ONE BOYFRIEND. SHE'S NOT LIKE THAT ANYMORE.
THAT NEWS ABOUT SUPES BLIND-SIDED ME.
LOOK AT IT--GATHERING DUST...
...WHILE SUPES WAS PUTTING HIS BUTT ON THE LINE FOR THIS CITY, I HAD MY BUTT ON A COMFY COUCH...
...BABYSITTING A SELFISH KID WHO CARES ABOUT NO ONE BUT HIMSELF!
AFTER MY LAST OUTING LANDED ME IN THE HOSPITAL...*
*AGAINST METALLO, IN ADVENTURES #491
...CAT BEGGED ME TO RETIRE-- TO PUT GANGBUSTER TO REST, BUT I--EH?
...SO I GUESS THAT SUPERMAN WASN'T SO SUPER AFTER ALL! THIS HAS BEEN A WMET NEWSBREAK.
WHY, YOU HAPPY-TALKING SON OF A--
WE NOW RETURN YOU TO "RAT-TAT-TOOEY" ALREADY IN PROGRE--¡SKEEEEE¡
KRESHH!
"PLEASE. TURN IT OFF, JONATHAN."

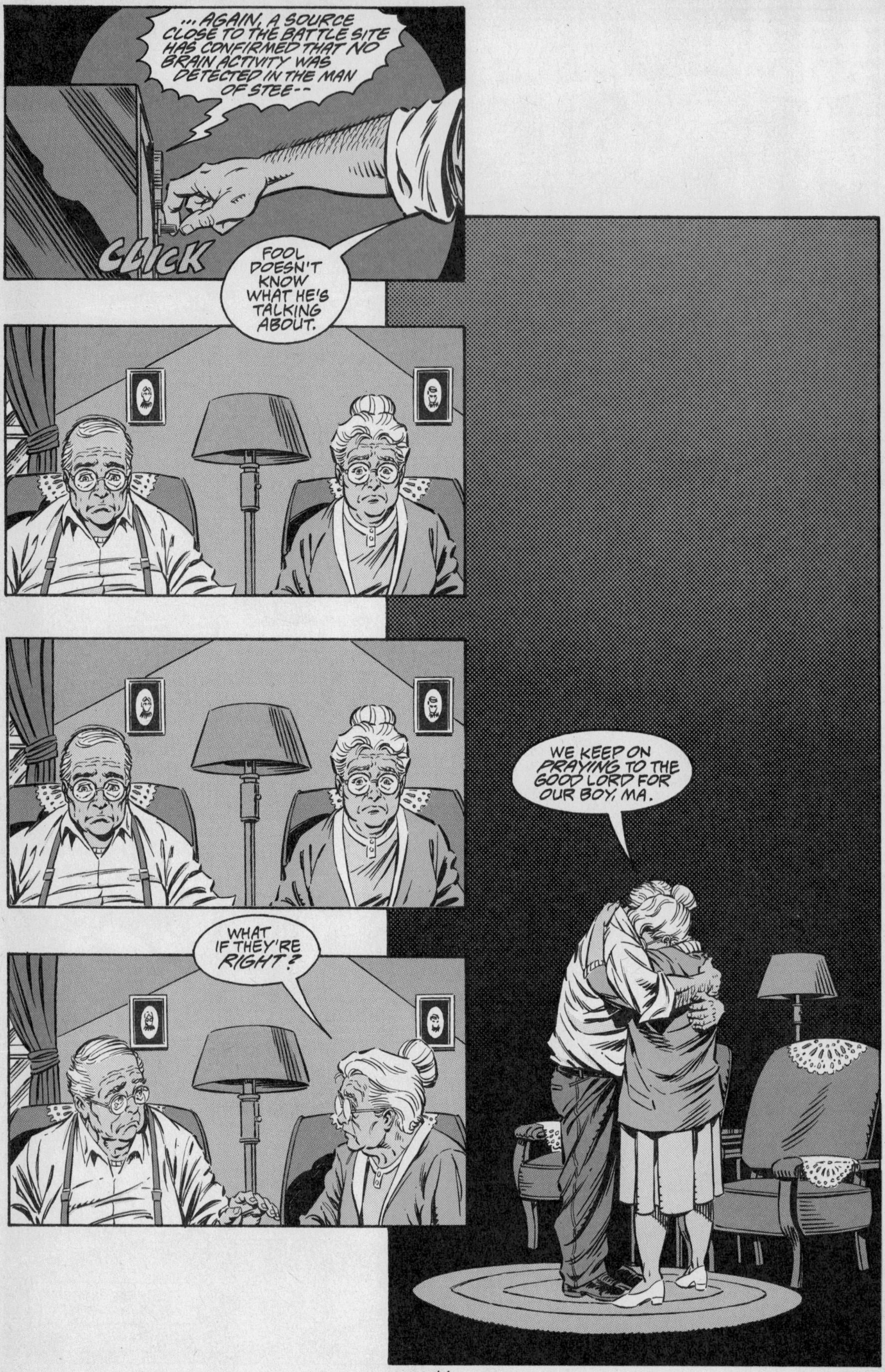
...AGAIN, A SOURCE CLOSE TO THE BATTLE SITE HAS CONFIRMED THAT NO BRAIN ACTIVITY WAS DETECTED IN THE MAN OF STEE--
CLICK
FOOL DOESN'T KNOW WHAT HE'S TALKING ABOUT.
WHAT IF THEY'RE RIGHT?
WE KEEP ON PRAYING TO THE GOOD LORD FOR OUR BOY, MA.

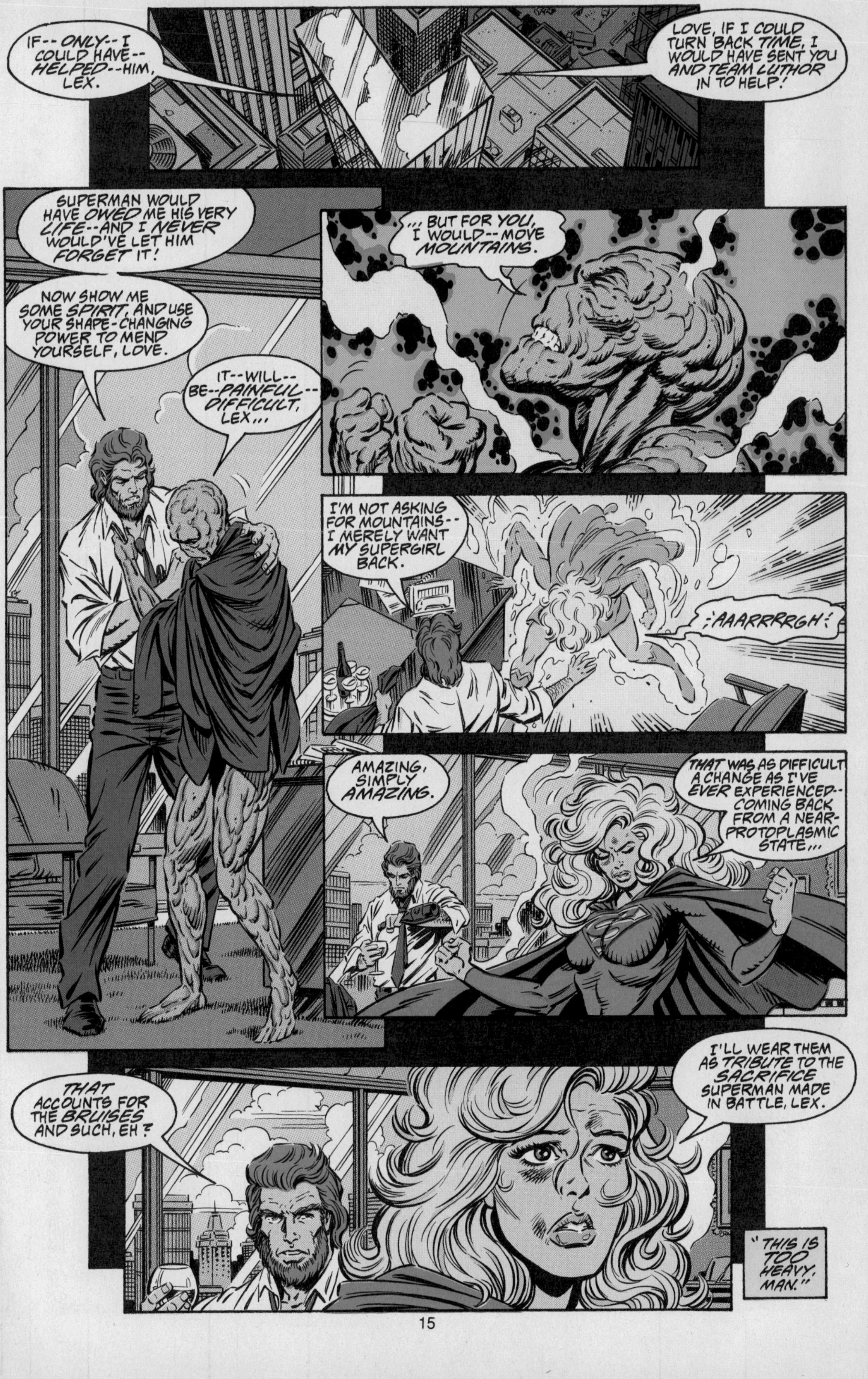

IF-- ONLY-- I COULD HAVE-- HELPED--HIM, LEX.
LOVE, IF I COULD TURN BACK TIME, I WOULD HAVE SENT YOU AND TEAM LUTHOR IN TO HELP!
SUPERMAN WOULD HAVE OWED ME HIS VERY LIFE--AND I NEVER WOULD'VE LET HIM FORGET IT!
NOW SHOW ME SOME SPIRIT, AND USE YOUR SHAPE-CHANGING POWER TO MEND YOURSELF, LOVE.
IT--WILL--BE--PAINFUL--DIFFICULT, LEX...
...BUT FOR YOU, I WOULD--MOVE MOUNTAINS.
I'M NOT ASKING FOR MOUNTAINS--I MERELY WANT MY SUPERGIRL BACK.
¡AAARRRRGH!
AMAZING. SIMPLY AMAZING.
THAT WAS AS DIFFICULT A CHANGE AS I'VE EVER EXPERIENCED--COMING BACK FROM A NEAR-PROTOPLASMIC STATE...
THAT ACCOUNTS FOR THE BRUISES AND SUCH, EH?
I'LL WEAR THEM AS TRIBUTE TO THE SACRIFICE SUPERMAN MADE IN BATTLE, LEX.
"THIS IS TOO HEAVY, MAN."

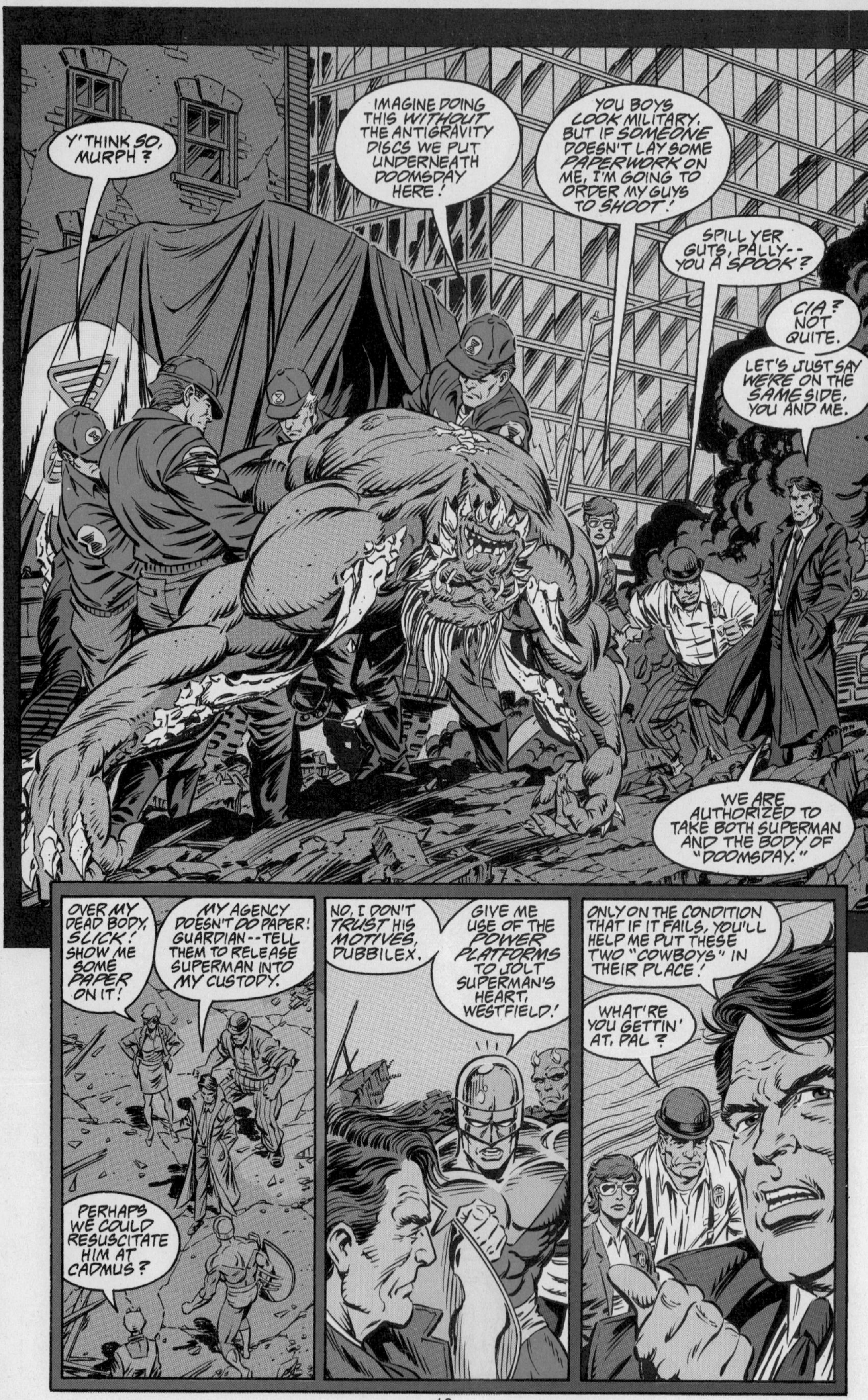
Y'THINK SO, MURPH?
IMAGINE DOING THIS WITHOUT THE ANTIGRAVITY DISCS WE PUT UNDERNEATH DOOMSDAY HERE!
YOU BOYS LOOK MILITARY. BUT IF SOMEONE DOESN'T LAY SOME PAPERWORK ON ME, I'M GOING TO ORDER MY GUYS TO SHOOT!
SPILL YER GUTS, PALLY-- YOU A SPOOK?
CIA? NOT QUITE.
LET'S JUST SAY WE'RE ON THE SAME SIDE, YOU AND ME.
WE ARE AUTHORIZED TO TAKE BOTH SUPERMAN AND THE BODY OF "DOOMSDAY."
OVER MY DEAD BODY, SLICK! SHOW ME SOME PAPER ON IT!
MY AGENCY DOESN'T DO PAPER! GUARDIAN--TELL THEM TO RELEASE SUPERMAN INTO MY CUSTODY.
PERHAPS WE COULD RESUSCITATE HIM AT CADMUS?
NO, I DON'T TRUST HIS MOTIVES, DUBBILEX.
GIVE ME USE OF THE POWER PLATFORMS TO JOLT SUPERMAN'S HEART, WESTFIELD!
ONLY ON THE CONDITION THAT IF IT FAILS, YOU'LL HELP ME PUT THESE TWO "COWBOYS" IN THEIR PLACE!
WHAT'RE YOU GETTIN' AT, PAL?

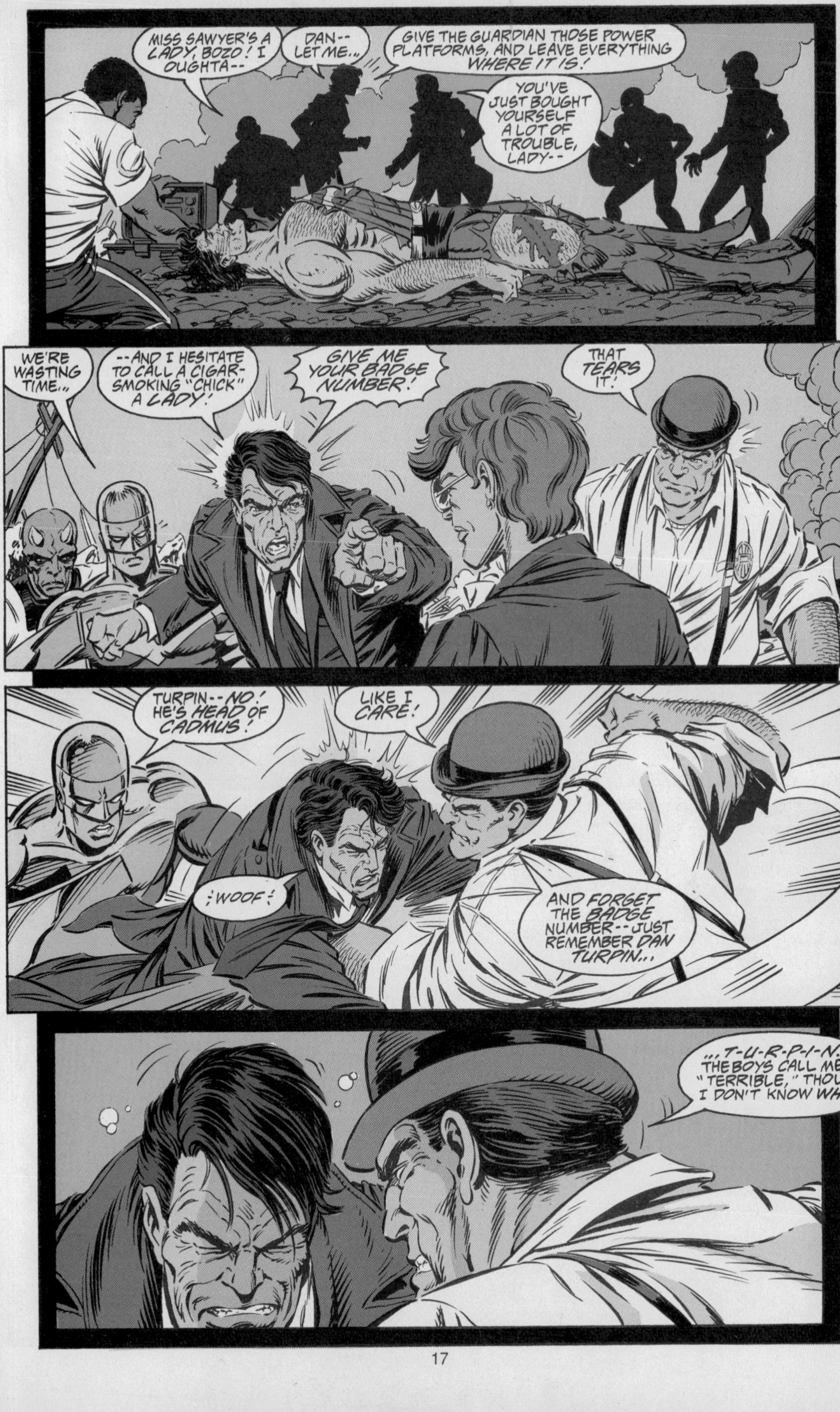
MISS SAWYER'S A LADY, BOZO! I OUGHTA--
DAN-- LET ME...
GIVE THE GUARDIAN THOSE POWER PLATFORMS, AND LEAVE EVERYTHING WHERE IT IS!
YOU'VE JUST BOUGHT YOURSELF A LOT OF TROUBLE, LADY--
WE'RE WASTING TIME...
--AND I HESITATE TO CALL A CIGAR-SMOKING "CHICK" A LADY!
GIVE ME YOUR BADGE NUMBER!
THAT TEARS IT!
TURPIN--NO! HE'S HEAD OF CADMUS!
LIKE I CARE!
WOOF!
AND FORGET THE BADGE NUMBER--JUST REMEMBER DAN TURPIN...
...T-U-R-P-I-N. THE BOYS CALL ME "TERRIBLE," THOUGH I DON'T KNOW WHY.

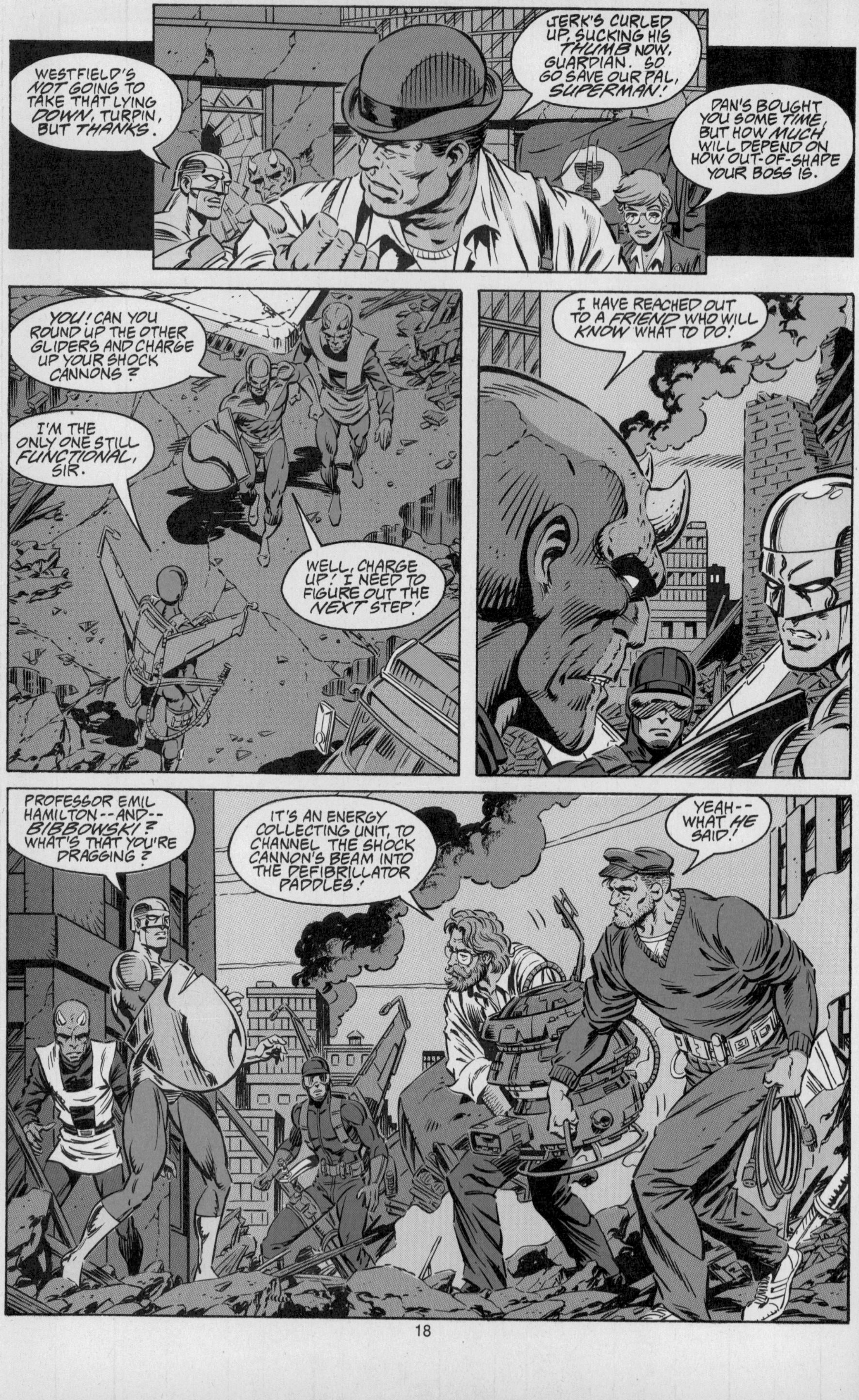
WESTFIELD'S NOT GOING TO TAKE THAT LYING DOWN, TURPIN, BUT THANKS.
JERK'S CURLED UP, SUCKING HIS THUMB NOW, GUARDIAN. SO GO SAVE OUR PAL, SUPERMAN!
DAN'S BOUGHT YOU SOME TIME, BUT HOW MUCH WILL DEPEND ON HOW OUT-OF-SHAPE YOUR BOSS IS.
YOU! CAN YOU ROUND UP THE OTHER GLIDERS AND CHARGE UP YOUR SHOCK CANNONS?
I'M THE ONLY ONE STILL FUNCTIONAL, SIR.
WELL, CHARGE UP! I NEED TO FIGURE OUT THE NEXT STEP!
I HAVE REACHED OUT TO A FRIEND WHO WILL KNOW WHAT TO DO!
PROFESSOR EMIL HAMILTON--AND--BIBBOWSKI? WHAT'S THAT YOU'RE DRAGGING?
IT'S AN ENERGY COLLECTING UNIT, TO CHANNEL THE SHOCK CANNON'S BEAM INTO THE DEFIBRILLATOR PADDLES!
YEAH--WHAT HE SAID!

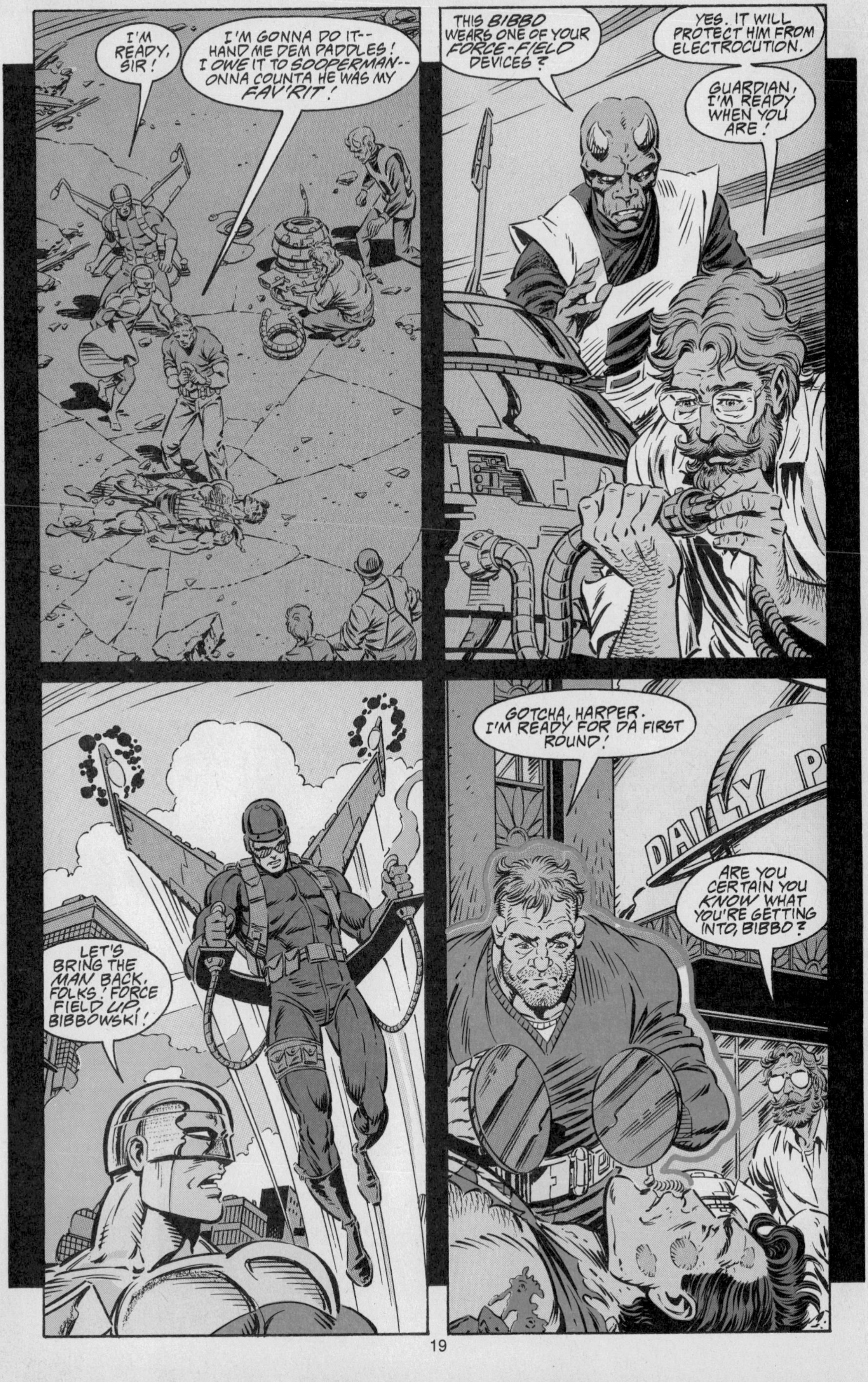
I'M READY, SIR!
I'M GONNA DO IT-- HAND ME DEM PADDLES! I OWE IT TO SOOPERMAN-- ONNA COUNTA HE WAS MY FAV'RIT!
THIS BIBBO WEARS ONE OF YOUR FORCE-FIELD DEVICES?
YES. IT WILL PROTECT HIM FROM ELECTROCUTION.
GUARDIAN, I'M READY WHEN YOU ARE!
LET'S BRING THE MAN BACK, FOLKS! FORCE FIELD UP, BIBBOWSKI!
GOTCHA, HARPER. I'M READY FOR DA FIRST ROUND!
DAILY P
ARE YOU CERTAIN YOU KNOW WHAT YOU'RE GETTING INTO, BIBBO?

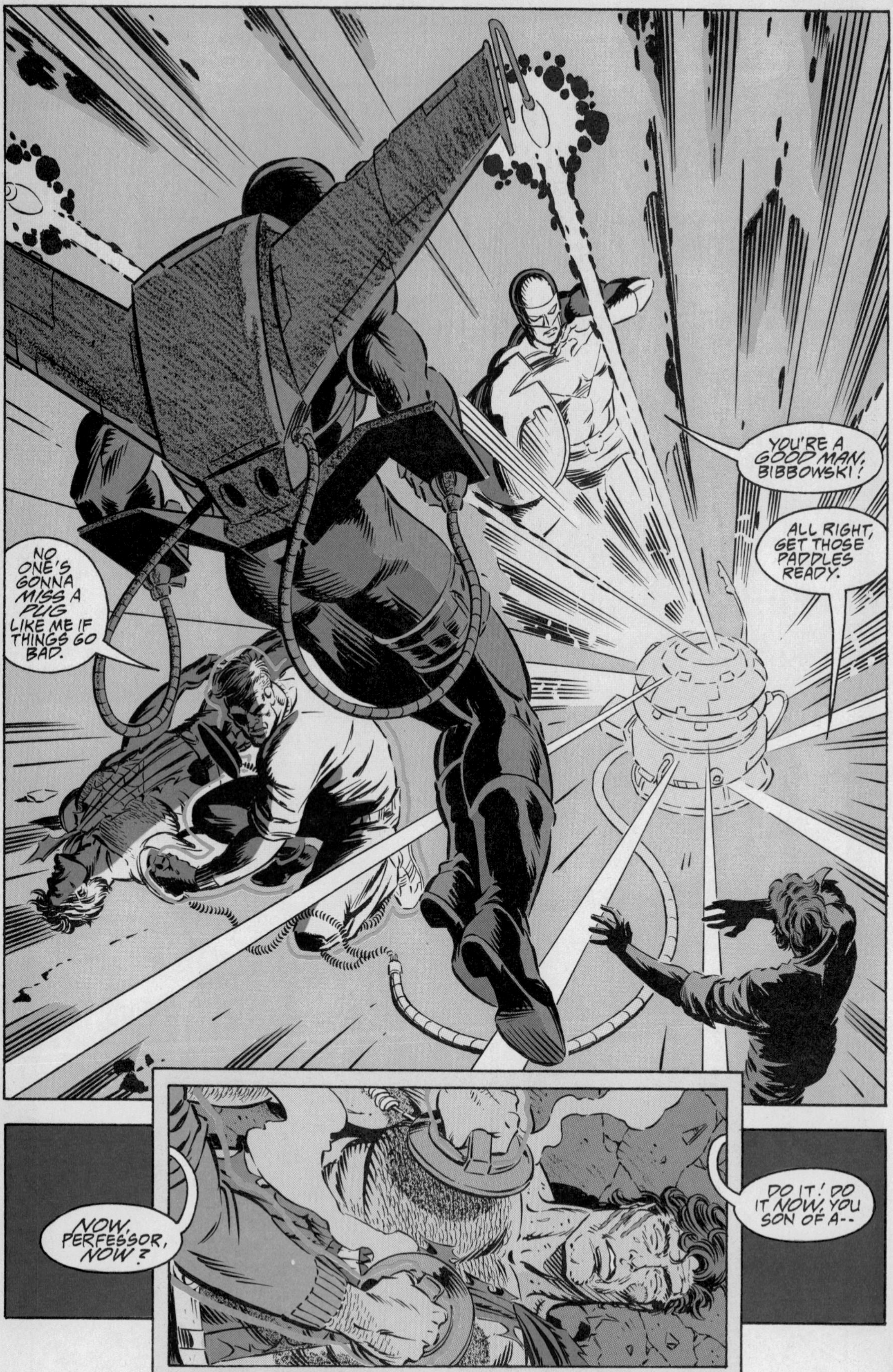
NO ONE'S GONNA MISS A PUG LIKE ME IF THINGS GO BAD.
YOU'RE A GOOD MAN, BIBBOWSKI!
ALL RIGHT, GET THOSE PADDLES READY.
NOW, PERFESSOR, NOW?
DO IT! DO IT NOW, YOU SON OF A--

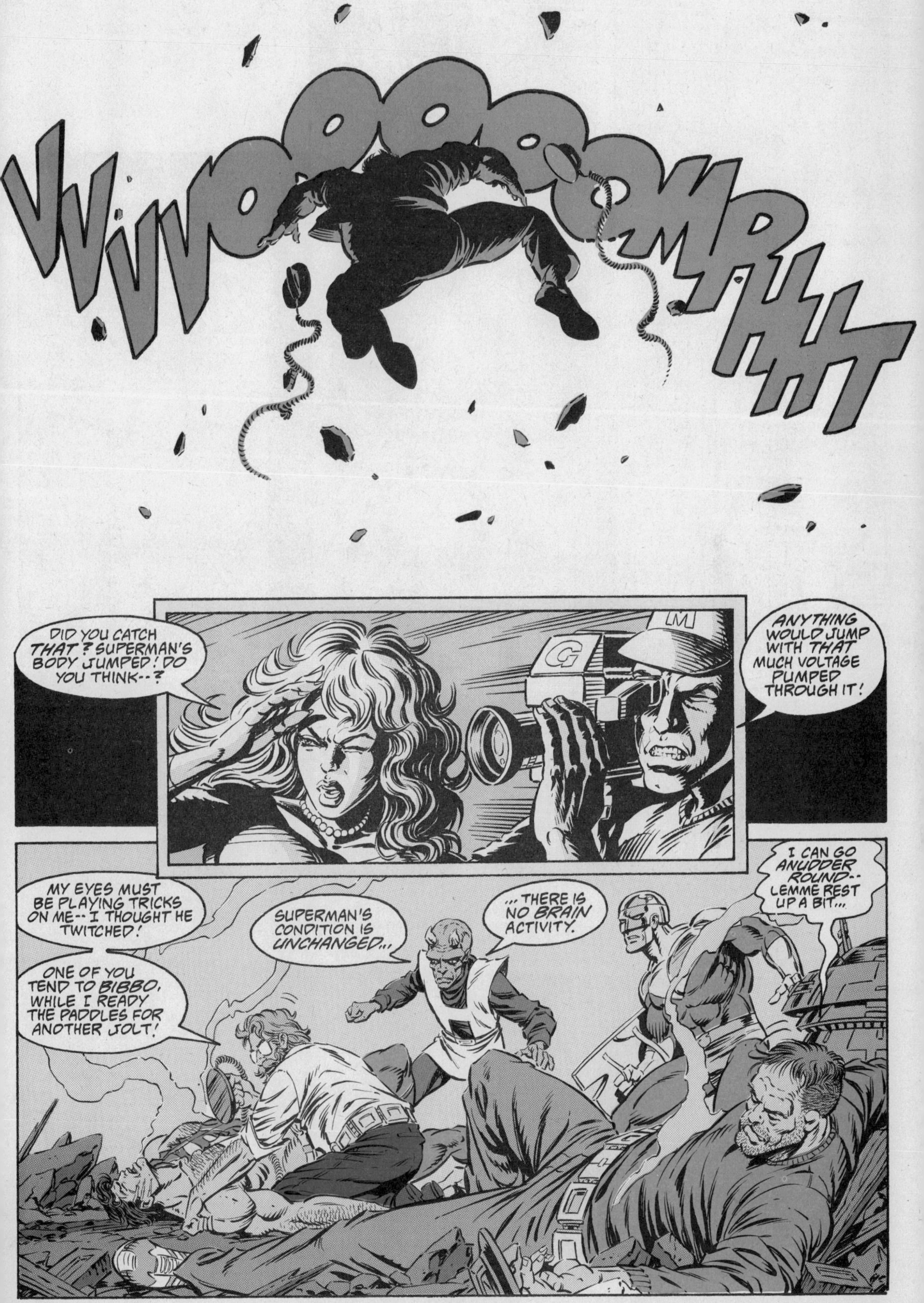
VVVVOOOOOOMRHHT
DID YOU CATCH THAT? SUPERMAN'S BODY JUMPED! DO YOU THINK--?
ANYTHING WOULD JUMP WITH THAT MUCH VOLTAGE PUMPED THROUGH IT!
MY EYES MUST BE PLAYING TRICKS ON ME-- I THOUGHT HE TWITCHED!
ONE OF YOU TEND TO BIBBO, WHILE I READY THE PADDLES FOR ANOTHER JOLT!
SUPERMAN'S CONDITION IS UNCHANGED...
...THERE IS NO BRAIN ACTIVITY.
I CAN GO ANUDDER ROUND-- LEMME REST UP A BIT...

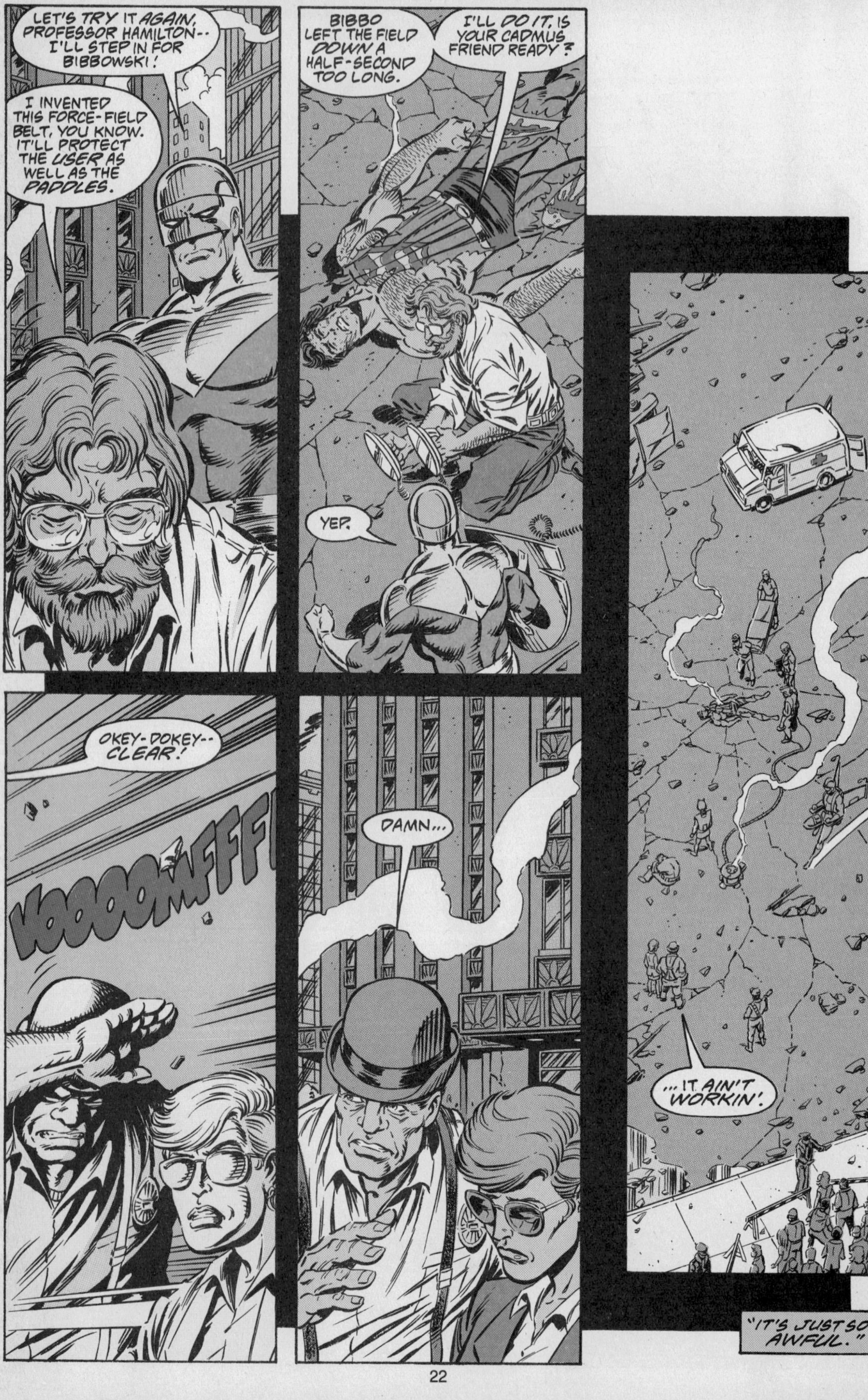
LET'S TRY IT AGAIN, PROFESSOR HAMILTON-- I'LL STEP IN FOR BIBBOWSKI!
I INVENTED THIS FORCE-FIELD BELT, YOU KNOW. IT'LL PROTECT THE USER AS WELL AS THE PADDLES.
BIBBO LEFT THE FIELD DOWN A HALF-SECOND TOO LONG.
I'LL DO IT, IS YOUR CADMUS FRIEND READY?
YEP.
OKEY-DOKEY-- CLEAR!
VOOOOMFFF
DAMN...
...IT AIN'T WORKIN'.
"IT'S JUST SO-- AWFUL."

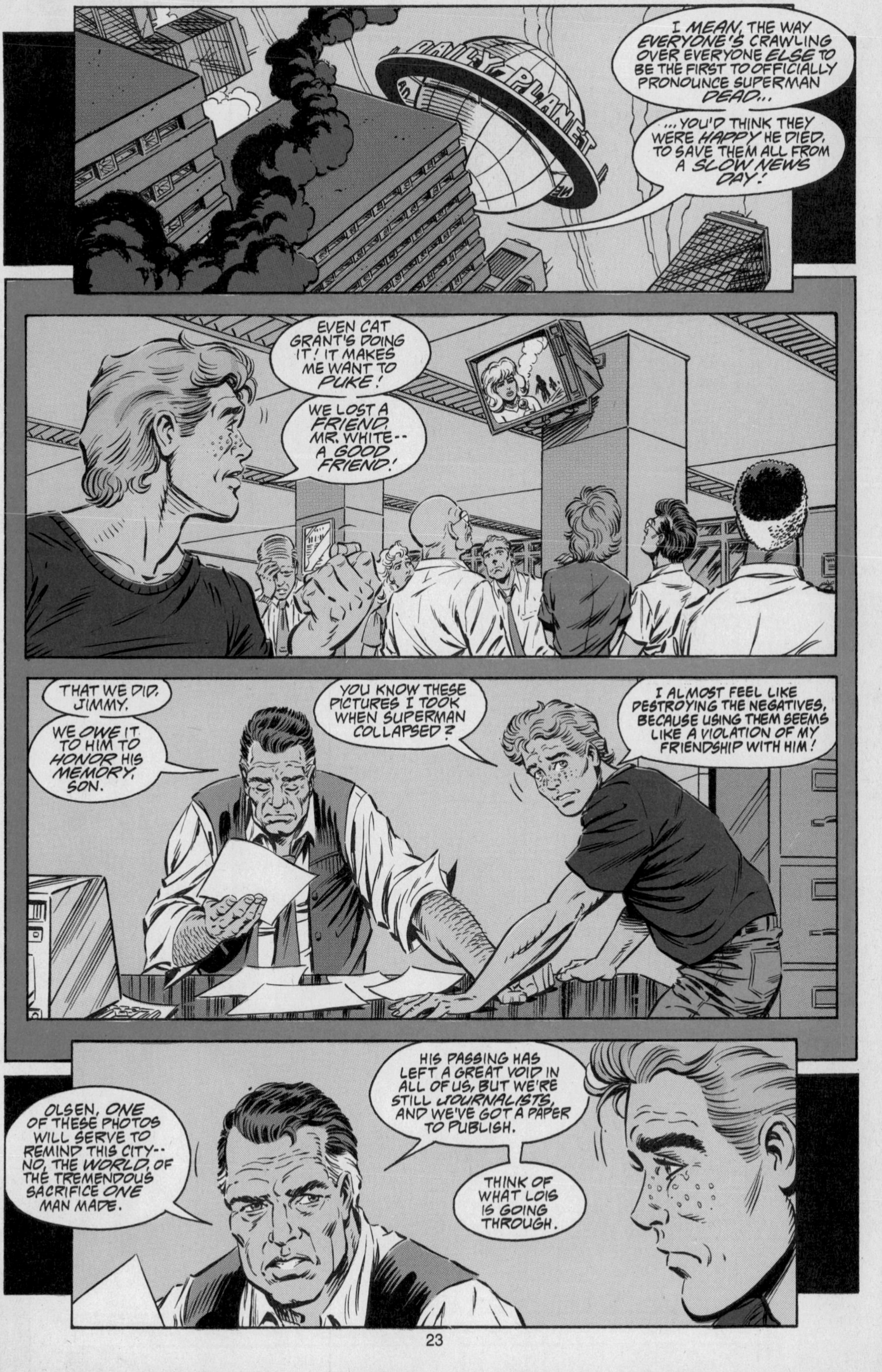

I MEAN, THE WAY EVERYONE'S CRAWLING OVER EVERYONE ELSE TO BE THE FIRST TO OFFICIALLY PRONOUNCE SUPERMAN DEAD...
...YOU'D THINK THEY WERE HAPPY HE DIED, TO SAVE THEM ALL FROM A SLOW NEWS DAY!
EVEN CAT GRANT'S DOING IT! IT MAKES ME WANT TO PUKE!
WE LOST A FRIEND, MR. WHITE-- A GOOD FRIEND!
THAT WE DID, JIMMY.
WE OWE IT TO HIM TO HONOR HIS MEMORY, SON.
YOU KNOW THESE PICTURES I TOOK WHEN SUPERMAN COLLAPSED?
I ALMOST FEEL LIKE DESTROYING THE NEGATIVES, BECAUSE USING THEM SEEMS LIKE A VIOLATION OF MY FRIENDSHIP WITH HIM!
OLSEN, ONE OF THESE PHOTOS WILL SERVE TO REMIND THIS CITY-- NO, THE WORLD, OF THE TREMENDOUS SACRIFICE ONE MAN MADE.
HIS PASSING HAS LEFT A GREAT VOID IN ALL OF US, BUT WE'RE STILL JOURNALISTS, AND WE'VE GOT A PAPER TO PUBLISH.
THINK OF WHAT LOIS IS GOING THROUGH.

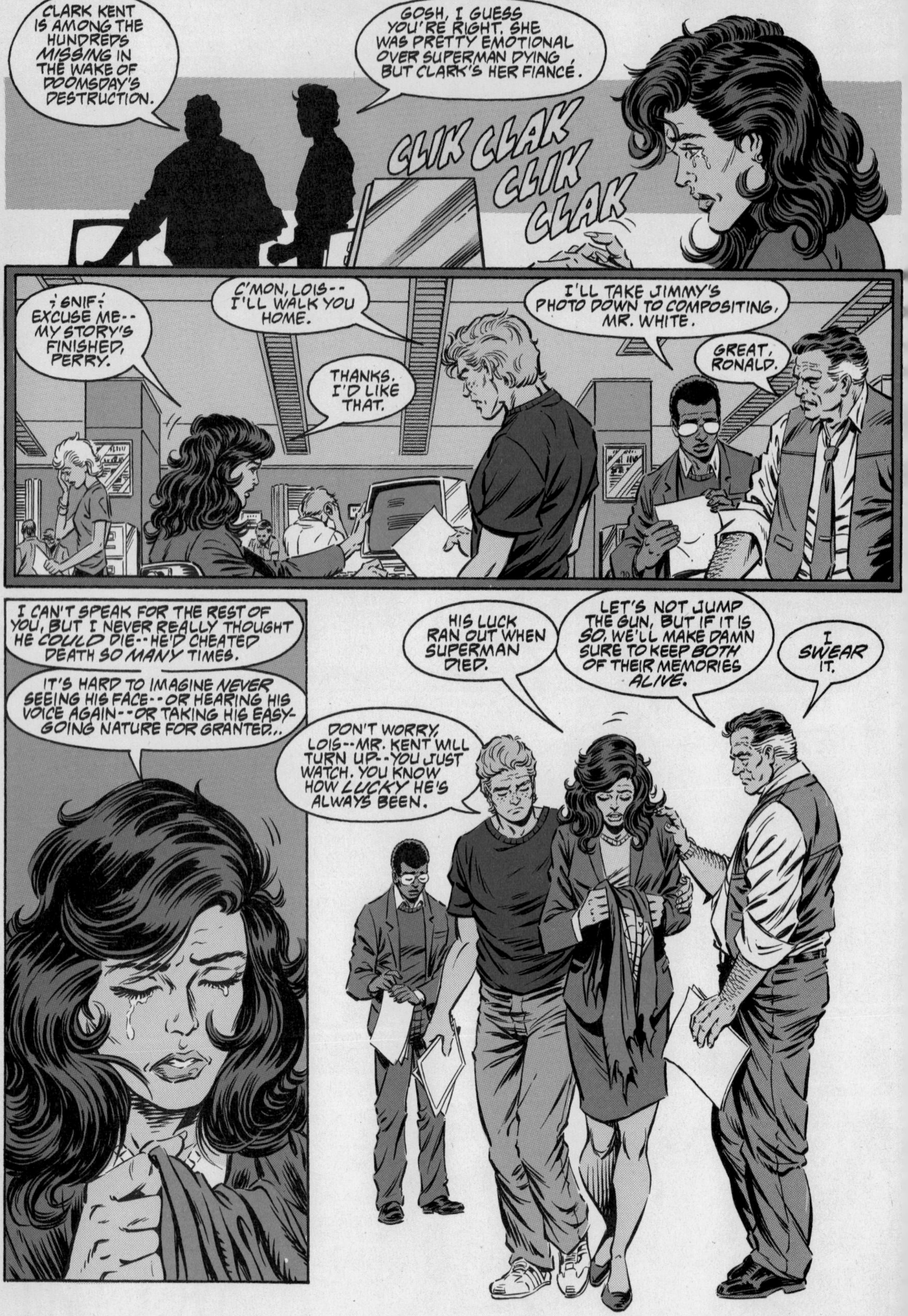
CLARK KENT IS AMONG THE HUNDREDS MISSING IN THE WAKE OF DOOMSDAY'S DESTRUCTION.
GOSH, I GUESS YOU'RE RIGHT. SHE WAS PRETTY EMOTIONAL OVER SUPERMAN DYING, BUT CLARK'S HER FIANCÉ.
CLIK CLAK CLIK CLAK
;SNIF; EXCUSE ME-- MY STORY'S FINISHED, PERRY.
C'MON, LOIS-- I'LL WALK YOU HOME.
THANKS. I'D LIKE THAT.
I'LL TAKE JIMMY'S PHOTO DOWN TO COMPOSITING, MR. WHITE.
GREAT, RONALD.
I CAN'T SPEAK FOR THE REST OF YOU, BUT I NEVER REALLY THOUGHT HE COULD DIE--HE'D CHEATED DEATH SO MANY TIMES.
IT'S HARD TO IMAGINE NEVER SEEING HIS FACE--OR HEARING HIS VOICE AGAIN--OR TAKING HIS EASY-GOING NATURE FOR GRANTED...
DON'T WORRY, LOIS--MR. KENT WILL TURN UP--YOU JUST WATCH. YOU KNOW HOW LUCKY HE'S ALWAYS BEEN.
HIS LUCK RAN OUT WHEN SUPERMAN DIED.
LET'S NOT JUMP THE GUN, BUT IF IT IS SO, WE'LL MAKE DAMN SURE TO KEEP BOTH OF THEIR MEMORIES ALIVE.
I SWEAR IT.

This issue dedicated to the memory of JOE SHUSTER.

A GREAT METROPOLITAN NEWSPAPER   METROPOLIS   TUESDAY, NOVEMBER 15, 1992   50 CENTS

SUPERMAN --DEAD

METROPOLIS MARVEL KILLED IN ACTION

By LOIS LANE

SPECIAL TO THE DAILY PLANET

Superman, our world's greatest hero, was declared dead late this afternoon.

He died of injuries sustained in the defense of the [wor]ld and her people. His

- **'DOOMSDAY' KILLER ALSO SLAIN**
  PAGE A2

- **JUSTICE LEAGUE IN MOURNING**
  PAGE A2

- **MAYOR DECLARES STATE OF EMERGENCY**
  [P]AGE A3

JAMES OLSEN/DAILY PLANET

FOR THOSE OF YOU JUST JOINING US... MUCH OF METROPOLIS REMAINS UNDER A DUSK-TO-DAWN CURFEW FOLLOWING THE DEATH OF SUPERMAN.

THE WORLD-RENOWNED HERO LAID DOWN HIS LIFE TO STOP A BERSERKER MONSTER CALLED DOOMSDAY WHO THREATENED TO LEVEL THE CITY--

R.I.P.

--FOLLOWING A SEVERAL-STATE RAMPAGE WHICH RESULTED IN OVER 500 DEATHS AND LEFT JUSTICE LEAGUE AMERICA IN DISARRAY. SUPERMAN JOINED THE BATTLE AT MIDDAY, BUT THOUGH HE FOUGHT VALIANTLY--

WLEX EXCLUSIVE FOOTAGE

--HE SEEMED UNABLE TO STOP DOOMSDAY'S ODYSSEY OF DEATH AND DESTRUCTION. IT WAS, TRAGICALLY, A FIGHT TO THE FINISH...

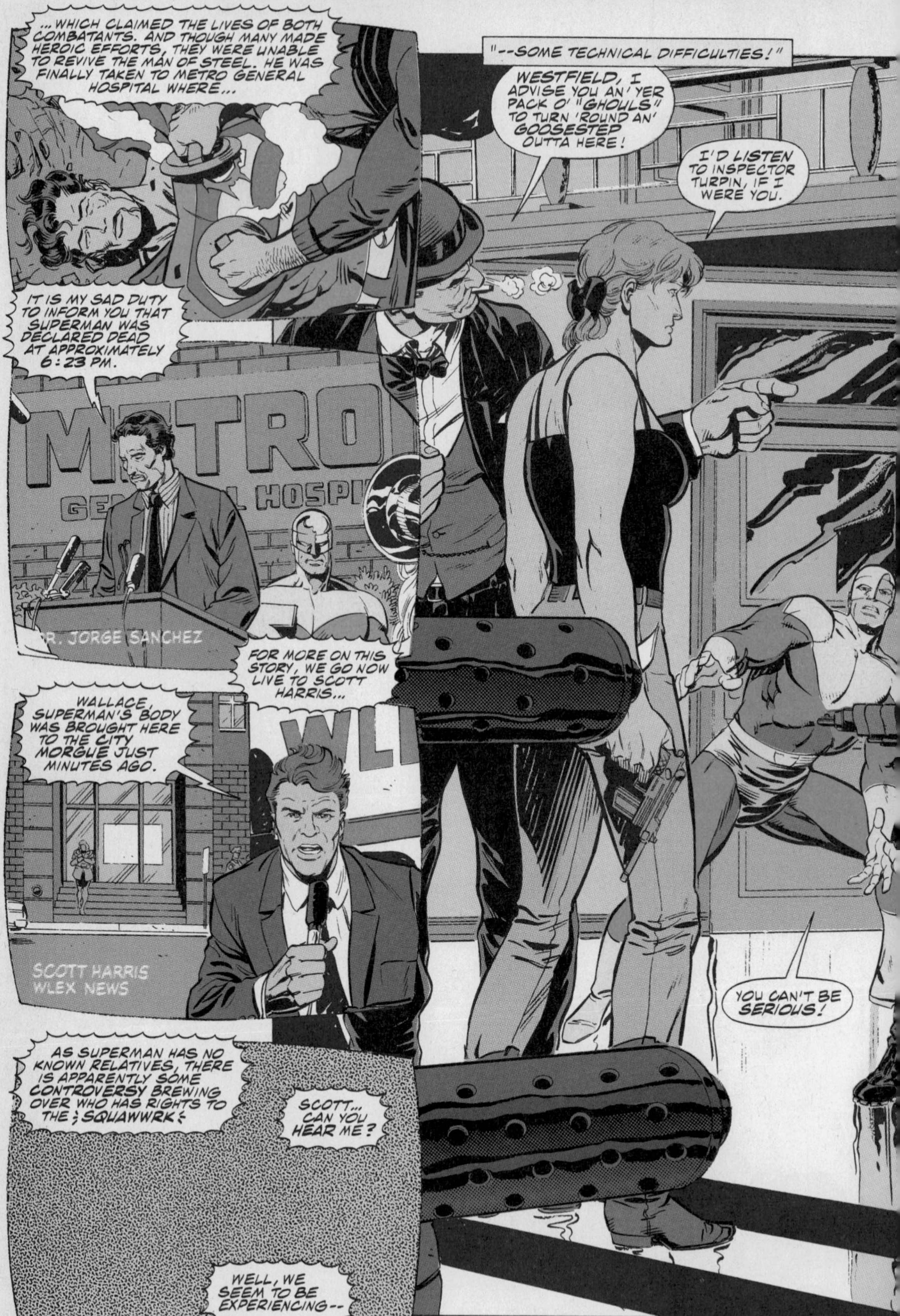
...WHICH CLAIMED THE LIVES OF BOTH COMBATANTS. AND THOUGH MANY MADE HEROIC EFFORTS, THEY WERE UNABLE TO REVIVE THE MAN OF STEEL. HE WAS FINALLY TAKEN TO METRO GENERAL HOSPITAL WHERE...
IT IS MY SAD DUTY TO INFORM YOU THAT SUPERMAN WAS DECLARED DEAD AT APPROXIMATELY 6:23 PM.
R. JORGE SANCHEZ
FOR MORE ON THIS STORY, WE GO NOW LIVE TO SCOTT HARRIS...
WALLACE, SUPERMAN'S BODY WAS BROUGHT HERE TO THE CITY MORGUE JUST MINUTES AGO.
SCOTT HARRIS
WLEX NEWS
AS SUPERMAN HAS NO KNOWN RELATIVES, THERE IS APPARENTLY SOME CONTROVERSY BREWING OVER WHO HAS RIGHTS TO THE ;SQUAWRK;
SCOTT... CAN YOU HEAR ME?
WELL, WE SEEM TO BE EXPERIENCING--
"--SOME TECHNICAL DIFFICULTIES!"
WESTFIELD, I ADVISE YOU AN' YER PACK O' "GHOULS" TO TURN 'ROUND AN' GOOSESTEP OUTTA HERE!
I'D LISTEN TO INSPECTOR TURPIN, IF I WERE YOU.
YOU CAN'T BE SERIOUS!

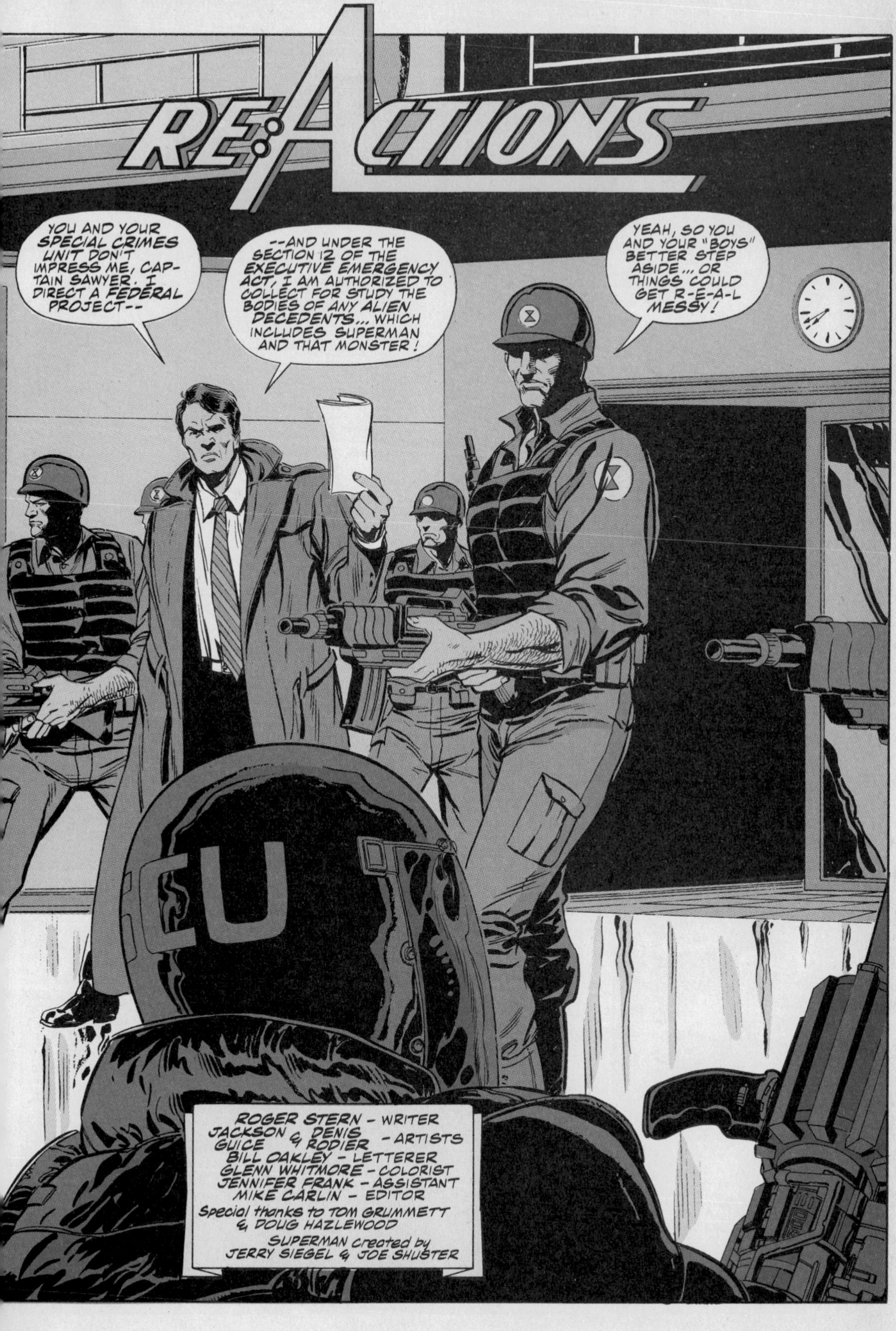
RE:ACTIONS
YOU AND YOUR SPECIAL CRIMES UNIT DON'T IMPRESS ME, CAPTAIN SAWYER. I DIRECT A FEDERAL PROJECT--
--AND UNDER THE SECTION 12 OF THE EXECUTIVE EMERGENCY ACT, I AM AUTHORIZED TO COLLECT FOR STUDY THE BODIES OF ANY ALIEN DECEDENTS... WHICH INCLUDES SUPERMAN AND THAT MONSTER!
YEAH, SO YOU AND YOUR "BOYS" BETTER STEP ASIDE... OR THINGS COULD GET R-E-A-L MESSY!
ROGER STERN - WRITER
JACKSON GUICE & DENIS RODIER - ARTISTS
BILL OAKLEY - LETTERER
GLENN WHITMORE - COLORIST
JENNIFER FRANK - ASSISTANT
MIKE CARLIN - EDITOR
Special thanks to TOM GRUMMETT & DOUG HAZLEWOOD
SUPERMAN created by JERRY SIEGEL & JOE SHUSTER

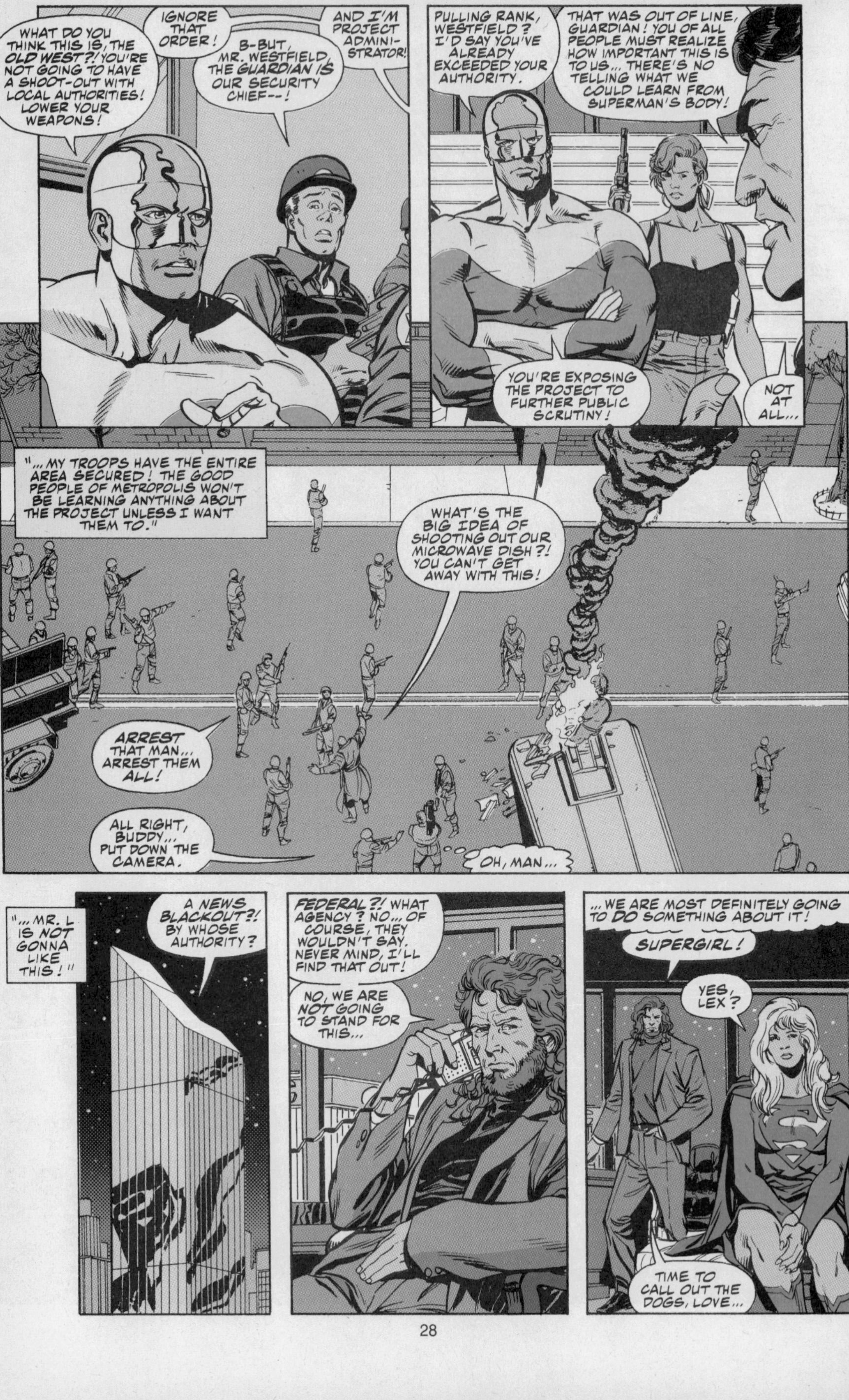
WHAT DO YOU THINK THIS IS, THE OLD WEST?! YOU'RE NOT GOING TO HAVE A SHOOT-OUT WITH LOCAL AUTHORITIES! LOWER YOUR WEAPONS!
IGNORE THAT ORDER!
B-BUT, MR. WESTFIELD, THE GUARDIAN IS OUR SECURITY CHIEF--!
AND I'M PROJECT ADMINISTRATOR!
PULLING RANK, WESTFIELD? I'D SAY YOU'VE ALREADY EXCEEDED YOUR AUTHORITY.
THAT WAS OUT OF LINE, GUARDIAN! YOU OF ALL PEOPLE MUST REALIZE HOW IMPORTANT THIS IS TO US... THERE'S NO TELLING WHAT WE COULD LEARN FROM SUPERMAN'S BODY!
YOU'RE EXPOSING THE PROJECT TO FURTHER PUBLIC SCRUTINY!
NOT AT ALL...
"...MY TROOPS HAVE THE ENTIRE AREA SECURED! THE GOOD PEOPLE OF METROPOLIS WON'T BE LEARNING ANYTHING ABOUT THE PROJECT UNLESS I WANT THEM TO."
WHAT'S THE BIG IDEA OF SHOOTING OUT OUR MICROWAVE DISH?! YOU CAN'T GET AWAY WITH THIS!
ARREST THAT MAN... ARREST THEM ALL!
ALL RIGHT, BUDDY... PUT DOWN THE CAMERA.
OH, MAN...
"...MR. L IS NOT GONNA LIKE THIS!"
A NEWS BLACKOUT?! BY WHOSE AUTHORITY?
FEDERAL?! WHAT AGENCY? NO... OF COURSE, THEY WOULDN'T SAY. NEVER MIND, I'LL FIND THAT OUT!
NO, WE ARE NOT GOING TO STAND FOR THIS...
...WE ARE MOST DEFINITELY GOING TO DO SOMETHING ABOUT IT!
SUPERGIRL!
YES, LEX?
TIME TO CALL OUT THE DOGS, LOVE...

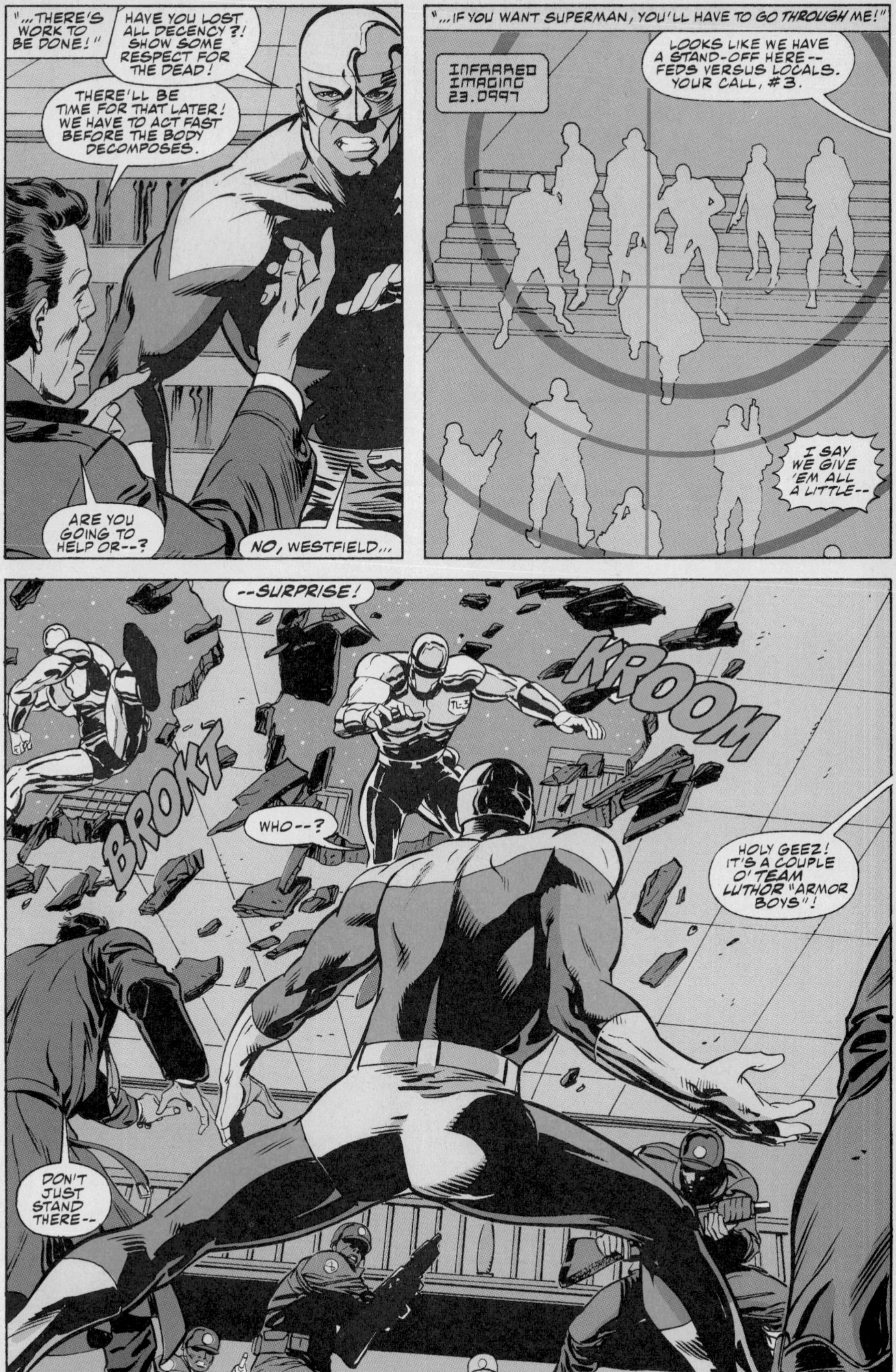
"...THERE'S WORK TO BE DONE!"
HAVE YOU LOST ALL DECENCY?! SHOW SOME RESPECT FOR THE DEAD!
THERE'LL BE TIME FOR THAT LATER! WE HAVE TO ACT FAST BEFORE THE BODY DECOMPOSES.
ARE YOU GOING TO HELP OR--?
NO, WESTFIELD...
"...IF YOU WANT SUPERMAN, YOU'LL HAVE TO GO THROUGH ME!"
INFRARED IMAGING 23.0997
LOOKS LIKE WE HAVE A STAND-OFF HERE-- FEDS VERSUS LOCALS. YOUR CALL, #3.
I SAY WE GIVE 'EM ALL A LITTLE--
--SURPRISE!
KROOM
BROKT
WHO--?
HOLY GEEZ! IT'S A COUPLE O' TEAM LUTHOR "ARMOR BOYS"!
DON'T JUST STAND THERE--

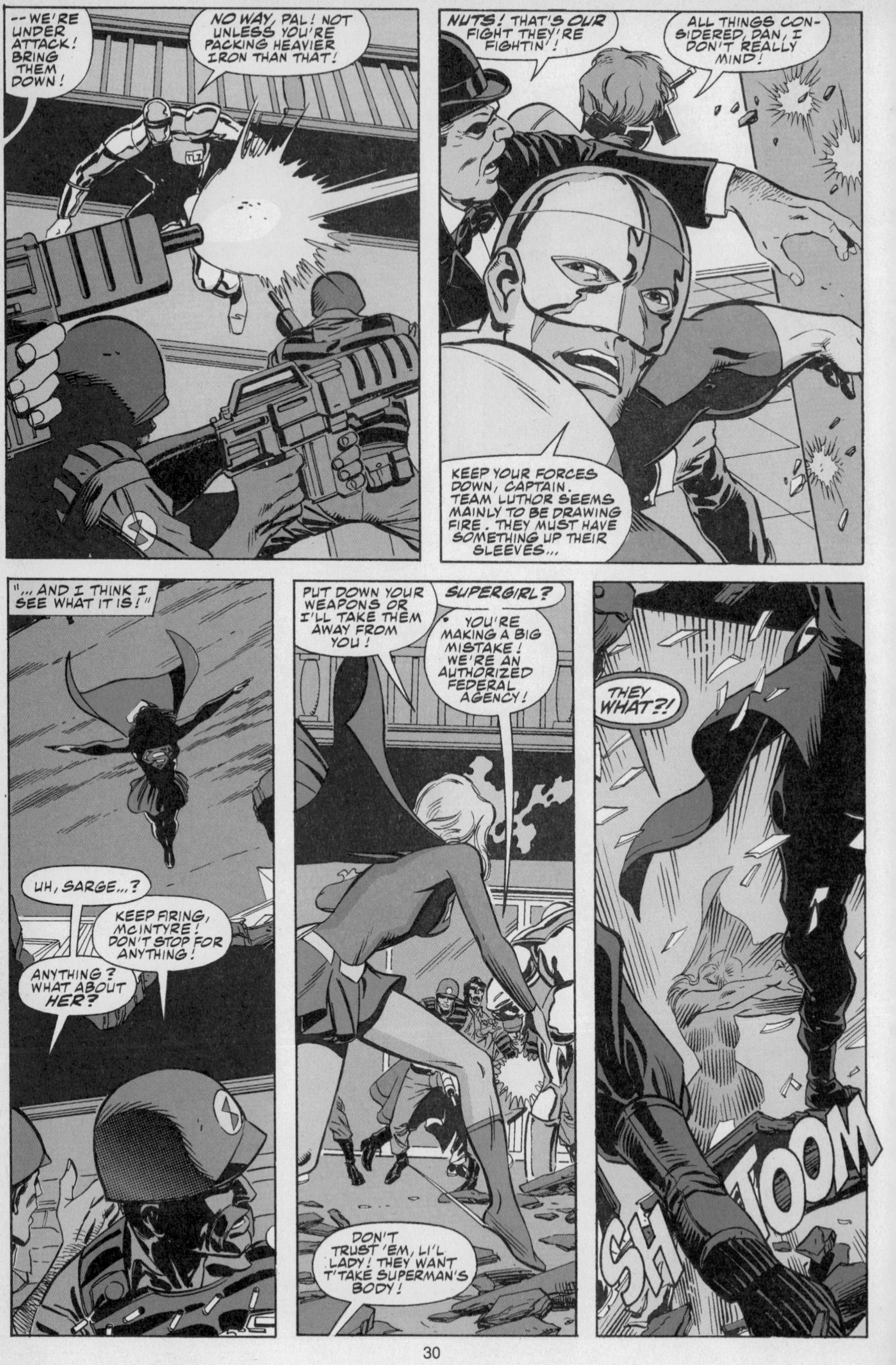
--WE'RE UNDER ATTACK! BRING THEM DOWN!
NO WAY, PAL! NOT UNLESS YOU'RE PACKING HEAVIER IRON THAN THAT!
NUTS! THAT'S OUR FIGHT THEY'RE FIGHTIN'!
ALL THINGS CONSIDERED, DAN, I DON'T REALLY MIND!
KEEP YOUR FORCES DOWN, CAPTAIN. TEAM LUTHOR SEEMS MAINLY TO BE DRAWING FIRE. THEY MUST HAVE SOMETHING UP THEIR SLEEVES...
"...AND I THINK I SEE WHAT IT IS!"
UH, SARGE...?
KEEP FIRING, McINTYRE! DON'T STOP FOR ANYTHING!
ANYTHING? WHAT ABOUT HER?
PUT DOWN YOUR WEAPONS OR I'LL TAKE THEM AWAY FROM YOU!
SUPERGIRL?
YOU'RE MAKING A BIG MISTAKE! WE'RE AN AUTHORIZED FEDERAL AGENCY!
DON'T TRUST 'EM, LI'L LADY! THEY WANT T'TAKE SUPERMAN'S BODY!
THEY WHAT?!
SH
TOOM

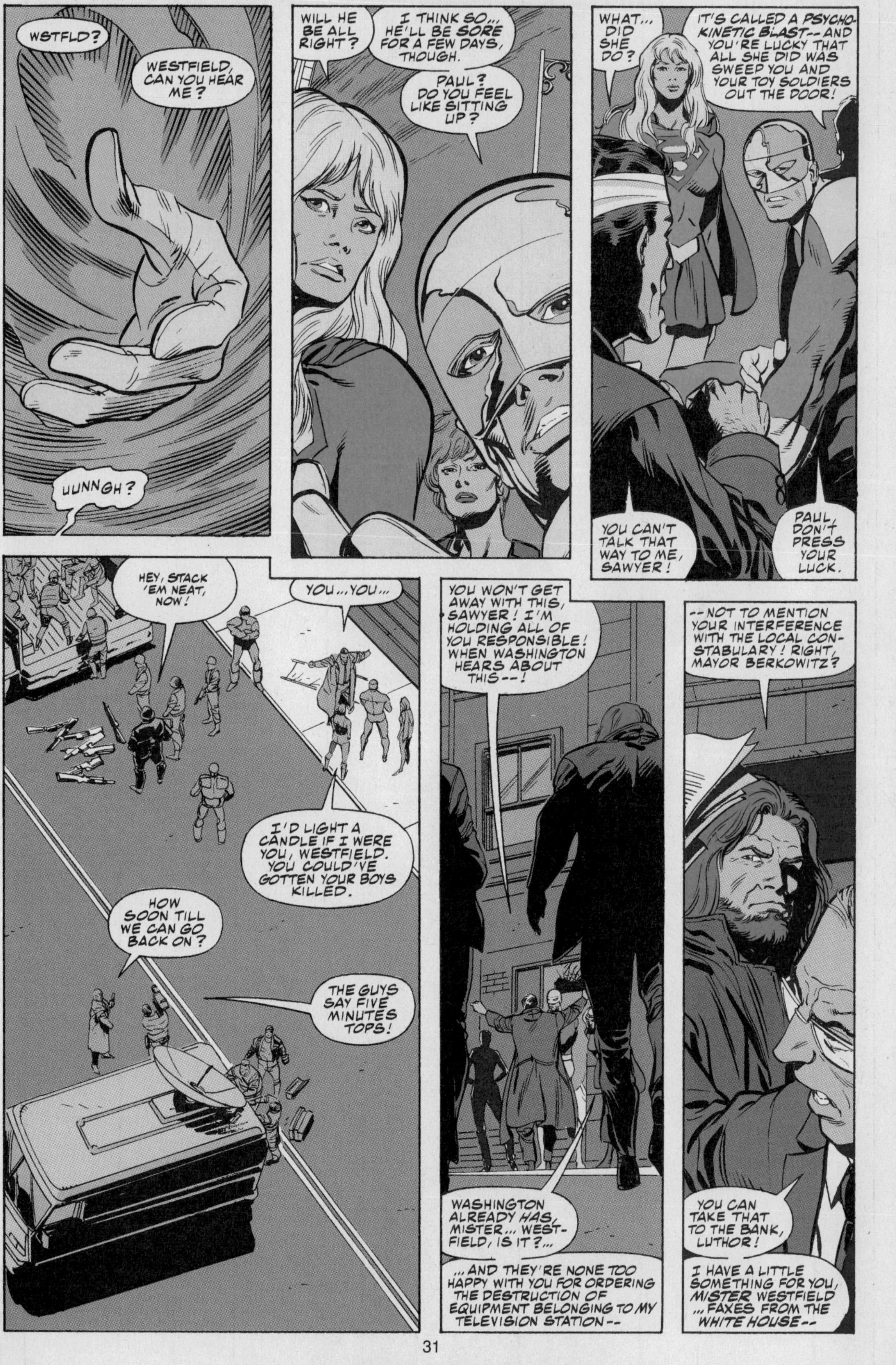
WSTFLD?
WESTFIELD, CAN YOU HEAR ME?
UUNNGH?
WILL HE BE ALL RIGHT?
I THINK SO... HE'LL BE SORE FOR A FEW DAYS, THOUGH.
PAUL? DO YOU FEEL LIKE SITTING UP?
WHAT... DID SHE DO?
IT'S CALLED A PSYCHO-KINETIC BLAST-- AND YOU'RE LUCKY THAT ALL SHE DID WAS SWEEP YOU AND YOUR TOY SOLDIERS OUT THE DOOR!
YOU CAN'T TALK THAT WAY TO ME, SAWYER!
PAUL, DON'T PRESS YOUR LUCK.
HEY, STACK 'EM NEAT, NOW!
YOU... YOU...
I'D LIGHT A CANDLE IF I WERE YOU, WESTFIELD. YOU COULD'VE GOTTEN YOUR BOYS KILLED.
HOW SOON TILL WE CAN GO BACK ON?
THE GUYS SAY FIVE MINUTES TOPS!
YOU WON'T GET AWAY WITH THIS, SAWYER! I'M HOLDING ALL OF YOU RESPONSIBLE! WHEN WASHINGTON HEARS ABOUT THIS--!
WASHINGTON ALREADY HAS, MISTER... WEST-FIELD, IS IT?...
...AND THEY'RE NONE TOO HAPPY WITH YOU FOR ORDERING THE DESTRUCTION OF EQUIPMENT BELONGING TO MY TELEVISION STATION--
--NOT TO MENTION YOUR INTERFERENCE WITH THE LOCAL CON-STABULARY! RIGHT, MAYOR BERKOWITZ?
YOU CAN TAKE THAT TO THE BANK, LUTHOR!
I HAVE A LITTLE SOMETHING FOR YOU, MISTER WESTFIELD ...FAXES FROM THE WHITE HOUSE--

-- RESCINDING YOUR AUTHORITY IN THIS MATTER! SUPERMAN'S HERITAGE MAY BE ALIEN, BUT AS FAR AS WE'RE CONCERNED -- AND THE PRESIDENT AGREES -- HE'S AN *AMERICAN!*

I... I...

AND, BY GOD, WE INTEND TO SEE THAT HE'S GIVEN A DECENT BURIAL... IN METROPOLIS!

I'D SAY YOU PUT YOUR FOOT IN IT, MATE. OH, AND DON'T TRY TO GO CLAIMING THAT DOOMS-DAY BEASTIE. S.T.A.R. LABS'LL DISPOSE OF 'IM!

NOW, AS A PATRIOTIC CITIZEN, I'M WILLING TO OVERLOOK THE DAMAGE TO MY PROPERTY--

--AND TO KEEP MENTION O' YOUR LITTLE PROJECT OUT OF THE NEWS... IF YOU GET IN YOUR TRUCKS AND RETURN TO YOUR BASE... *NOW!*

"TEAM LUTHOR WILL HELP THE GUARDIAN *'ESCORT'* YOU TO THE COUNTY LINE!"

I KNOW THAT WESTFIELD HAD IT IN FOR SUPERMAN, * BUT I NEVER THOUGHT HE'D STOOP SO LOW AS TO PICK A FIGHT OVER THE MAN'S BODY!

THAT'S THE SORT OF LUNATIC STUNT I'D HAVE EXPECTED FROM DABNEY DONOVAN!

THERE'D BETTER BE SOME CHANGES MADE AT THE CADMUS PROJECT AFTER THIS!

I'M TOLD THAT OUR REMOTE CREW HAS CORRECTED THEIR TECHNICAL PROB-LEMS. SCOTT, ARE YOU THERE?

* SINCE SUPERMAN #58.

YES, WALLACE. EVERYTHING IS... UNDER CONTROL NOW.

LEXCORP C.E.O. LEX LUTHOR THE SECOND HAS ARRIVED... WITH SUPERGIRL! I BELIEVE HE'S ABOUT TO MAKE A STATEMENT...

WLEX NEWS

LADIES AND GENTLEMEN... THE DEATH OF SUPERMAN ... HAS AFFECTED US ALL... DEEPLY. A LEGEND HAS BEEN TAKEN FROM US.

IT IS FITTING AND PROPER THAT WE MOURN HIS PASSING... ESPECI-ALLY THOSE OF US IN METROPOLIS... WHO KNEW HIM SO WELL...

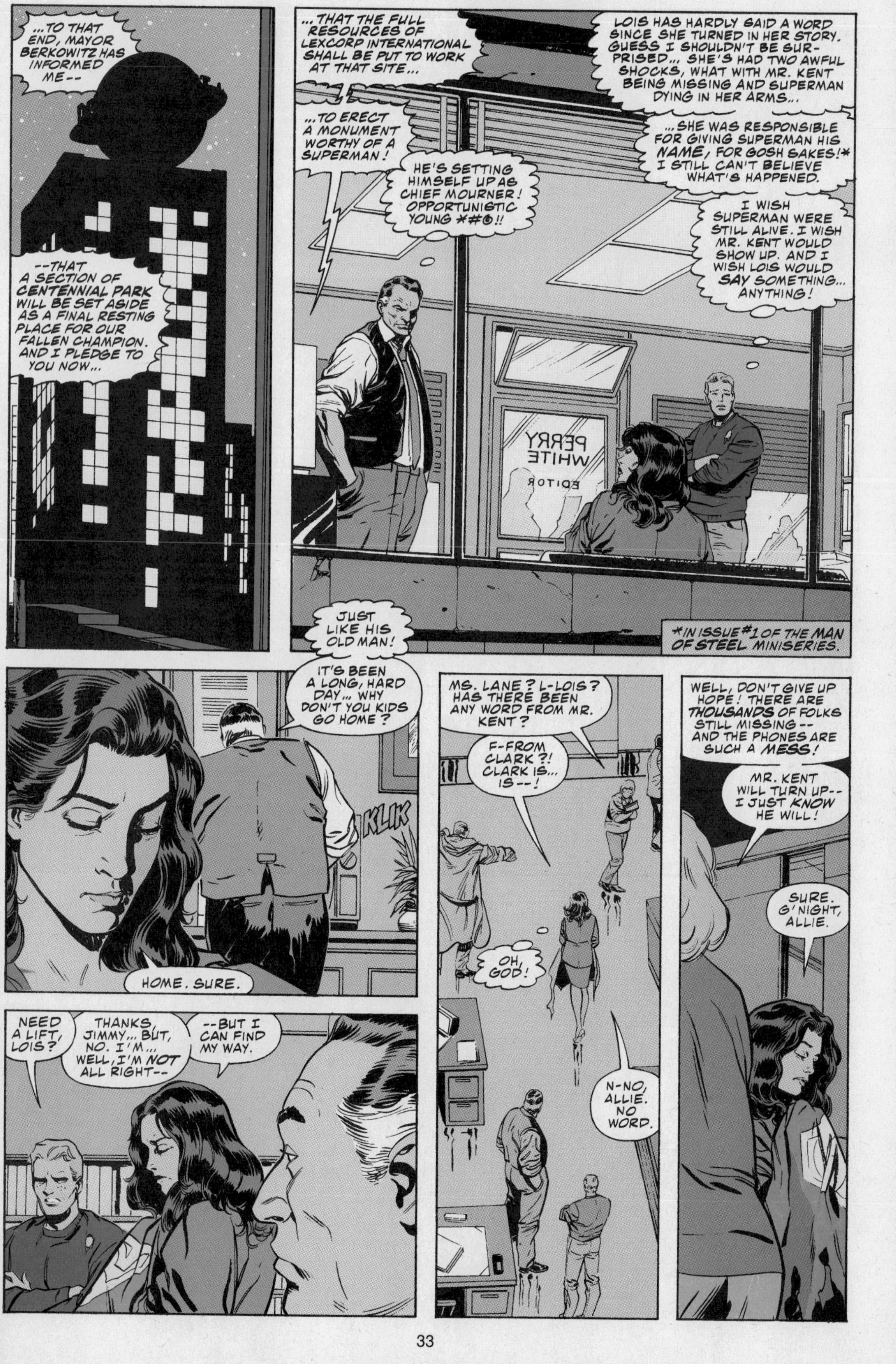

...TO THAT END, MAYOR BERKOWITZ HAS INFORMED ME--
--THAT A SECTION OF CENTENNIAL PARK WILL BE SET ASIDE AS A FINAL RESTING PLACE FOR OUR FALLEN CHAMPION. AND I PLEDGE TO YOU NOW...
...THAT THE FULL RESOURCES OF LEXCORP INTERNATIONAL SHALL BE PUT TO WORK AT THAT SITE...
...TO ERECT A MONUMENT WORTHY OF A SUPERMAN!
HE'S SETTING HIMSELF UP AS CHIEF MOURNER! OPPORTUNISTIC YOUNG *#©!!
JUST LIKE HIS OLD MAN!
LOIS HAS HARDLY SAID A WORD SINCE SHE TURNED IN HER STORY. GUESS I SHOULDN'T BE SURPRISED... SHE'S HAD TWO AWFUL SHOCKS, WHAT WITH MR. KENT BEING MISSING AND SUPERMAN DYING IN HER ARMS...
...SHE WAS RESPONSIBLE FOR GIVING SUPERMAN HIS NAME, FOR GOSH SAKES!* I STILL CAN'T BELIEVE WHAT'S HAPPENED.
I WISH SUPERMAN WERE STILL ALIVE. I WISH MR. KENT WOULD SHOW UP. AND I WISH LOIS WOULD SAY SOMETHING... ANYTHING!
PERRY WHITE EDITOR
*IN ISSUE #1 OF THE MAN OF STEEL MINISERIES.
IT'S BEEN A LONG, HARD DAY... WHY DON'T YOU KIDS GO HOME?
KLIK
HOME. SURE.
NEED A LIFT, LOIS?
THANKS, JIMMY... BUT, NO. I'M... WELL, I'M NOT ALL RIGHT--
--BUT I CAN FIND MY WAY.
MS. LANE? L-LOIS? HAS THERE BEEN ANY WORD FROM MR. KENT?
F-FROM CLARK?! CLARK IS... IS--!
OH, GOD!
N-NO, ALLIE. NO WORD.
WELL, DON'T GIVE UP HOPE! THERE ARE THOUSANDS OF FOLKS STILL MISSING--AND THE PHONES ARE SUCH A MESS!
MR. KENT WILL TURN UP--I JUST KNOW HE WILL!
SURE. G'NIGHT, ALLIE.

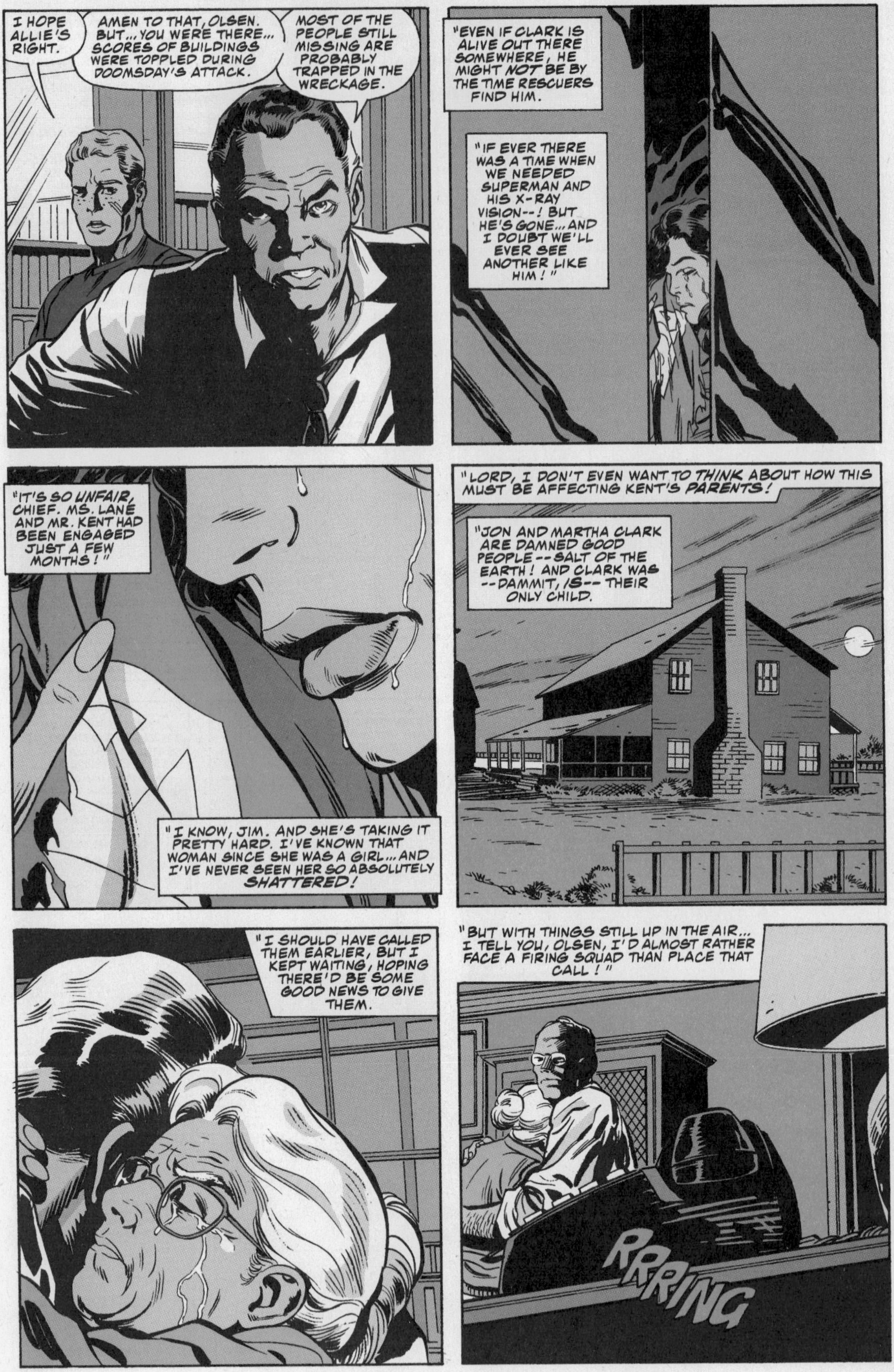
I HOPE ALLIE'S RIGHT.
AMEN TO THAT, OLSEN. BUT... YOU WERE THERE... SCORES OF BUILDINGS WERE TOPPLED DURING DOOMSDAY'S ATTACK.
MOST OF THE PEOPLE STILL MISSING ARE PROBABLY TRAPPED IN THE WRECKAGE.
"EVEN IF CLARK IS ALIVE OUT THERE SOMEWHERE, HE MIGHT NOT BE BY THE TIME RESCUERS FIND HIM.
"IF EVER THERE WAS A TIME WHEN WE NEEDED SUPERMAN AND HIS X-RAY VISION--! BUT HE'S GONE... AND I DOUBT WE'LL EVER SEE ANOTHER LIKE HIM!"
"IT'S SO UNFAIR, CHIEF. MS. LANE AND MR. KENT HAD BEEN ENGAGED JUST A FEW MONTHS!"
"I KNOW, JIM. AND SHE'S TAKING IT PRETTY HARD. I'VE KNOWN THAT WOMAN SINCE SHE WAS A GIRL... AND I'VE NEVER SEEN HER SO ABSOLUTELY SHATTERED!
"LORD, I DON'T EVEN WANT TO THINK ABOUT HOW THIS MUST BE AFFECTING KENT'S PARENTS!
"JON AND MARTHA CLARK ARE DAMNED GOOD PEOPLE -- SALT OF THE EARTH! AND CLARK WAS --DAMMIT, IS-- THEIR ONLY CHILD.
"I SHOULD HAVE CALLED THEM EARLIER, BUT I KEPT WAITING, HOPING THERE'D BE SOME GOOD NEWS TO GIVE THEM.
"BUT WITH THINGS STILL UP IN THE AIR... I TELL YOU, OLSEN, I'D ALMOST RATHER FACE A FIRING SQUAD THAN PLACE THAT CALL!"
RRRING

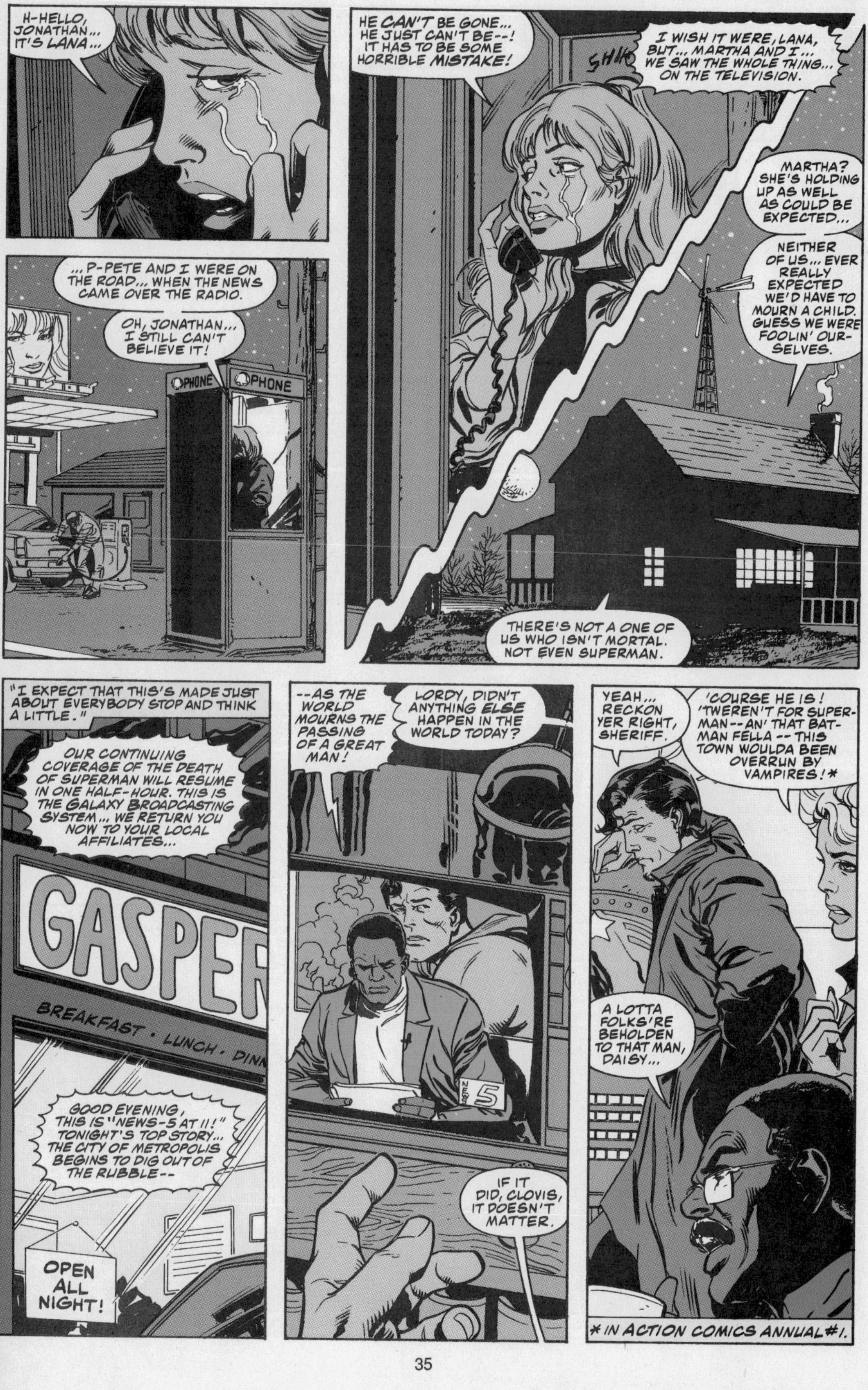

H-HELLO, JONATHAN... IT'S LANA...
HE CAN'T BE GONE... HE JUST CAN'T BE--! IT HAS TO BE SOME HORRIBLE MISTAKE!
SHHK
I WISH IT WERE, LANA, BUT... MARTHA AND I... WE SAW THE WHOLE THING... ON THE TELEVISION.
...P-PETE AND I WERE ON THE ROAD... WHEN THE NEWS CAME OVER THE RADIO.
OH, JONATHAN... I STILL CAN'T BELIEVE IT!
PHONE
PHONE
MARTHA? SHE'S HOLDING UP AS WELL AS COULD BE EXPECTED...
NEITHER OF US... EVER REALLY EXPECTED WE'D HAVE TO MOURN A CHILD. GUESS WE WERE FOOLIN' OURSELVES.
THERE'S NOT A ONE OF US WHO ISN'T MORTAL. NOT EVEN SUPERMAN.
"I EXPECT THAT THIS'S MADE JUST ABOUT EVERYBODY STOP AND THINK A LITTLE."
OUR CONTINUING COVERAGE OF THE DEATH OF SUPERMAN WILL RESUME IN ONE HALF-HOUR. THIS IS THE GALAXY BROADCASTING SYSTEM... WE RETURN YOU NOW TO YOUR LOCAL AFFILIATES...
GASPER
BREAKFAST • LUNCH • DINN
GOOD EVENING, THIS IS "NEWS-5 AT 11!" TONIGHT'S TOP STORY... THE CITY OF METROPOLIS BEGINS TO DIG OUT OF THE RUBBLE--
OPEN ALL NIGHT!
--AS THE WORLD MOURNS THE PASSING OF A GREAT MAN!
LORDY, DIDN'T ANYTHING ELSE HAPPEN IN THE WORLD TODAY?
5
IF IT DID, CLOVIS, IT DOESN'T MATTER.
YEAH... RECKON YER RIGHT, SHERIFF.
'COURSE HE IS! 'TWEREN'T FOR SUPERMAN--AN' THAT BATMAN FELLA--THIS TOWN WOULDA BEEN OVERRUN BY VAMPIRES!*
A LOTTA FOLKS'RE BEHOLDEN TO THAT MAN, DAISY...
*IN ACTION COMICS ANNUAL #1.

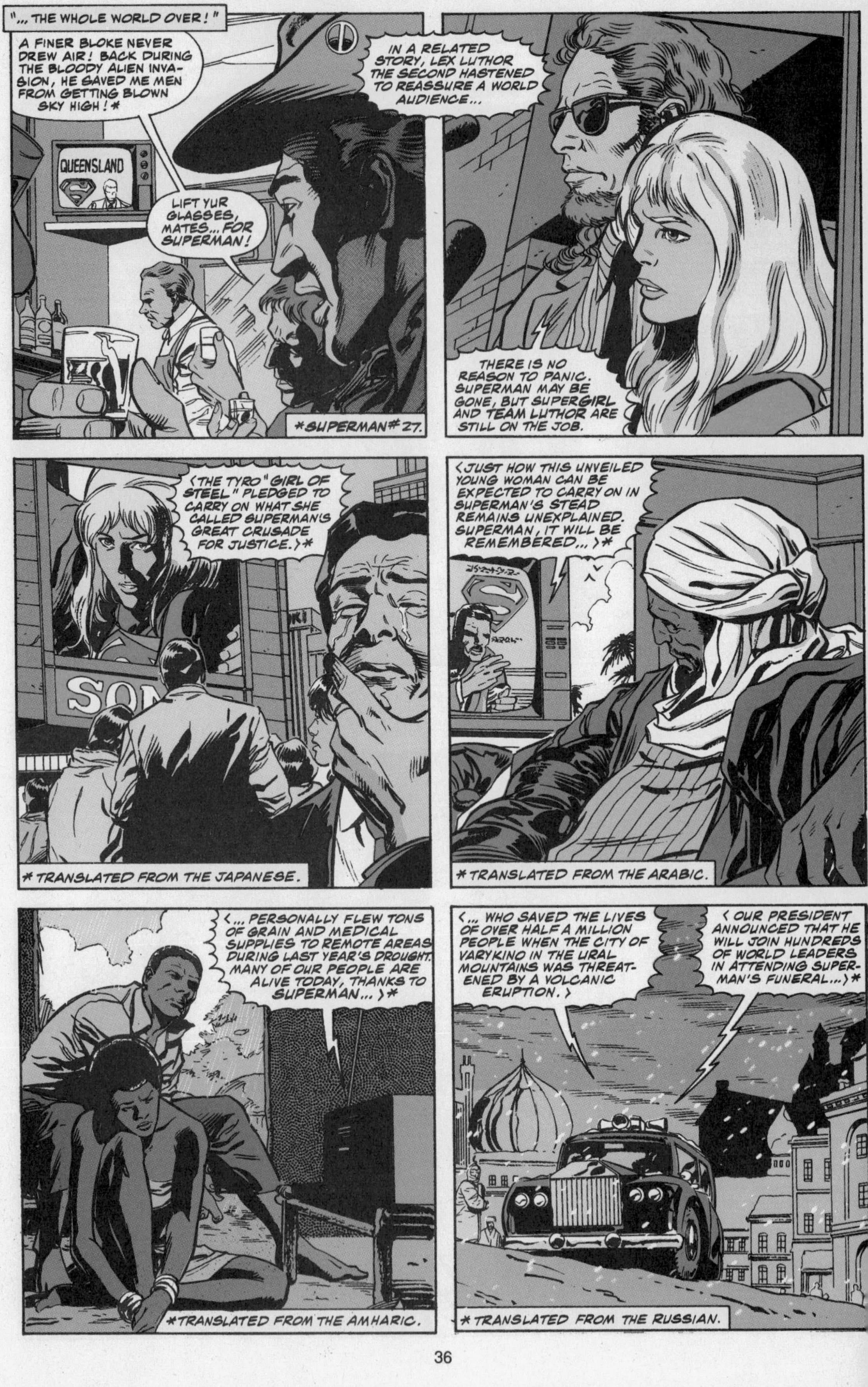
"... THE WHOLE WORLD OVER!"
A FINER BLOKE NEVER DREW AIR! BACK DURING THE BLOODY ALIEN INVASION, HE SAVED ME MEN FROM GETTING BLOWN SKY HIGH! *
QUEENSLAND
LIFT YUR GLASSES, MATES... FOR SUPERMAN!
*SUPERMAN #27.
IN A RELATED STORY, LEX LUTHOR THE SECOND HASTENED TO REASSURE A WORLD AUDIENCE...
THERE IS NO REASON TO PANIC. SUPERMAN MAY BE GONE, BUT SUPERGIRL AND TEAM LUTHOR ARE STILL ON THE JOB.
<THE TYRO "GIRL OF STEEL" PLEDGED TO CARRY ON WHAT SHE CALLED SUPERMAN'S GREAT CRUSADE FOR JUSTICE.>*
SO
*TRANSLATED FROM THE JAPANESE.
<JUST HOW THIS UNVEILED YOUNG WOMAN CAN BE EXPECTED TO CARRY ON IN SUPERMAN'S STEAD REMAINS UNEXPLAINED. SUPERMAN, IT WILL BE REMEMBERED...>*
*TRANSLATED FROM THE ARABIC.
<...PERSONALLY FLEW TONS OF GRAIN AND MEDICAL SUPPLIES TO REMOTE AREAS DURING LAST YEAR'S DROUGHT. MANY OF OUR PEOPLE ARE ALIVE TODAY, THANKS TO SUPERMAN...>*
*TRANSLATED FROM THE AMHARIC.
<...WHO SAVED THE LIVES OF OVER HALF A MILLION PEOPLE WHEN THE CITY OF VARYKINO IN THE URAL MOUNTAINS WAS THREATENED BY A VOLCANIC ERUPTION.>
<OUR PRESIDENT ANNOUNCED THAT HE WILL JOIN HUNDREDS OF WORLD LEADERS IN ATTENDING SUPERMAN'S FUNERAL...>*
*TRANSLATED FROM THE RUSSIAN.

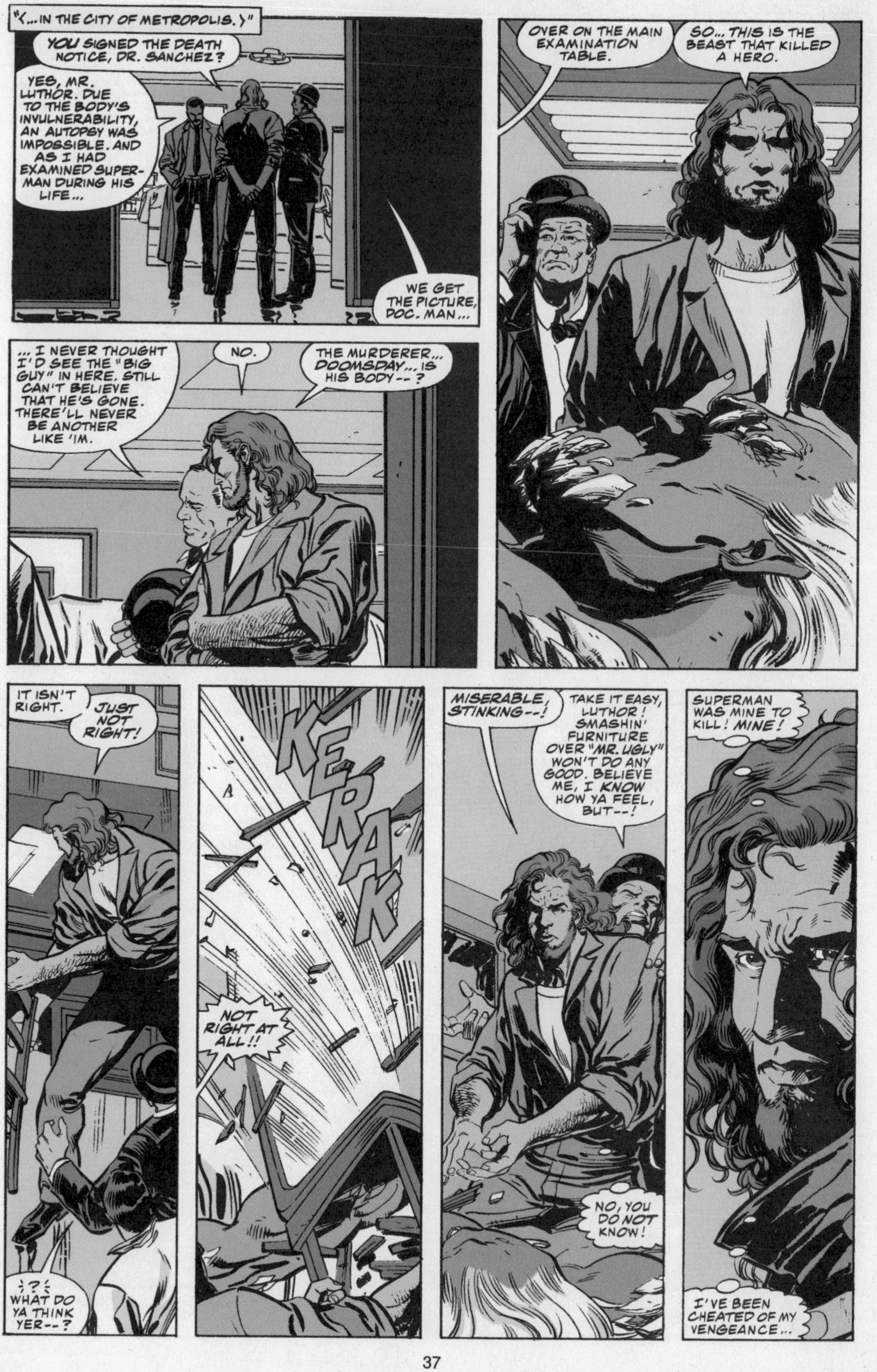
"‹...IN THE CITY OF METROPOLIS.›"
YOU SIGNED THE DEATH NOTICE, DR. SANCHEZ?
YES, MR. LUTHOR. DUE TO THE BODY'S INVULNERABILITY, AN AUTOPSY WAS IMPOSSIBLE. AND AS I HAD EXAMINED SUPERMAN DURING HIS LIFE...
WE GET THE PICTURE, DOC. MAN...
OVER ON THE MAIN EXAMINATION TABLE.
SO... THIS IS THE BEAST THAT KILLED A HERO.
...I NEVER THOUGHT I'D SEE THE "BIG GUY" IN HERE. STILL CAN'T BELIEVE THAT HE'S GONE. THERE'LL NEVER BE ANOTHER LIKE 'IM.
NO.
THE MURDERER... DOOMSDAY... IS HIS BODY--?
IT ISN'T RIGHT.
JUST NOT RIGHT!
?!?
WHAT DO YA THINK YER--?
KERAK
NOT RIGHT AT ALL!!
MISERABLE, STINKING--!
TAKE IT EASY, LUTHOR! SMASHIN' FURNITURE OVER "MR. UGLY" WON'T DO ANY GOOD. BELIEVE ME, I KNOW HOW YA FEEL, BUT--!
NO, YOU DO NOT KNOW!
SUPERMAN WAS MINE TO KILL! MINE!
I'VE BEEN CHEATED OF MY VENGEANCE...

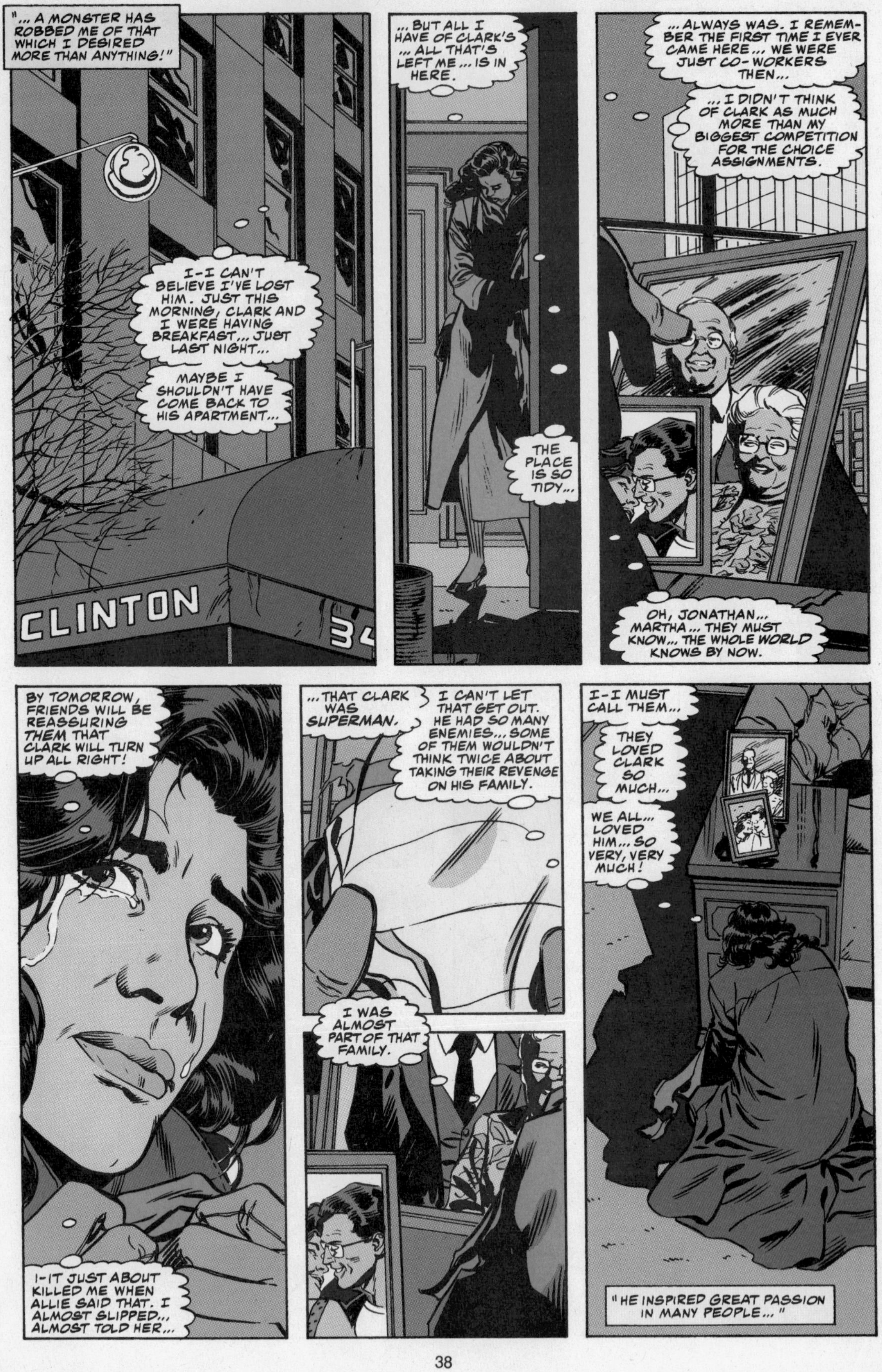
"... A MONSTER HAS ROBBED ME OF THAT WHICH I DESIRED MORE THAN ANYTHING!"
I-I CAN'T BELIEVE I'VE LOST HIM. JUST THIS MORNING, CLARK AND I WERE HAVING BREAKFAST... JUST LAST NIGHT...
MAYBE I SHOULDN'T HAVE COME BACK TO HIS APARTMENT...
CLINTON
... BUT ALL I HAVE OF CLARK'S ... ALL THAT'S LEFT ME ... IS IN HERE.
THE PLACE IS SO TIDY...
... ALWAYS WAS. I REMEMBER THE FIRST TIME I EVER CAME HERE... WE WERE JUST CO-WORKERS THEN...
... I DIDN'T THINK OF CLARK AS MUCH MORE THAN MY BIGGEST COMPETITION FOR THE CHOICE ASSIGNMENTS.
OH, JONATHAN... MARTHA... THEY MUST KNOW... THE WHOLE WORLD KNOWS BY NOW.
BY TOMORROW, FRIENDS WILL BE REASSURING THEM THAT CLARK WILL TURN UP ALL RIGHT!
I-IT JUST ABOUT KILLED ME WHEN ALLIE SAID THAT. I ALMOST SLIPPED... ALMOST TOLD HER...
... THAT CLARK WAS SUPERMAN.
I CAN'T LET THAT GET OUT. HE HAD SO MANY ENEMIES... SOME OF THEM WOULDN'T THINK TWICE ABOUT TAKING THEIR REVENGE ON HIS FAMILY.
I WAS ALMOST PART OF THAT FAMILY.
I-I MUST CALL THEM...
THEY LOVED CLARK SO MUCH...
WE ALL... LOVED HIM... SO VERY, VERY MUCH!
"HE INSPIRED GREAT PASSION IN MANY PEOPLE..."

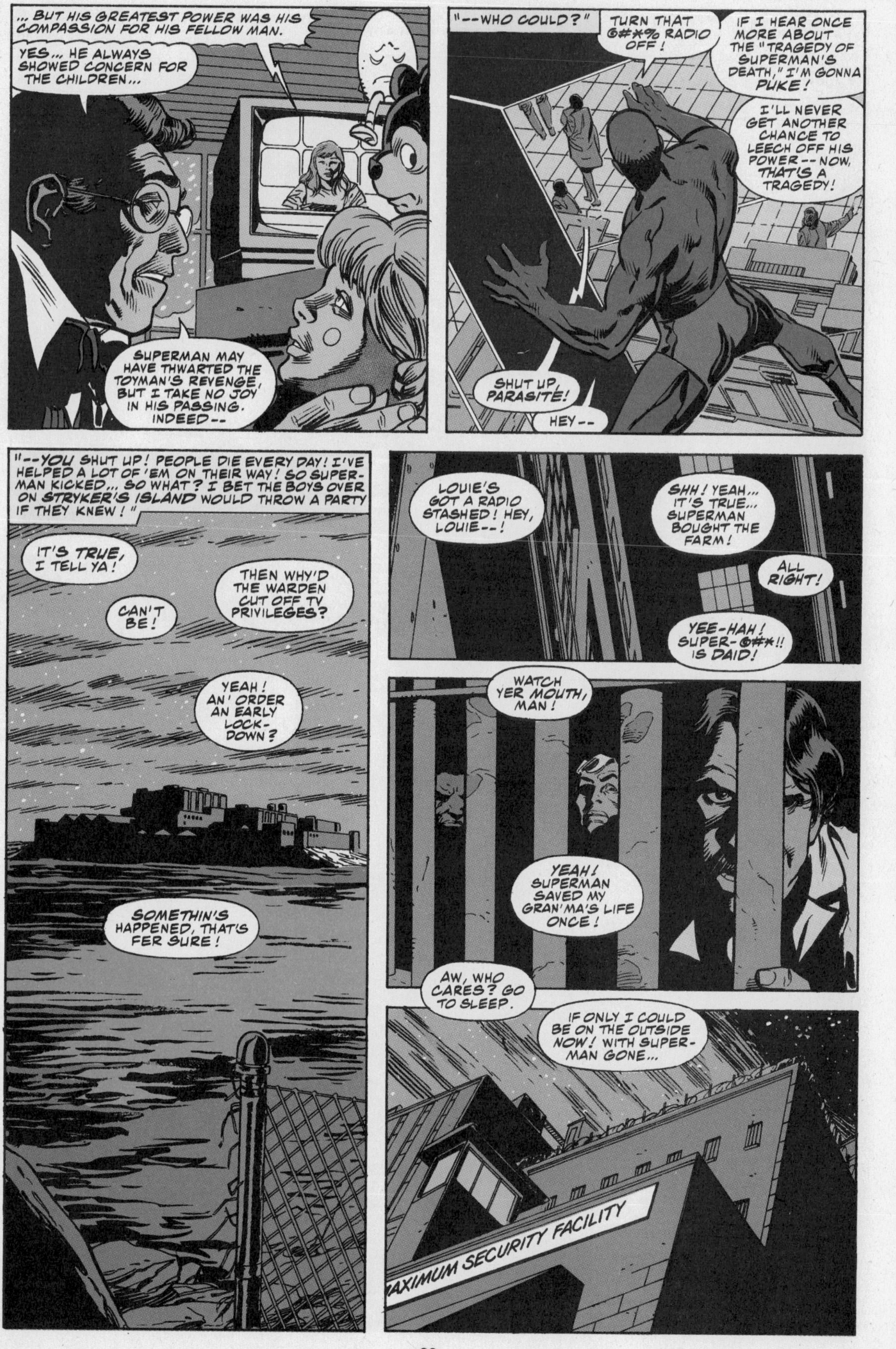
...BUT HIS GREATEST POWER WAS HIS COMPASSION FOR HIS FELLOW MAN.
YES... HE ALWAYS SHOWED CONCERN FOR THE CHILDREN...
SUPERMAN MAY HAVE THWARTED THE TOYMAN'S REVENGE, BUT I TAKE NO JOY IN HIS PASSING. INDEED--
"--WHO COULD?"
TURN THAT @#*% RADIO OFF!
IF I HEAR ONCE MORE ABOUT THE "TRAGEDY OF SUPERMAN'S DEATH," I'M GONNA PUKE!
I'LL NEVER GET ANOTHER CHANCE TO LEECH OFF HIS POWER--NOW, THAT'S A TRAGEDY!
SHUT UP, PARASITE!
HEY--
"--YOU SHUT UP! PEOPLE DIE EVERY DAY! I'VE HELPED A LOT OF 'EM ON THEIR WAY! SO SUPERMAN KICKED... SO WHAT? I BET THE BOYS OVER ON STRYKER'S ISLAND WOULD THROW A PARTY IF THEY KNEW!"
IT'S TRUE, I TELL YA!
CAN'T BE!
THEN WHY'D THE WARDEN CUT OFF TV PRIVILEGES?
YEAH! AN' ORDER AN EARLY LOCK-DOWN?
SOMETHIN'S HAPPENED, THAT'S FER SURE!
LOUIE'S GOT A RADIO STASHED! HEY, LOUIE--!
SHH! YEAH... IT'S TRUE... SUPERMAN BOUGHT THE FARM!
ALL RIGHT!
YEE-HAH! SUPER-@#*!! IS DAID!
WATCH YER MOUTH, MAN!
YEAH! SUPERMAN SAVED MY GRAN'MA'S LIFE ONCE!
AW, WHO CARES? GO TO SLEEP.
IF ONLY I COULD BE ON THE OUTSIDE NOW! WITH SUPERMAN GONE...
MAXIMUM SECURITY FACILITY

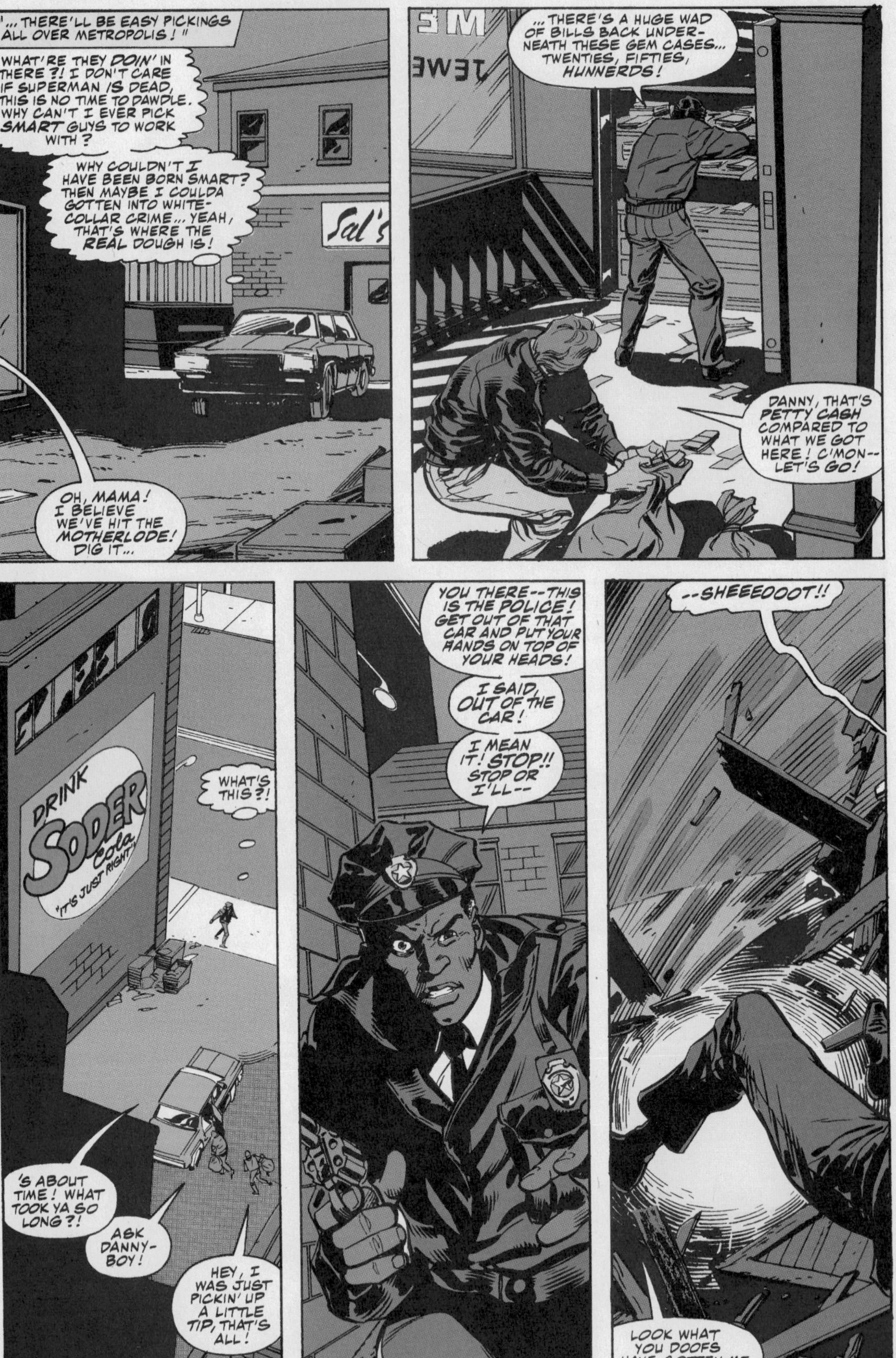
"... THERE'LL BE EASY PICKINGS ALL OVER METROPOLIS!"
WHAT'RE THEY DOIN' IN THERE?! I DON'T CARE IF SUPERMAN IS DEAD, THIS IS NO TIME TO DAWDLE. WHY CAN'T I EVER PICK SMART GUYS TO WORK WITH?
WHY COULDN'T I HAVE BEEN BORN SMART? THEN MAYBE I COULDA GOTTEN INTO WHITE-COLLAR CRIME... YEAH, THAT'S WHERE THE REAL DOUGH IS!
Sal's
OH, MAMA! I BELIEVE WE'VE HIT THE MOTHERLODE! DIG IT...
... THERE'S A HUGE WAD OF BILLS BACK UNDER-NEATH THESE GEM CASES... TWENTIES, FIFTIES, HUNNERDS!
DANNY, THAT'S PETTY CASH COMPARED TO WHAT WE GOT HERE! C'MON-- LET'S GO!
DRINK SODER Cola "IT'S JUST RIGHT!"
WHAT'S THIS?!
'S ABOUT TIME! WHAT TOOK YA SO LONG?!
ASK DANNY-BOY!
HEY, I WAS JUST PICKIN' UP A LITTLE TIP, THAT'S ALL!
YOU THERE--THIS IS THE POLICE! GET OUT OF THAT CAR AND PUT YOUR HANDS ON TOP OF YOUR HEADS!
I SAID, OUT OF THE CAR!
I MEAN IT! STOP!! STOP OR I'LL--
--SHEEEOOOT!!
LOOK WHAT YOU DOOFS HAVE GOTTEN ME INTO NOW!

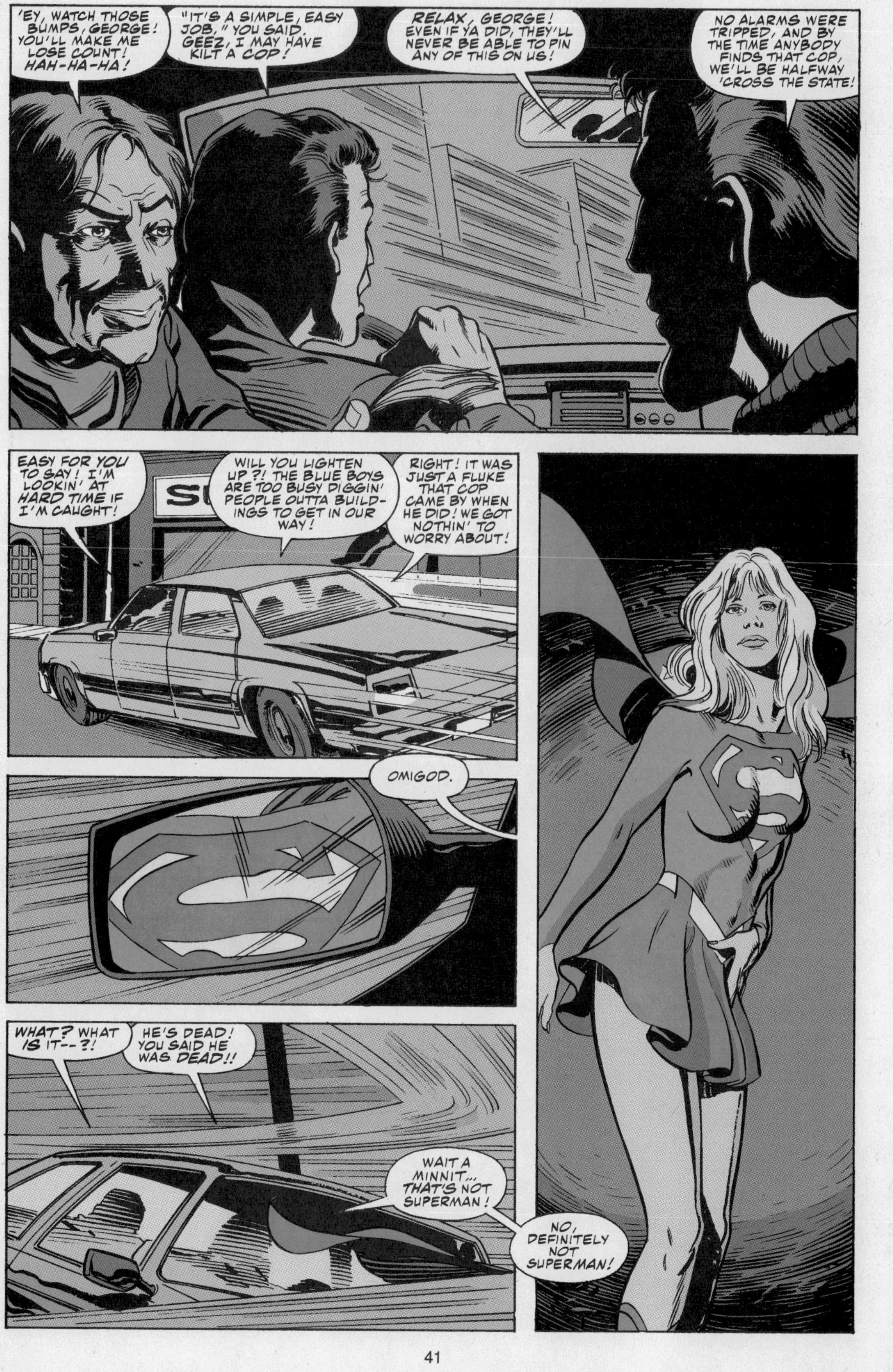
'EY, WATCH THOSE BUMPS, GEORGE! YOU'LL MAKE ME LOSE COUNT! HAH-HA-HA!
"IT'S A SIMPLE, EASY JOB," YOU SAID. GEEZ, I MAY HAVE KILT A COP!
RELAX, GEORGE! EVEN IF YA DID, THEY'LL NEVER BE ABLE TO PIN ANY OF THIS ON US!
NO ALARMS WERE TRIPPED, AND BY THE TIME ANYBODY FINDS THAT COP, WE'LL BE HALFWAY 'CROSS THE STATE!
EASY FOR YOU TO SAY! I'M LOOKIN' AT HARD TIME IF I'M CAUGHT!
WILL YOU LIGHTEN UP?! THE BLUE BOYS ARE TOO BUSY DIGGIN' PEOPLE OUTTA BUILD-INGS TO GET IN OUR WAY!
RIGHT! IT WAS JUST A FLUKE THAT COP CAME BY WHEN HE DID! WE GOT NOTHIN' TO WORRY ABOUT!
OMIGOD.
WHAT? WHAT IS IT--?!
HE'S DEAD! YOU SAID HE WAS DEAD!!
WAIT A MINNIT... THAT'S NOT SUPERMAN!
NO, DEFINITELY NOT SUPERMAN!

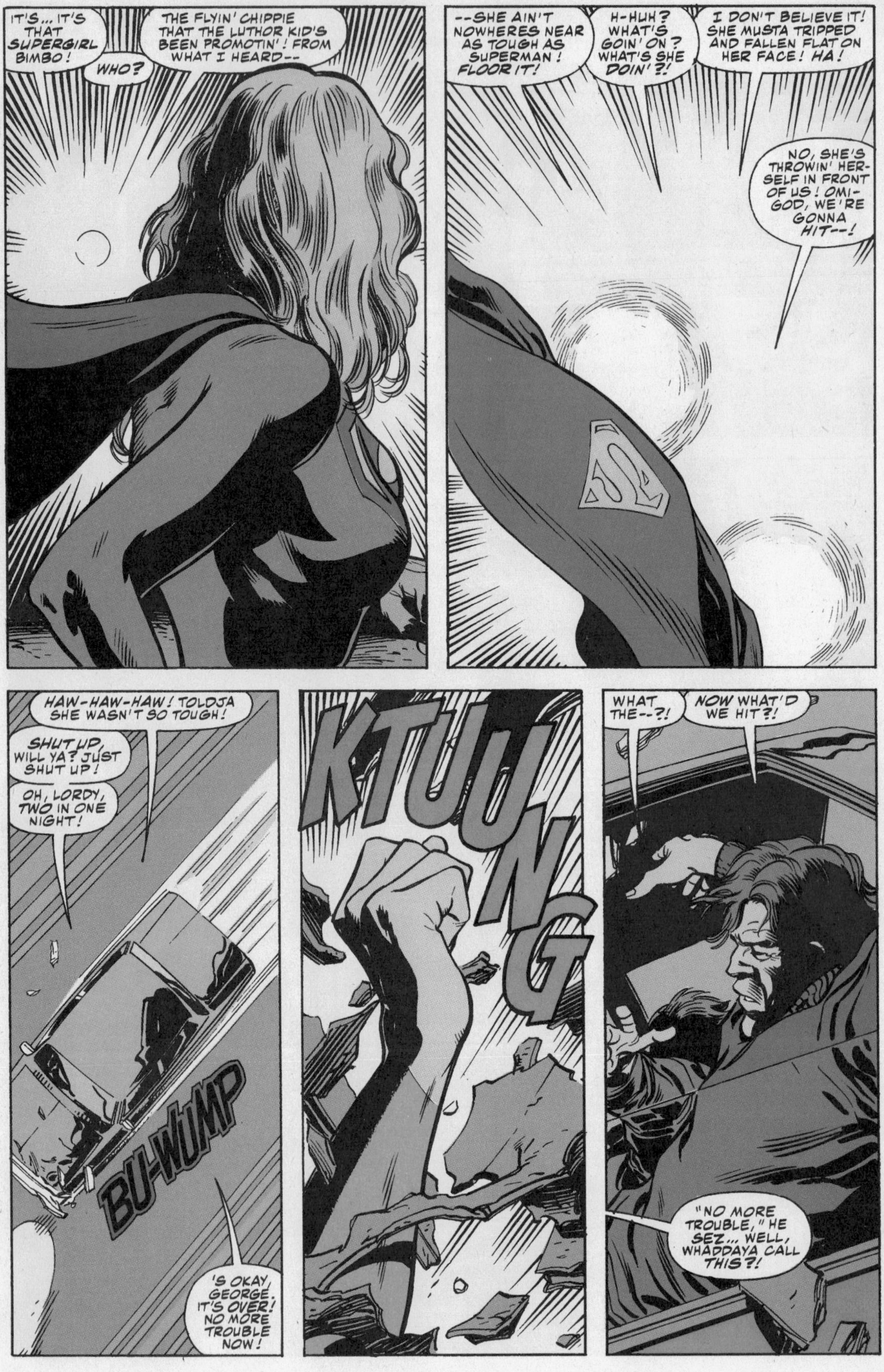
IT'S... IT'S THAT SUPERGIRL BIMBO!
WHO?
THE FLYIN' CHIPPIE THAT THE LUTHOR KID'S BEEN PROMOTIN'! FROM WHAT I HEARD--
--SHE AIN'T NOWHERES NEAR AS TOUGH AS SUPERMAN! FLOOR IT!
H-HUH? WHAT'S GOIN' ON? WHAT'S SHE DOIN'?!
I DON'T BELIEVE IT! SHE MUSTA TRIPPED AND FALLEN FLAT ON HER FACE! HA!
NO, SHE'S THROWIN' HERSELF IN FRONT OF US! OMIGOD, WE'RE GONNA HIT--!
HAW-HAW-HAW! TOLDJA SHE WASN'T SO TOUGH!
SHUT UP, WILL YA? JUST SHUT UP!
OH, LORDY, TWO IN ONE NIGHT!
BU-WUMP
'S OKAY, GEORGE. IT'S OVER! NO MORE TROUBLE NOW!
KTUUNG
WHAT THE--?!
NOW WHAT'D WE HIT?!
"NO MORE TROUBLE," HE SEZ... WELL, WHADDAYA CALL THIS?!

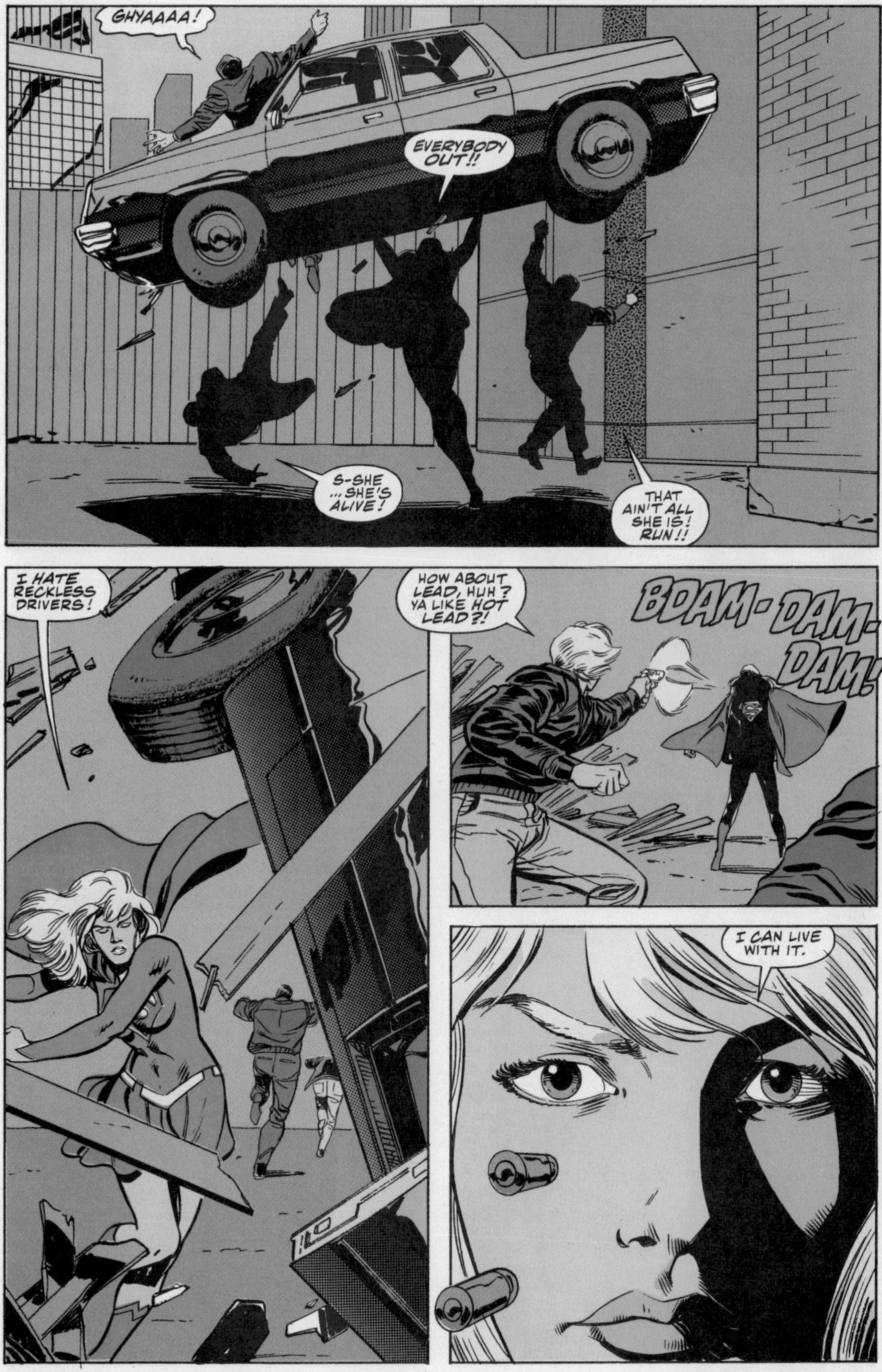
GHYAAAA!
EVERYBODY OUT!!
S-SHE ...SHE'S ALIVE!
THAT AIN'T ALL SHE IS! RUN!!
I HATE RECKLESS DRIVERS!
HOW ABOUT LEAD, HUH? YA LIKE HOT LEAD?!
BDAM-DAM-DAM-DAM!
I CAN LIVE WITH IT.

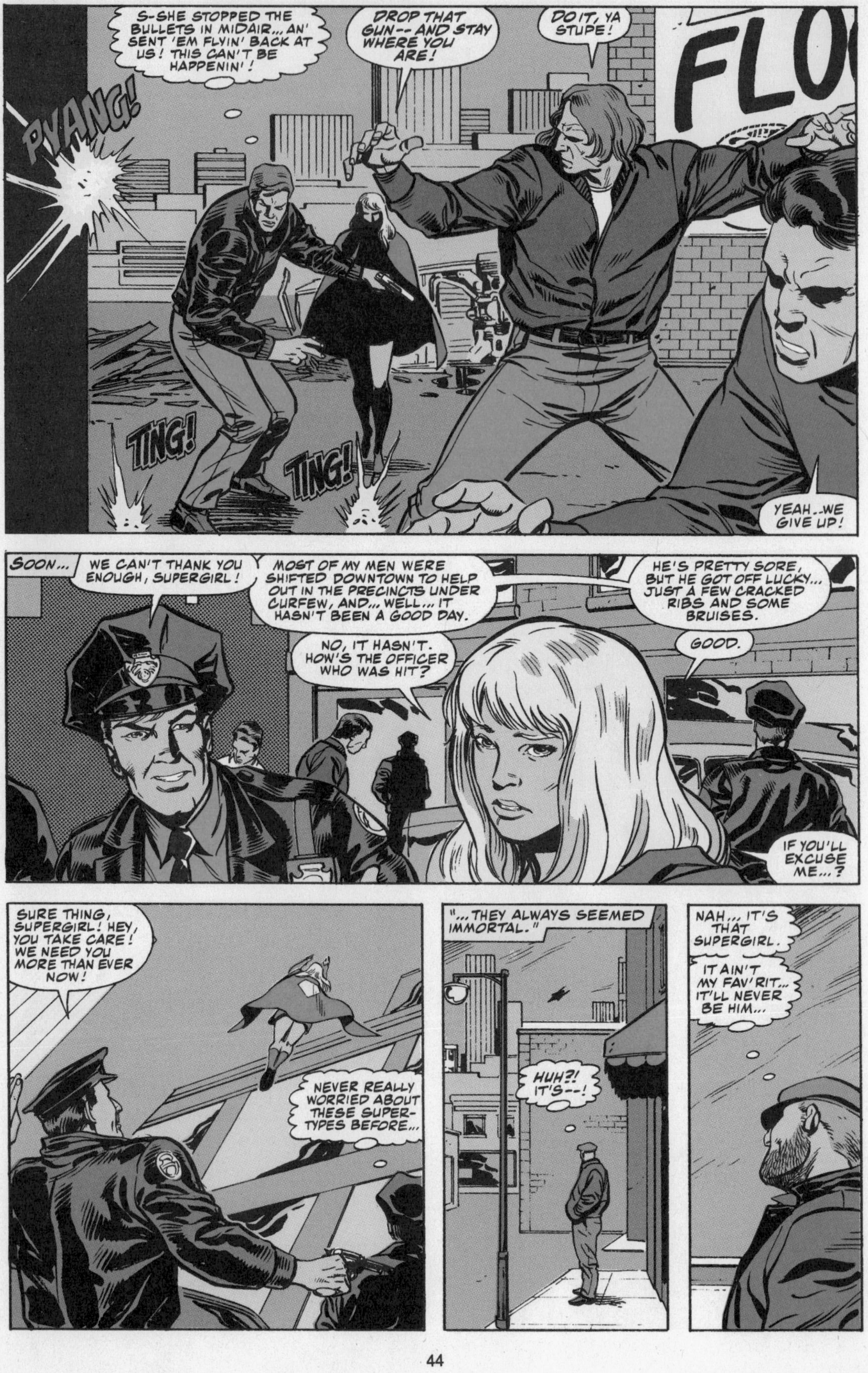
S-SHE STOPPED THE BULLETS IN MIDAIR... AN' SENT 'EM FLYIN' BACK AT US! THIS CAN'T BE HAPPENIN'!
PYANG!
DROP THAT GUN-- AND STAY WHERE YOU ARE!
DO IT, YA STUPE!
FLO
TING!
TING!
YEAH..WE GIVE UP!
SOON...
WE CAN'T THANK YOU ENOUGH, SUPERGIRL!
MOST OF MY MEN WERE SHIFTED DOWNTOWN TO HELP OUT IN THE PRECINCTS UNDER CURFEW, AND... WELL... IT HASN'T BEEN A GOOD DAY.
NO, IT HASN'T. HOW'S THE OFFICER WHO WAS HIT?
HE'S PRETTY SORE, BUT HE GOT OFF LUCKY... JUST A FEW CRACKED RIBS AND SOME BRUISES.
GOOD.
IF YOU'LL EXCUSE ME...?
SURE THING, SUPERGIRL! HEY, YOU TAKE CARE! WE NEED YOU MORE THAN EVER NOW!
NEVER REALLY WORRIED ABOUT THESE SUPER-TYPES BEFORE...
"...THEY ALWAYS SEEMED IMMORTAL."
HUH?! IT'S--!
NAH... IT'S THAT SUPERGIRL.
IT AIN'T MY FAV'RIT... IT'LL NEVER BE HIM...

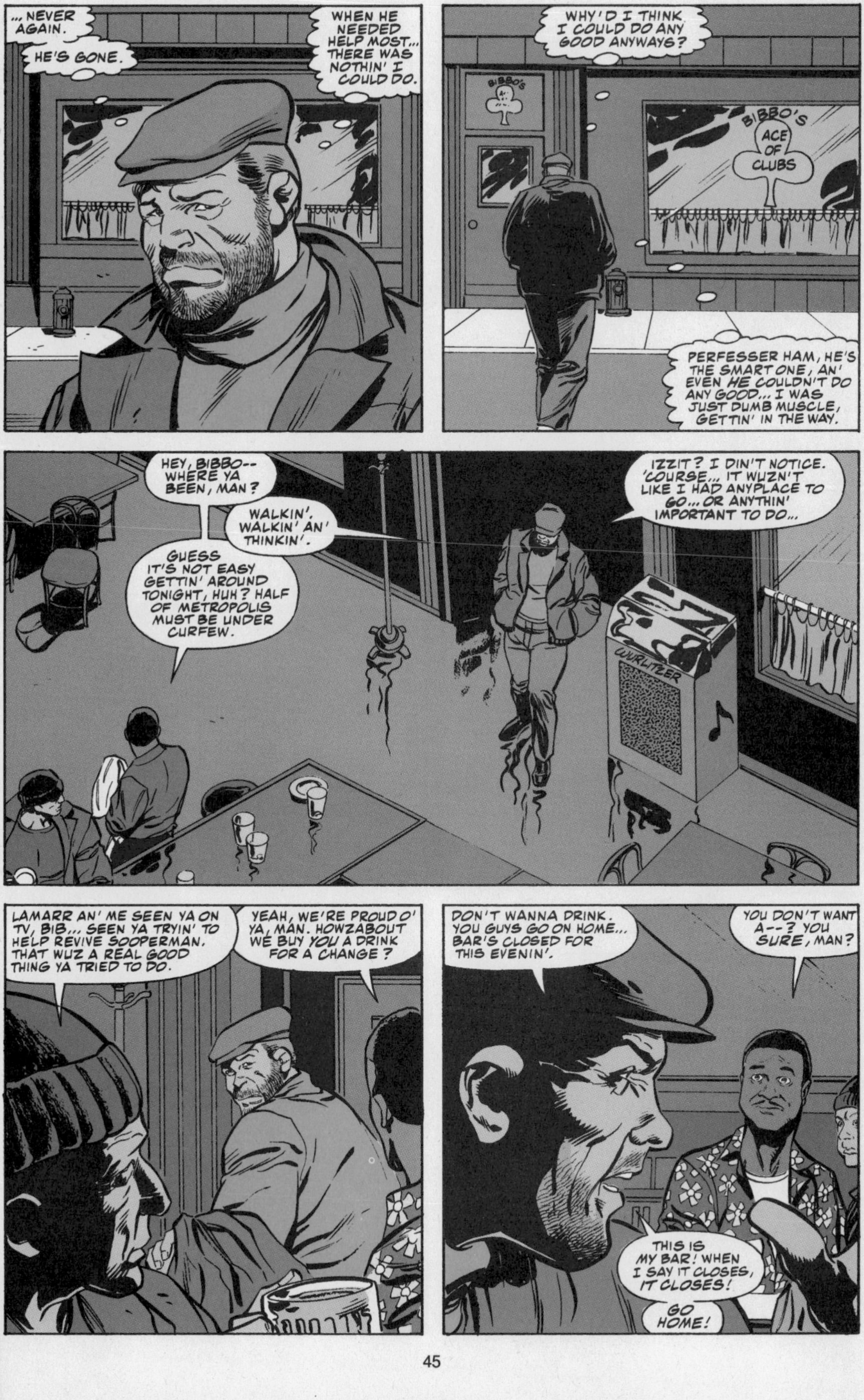
...NEVER AGAIN.
HE'S GONE.
WHEN HE NEEDED HELP MOST... THERE WAS NOTHIN' I COULD DO.
WHY'D I THINK I COULD DO ANY GOOD ANYWAYS?
BIBBO'S
BIBBO'S ACE OF CLUBS
PERFESSER HAM, HE'S THE SMART ONE, AN' EVEN HE COULDN'T DO ANY GOOD... I WAS JUST DUMB MUSCLE, GETTIN' IN THE WAY.
HEY, BIBBO-- WHERE YA BEEN, MAN?
WALKIN'. WALKIN' AN' THINKIN'.
GUESS IT'S NOT EASY GETTIN' AROUND TONIGHT, HUH? HALF OF METROPOLIS MUST BE UNDER CURFEW.
IZZIT? I DIN'T NOTICE. 'COURSE... IT WUZN'T LIKE I HAD ANYPLACE TO GO... OR ANYTHIN' IMPORTANT TO DO...
WURLITZER
LAMARR AN' ME SEEN YA ON TV, BIB... SEEN YA TRYIN' TO HELP REVIVE SOOPERMAN. THAT WUZ A REAL GOOD THING YA TRIED TO DO.
YEAH, WE'RE PROUD O' YA, MAN. HOWZABOUT WE BUY YOU A DRINK FOR A CHANGE?
DON'T WANNA DRINK. YOU GUYS GO ON HOME... BAR'S CLOSED FOR THIS EVENIN'.
YOU DON'T WANT A--? YOU SURE, MAN?
THIS IS MY BAR! WHEN I SAY IT CLOSES, IT CLOSES!
GO HOME!

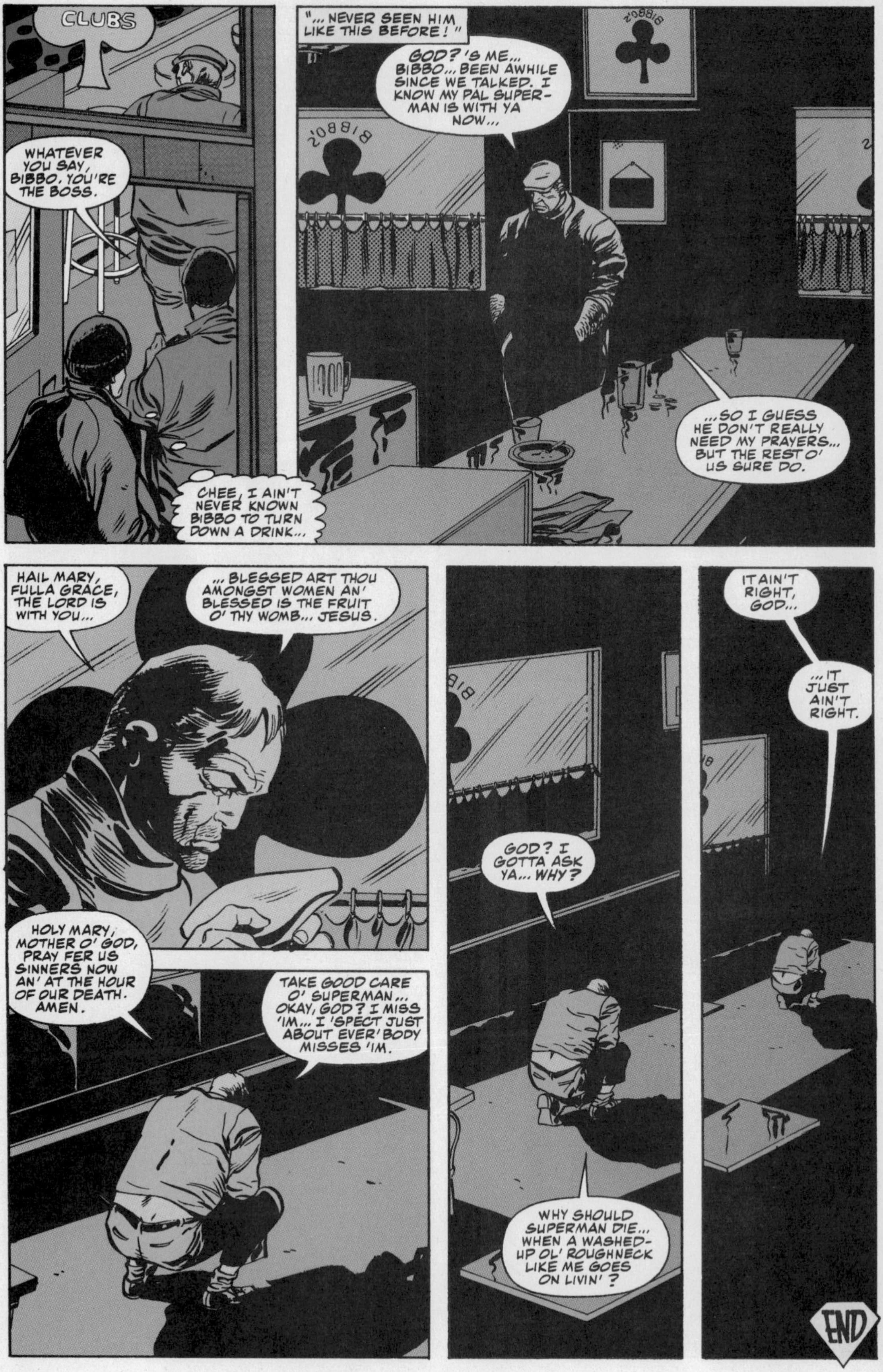
CLUBS
WHATEVER YOU SAY, BIBBO. YOU'RE THE BOSS.
CHEE, I AIN'T NEVER KNOWN BIBBO TO TURN DOWN A DRINK...
"... NEVER SEEN HIM LIKE THIS BEFORE!"
GOD? 'S ME... BIBBO... BEEN AWHILE SINCE WE TALKED. I KNOW MY PAL SUPER-MAN IS WITH YA NOW...
...SO I GUESS HE DON'T REALLY NEED MY PRAYERS... BUT THE REST O' US SURE DO.
HAIL MARY, FULLA GRACE, THE LORD IS WITH YOU...
... BLESSED ART THOU AMONGST WOMEN AN' BLESSED IS THE FRUIT O' THY WOMB... JESUS.
HOLY MARY, MOTHER O' GOD, PRAY FER US SINNERS NOW AN' AT THE HOUR OF OUR DEATH. AMEN.
TAKE GOOD CARE O' SUPERMAN... OKAY, GOD? I MISS 'IM... I 'SPECT JUST ABOUT EVER' BODY MISSES 'IM.
GOD? I GOTTA ASK YA... WHY?
WHY SHOULD SUPERMAN DIE... WHEN A WASHED-UP OL' ROUGHNECK LIKE ME GOES ON LIVIN'?
IT AIN'T RIGHT, GOD...
...IT JUST AIN'T RIGHT.
END

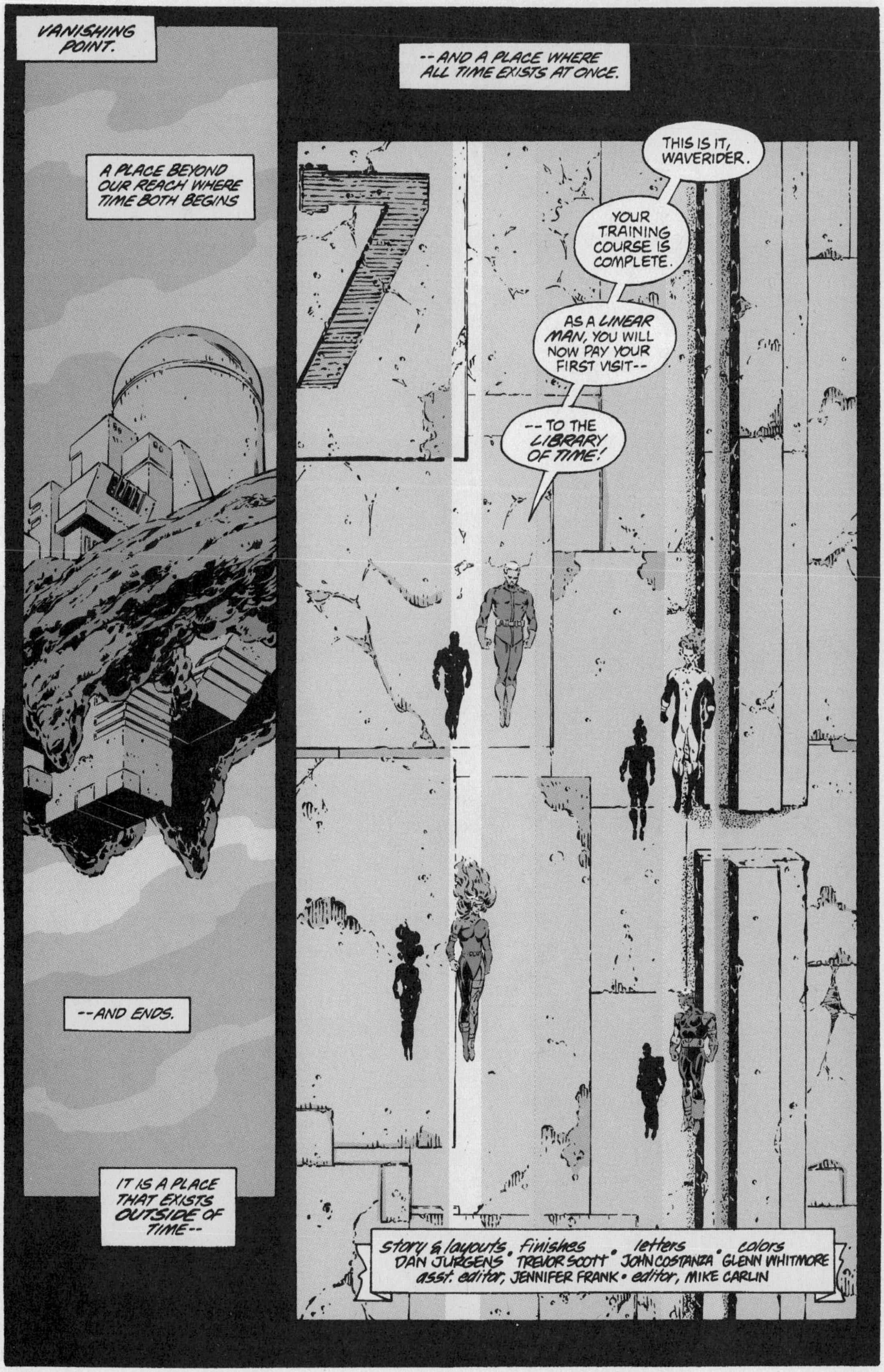
VANISHING POINT.
A PLACE BEYOND OUR REACH WHERE TIME BOTH BEGINS
--AND ENDS.
IT IS A PLACE THAT EXISTS OUTSIDE OF TIME--
--AND A PLACE WHERE ALL TIME EXISTS AT ONCE.
THIS IS IT, WAVERIDER.
YOUR TRAINING COURSE IS COMPLETE.
AS A LINEAR MAN, YOU WILL NOW PAY YOUR FIRST VISIT--
--TO THE LIBRARY OF TIME!
story & layouts DAN JURGENS • finishes TREVOR SCOTT • letters JOHN COSTANZA • colors GLENN WHITMORE
asst. editor, JENNIFER FRANK • editor, MIKE CARLIN

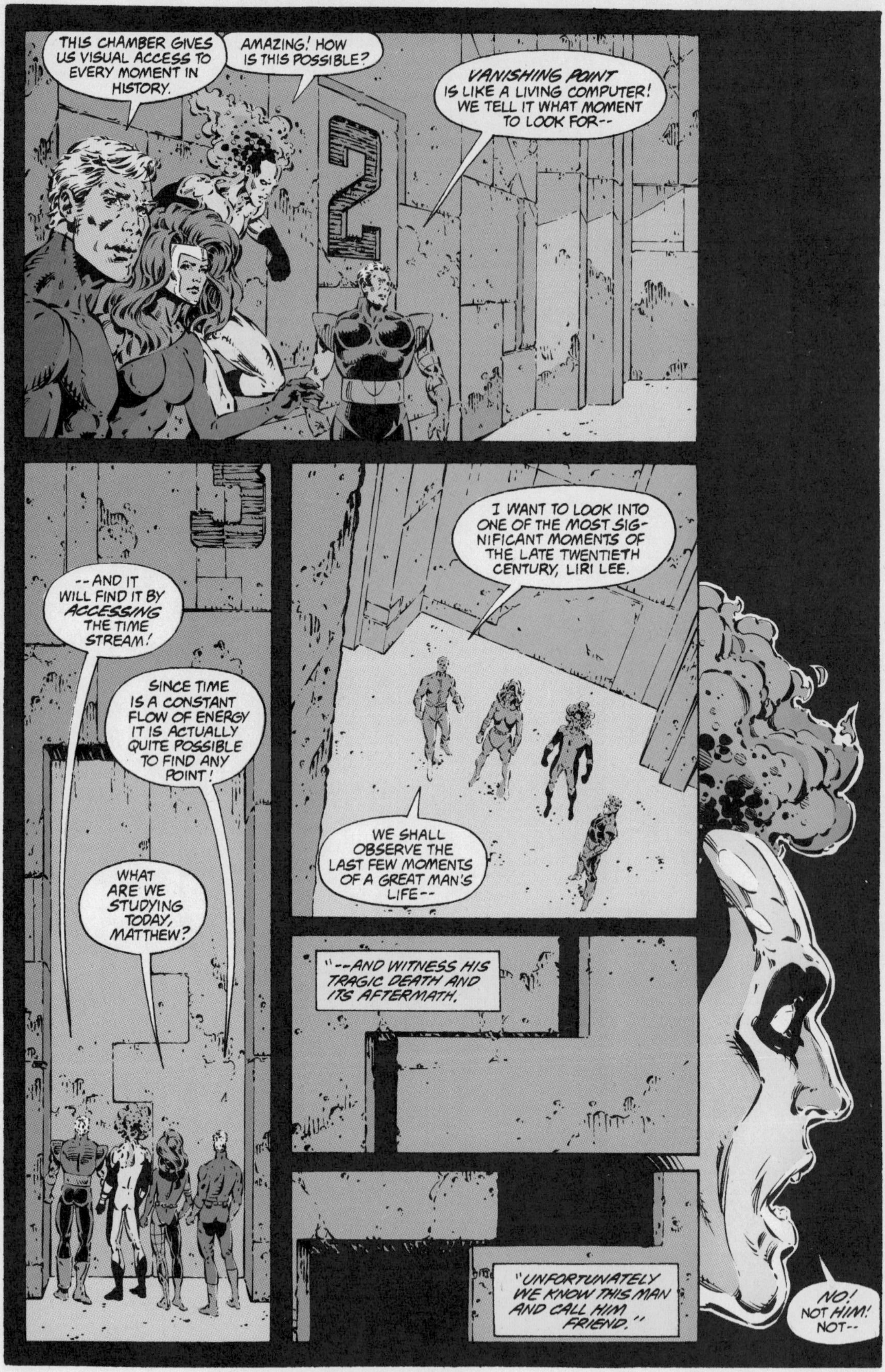
THIS CHAMBER GIVES US VISUAL ACCESS TO EVERY MOMENT IN HISTORY.
AMAZING! HOW IS THIS POSSIBLE?
VANISHING POINT IS LIKE A LIVING COMPUTER! WE TELL IT WHAT MOMENT TO LOOK FOR--
--AND IT WILL FIND IT BY ACCESSING THE TIME STREAM!
SINCE TIME IS A CONSTANT FLOW OF ENERGY IT IS ACTUALLY QUITE POSSIBLE TO FIND ANY POINT!
WHAT ARE WE STUDYING TODAY, MATTHEW?
I WANT TO LOOK INTO ONE OF THE MOST SIGNIFICANT MOMENTS OF THE LATE TWENTIETH CENTURY, LIRI LEE.
WE SHALL OBSERVE THE LAST FEW MOMENTS OF A GREAT MAN'S LIFE--
"--AND WITNESS HIS TRAGIC DEATH AND ITS AFTERMATH.
"UNFORTUNATELY WE KNOW THIS MAN AND CALL HIM FRIEND."
NO! NOT HIM! NOT--

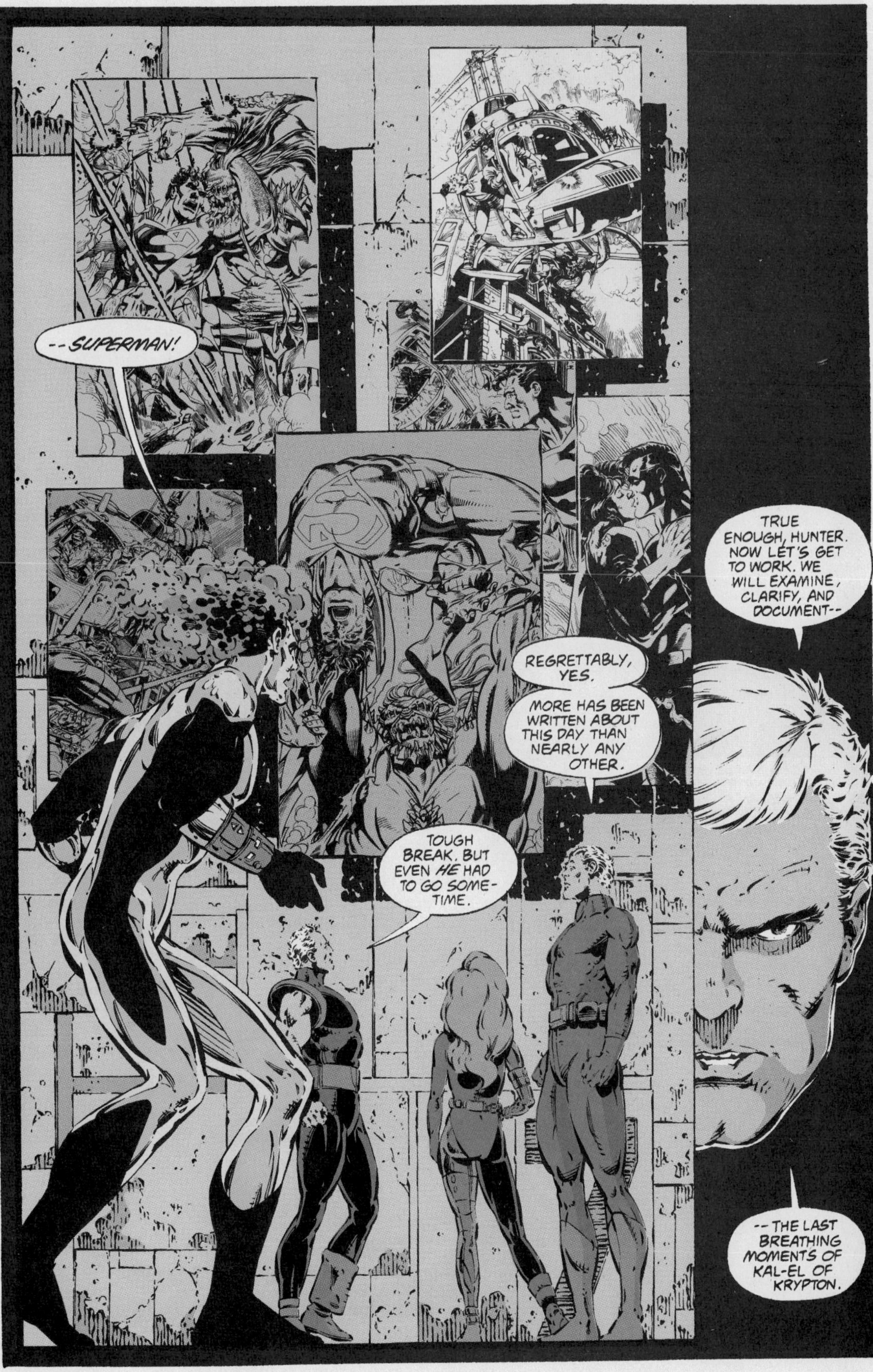
--SUPERMAN!
TRUE ENOUGH, HUNTER. NOW LET'S GET TO WORK. WE WILL EXAMINE, CLARIFY, AND DOCUMENT--
REGRETTABLY, YES.
MORE HAS BEEN WRITTEN ABOUT THIS DAY THAN NEARLY ANY OTHER.
TOUGH BREAK. BUT EVEN HE HAD TO GO SOMETIME.
--THE LAST BREATHING MOMENTS OF KAL-EL OF KRYPTON.

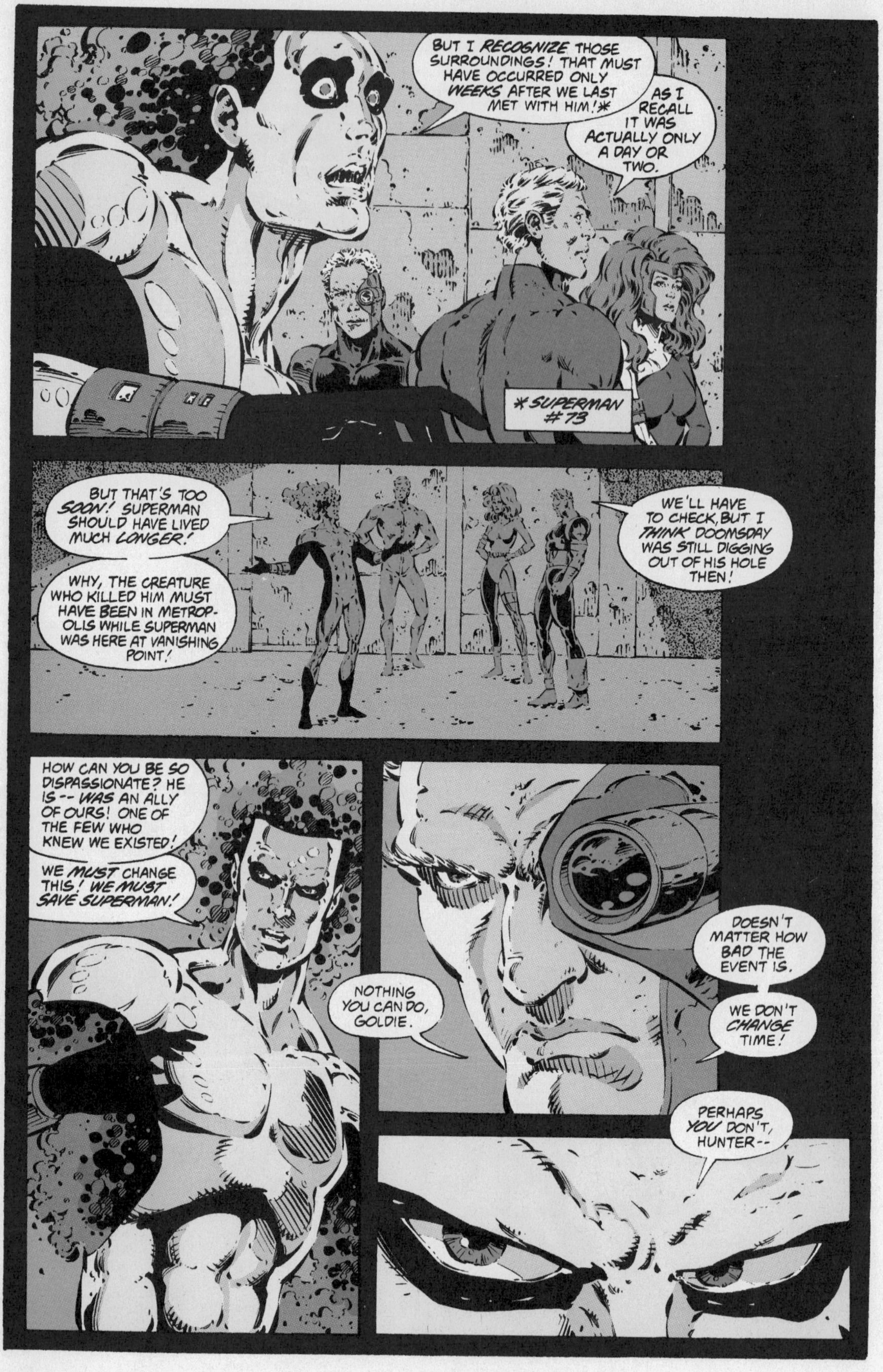
BUT I RECOGNIZE THOSE SURROUNDINGS! THAT MUST HAVE OCCURRED ONLY WEEKS AFTER WE LAST MET WITH HIM!*
AS I RECALL IT WAS ACTUALLY ONLY A DAY OR TWO.
*SUPERMAN #73
BUT THAT'S TOO SOON! SUPERMAN SHOULD HAVE LIVED MUCH LONGER!
WHY, THE CREATURE WHO KILLED HIM MUST HAVE BEEN IN METROPOLIS WHILE SUPERMAN WAS HERE AT VANISHING POINT!
WE'LL HAVE TO CHECK, BUT I THINK DOOMSDAY WAS STILL DIGGING OUT OF HIS HOLE THEN!
HOW CAN YOU BE SO DISPASSIONATE? HE IS -- WAS AN ALLY OF OURS! ONE OF THE FEW WHO KNEW WE EXISTED!
WE MUST CHANGE THIS! WE MUST SAVE SUPERMAN!
NOTHING YOU CAN DO, GOLDIE.
DOESN'T MATTER HOW BAD THE EVENT IS.
WE DON'T CHANGE TIME!
PERHAPS YOU DON'T, HUNTER--

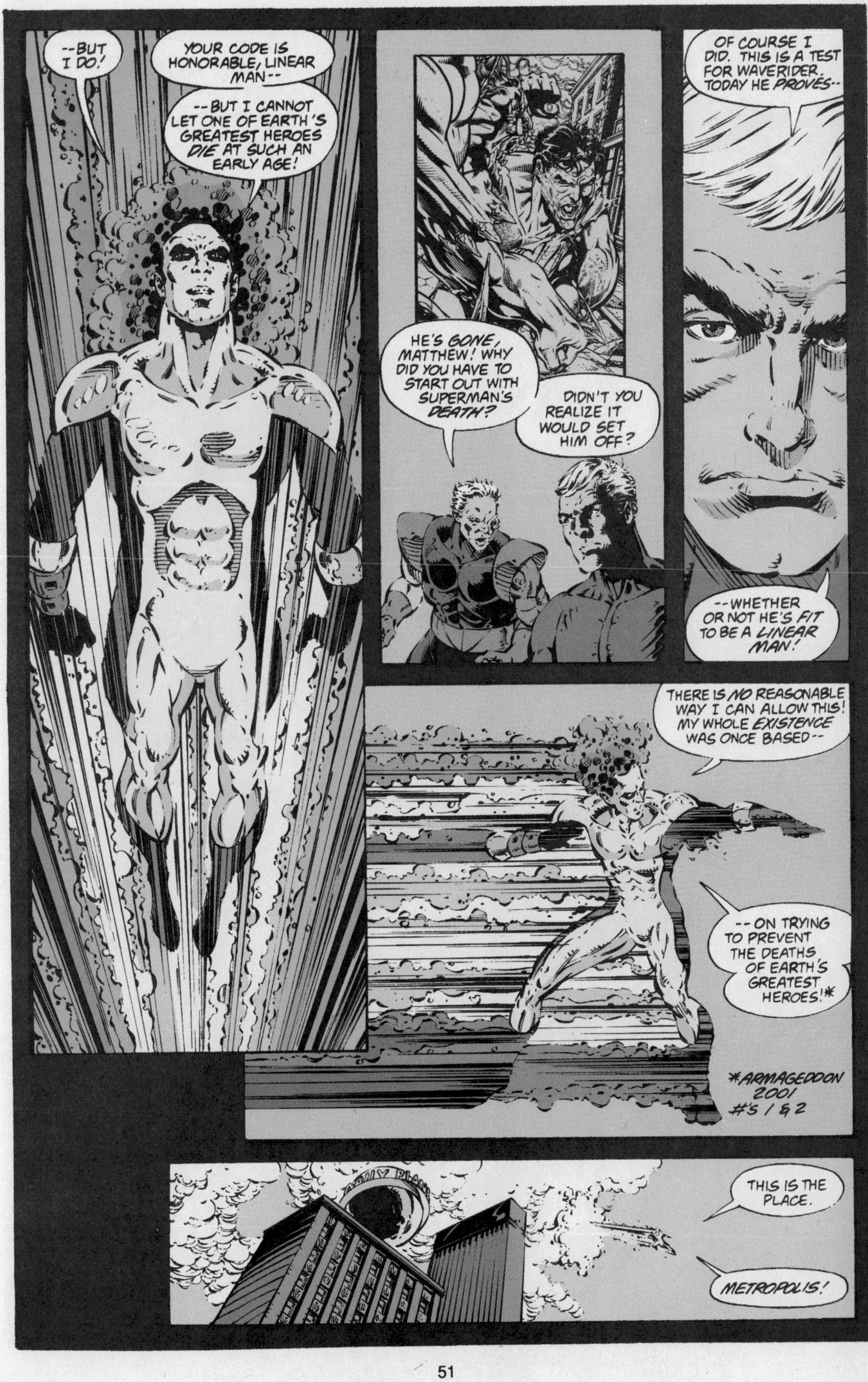
--BUT I DO!
YOUR CODE IS HONORABLE, LINEAR MAN--
--BUT I CANNOT LET ONE OF EARTH'S GREATEST HEROES DIE AT SUCH AN EARLY AGE!
HE'S GONE, MATTHEW! WHY DID YOU HAVE TO START OUT WITH SUPERMAN'S DEATH?
DIDN'T YOU REALIZE IT WOULD SET HIM OFF?
OF COURSE I DID. THIS IS A TEST FOR WAVERIDER. TODAY HE PROVES--
--WHETHER OR NOT HE'S FIT TO BE A LINEAR MAN!
THERE IS NO REASONABLE WAY I CAN ALLOW THIS! MY WHOLE EXISTENCE WAS ONCE BASED--
--ON TRYING TO PREVENT THE DEATHS OF EARTH'S GREATEST HEROES!*
*ARMAGEDDON 2001 #'S 1 & 2
THIS IS THE PLACE.
METROPOLIS!

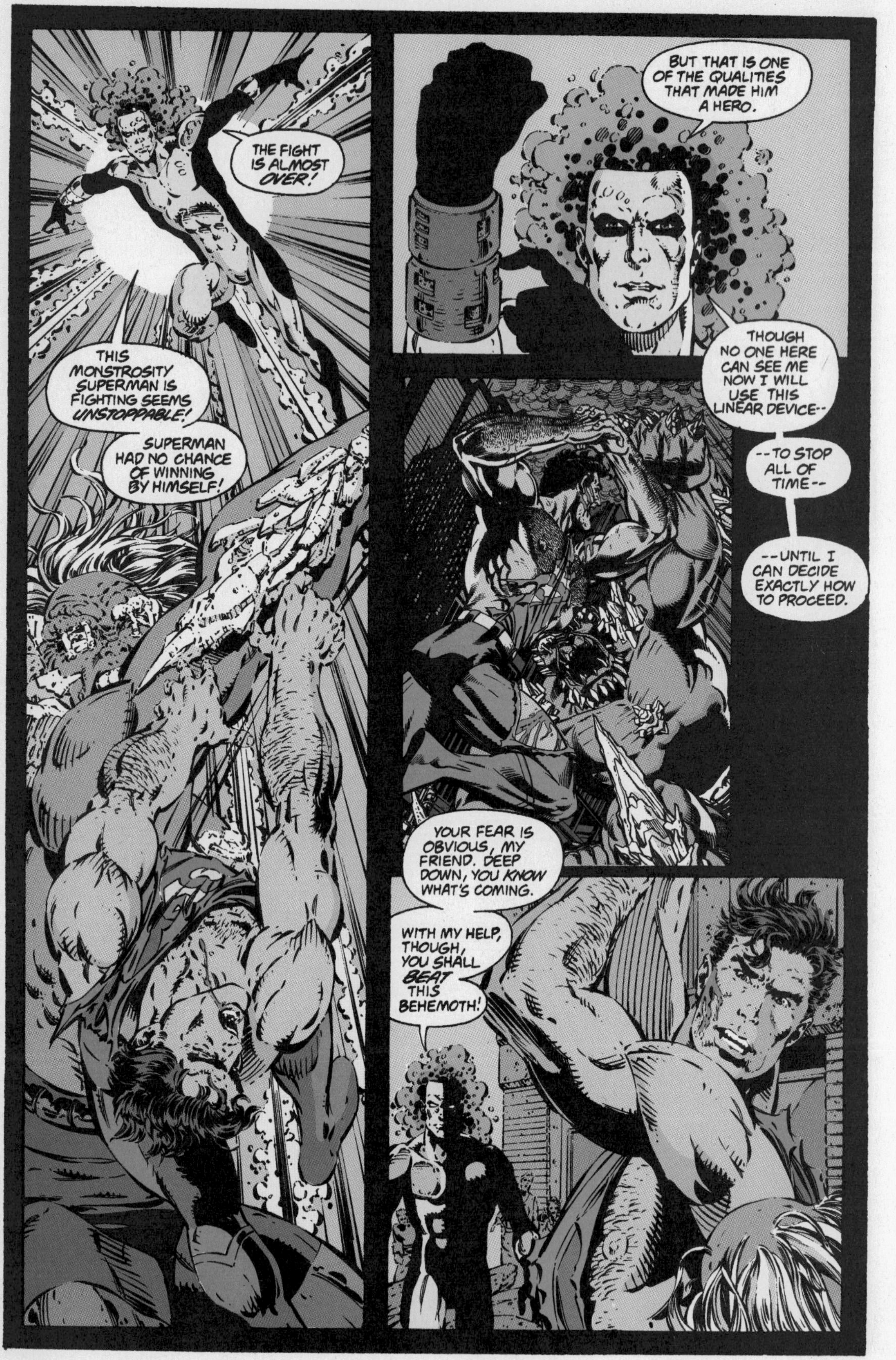
THE FIGHT IS ALMOST OVER!
THIS MONSTROSITY SUPERMAN IS FIGHTING SEEMS UNSTOPPABLE!
SUPERMAN HAD NO CHANCE OF WINNING BY HIMSELF!
BUT THAT IS ONE OF THE QUALITIES THAT MADE HIM A HERO.
THOUGH NO ONE HERE CAN SEE ME NOW I WILL USE THIS LINEAR DEVICE--
--TO STOP ALL OF TIME--
--UNTIL I CAN DECIDE EXACTLY HOW TO PROCEED.
YOUR FEAR IS OBVIOUS, MY FRIEND. DEEP DOWN, YOU KNOW WHAT'S COMING.
WITH MY HELP, THOUGH, YOU SHALL BEAT THIS BEHEMOTH!

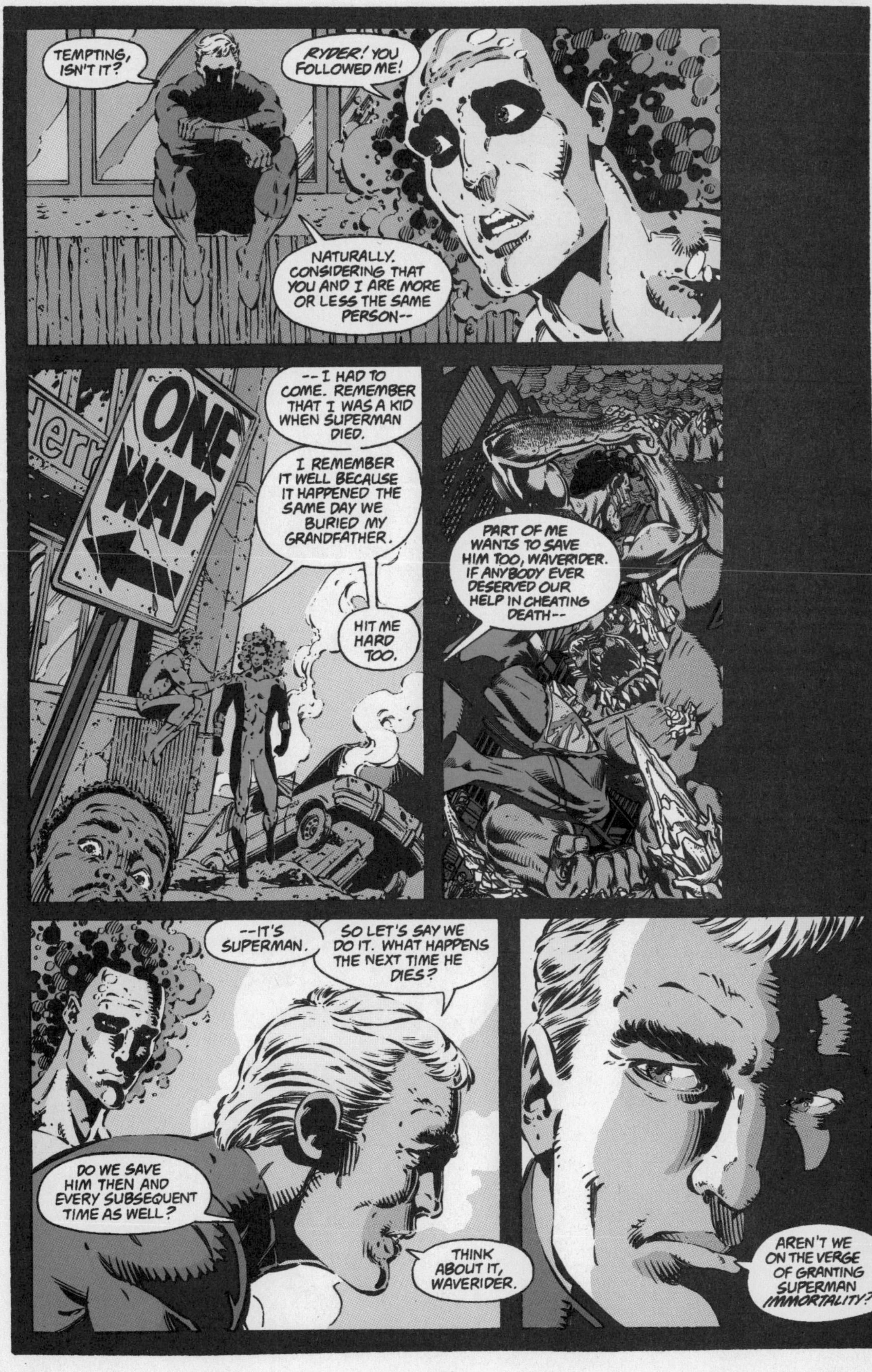
TEMPTING, ISN'T IT?
RYDER! YOU FOLLOWED ME!
NATURALLY. CONSIDERING THAT YOU AND I ARE MORE OR LESS THE SAME PERSON--
ONE WAY
--I HAD TO COME. REMEMBER THAT I WAS A KID WHEN SUPERMAN DIED.
I REMEMBER IT WELL BECAUSE IT HAPPENED THE SAME DAY WE BURIED MY GRANDFATHER.
HIT ME HARD TOO.
PART OF ME WANTS TO SAVE HIM TOO, WAVERIDER. IF ANYBODY EVER DESERVED OUR HELP IN CHEATING DEATH--
--IT'S SUPERMAN.
SO LET'S SAY WE DO IT. WHAT HAPPENS THE NEXT TIME HE DIES?
DO WE SAVE HIM THEN AND EVERY SUBSEQUENT TIME AS WELL?
THINK ABOUT IT, WAVERIDER.
AREN'T WE ON THE VERGE OF GRANTING SUPERMAN *IMMORTALITY*?

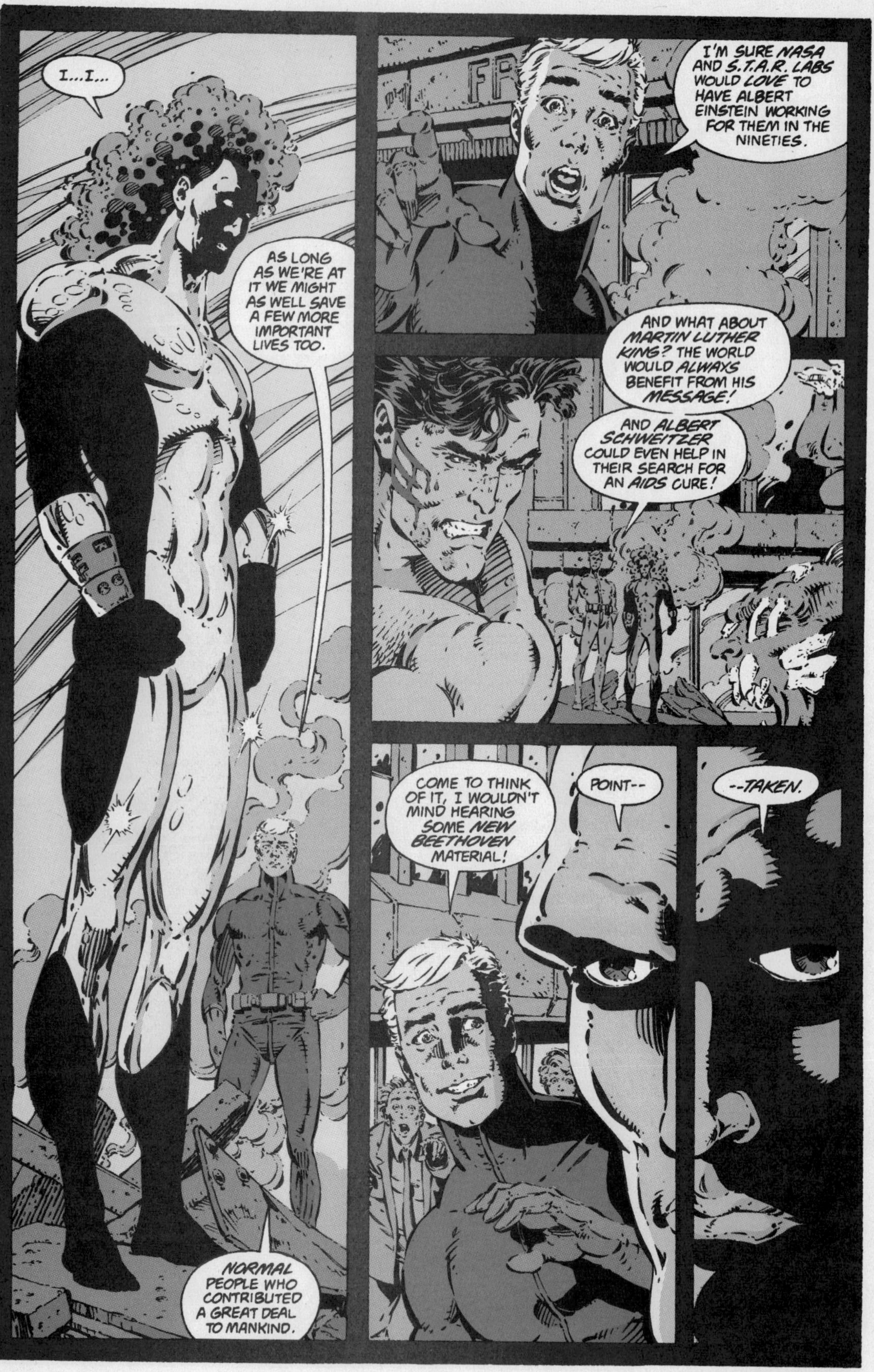
I...I...
AS LONG AS WE'RE AT IT WE MIGHT AS WELL SAVE A FEW MORE IMPORTANT LIVES TOO.
NORMAL PEOPLE WHO CONTRIBUTED A GREAT DEAL TO MANKIND.
I'M SURE NASA AND S.T.A.R. LABS WOULD LOVE TO HAVE ALBERT EINSTEIN WORKING FOR THEM IN THE NINETIES.
AND WHAT ABOUT MARTIN LUTHER KING? THE WORLD WOULD ALWAYS BENEFIT FROM HIS MESSAGE!
AND ALBERT SCHWEITZER COULD EVEN HELP IN THEIR SEARCH FOR AN AIDS CURE!
COME TO THINK OF IT, I WOULDN'T MIND HEARING SOME NEW BEETHOVEN MATERIAL!
POINT--
--TAKEN.

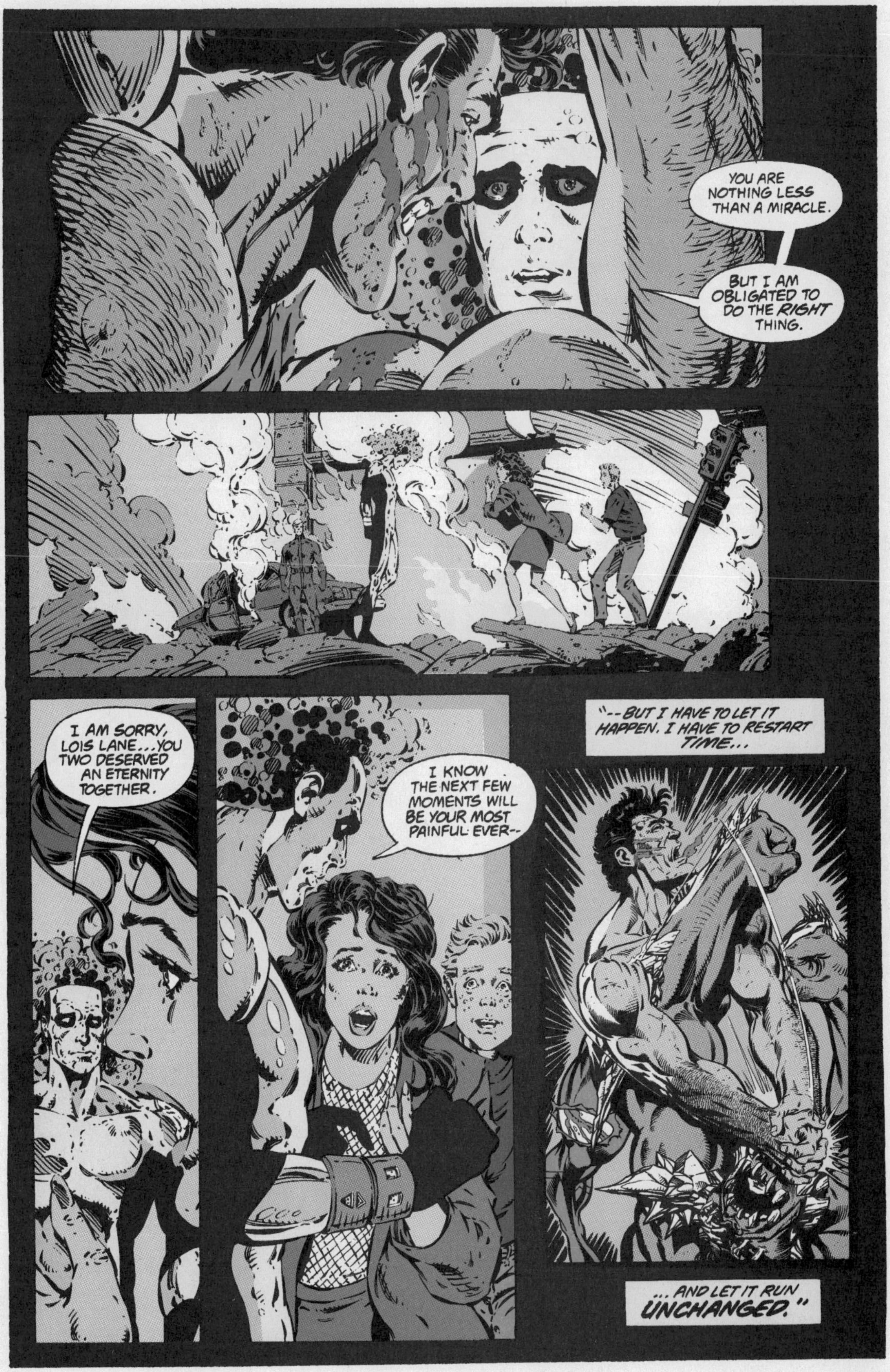
YOU ARE NOTHING LESS THAN A MIRACLE.
BUT I AM OBLIGATED TO DO THE RIGHT THING.
I AM SORRY, LOIS LANE...YOU TWO DESERVED AN ETERNITY TOGETHER.
I KNOW THE NEXT FEW MOMENTS WILL BE YOUR MOST PAINFUL EVER--
"--BUT I HAVE TO LET IT HAPPEN. I HAVE TO RESTART TIME...
...AND LET IT RUN UNCHANGED."

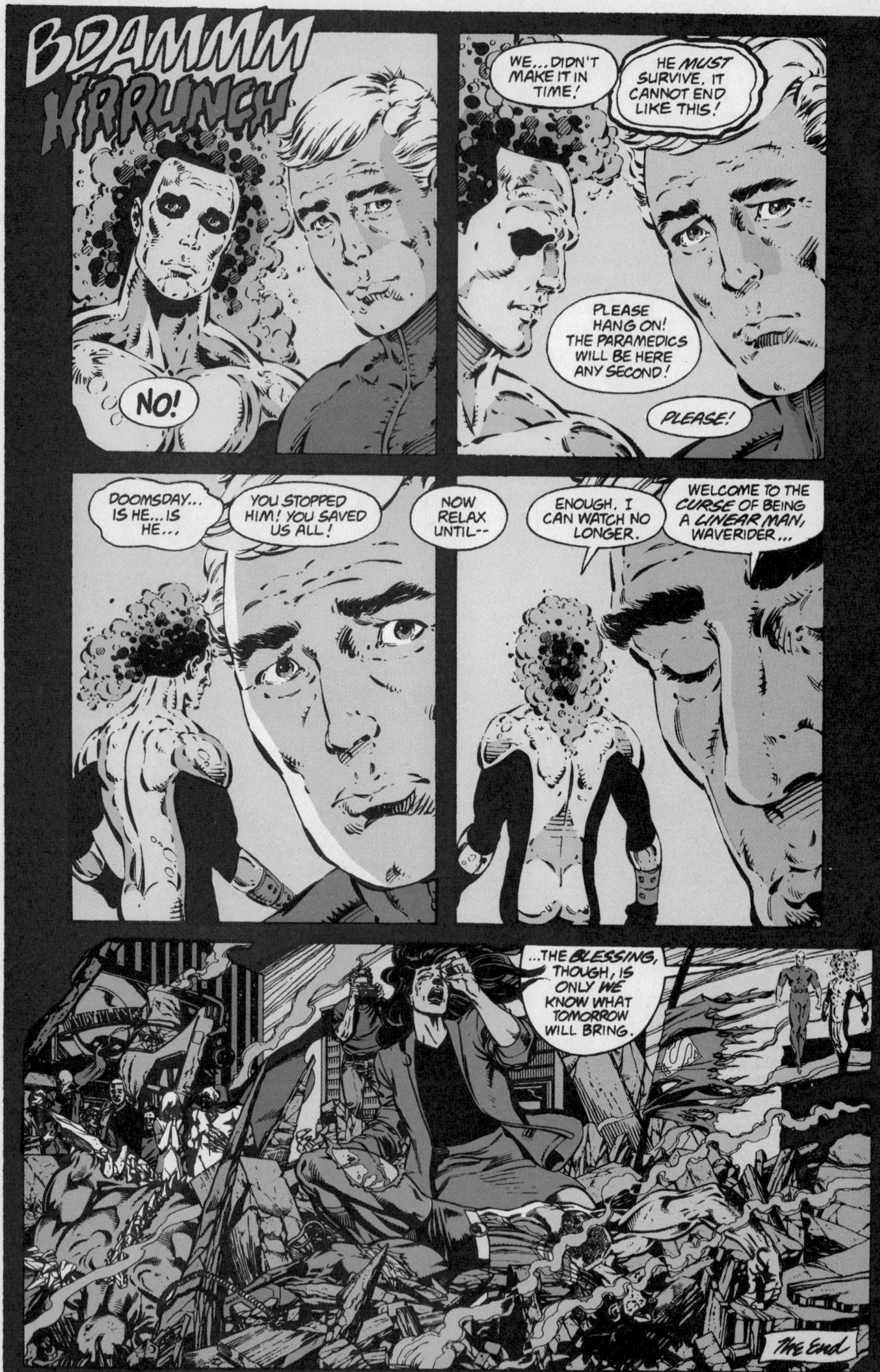
BDAMMM
KRRUNCH
NO!
WE... DIDN'T MAKE IT IN TIME!
HE MUST SURVIVE. IT CANNOT END LIKE THIS!
PLEASE HANG ON! THE PARAMEDICS WILL BE HERE ANY SECOND!
PLEASE!
DOOMSDAY... IS HE... IS HE...
YOU STOPPED HIM! YOU SAVED US ALL!
NOW RELAX UNTIL--
ENOUGH. I CAN WATCH NO LONGER.
WELCOME TO THE CURSE OF BEING A LINEAR MAN, WAVERIDER...
...THE BLESSING, THOUGH, IS ONLY WE KNOW WHAT TOMORROW WILL BRING.
The End

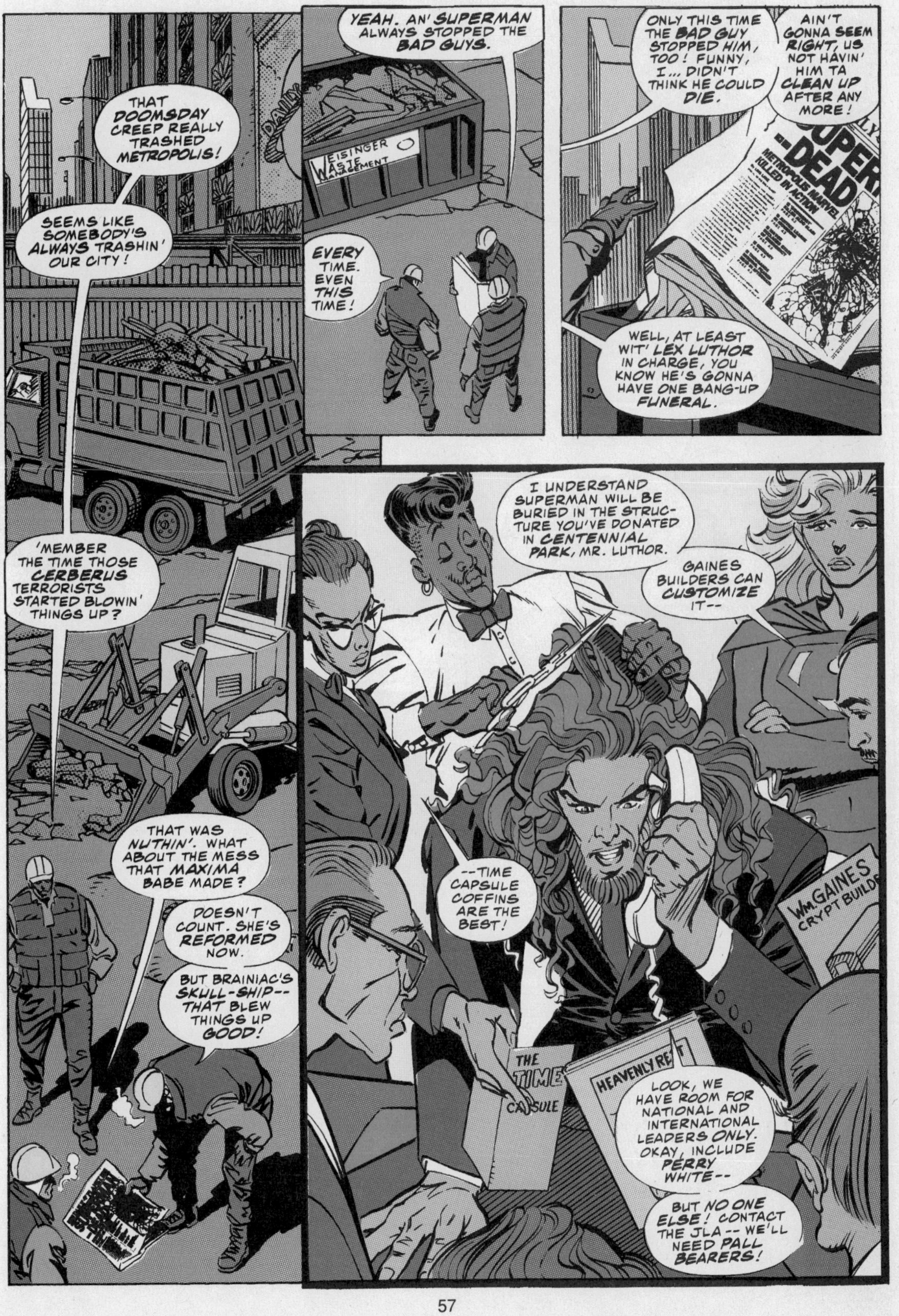

THAT DOOMSDAY CREEP REALLY TRASHED METROPOLIS!
SEEMS LIKE SOMEBODY'S ALWAYS TRASHIN' OUR CITY!
'MEMBER THE TIME THOSE CERBERUS TERRORISTS STARTED BLOWIN' THINGS UP?
THAT WAS NUTHIN'. WHAT ABOUT THE MESS THAT MAXIMA BABE MADE?
DOESN'T COUNT. SHE'S REFORMED NOW.
BUT BRAINIAC'S SKULL-SHIP-- THAT BLEW THINGS UP GOOD!
YEAH. AN' SUPERMAN ALWAYS STOPPED THE BAD GUYS.
WEISINGER WASTE MANAGEMENT
EVERY TIME. EVEN THIS TIME!
ONLY THIS TIME THE BAD GUY STOPPED HIM, TOO! FUNNY, I... DIDN'T THINK HE COULD DIE.
AIN'T GONNA SEEM RIGHT, US NOT HAVIN' HIM TA CLEAN UP AFTER ANY MORE!
SUPER DEAD
METROPOLIS MARVEL KILLED IN ACTION
WELL, AT LEAST WIT' LEX LUTHOR IN CHARGE, YOU KNOW HE'S GONNA HAVE ONE BANG-UP FUNERAL.
I UNDERSTAND SUPERMAN WILL BE BURIED IN THE STRUCTURE YOU'VE DONATED IN CENTENNIAL PARK, MR. LUTHOR.
GAINES BUILDERS CAN CUSTOMIZE IT--
--TIME CAPSULE COFFINS ARE THE BEST!
Wm. GAINES CRYPT BUILDE
THE TIME CAPSULE
HEAVENLY REST
LOOK, WE HAVE ROOM FOR NATIONAL AND INTERNATIONAL LEADERS ONLY. OKAY, INCLUDE PERRY WHITE--
BUT NO ONE ELSE! CONTACT THE JLA -- WE'LL NEED PALL BEARERS!

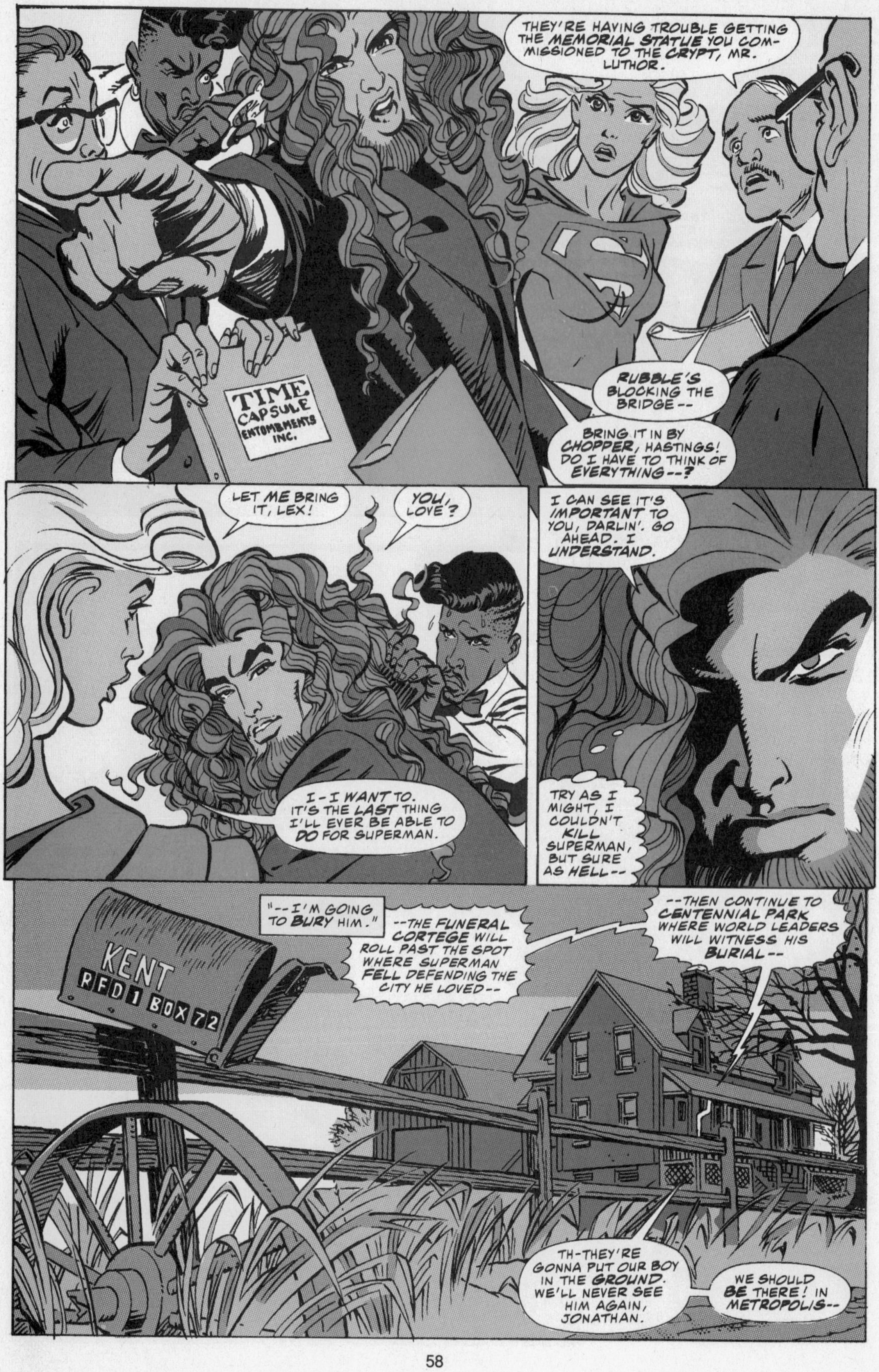
THEY'RE HAVING TROUBLE GETTING THE MEMORIAL STATUE YOU COMMISSIONED TO THE CRYPT, MR. LUTHOR.
TIME CAPSULE ENTOMBMENTS INC.
RUBBLE'S BLOCKING THE BRIDGE--
BRING IT IN BY CHOPPER, HASTINGS! DO I HAVE TO THINK OF EVERYTHING--?
LET ME BRING IT, LEX!
YOU, LOVE?
I-I WANT TO. IT'S THE LAST THING I'LL EVER BE ABLE TO DO FOR SUPERMAN.
I CAN SEE IT'S IMPORTANT TO YOU, DARLIN'. GO AHEAD. I UNDERSTAND.
TRY AS I MIGHT, I COULDN'T KILL SUPERMAN, BUT SURE AS HELL--
"--I'M GOING TO BURY HIM."
KENT
RFD 1 BOX 72
--THE FUNERAL CORTEGE WILL ROLL PAST THE SPOT WHERE SUPERMAN FELL DEFENDING THE CITY HE LOVED--
--THEN CONTINUE TO CENTENNIAL PARK WHERE WORLD LEADERS WILL WITNESS HIS BURIAL--
TH-THEY'RE GONNA PUT OUR BOY IN THE GROUND. WE'LL NEVER SEE HIM AGAIN, JONATHAN.
WE SHOULD BE THERE! IN METROPOLIS--

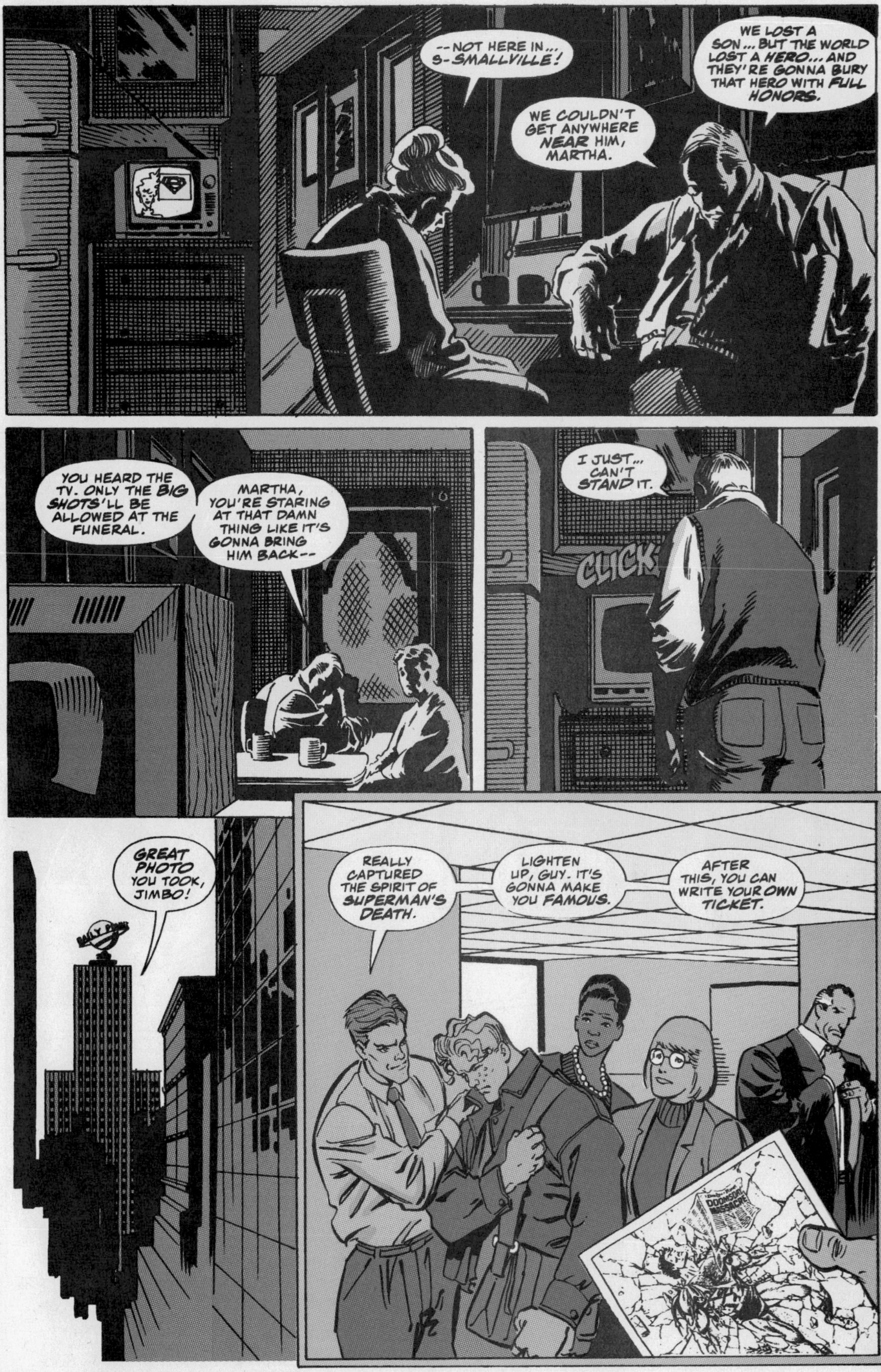
--NOT HERE IN... S-SMALLVILLE!
WE COULDN'T GET ANYWHERE NEAR HIM, MARTHA.
WE LOST A SON... BUT THE WORLD LOST A HERO... AND THEY'RE GONNA BURY THAT HERO WITH FULL HONORS.
YOU HEARD THE TV. ONLY THE BIG SHOTS'LL BE ALLOWED AT THE FUNERAL.
MARTHA, YOU'RE STARING AT THAT DAMN THING LIKE IT'S GONNA BRING HIM BACK--
I JUST... CAN'T STAND IT.
CLICK
GREAT PHOTO YOU TOOK, JIMBO!
REALLY CAPTURED THE SPIRIT OF SUPERMAN'S DEATH.
LIGHTEN UP, GUY. IT'S GONNA MAKE YOU FAMOUS.
AFTER THIS, YOU CAN WRITE YOUR OWN TICKET.

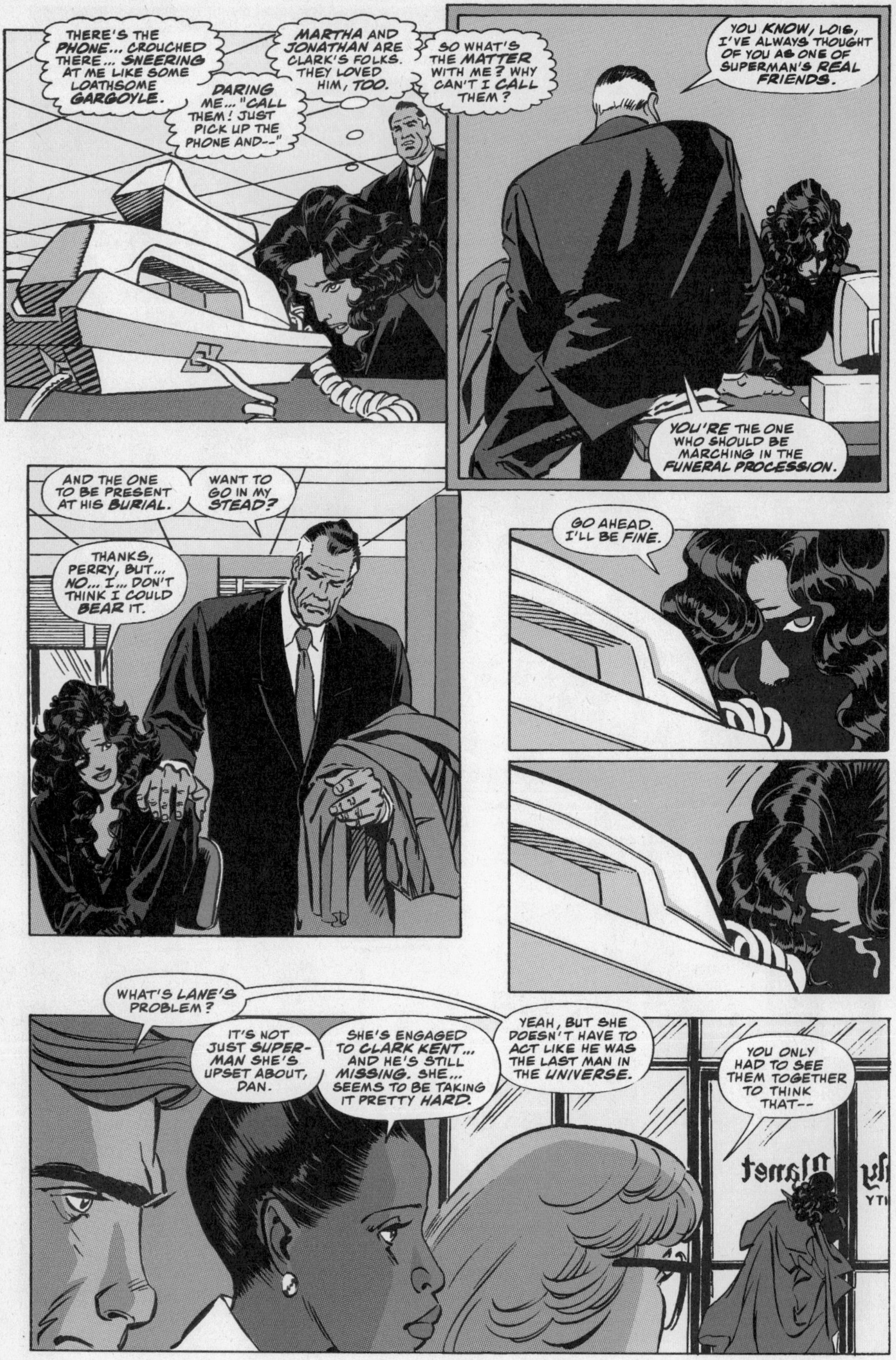
THERE'S THE PHONE... CROUCHED THERE... SNEERING AT ME LIKE SOME LOATHSOME GARGOYLE.
DARING ME... "CALL THEM! JUST PICK UP THE PHONE AND--"
MARTHA AND JONATHAN ARE CLARK'S FOLKS. THEY LOVED HIM, TOO.
SO WHAT'S THE MATTER WITH ME? WHY CAN'T I CALL THEM?
YOU KNOW, LOIS, I'VE ALWAYS THOUGHT OF YOU AS ONE OF SUPERMAN'S REAL FRIENDS.
YOU'RE THE ONE WHO SHOULD BE MARCHING IN THE FUNERAL PROCESSION.
AND THE ONE TO BE PRESENT AT HIS BURIAL.
WANT TO GO IN MY STEAD?
THANKS, PERRY, BUT... NO... I... DON'T THINK I COULD BEAR IT.
GO AHEAD. I'LL BE FINE.
WHAT'S LANE'S PROBLEM?
IT'S NOT JUST SUPERMAN SHE'S UPSET ABOUT, DAN.
SHE'S ENGAGED TO CLARK KENT... AND HE'S STILL MISSING. SHE... SEEMS TO BE TAKING IT PRETTY HARD.
YEAH, BUT SHE DOESN'T HAVE TO ACT LIKE HE WAS THE LAST MAN IN THE UNIVERSE.
YOU ONLY HAD TO SEE THEM TOGETHER TO THINK THAT--

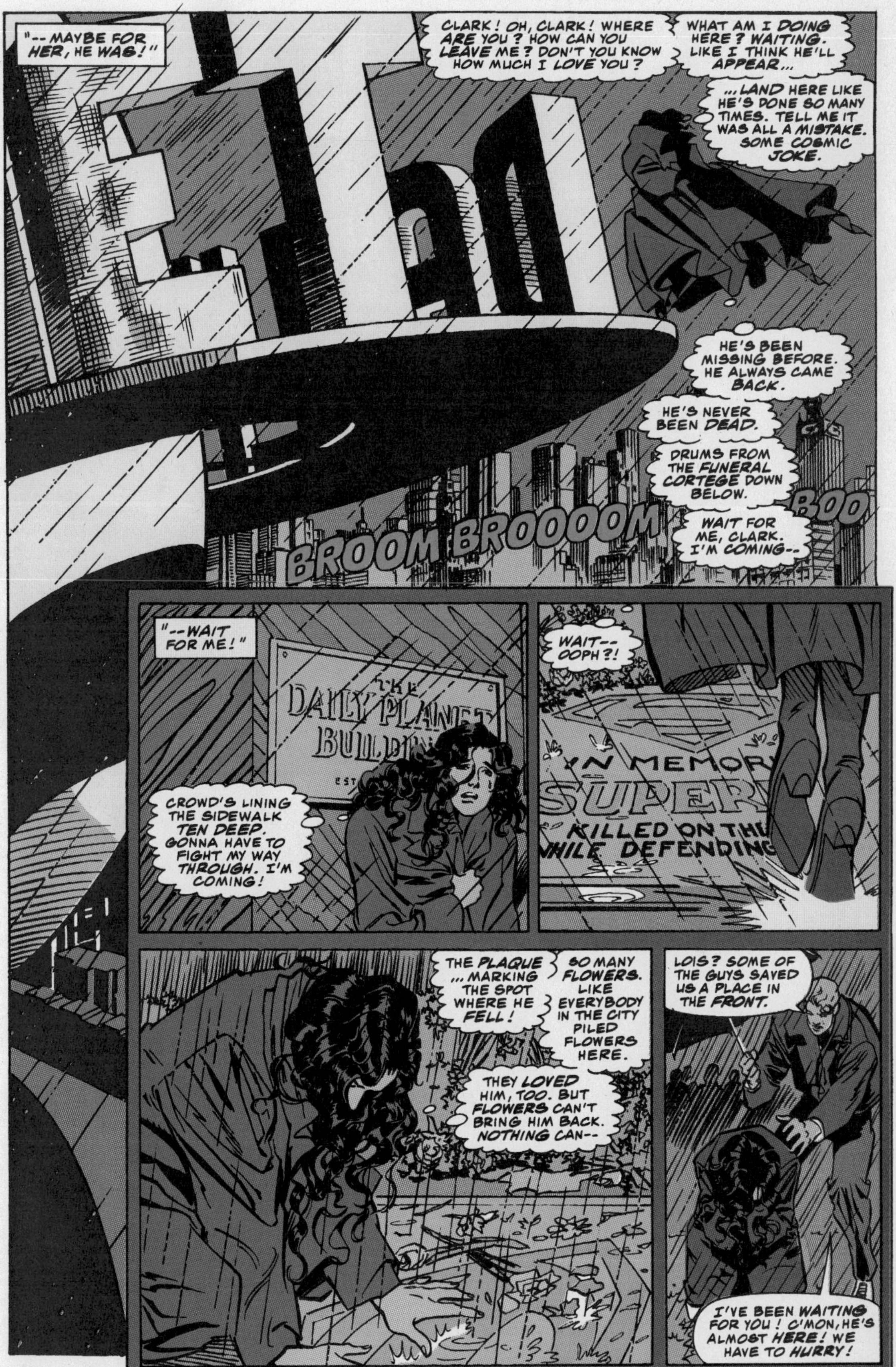
"--MAYBE FOR HER, HE WAS!"
CLARK! OH, CLARK! WHERE ARE YOU? HOW CAN YOU LEAVE ME? DON'T YOU KNOW HOW MUCH I LOVE YOU?
WHAT AM I DOING HERE? WAITING. LIKE I THINK HE'LL APPEAR...
...LAND HERE LIKE HE'S DONE SO MANY TIMES. TELL ME IT WAS ALL A MISTAKE. SOME COSMIC JOKE.
HE'S BEEN MISSING BEFORE. HE ALWAYS CAME BACK.
HE'S NEVER BEEN DEAD.
DRUMS FROM THE FUNERAL CORTEGE DOWN BELOW.
BROOM BROOOOM BOO
WAIT FOR ME, CLARK. I'M COMING--
"--WAIT FOR ME!"
THE DAILY PLANET BUILDIN
CROWD'S LINING THE SIDEWALK TEN DEEP. GONNA HAVE TO FIGHT MY WAY THROUGH. I'M COMING!
WAIT-- OOPH?!
IN MEMOR
SUPER
KILLED ON THE
WHILE DEFENDING
THE PLAQUE ...MARKING THE SPOT WHERE HE FELL!
SO MANY FLOWERS. LIKE EVERYBODY IN THE CITY PILED FLOWERS HERE.
THEY LOVED HIM, TOO. BUT FLOWERS CAN'T BRING HIM BACK. NOTHING CAN--
LOIS? SOME OF THE GUYS SAVED US A PLACE IN THE FRONT.
I'VE BEEN WAITING FOR YOU! C'MON, HE'S ALMOST HERE! WE HAVE TO HURRY!

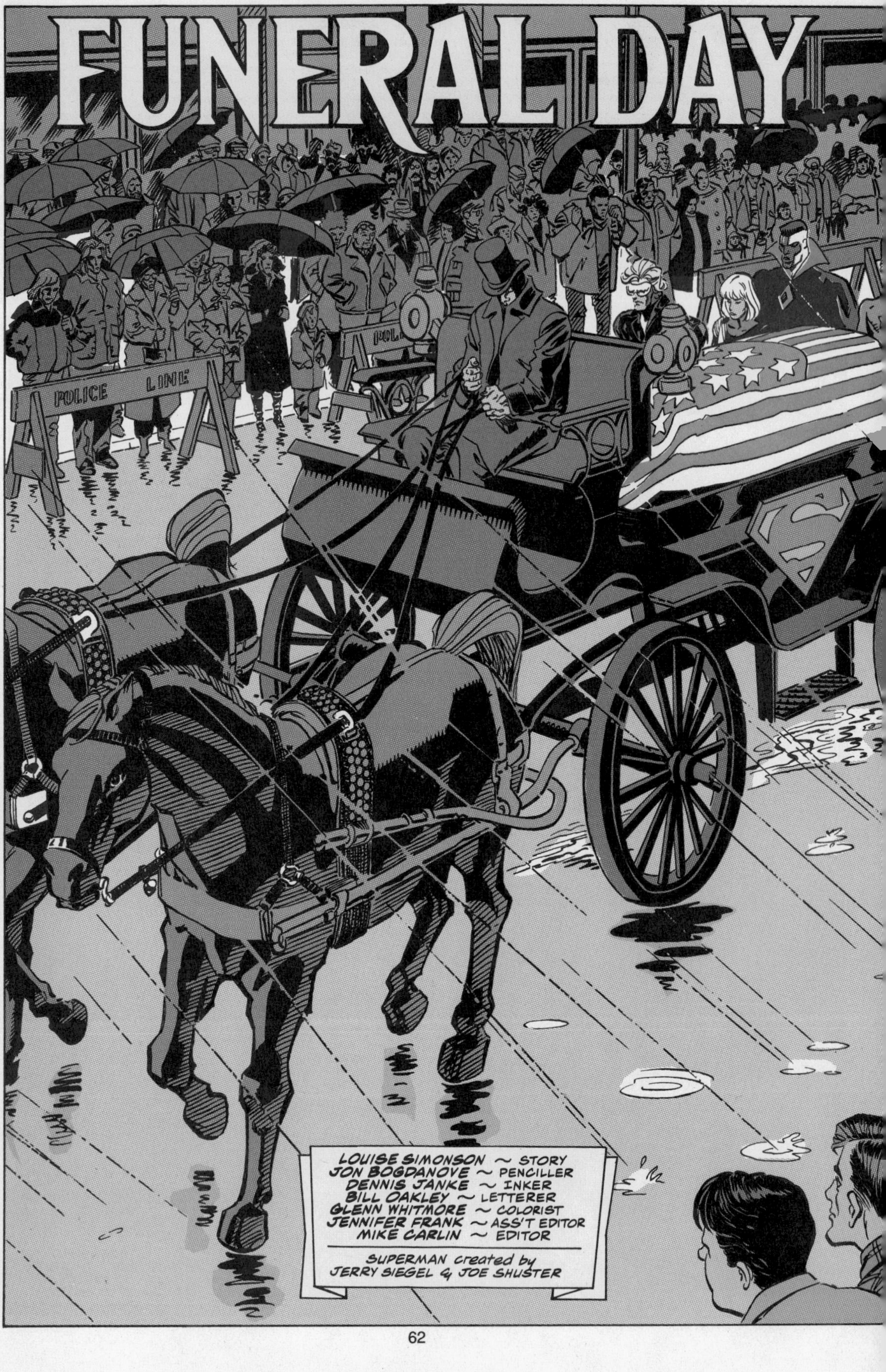
FUNERAL DAY
POLICE LINE
LOUISE SIMONSON ~ STORY
JON BOGDANOVE ~ PENCILLER
DENNIS JANKE ~ INKER
BILL OAKLEY ~ LETTERER
GLENN WHITMORE ~ COLORIST
JENNIFER FRANK ~ ASS'T EDITOR
MIKE CARLIN ~ EDITOR
SUPERMAN created by
JERRY SIEGEL & JOE SHUSTER

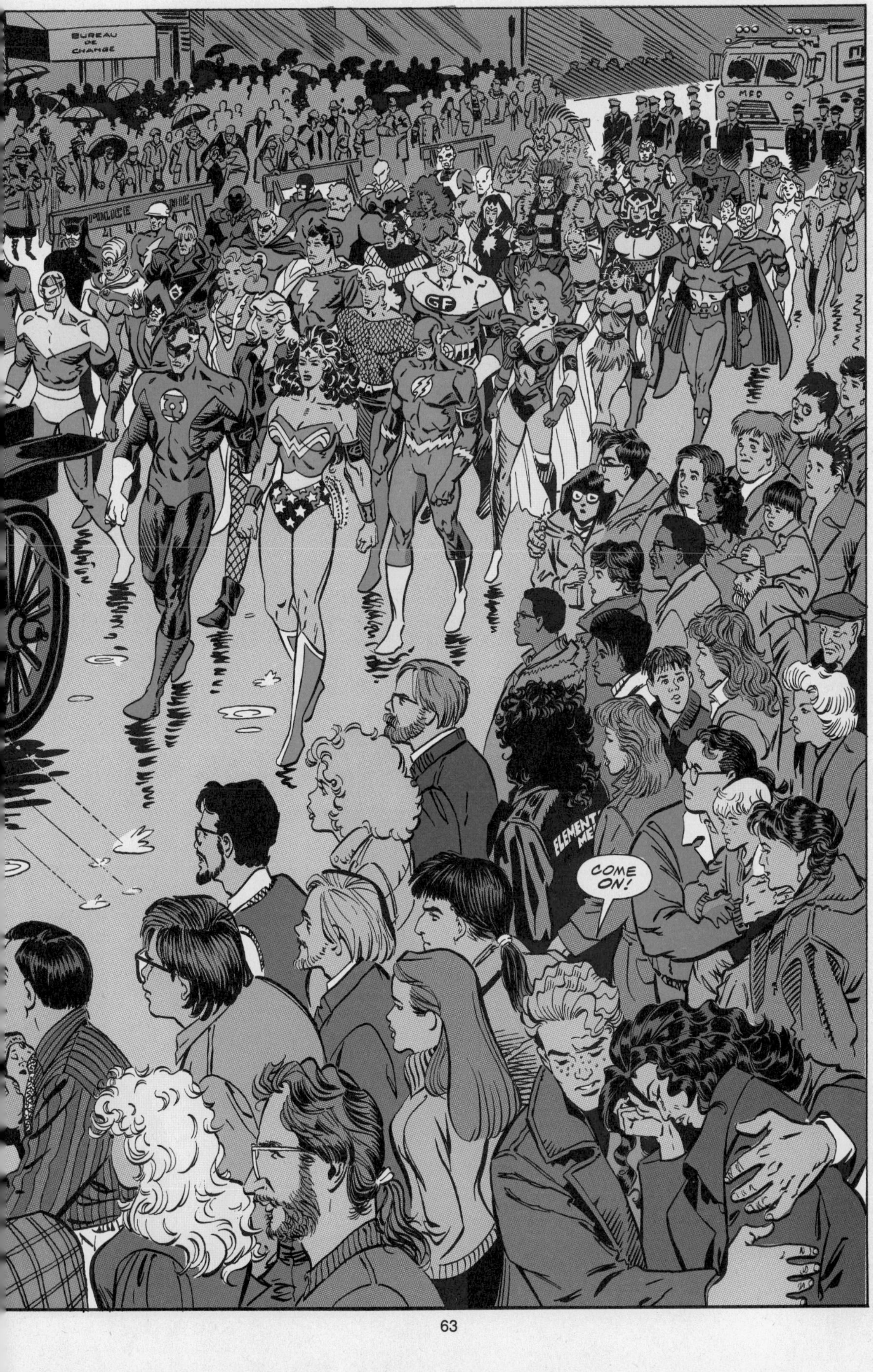
BUREAU DE CHANGE
POLICE
COME ON!

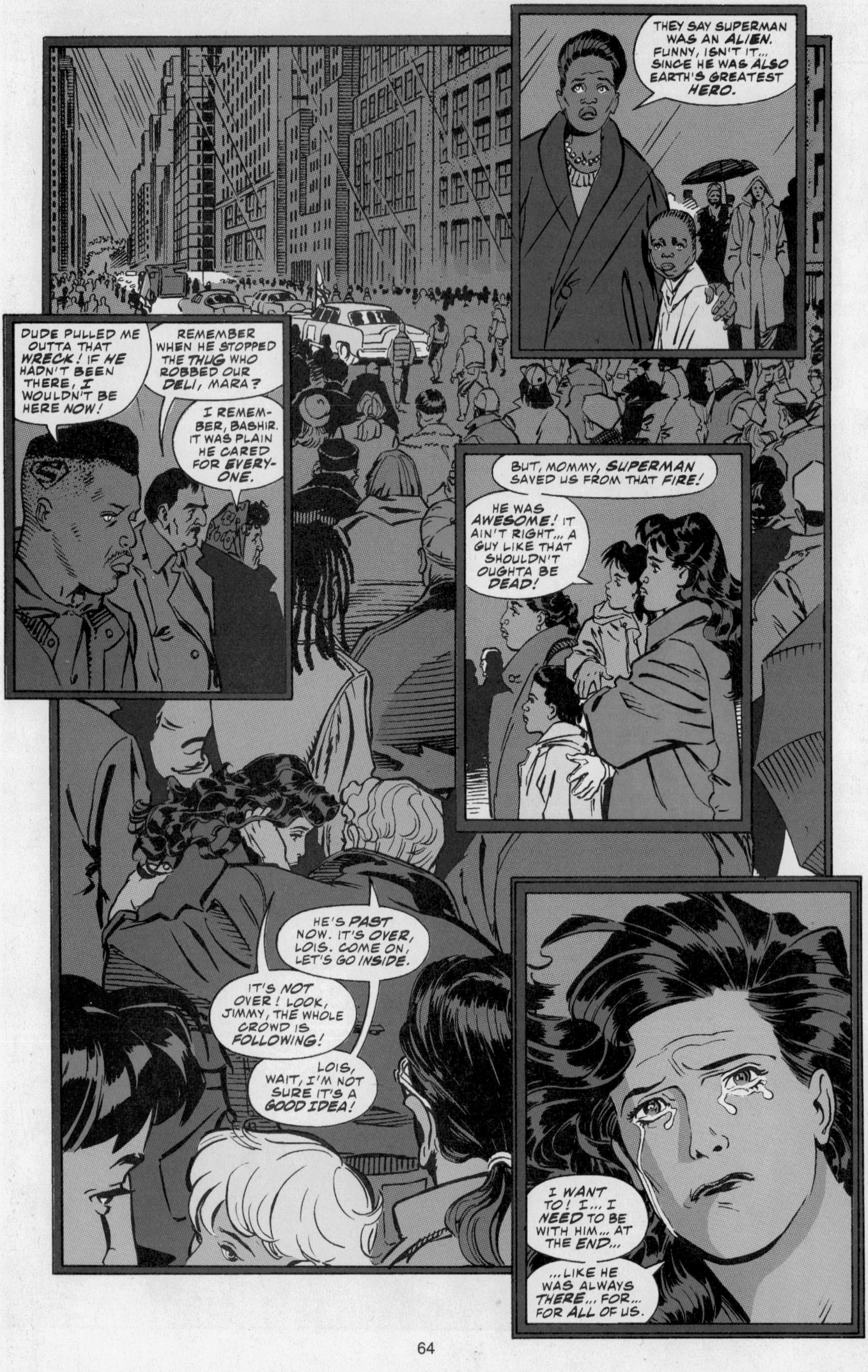
THEY SAY SUPERMAN WAS AN ALIEN. FUNNY, ISN'T IT... SINCE HE WAS ALSO EARTH'S GREATEST HERO.
DUDE PULLED ME OUTTA THAT WRECK! IF HE HADN'T BEEN THERE, I WOULDN'T BE HERE NOW!
REMEMBER WHEN HE STOPPED THE THUG WHO ROBBED OUR DELI, MARA?
I REMEMBER, BASHIR. IT WAS PLAIN HE CARED FOR EVERYONE.
BUT, MOMMY, SUPERMAN SAVED US FROM THAT FIRE!
HE WAS AWESOME! IT AIN'T RIGHT... A GUY LIKE THAT SHOULDN'T OUGHTA BE DEAD!
HE'S PAST NOW. IT'S OVER, LOIS. COME ON, LET'S GO INSIDE.
IT'S NOT OVER! LOOK, JIMMY, THE WHOLE CROWD IS FOLLOWING!
LOIS, WAIT, I'M NOT SURE IT'S A GOOD IDEA!
I WANT TO! I... I NEED TO BE WITH HIM... AT THE END...
...LIKE HE WAS ALWAYS THERE... FOR... FOR ALL OF US.

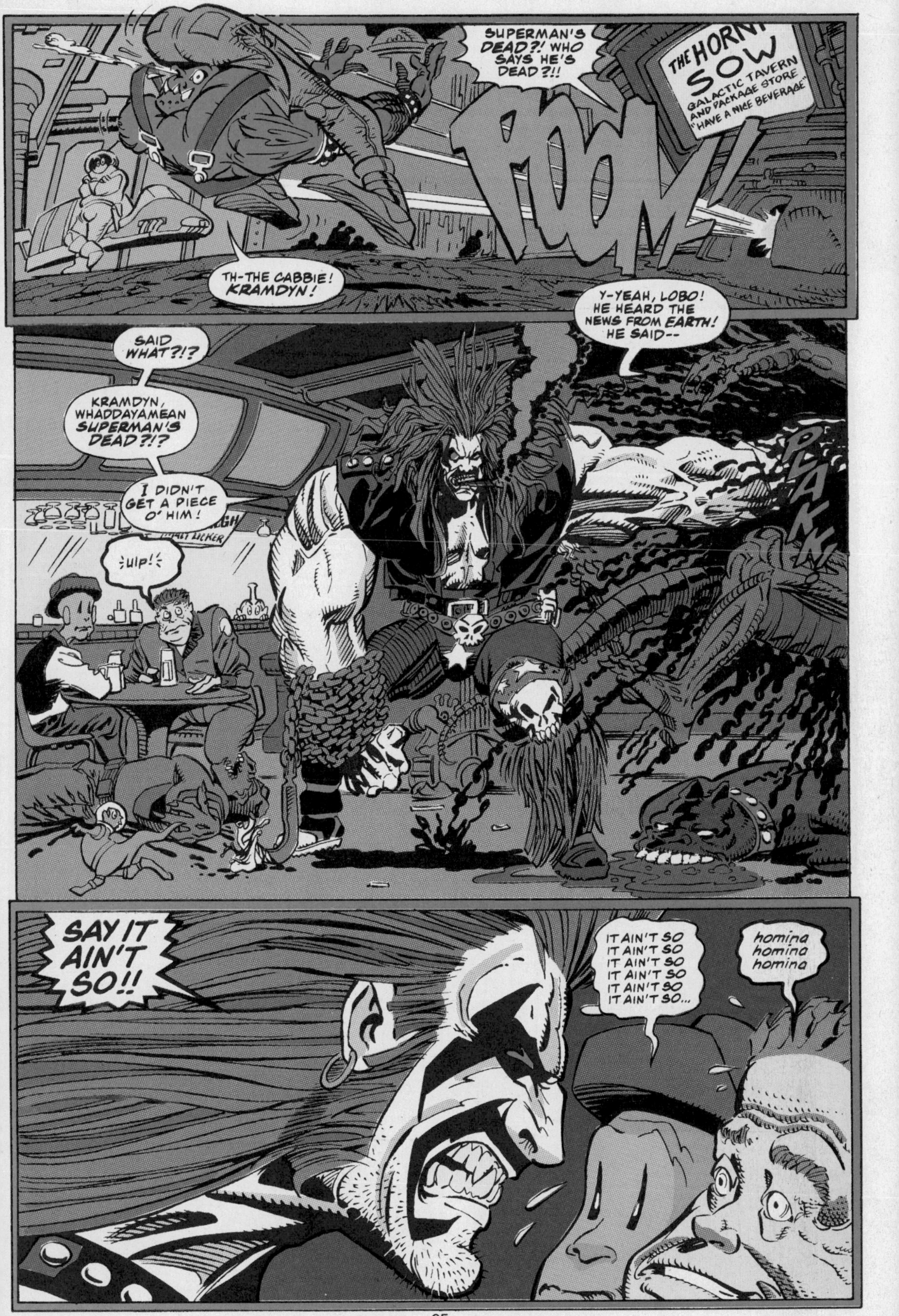
SUPERMAN'S DEAD?! WHO SAYS HE'S DEAD?!!
THE HORN SOW GALACTIC TAVERN AND PACKAGE STORE "HAVE A NICE BEVERAGE"
POOM!
TH-THE CABBIE! KRAMDYN!
Y-YEAH, LOBO! HE HEARD THE NEWS FROM EARTH! HE SAID--
SAID WHAT?!?
KRAMDYN, WHADDAYAMEAN SUPERMAN'S DEAD?!?
I DIDN'T GET A PIECE O' HIM!
PLAKK!
ulp!
SAY IT AIN'T SO!!
IT AIN'T SO IT AIN'T SO IT AIN'T SO IT AIN'T SO IT AIN'T SO IT AIN'T SO...
homina homina homina

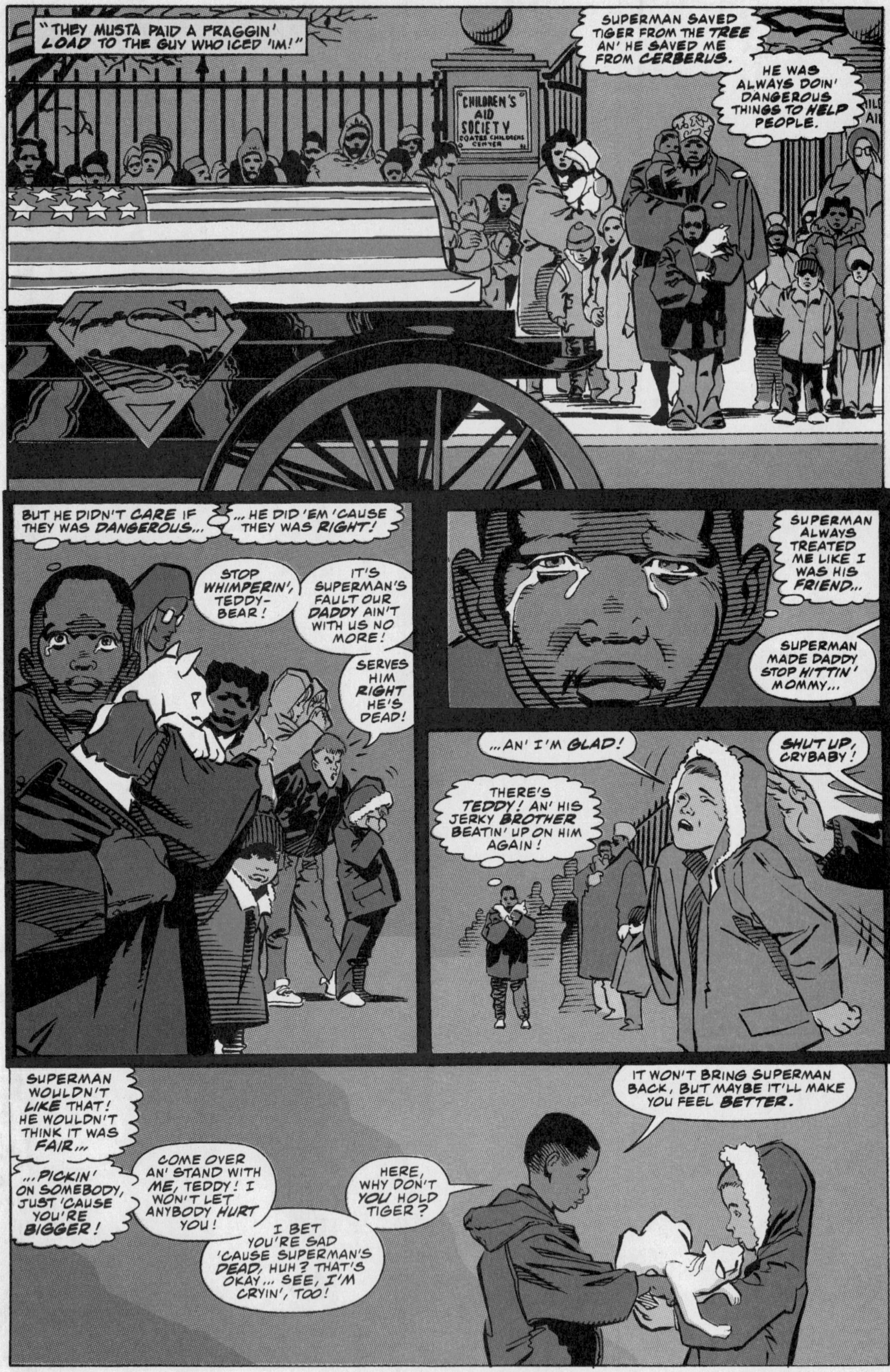
"THEY MUSTA PAID A FRAGGIN' LOAD TO THE GUY WHO ICED 'IM!"
CHILDREN'S AID SOCIETY
SUPERMAN SAVED TIGER FROM THE TREE AN' HE SAVED ME FROM CERBERUS.
HE WAS ALWAYS DOIN' DANGEROUS THINGS TO HELP PEOPLE.
BUT HE DIDN'T CARE IF THEY WAS DANGEROUS...
...HE DID 'EM 'CAUSE THEY WAS RIGHT!
STOP WHIMPERIN', TEDDY-BEAR!
IT'S SUPERMAN'S FAULT OUR DADDY AIN'T WITH US NO MORE!
SERVES HIM RIGHT HE'S DEAD!
SUPERMAN ALWAYS TREATED ME LIKE I WAS HIS FRIEND...
SUPERMAN MADE DADDY STOP HITTIN' MOMMY...
...AN' I'M GLAD!
SHUT UP, CRYBABY!
THERE'S TEDDY! AN' HIS JERKY BROTHER BEATIN' UP ON HIM AGAIN!
SUPERMAN WOULDN'T LIKE THAT! HE WOULDN'T THINK IT WAS FAIR...
...PICKIN' ON SOMEBODY, JUST 'CAUSE YOU'RE BIGGER!
COME OVER AN' STAND WITH ME, TEDDY! I WON'T LET ANYBODY HURT YOU!
I BET YOU'RE SAD 'CAUSE SUPERMAN'S DEAD, HUH? THAT'S OKAY... SEE, I'M CRYIN', TOO!
HERE, WHY DON'T YOU HOLD TIGER?
IT WON'T BRING SUPERMAN BACK, BUT MAYBE IT'LL MAKE YOU FEEL BETTER.

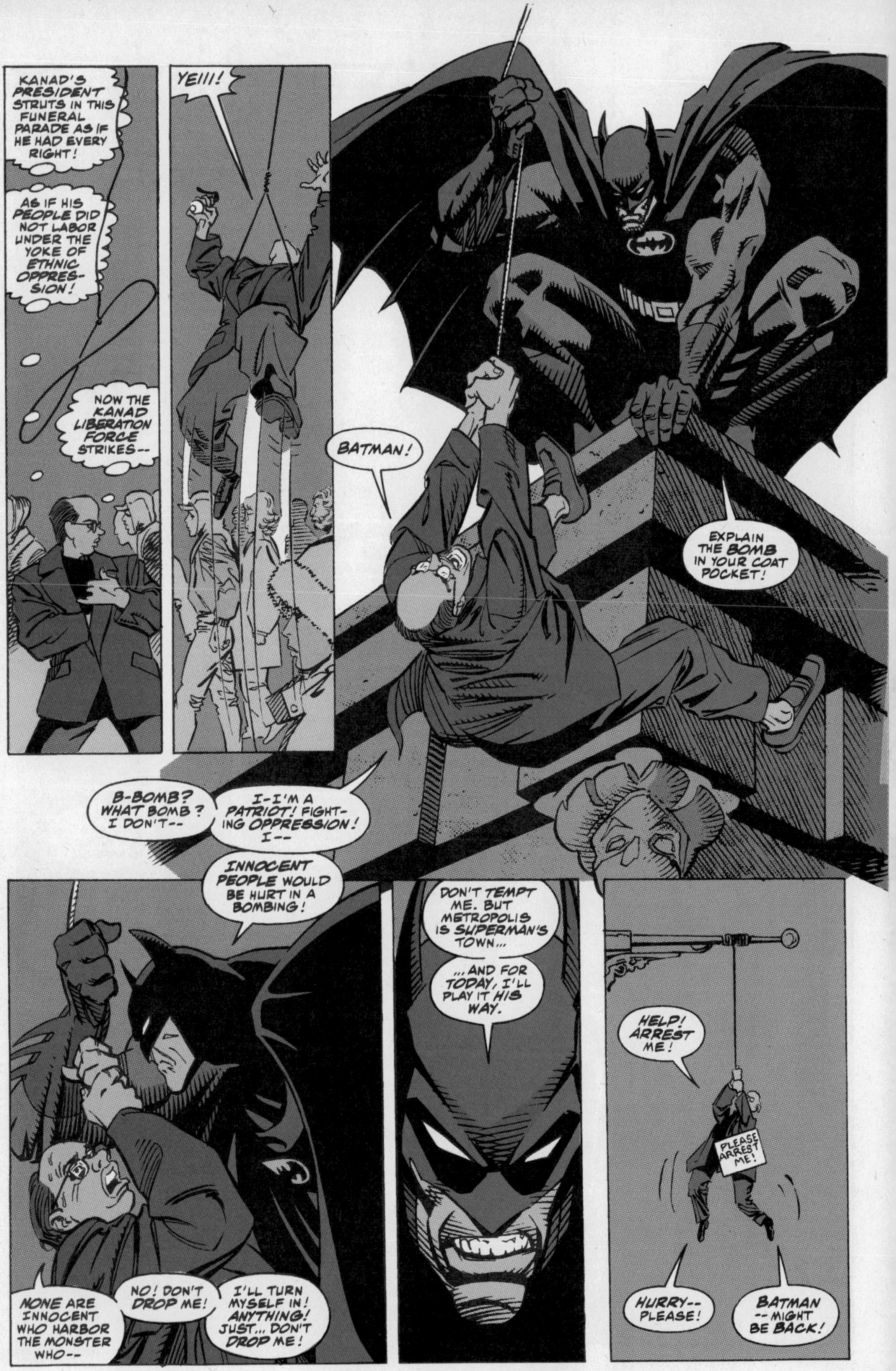
KANAD'S PRESIDENT STRUTS IN THIS FUNERAL PARADE AS IF HE HAD EVERY RIGHT!
AS IF HIS PEOPLE DID NOT LABOR UNDER THE YOKE OF ETHNIC OPPRESSION!
NOW THE KANAD LIBERATION FORCE STRIKES--
YEIII!
BATMAN!
EXPLAIN THE BOMB IN YOUR COAT POCKET!
B-BOMB? WHAT BOMB? I DON'T--
I-I'M A PATRIOT! FIGHTING OPPRESSION! I--
INNOCENT PEOPLE WOULD BE HURT IN A BOMBING!
NONE ARE INNOCENT WHO HARBOR THE MONSTER WHO--
NO! DON'T DROP ME!
I'LL TURN MYSELF IN! ANYTHING! JUST... DON'T DROP ME!
DON'T TEMPT ME. BUT METROPOLIS IS SUPERMAN'S TOWN...
...AND FOR TODAY, I'LL PLAY IT HIS WAY.
HELP! ARREST ME!
PLEASE ARREST ME!
HURRY-- PLEASE!
BATMAN --MIGHT BE BACK!

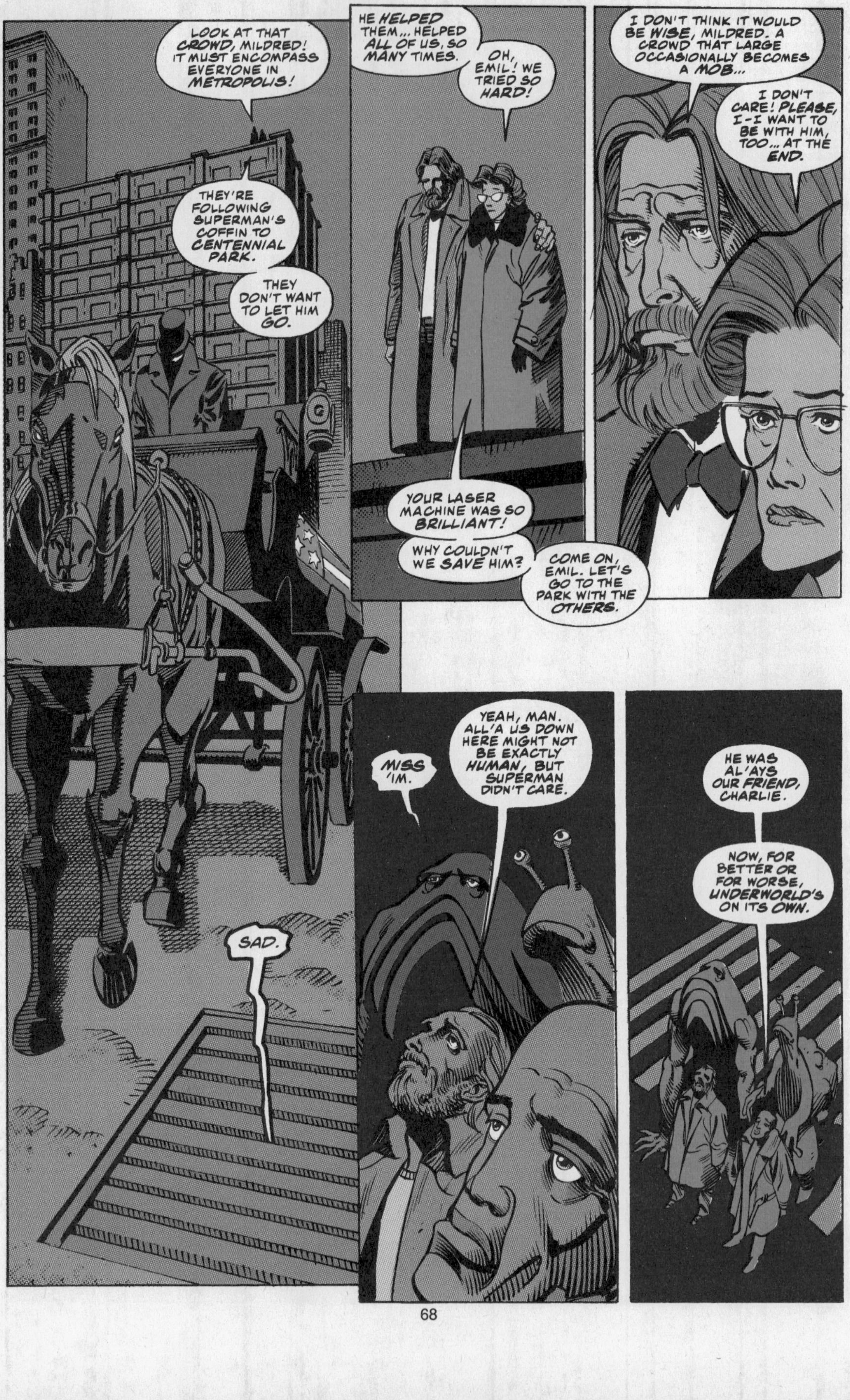
LOOK AT THAT CROWD, MILDRED! IT MUST ENCOMPASS EVERYONE IN METROPOLIS!
THEY'RE FOLLOWING SUPERMAN'S COFFIN TO CENTENNIAL PARK.
THEY DON'T WANT TO LET HIM GO.
HE HELPED THEM... HELPED ALL OF US, SO MANY TIMES.
OH, EMIL! WE TRIED SO HARD!
YOUR LASER MACHINE WAS SO BRILLIANT!
WHY COULDN'T WE SAVE HIM?
COME ON, EMIL. LET'S GO TO THE PARK WITH THE OTHERS.
I DON'T THINK IT WOULD BE WISE, MILDRED. A CROWD THAT LARGE OCCASIONALLY BECOMES A MOB...
I DON'T CARE! PLEASE, I-I WANT TO BE WITH HIM, TOO... AT THE END.
SAD.
MISS 'IM.
YEAH, MAN. ALL'A US DOWN HERE MIGHT NOT BE EXACTLY HUMAN, BUT SUPERMAN DIDN'T CARE.
HE WAS AL'AYS OUR FRIEND, CHARLIE.
NOW, FOR BETTER OR FOR WORSE, UNDERWORLD'S ON ITS OWN.

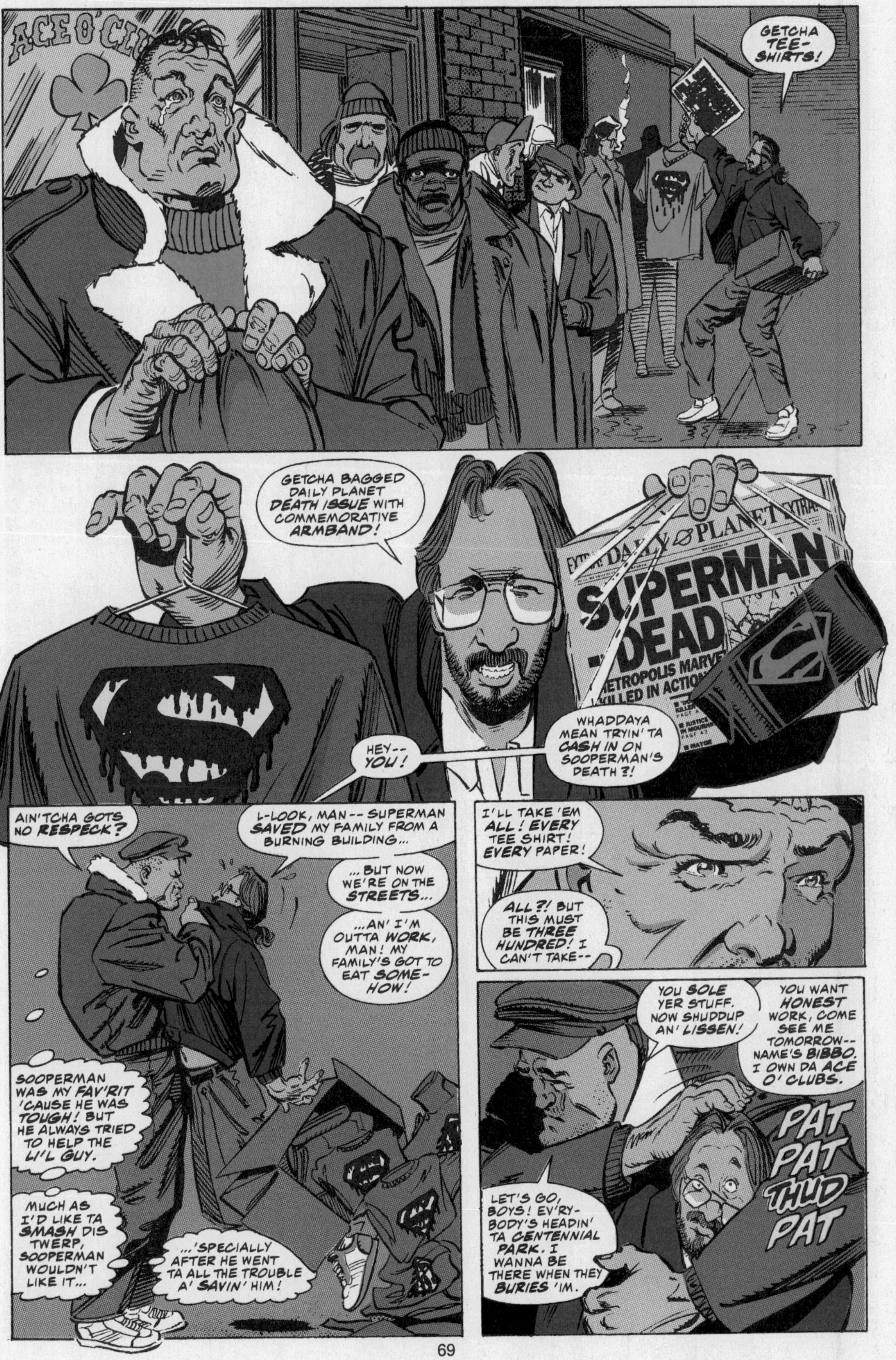
GETCHA TEE-SHIRTS!
GETCHA BAGGED DAILY PLANET DEATH ISSUE WITH COMMEMORATIVE ARMBAND!
DAILY PLANET EXTRA!
SUPERMAN DEAD
METROPOLIS MARVEL KILLED IN ACTION
HEY-- YOU!
WHADDAYA MEAN TRYIN' TA CASH IN ON SOOPERMAN'S DEATH ?!
AIN'TCHA GOTS NO RESPECK?
L-LOOK, MAN-- SUPERMAN SAVED MY FAMILY FROM A BURNING BUILDING...
...BUT NOW WE'RE ON THE STREETS...
...AN' I'M OUTTA WORK, MAN! MY FAMILY'S GOT TO EAT SOME-HOW!
SOOPERMAN WAS MY FAV'RIT 'CAUSE HE WAS TOUGH! BUT HE ALWAYS TRIED TO HELP THE LI'L GUY.
MUCH AS I'D LIKE TA SMASH DIS TWERP, SOOPERMAN WOULDN'T LIKE IT...
...'SPECIALLY AFTER HE WENT TA ALL THE TROUBLE A' SAVIN' HIM!
I'LL TAKE 'EM ALL! EVERY TEE SHIRT! EVERY PAPER!
ALL?! BUT THIS MUST BE THREE HUNDRED! I CAN'T TAKE--
YOU SOLE YER STUFF. NOW SHUDDUP AN' LISSEN!
YOU WANT HONEST WORK, COME SEE ME TOMORROW-- NAME'S BIBBO. I OWN DA ACE O' CLUBS.
PAT PAT THUD PAT
LET'S GO, BOYS! EV'RY-BODY'S HEADIN' TA CENTENNIAL PARK. I WANNA BE THERE WHEN THEY BURIES 'IM.

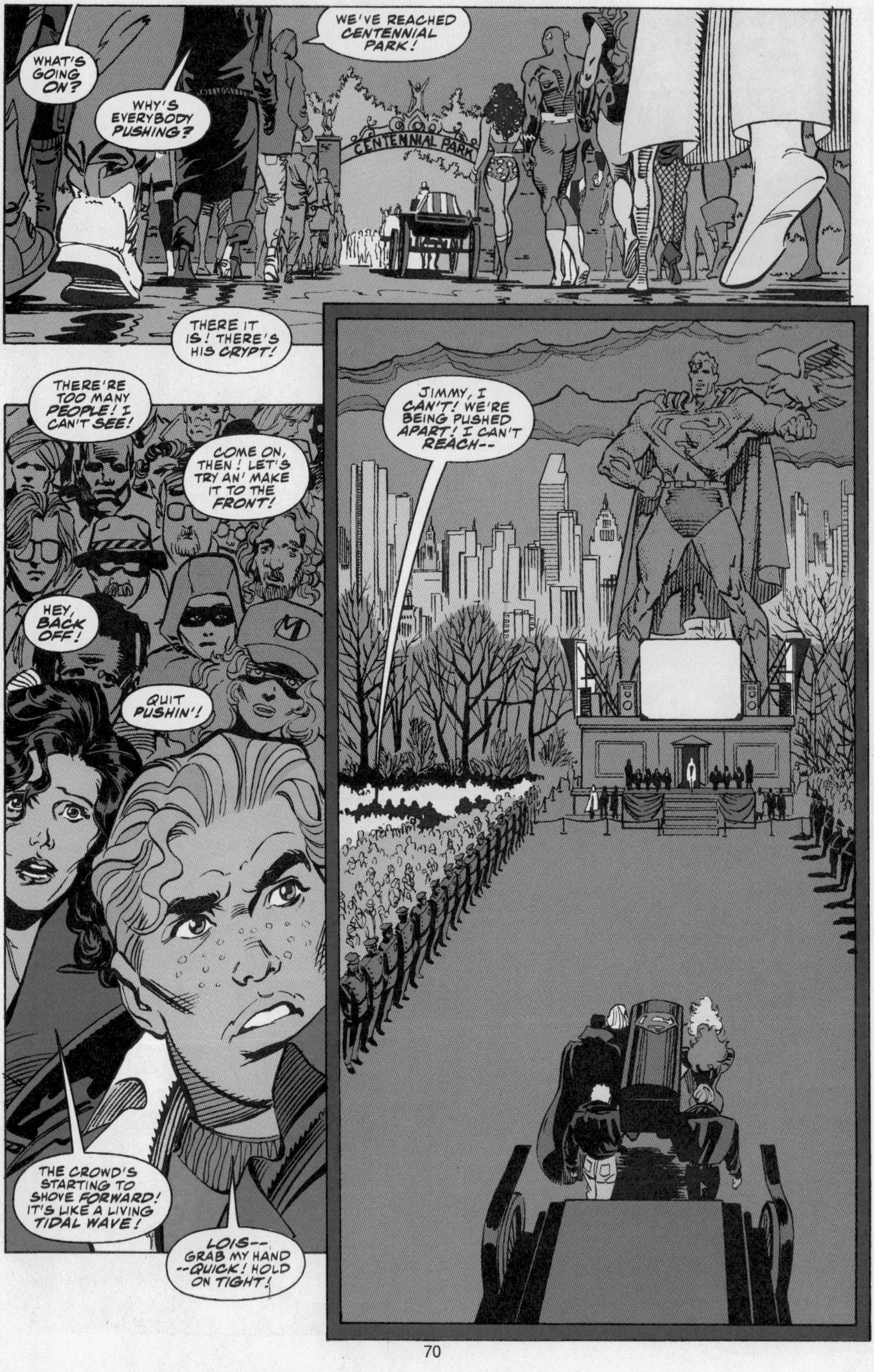
WHAT'S GOING ON?
WHY'S EVERYBODY PUSHING?
WE'VE REACHED CENTENNIAL PARK!
CENTENNIAL PARK
THERE IT IS! THERE'S HIS CRYPT!
THERE'RE TOO MANY PEOPLE! I CAN'T SEE!
COME ON, THEN! LET'S TRY AN' MAKE IT TO THE FRONT!
HEY, BACK OFF!
QUIT PUSHIN'!
THE CROWD'S STARTING TO SHOVE FORWARD! IT'S LIKE A LIVING TIDAL WAVE!
LOIS-- GRAB MY HAND --QUICK! HOLD ON TIGHT!
JIMMY, I CAN'T! WE'RE BEING PUSHED APART! I CAN'T REACH--

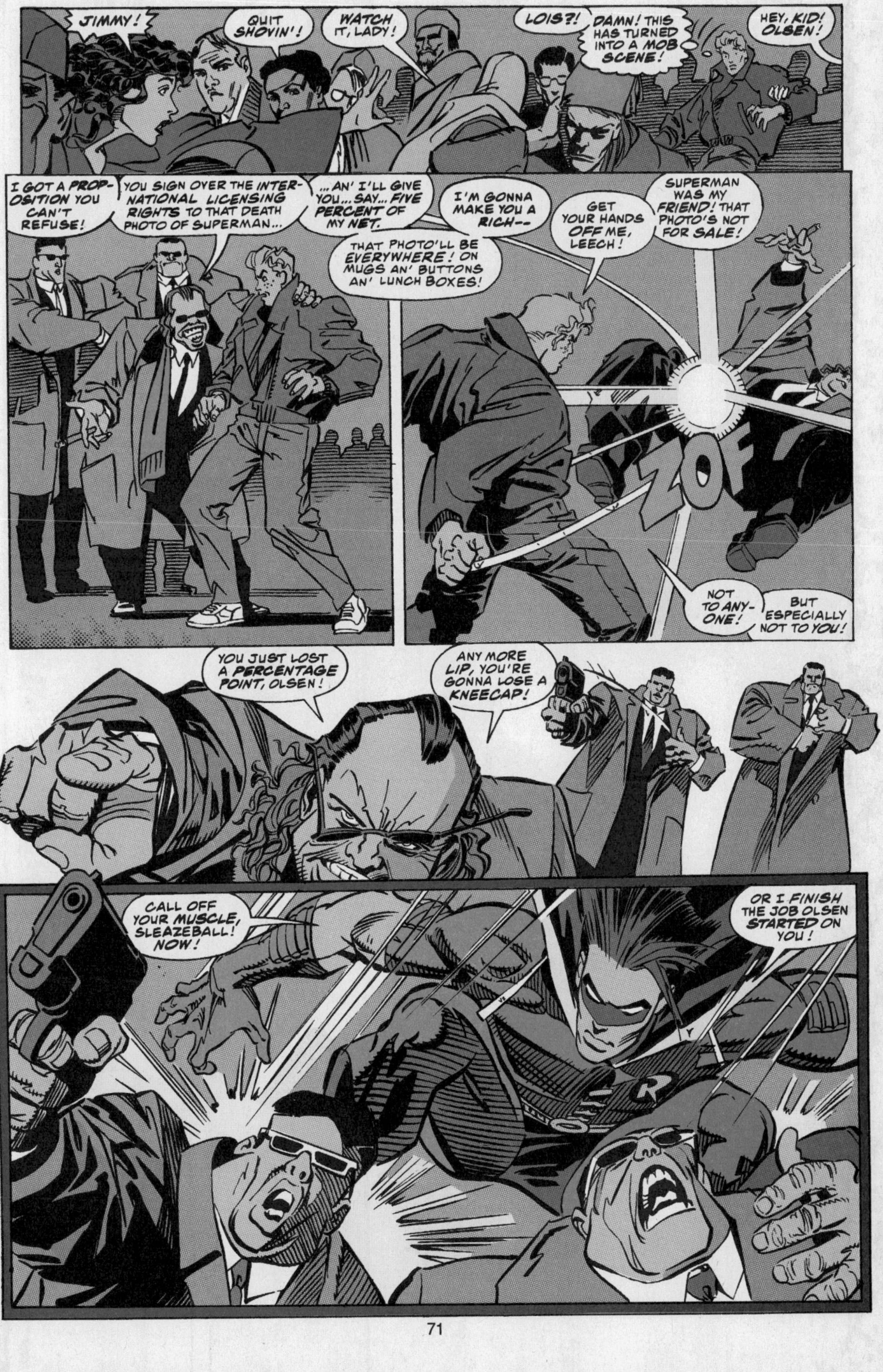
JIMMY!
QUIT SHOVIN'!
WATCH IT, LADY!
LOIS?!
DAMN! THIS HAS TURNED INTO A MOB SCENE!
HEY, KID! OLSEN!
I GOT A PROPOSITION YOU CAN'T REFUSE!
YOU SIGN OVER THE INTERNATIONAL LICENSING RIGHTS TO THAT DEATH PHOTO OF SUPERMAN...
...AN' I'LL GIVE YOU... SAY... FIVE PERCENT OF MY NET.
THAT PHOTO'LL BE EVERYWHERE! ON MUGS AN' BUTTONS AN' LUNCH BOXES!
I'M GONNA MAKE YOU A RICH--
GET YOUR HANDS OFF ME, LEECH!
SUPERMAN WAS MY FRIEND! THAT PHOTO'S NOT FOR SALE!
ZOF
NOT TO ANYONE!
BUT ESPECIALLY NOT TO YOU!
YOU JUST LOST A PERCENTAGE POINT, OLSEN!
ANY MORE LIP, YOU'RE GONNA LOSE A KNEECAP!
CALL OFF YOUR MUSCLE, SLEAZEBALL! NOW!
OR I FINISH THE JOB OLSEN STARTED ON YOU!

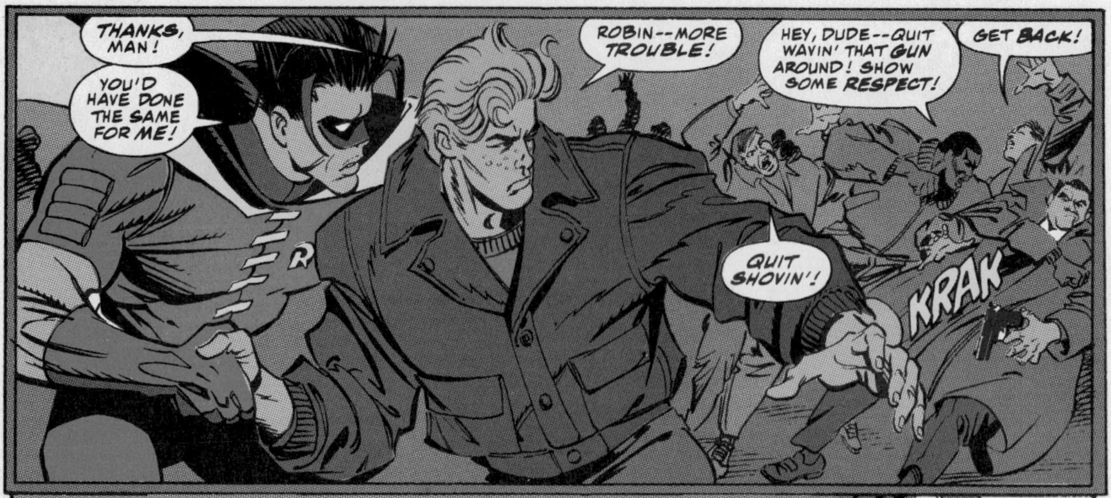
THANKS, MAN!
YOU'D HAVE DONE THE SAME FOR ME!
ROBIN--MORE TROUBLE!
HEY, DUDE--QUIT WAVIN' THAT GUN AROUND! SHOW SOME RESPECT!
GET BACK!
QUIT SHOVIN'!
KRAK

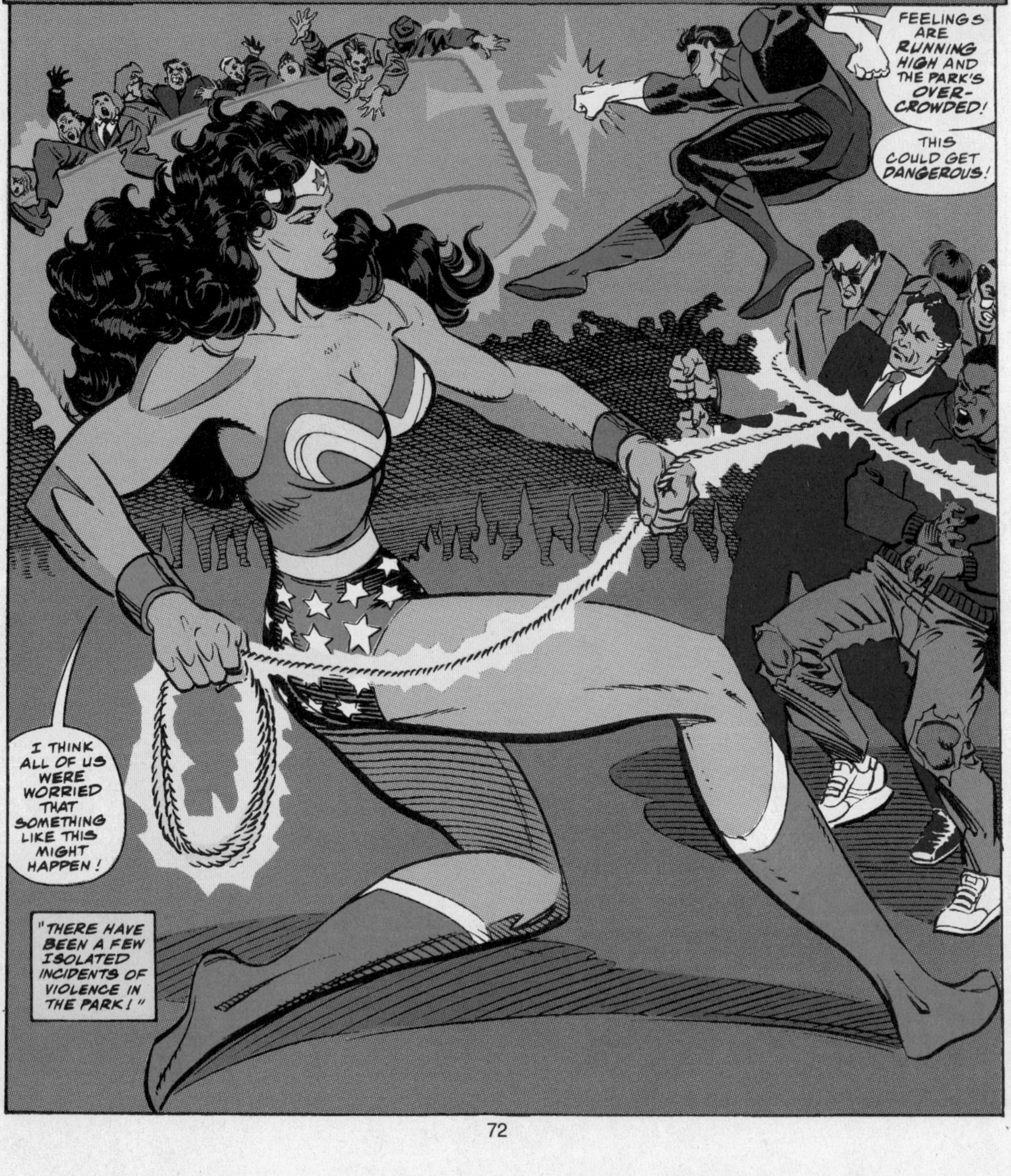
FEELINGS ARE RUNNING HIGH AND THE PARK'S OVER-CROWDED!
THIS COULD GET DANGEROUS!
I THINK ALL OF US WERE WORRIED THAT SOMETHING LIKE THIS MIGHT HAPPEN!
"THERE HAVE BEEN A FEW ISOLATED INCIDENTS OF VIOLENCE IN THE PARK!"

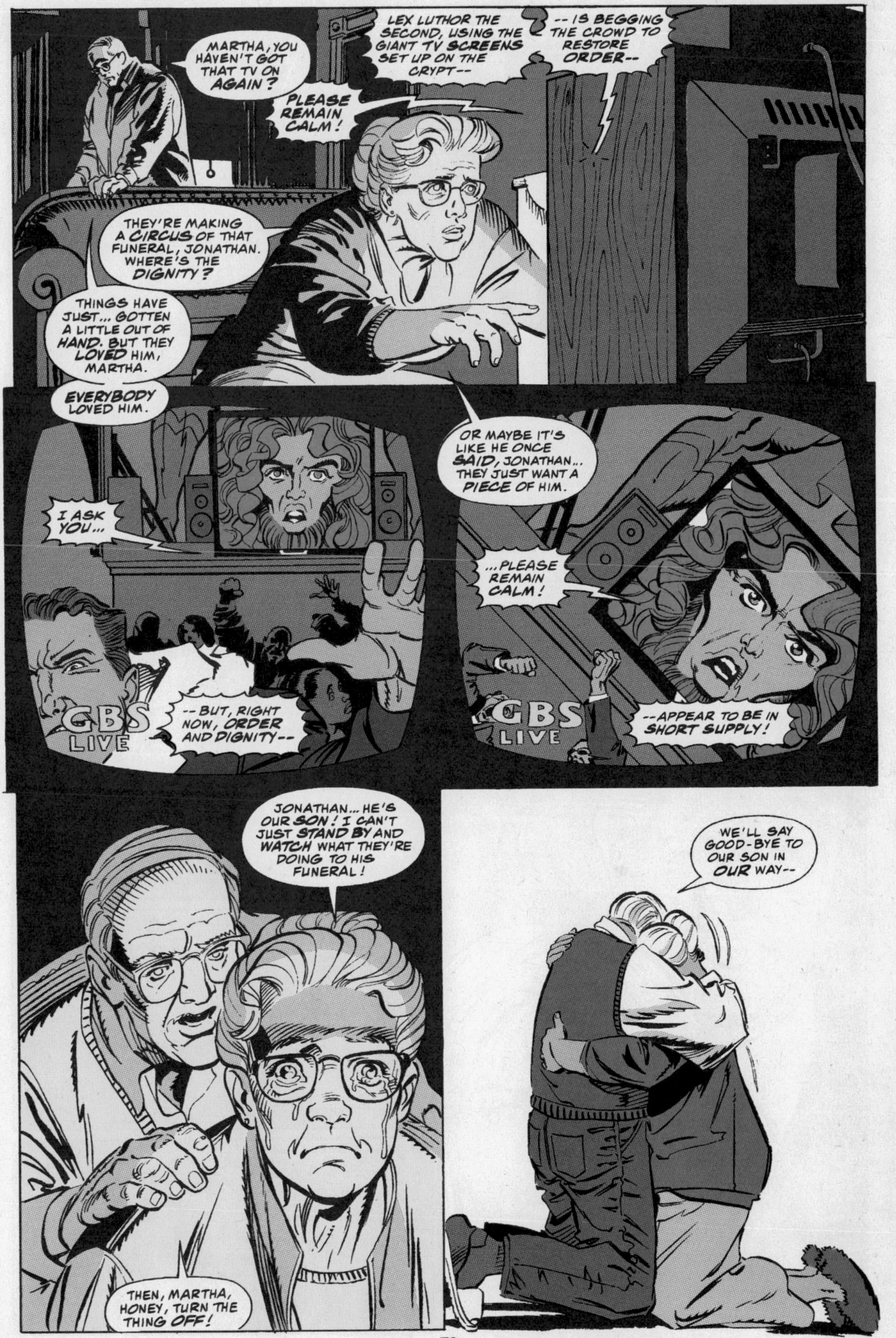

MARTHA, YOU HAVEN'T GOT THAT TV ON AGAIN?
LEX LUTHOR THE SECOND, USING THE GIANT TV SCREENS SET UP ON THE CRYPT--
-- IS BEGGING THE CROWD TO RESTORE ORDER--
PLEASE REMAIN CALM!
THEY'RE MAKING A CIRCUS OF THAT FUNERAL, JONATHAN. WHERE'S THE DIGNITY?
THINGS HAVE JUST... GOTTEN A LITTLE OUT OF HAND. BUT THEY LOVED HIM, MARTHA.
EVERYBODY LOVED HIM.
I ASK YOU...
--BUT, RIGHT NOW, ORDER AND DIGNITY--
GBS LIVE
OR MAYBE IT'S LIKE HE ONCE SAID, JONATHAN... THEY JUST WANT A PIECE OF HIM.
...PLEASE REMAIN CALM!
--APPEAR TO BE IN SHORT SUPPLY!
GBS LIVE
JONATHAN... HE'S OUR SON! I CAN'T JUST STAND BY AND WATCH WHAT THEY'RE DOING TO HIS FUNERAL!
THEN, MARTHA, HONEY, TURN THE THING OFF!
WE'LL SAY GOOD-BYE TO OUR SON IN OUR WAY--

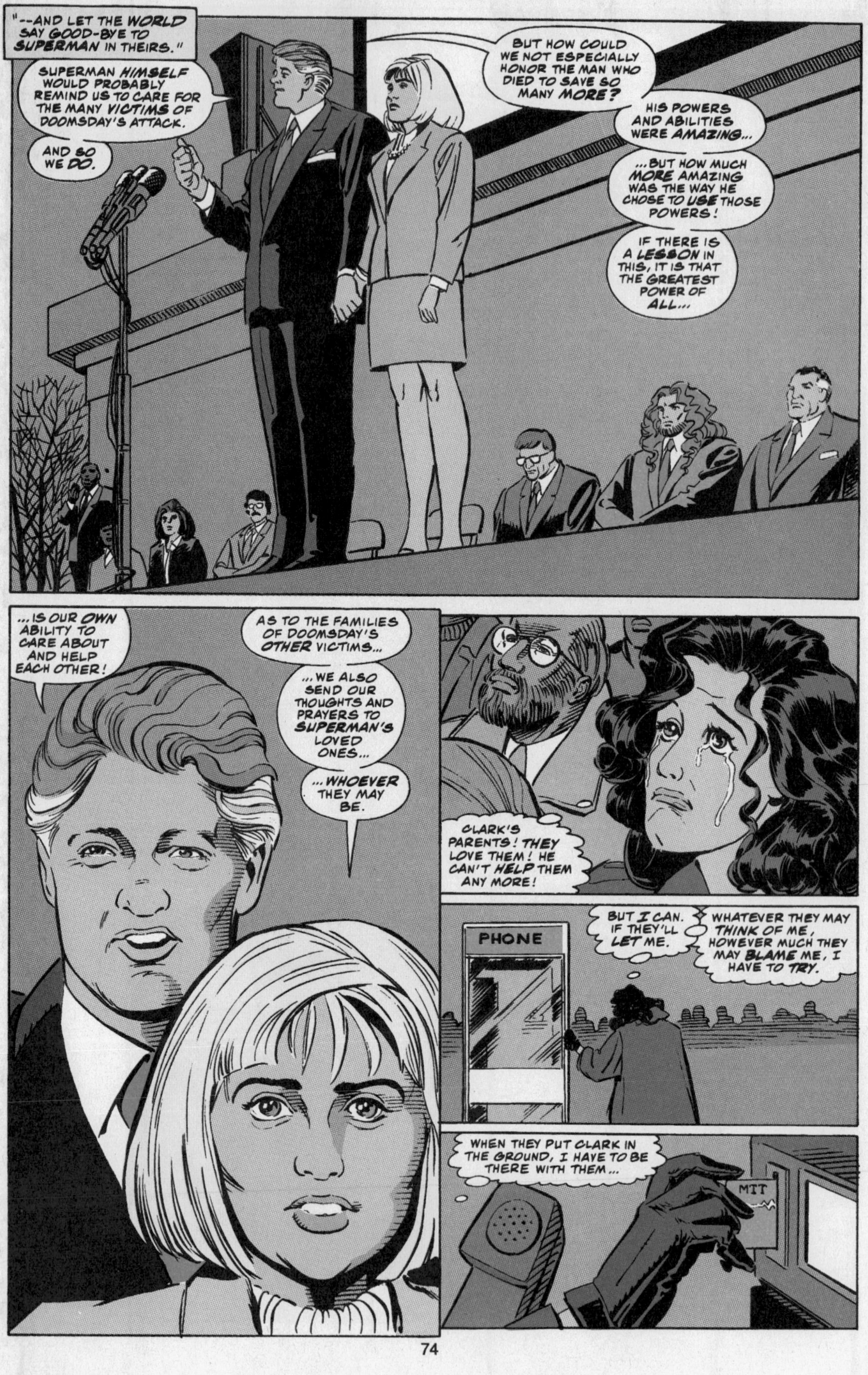
"--AND LET THE WORLD SAY GOOD-BYE TO SUPERMAN IN THEIRS."
SUPERMAN HIMSELF WOULD PROBABLY REMIND US TO CARE FOR THE MANY VICTIMS OF DOOMSDAY'S ATTACK.
AND SO WE DO.
BUT HOW COULD WE NOT ESPECIALLY HONOR THE MAN WHO DIED TO SAVE SO MANY MORE?
HIS POWERS AND ABILITIES WERE AMAZING...
...BUT HOW MUCH MORE AMAZING WAS THE WAY HE CHOSE TO USE THOSE POWERS!
IF THERE IS A LESSON IN THIS, IT IS THAT THE GREATEST POWER OF ALL...
...IS OUR OWN ABILITY TO CARE ABOUT AND HELP EACH OTHER!
AS TO THE FAMILIES OF DOOMSDAY'S OTHER VICTIMS...
...WE ALSO SEND OUR THOUGHTS AND PRAYERS TO SUPERMAN'S LOVED ONES...
...WHOEVER THEY MAY BE.
CLARK'S PARENTS! THEY LOVE THEM! HE CAN'T HELP THEM ANY MORE!
PHONE
BUT I CAN. IF THEY'LL LET ME.
WHATEVER THEY MAY THINK OF ME, HOWEVER MUCH THEY MAY BLAME ME, I HAVE TO TRY.
WHEN THEY PUT CLARK IN THE GROUND, I HAVE TO BE THERE WITH THEM...
MTT

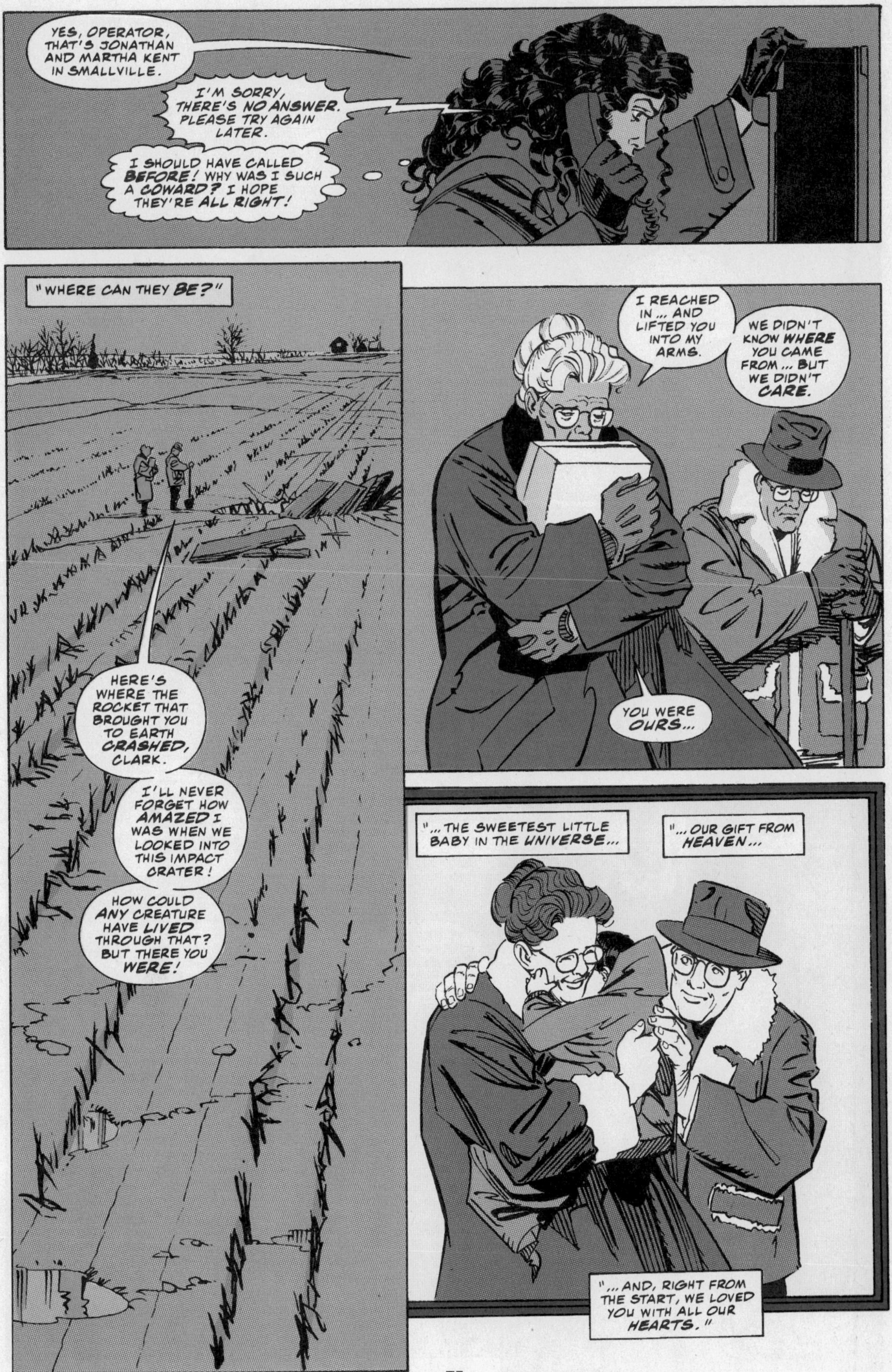
YES, OPERATOR, THAT'S JONATHAN AND MARTHA KENT IN SMALLVILLE.
I'M SORRY, THERE'S NO ANSWER. PLEASE TRY AGAIN LATER.
I SHOULD HAVE CALLED BEFORE! WHY WAS I SUCH A COWARD? I HOPE THEY'RE ALL RIGHT!
"WHERE CAN THEY BE?"
HERE'S WHERE THE ROCKET THAT BROUGHT YOU TO EARTH CRASHED, CLARK.
I'LL NEVER FORGET HOW AMAZED I WAS WHEN WE LOOKED INTO THIS IMPACT CRATER!
HOW COULD ANY CREATURE HAVE LIVED THROUGH THAT? BUT THERE YOU WERE!
I REACHED IN ... AND LIFTED YOU INTO MY ARMS.
WE DIDN'T KNOW WHERE YOU CAME FROM ... BUT WE DIDN'T CARE.
YOU WERE OURS...
"... THE SWEETEST LITTLE BABY IN THE UNIVERSE...
"... OUR GIFT FROM HEAVEN...
"... AND, RIGHT FROM THE START, WE LOVED YOU WITH ALL OUR HEARTS."

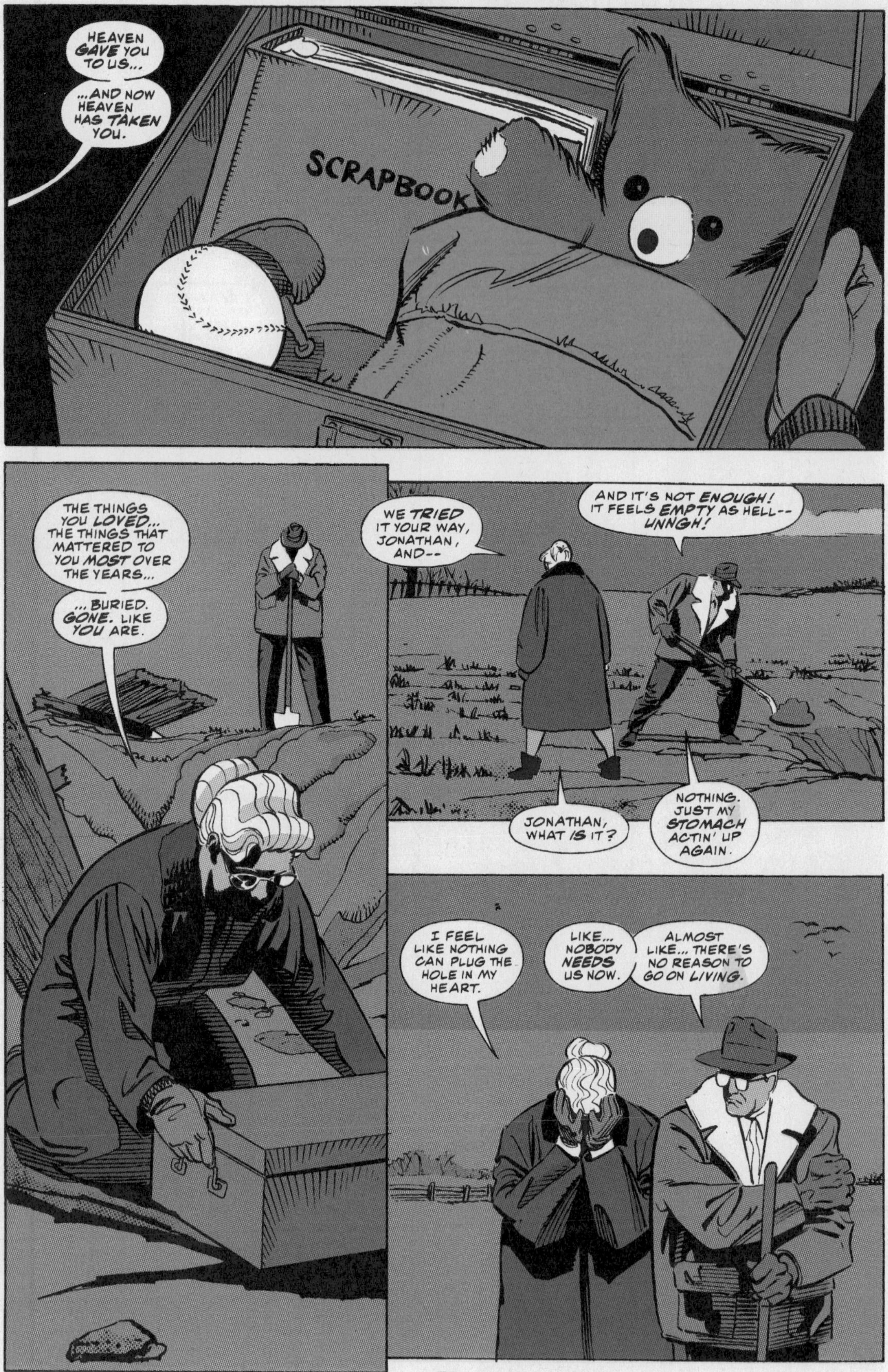
HEAVEN GAVE YOU TO US...
...AND NOW HEAVEN HAS TAKEN YOU.
SCRAPBOOK
THE THINGS YOU LOVED... THE THINGS THAT MATTERED TO YOU MOST OVER THE YEARS...
...BURIED. GONE. LIKE YOU ARE.
WE TRIED IT YOUR WAY, JONATHAN, AND--
AND IT'S NOT ENOUGH! IT FEELS EMPTY AS HELL-- UNNGH!
JONATHAN, WHAT IS IT?
NOTHING. JUST MY STOMACH ACTIN' UP AGAIN.
I FEEL LIKE NOTHING CAN PLUG THE HOLE IN MY HEART.
LIKE... NOBODY NEEDS US NOW.
ALMOST LIKE... THERE'S NO REASON TO GO ON LIVING.

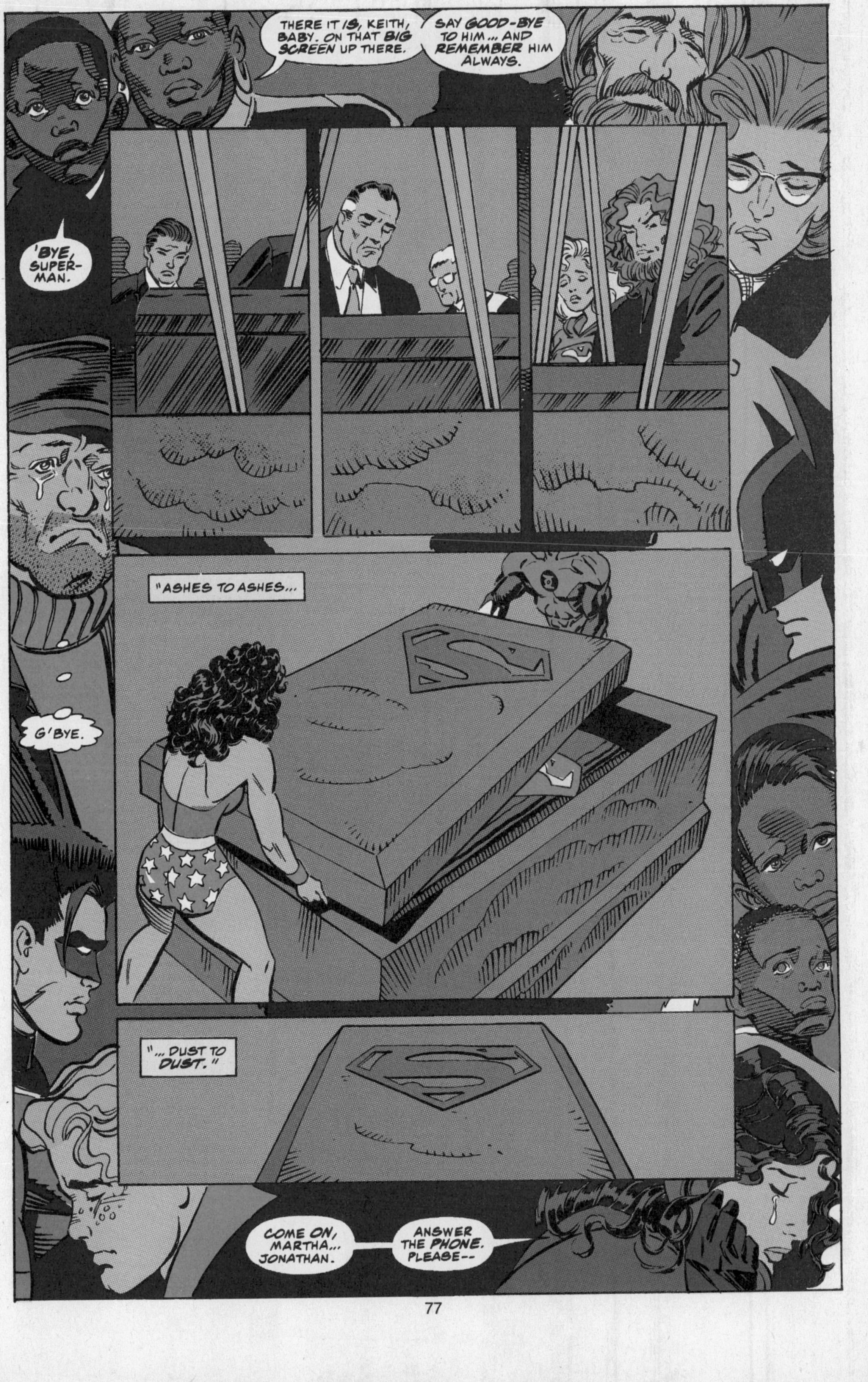

THERE IT IS, KEITH, BABY. ON THAT BIG SCREEN UP THERE.
SAY GOOD-BYE TO HIM... AND REMEMBER HIM ALWAYS.
'BYE, SUPER-MAN.
"ASHES TO ASHES...
G'BYE.
"...DUST TO DUST."
COME ON, MARTHA... JONATHAN.
ANSWER THE PHONE. PLEASE--

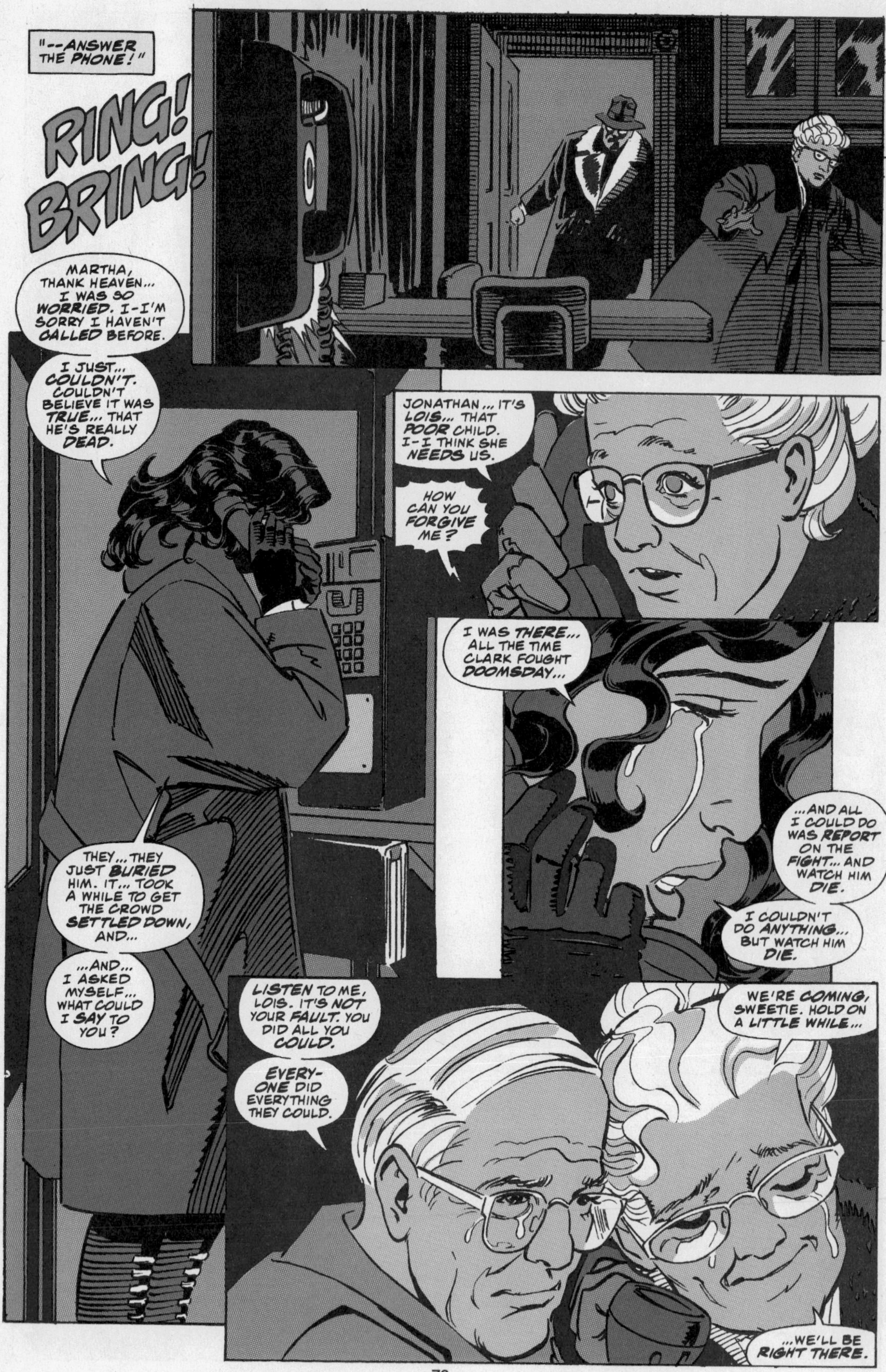
"--ANSWER THE PHONE!"
RING! BRING!
MARTHA, THANK HEAVEN... I WAS SO WORRIED. I-I'M SORRY I HAVEN'T CALLED BEFORE.
I JUST... COULDN'T. COULDN'T BELIEVE IT WAS TRUE... THAT HE'S REALLY DEAD.
JONATHAN... IT'S LOIS... THAT POOR CHILD. I-I THINK SHE NEEDS US.
HOW CAN YOU FORGIVE ME?
THEY... THEY JUST BURIED HIM. IT... TOOK A WHILE TO GET THE CROWD SETTLED DOWN, AND...
...AND... I ASKED MYSELF... WHAT COULD I SAY TO YOU?
I WAS THERE... ALL THE TIME CLARK FOUGHT DOOMSDAY...
...AND ALL I COULD DO WAS REPORT ON THE FIGHT... AND WATCH HIM DIE.
I COULDN'T DO ANYTHING... BUT WATCH HIM DIE.
LISTEN TO ME, LOIS. IT'S NOT YOUR FAULT. YOU DID ALL YOU COULD.
EVERY-ONE DID EVERYTHING THEY COULD.
WE'RE COMING, SWEETIE. HOLD ON A LITTLE WHILE...
...WE'LL BE RIGHT THERE.

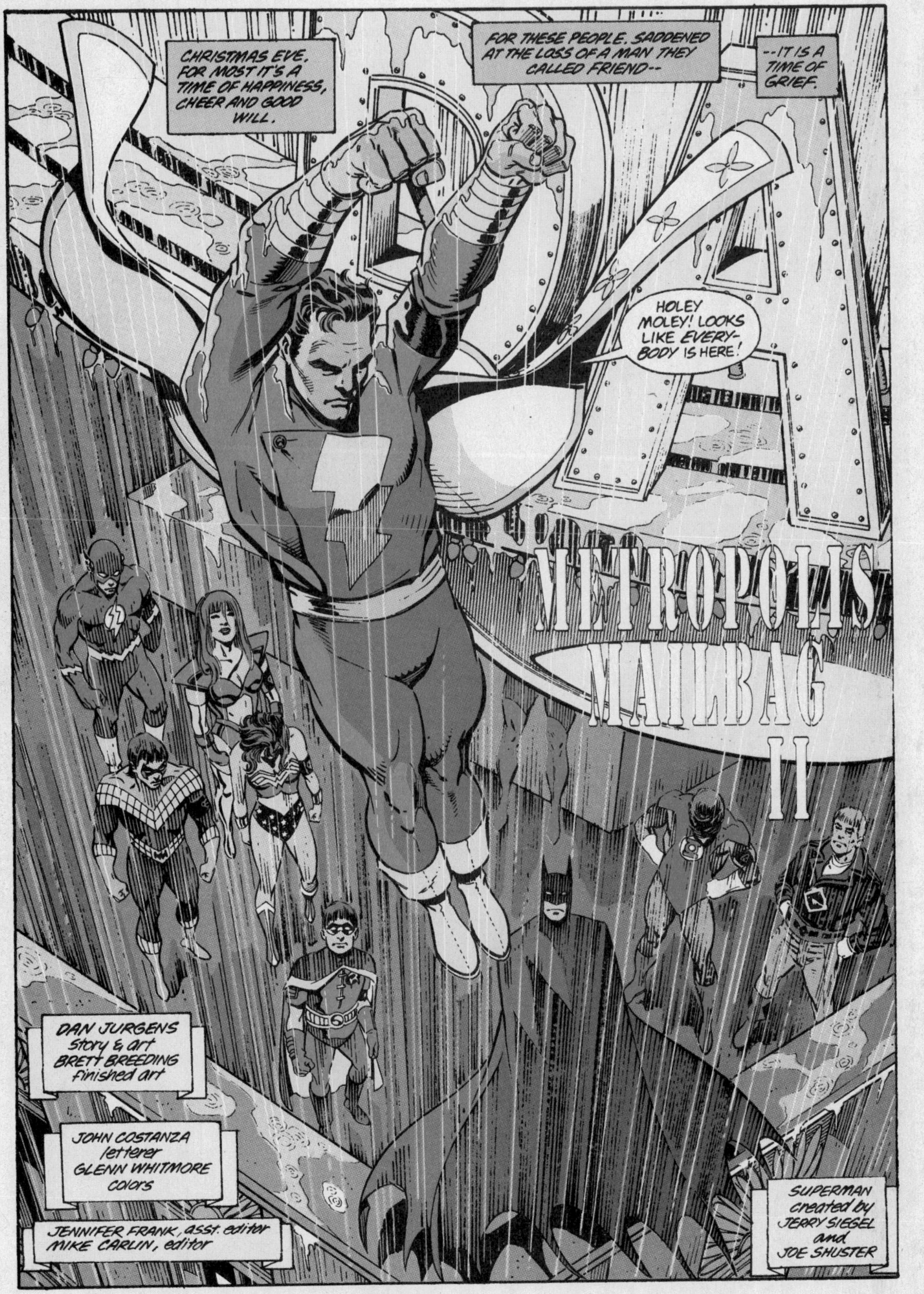
CHRISTMAS EVE. FOR MOST IT'S A TIME OF HAPPINESS, CHEER AND GOOD WILL.
FOR THESE PEOPLE. SADDENED AT THE LOSS OF A MAN THEY CALLED FRIEND--
--IT IS A TIME OF GRIEF.
HOLEY MOLEY! LOOKS LIKE EVERY-BODY IS HERE!
METROPOLIS MAILBAG II
DAN JURGENS Story & art
BRETT BREEDING finished art
JOHN COSTANZA letterer
GLENN WHITMORE colors
JENNIFER FRANK, asst. editor
MIKE CARLIN, editor
SUPERMAN created by JERRY SIEGEL and JOE SHUSTER

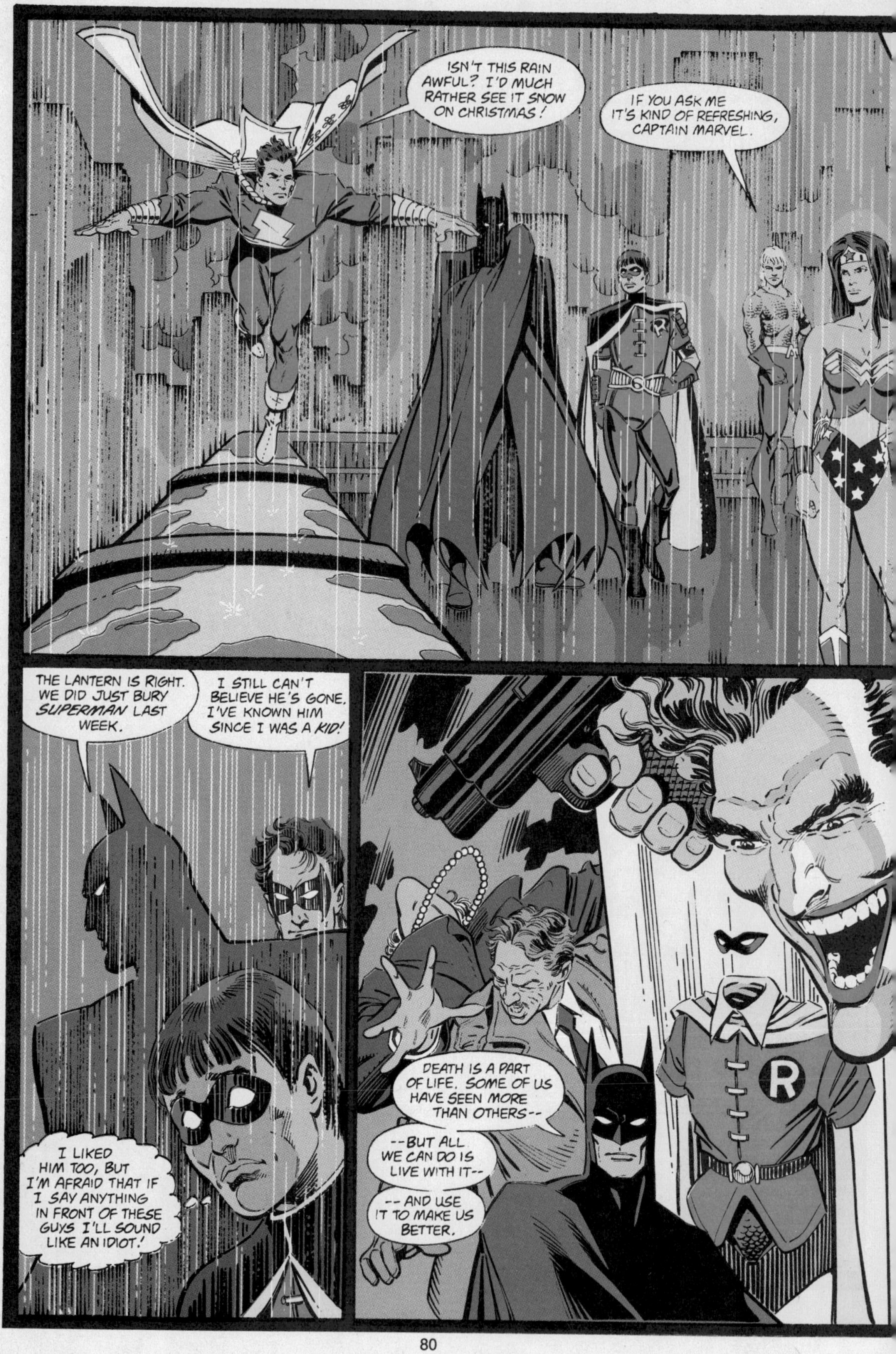

ISN'T THIS RAIN AWFUL? I'D MUCH RATHER SEE IT SNOW ON CHRISTMAS!
IF YOU ASK ME IT'S KIND OF REFRESHING, CAPTAIN MARVEL.
THE LANTERN IS RIGHT. WE DID JUST BURY SUPERMAN LAST WEEK.
I STILL CAN'T BELIEVE HE'S GONE. I'VE KNOWN HIM SINCE I WAS A KID!
I LIKED HIM TOO, BUT I'M AFRAID THAT IF I SAY ANYTHING IN FRONT OF THESE GUYS I'LL SOUND LIKE AN IDIOT!
DEATH IS A PART OF LIFE. SOME OF US HAVE SEEN MORE THAN OTHERS--
--BUT ALL WE CAN DO IS LIVE WITH IT--
--AND USE IT TO MAKE US BETTER.

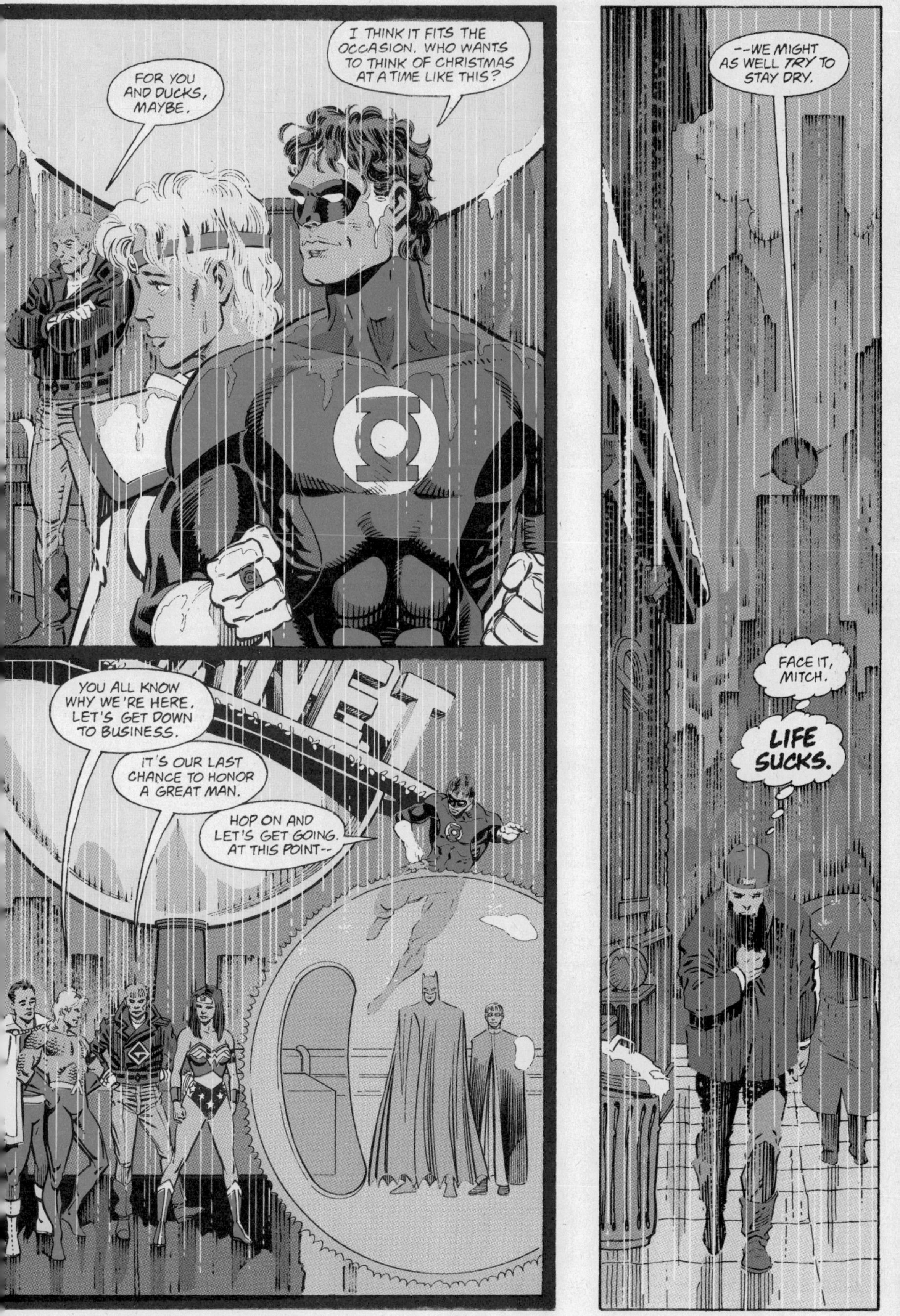
FOR YOU AND DUCKS, MAYBE.
I THINK IT FITS THE OCCASION. WHO WANTS TO THINK OF CHRISTMAS AT A TIME LIKE THIS?
YOU ALL KNOW WHY WE'RE HERE. LET'S GET DOWN TO BUSINESS.
IT'S OUR LAST CHANCE TO HONOR A GREAT MAN.
HOP ON AND LET'S GET GOING. AT THIS POINT--
--WE MIGHT AS WELL TRY TO STAY DRY.
FACE IT, MITCH.
LIFE SUCKS.

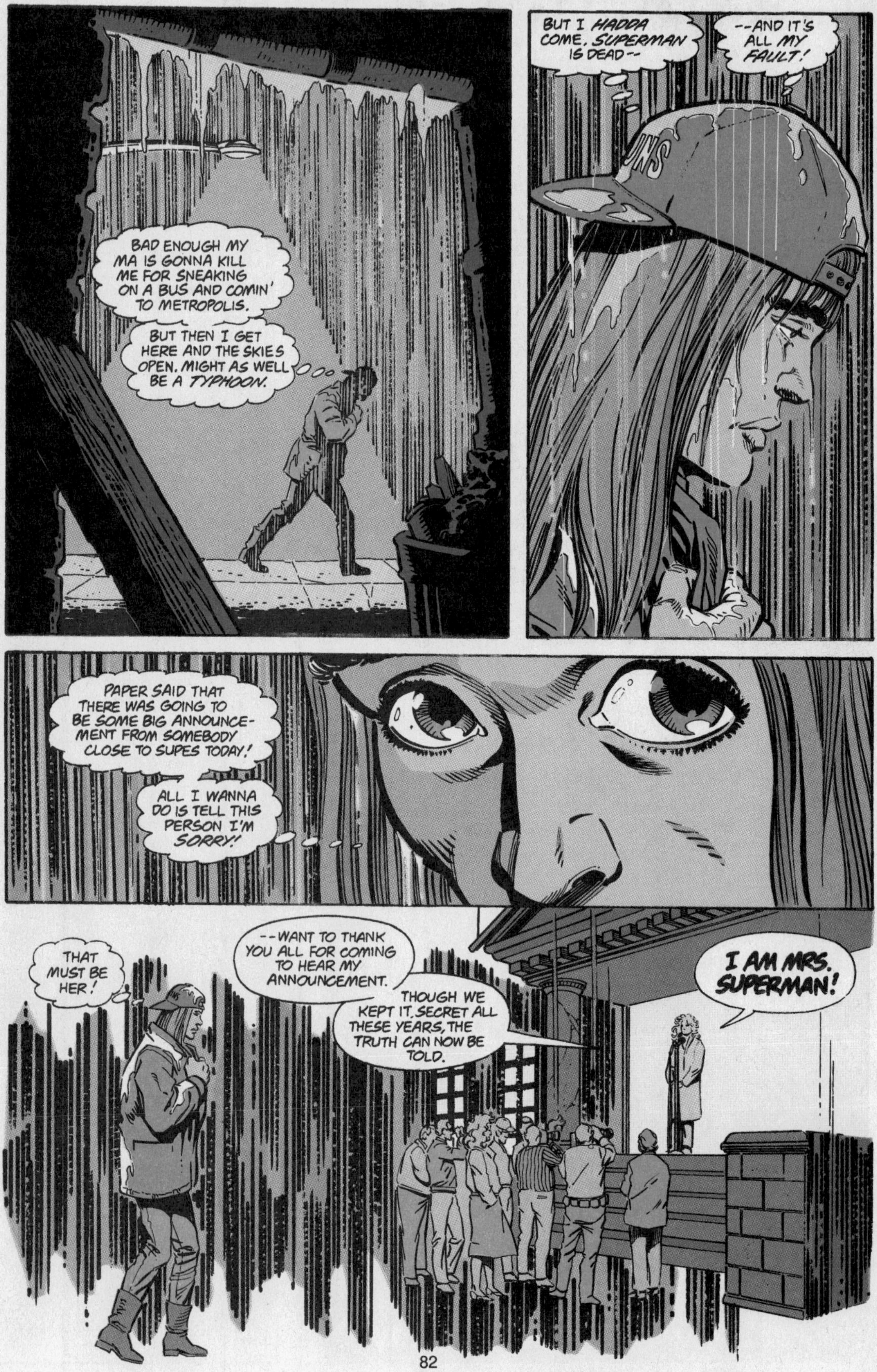

BAD ENOUGH MY MA IS GONNA KILL ME FOR SNEAKING ON A BUS AND COMIN' TO METROPOLIS.
BUT THEN I GET HERE AND THE SKIES OPEN. MIGHT AS WELL BE A TYPHOON.
BUT I HADDA COME. SUPERMAN IS DEAD--
--AND IT'S ALL MY FAULT!
PAPER SAID THAT THERE WAS GOING TO BE SOME BIG ANNOUNCE-MENT FROM SOMEBODY CLOSE TO SUPES TODAY!
ALL I WANNA DO IS TELL THIS PERSON I'M SORRY!
THAT MUST BE HER!
--WANT TO THANK YOU ALL FOR COMING TO HEAR MY ANNOUNCEMENT.
THOUGH WE KEPT IT SECRET ALL THESE YEARS, THE TRUTH CAN NOW BE TOLD.
I AM MRS. SUPERMAN!

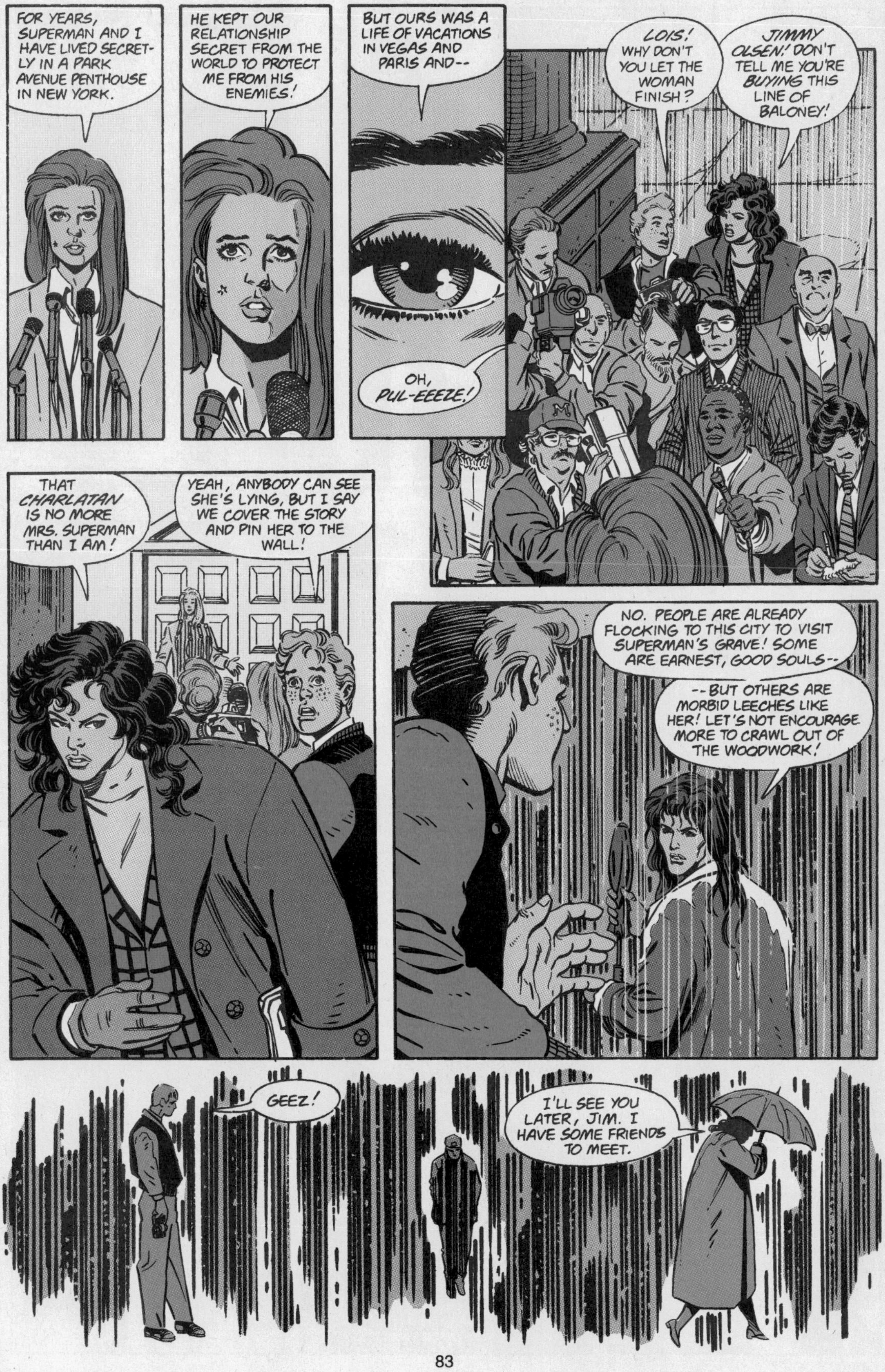
FOR YEARS, SUPERMAN AND I HAVE LIVED SECRETLY IN A PARK AVENUE PENTHOUSE IN NEW YORK.
HE KEPT OUR RELATIONSHIP SECRET FROM THE WORLD TO PROTECT ME FROM HIS ENEMIES!
BUT OURS WAS A LIFE OF VACATIONS IN VEGAS AND PARIS AND--
OH, PUL-EEEZE!
LOIS! WHY DON'T YOU LET THE WOMAN FINISH?
JIMMY OLSEN! DON'T TELL ME YOU'RE BUYING THIS LINE OF BALONEY!
THAT CHARLATAN IS NO MORE MRS. SUPERMAN THAN I AM!
YEAH, ANYBODY CAN SEE SHE'S LYING, BUT I SAY WE COVER THE STORY AND PIN HER TO THE WALL!
NO. PEOPLE ARE ALREADY FLOCKING TO THIS CITY TO VISIT SUPERMAN'S GRAVE! SOME ARE EARNEST, GOOD SOULS--
--BUT OTHERS ARE MORBID LEECHES LIKE HER! LET'S NOT ENCOURAGE MORE TO CRAWL OUT OF THE WOODWORK!
GEEZ!
I'LL SEE YOU LATER, JIM. I HAVE SOME FRIENDS TO MEET.

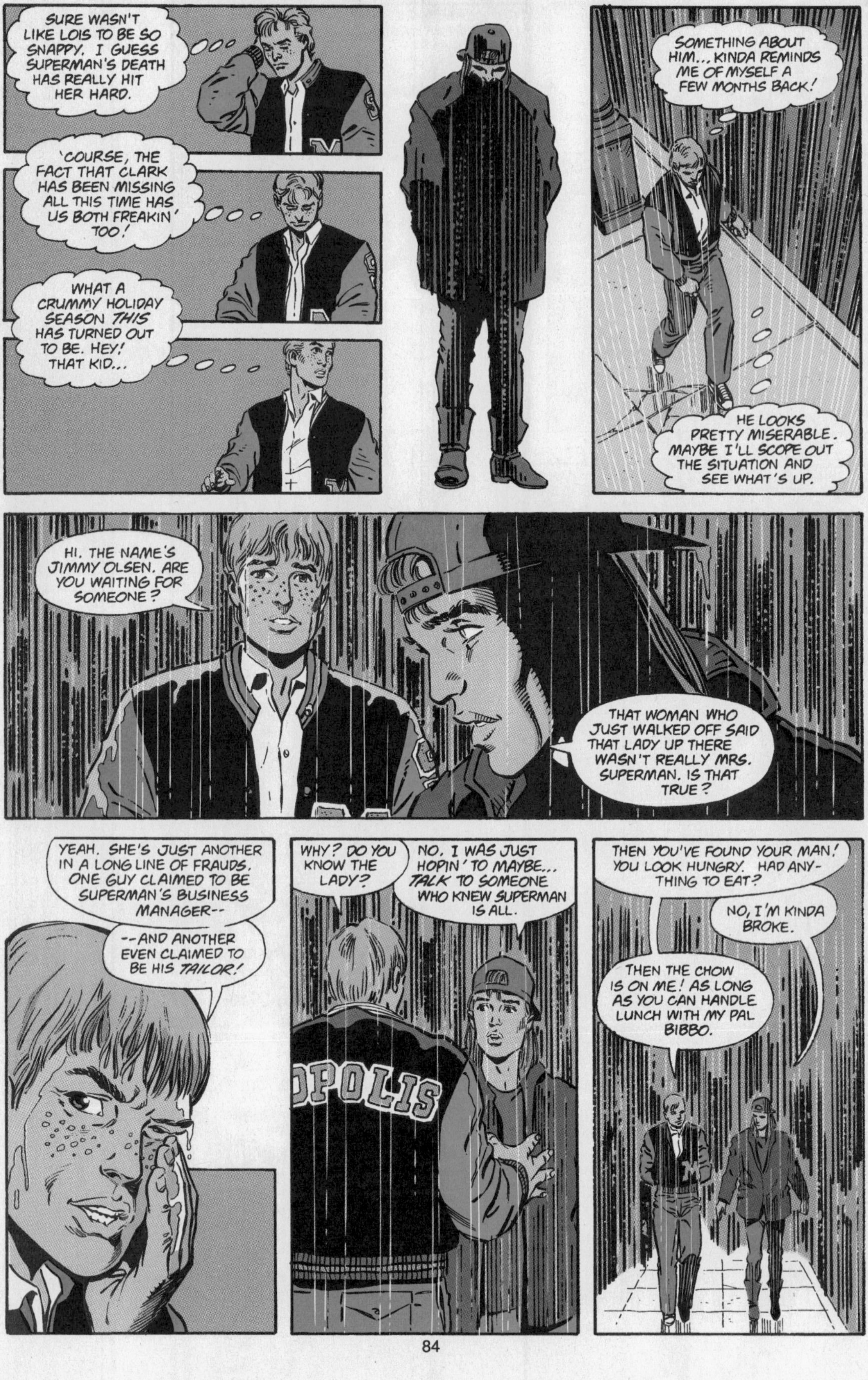
SURE WASN'T LIKE LOIS TO BE SO SNAPPY. I GUESS SUPERMAN'S DEATH HAS REALLY HIT HER HARD.
'COURSE, THE FACT THAT CLARK HAS BEEN MISSING ALL THIS TIME HAS US BOTH FREAKIN' TOO!
WHAT A CRUMMY HOLIDAY SEASON THIS HAS TURNED OUT TO BE. HEY! THAT KID...
SOMETHING ABOUT HIM... KINDA REMINDS ME OF MYSELF A FEW MONTHS BACK!
HE LOOKS PRETTY MISERABLE. MAYBE I'LL SCOPE OUT THE SITUATION AND SEE WHAT'S UP.
HI. THE NAME'S JIMMY OLSEN. ARE YOU WAITING FOR SOMEONE?
THAT WOMAN WHO JUST WALKED OFF SAID THAT LADY UP THERE WASN'T REALLY MRS. SUPERMAN. IS THAT TRUE?
YEAH. SHE'S JUST ANOTHER IN A LONG LINE OF FRAUDS. ONE GUY CLAIMED TO BE SUPERMAN'S BUSINESS MANAGER--
--AND ANOTHER EVEN CLAIMED TO BE HIS TAILOR!
WHY? DO YOU KNOW THE LADY?
NO. I WAS JUST HOPIN' TO MAYBE... TALK TO SOMEONE WHO KNEW SUPERMAN IS ALL.
OPOLIS
THEN YOU'VE FOUND YOUR MAN! YOU LOOK HUNGRY. HAD ANY-THING TO EAT?
NO, I'M KINDA BROKE.
THEN THE CHOW IS ON ME! AS LONG AS YOU CAN HANDLE LUNCH WITH MY PAL BIBBO.

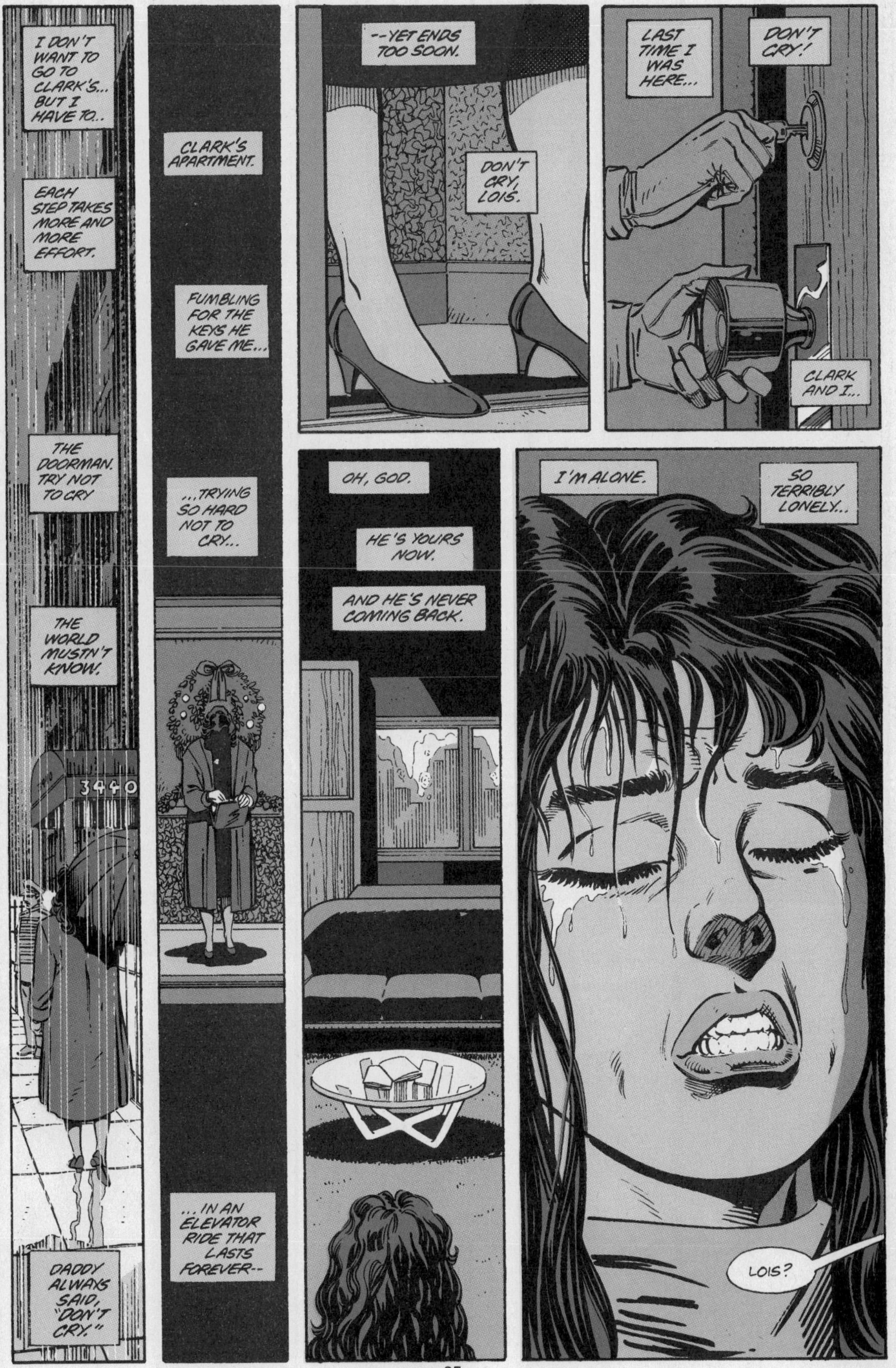
I DON'T WANT TO GO TO CLARK'S... BUT I HAVE TO...
EACH STEP TAKES MORE AND MORE EFFORT.
THE DOORMAN. TRY NOT TO CRY
THE WORLD MUSTN'T KNOW.
3440
DADDY ALWAYS SAID, "DON'T CRY."
CLARK'S APARTMENT.
FUMBLING FOR THE KEYS HE GAVE ME...
...TRYING SO HARD NOT TO CRY...
...IN AN ELEVATOR RIDE THAT LASTS FOREVER--
--YET ENDS TOO SOON.
DON'T CRY, LOIS.
LAST TIME I WAS HERE...
DON'T CRY!
CLARK AND I...
OH, GOD.
HE'S YOURS NOW.
AND HE'S NEVER COMING BACK.
I'M ALONE.
SO TERRIBLY LONELY...
LOIS?

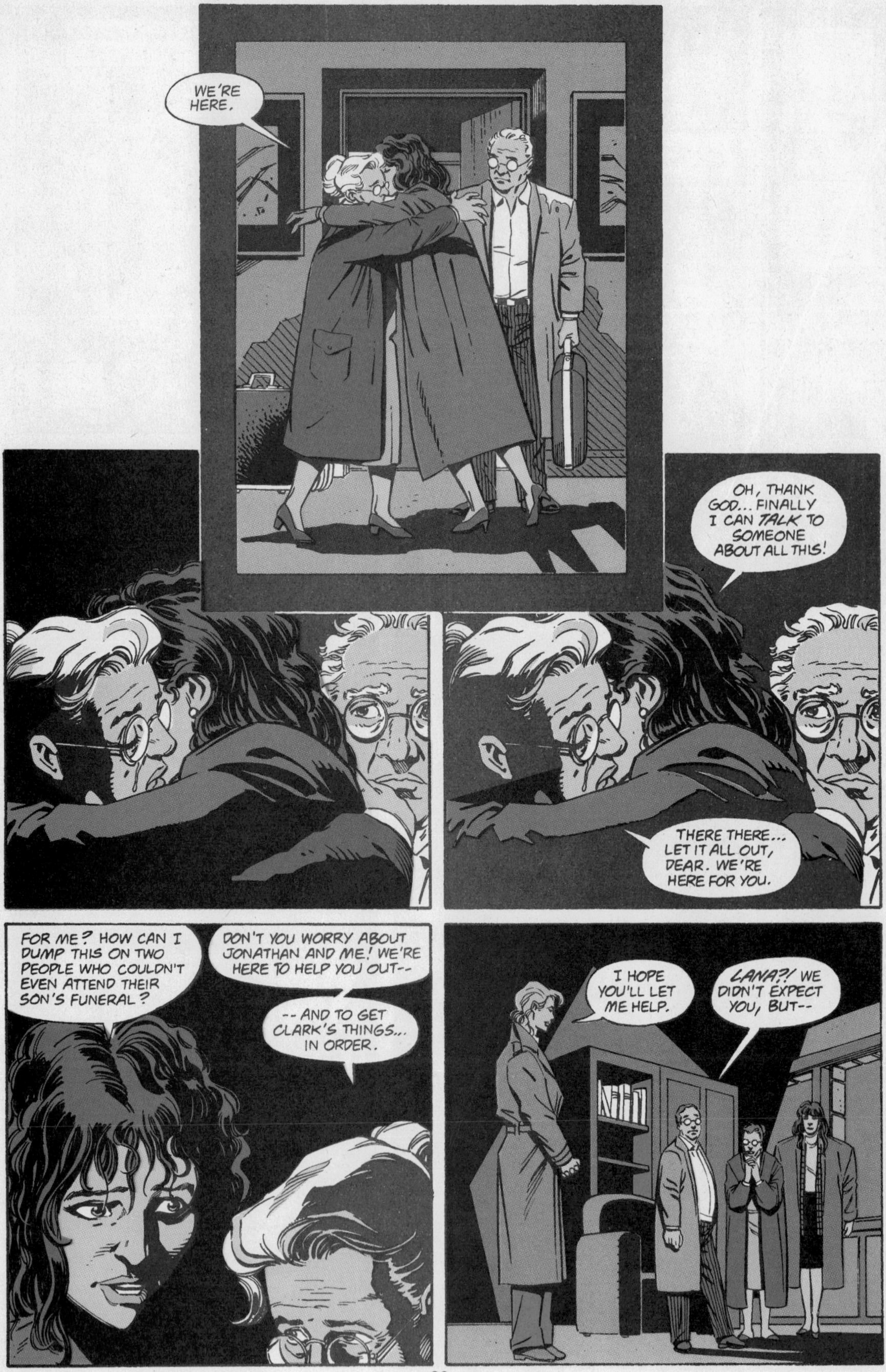
WE'RE HERE.
OH, THANK GOD... FINALLY I CAN TALK TO SOMEONE ABOUT ALL THIS!
THERE THERE... LET IT ALL OUT, DEAR. WE'RE HERE FOR YOU.
FOR ME? HOW CAN I DUMP THIS ON TWO PEOPLE WHO COULDN'T EVEN ATTEND THEIR SON'S FUNERAL?
DON'T YOU WORRY ABOUT JONATHAN AND ME! WE'RE HERE TO HELP YOU OUT--
--AND TO GET CLARK'S THINGS... IN ORDER.
I HOPE YOU'LL LET ME HELP.
LANA?! WE DIDN'T EXPECT YOU, BUT--

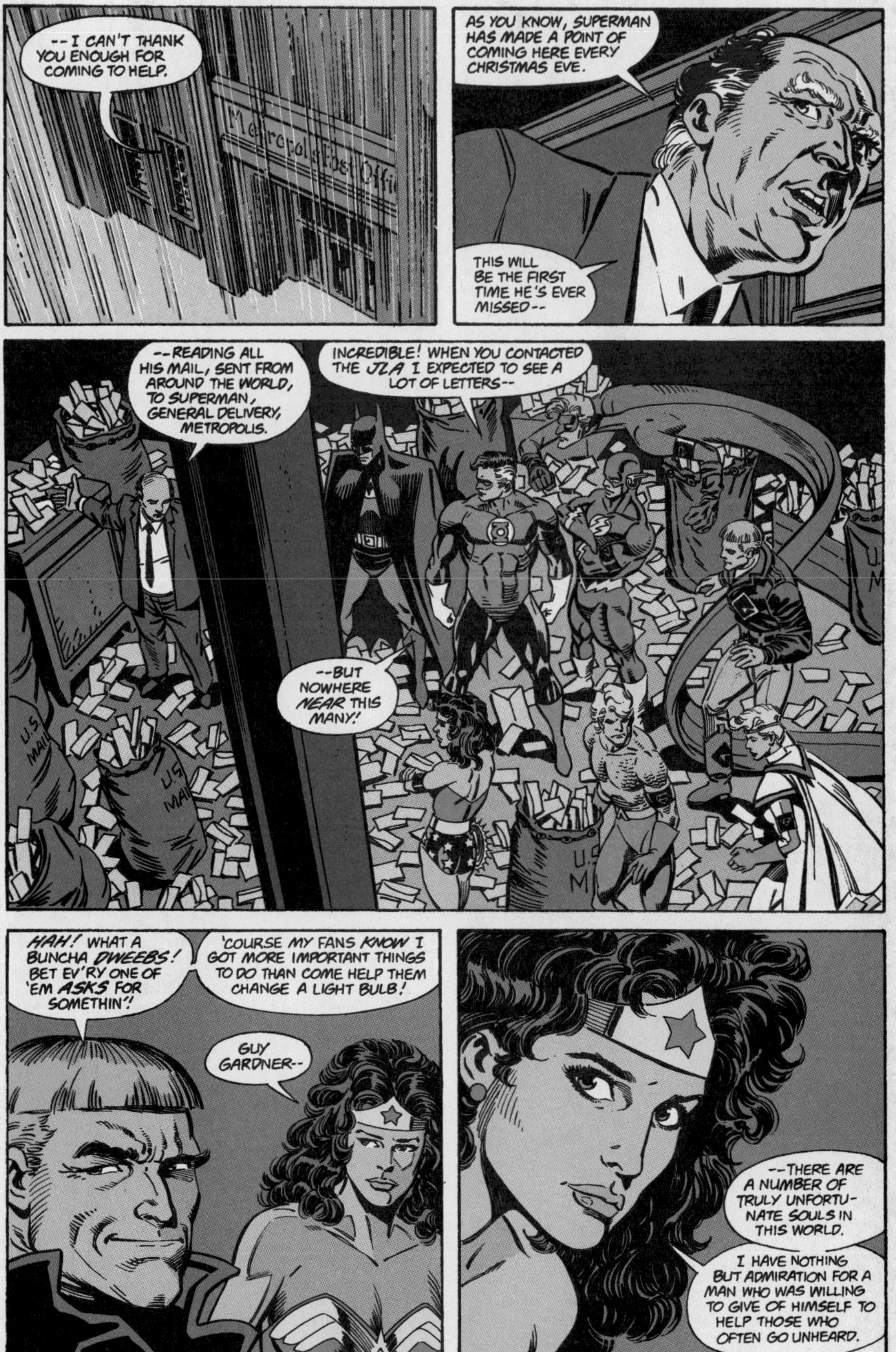

-- I CAN'T THANK YOU ENOUGH FOR COMING TO HELP.
AS YOU KNOW, SUPERMAN HAS MADE A POINT OF COMING HERE EVERY CHRISTMAS EVE.
THIS WILL BE THE FIRST TIME HE'S EVER MISSED--
--READING ALL HIS MAIL, SENT FROM AROUND THE WORLD, TO SUPERMAN, GENERAL DELIVERY, METROPOLIS.
INCREDIBLE! WHEN YOU CONTACTED THE JLA I EXPECTED TO SEE A LOT OF LETTERS--
--BUT NOWHERE NEAR THIS MANY!
HAH! WHAT A BUNCHA DWEEBS! BET EV'RY ONE OF 'EM ASKS FOR SOMETHIN'!
'COURSE MY FANS KNOW I GOT MORE IMPORTANT THINGS TO DO THAN COME HELP THEM CHANGE A LIGHT BULB!
GUY GARDNER--
--THERE ARE A NUMBER OF TRULY UNFORTU-NATE SOULS IN THIS WORLD.
I HAVE NOTHING BUT ADMIRATION FOR A MAN WHO WAS WILLING TO GIVE OF HIMSELF TO HELP THOSE WHO OFTEN GO UNHEARD.

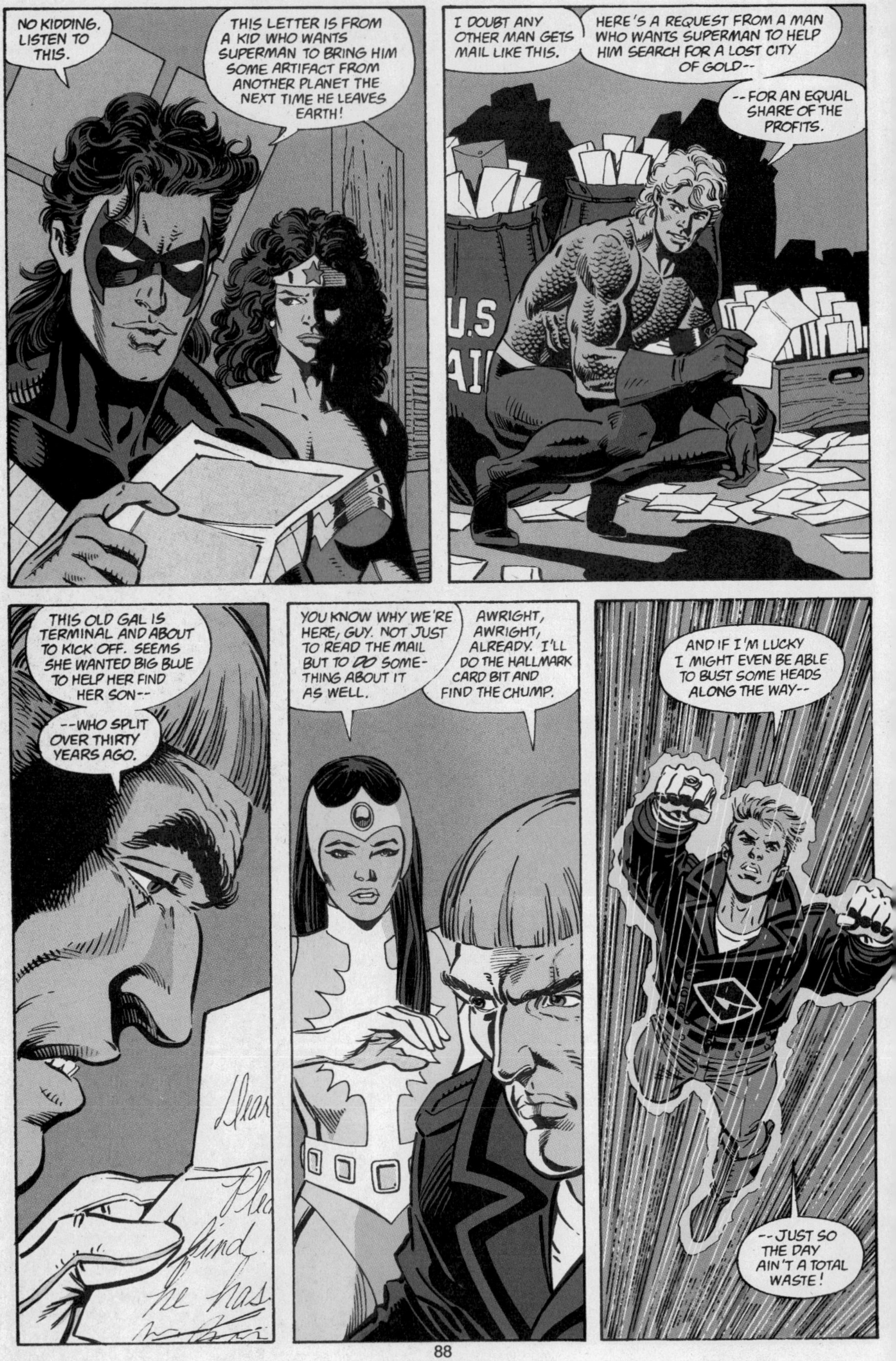
NO KIDDING. LISTEN TO THIS.
THIS LETTER IS FROM A KID WHO WANTS SUPERMAN TO BRING HIM SOME ARTIFACT FROM ANOTHER PLANET THE NEXT TIME HE LEAVES EARTH!
I DOUBT ANY OTHER MAN GETS MAIL LIKE THIS.
HERE'S A REQUEST FROM A MAN WHO WANTS SUPERMAN TO HELP HIM SEARCH FOR A LOST CITY OF GOLD--
--FOR AN EQUAL SHARE OF THE PROFITS.
U.S
THIS OLD GAL IS TERMINAL AND ABOUT TO KICK OFF. SEEMS SHE WANTED BIG BLUE TO HELP HER FIND HER SON--
--WHO SPLIT OVER THIRTY YEARS AGO.
YOU KNOW WHY WE'RE HERE, GUY. NOT JUST TO READ THE MAIL BUT TO DO SOMETHING ABOUT IT AS WELL.
AWRIGHT, AWRIGHT, ALREADY. I'LL DO THE HALLMARK CARD BIT AND FIND THE CHUMP.
AND IF I'M LUCKY I MIGHT EVEN BE ABLE TO BUST SOME HEADS ALONG THE WAY--
--JUST SO THE DAY AIN'T A TOTAL WASTE!

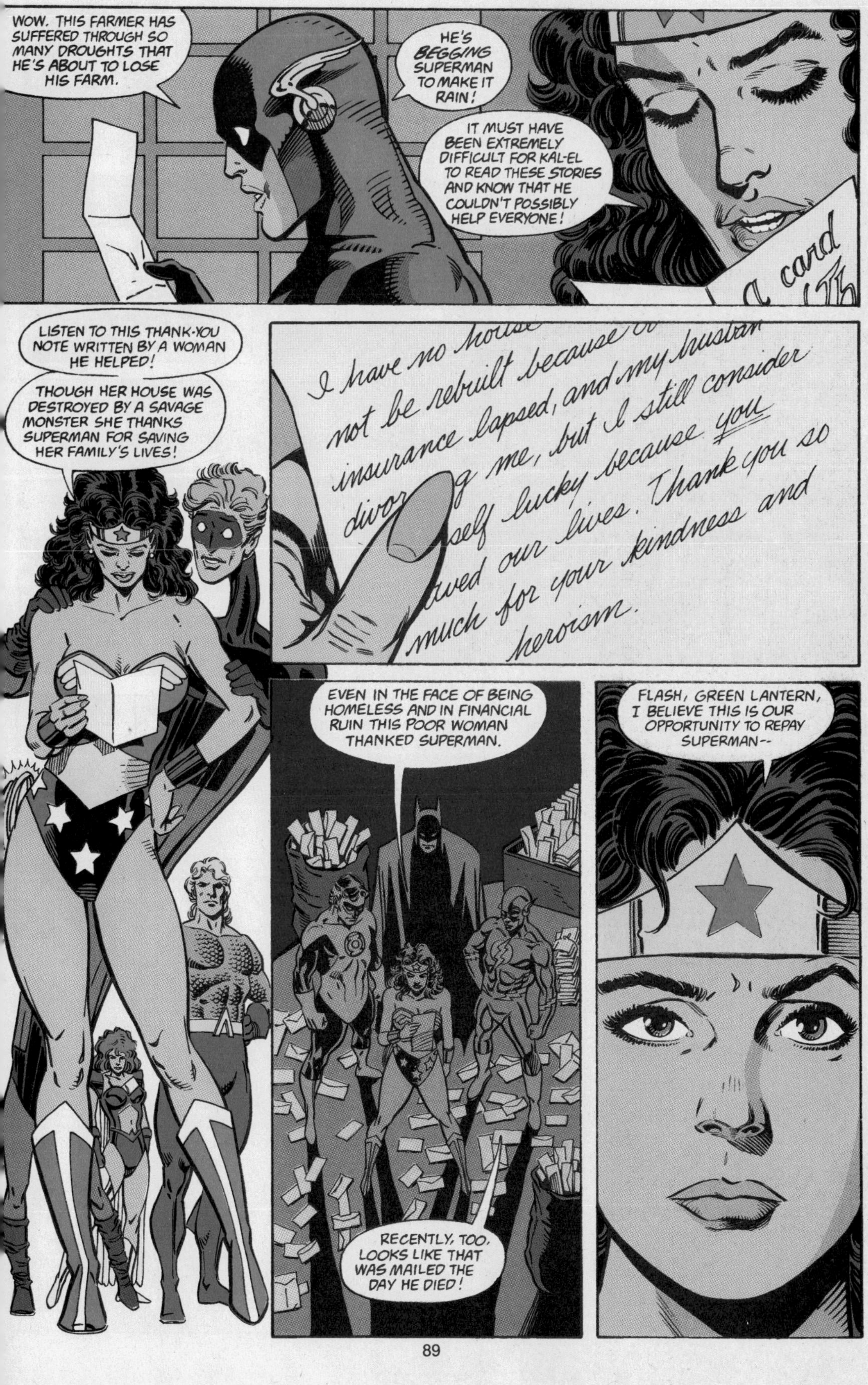
WOW. THIS FARMER HAS SUFFERED THROUGH SO MANY DROUGHTS THAT HE'S ABOUT TO LOSE HIS FARM.
HE'S BEGGING SUPERMAN TO MAKE IT RAIN!
IT MUST HAVE BEEN EXTREMELY DIFFICULT FOR KAL-EL TO READ THESE STORIES AND KNOW THAT HE COULDN'T POSSIBLY HELP EVERYONE!
LISTEN TO THIS THANK-YOU NOTE WRITTEN BY A WOMAN HE HELPED!
THOUGH HER HOUSE WAS DESTROYED BY A SAVAGE MONSTER SHE THANKS SUPERMAN FOR SAVING HER FAMILY'S LIVES!
I have no house
not be rebuilt because of
insurance lapsed, and my husban
divor g me, but I still consider
self lucky because you
ved our lives. Thank you so
much for your kindness and
heroism.
EVEN IN THE FACE OF BEING HOMELESS AND IN FINANCIAL RUIN THIS POOR WOMAN THANKED SUPERMAN.
RECENTLY, TOO. LOOKS LIKE THAT WAS MAILED THE DAY HE DIED!
FLASH, GREEN LANTERN, I BELIEVE THIS IS OUR OPPORTUNITY TO REPAY SUPERMAN--

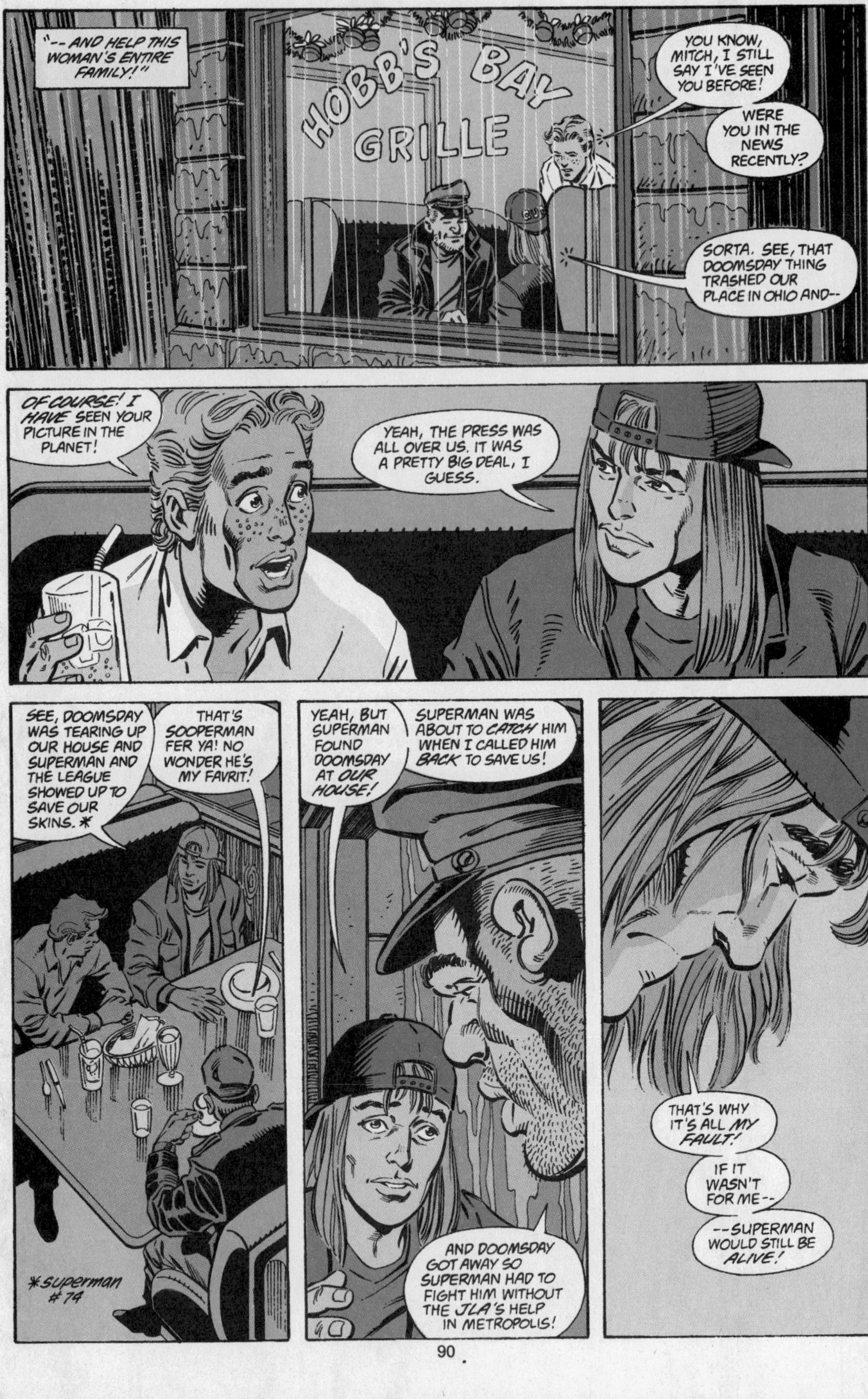
"--AND HELP THIS WOMAN'S ENTIRE FAMILY!"
HOBB'S BAY GRILLE
YOU KNOW, MITCH, I STILL SAY I'VE SEEN YOU BEFORE!
WERE YOU IN THE NEWS RECENTLY?
SORTA. SEE, THAT DOOMSDAY THING TRASHED OUR PLACE IN OHIO AND--
OF COURSE! I HAVE SEEN YOUR PICTURE IN THE PLANET!
YEAH, THE PRESS WAS ALL OVER US. IT WAS A PRETTY BIG DEAL, I GUESS.
SEE, DOOMSDAY WAS TEARING UP OUR HOUSE AND SUPERMAN AND THE LEAGUE SHOWED UP TO SAVE OUR SKINS. *
THAT'S SOOPERMAN FER YA! NO WONDER HE'S MY FAVRIT!
*Superman #74
YEAH, BUT SUPERMAN FOUND DOOMSDAY AT OUR HOUSE!
SUPERMAN WAS ABOUT TO CATCH HIM WHEN I CALLED HIM BACK TO SAVE US!
AND DOOMSDAY GOT AWAY SO SUPERMAN HAD TO FIGHT HIM WITHOUT THE JLA'S HELP IN METROPOLIS!
THAT'S WHY IT'S ALL MY FAULT!
IF IT WASN'T FOR ME--
--SUPERMAN WOULD STILL BE ALIVE!

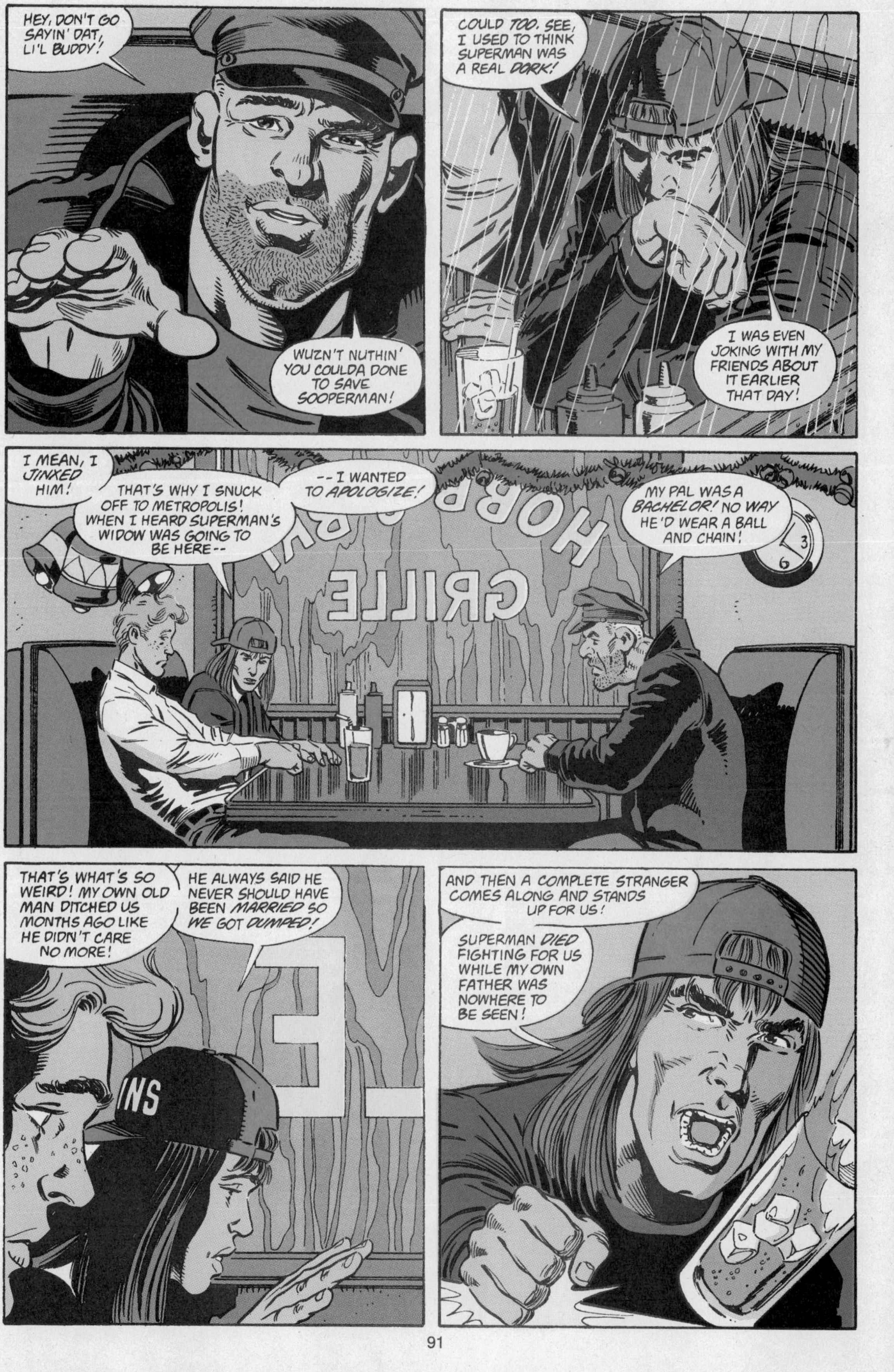
HEY, DON'T GO SAYIN' DAT, LI'L BUDDY!
WUZN'T NUTHIN' YOU COULDA DONE TO SAVE SOOPERMAN!
COULD TOO. SEE, I USED TO THINK SUPERMAN WAS A REAL DORK!
I WAS EVEN JOKING WITH MY FRIENDS ABOUT IT EARLIER THAT DAY!
I MEAN, I JINXED HIM!
THAT'S WHY I SNUCK OFF TO METROPOLIS! WHEN I HEARD SUPERMAN'S WIDOW WAS GOING TO BE HERE--
--I WANTED TO APOLOGIZE!
MY PAL WAS A BACHELOR! NO WAY HE'D WEAR A BALL AND CHAIN!
GRILLE
THAT'S WHAT'S SO WEIRD! MY OWN OLD MAN DITCHED US MONTHS AGO LIKE HE DIDN'T CARE NO MORE!
HE ALWAYS SAID HE NEVER SHOULD HAVE BEEN MARRIED SO WE GOT DUMPED!
AND THEN A COMPLETE STRANGER COMES ALONG AND STANDS UP FOR US!
SUPERMAN DIED FIGHTING FOR US WHILE MY OWN FATHER WAS NOWHERE TO BE SEEN!

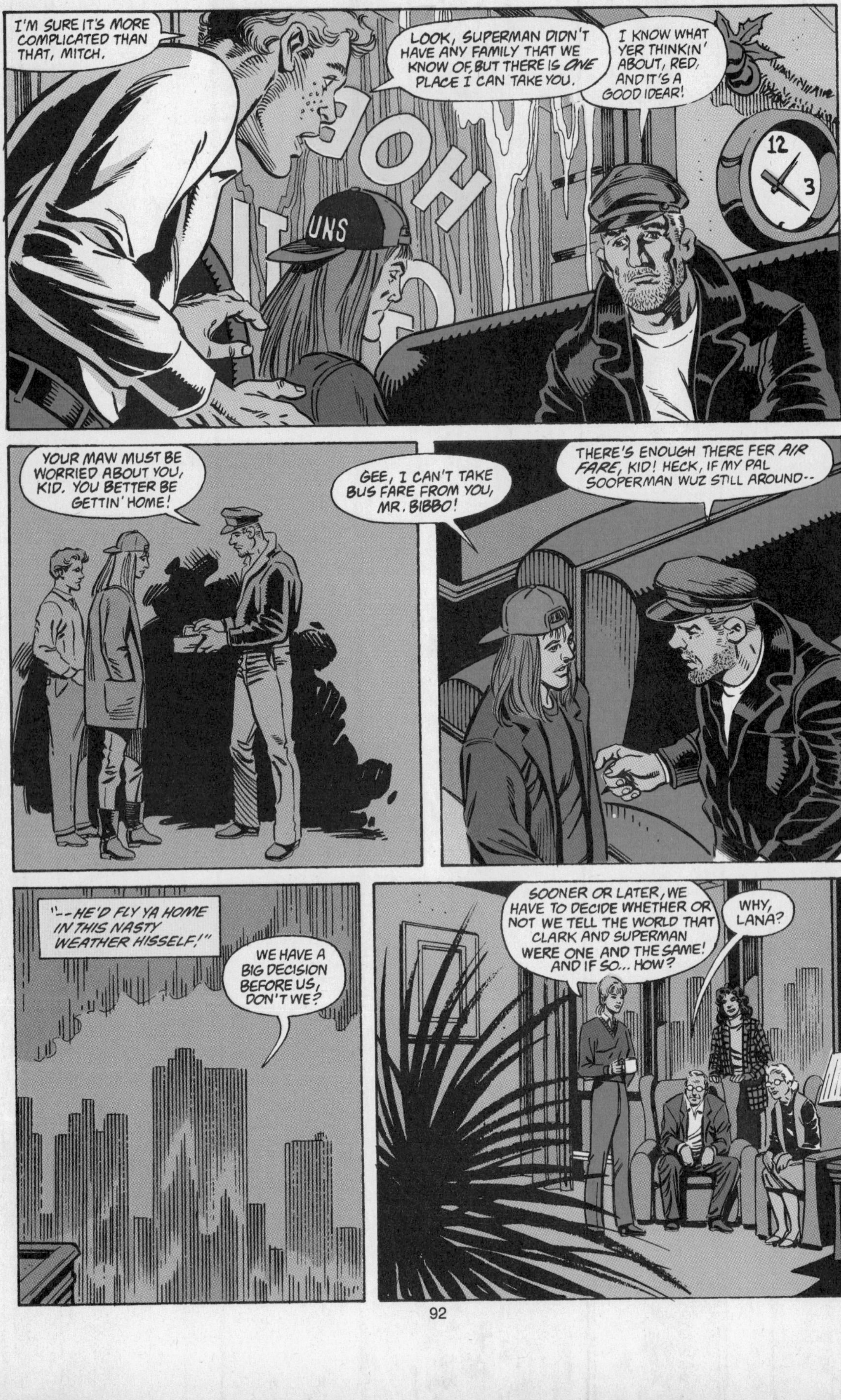
I'M SURE IT'S MORE COMPLICATED THAN THAT, MITCH.
LOOK, SUPERMAN DIDN'T HAVE ANY FAMILY THAT WE KNOW OF, BUT THERE IS *ONE* PLACE I CAN TAKE YOU.
I KNOW WHAT YER THINKIN' ABOUT, RED, AND IT'S A GOOD IDEAR!
12
3
UNS
YOUR MAW MUST BE WORRIED ABOUT YOU, KID. YOU BETTER BE GETTIN' HOME!
GEE, I CAN'T TAKE BUS FARE FROM YOU, MR. BIBBO!
THERE'S ENOUGH THERE FER *AIR FARE*, KID! HECK, IF MY PAL SOOPERMAN WUZ STILL AROUND--
"--HE'D FLY YA HOME IN THIS NASTY WEATHER HISSELF!"
WE HAVE A BIG DECISION BEFORE US, DON'T WE?
SOONER OR LATER, WE HAVE TO DECIDE WHETHER OR NOT WE TELL THE WORLD THAT CLARK AND SUPERMAN WERE ONE AND THE SAME! AND IF SO... HOW?
WHY, LANA?

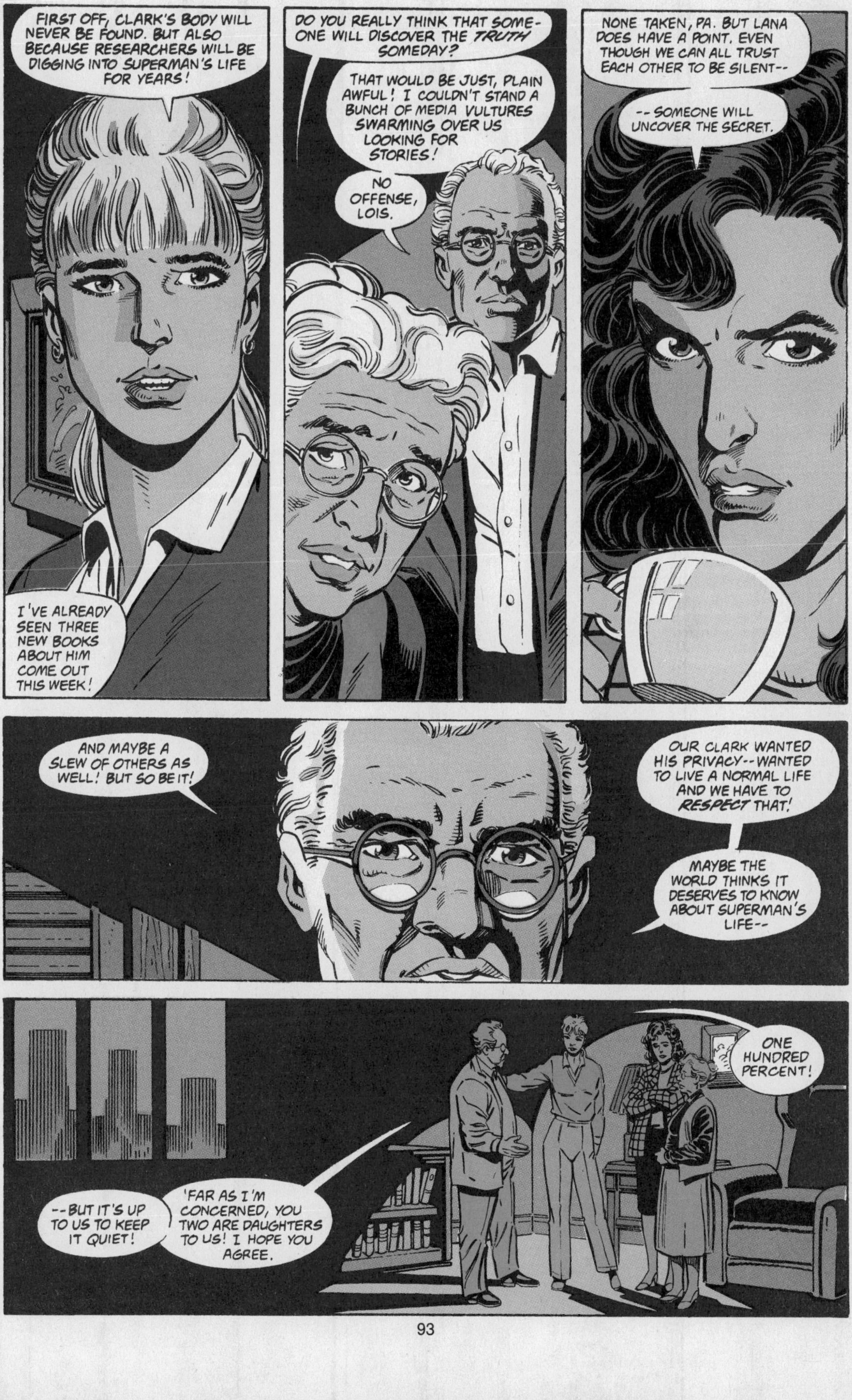
FIRST OFF, CLARK'S BODY WILL NEVER BE FOUND. BUT ALSO BECAUSE RESEARCHERS WILL BE DIGGING INTO SUPERMAN'S LIFE FOR YEARS!
I'VE ALREADY SEEN THREE NEW BOOKS ABOUT HIM COME OUT THIS WEEK!
DO YOU REALLY THINK THAT SOMEONE WILL DISCOVER THE TRUTH SOMEDAY?
THAT WOULD BE JUST, PLAIN AWFUL! I COULDN'T STAND A BUNCH OF MEDIA VULTURES SWARMING OVER US LOOKING FOR STORIES!
NO OFFENSE, LOIS.
NONE TAKEN, PA. BUT LANA DOES HAVE A POINT. EVEN THOUGH WE CAN ALL TRUST EACH OTHER TO BE SILENT--
--SOMEONE WILL UNCOVER THE SECRET.
AND MAYBE A SLEW OF OTHERS AS WELL! BUT SO BE IT!
OUR CLARK WANTED HIS PRIVACY--WANTED TO LIVE A NORMAL LIFE AND WE HAVE TO RESPECT THAT!
MAYBE THE WORLD THINKS IT DESERVES TO KNOW ABOUT SUPERMAN'S LIFE--
--BUT IT'S UP TO US TO KEEP IT QUIET!
'FAR AS I'M CONCERNED, YOU TWO ARE DAUGHTERS TO US! I HOPE YOU AGREE.
ONE HUNDRED PERCENT!

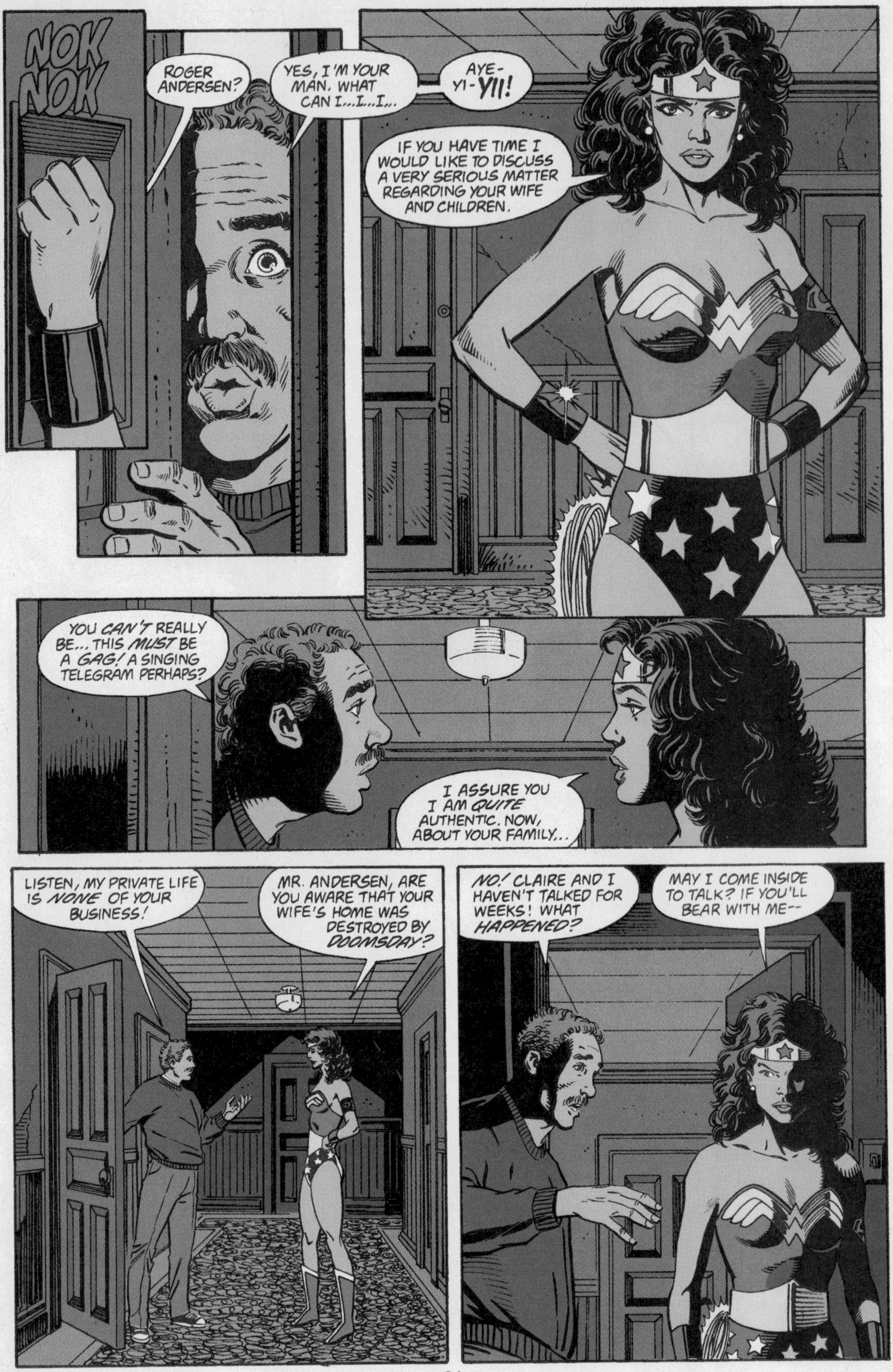
NOK NOK
ROGER ANDERSEN?
YES, I'M YOUR MAN. WHAT CAN I...I...I...
AYE-YI-YII!
IF YOU HAVE TIME I WOULD LIKE TO DISCUSS A VERY SERIOUS MATTER REGARDING YOUR WIFE AND CHILDREN.
YOU CAN'T REALLY BE... THIS MUST BE A GAG! A SINGING TELEGRAM PERHAPS?
I ASSURE YOU I AM QUITE AUTHENTIC. NOW, ABOUT YOUR FAMILY...
LISTEN, MY PRIVATE LIFE IS NONE OF YOUR BUSINESS!
MR. ANDERSEN, ARE YOU AWARE THAT YOUR WIFE'S HOME WAS DESTROYED BY DOOMSDAY?
NO! CLAIRE AND I HAVEN'T TALKED FOR WEEKS! WHAT HAPPENED?
MAY I COME INSIDE TO TALK? IF YOU'LL BEAR WITH ME--

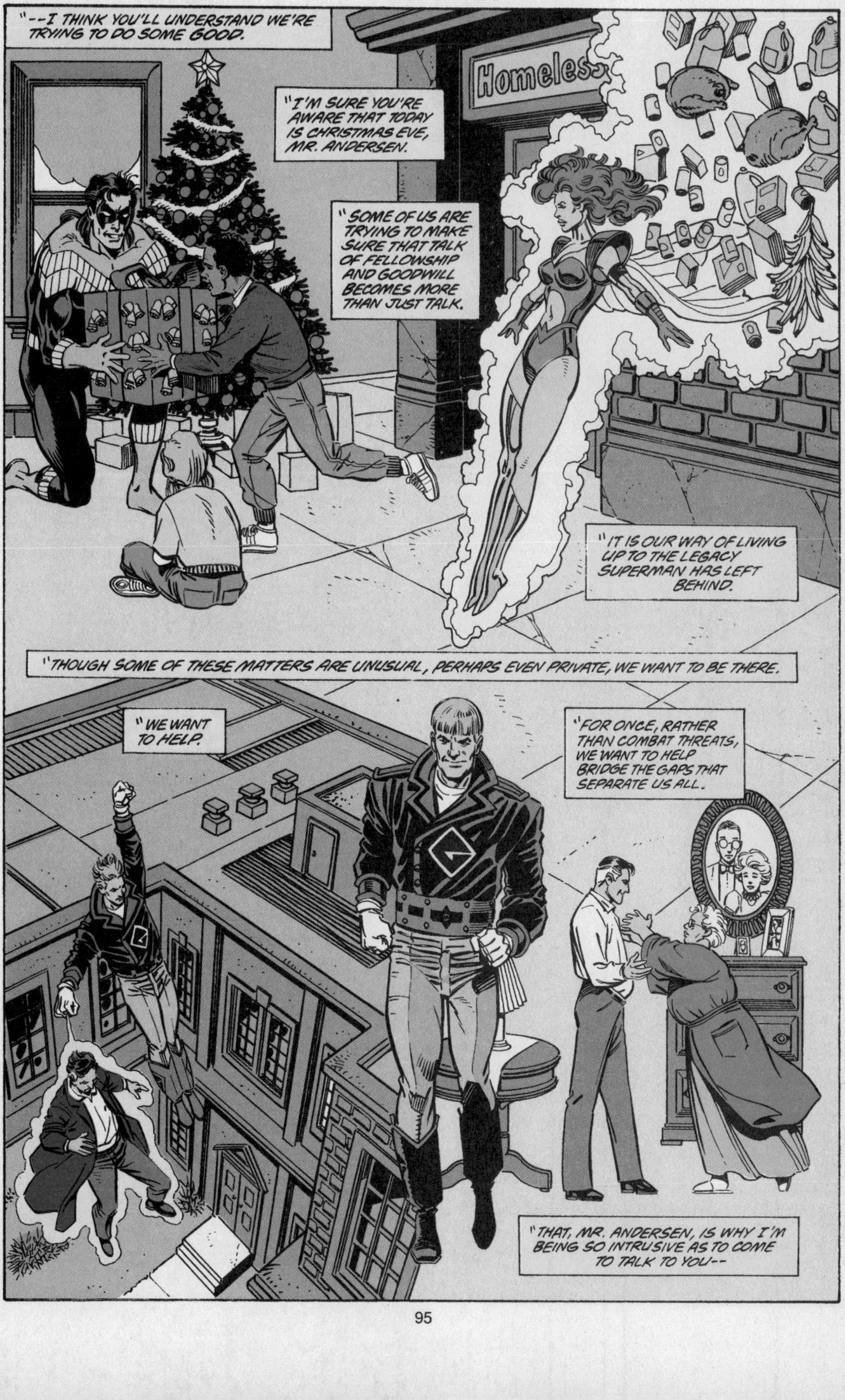
"--I THINK YOU'LL UNDERSTAND WE'RE TRYING TO DO SOME GOOD.
Homeless
"I'M SURE YOU'RE AWARE THAT TODAY IS CHRISTMAS EVE, MR. ANDERSEN.
"SOME OF US ARE TRYING TO MAKE SURE THAT TALK OF FELLOWSHIP AND GOODWILL BECOMES MORE THAN JUST TALK.
"IT IS OUR WAY OF LIVING UP TO THE LEGACY SUPERMAN HAS LEFT BEHIND.
"THOUGH SOME OF THESE MATTERS ARE UNUSUAL, PERHAPS EVEN PRIVATE, WE WANT TO BE THERE.
"WE WANT TO HELP.
"FOR ONCE, RATHER THAN COMBAT THREATS, WE WANT TO HELP BRIDGE THE GAPS THAT SEPARATE US ALL.
"THAT, MR. ANDERSEN, IS WHY I'M BEING SO INTRUSIVE AS TO COME TO TALK TO YOU--

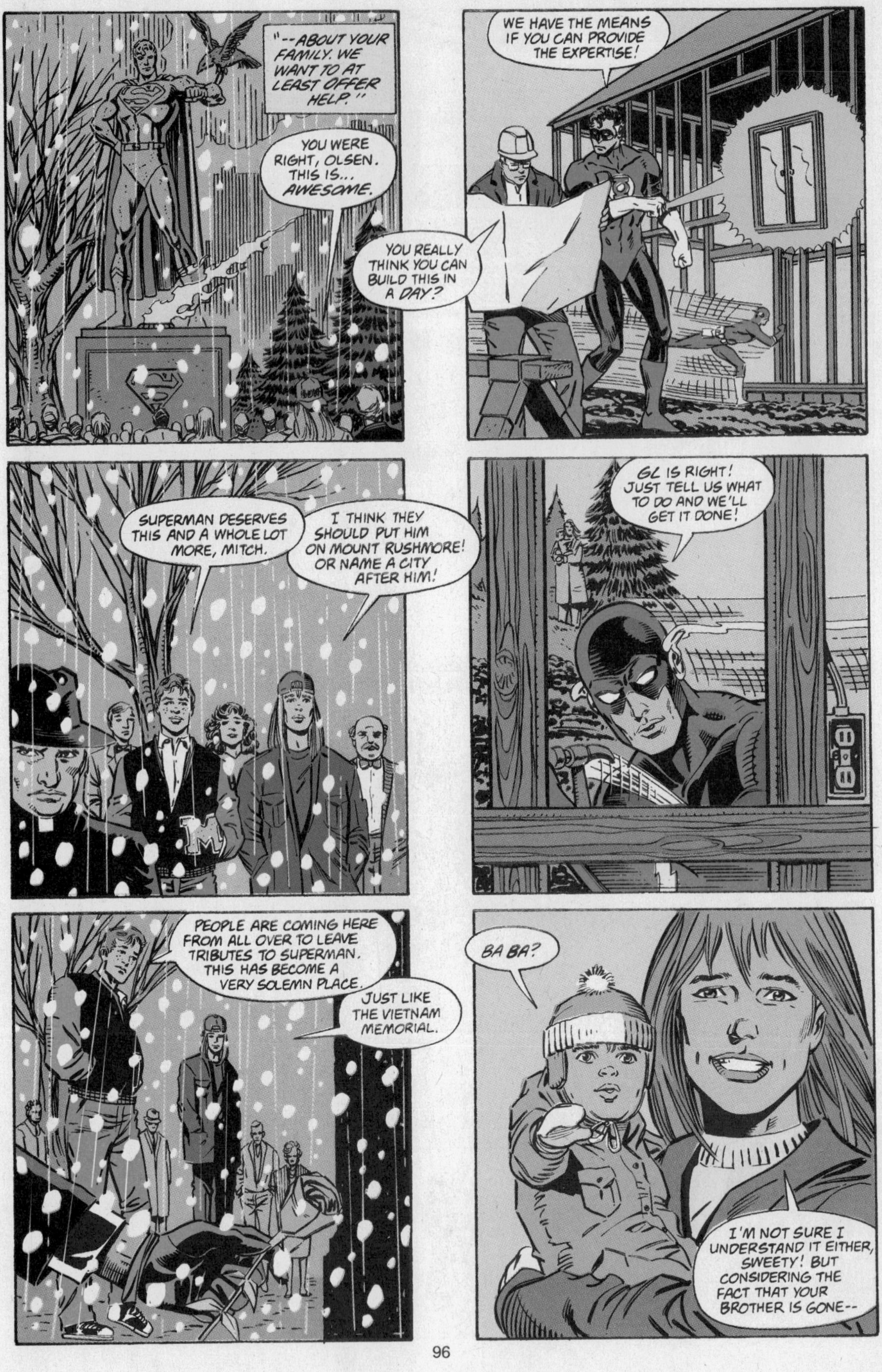
"--ABOUT YOUR FAMILY. WE WANT TO AT LEAST OFFER HELP."
YOU WERE RIGHT, OLSEN. THIS IS... AWESOME.
WE HAVE THE MEANS IF YOU CAN PROVIDE THE EXPERTISE!
YOU REALLY THINK YOU CAN BUILD THIS IN A DAY?
SUPERMAN DESERVES THIS AND A WHOLE LOT MORE, MITCH.
I THINK THEY SHOULD PUT HIM ON MOUNT RUSHMORE! OR NAME A CITY AFTER HIM!
GL IS RIGHT! JUST TELL US WHAT TO DO AND WE'LL GET IT DONE!
PEOPLE ARE COMING HERE FROM ALL OVER TO LEAVE TRIBUTES TO SUPERMAN. THIS HAS BECOME A VERY SOLEMN PLACE.
JUST LIKE THE VIETNAM MEMORIAL.
BA BA?
I'M NOT SURE I UNDERSTAND IT EITHER, SWEETY! BUT CONSIDERING THE FACT THAT YOUR BROTHER IS GONE--

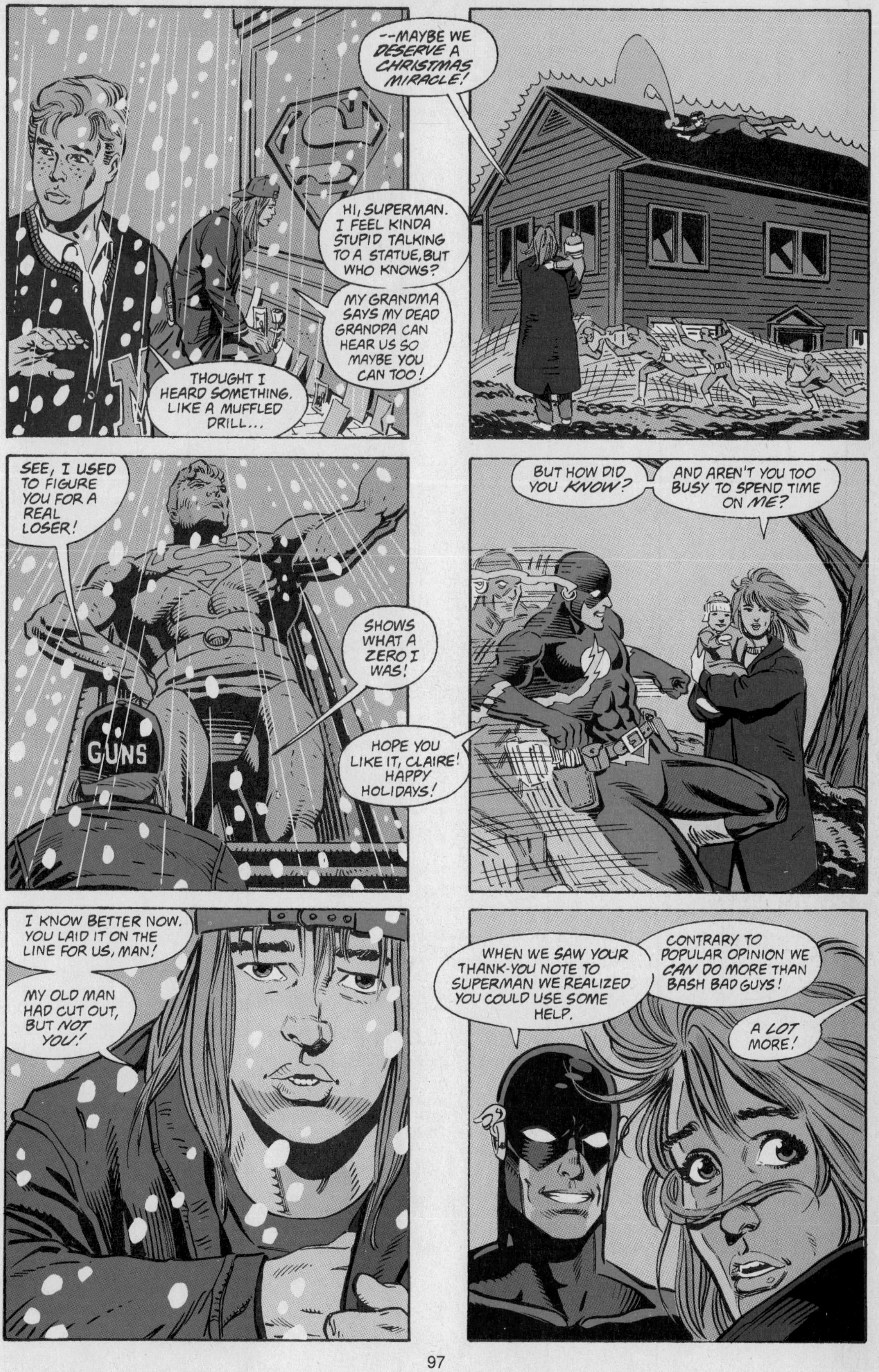
--MAYBE WE DESERVE A CHRISTMAS MIRACLE!
HI, SUPERMAN. I FEEL KINDA STUPID TALKING TO A STATUE, BUT WHO KNOWS?
MY GRANDMA SAYS MY DEAD GRANDPA CAN HEAR US SO MAYBE YOU CAN TOO!
THOUGHT I HEARD SOMETHING. LIKE A MUFFLED DRILL...
SEE, I USED TO FIGURE YOU FOR A REAL LOSER!
SHOWS WHAT A ZERO I WAS!
GUNS
BUT HOW DID YOU KNOW?
AND AREN'T YOU TOO BUSY TO SPEND TIME ON ME?
HOPE YOU LIKE IT, CLAIRE! HAPPY HOLIDAYS!
I KNOW BETTER NOW. YOU LAID IT ON THE LINE FOR US, MAN!
MY OLD MAN HAD CUT OUT, BUT NOT YOU!
WHEN WE SAW YOUR THANK-YOU NOTE TO SUPERMAN WE REALIZED YOU COULD USE SOME HELP.
CONTRARY TO POPULAR OPINION WE CAN DO MORE THAN BASH BAD GUYS!
A LOT MORE!

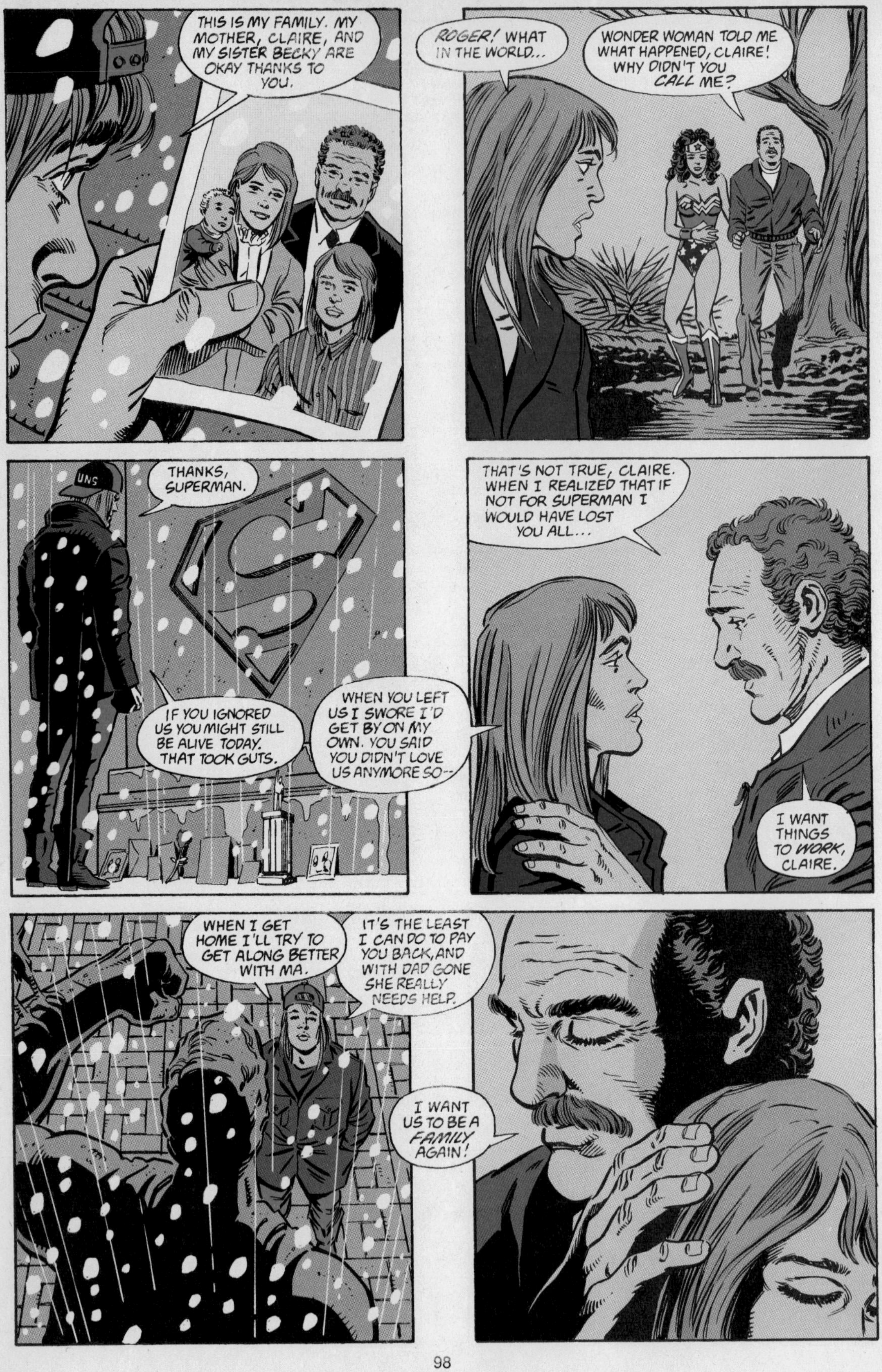
THIS IS MY FAMILY. MY MOTHER, CLAIRE, AND MY SISTER BECKY ARE OKAY THANKS TO YOU.
ROGER! WHAT IN THE WORLD...
WONDER WOMAN TOLD ME WHAT HAPPENED, CLAIRE! WHY DIDN'T YOU CALL ME?
THANKS, SUPERMAN.
IF YOU IGNORED US YOU MIGHT STILL BE ALIVE TODAY. THAT TOOK GUTS.
WHEN YOU LEFT US I SWORE I'D GET BY ON MY OWN. YOU SAID YOU DIDN'T LOVE US ANYMORE SO--
THAT'S NOT TRUE, CLAIRE. WHEN I REALIZED THAT IF NOT FOR SUPERMAN I WOULD HAVE LOST YOU ALL...
I WANT THINGS TO WORK, CLAIRE.
WHEN I GET HOME I'LL TRY TO GET ALONG BETTER WITH MA.
IT'S THE LEAST I CAN DO TO PAY YOU BACK, AND WITH DAD GONE SHE REALLY NEEDS HELP.
I WANT US TO BE A FAMILY AGAIN!

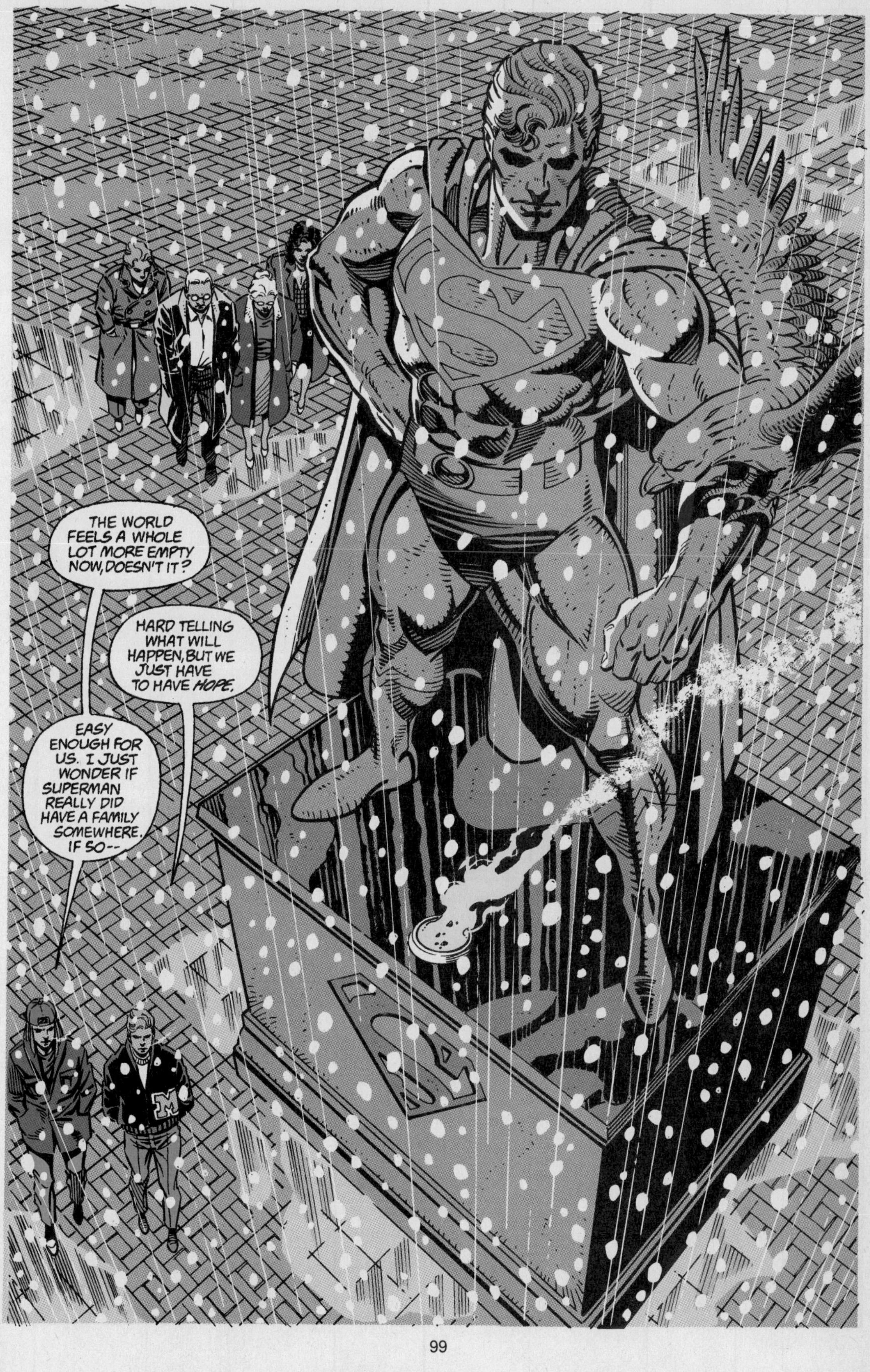
THE WORLD FEELS A WHOLE LOT MORE EMPTY NOW, DOESN'T IT?
HARD TELLING WHAT WILL HAPPEN, BUT WE JUST HAVE TO HAVE *HOPE*.
EASY ENOUGH FOR US. I JUST WONDER IF SUPERMAN REALLY DID HAVE A FAMILY SOMEWHERE. IF SO--

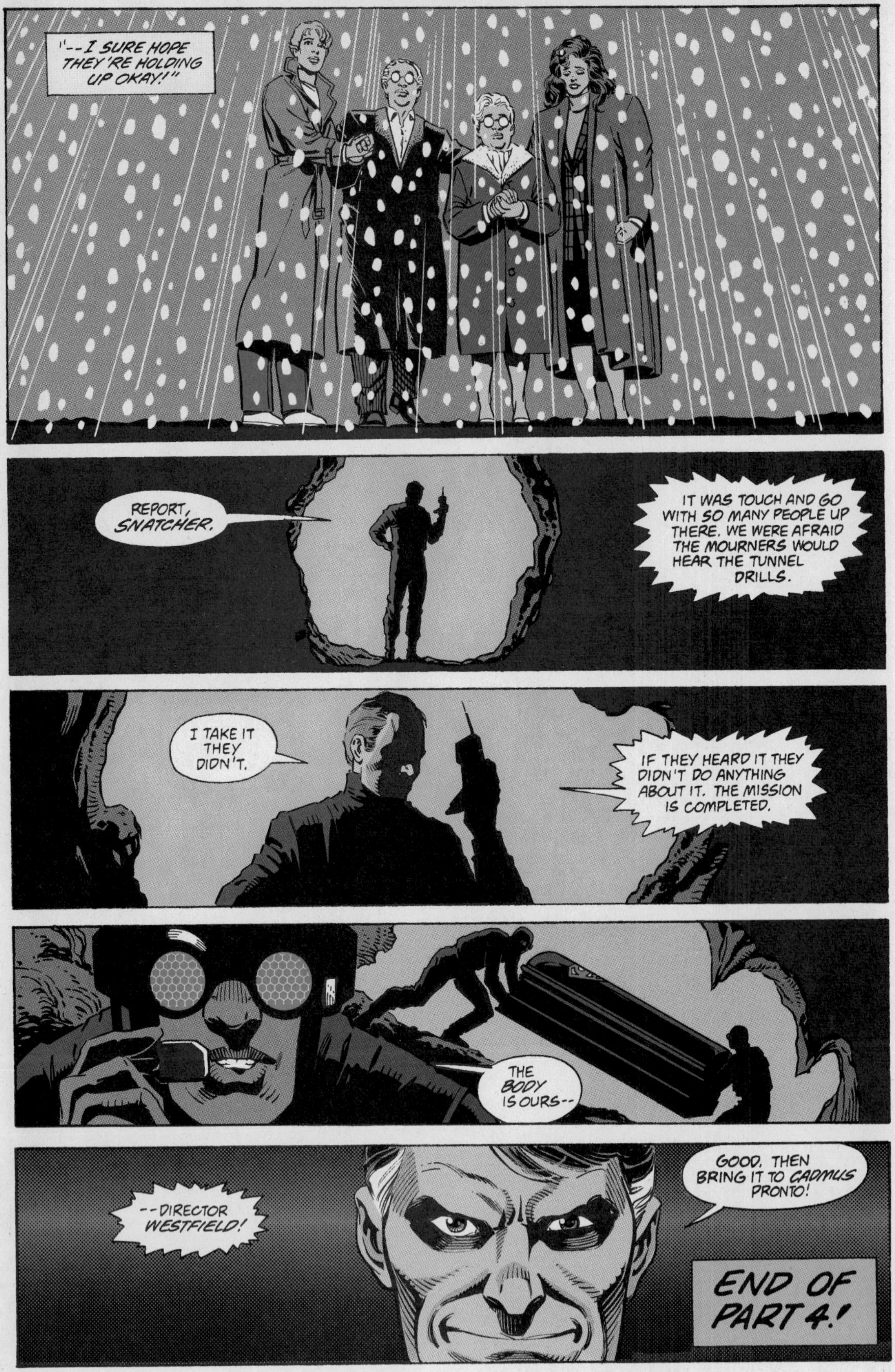
"--I SURE HOPE THEY'RE HOLDING UP OKAY!"
REPORT, SNATCHER.
IT WAS TOUCH AND GO WITH SO MANY PEOPLE UP THERE. WE WERE AFRAID THE MOURNERS WOULD HEAR THE TUNNEL DRILLS.
I TAKE IT THEY DIDN'T.
IF THEY HEARD IT THEY DIDN'T DO ANYTHING ABOUT IT. THE MISSION IS COMPLETED.
THE BODY IS OURS--
--DIRECTOR WESTFIELD!
GOOD. THEN BRING IT TO CADMUS PRONTO!
END OF PART 4!

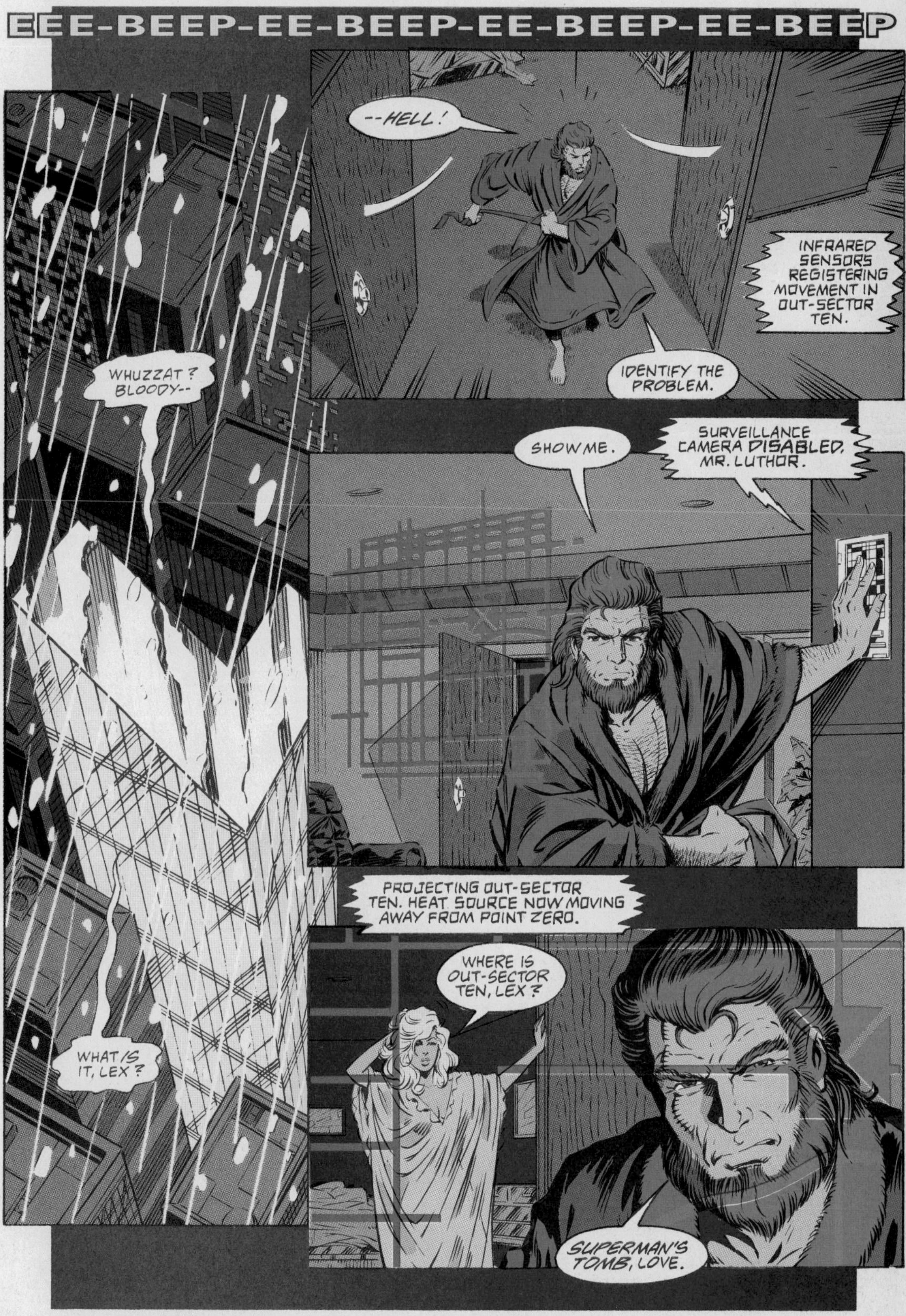
EEE-BEEP-EE-BEEP-EE-BEEP-EE-BEEP
WHUZZAT? BLOODY--
WHAT IS IT, LEX?
--HELL!
INFRARED SENSORS REGISTERING MOVEMENT IN OUT-SECTOR TEN.
IDENTIFY THE PROBLEM.
SURVEILLANCE CAMERA DISABLED, MR. LUTHOR.
SHOW ME.
PROJECTING OUT-SECTOR TEN. HEAT SOURCE NOW MOVING AWAY FROM POINT ZERO.
WHERE IS OUT-SECTOR TEN, LEX?
SUPERMAN'S TOMB, LOVE.

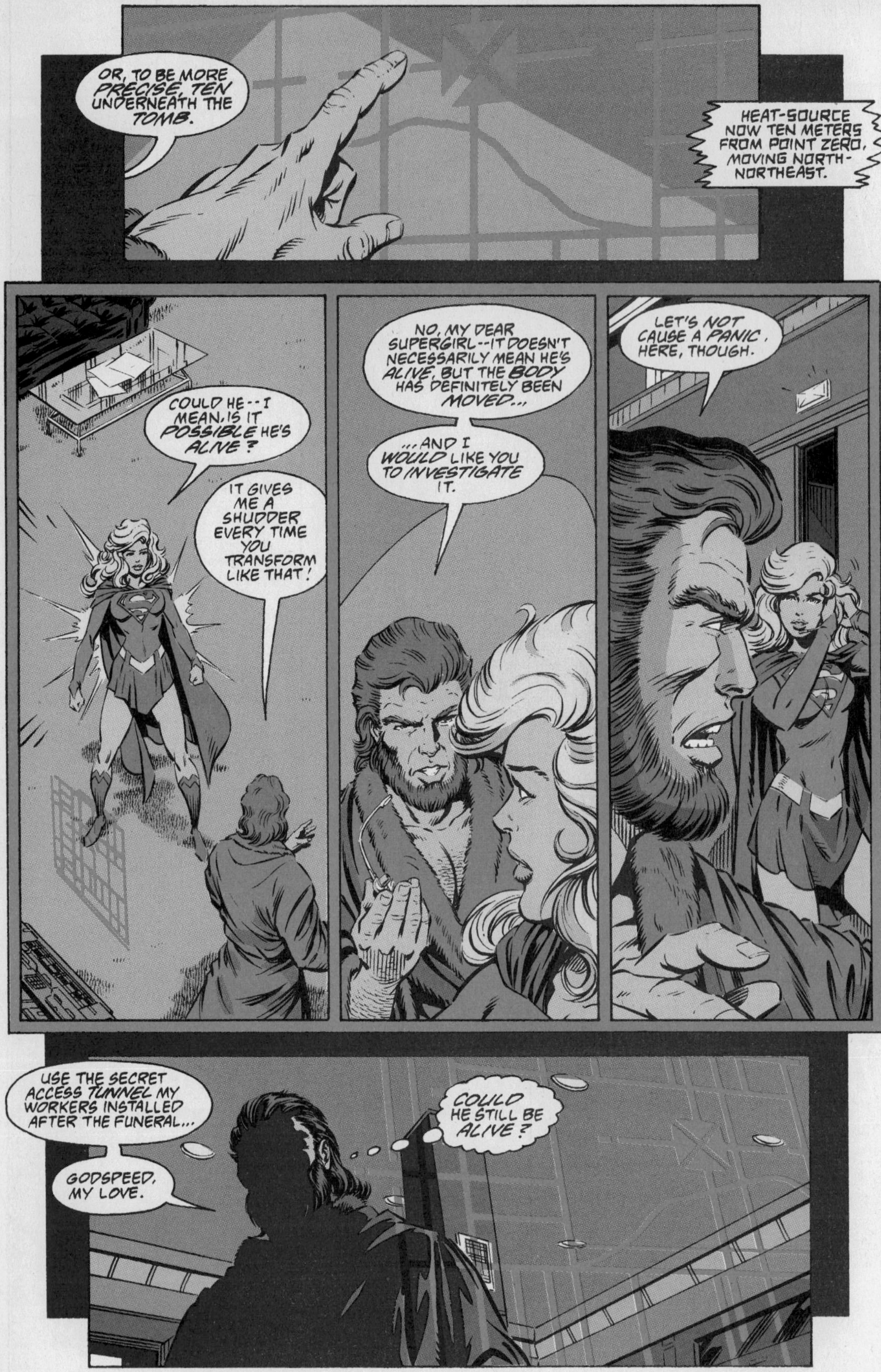
OR, TO BE MORE PRECISE, TEN UNDERNEATH THE TOMB.
HEAT-SOURCE NOW TEN METERS FROM POINT ZERO, MOVING NORTH-NORTHEAST.
COULD HE--I MEAN, IS IT POSSIBLE HE'S ALIVE?
IT GIVES ME A SHUDDER EVERY TIME YOU TRANSFORM LIKE THAT!
NO, MY DEAR SUPERGIRL--IT DOESN'T NECESSARILY MEAN HE'S ALIVE, BUT THE BODY HAS DEFINITELY BEEN MOVED...
...AND I WOULD LIKE YOU TO INVESTIGATE IT.
LET'S NOT CAUSE A PANIC, HERE, THOUGH.
USE THE SECRET ACCESS TUNNEL MY WORKERS INSTALLED AFTER THE FUNERAL...
GODSPEED, MY LOVE.
COULD HE STILL BE ALIVE?

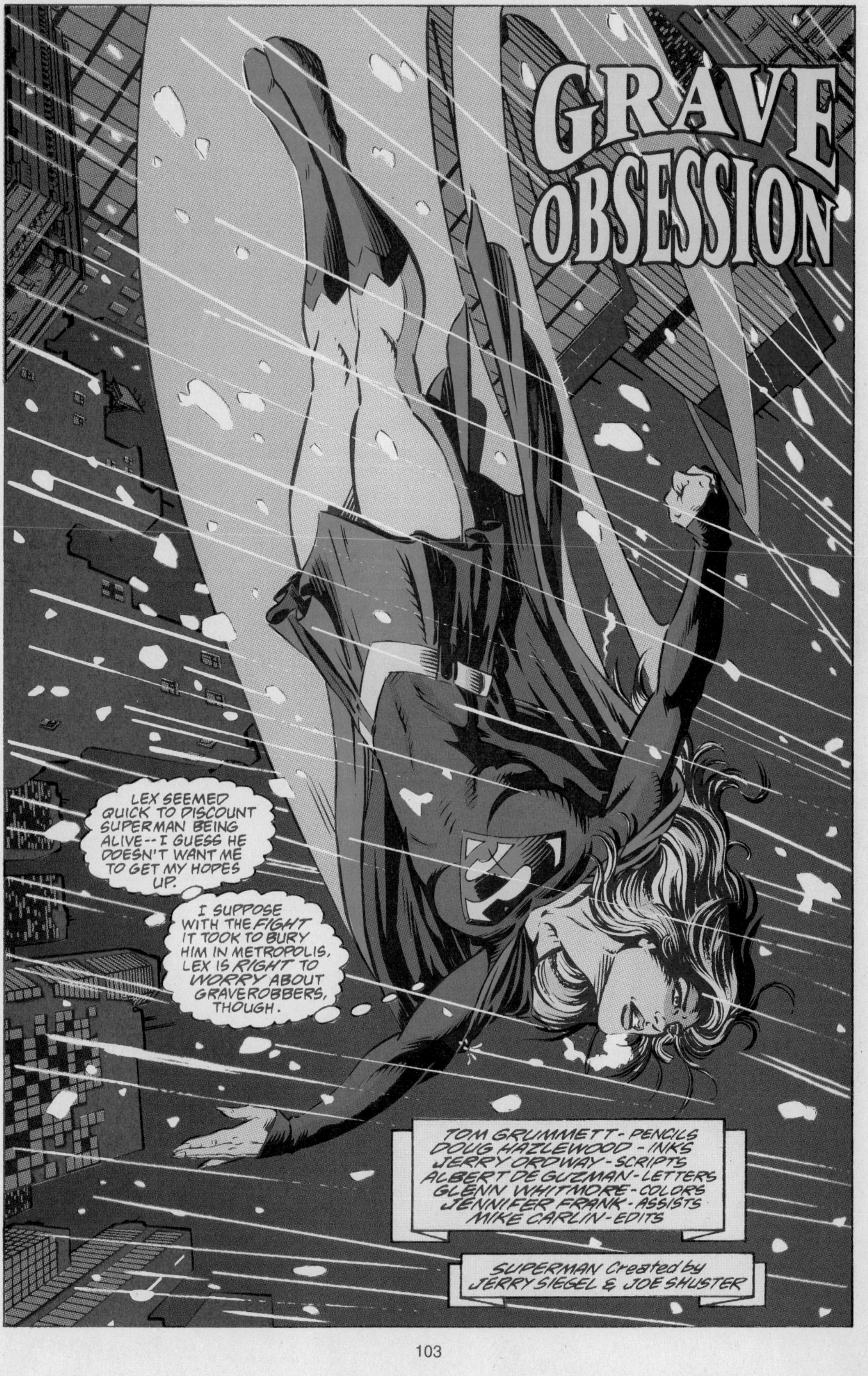
GRAVE OBSESSION
LEX SEEMED QUICK TO DISCOUNT SUPERMAN BEING ALIVE--I GUESS HE DOESN'T WANT ME TO GET MY HOPES UP.
I SUPPOSE WITH THE FIGHT IT TOOK TO BURY HIM IN METROPOLIS, LEX IS RIGHT TO WORRY ABOUT GRAVEROBBERS, THOUGH.
TOM GRUMMETT - PENCILS
DOUG HAZLEWOOD - INKS
JERRY ORDWAY - SCRIPTS
ALBERT DE GUZMAN - LETTERS
GLENN WHITMORE - COLORS
JENNIFER FRANK - ASSISTS
MIKE CARLIN - EDITS
SUPERMAN Created by
JERRY SIEGEL & JOE SHUSTER

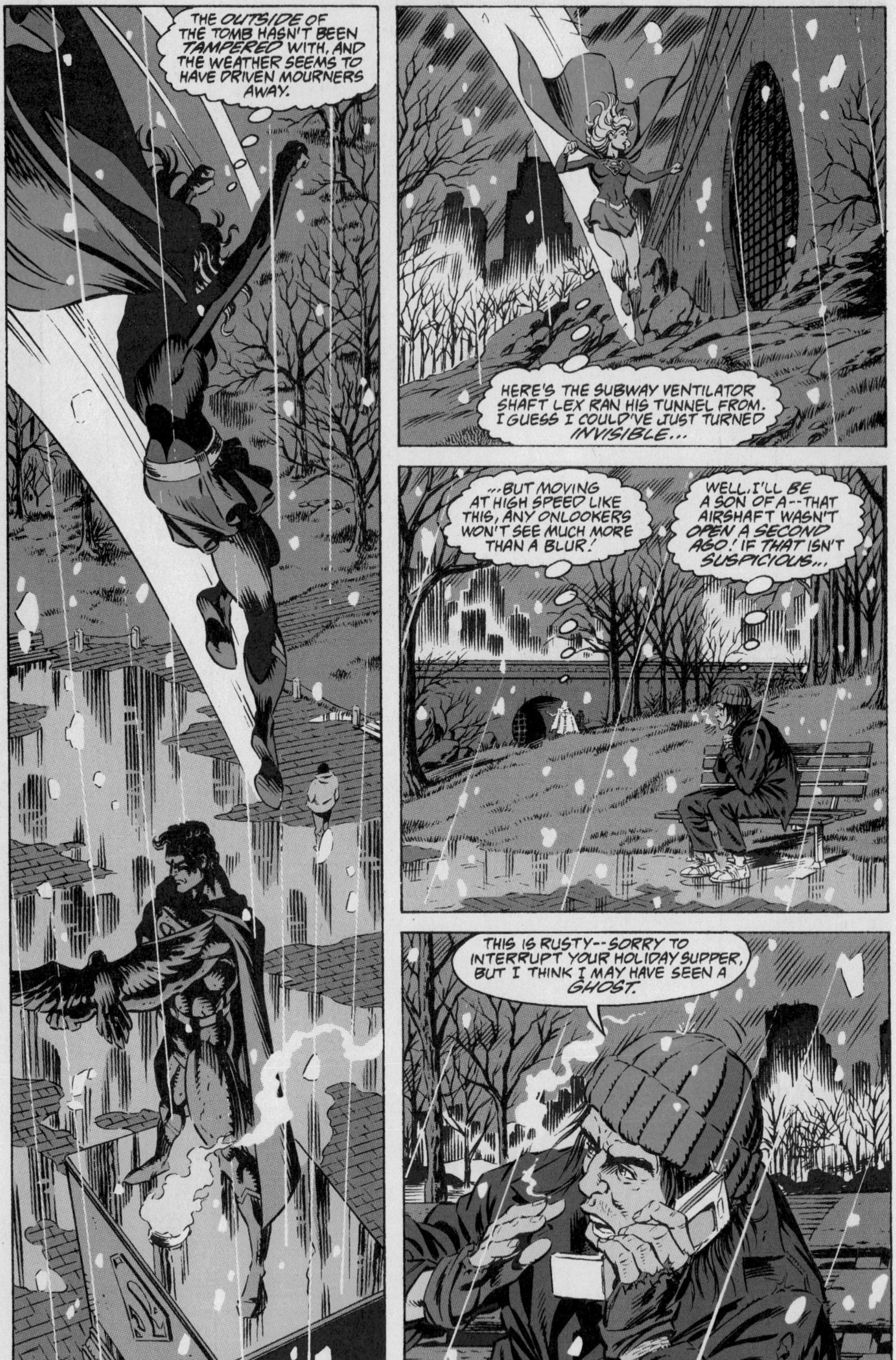

THE OUTSIDE OF THE TOMB HASN'T BEEN TAMPERED WITH, AND THE WEATHER SEEMS TO HAVE DRIVEN MOURNERS AWAY.
HERE'S THE SUBWAY VENTILATOR SHAFT LEX RAN HIS TUNNEL FROM. I GUESS I COULD'VE JUST TURNED INVISIBLE...
...BUT MOVING AT HIGH SPEED LIKE THIS, ANY ONLOOKERS WON'T SEE MUCH MORE THAN A BLUR!
WELL, I'LL BE A SON OF A--THAT AIRSHAFT WASN'T OPEN A SECOND AGO! IF THAT ISN'T SUSPICIOUS...
THIS IS RUSTY--SORRY TO INTERRUPT YOUR HOLIDAY SUPPER, BUT I THINK I MAY HAVE SEEN A GHOST.

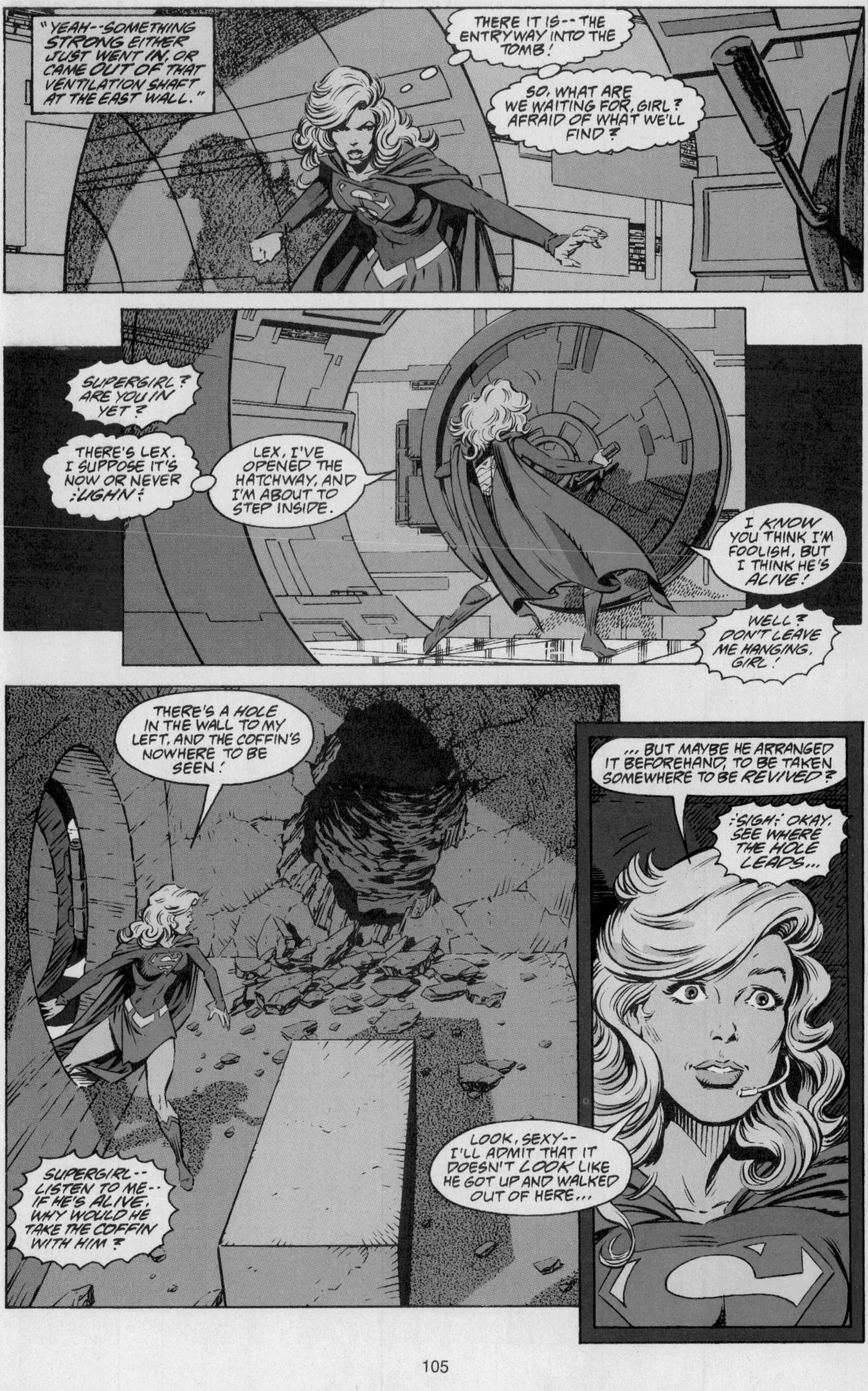
"YEAH--SOMETHING STRONG EITHER JUST WENT IN, OR CAME OUT OF THAT VENTILATION SHAFT AT THE EAST WALL."
THERE IT IS--THE ENTRYWAY INTO THE TOMB!
SO, WHAT ARE WE WAITING FOR, GIRL? AFRAID OF WHAT WE'LL FIND?
SUPERGIRL? ARE YOU IN YET?
THERE'S LEX. I SUPPOSE IT'S NOW OR NEVER :UGHN:
LEX, I'VE OPENED THE HATCHWAY, AND I'M ABOUT TO STEP INSIDE.
I KNOW YOU THINK I'M FOOLISH, BUT I THINK HE'S ALIVE!
WELL? DON'T LEAVE ME HANGING, GIRL!
THERE'S A HOLE IN THE WALL TO MY LEFT, AND THE COFFIN'S NOWHERE TO BE SEEN.
SUPERGIRL--LISTEN TO ME--IF HE'S ALIVE, WHY WOULD HE TAKE THE COFFIN WITH HIM?
LOOK, SEXY--I'LL ADMIT THAT IT DOESN'T LOOK LIKE HE GOT UP AND WALKED OUT OF HERE...
...BUT MAYBE HE ARRANGED IT BEFOREHAND, TO BE TAKEN SOMEWHERE TO BE REVIVED?
:SIGH: OKAY. SEE WHERE THE HOLE LEADS...

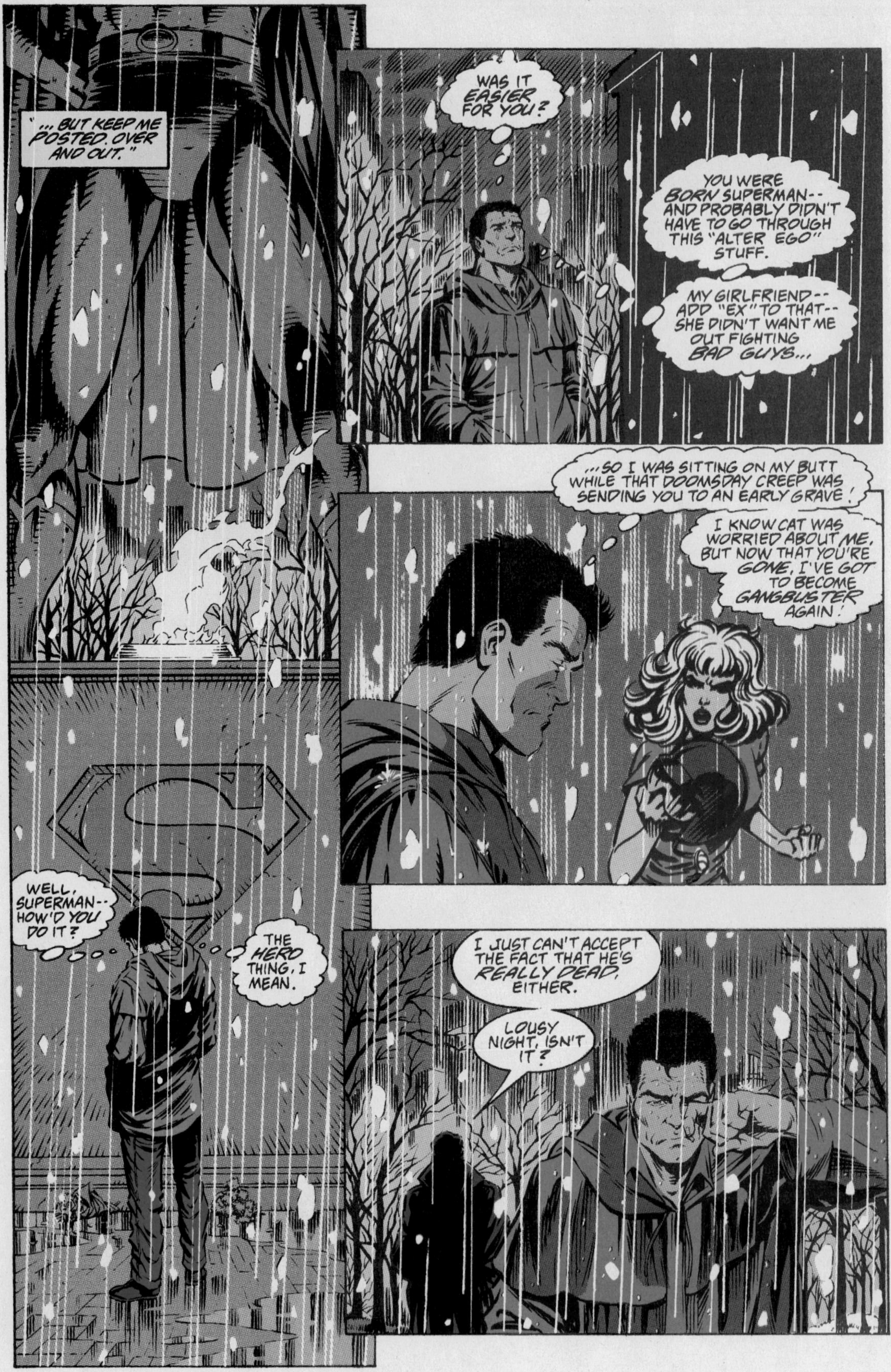
"...BUT KEEP ME POSTED. OVER AND OUT."
WAS IT EASIER FOR YOU?
YOU WERE BORN SUPERMAN-- AND PROBABLY DIDN'T HAVE TO GO THROUGH THIS "ALTER EGO" STUFF.
MY GIRLFRIEND-- ADD "EX" TO THAT-- SHE DIDN'T WANT ME OUT FIGHTING BAD GUYS...
...SO I WAS SITTING ON MY BUTT WHILE THAT DOOMSDAY CREEP WAS SENDING YOU TO AN EARLY GRAVE!
I KNOW CAT WAS WORRIED ABOUT ME, BUT NOW THAT YOU'RE GONE, I'VE GOT TO BECOME GANGBUSTER AGAIN!
WELL, SUPERMAN-- HOW'D YOU DO IT?
THE HERO THING, I MEAN.
I JUST CAN'T ACCEPT THE FACT THAT HE'S REALLY DEAD, EITHER.
LOUSY NIGHT, ISN'T IT?

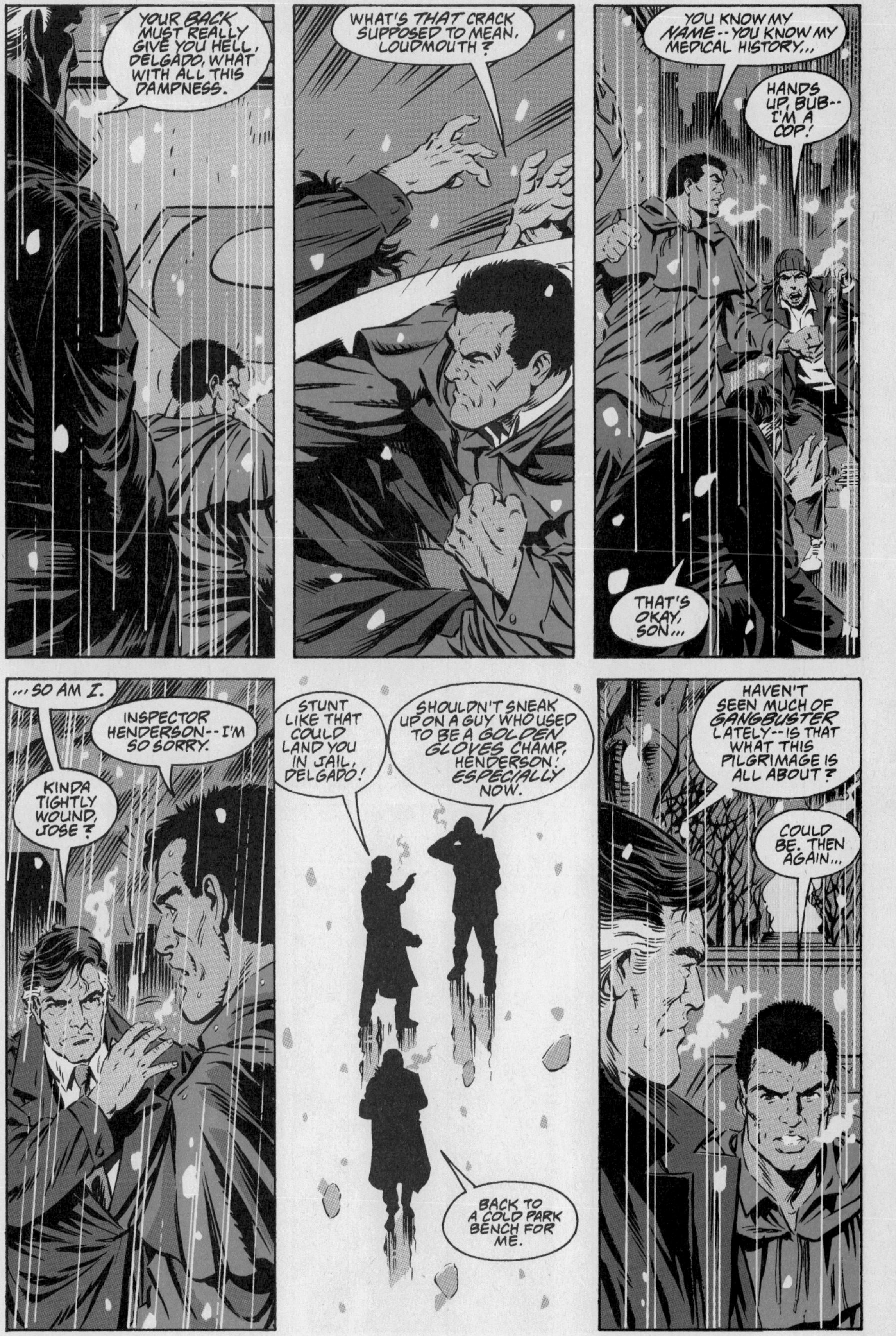
YOUR BACK MUST REALLY GIVE YOU HELL, DELGADO, WHAT WITH ALL THIS DAMPNESS.
WHAT'S THAT CRACK SUPPOSED TO MEAN, LOUDMOUTH?
YOU KNOW MY NAME--YOU KNOW MY MEDICAL HISTORY...
HANDS UP, BUB--I'M A COP!
THAT'S OKAY, SON...
...SO AM I.
INSPECTOR HENDERSON--I'M SO SORRY.
KINDA TIGHTLY WOUND, JOSE?
STUNT LIKE THAT COULD LAND YOU IN JAIL, DELGADO!
SHOULDN'T SNEAK UP ON A GUY WHO USED TO BE A GOLDEN GLOVES CHAMP, HENDERSON! ESPECIALLY NOW.
BACK TO A COLD PARK BENCH FOR ME.
HAVEN'T SEEN MUCH OF GANGBUSTER LATELY--IS THAT WHAT THIS PILGRIMAGE IS ALL ABOUT?
COULD BE. THEN AGAIN...

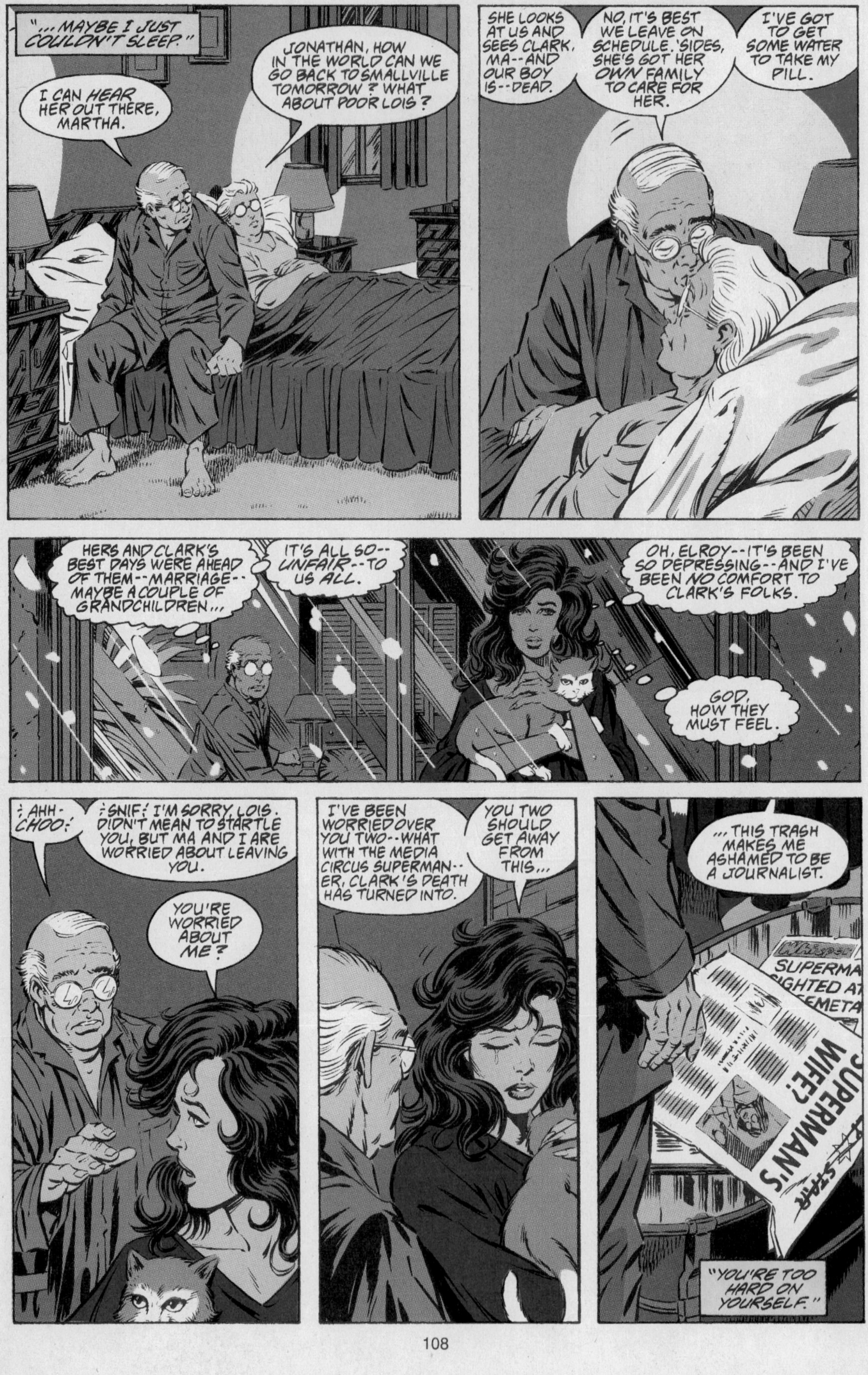
"...MAYBE I JUST COULDN'T SLEEP."
I CAN HEAR HER OUT THERE, MARTHA.
JONATHAN, HOW IN THE WORLD CAN WE GO BACK TO SMALLVILLE TOMORROW? WHAT ABOUT POOR LOIS?
SHE LOOKS AT US AND SEES CLARK, MA--AND OUR BOY IS--DEAD.
NO, IT'S BEST WE LEAVE ON SCHEDULE. 'SIDES, SHE'S GOT HER OWN FAMILY TO CARE FOR HER.
I'VE GOT TO GET SOME WATER TO TAKE MY PILL.
HERS AND CLARK'S BEST DAYS WERE AHEAD OF THEM--MARRIAGE--MAYBE A COUPLE OF GRANDCHILDREN...
IT'S ALL SO--UNFAIR--TO US ALL.
OH, ELROY--IT'S BEEN SO DEPRESSING--AND I'VE BEEN NO COMFORT TO CLARK'S FOLKS.
GOD, HOW THEY MUST FEEL.
AHH-CHOO!
SNIF! I'M SORRY, LOIS. DIDN'T MEAN TO STARTLE YOU, BUT MA AND I ARE WORRIED ABOUT LEAVING YOU.
YOU'RE WORRIED ABOUT ME?
I'VE BEEN WORRIED OVER YOU TWO--WHAT WITH THE MEDIA CIRCUS SUPERMAN--ER, CLARK'S DEATH HAS TURNED INTO.
YOU TWO SHOULD GET AWAY FROM THIS...
...THIS TRASH MAKES ME ASHAMED TO BE A JOURNALIST.
SUPERMAN SIGHTED AT CEMETA
SUPERMAN'S WIFE?
STAR
"YOU'RE TOO HARD ON YOURSELF."

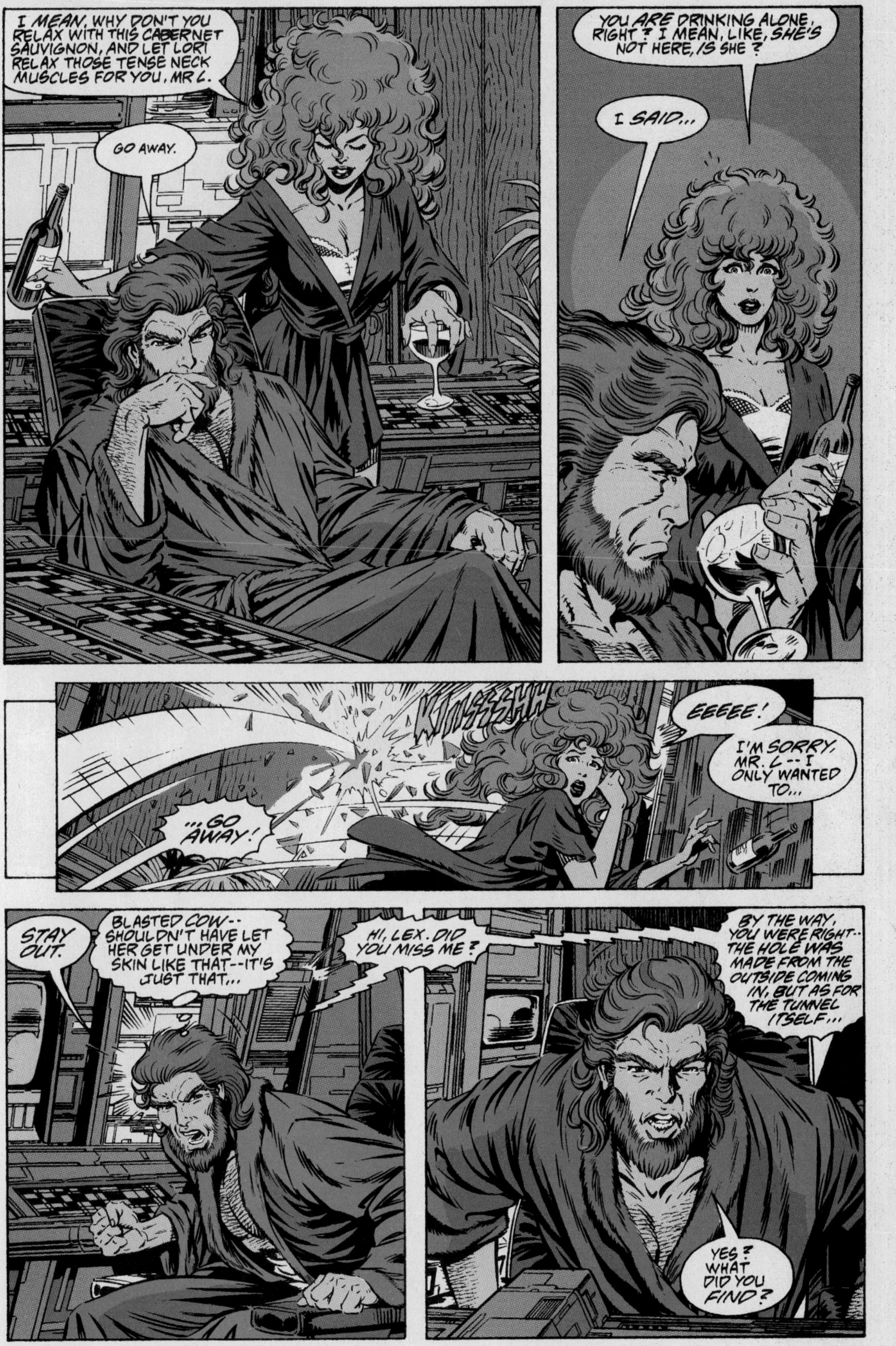
I MEAN, WHY DON'T YOU RELAX WITH THIS CABERNET SAUVIGNON, AND LET LORI RELAX THOSE TENSE NECK MUSCLES FOR YOU, MR L.
GO AWAY.
YOU ARE DRINKING ALONE, RIGHT? I MEAN, LIKE, SHE'S NOT HERE, IS SHE?
I SAID...
KRASSSHH
EEEEE!
I'M SORRY, MR. L -- I ONLY WANTED TO...
...GO AWAY!
STAY OUT.
BLASTED COW-- SHOULDN'T HAVE LET HER GET UNDER MY SKIN LIKE THAT--IT'S JUST THAT...
HI, LEX. DID YOU MISS ME?
BY THE WAY, YOU WERE RIGHT.. THE HOLE WAS MADE FROM THE OUTSIDE COMING IN, BUT AS FOR THE TUNNEL ITSELF...
YES? WHAT DID YOU FIND?

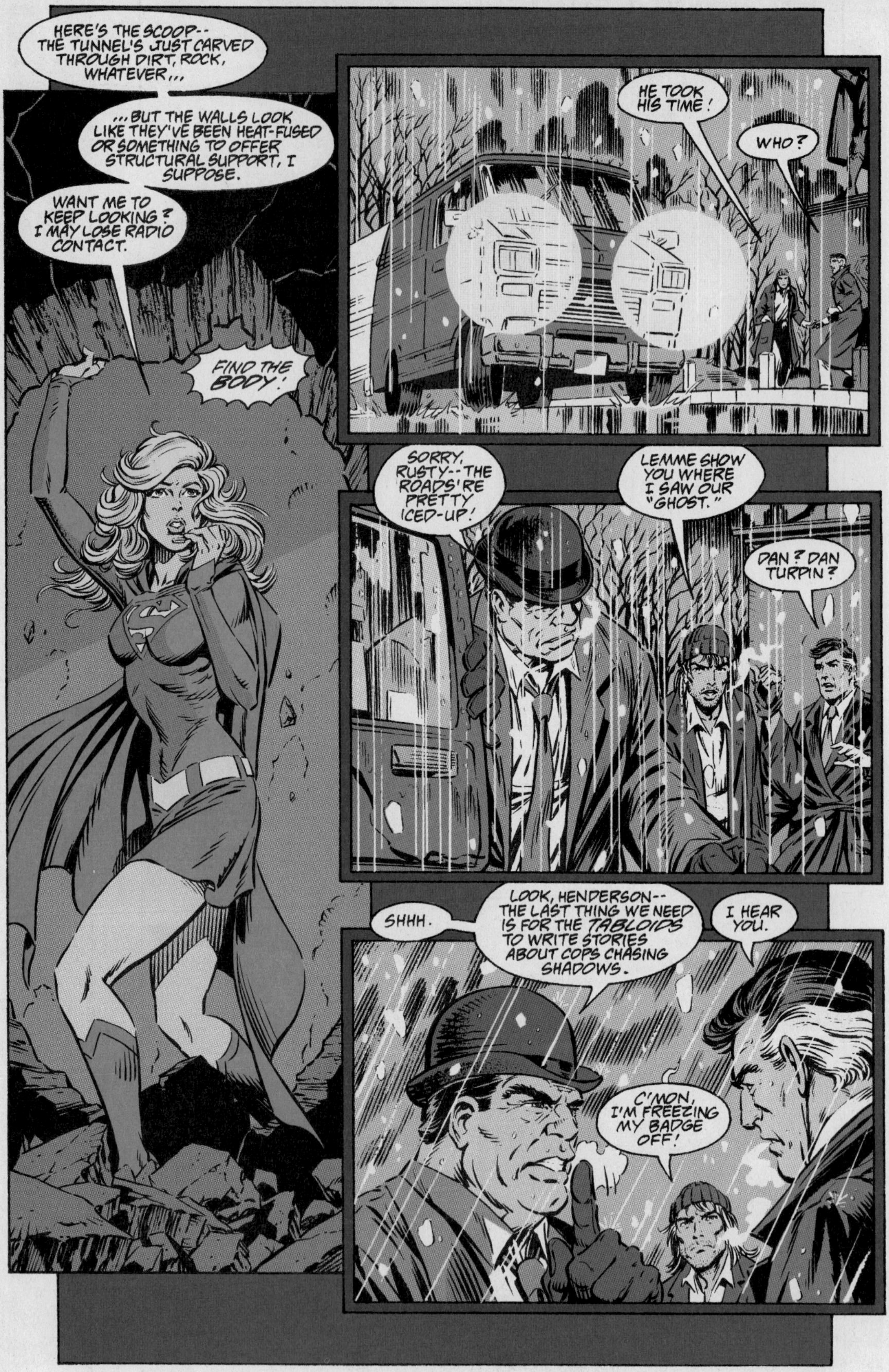
HERE'S THE SCOOP-- THE TUNNEL'S JUST CARVED THROUGH DIRT, ROCK, WHATEVER...
...BUT THE WALLS LOOK LIKE THEY'VE BEEN HEAT-FUSED OR SOMETHING TO OFFER STRUCTURAL SUPPORT, I SUPPOSE.
WANT ME TO KEEP LOOKING? I MAY LOSE RADIO CONTACT.
FIND THE BODY!
HE TOOK HIS TIME!
WHO?
SORRY, RUSTY--THE ROADS'RE PRETTY ICED-UP!
LEMME SHOW YOU WHERE I SAW OUR "GHOST."
DAN? DAN TURPIN?
SHHH.
LOOK, HENDERSON-- THE LAST THING WE NEED IS FOR THE TABLOIDS TO WRITE STORIES ABOUT COPS CHASING SHADOWS.
I HEAR YOU.
C'MON, I'M FREEZING MY BADGE OFF!

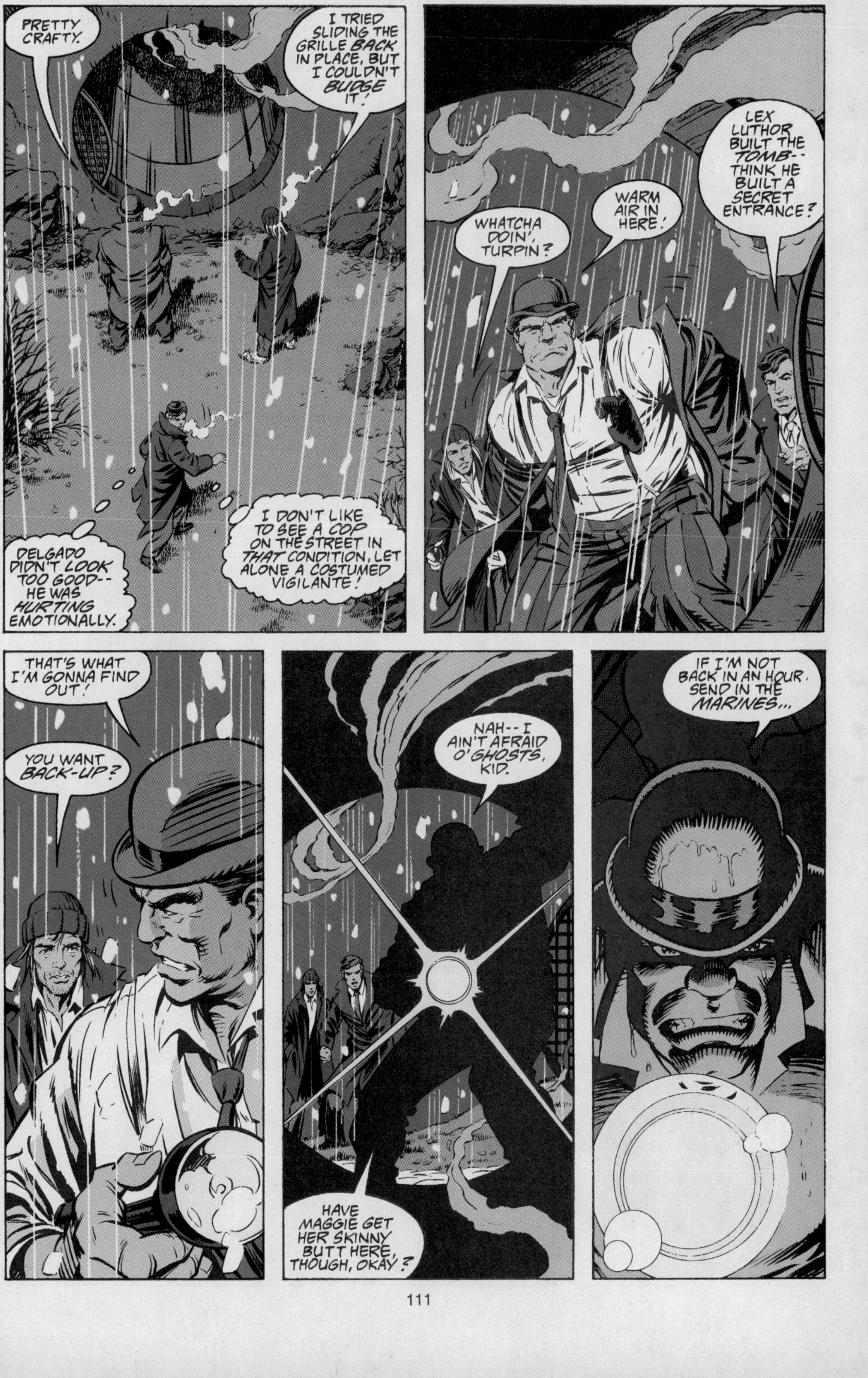
PRETTY CRAFTY.
I TRIED SLIDING THE GRILLE BACK IN PLACE, BUT I COULDN'T BUDGE IT!
DELGADO DIDN'T LOOK TOO GOOD-- HE WAS HURTING EMOTIONALLY.
I DON'T LIKE TO SEE A COP ON THE STREET IN THAT CONDITION, LET ALONE A COSTUMED VIGILANTE!
LEX LUTHOR BUILT THE TOMB-- THINK HE BUILT A SECRET ENTRANCE?
WARM AIR IN HERE!
WHATCHA DOIN', TURPIN?
THAT'S WHAT I'M GONNA FIND OUT!
YOU WANT BACK-UP?
NAH-- I AIN'T AFRAID O' GHOSTS, KID.
HAVE MAGGIE GET HER SKINNY BUTT HERE, THOUGH, OKAY?
IF I'M NOT BACK IN AN HOUR, SEND IN THE MARINES...

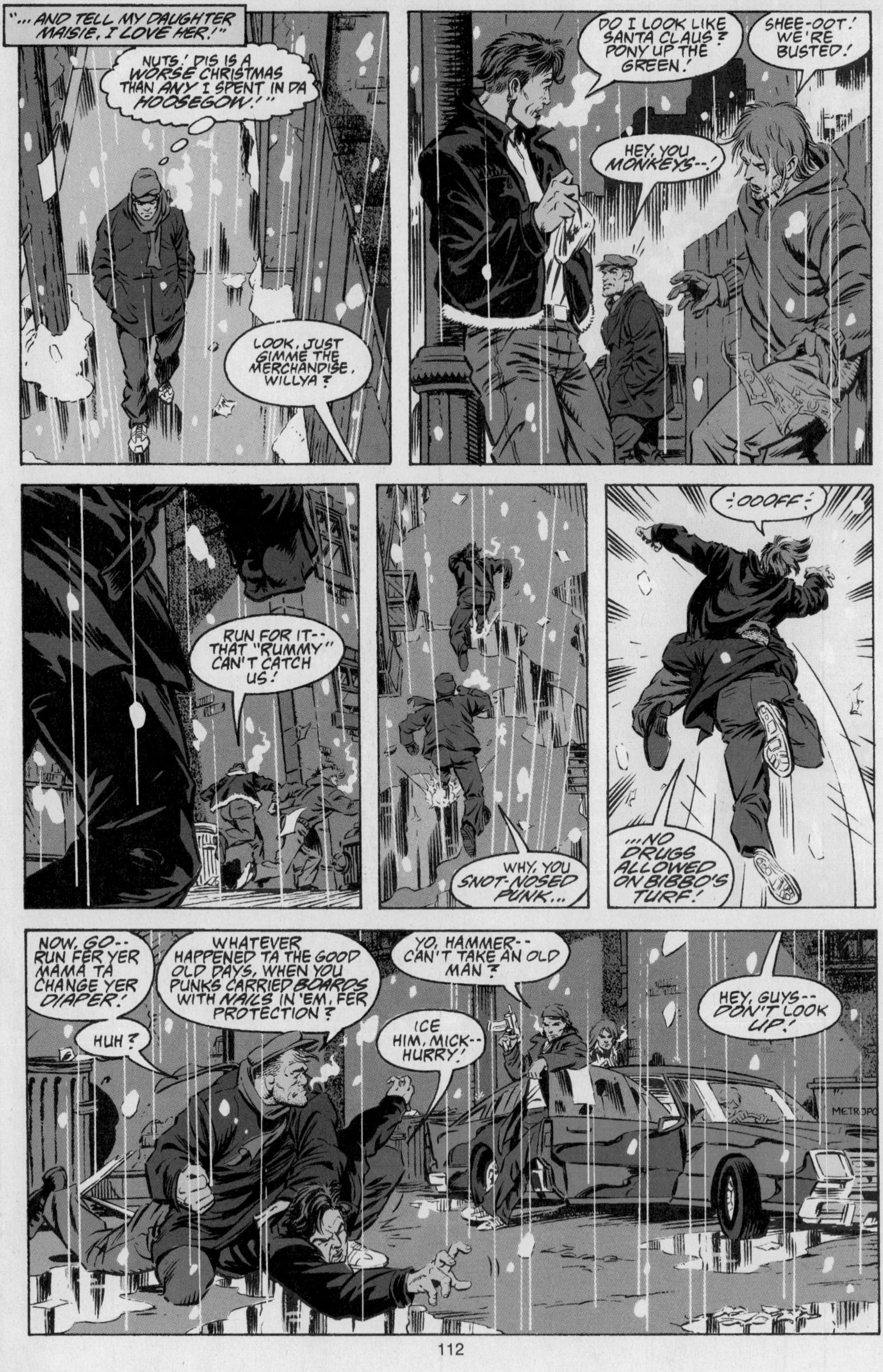
"...AND TELL MY DAUGHTER MAISIE, I LOVE HER!"
NUTS! DIS IS A WORSE CHRISTMAS THAN ANY I SPENT IN DA HOOSEGOW!"
LOOK, JUST GIMME THE MERCHANDISE, WILLYA?
DO I LOOK LIKE SANTA CLAUS? PONY UP THE GREEN!
SHEE-OOT! WE'RE BUSTED!
HEY, YOU MONKEYS--!
RUN FOR IT-- THAT "RUMMY" CAN'T CATCH US!
WHY, YOU SNOT-NOSED PUNK...
OOOFF
...NO DRUGS ALLOWED ON BIBBO'S TURF!
NOW, GO-- RUN FER YER MAMA TA CHANGE YER DIAPER!
HUH?
WHATEVER HAPPENED TA THE GOOD OLD DAYS, WHEN YOU PUNKS CARRIED BOARDS WITH NAILS IN 'EM, FER PROTECTION?
YO, HAMMER-- CAN'T TAKE AN OLD MAN?
ICE HIM, MICK-- HURRY!
HEY, GUYS-- DON'T LOOK UP!
METROPO

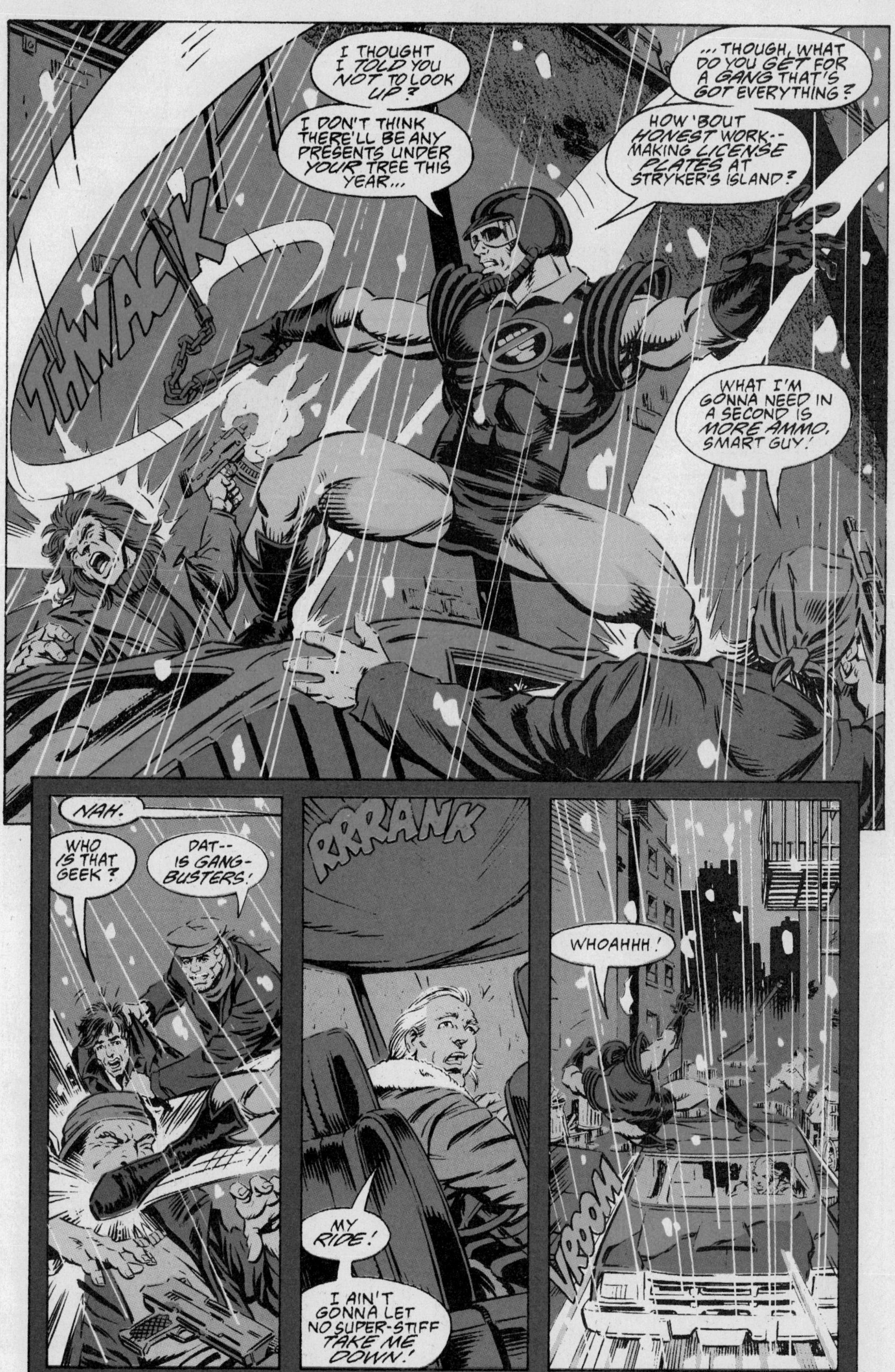
I THOUGHT I TOLD YOU NOT TO LOOK UP?
I DON'T THINK THERE'LL BE ANY PRESENTS UNDER YOUR TREE THIS YEAR...
...THOUGH, WHAT DO YOU GET FOR A GANG THAT'S GOT EVERYTHING?
HOW 'BOUT HONEST WORK-- MAKING LICENSE PLATES AT STRYKER'S ISLAND?
THWACK
WHAT I'M GONNA NEED IN A SECOND IS MORE AMMO, SMART GUY!
NAH.
WHO IS THAT GEEK?
DAT-- IS GANG-BUSTERS!
RRRANK
MY RIDE!
I AIN'T GONNA LET NO SUPER-STIFF TAKE ME DOWN!
WHOAHHH!
VROOM

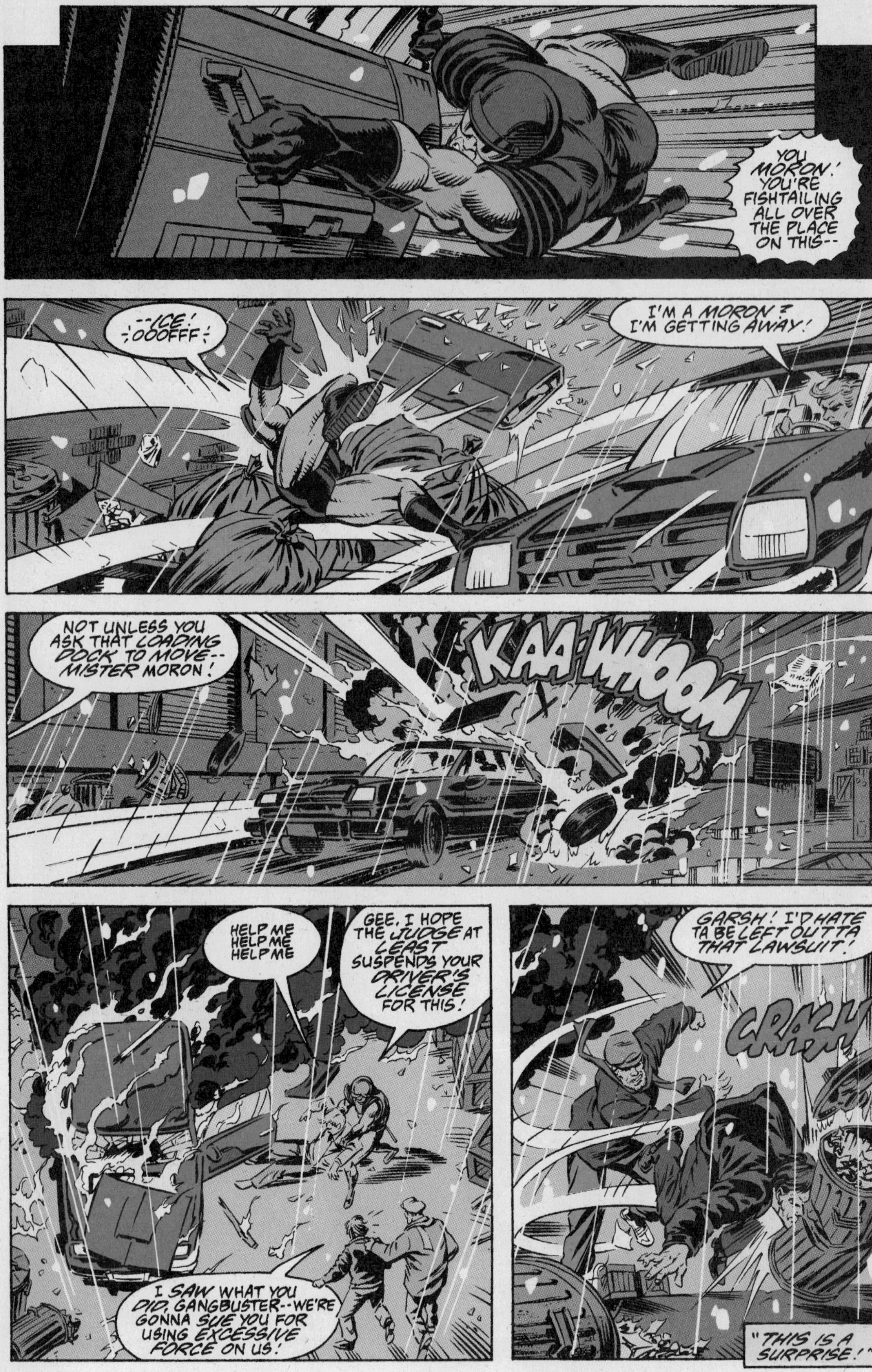
YOU MORON! YOU'RE FISHTAILING ALL OVER THE PLACE ON THIS--
--ICE! OOOFFF!
I'M A MORON? I'M GETTING AWAY!
NOT UNLESS YOU ASK THAT LOADING DOCK TO MOVE-- MISTER MORON!
KAA-WHOOM
HELP ME HELP ME HELP ME
GEE, I HOPE THE JUDGE AT LEAST SUSPENDS YOUR DRIVER'S LICENSE FOR THIS!
I SAW WHAT YOU DID, GANGBUSTER--WE'RE GONNA SUE YOU FOR USING EXCESSIVE FORCE ON US!
GARSH! I'D HATE TA BE LEFT OUTTA THAT LAWSUIT!
CRASH
"THIS IS A SURPRISE!"

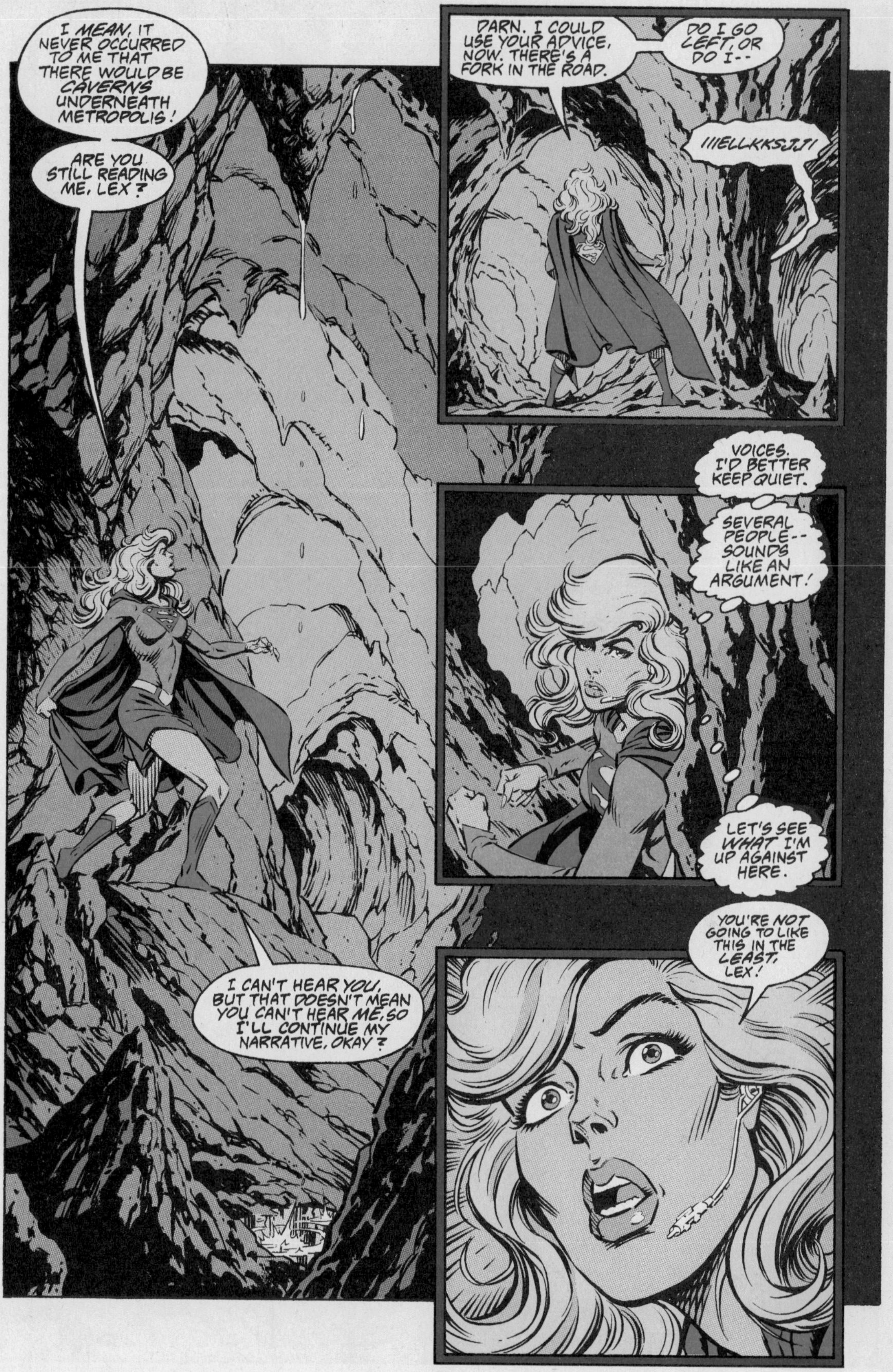

I MEAN, IT NEVER OCCURRED TO ME THAT THERE WOULD BE CAVERNS UNDERNEATH METROPOLIS!
ARE YOU STILL READING ME, LEX?
I CAN'T HEAR YOU, BUT THAT DOESN'T MEAN YOU CAN'T HEAR ME, SO I'LL CONTINUE MY NARRATIVE, OKAY?
DARN. I COULD USE YOUR ADVICE, NOW. THERE'S A FORK IN THE ROAD.
DO I GO LEFT, OR DO I--
!!!ELLKKSJJ!
VOICES. I'D BETTER KEEP QUIET.
SEVERAL PEOPLE-- SOUNDS LIKE AN ARGUMENT!
LET'S SEE WHAT I'M UP AGAINST HERE.
YOU'RE NOT GOING TO LIKE THIS IN THE LEAST, LEX!

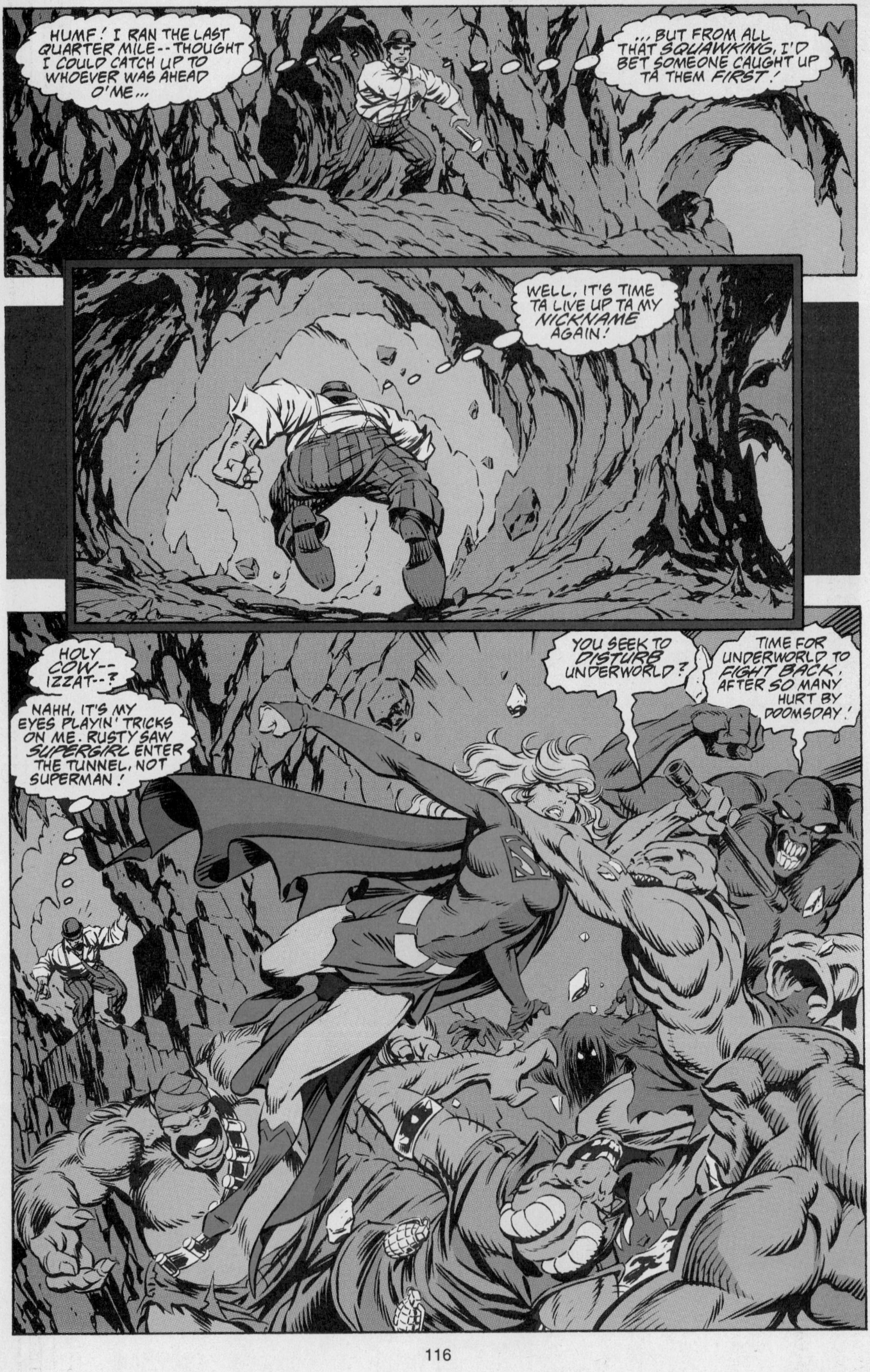
HUMF! I RAN THE LAST QUARTER MILE-- THOUGHT I COULD CATCH UP TO WHOEVER WAS AHEAD O'ME...
...BUT FROM ALL THAT SQUAWKING, I'D BET SOMEONE CAUGHT UP TA THEM FIRST!
WELL, IT'S TIME TA LIVE UP TA MY NICKNAME AGAIN!
HOLY COW-- IZZAT--?
NAHH, IT'S MY EYES PLAYIN' TRICKS ON ME. RUSTY SAW SUPERGIRL ENTER THE TUNNEL, NOT SUPERMAN!
YOU SEEK TO DISTURB UNDERWORLD?
TIME FOR UNDERWORLD TO FIGHT BACK, AFTER SO MANY HURT BY DOOMSDAY!

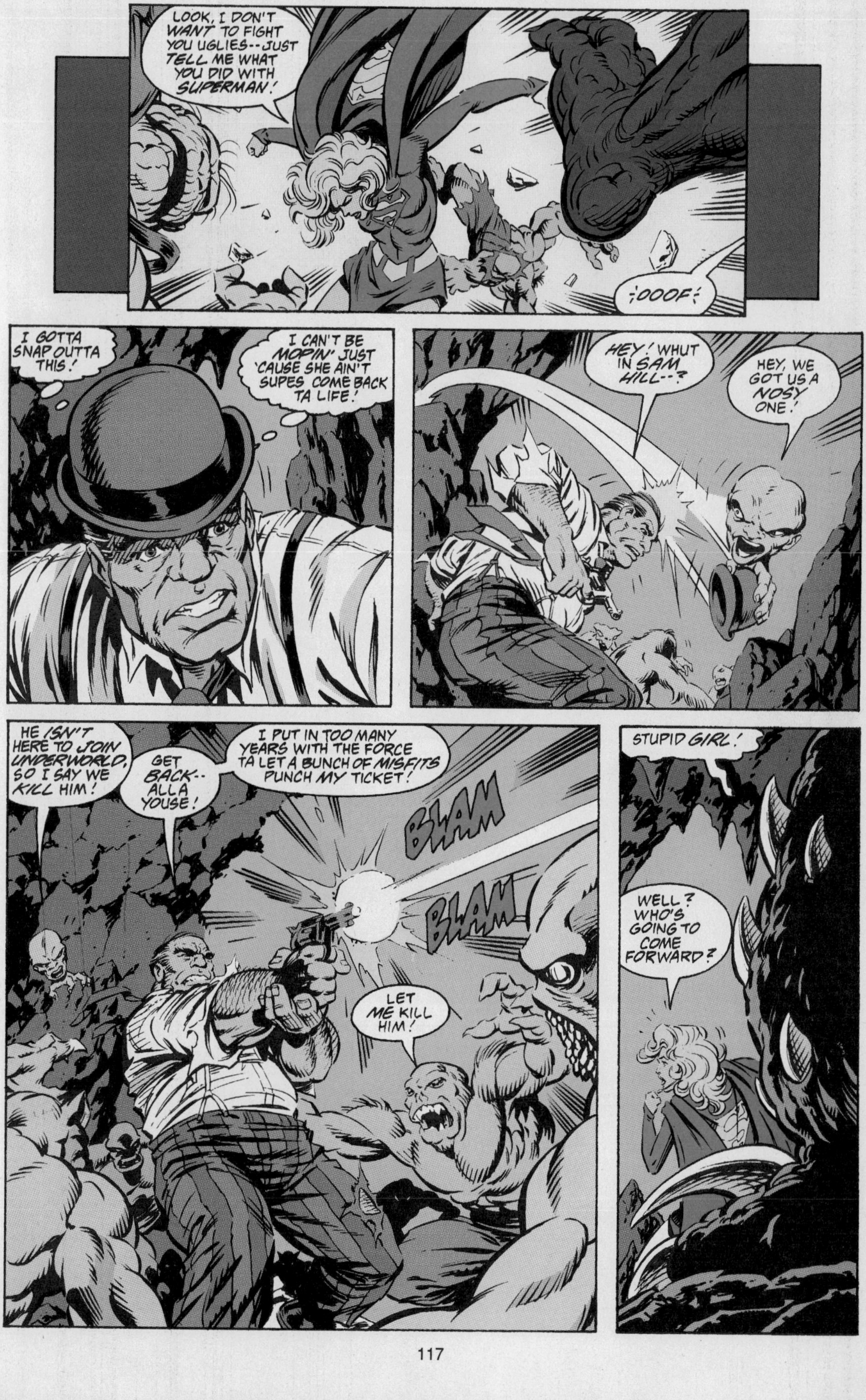
LOOK, I DON'T WANT TO FIGHT YOU UGLIES--JUST TELL ME WHAT YOU DID WITH SUPERMAN!
¡OOOF!
I GOTTA SNAP OUTTA THIS!
I CAN'T BE MOPIN' JUST 'CAUSE SHE AIN'T SUPES COME BACK TA LIFE!
HEY! WHUT IN SAM HILL--?
HEY, WE GOT US A NOSY ONE!
HE ISN'T HERE TO JOIN UNDERWORLD, SO I SAY WE KILL HIM!
GET BACK-- ALL A YOUSE!
I PUT IN TOO MANY YEARS WITH THE FORCE TA LET A BUNCH OF MISFITS PUNCH MY TICKET!
BLAM
BLAM
LET ME KILL HIM!
STUPID GIRL!
WELL? WHO'S GOING TO COME FORWARD?

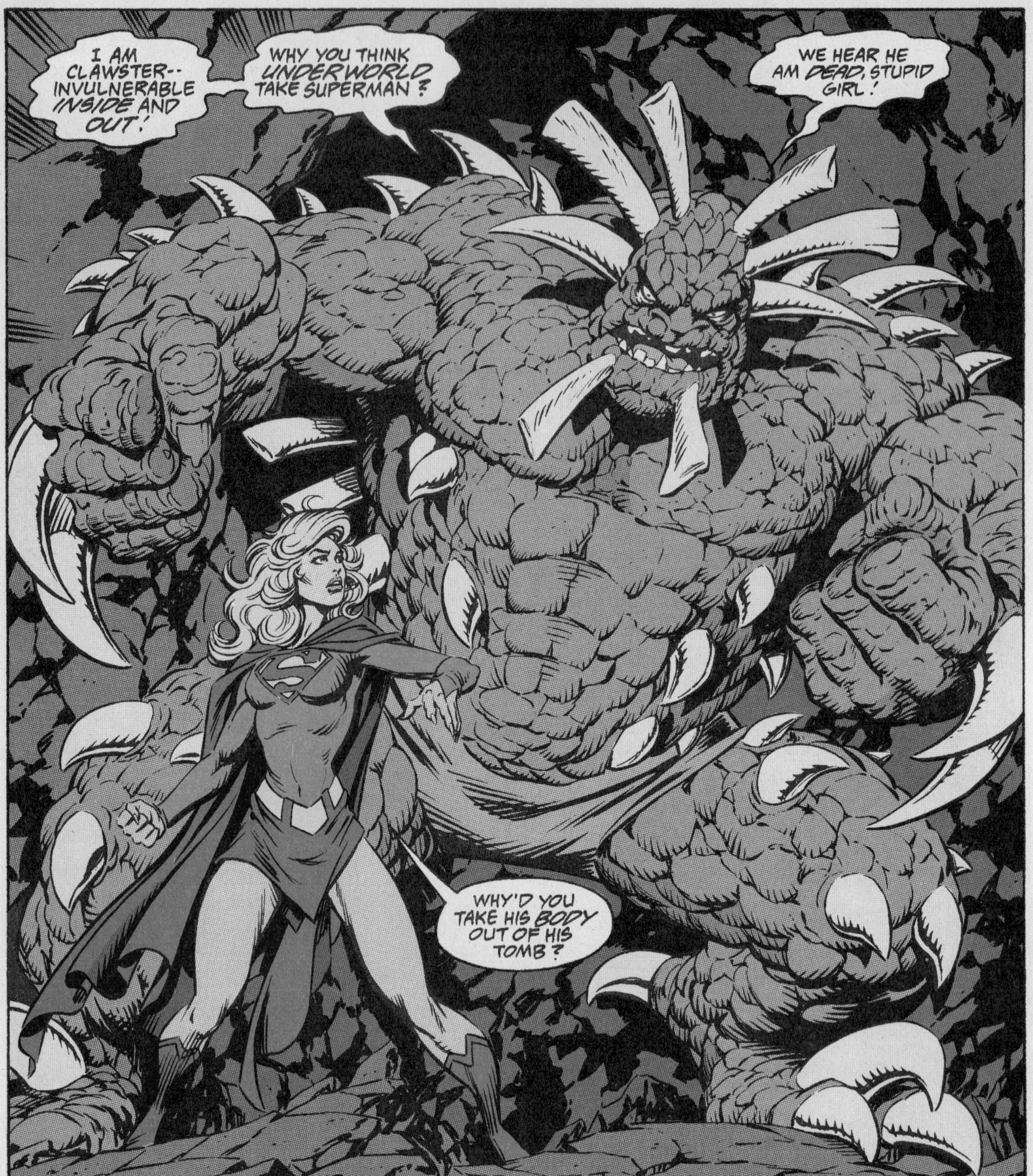
I AM CLAWSTER-- INVULNERABLE INSIDE AND OUT!
WHY YOU THINK UNDERWORLD TAKE SUPERMAN?
WE HEAR HE AM DEAD, STUPID GIRL!
WHY'D YOU TAKE HIS BODY OUT OF HIS TOMB?

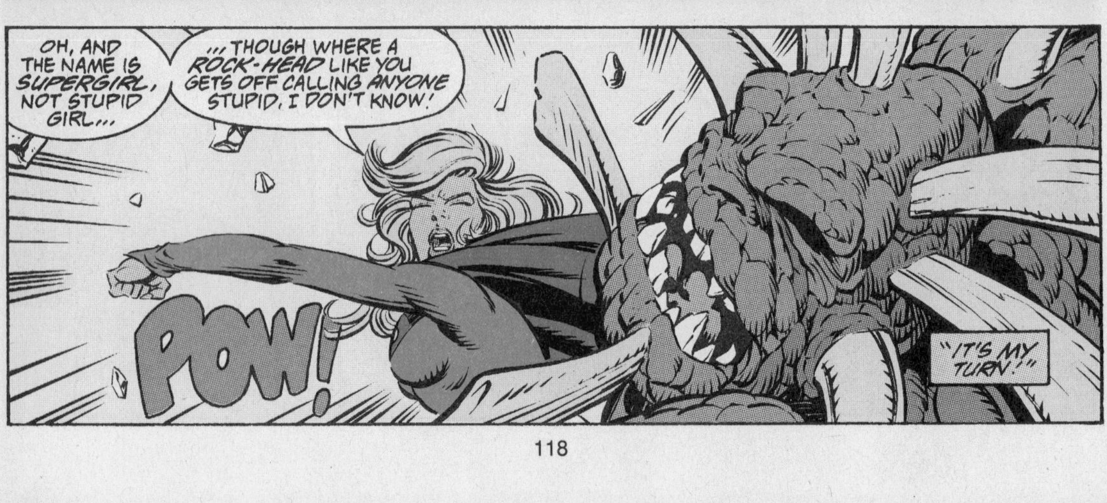
OH, AND THE NAME IS SUPERGIRL, NOT STUPID GIRL...
...THOUGH WHERE A ROCK-HEAD LIKE YOU GETS OFF CALLING ANYONE STUPID, I DON'T KNOW!
POW!
"IT'S MY TURN!"

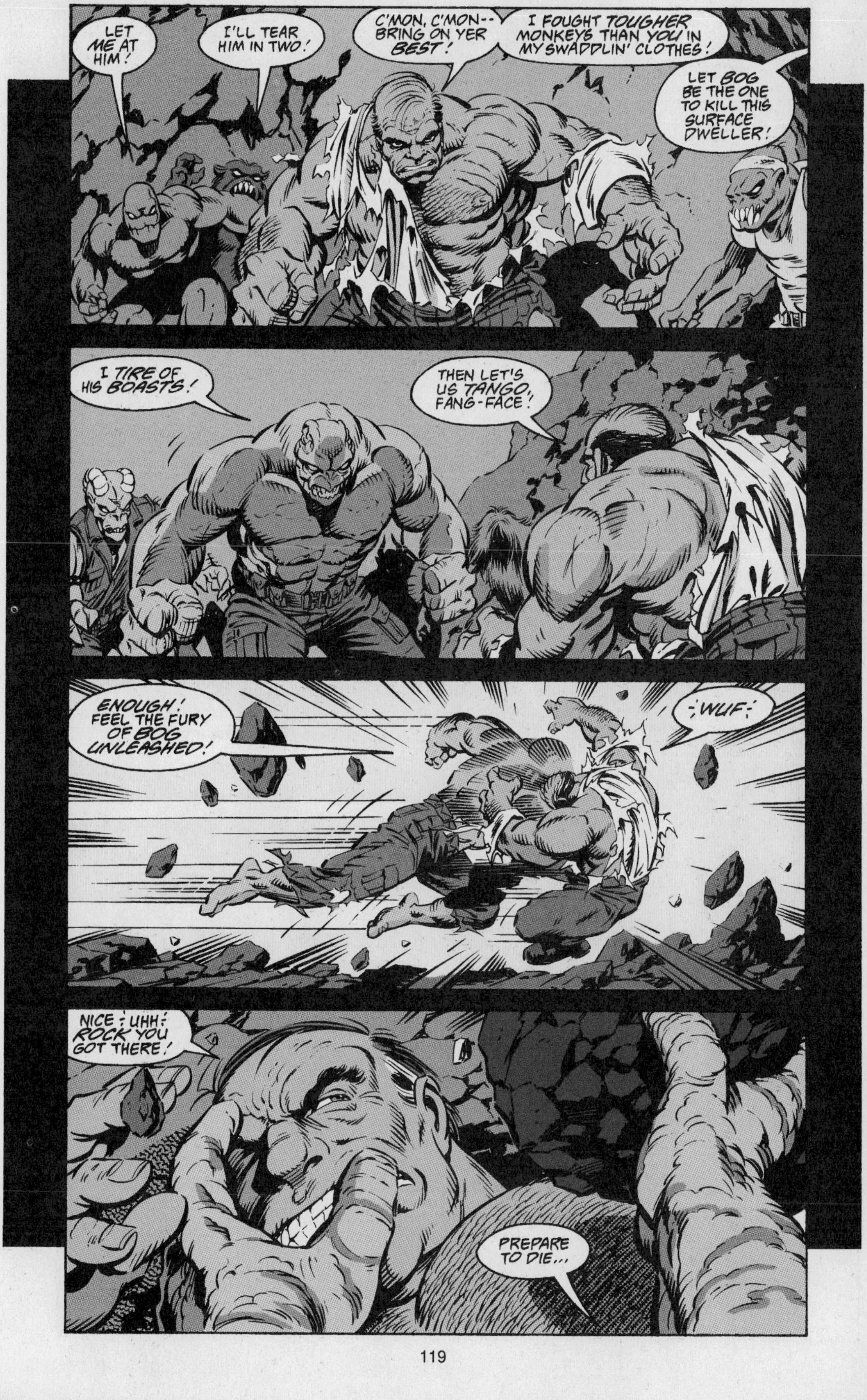
LET ME AT HIM!
I'LL TEAR HIM IN TWO!
C'MON, C'MON-- BRING ON YER BEST!
I FOUGHT TOUGHER MONKEYS THAN YOU IN MY SWADDLIN' CLOTHES!
LET BOG BE THE ONE TO KILL THIS SURFACE DWELLER!
I TIRE OF HIS BOASTS!
THEN LET'S US TANGO, FANG-FACE!
ENOUGH! FEEL THE FURY OF BOG UNLEASHED!
WUF
NICE -- UHH -- ROCK YOU GOT THERE!
PREPARE TO DIE...

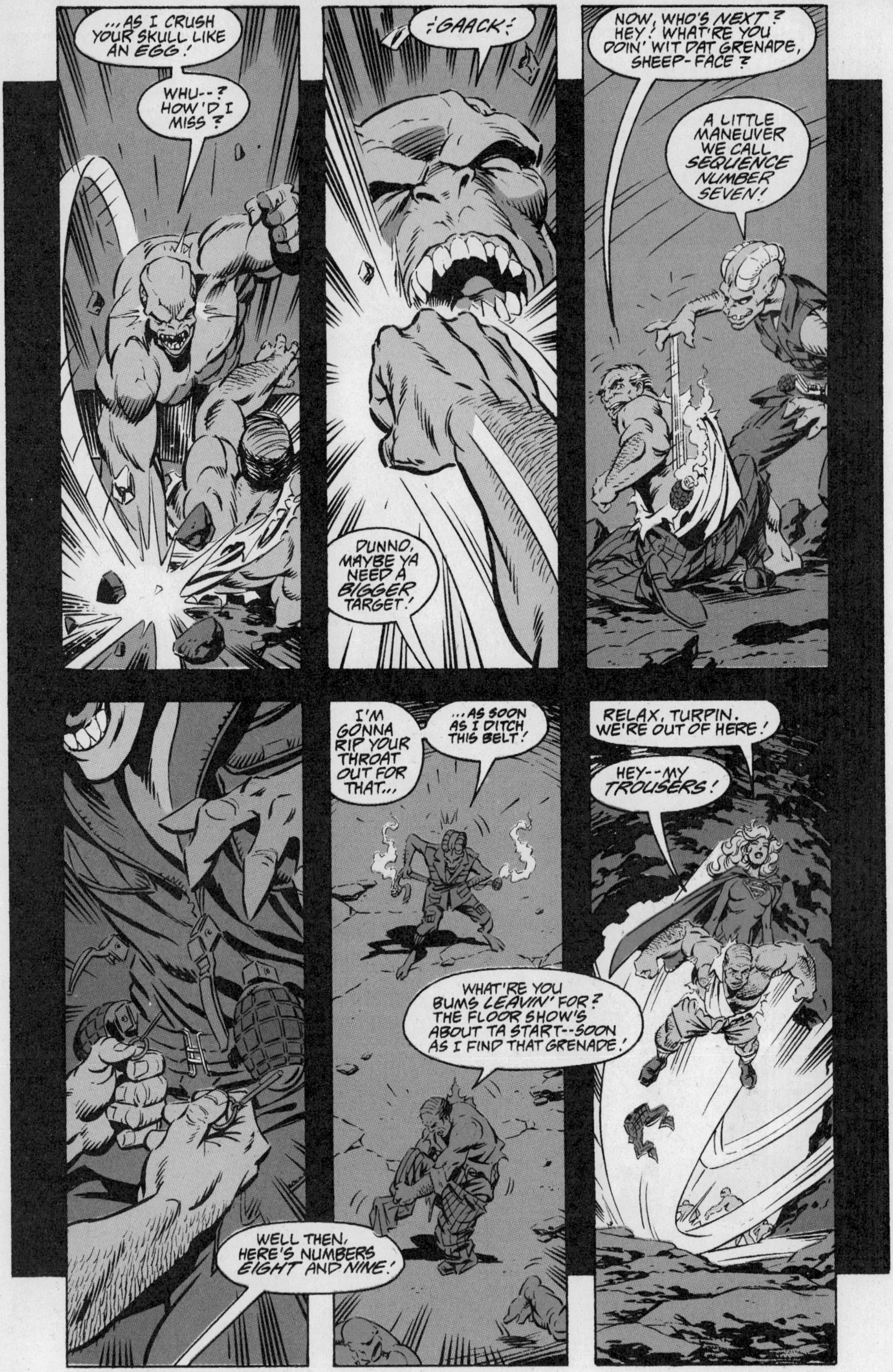
...AS I CRUSH YOUR SKULL LIKE AN EGG!
WHU--? HOW'D I MISS?
-GAACK-
DUNNO, MAYBE YA NEED A BIGGER TARGET!
NOW, WHO'S NEXT? HEY! WHAT'RE YOU DOIN' WIT DAT GRENADE, SHEEP-FACE?
A LITTLE MANEUVER WE CALL SEQUENCE NUMBER SEVEN!
WELL THEN, HERE'S NUMBERS EIGHT AND NINE!
I'M GONNA RIP YOUR THROAT OUT FOR THAT...
...AS SOON AS I DITCH THIS BELT!
WHAT'RE YOU BUMS LEAVIN' FOR? THE FLOOR SHOW'S ABOUT TA START--SOON AS I FIND THAT GRENADE!
RELAX, TURPIN. WE'RE OUT OF HERE!
HEY--MY TROUSERS!

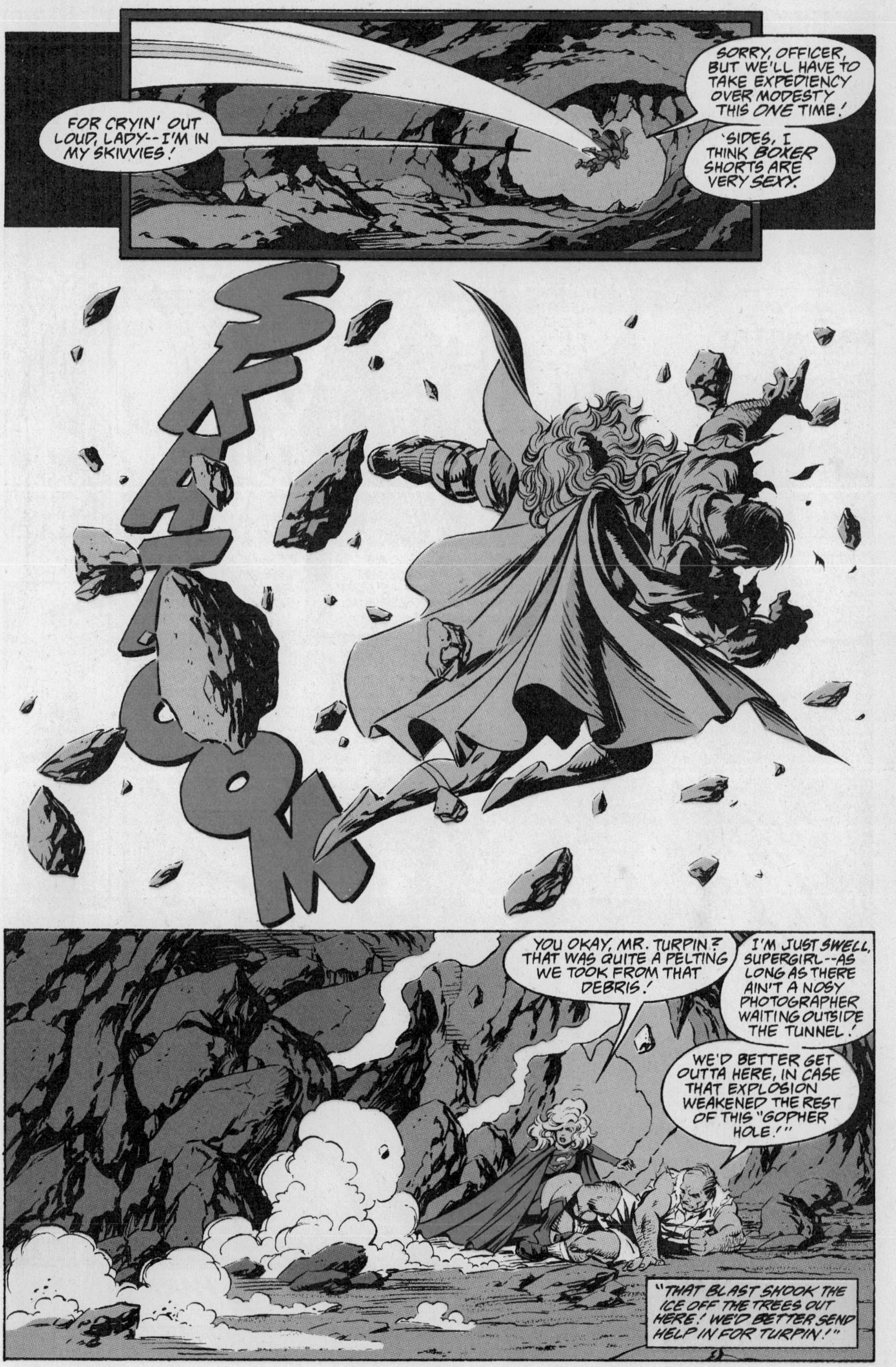
FOR CRYIN' OUT LOUD, LADY--I'M IN MY SKIVVIES!
SORRY, OFFICER, BUT WE'LL HAVE TO TAKE EXPEDIENCY OVER MODESTY THIS ONE TIME!
'SIDES, I THINK BOXER SHORTS ARE VERY SEXY.
SKRAKATOOM
YOU OKAY, MR. TURPIN? THAT WAS QUITE A PELTING WE TOOK FROM THAT DEBRIS!
I'M JUST SWELL, SUPERGIRL--AS LONG AS THERE AIN'T A NOSY PHOTOGRAPHER WAITING OUTSIDE THE TUNNEL!
WE'D BETTER GET OUTTA HERE, IN CASE THAT EXPLOSION WEAKENED THE REST OF THIS "GOPHER HOLE!"
"THAT BLAST SHOOK THE ICE OFF THE TREES OUT HERE! WE'D BETTER SEND HELP IN FOR TURPIN!"

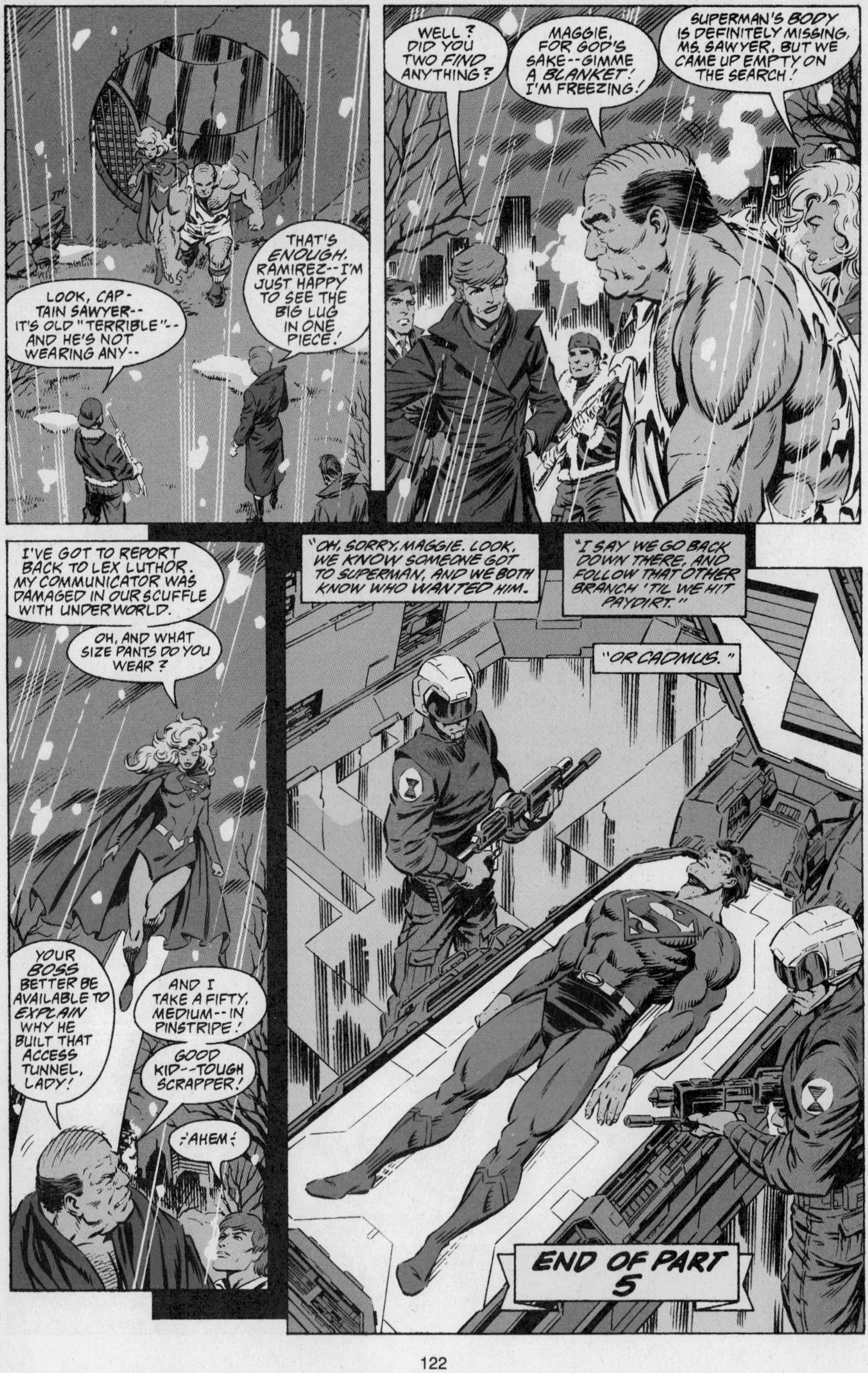
LOOK, CAPTAIN SAWYER-- IT'S OLD "TERRIBLE"-- AND HE'S NOT WEARING ANY--
THAT'S ENOUGH, RAMIREZ--I'M JUST HAPPY TO SEE THE BIG LUG IN ONE PIECE!
WELL? DID YOU TWO FIND ANYTHING?
MAGGIE, FOR GOD'S SAKE--GIMME A BLANKET! I'M FREEZING!
SUPERMAN'S BODY IS DEFINITELY MISSING, MS. SAWYER, BUT WE CAME UP EMPTY ON THE SEARCH!
I'VE GOT TO REPORT BACK TO LEX LUTHOR. MY COMMUNICATOR WAS DAMAGED IN OUR SCUFFLE WITH UNDERWORLD.
OH, AND WHAT SIZE PANTS DO YOU WEAR?
YOUR BOSS BETTER BE AVAILABLE TO EXPLAIN WHY HE BUILT THAT ACCESS TUNNEL, LADY!
AND I TAKE A FIFTY, MEDIUM--IN PINSTRIPE!
GOOD KID--TOUGH SCRAPPER!
AHEM
"OH, SORRY, MAGGIE. LOOK, WE KNOW SOMEONE GOT TO SUPERMAN, AND WE BOTH KNOW WHO WANTED HIM.
"I SAY WE GO BACK DOWN THERE, AND FOLLOW THAT OTHER BRANCH 'TIL WE HIT PAYDIRT."
"OR CADMUS."
END OF PART 5

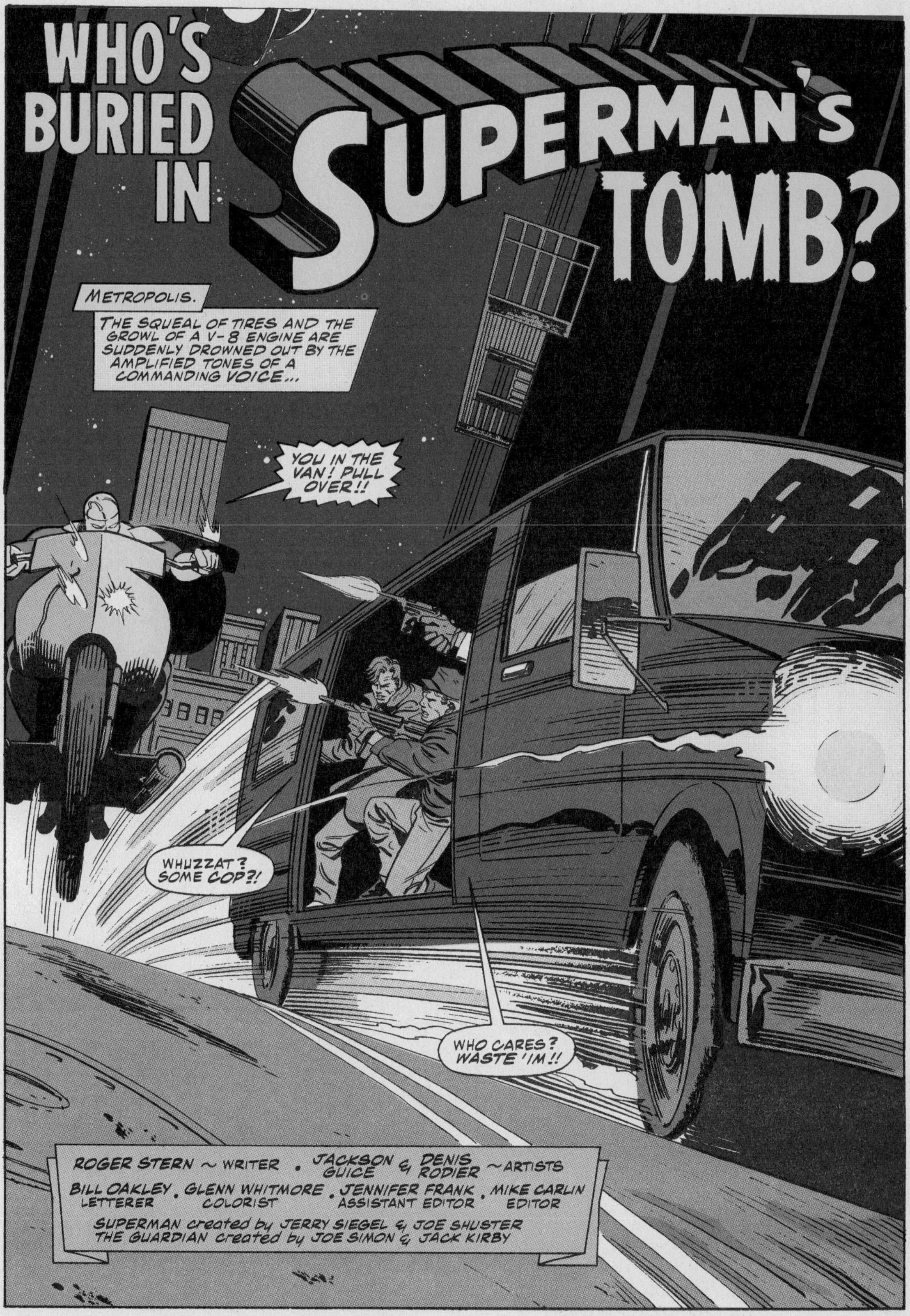
WHO'S BURIED IN SUPERMAN'S TOMB?
METROPOLIS.
THE SQUEAL OF TIRES AND THE GROWL OF A V-8 ENGINE ARE SUDDENLY DROWNED OUT BY THE AMPLIFIED TONES OF A COMMANDING VOICE...
YOU IN THE VAN! PULL OVER!!
WHUZZAT? SOME COP?!
WHO CARES? WASTE 'IM!!
ROGER STERN ~ WRITER • JACKSON GUICE & DENIS RODIER ~ ARTISTS
BILL OAKLEY LETTERER • GLENN WHITMORE COLORIST • JENNIFER FRANK ASSISTANT EDITOR • MIKE CARLIN EDITOR
SUPERMAN created by JERRY SIEGEL & JOE SHUSTER
THE GUARDIAN created by JOE SIMON & JACK KIRBY

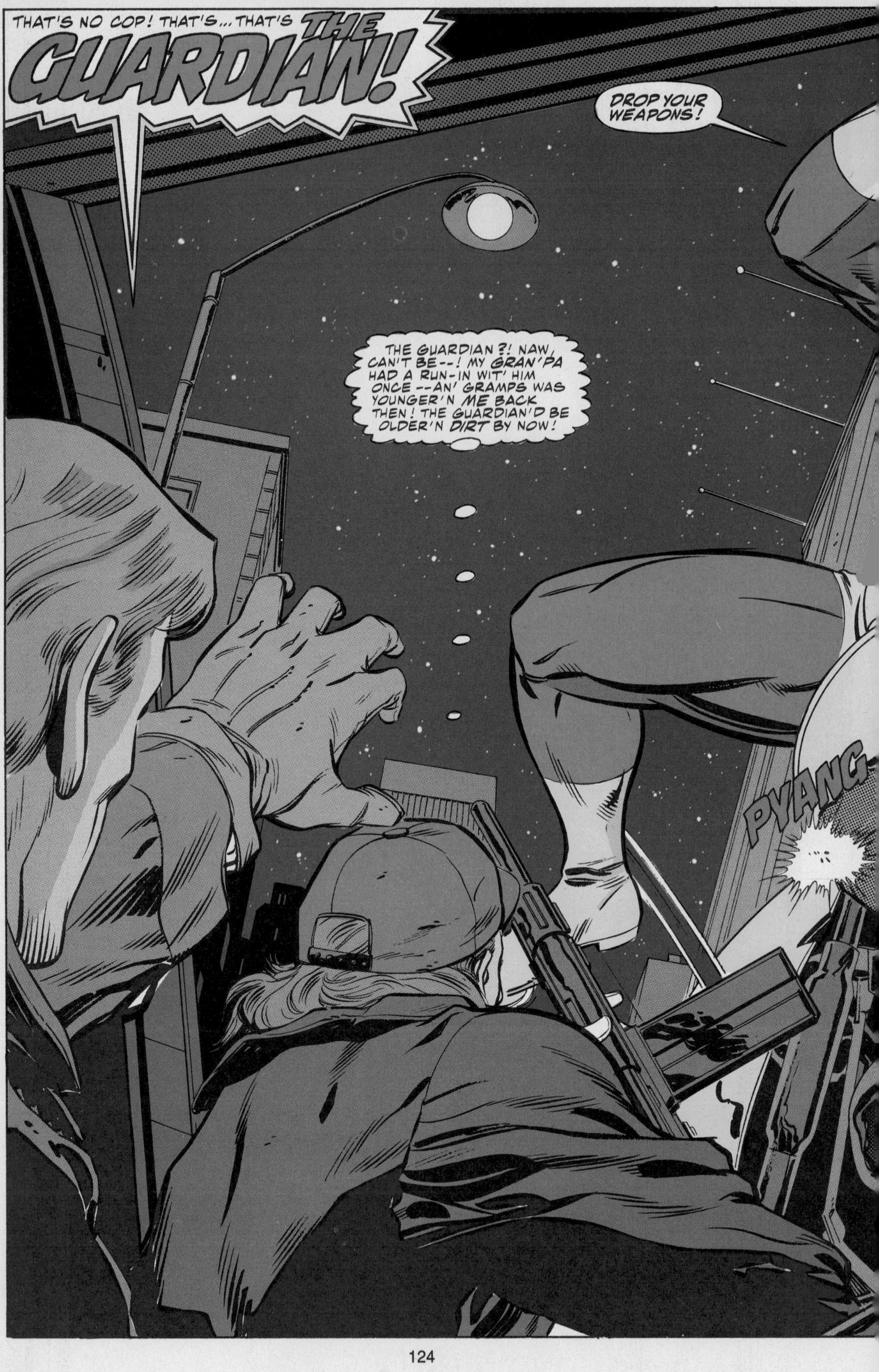
THAT'S NO COP! THAT'S... THAT'S THE GUARDIAN!
DROP YOUR WEAPONS!
THE GUARDIAN?! NAW, CAN'T BE--! MY GRAN'PA HAD A RUN-IN WIT' HIM ONCE --AN' GRAMPS WAS YOUNGER'N ME BACK THEN! THE GUARDIAN'D BE OLDER'N DIRT BY NOW!
PYANG

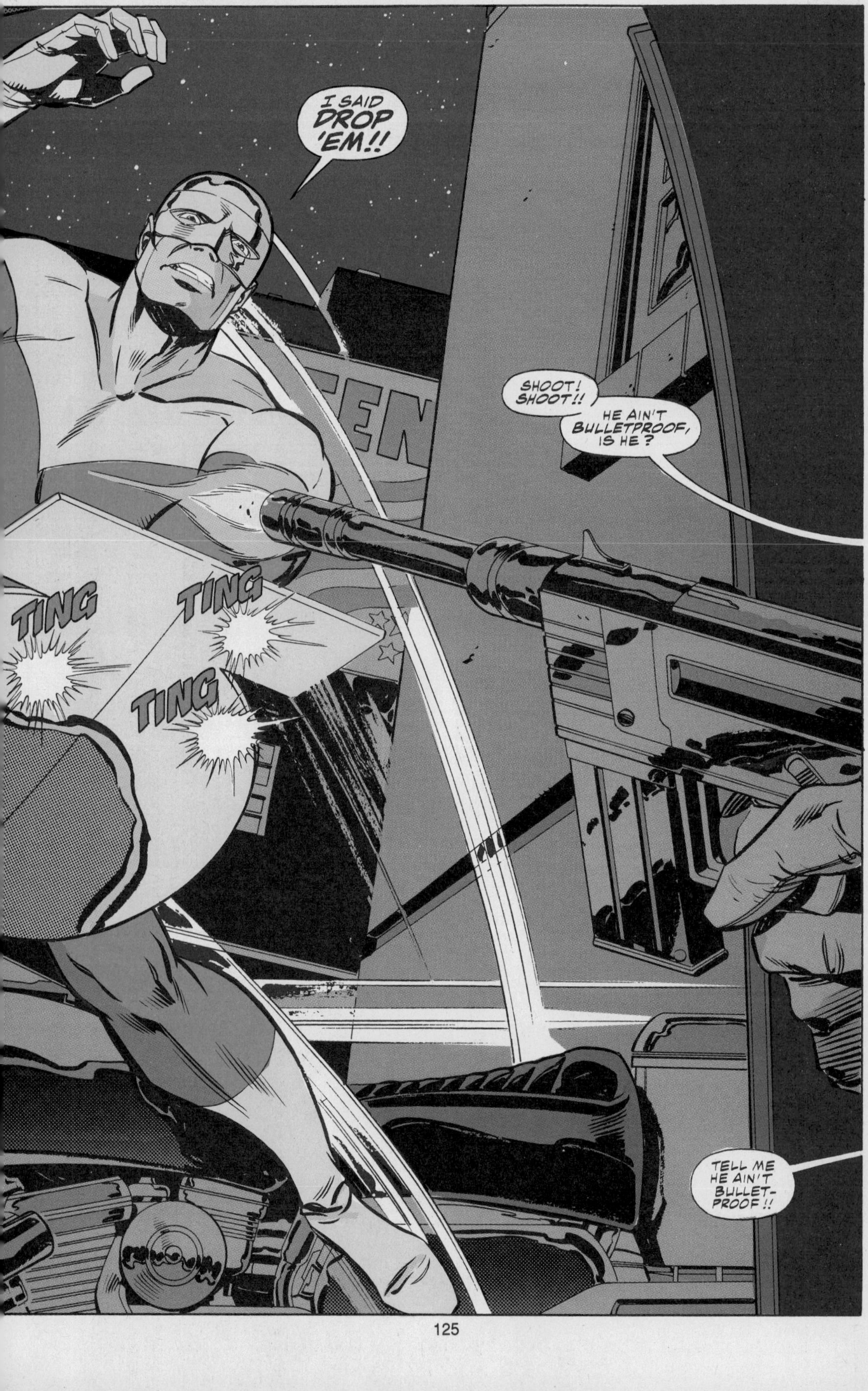

I SAID DROP 'EM!!
SHOOT! SHOOT!!
HE AIN'T BULLETPROOF, IS HE?
TING
TING
TING
TELL ME HE AIN'T BULLET-PROOF!!

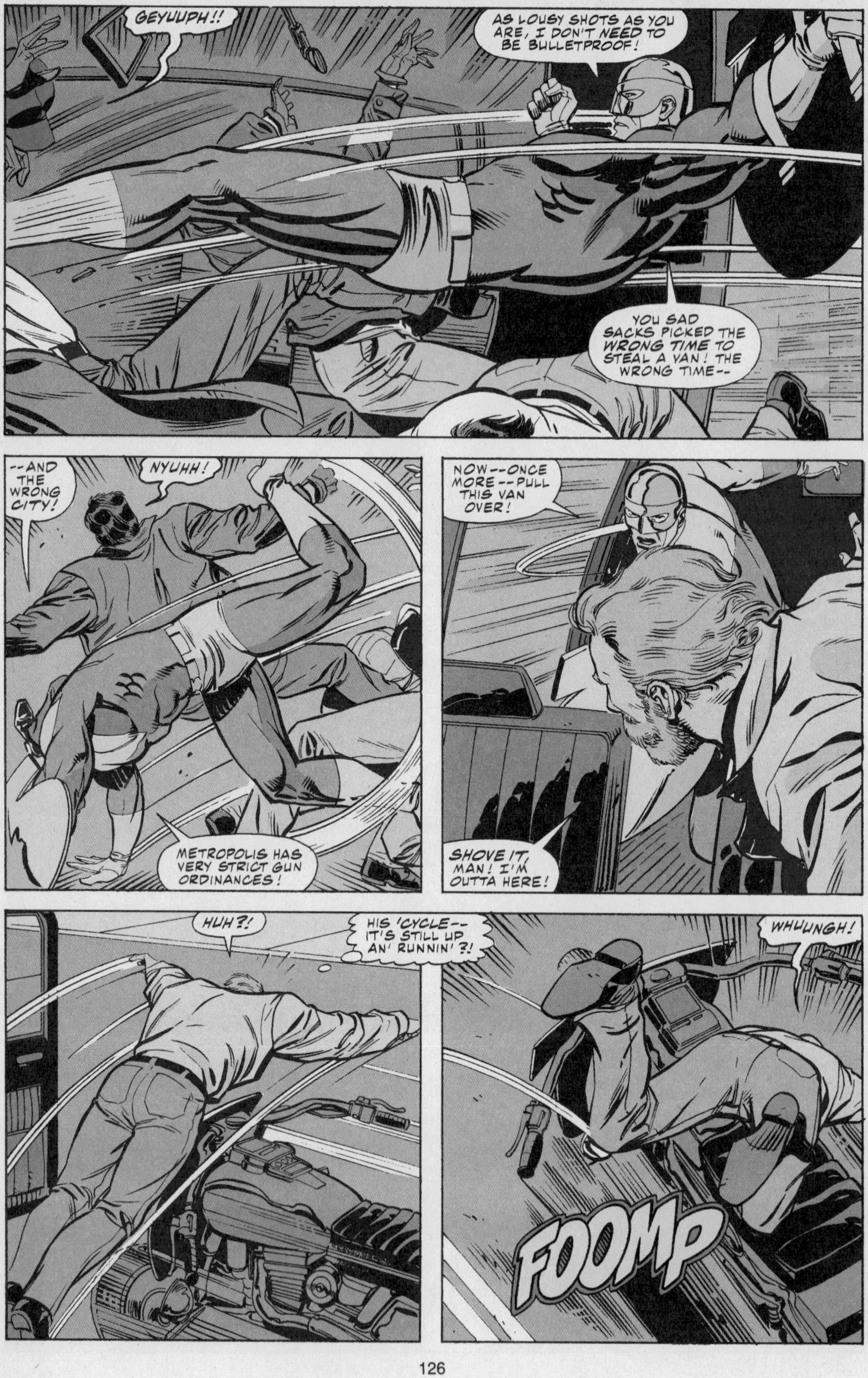
GEYUUPH!!
AS LOUSY SHOTS AS YOU ARE, I DON'T NEED TO BE BULLETPROOF!
YOU SAD SACKS PICKED THE WRONG TIME TO STEAL A VAN! THE WRONG TIME--
--AND THE WRONG CITY!
NYUHH!
METROPOLIS HAS VERY STRICT GUN ORDINANCES!
NOW--ONCE MORE--PULL THIS VAN OVER!
SHOVE IT, MAN! I'M OUTTA HERE!
HUH?!
HIS 'CYCLE-- IT'S STILL UP AN' RUNNIN'?!
WHUUNGH!
FOOMP

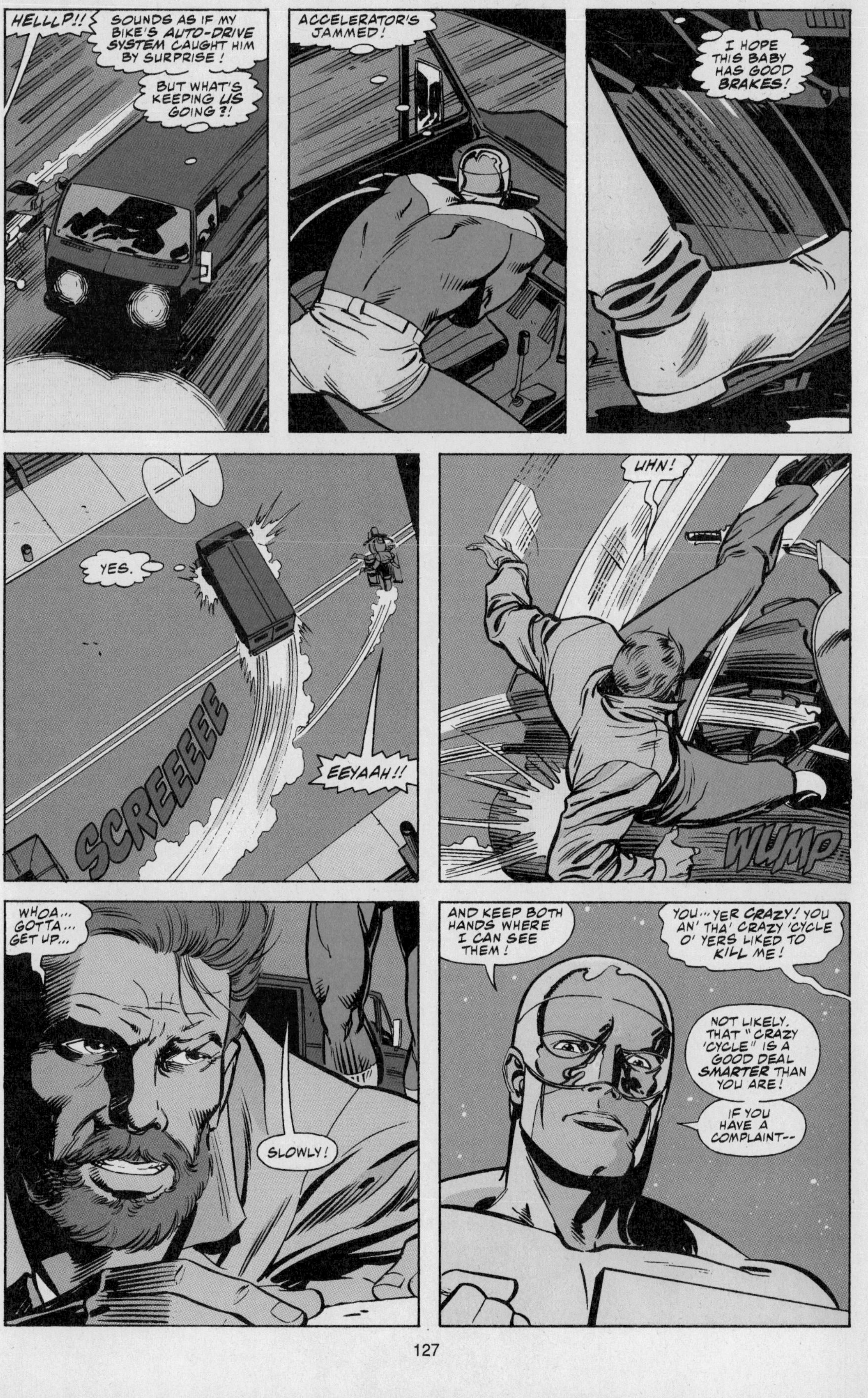
HELLLP!!
SOUNDS AS IF MY BIKE'S AUTO-DRIVE SYSTEM CAUGHT HIM BY SURPRISE!
BUT WHAT'S KEEPING US GOING?!
ACCELERATOR'S JAMMED!
I HOPE THIS BABY HAS GOOD BRAKES!
YES.
SCREEEEE
EEYAAH!!
UHN!
WUMP
WHOA... GOTTA... GET UP...
SLOWLY!
AND KEEP BOTH HANDS WHERE I CAN SEE THEM!
YOU... YER CRAZY! YOU AN' THA' CRAZY 'CYCLE O' YERS LIKED TO KILL ME!
NOT LIKELY. THAT "CRAZY 'CYCLE" IS A GOOD DEAL SMARTER THAN YOU ARE!
IF YOU HAVE A COMPLAINT--

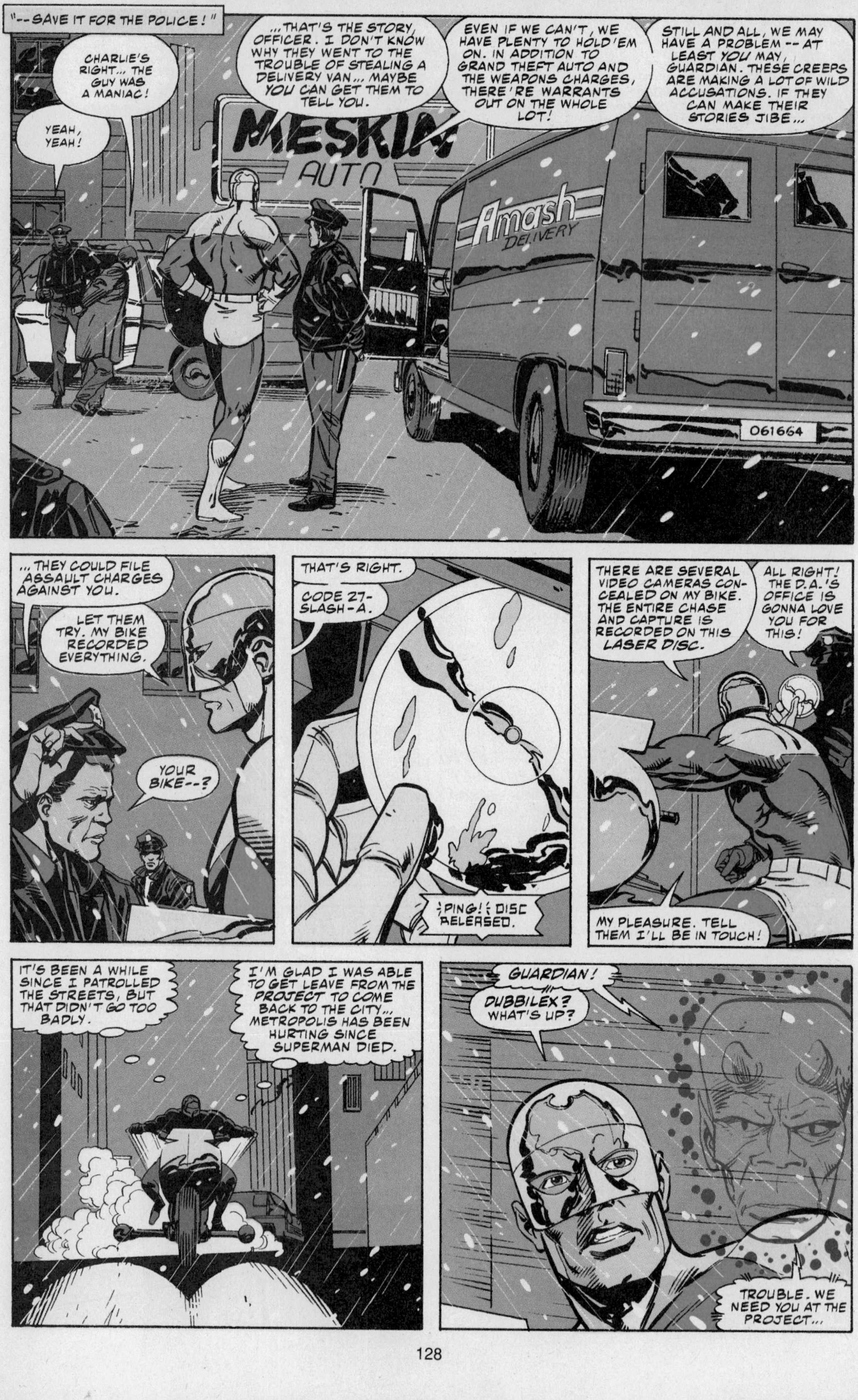
"--SAVE IT FOR THE POLICE!"
CHARLIE'S RIGHT... THE GUY WAS A MANIAC!
YEAH, YEAH!
...THAT'S THE STORY, OFFICER. I DON'T KNOW WHY THEY WENT TO THE TROUBLE OF STEALING A DELIVERY VAN... MAYBE YOU CAN GET THEM TO TELL YOU.
EVEN IF WE CAN'T, WE HAVE PLENTY TO HOLD 'EM ON. IN ADDITION TO GRAND THEFT AUTO AND THE WEAPONS CHARGES, THERE'RE WARRANTS OUT ON THE WHOLE LOT!
STILL AND ALL, WE MAY HAVE A PROBLEM -- AT LEAST YOU MAY, GUARDIAN. THESE CREEPS ARE MAKING A LOT OF WILD ACCUSATIONS. IF THEY CAN MAKE THEIR STORIES JIBE...
MESKIN
AUTO
Amash
DELIVERY
061664
...THEY COULD FILE ASSAULT CHARGES AGAINST YOU.
LET THEM TRY. MY BIKE RECORDED EVERYTHING.
YOUR BIKE--?
THAT'S RIGHT.
CODE 27-SLASH-A.
‡PING!‡ DISC RELEASED.
THERE ARE SEVERAL VIDEO CAMERAS CONCEALED ON MY BIKE. THE ENTIRE CHASE AND CAPTURE IS RECORDED ON THIS LASER DISC.
ALL RIGHT! THE D.A.'S OFFICE IS GONNA LOVE YOU FOR THIS!
MY PLEASURE. TELL THEM I'LL BE IN TOUCH!
IT'S BEEN A WHILE SINCE I PATROLLED THE STREETS, BUT THAT DIDN'T GO TOO BADLY.
I'M GLAD I WAS ABLE TO GET LEAVE FROM THE PROJECT TO COME BACK TO THE CITY... METROPOLIS HAS BEEN HURTING SINCE SUPERMAN DIED.
GUARDIAN!
DUBBILEX? WHAT'S UP?
TROUBLE. WE NEED YOU AT THE PROJECT...

...HURRY! I MUST GATHER THE OTHERS...!

IT MUST BE SERIOUS FOR DUBBILEX TO SEND A *TELEPATHIC* MESSAGE ALL THE WAY FROM THE *PROJECT.* I KNOW IT'S A DRAIN FOR HIM TO CAST HIS MIND ACROSS SO MANY MILES.

BETTER TAKE THE BOULEVARD... IT'LL GET ME THERE FASTEST!

REALLY, MISTER L... THERE'S PROBABLY NOTHING TO WORRY ABOUT!

NOTHING, HAPPERSEN? SUPERMAN'S BODY IS MISSING FROM ITS TOMB!

GRAVE ROBBERS-- SOME NUT CASES HAVE STOLEN THE BODY -- THAT'S THE ANSWER-- PURE AND SIMPLE! THE MAN HAD A LOT OF ENEMIES, AFTER ALL... YOU WEREN'T THE ONLY ONE WHO WANTED HIM DEAD, SIR!

YOU SAW THE NEWS FOOTAGE OF HIS BATTLE WITH THAT *DOOMSDAY* CREATURE... SUPERMAN COULDN'T POSSIBLY HAVE FAKED HIS DEATH!

NO, HAPPERSEN? I FAKED MINE!

COULD HE HAVE FOUND THAT OUT?

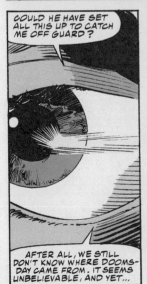

COULD HE HAVE SET ALL THIS UP TO CATCH ME OFF GUARD?

AFTER ALL, WE STILL DON'T KNOW WHERE DOOMS-DAY CAME FROM. IT SEEMS UNBELIEVABLE, AND YET...

"...KELLEY'S DIAGNOSIS SEEMED UNBELIEVABLE!"

I'M SORRY, LEX... YOU HAVE NO MORE THAN A YEAR TO LIVE.

"LEX LUTHOR... THE WORLD'S MOST POWERFUL BUSINESS-MAN... DYING OF RADIATION POISONING. I NEEDED A MIRACLE, HAPPERSEN--!"

"AND YOU *MADE* ONE, SIR! WE LET EVERY-ONE THINK THAT YOU DIED IN THAT PLANE CRASH!

"WE LET THE CORPORA-TION FOUNDER... IN-SURING THAT THE WORLD WOULD MOURN THE PASSING OF THE OLD LEX LUTHOR..."

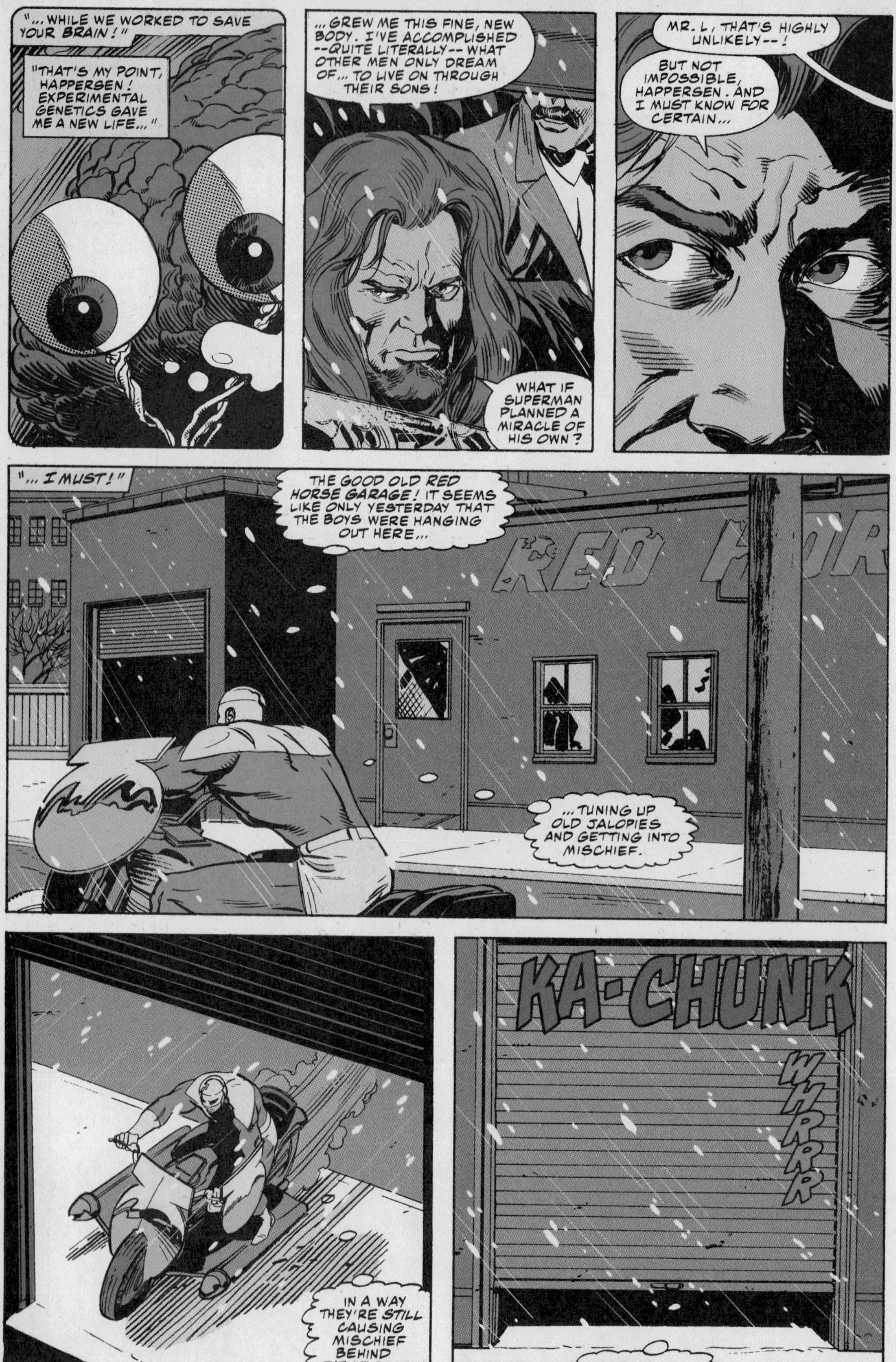
"... WHILE WE WORKED TO SAVE YOUR BRAIN!"
"THAT'S MY POINT, HAPPERSEN! EXPERIMENTAL GENETICS GAVE ME A NEW LIFE..."
... GREW ME THIS FINE, NEW BODY. I'VE ACCOMPLISHED --QUITE LITERALLY-- WHAT OTHER MEN ONLY DREAM OF... TO LIVE ON THROUGH THEIR SONS!
MR. L, THAT'S HIGHLY UNLIKELY--!
BUT NOT IMPOSSIBLE, HAPPERSEN. AND I MUST KNOW FOR CERTAIN...
WHAT IF SUPERMAN PLANNED A MIRACLE OF HIS OWN?
"... I MUST!"
THE GOOD OLD RED HORSE GARAGE! IT SEEMS LIKE ONLY YESTERDAY THAT THE BOYS WERE HANGING OUT HERE...
RED
... TUNING UP OLD JALOPIES AND GETTING INTO MISCHIEF.
IN A WAY THEY'RE STILL CAUSING MISCHIEF BEHIND THESE DOORS!
KA-CHUNK
WHRRRR
FAR BEHIND...

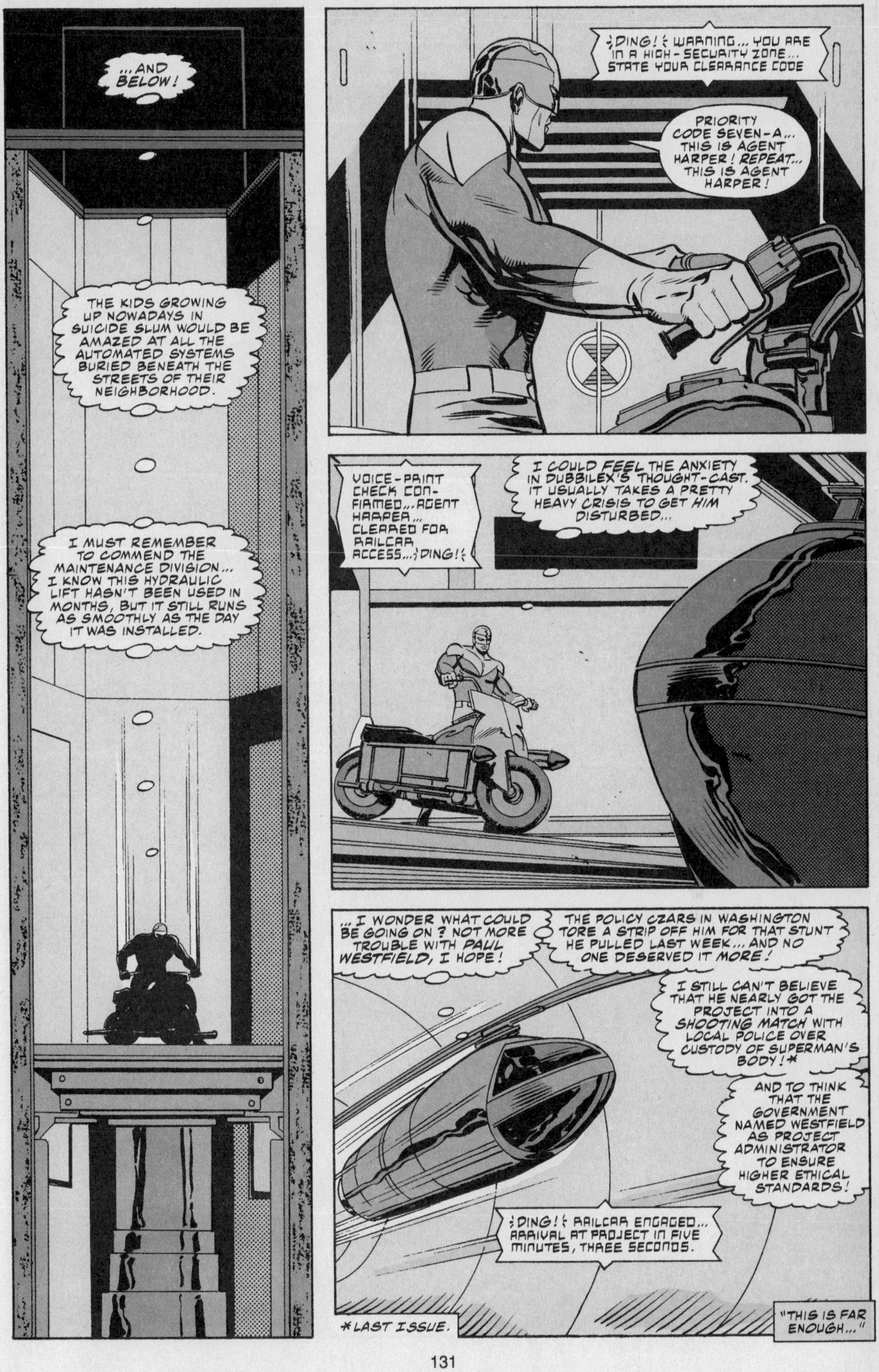
...AND BELOW!
THE KIDS GROWING UP NOWADAYS IN SUICIDE SLUM WOULD BE AMAZED AT ALL THE AUTOMATED SYSTEMS BURIED BENEATH THE STREETS OF THEIR NEIGHBORHOOD.
I MUST REMEMBER TO COMMEND THE MAINTENANCE DIVISION... I KNOW THIS HYDRAULIC LIFT HASN'T BEEN USED IN MONTHS, BUT IT STILL RUNS AS SMOOTHLY AS THE DAY IT WAS INSTALLED.
DING! WARNING... YOU ARE IN A HIGH-SECURITY ZONE... STATE YOUR CLEARANCE CODE
PRIORITY CODE SEVEN-A... THIS IS AGENT HARPER! REPEAT... THIS IS AGENT HARPER!
VOICE-PRINT CHECK CON-FIRMED... AGENT HARPER... CLEARED FOR RAILCAR ACCESS... DING!
I COULD FEEL THE ANXIETY IN DUBBILEX'S THOUGHT-CAST. IT USUALLY TAKES A PRETTY HEAVY CRISIS TO GET HIM DISTURBED...
...I WONDER WHAT COULD BE GOING ON? NOT MORE TROUBLE WITH PAUL WESTFIELD, I HOPE!
THE POLICY CZARS IN WASHINGTON TORE A STRIP OFF HIM FOR THAT STUNT HE PULLED LAST WEEK... AND NO ONE DESERVED IT MORE!
I STILL CAN'T BELIEVE THAT HE NEARLY GOT THE PROJECT INTO A SHOOTING MATCH WITH LOCAL POLICE OVER CUSTODY OF SUPERMAN'S BODY!*
AND TO THINK THAT THE GOVERNMENT NAMED WESTFIELD AS PROJECT ADMINISTRATOR TO ENSURE HIGHER ETHICAL STANDARDS!
DING! RAILCAR ENGAGED... ARRIVAL AT PROJECT IN FIVE MINUTES, THREE SECONDS.
*LAST ISSUE.
"THIS IS FAR ENOUGH..."

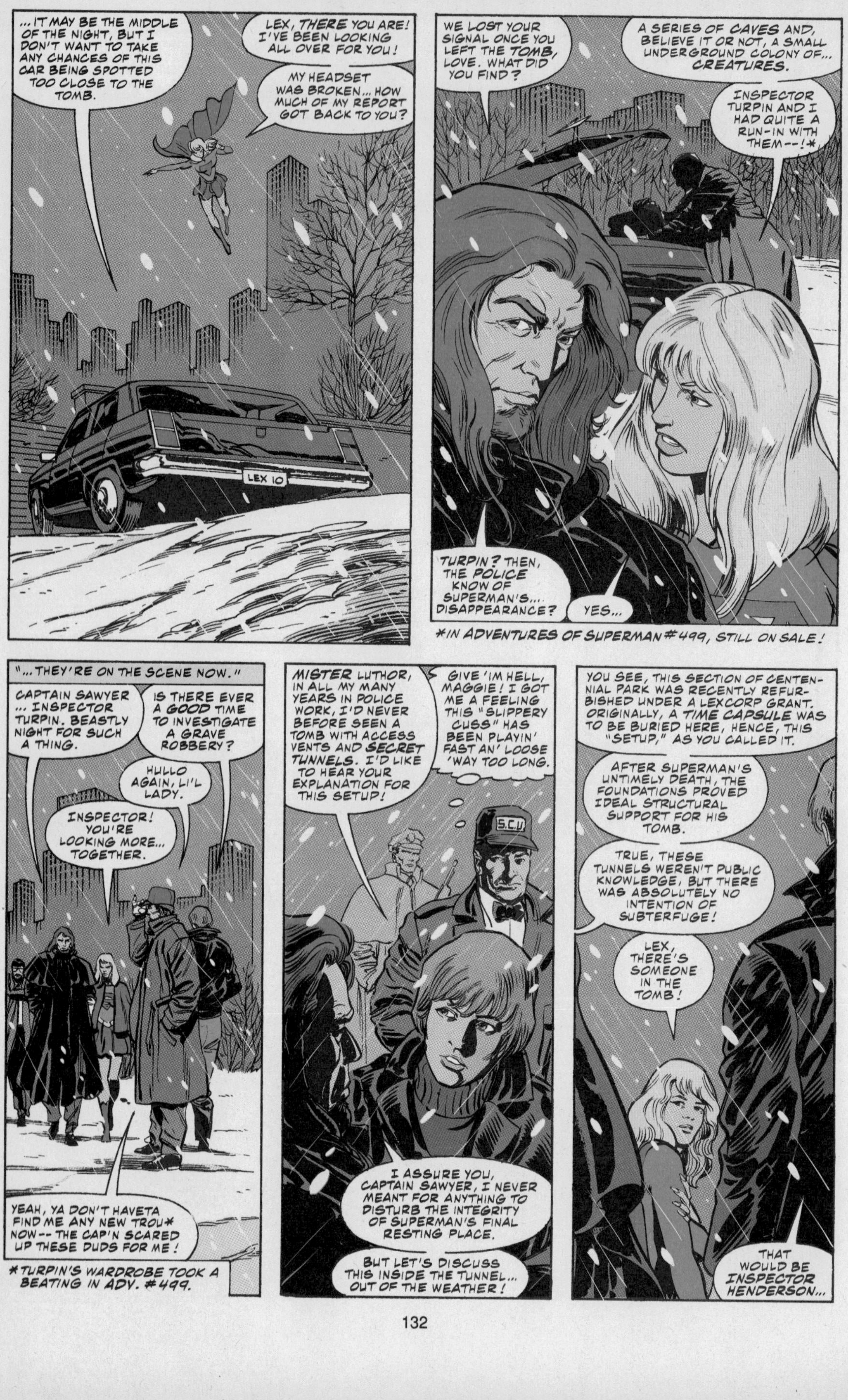
...IT MAY BE THE MIDDLE OF THE NIGHT, BUT I DON'T WANT TO TAKE ANY CHANCES OF THIS CAR BEING SPOTTED TOO CLOSE TO THE TOMB.
LEX, THERE YOU ARE! I'VE BEEN LOOKING ALL OVER FOR YOU!
MY HEADSET WAS BROKEN... HOW MUCH OF MY REPORT GOT BACK TO YOU?
LEX 10
WE LOST YOUR SIGNAL ONCE YOU LEFT THE TOMB, LOVE. WHAT DID YOU FIND?
A SERIES OF CAVES AND, BELIEVE IT OR NOT, A SMALL UNDERGROUND COLONY OF... CREATURES.
INSPECTOR TURPIN AND I HAD QUITE A RUN-IN WITH THEM--!*
TURPIN? THEN, THE POLICE KNOW OF SUPERMAN'S... DISAPPEARANCE?
YES...
*IN ADVENTURES OF SUPERMAN #499, STILL ON SALE!
"...THEY'RE ON THE SCENE NOW."
CAPTAIN SAWYER ...INSPECTOR TURPIN. BEASTLY NIGHT FOR SUCH A THING.
IS THERE EVER A GOOD TIME TO INVESTIGATE A GRAVE ROBBERY?
HULLO AGAIN, LI'L LADY.
INSPECTOR! YOU'RE LOOKING MORE... TOGETHER.
YEAH, YA DON'T HAVETA FIND ME ANY NEW TROU* NOW-- THE CAP'N SCARED UP THESE DUDS FOR ME!
*TURPIN'S WARDROBE TOOK A BEATING IN ADV. #499.
MISTER LUTHOR, IN ALL MY MANY YEARS IN POLICE WORK, I'D NEVER BEFORE SEEN A TOMB WITH ACCESS VENTS AND SECRET TUNNELS. I'D LIKE TO HEAR YOUR EXPLANATION FOR THIS SETUP!
GIVE 'IM HELL, MAGGIE! I GOT ME A FEELING THIS "SLIPPERY CUSS" HAS BEEN PLAYIN' FAST AN' LOOSE 'WAY TOO LONG.
S.C.U.
I ASSURE YOU, CAPTAIN SAWYER, I NEVER MEANT FOR ANYTHING TO DISTURB THE INTEGRITY OF SUPERMAN'S FINAL RESTING PLACE.
BUT LET'S DISCUSS THIS INSIDE THE TUNNEL... OUT OF THE WEATHER!
YOU SEE, THIS SECTION OF CENTENNIAL PARK WAS RECENTLY REFURBISHED UNDER A LEXCORP GRANT. ORIGINALLY, A TIME CAPSULE WAS TO BE BURIED HERE, HENCE, THIS "SETUP," AS YOU CALLED IT.
AFTER SUPERMAN'S UNTIMELY DEATH, THE FOUNDATIONS PROVED IDEAL STRUCTURAL SUPPORT FOR HIS TOMB.
TRUE, THESE TUNNELS WEREN'T PUBLIC KNOWLEDGE, BUT THERE WAS ABSOLUTELY NO INTENTION OF SUBTERFUGE!
LEX, THERE'S SOMEONE IN THE TOMB!
THAT WOULD BE INSPECTOR HENDERSON...

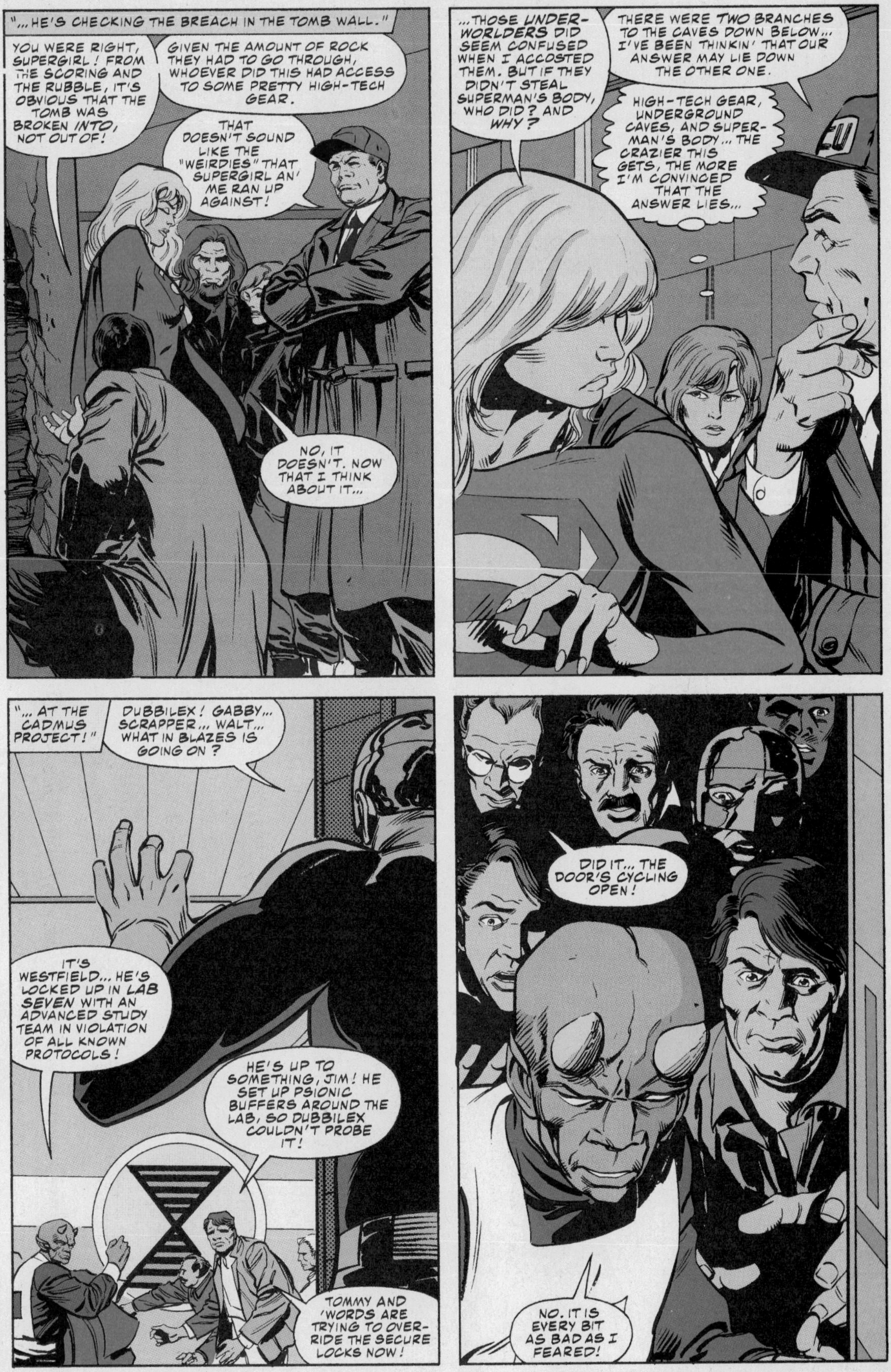
"... HE'S CHECKING THE BREACH IN THE TOMB WALL."
YOU WERE RIGHT, SUPERGIRL! FROM THE SCORING AND THE RUBBLE, IT'S OBVIOUS THAT THE TOMB WAS BROKEN INTO, NOT OUT OF!
GIVEN THE AMOUNT OF ROCK THEY HAD TO GO THROUGH, WHOEVER DID THIS HAD ACCESS TO SOME PRETTY HIGH-TECH GEAR.
THAT DOESN'T SOUND LIKE THE "WEIRDIES" THAT SUPERGIRL AN' ME RAN UP AGAINST!
NO, IT DOESN'T. NOW THAT I THINK ABOUT IT...
...THOSE UNDER-WORLDERS DID SEEM CONFUSED WHEN I ACCOSTED THEM. BUT IF THEY DIDN'T STEAL SUPERMAN'S BODY, WHO DID? AND WHY?
THERE WERE TWO BRANCHES TO THE CAVES DOWN BELOW... I'VE BEEN THINKIN' THAT OUR ANSWER MAY LIE DOWN THE OTHER ONE.
HIGH-TECH GEAR, UNDERGROUND CAVES, AND SUPER-MAN'S BODY... THE CRAZIER THIS GETS, THE MORE I'M CONVINCED THAT THE ANSWER LIES...
"... AT THE CADMUS PROJECT!"
DUBBILEX! GABBY... SCRAPPER... WALT... WHAT IN BLAZES IS GOING ON?
IT'S WESTFIELD... HE'S LOCKED UP IN LAB SEVEN WITH AN ADVANCED STUDY TEAM IN VIOLATION OF ALL KNOWN PROTOCOLS!
HE'S UP TO SOMETHING, JIM! HE SET UP PSIONIC BUFFERS AROUND THE LAB, SO DUBBILEX COULDN'T PROBE IT!
TOMMY AND 'WORDS ARE TRYING TO OVER-RIDE THE SECURE LOCKS NOW!
DID IT... THE DOOR'S CYCLING OPEN!
NO. IT IS EVERY BIT AS BAD AS I FEARED!

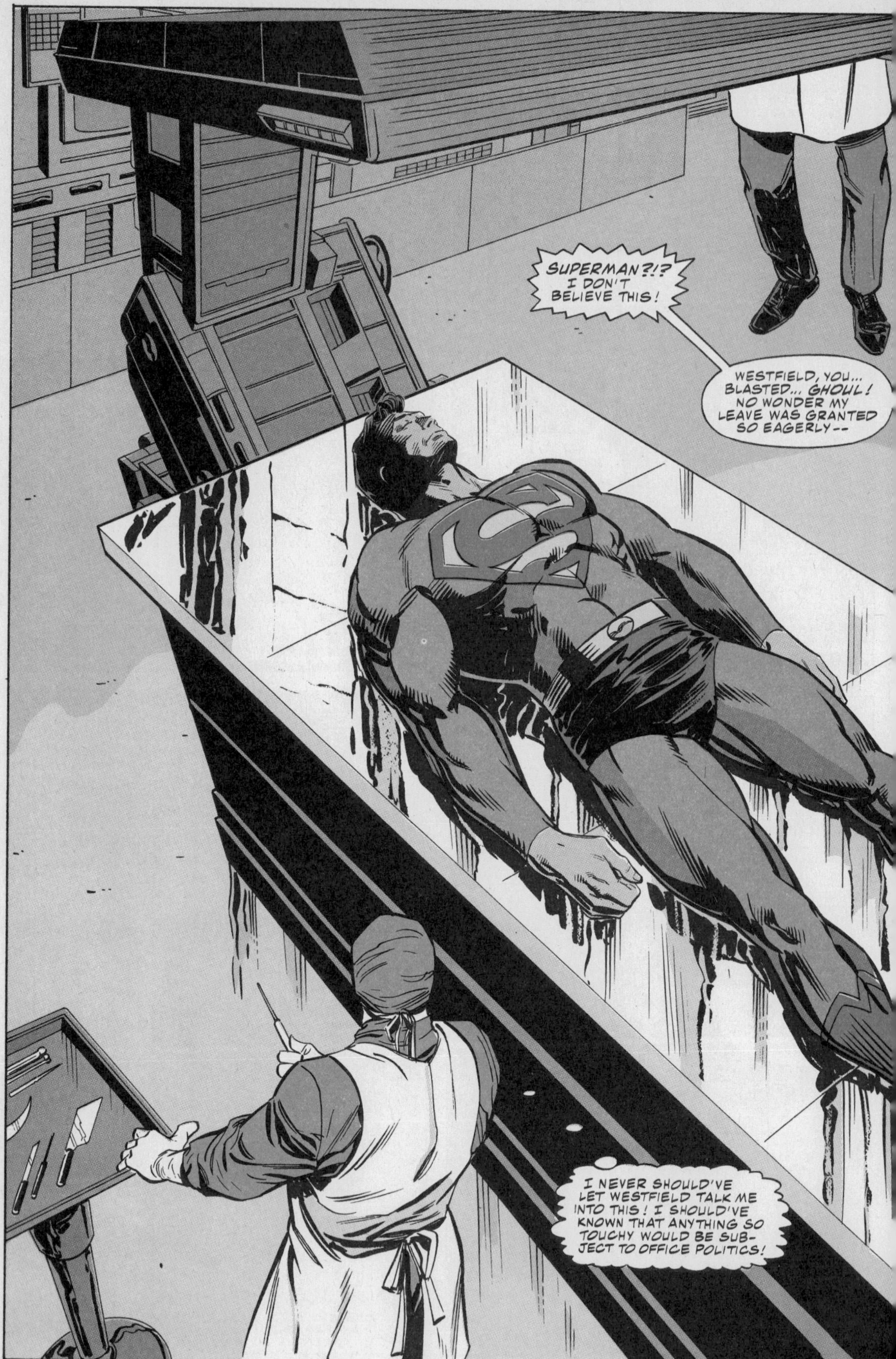
SUPERMAN?!? I DON'T BELIEVE THIS!
WESTFIELD, YOU... BLASTED... GHOUL! NO WONDER MY LEAVE WAS GRANTED SO EAGERLY--
I NEVER SHOULD'VE LET WESTFIELD TALK ME INTO THIS! I SHOULD'VE KNOWN THAT ANYTHING SO TOUCHY WOULD BE SUBJECT TO OFFICE POLITICS!

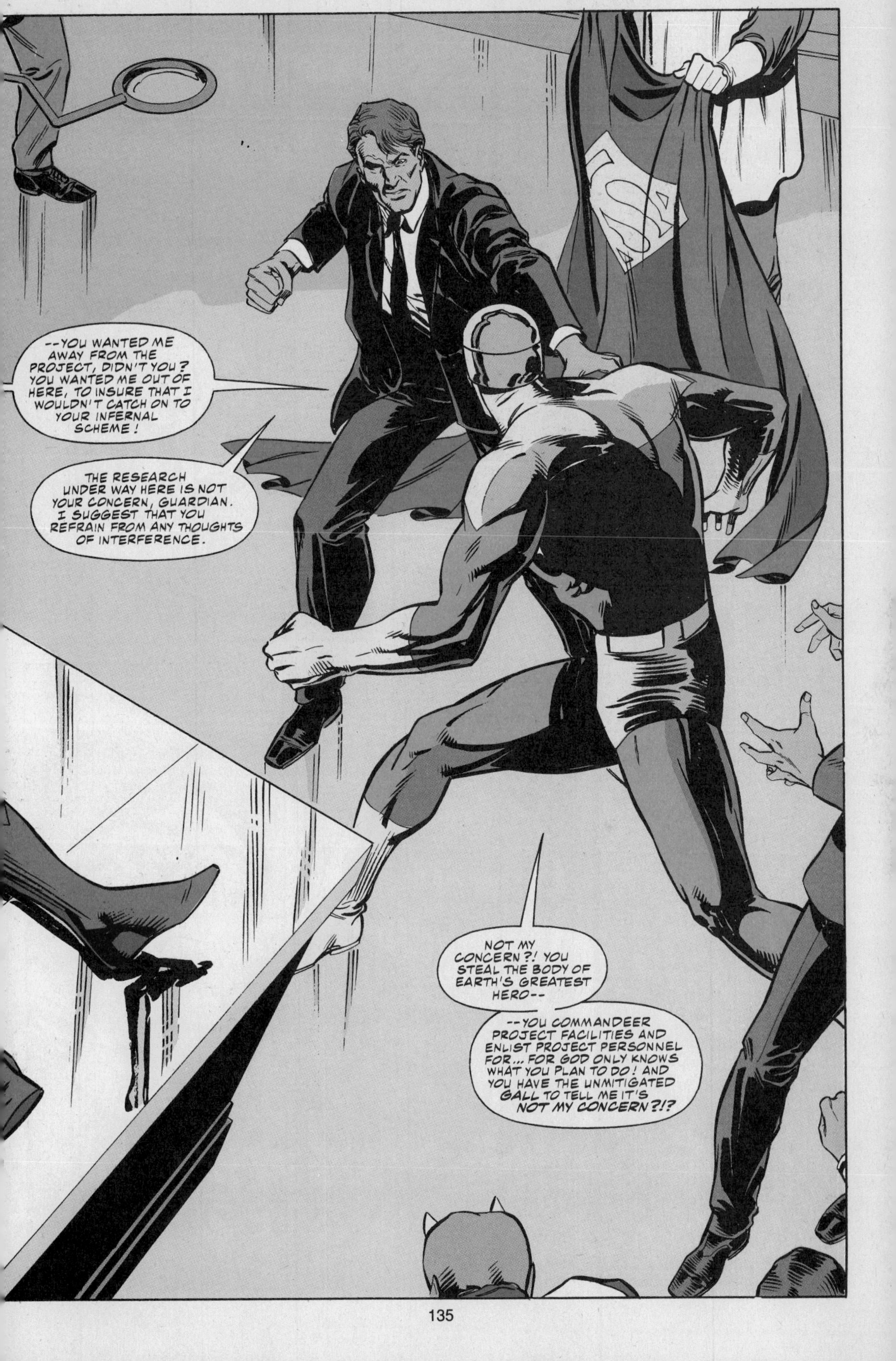

--YOU WANTED ME AWAY FROM THE PROJECT, DIDN'T YOU? YOU WANTED ME OUT OF HERE, TO INSURE THAT I WOULDN'T CATCH ON TO YOUR INFERNAL SCHEME!
THE RESEARCH UNDER WAY HERE IS NOT YOUR CONCERN, GUARDIAN. I SUGGEST THAT YOU REFRAIN FROM ANY THOUGHTS OF INTERFERENCE.
NOT MY CONCERN?! YOU STEAL THE BODY OF EARTH'S GREATEST HERO--
--YOU COMMANDEER PROJECT FACILITIES AND ENLIST PROJECT PERSONNEL FOR... FOR GOD ONLY KNOWS WHAT YOU PLAN TO DO! AND YOU HAVE THE UNMITIGATED GALL TO TELL ME IT'S NOT MY CONCERN?!?

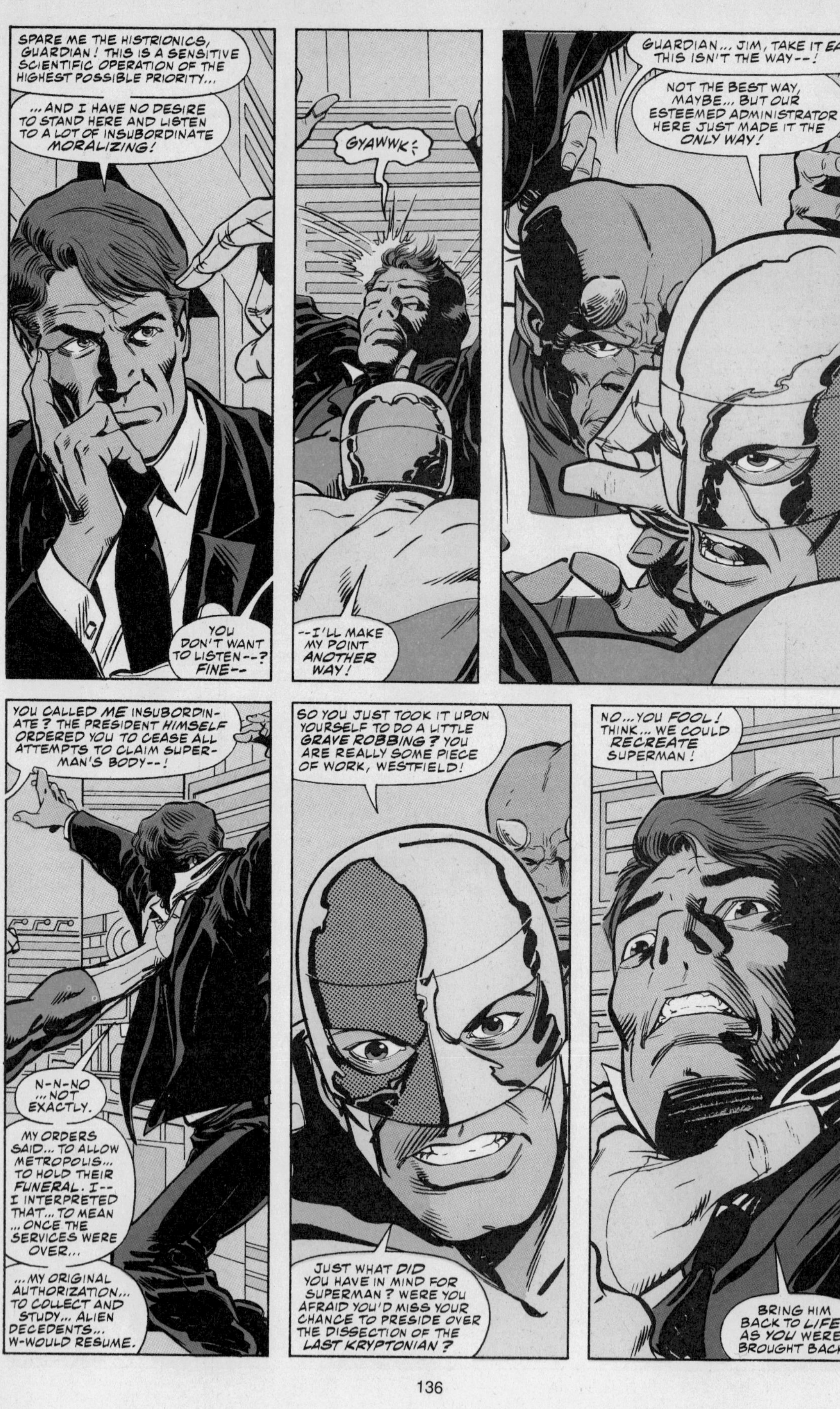
SPARE ME THE HISTRIONICS, GUARDIAN! THIS IS A SENSITIVE SCIENTIFIC OPERATION OF THE HIGHEST POSSIBLE PRIORITY...
...AND I HAVE NO DESIRE TO STAND HERE AND LISTEN TO A LOT OF INSUBORDINATE MORALIZING!
YOU DON'T WANT TO LISTEN--? FINE--
GYAWWK!
--I'LL MAKE MY POINT ANOTHER WAY!
GUARDIAN... JIM, TAKE IT EASY! THIS ISN'T THE WAY--!
NOT THE BEST WAY, MAYBE... BUT OUR ESTEEMED ADMINISTRATOR HERE JUST MADE IT THE ONLY WAY!
YOU CALLED ME INSUBORDINATE? THE PRESIDENT HIMSELF ORDERED YOU TO CEASE ALL ATTEMPTS TO CLAIM SUPERMAN'S BODY--!
N-N-NO ...NOT EXACTLY.
MY ORDERS SAID... TO ALLOW METROPOLIS... TO HOLD THEIR FUNERAL. I--I INTERPRETED THAT... TO MEAN ...ONCE THE SERVICES WERE OVER...
...MY ORIGINAL AUTHORIZATION... TO COLLECT AND STUDY... ALIEN DECEDENTS... W-WOULD RESUME.
SO YOU JUST TOOK IT UPON YOURSELF TO DO A LITTLE GRAVE ROBBING? YOU ARE REALLY SOME PIECE OF WORK, WESTFIELD!
JUST WHAT DID YOU HAVE IN MIND FOR SUPERMAN? WERE YOU AFRAID YOU'D MISS YOUR CHANCE TO PRESIDE OVER THE DISSECTION OF THE LAST KRYPTONIAN?
NO... YOU FOOL! THINK... WE COULD RECREATE SUPERMAN!
BRING HIM BACK TO LIFE... AS YOU WERE BROUGHT BACK!

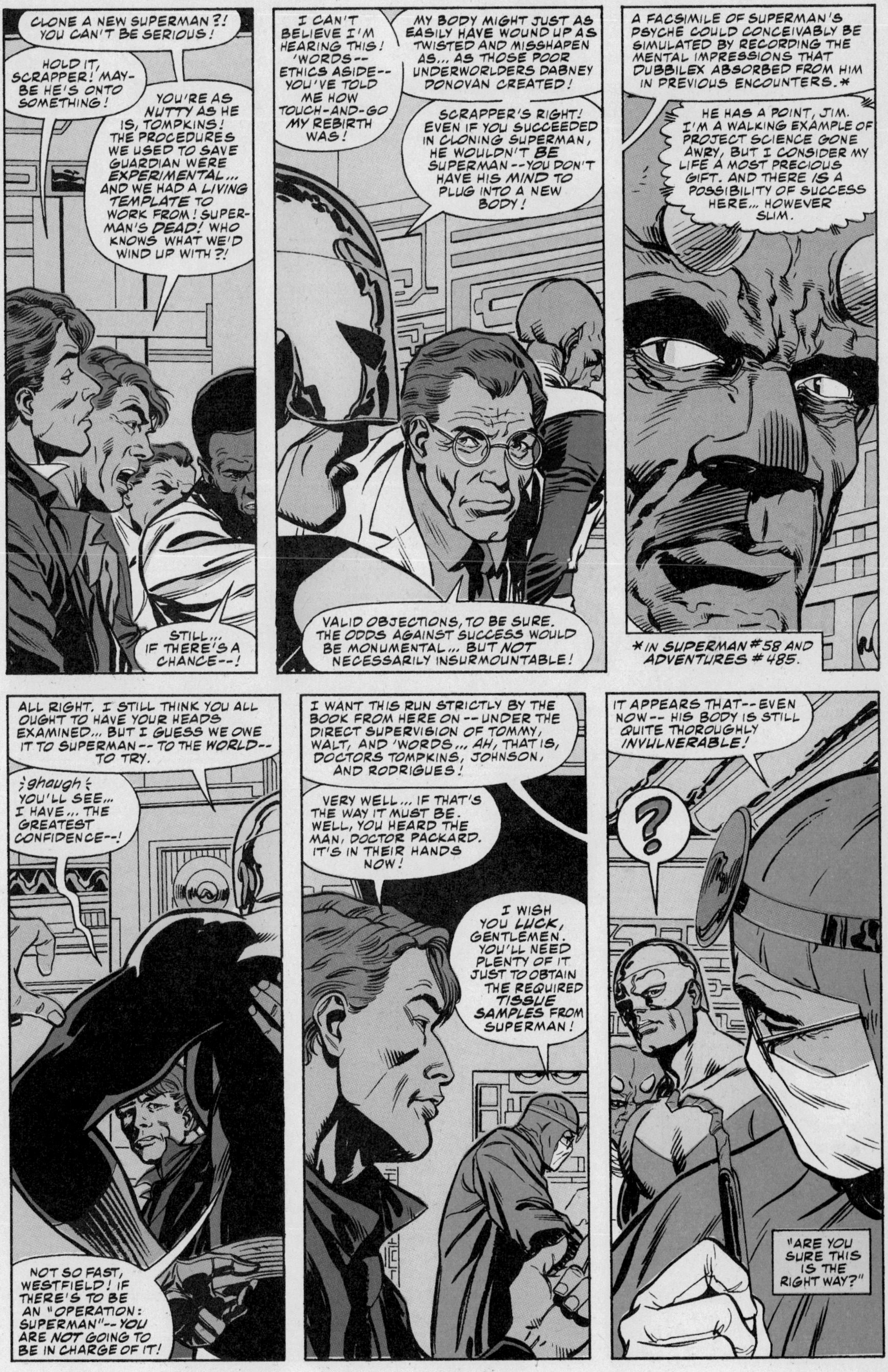
CLONE A NEW SUPERMAN?! YOU CAN'T BE SERIOUS!
HOLD IT, SCRAPPER! MAY-BE HE'S ONTO SOMETHING!
YOU'RE AS NUTTY AS HE IS, TOMPKINS! THE PROCEDURES WE USED TO SAVE GUARDIAN WERE EXPERIMENTAL... AND WE HAD A LIVING TEMPLATE TO WORK FROM! SUPER-MAN'S DEAD! WHO KNOWS WHAT WE'D WIND UP WITH?!
STILL... IF THERE'S A CHANCE--!
I CAN'T BELIEVE I'M HEARING THIS! 'WORDS-- ETHICS ASIDE-- YOU'VE TOLD ME HOW TOUCH-AND-GO MY REBIRTH WAS!
MY BODY MIGHT JUST AS EASILY HAVE WOUND UP AS TWISTED AND MISSHAPEN AS... AS THOSE POOR UNDERWORLDERS DABNEY DONOVAN CREATED!
SCRAPPER'S RIGHT! EVEN IF YOU SUCCEEDED IN CLONING SUPERMAN, HE WOULDN'T BE SUPERMAN--YOU DON'T HAVE HIS MIND TO PLUG INTO A NEW BODY!
VALID OBJECTIONS, TO BE SURE. THE ODDS AGAINST SUCCESS WOULD BE MONUMENTAL... BUT NOT NECESSARILY INSURMOUNTABLE!
A FACSIMILE OF SUPERMAN'S PSYCHE COULD CONCEIVABLY BE SIMULATED BY RECORDING THE MENTAL IMPRESSIONS THAT DUBBILEX ABSORBED FROM HIM IN PREVIOUS ENCOUNTERS.*
HE HAS A POINT, JIM. I'M A WALKING EXAMPLE OF PROJECT SCIENCE GONE AWRY, BUT I CONSIDER MY LIFE A MOST PRECIOUS GIFT. AND THERE IS A POSSIBILITY OF SUCCESS HERE... HOWEVER SLIM.
*IN SUPERMAN #58 AND ADVENTURES #485.
ALL RIGHT. I STILL THINK YOU ALL OUGHT TO HAVE YOUR HEADS EXAMINED... BUT I GUESS WE OWE IT TO SUPERMAN-- TO THE WORLD-- TO TRY.
;ghaugh; YOU'LL SEE... I HAVE... THE GREATEST CONFIDENCE--!
NOT SO FAST, WESTFIELD! IF THERE'S TO BE AN "OPERATION: SUPERMAN"--YOU ARE NOT GOING TO BE IN CHARGE OF IT!
I WANT THIS RUN STRICTLY BY THE BOOK FROM HERE ON--UNDER THE DIRECT SUPERVISION OF TOMMY, WALT, AND 'WORDS... AH, THAT IS, DOCTORS TOMPKINS, JOHNSON, AND RODRIGUES!
VERY WELL... IF THAT'S THE WAY IT MUST BE. WELL, YOU HEARD THE MAN, DOCTOR PACKARD. IT'S IN THEIR HANDS NOW!
I WISH YOU LUCK, GENTLEMEN. YOU'LL NEED PLENTY OF IT JUST TO OBTAIN THE REQUIRED TISSUE SAMPLES FROM SUPERMAN!
IT APPEARS THAT--EVEN NOW-- HIS BODY IS STILL QUITE THOROUGHLY INVULNERABLE!
?
"ARE YOU SURE THIS IS THE RIGHT WAY?"

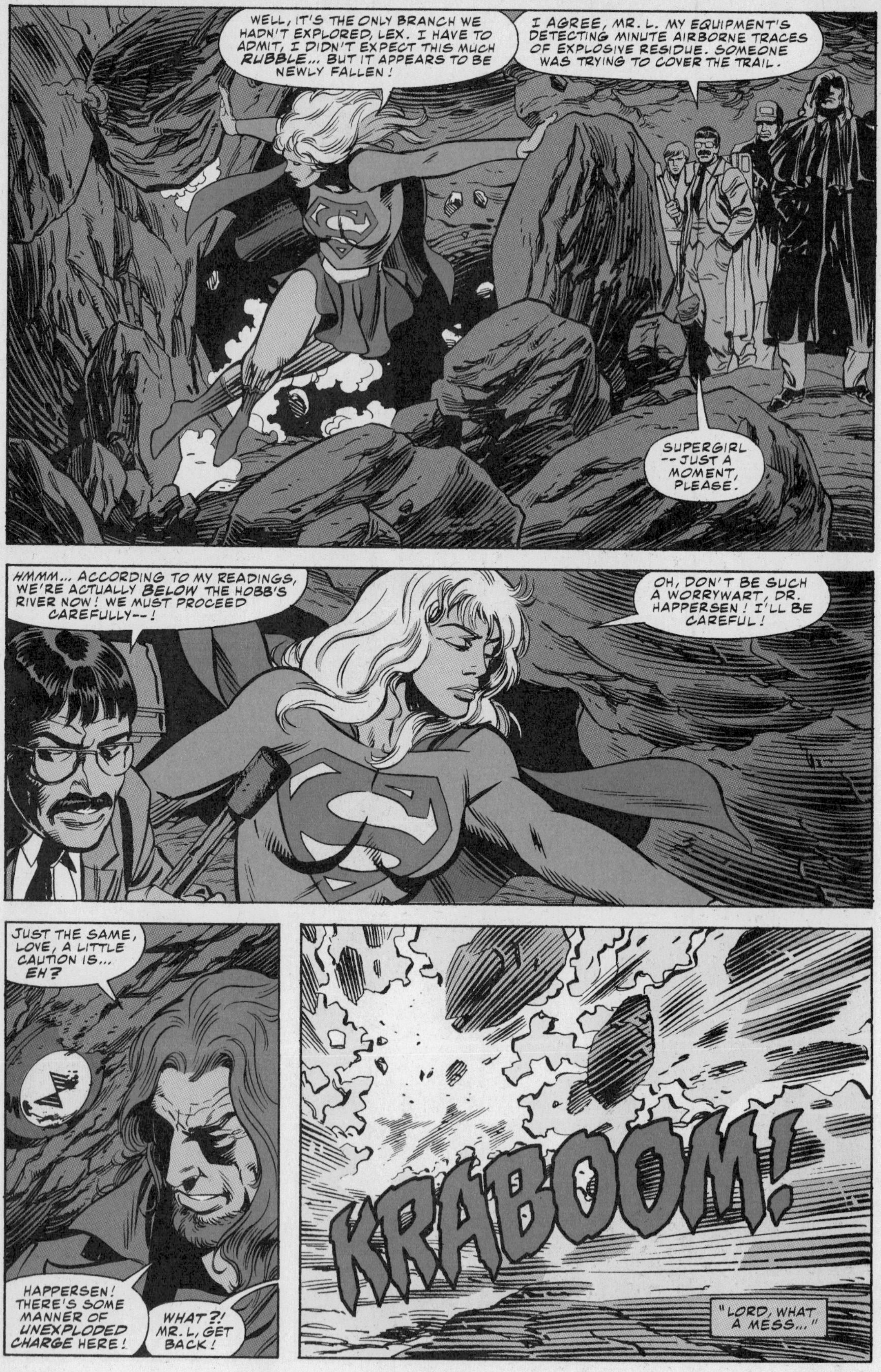
WELL, IT'S THE ONLY BRANCH WE HADN'T EXPLORED, LEX. I HAVE TO ADMIT, I DIDN'T EXPECT THIS MUCH RUBBLE... BUT IT APPEARS TO BE NEWLY FALLEN!
I AGREE, MR. L. MY EQUIPMENT'S DETECTING MINUTE AIRBORNE TRACES OF EXPLOSIVE RESIDUE. SOMEONE WAS TRYING TO COVER THE TRAIL.
SUPERGIRL--JUST A MOMENT, PLEASE.
HMMM... ACCORDING TO MY READINGS, WE'RE ACTUALLY BELOW THE HOBB'S RIVER NOW! WE MUST PROCEED CAREFULLY--!
OH, DON'T BE SUCH A WORRYWART, DR. HAPPERSEN! I'LL BE CAREFUL!
JUST THE SAME, LOVE, A LITTLE CAUTION IS... EH?
HAPPERSEN! THERE'S SOME MANNER OF UNEXPLODED CHARGE HERE!
WHAT?! MR. L, GET BACK!
KRABOOM!
"LORD, WHAT A MESS..."

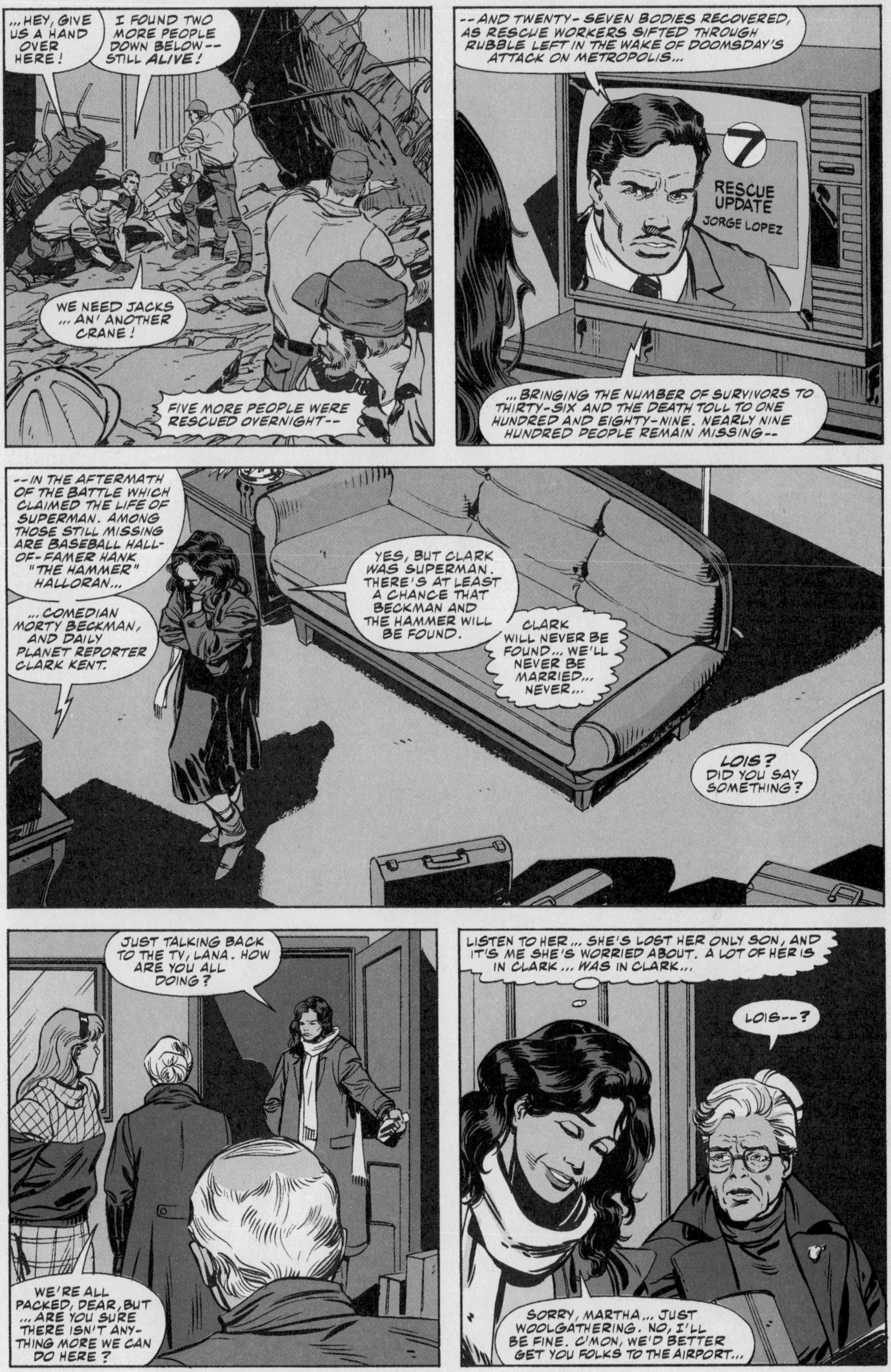
...HEY, GIVE US A HAND OVER HERE!
I FOUND TWO MORE PEOPLE DOWN BELOW-- STILL ALIVE!
WE NEED JACKS ...AN' ANOTHER CRANE!
FIVE MORE PEOPLE WERE RESCUED OVERNIGHT--
--AND TWENTY-SEVEN BODIES RECOVERED, AS RESCUE WORKERS SIFTED THROUGH RUBBLE LEFT IN THE WAKE OF DOOMSDAY'S ATTACK ON METROPOLIS...
7
RESCUE UPDATE
JORGE LOPEZ
...BRINGING THE NUMBER OF SURVIVORS TO THIRTY-SIX AND THE DEATH TOLL TO ONE HUNDRED AND EIGHTY-NINE. NEARLY NINE HUNDRED PEOPLE REMAIN MISSING--
--IN THE AFTERMATH OF THE BATTLE WHICH CLAIMED THE LIFE OF SUPERMAN. AMONG THOSE STILL MISSING ARE BASEBALL HALL-OF-FAMER HANK "THE HAMMER" HALLORAN...
...COMEDIAN MORTY BECKMAN, AND DAILY PLANET REPORTER CLARK KENT.
YES, BUT CLARK WAS SUPERMAN. THERE'S AT LEAST A CHANCE THAT BECKMAN AND THE HAMMER WILL BE FOUND.
CLARK WILL NEVER BE FOUND... WE'LL NEVER BE MARRIED... NEVER...
LOIS? DID YOU SAY SOMETHING?
JUST TALKING BACK TO THE TV, LANA. HOW ARE YOU ALL DOING?
WE'RE ALL PACKED, DEAR, BUT ...ARE YOU SURE THERE ISN'T ANYTHING MORE WE CAN DO HERE?
LISTEN TO HER... SHE'S LOST HER ONLY SON, AND IT'S ME SHE'S WORRIED ABOUT. A LOT OF HER IS IN CLARK... WAS IN CLARK...
LOIS--?
SORRY, MARTHA... JUST WOOLGATHERING. NO, I'LL BE FINE. C'MON, WE'D BETTER GET YOU FOLKS TO THE AIRPORT...

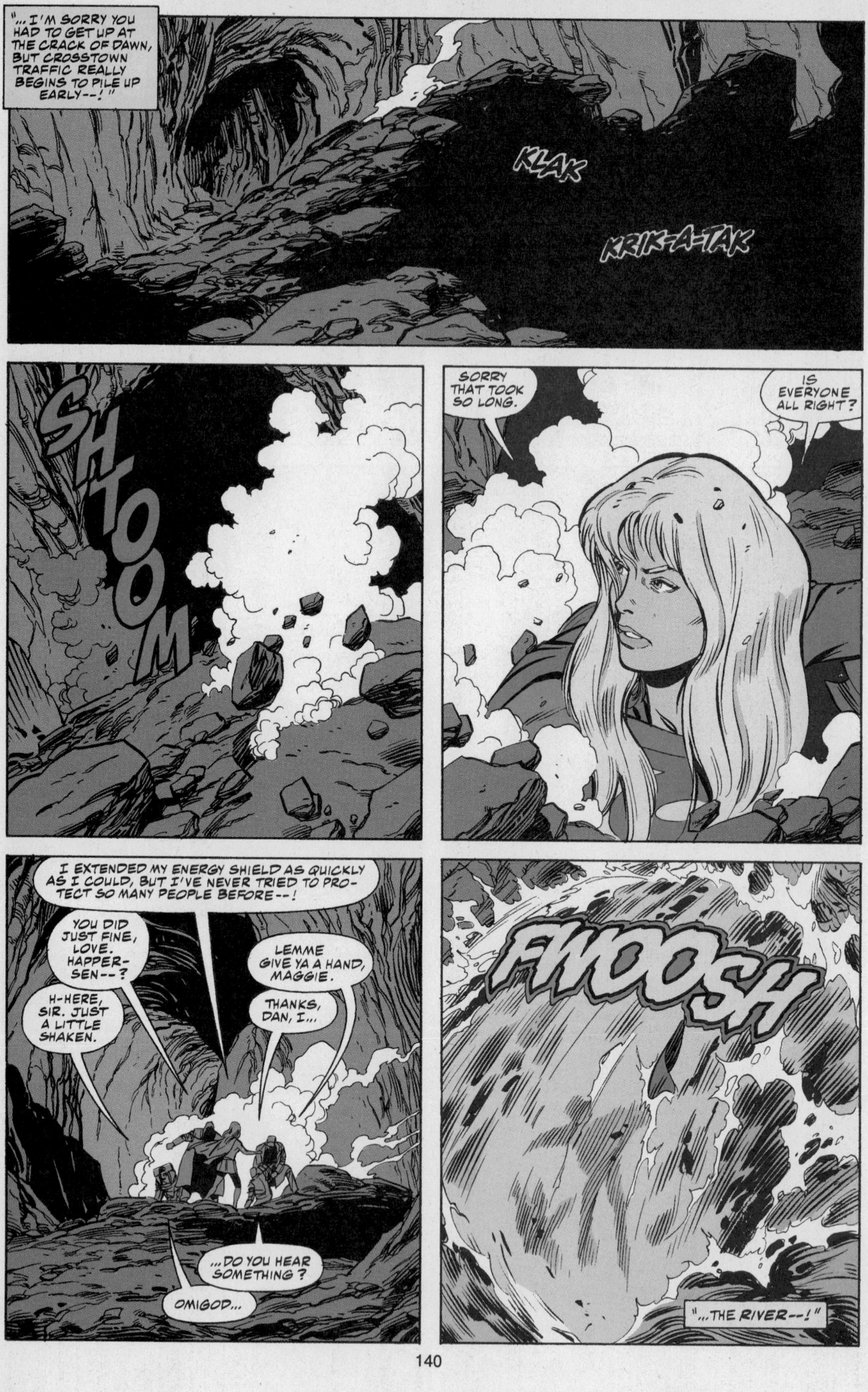
"...I'M SORRY YOU HAD TO GET UP AT THE CRACK OF DAWN, BUT CROSSTOWN TRAFFIC REALLY BEGINS TO PILE UP EARLY--!"
KLAK
KRIK-A-TAK
SHTOOM
SORRY THAT TOOK SO LONG.
IS EVERYONE ALL RIGHT?
I EXTENDED MY ENERGY SHIELD AS QUICKLY AS I COULD, BUT I'VE NEVER TRIED TO PROTECT SO MANY PEOPLE BEFORE--!
YOU DID JUST FINE, LOVE. HAPPERSEN--?
H-HERE, SIR. JUST A LITTLE SHAKEN.
LEMME GIVE YA A HAND, MAGGIE.
THANKS, DAN, I...
...DO YOU HEAR SOMETHING?
OMIGOD...
FWOOSH
"...THE RIVER--!"

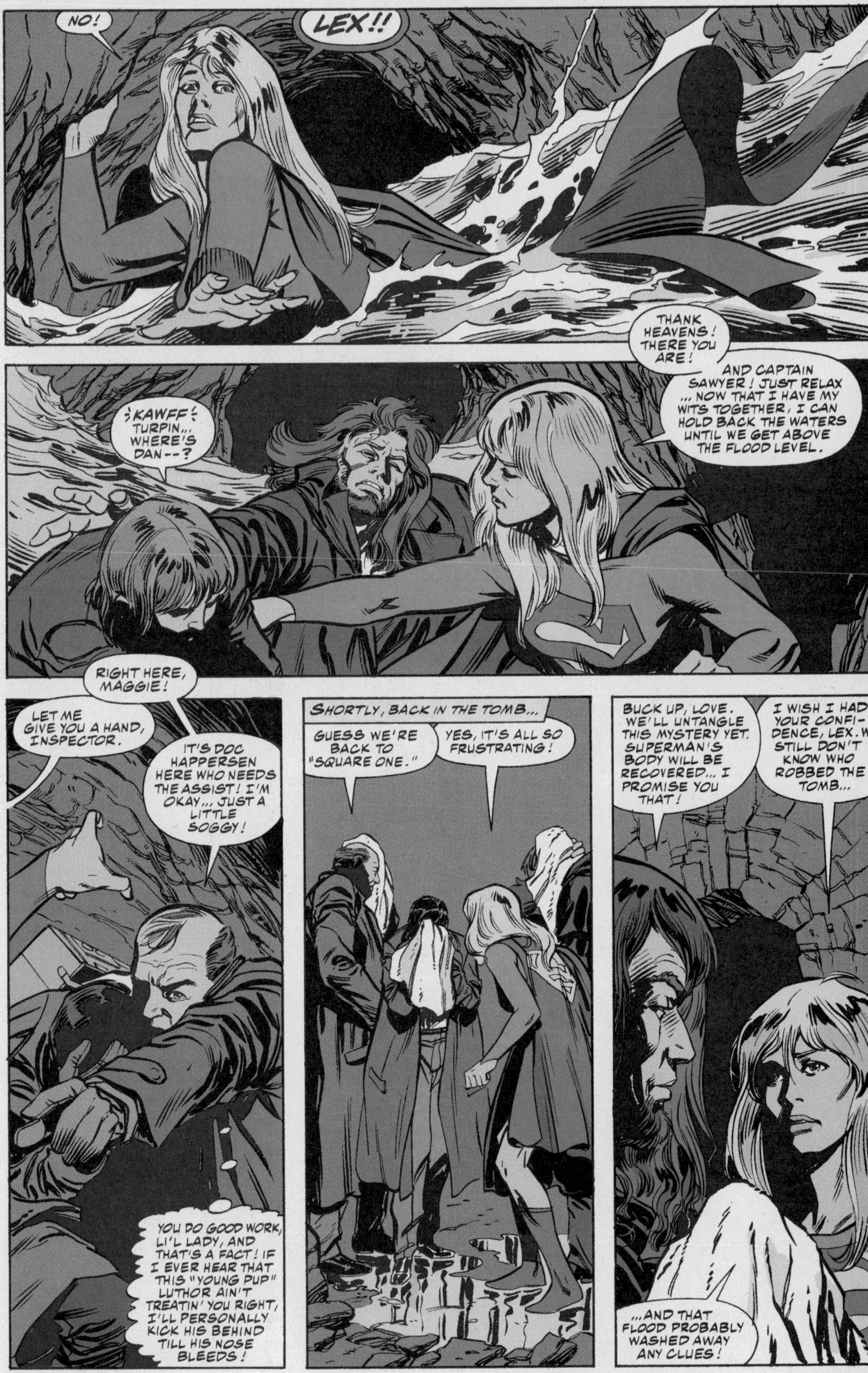
NO!
LEX!!
THANK HEAVENS! THERE YOU ARE!
AND CAPTAIN SAWYER! JUST RELAX ... NOW THAT I HAVE MY WITS TOGETHER, I CAN HOLD BACK THE WATERS UNTIL WE GET ABOVE THE FLOOD LEVEL.
KAWFF TURPIN... WHERE'S DAN--?
RIGHT HERE, MAGGIE!
LET ME GIVE YOU A HAND, INSPECTOR.
IT'S DOC HAPPERSEN HERE WHO NEEDS THE ASSIST! I'M OKAY... JUST A LITTLE SOGGY!
YOU DO GOOD WORK, LI'L LADY, AND THAT'S A FACT! IF I EVER HEAR THAT THIS "YOUNG PUP" LUTHOR AIN'T TREATIN' YOU RIGHT, I'LL PERSONALLY KICK HIS BEHIND TILL HIS NOSE BLEEDS!
SHORTLY, BACK IN THE TOMB...
GUESS WE'RE BACK TO "SQUARE ONE."
YES, IT'S ALL SO FRUSTRATING!
BUCK UP, LOVE. WE'LL UNTANGLE THIS MYSTERY YET. SUPERMAN'S BODY WILL BE RECOVERED... I PROMISE YOU THAT!
I WISH I HAD YOUR CONFI-DENCE, LEX. WE STILL DON'T KNOW WHO ROBBED THE TOMB...
...AND THAT FLOOD PROBABLY WASHED AWAY ANY CLUES!

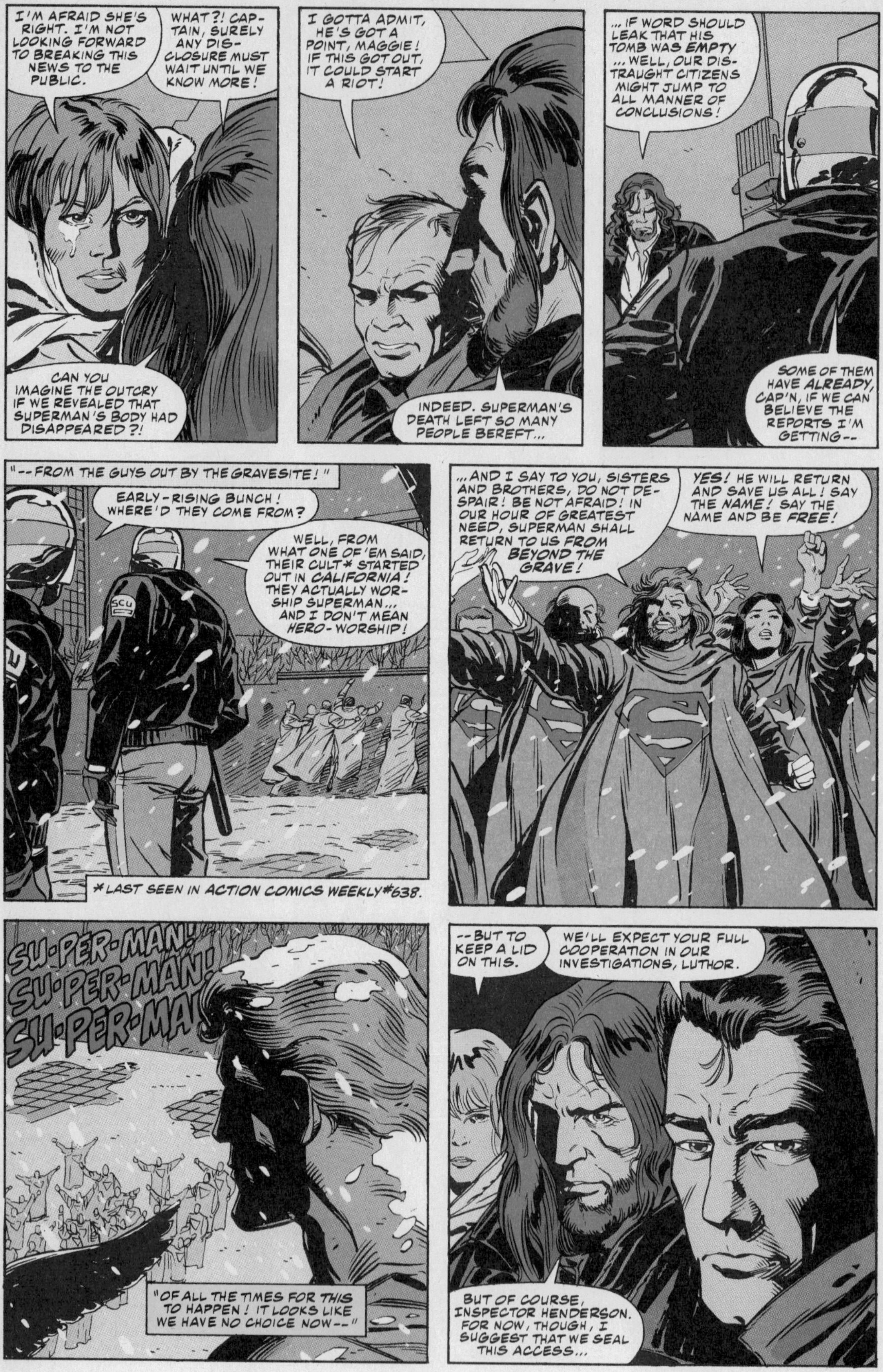
I'M AFRAID SHE'S RIGHT. I'M NOT LOOKING FORWARD TO BREAKING THIS NEWS TO THE PUBLIC.
WHAT?! CAPTAIN, SURELY ANY DISCLOSURE MUST WAIT UNTIL WE KNOW MORE!
CAN YOU IMAGINE THE OUTCRY IF WE REVEALED THAT SUPERMAN'S BODY HAD DISAPPEARED?!
I GOTTA ADMIT, HE'S GOT A POINT, MAGGIE! IF THIS GOT OUT, IT COULD START A RIOT!
INDEED. SUPERMAN'S DEATH LEFT SO MANY PEOPLE BEREFT...
...IF WORD SHOULD LEAK THAT HIS TOMB WAS EMPTY ...WELL, OUR DISTRAUGHT CITIZENS MIGHT JUMP TO ALL MANNER OF CONCLUSIONS!
SOME OF THEM HAVE ALREADY, CAP'N, IF WE CAN BELIEVE THE REPORTS I'M GETTING--
"--FROM THE GUYS OUT BY THE GRAVESITE!"
EARLY-RISING BUNCH! WHERE'D THEY COME FROM?
WELL, FROM WHAT ONE OF 'EM SAID, THEIR CULT* STARTED OUT IN CALIFORNIA! THEY ACTUALLY WORSHIP SUPERMAN... AND I DON'T MEAN HERO-WORSHIP!
SCU
*LAST SEEN IN ACTION COMICS WEEKLY #638.
...AND I SAY TO YOU, SISTERS AND BROTHERS, DO NOT DESPAIR! BE NOT AFRAID! IN OUR HOUR OF GREATEST NEED, SUPERMAN SHALL RETURN TO US FROM BEYOND THE GRAVE!
YES! HE WILL RETURN AND SAVE US ALL! SAY THE NAME! SAY THE NAME AND BE FREE!
SU-PER-MAN! SU-PER-MAN! SU-PER-MA
"OF ALL THE TIMES FOR THIS TO HAPPEN! IT LOOKS LIKE WE HAVE NO CHOICE NOW--"
--BUT TO KEEP A LID ON THIS.
WE'LL EXPECT YOUR FULL COOPERATION IN OUR INVESTIGATIONS, LUTHOR.
BUT OF COURSE, INSPECTOR HENDERSON. FOR NOW, THOUGH, I SUGGEST THAT WE SEAL THIS ACCESS...

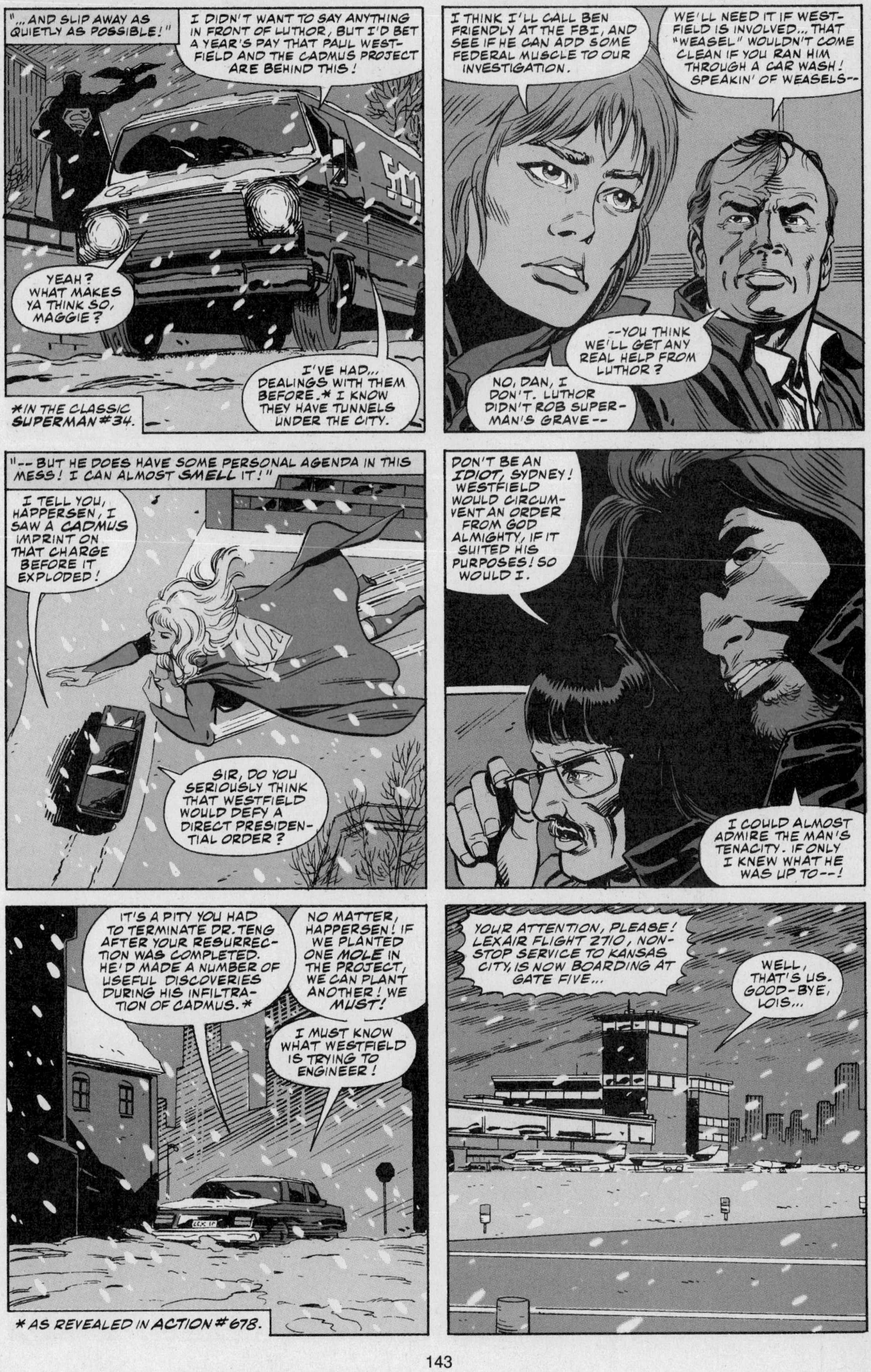
"...AND SLIP AWAY AS QUIETLY AS POSSIBLE!"
I DIDN'T WANT TO SAY ANYTHING IN FRONT OF LUTHOR, BUT I'D BET A YEAR'S PAY THAT PAUL WESTFIELD AND THE CADMUS PROJECT ARE BEHIND THIS!
YEAH? WHAT MAKES YA THINK SO, MAGGIE?
I'VE HAD... DEALINGS WITH THEM BEFORE.* I KNOW THEY HAVE TUNNELS UNDER THE CITY.
*IN THE CLASSIC SUPERMAN #34.
I THINK I'LL CALL BEN FRIENDLY AT THE FBI, AND SEE IF HE CAN ADD SOME FEDERAL MUSCLE TO OUR INVESTIGATION.
WE'LL NEED IT IF WESTFIELD IS INVOLVED... THAT "WEASEL" WOULDN'T COME CLEAN IF YOU RAN HIM THROUGH A CAR WASH! SPEAKIN' OF WEASELS--
--YOU THINK WE'LL GET ANY REAL HELP FROM LUTHOR?
NO, DAN, I DON'T. LUTHOR DIDN'T ROB SUPERMAN'S GRAVE--
"--BUT HE DOES HAVE SOME PERSONAL AGENDA IN THIS MESS! I CAN ALMOST SMELL IT!"
I TELL YOU, HAPPERSEN, I SAW A CADMUS IMPRINT ON THAT CHARGE BEFORE IT EXPLODED!
SIR, DO YOU SERIOUSLY THINK THAT WESTFIELD WOULD DEFY A DIRECT PRESIDENTIAL ORDER?
DON'T BE AN IDIOT, SYDNEY! WESTFIELD WOULD CIRCUMVENT AN ORDER FROM GOD ALMIGHTY, IF IT SUITED HIS PURPOSES! SO WOULD I.
I COULD ALMOST ADMIRE THE MAN'S TENACITY. IF ONLY I KNEW WHAT HE WAS UP TO--!
IT'S A PITY YOU HAD TO TERMINATE DR. TENG AFTER YOUR RESURRECTION WAS COMPLETED. HE'D MADE A NUMBER OF USEFUL DISCOVERIES DURING HIS INFILTRATION OF CADMUS.*
NO MATTER, HAPPERSEN! IF WE PLANTED ONE MOLE IN THE PROJECT, WE CAN PLANT ANOTHER! WE MUST!
I MUST KNOW WHAT WESTFIELD IS TRYING TO ENGINEER!
*AS REVEALED IN ACTION #678.
YOUR ATTENTION, PLEASE! LEXAIR FLIGHT 2710, NON-STOP SERVICE TO KANSAS CITY, IS NOW BOARDING AT GATE FIVE...
WELL, THAT'S US. GOOD-BYE, LOIS...

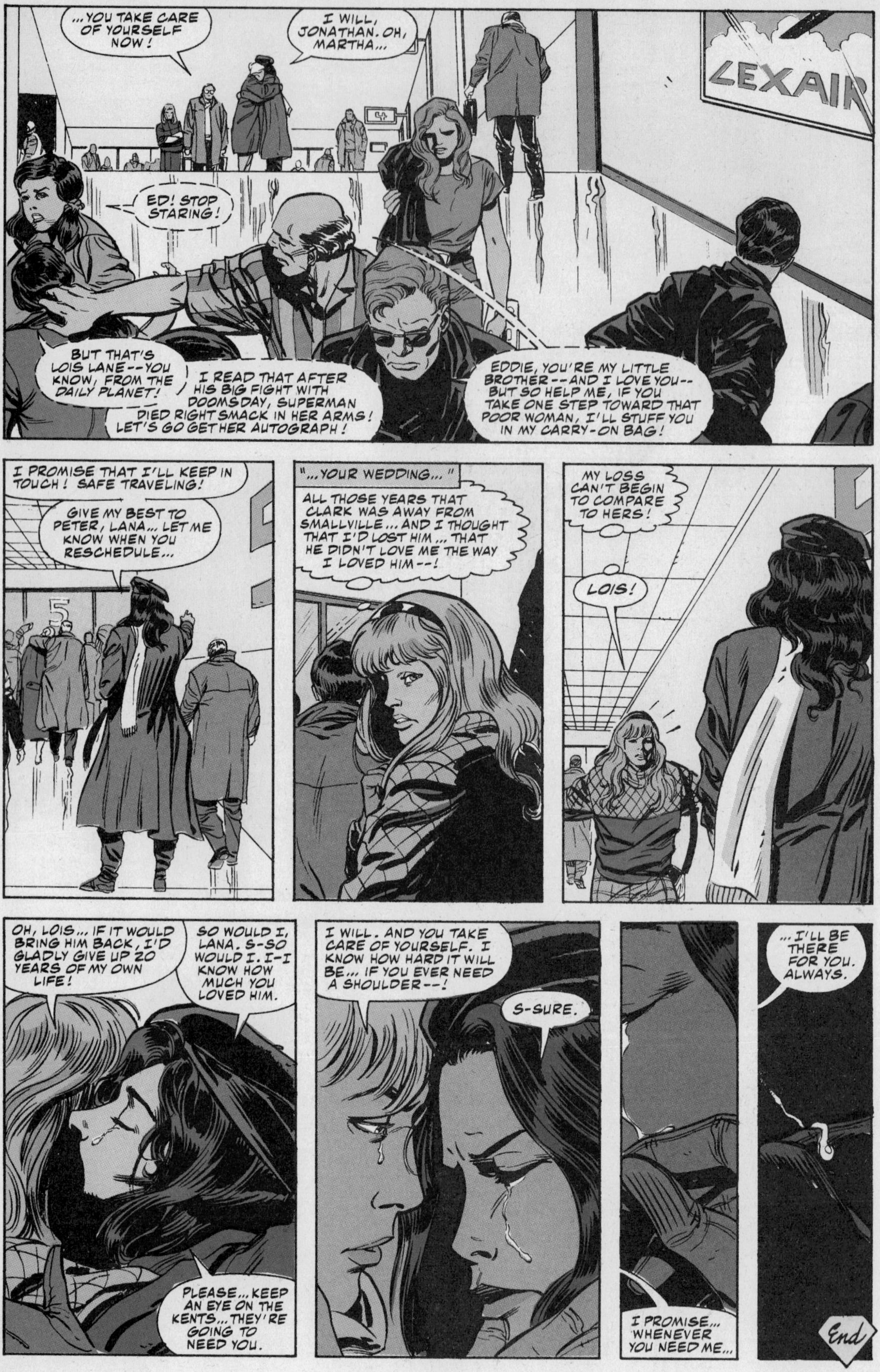
...YOU TAKE CARE OF YOURSELF NOW!
I WILL, JONATHAN. OH, MARTHA...
LEXAIR
ED! STOP STARING!
BUT THAT'S LOIS LANE--YOU KNOW, FROM THE DAILY PLANET!
I READ THAT AFTER HIS BIG FIGHT WITH DOOMSDAY, SUPERMAN DIED RIGHT SMACK IN HER ARMS! LET'S GO GET HER AUTOGRAPH!
EDDIE, YOU'RE MY LITTLE BROTHER--AND I LOVE YOU--BUT SO HELP ME, IF YOU TAKE ONE STEP TOWARD THAT POOR WOMAN, I'LL STUFF YOU IN MY CARRY-ON BAG!
I PROMISE THAT I'LL KEEP IN TOUCH! SAFE TRAVELING!
GIVE MY BEST TO PETER, LANA... LET ME KNOW WHEN YOU RESCHEDULE...
"...YOUR WEDDING..."
ALL THOSE YEARS THAT CLARK WAS AWAY FROM SMALLVILLE... AND I THOUGHT THAT I'D LOST HIM... THAT HE DIDN'T LOVE ME THE WAY I LOVED HIM--!
MY LOSS CAN'T BEGIN TO COMPARE TO HERS!
LOIS!
OH, LOIS... IF IT WOULD BRING HIM BACK, I'D GLADLY GIVE UP 20 YEARS OF MY OWN LIFE!
SO WOULD I, LANA. S-SO WOULD I. I-I KNOW HOW MUCH YOU LOVED HIM.
PLEASE... KEEP AN EYE ON THE KENTS... THEY'RE GOING TO NEED YOU.
I WILL. AND YOU TAKE CARE OF YOURSELF. I KNOW HOW HARD IT WILL BE... IF YOU EVER NEED A SHOULDER--!
S-SURE.
I PROMISE... WHENEVER YOU NEED ME...
...I'LL BE THERE FOR YOU. ALWAYS.
End

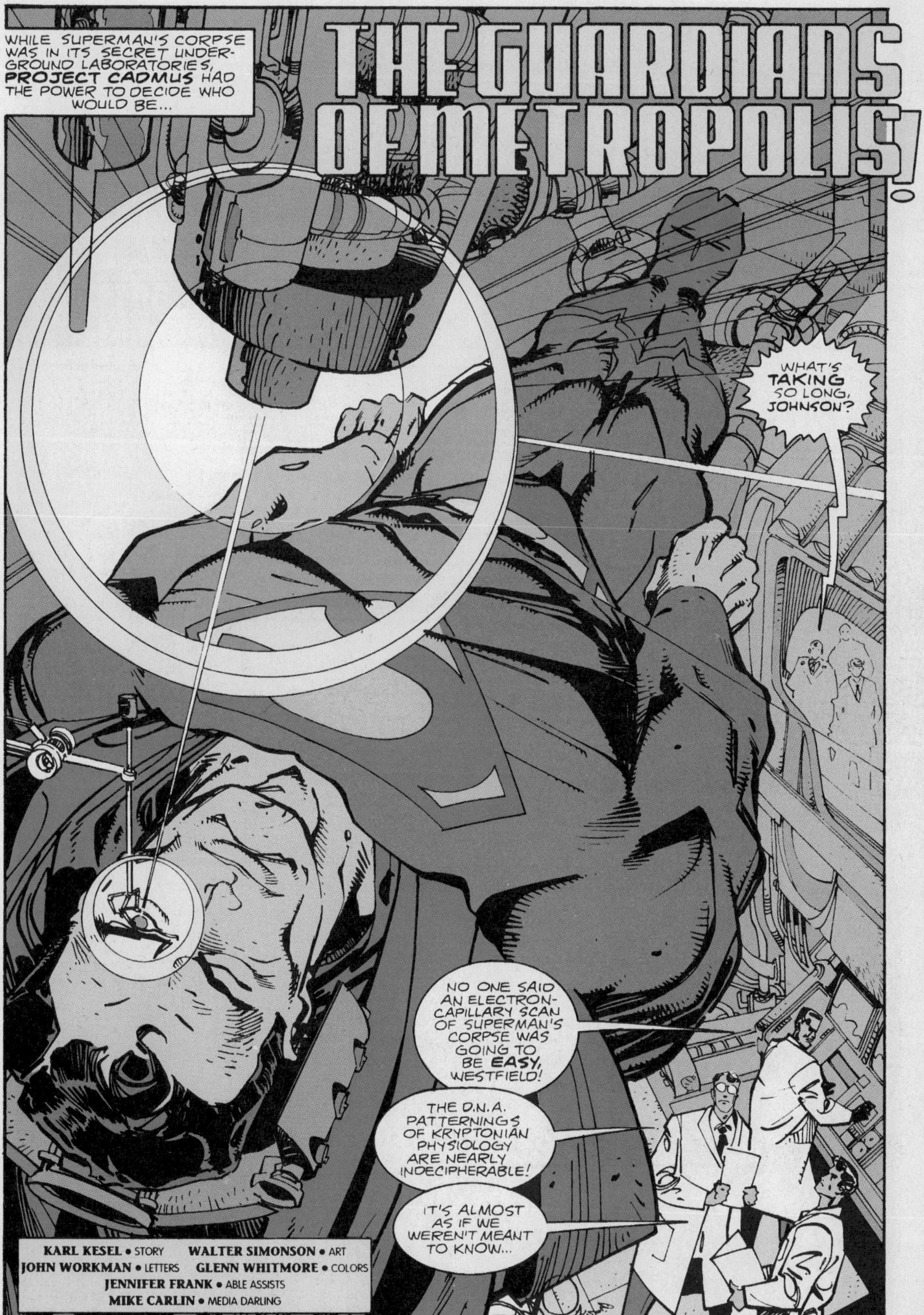
WHILE SUPERMAN'S CORPSE WAS IN ITS SECRET UNDERGROUND LABORATORIES, PROJECT CADMUS HAD THE POWER TO DECIDE WHO WOULD BE...
THE GUARDIANS OF METROPOLIS!
WHAT'S TAKING SO LONG, JOHNSON?
NO ONE SAID AN ELECTRON-CAPILLARY SCAN OF SUPERMAN'S CORPSE WAS GOING TO BE EASY, WESTFIELD!
THE D.N.A. PATTERNINGS OF KRYPTONIAN PHYSIOLOGY ARE NEARLY INDECIPHERABLE!
IT'S ALMOST AS IF WE WEREN'T MEANT TO KNOW...
KARL KESEL • STORY WALTER SIMONSON • ART
JOHN WORKMAN • LETTERS GLENN WHITMORE • COLORS
JENNIFER FRANK • ABLE ASSISTS
MIKE CARLIN • MEDIA DARLING

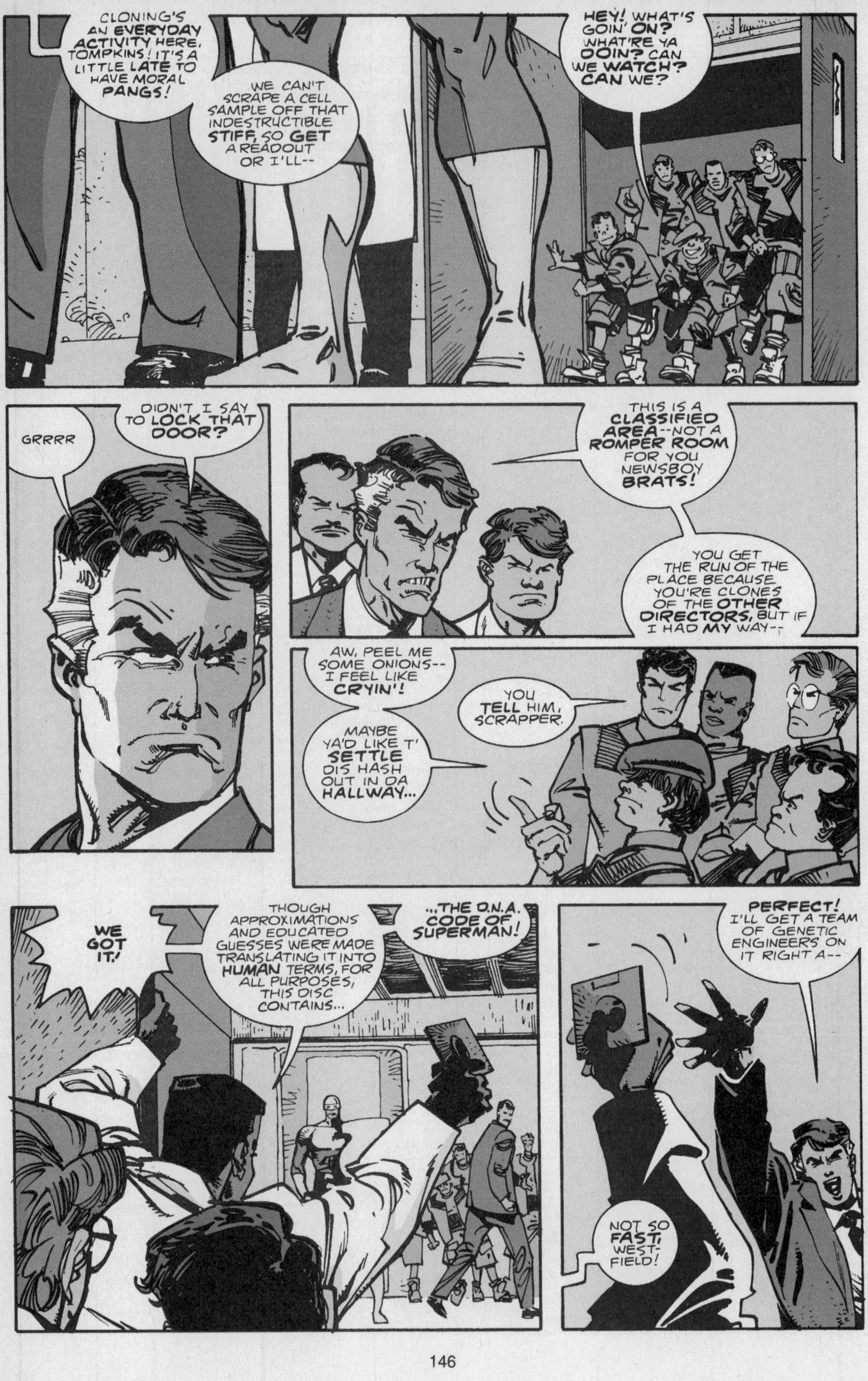
CLONING'S AN EVERYDAY ACTIVITY HERE, TOMPKINS! IT'S A LITTLE LATE TO HAVE MORAL PANGS!
WE CAN'T SCRAPE A CELL SAMPLE OFF THAT INDESTRUCTIBLE STIFF, SO GET A READOUT OR I'LL--
HEY! WHAT'S GOIN' ON? WHAT'RE YA DOIN? CAN WE WATCH? CAN WE?
GRRRR
DIDN'T I SAY TO LOCK THAT DOOR?
THIS IS A CLASSIFIED AREA--NOT A ROMPER ROOM FOR YOU NEWSBOY BRATS!
YOU GET THE RUN OF THE PLACE BECAUSE YOU'RE CLONES OF THE OTHER DIRECTORS, BUT IF I HAD MY WAY--
AW, PEEL ME SOME ONIONS-- I FEEL LIKE CRYIN'!
MAYBE YA'D LIKE T' SETTLE DIS HASH OUT IN DA HALLWAY...
YOU TELL HIM, SCRAPPER.
WE GOT IT!
THOUGH APPROXIMATIONS AND EDUCATED GUESSES WERE MADE TRANSLATING IT INTO HUMAN TERMS, FOR ALL PURPOSES, THIS DISC CONTAINS...
...THE D.N.A. CODE OF SUPERMAN!
PERFECT! I'LL GET A TEAM OF GENETIC ENGINEERS ON IT RIGHT A--
NOT SO FAST, WEST-FIELD!

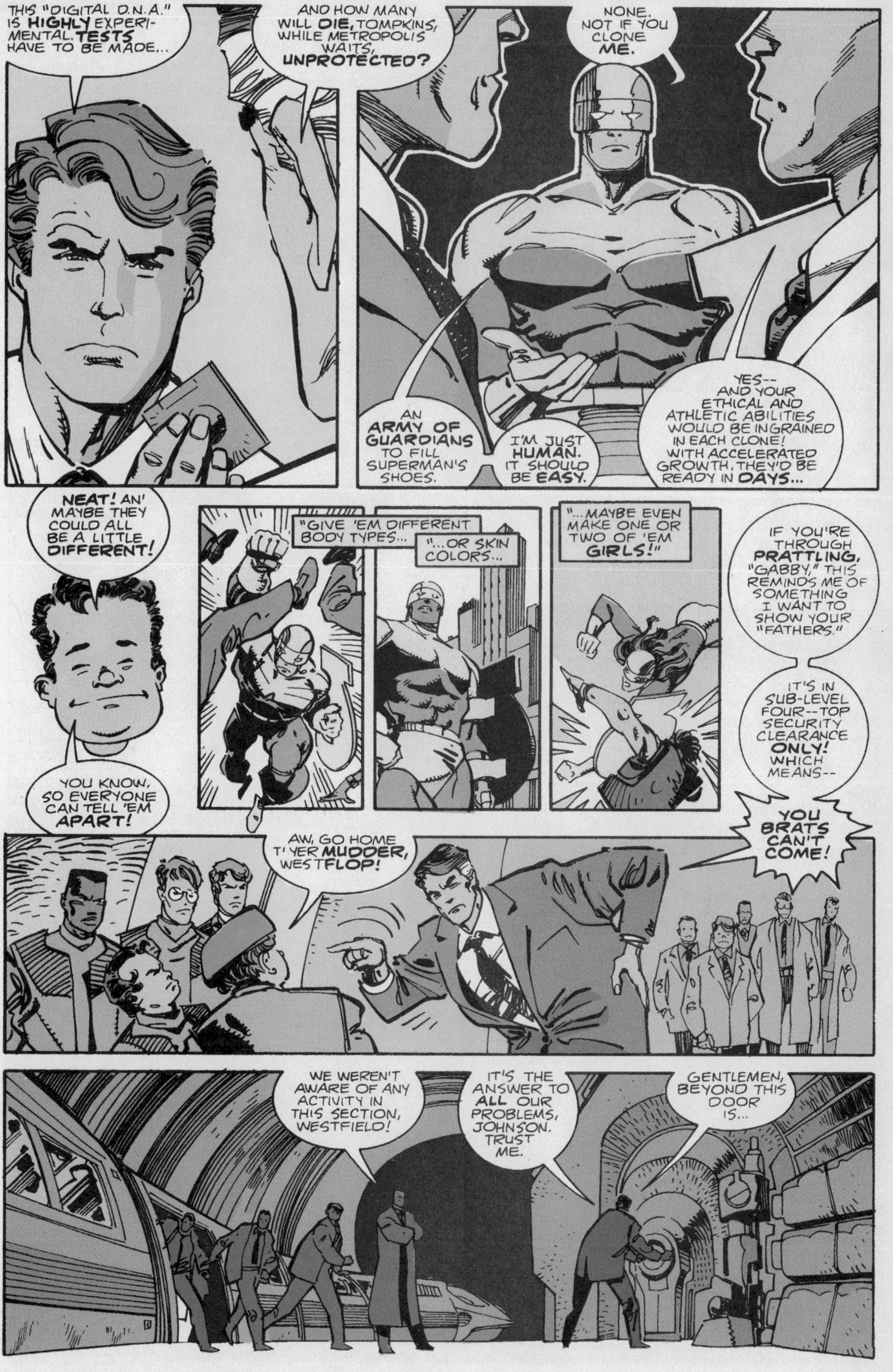

THIS "DIGITAL D.N.A." IS HIGHLY EXPERIMENTAL. TESTS HAVE TO BE MADE...
AND HOW MANY WILL DIE, TOMPKINS, WHILE METROPOLIS WAITS, UNPROTECTED?
NONE. NOT IF YOU CLONE ME.
AN ARMY OF GUARDIANS TO FILL SUPERMAN'S SHOES.
I'M JUST HUMAN. IT SHOULD BE EASY.
YES-- AND YOUR ETHICAL AND ATHLETIC ABILITIES WOULD BE INGRAINED IN EACH CLONE! WITH ACCELERATED GROWTH, THEY'D BE READY IN DAYS...
NEAT! AN' MAYBE THEY COULD ALL BE A LITTLE DIFFERENT!
YOU KNOW, SO EVERYONE CAN TELL 'EM APART!
"GIVE 'EM DIFFERENT BODY TYPES...
"...OR SKIN COLORS...
"...MAYBE EVEN MAKE ONE OR TWO OF 'EM GIRLS!"
IF YOU'RE THROUGH PRATTLING, "GABBY," THIS REMINDS ME OF SOMETHING I WANT TO SHOW YOUR "FATHERS."
IT'S IN SUB-LEVEL FOUR--TOP SECURITY CLEARANCE ONLY! WHICH MEANS--
YOU BRATS CAN'T COME!
AW, GO HOME T' YER MUDDER, WESTFLOP!
WE WEREN'T AWARE OF ANY ACTIVITY IN THIS SECTION, WESTFIELD!
IT'S THE ANSWER TO ALL OUR PROBLEMS, JOHNSON. TRUST ME.
GENTLEMEN, BEYOND THIS DOOR IS...

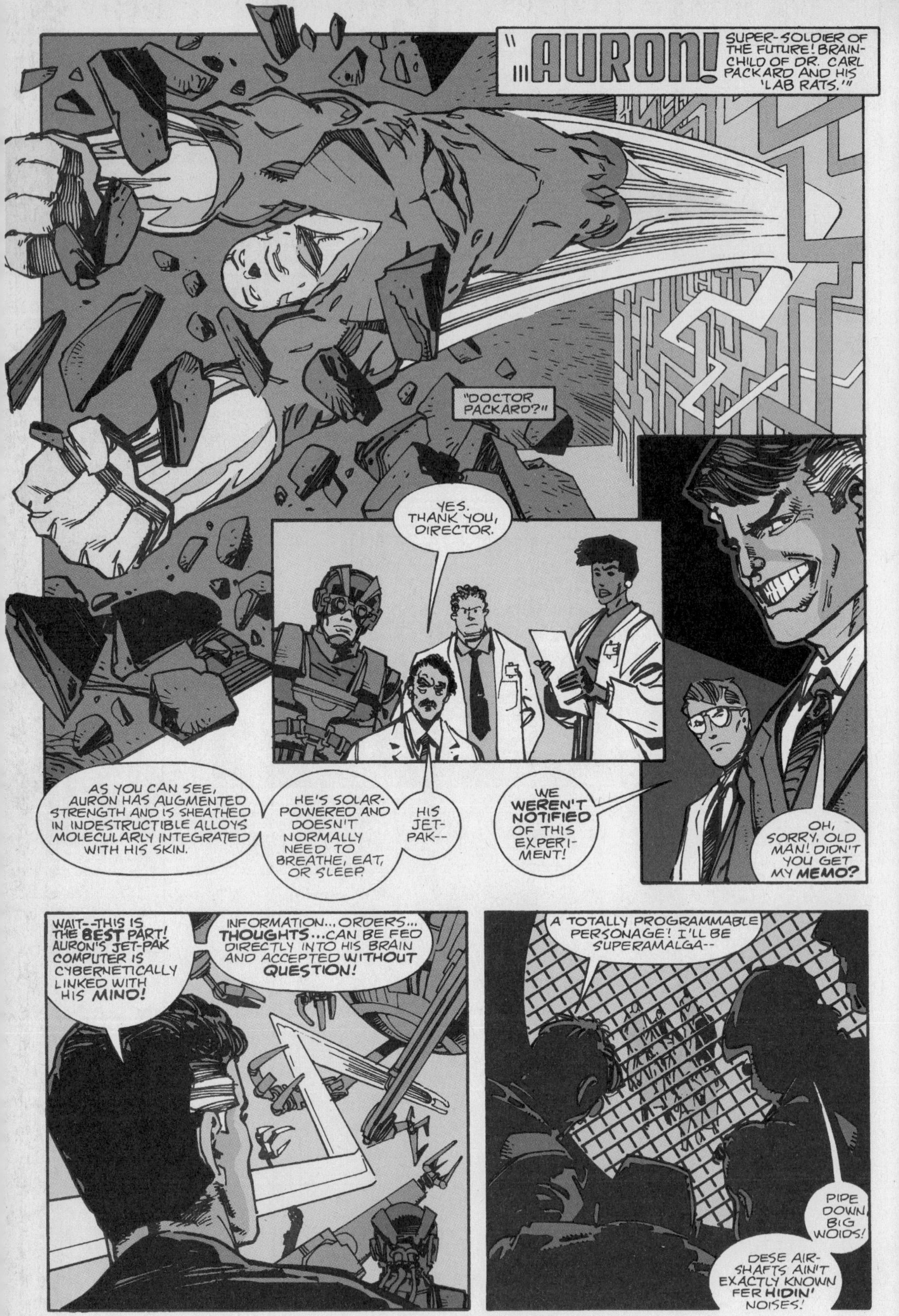
"...AURON! SUPER-SOLDIER OF THE FUTURE! BRAIN-CHILD OF DR. CARL PACKARD AND HIS 'LAB RATS.'"
"DOCTOR PACKARD?"
YES. THANK YOU, DIRECTOR.
AS YOU CAN SEE, AURON HAS AUGMENTED STRENGTH AND IS SHEATHED IN INDESTRUCTIBLE ALLOYS MOLECULARLY INTEGRATED WITH HIS SKIN.
HE'S SOLAR-POWERED AND DOESN'T NORMALLY NEED TO BREATHE, EAT, OR SLEEP.
HIS JET-PAK--
WE WEREN'T NOTIFIED OF THIS EXPERIMENT!
OH, SORRY, OLD MAN! DIDN'T YOU GET MY MEMO?
WAIT--THIS IS THE BEST PART! AURON'S JET-PAK COMPUTER IS CYBERNETICALLY LINKED WITH HIS MIND!
INFORMATION... ORDERS... THOUGHTS...CAN BE FED DIRECTLY INTO HIS BRAIN AND ACCEPTED WITHOUT QUESTION!
A TOTALLY PROGRAMMABLE PERSONAGE! I'LL BE SUPERAMALGA--
PIPE DOWN, BIG WOIDS!
DESE AIR-SHAFTS AIN'T EXACTLY KNOWN FER HIDIN' NOISES!

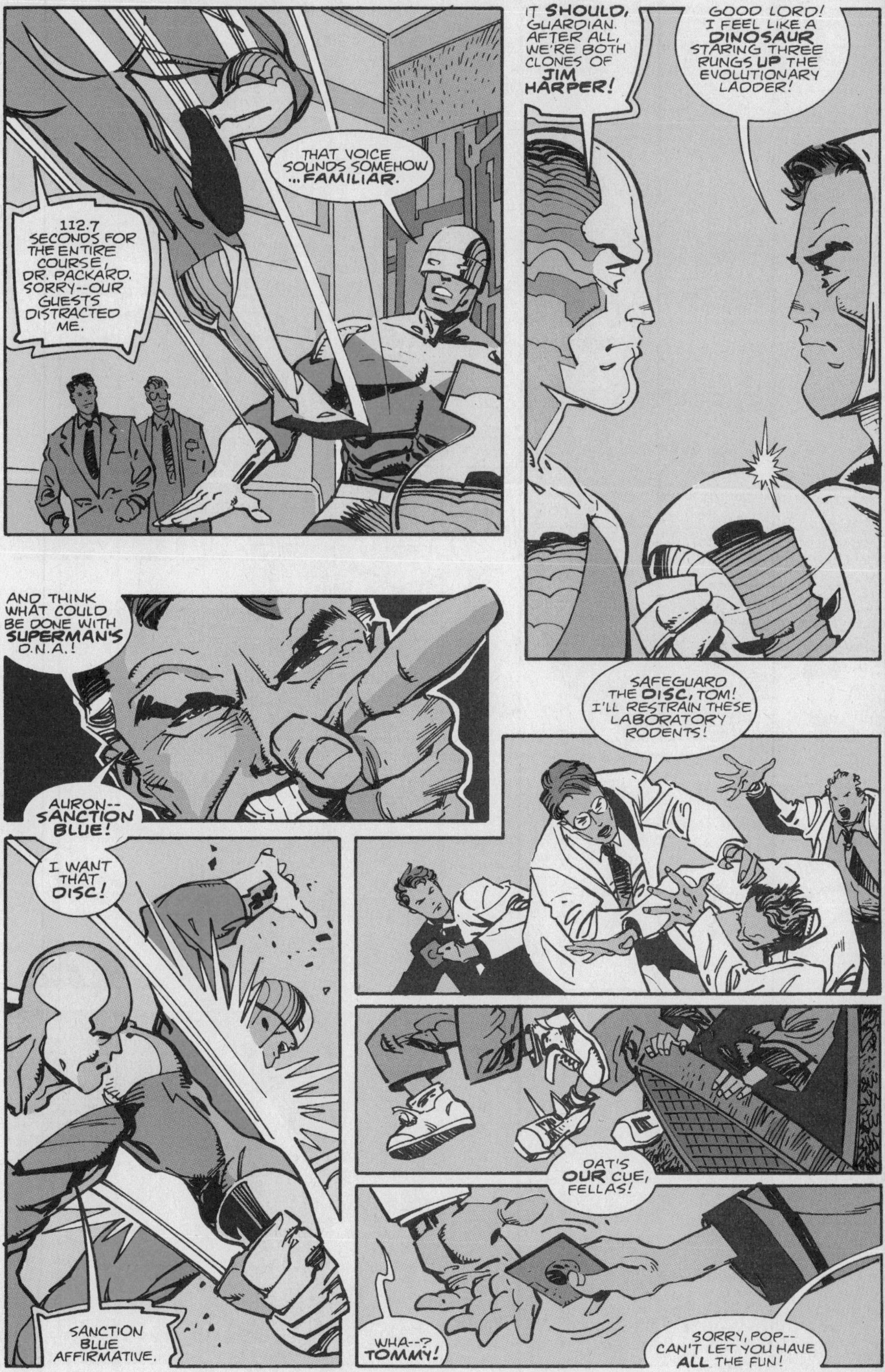
THAT VOICE SOUNDS SOMEHOW ...FAMILIAR.
112.7 SECONDS FOR THE ENTIRE COURSE, DR. PACKARD. SORRY--OUR GUESTS DISTRACTED ME.
IT SHOULD, GUARDIAN. AFTER ALL, WE'RE BOTH CLONES OF JIM HARPER!
GOOD LORD! I FEEL LIKE A DINOSAUR STARING THREE RUNGS UP THE EVOLUTIONARY LADDER!
AND THINK WHAT COULD BE DONE WITH SUPERMAN'S D.N.A.!
AURON-- SANCTION BLUE!
I WANT THAT DISC!
SAFEGUARD THE DISC, TOM! I'LL RESTRAIN THESE LABORATORY RODENTS!
DAT'S OUR CUE, FELLAS!
SANCTION BLUE AFFIRMATIVE.
WHA--? TOMMY!
SORRY, POP-- CAN'T LET YOU HAVE ALL THE FUN!

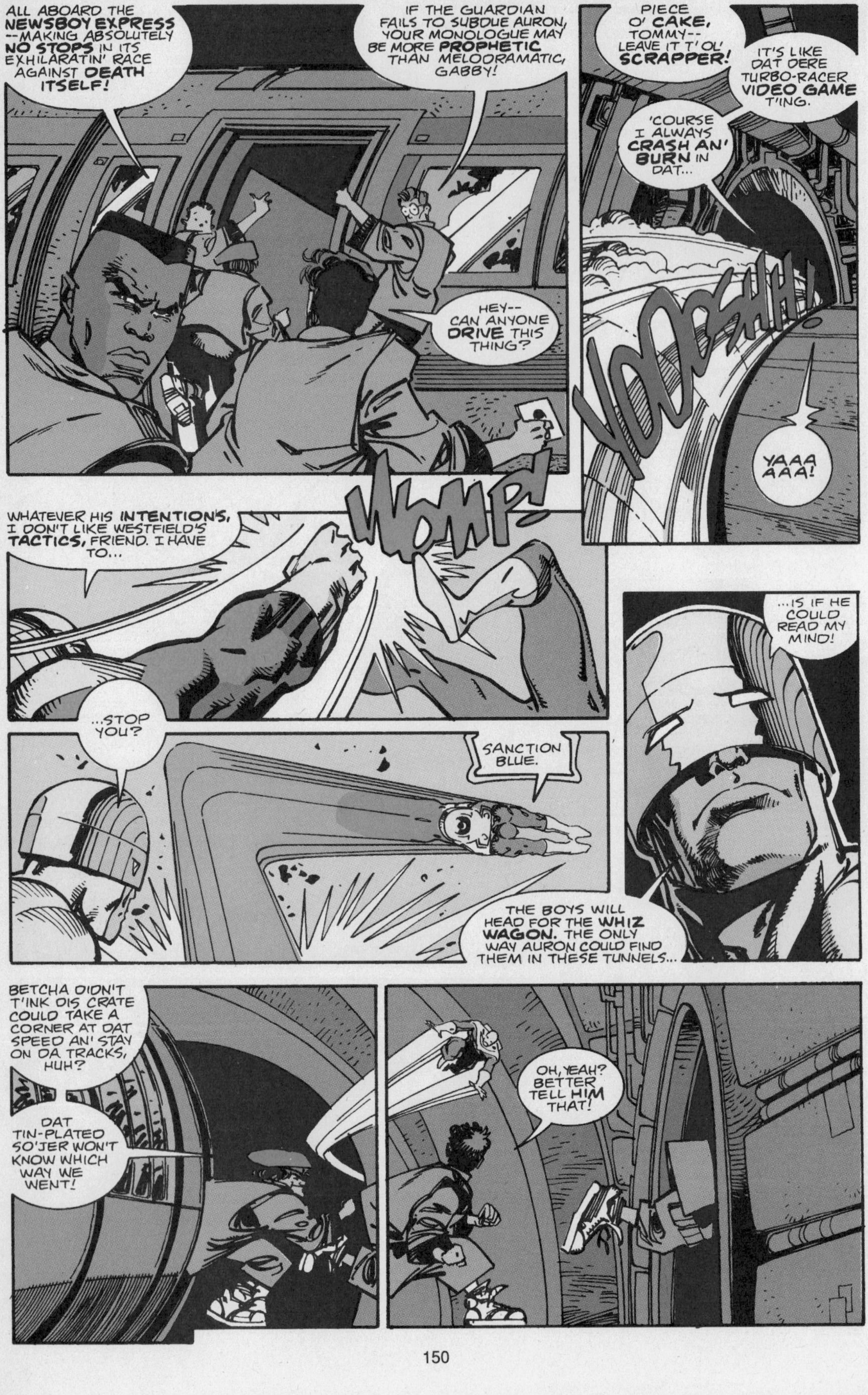
ALL ABOARD THE NEWSBOY EXPRESS --MAKING ABSOLUTELY NO STOPS IN ITS EXHILARATIN' RACE AGAINST DEATH ITSELF!
IF THE GUARDIAN FAILS TO SUBDUE AURON, YOUR MONOLOGUE MAY BE MORE PROPHETIC THAN MELODRAMATIC, GABBY!
HEY-- CAN ANYONE DRIVE THIS THING?
PIECE O' CAKE, TOMMY-- LEAVE IT T' OL' SCRAPPER!
IT'S LIKE DAT DERE TURBO-RACER VIDEO GAME T'ING.
'COURSE I ALWAYS CRASH AN' BURN IN DAT...
VOOOSHH!
YAAA AAA!
WHATEVER HIS INTENTIONS, I DON'T LIKE WESTFIELD'S TACTICS, FRIEND. I HAVE TO...
WOMP!
...STOP YOU?
SANCTION BLUE.
...IS IF HE COULD READ MY MIND!
THE BOYS WILL HEAD FOR THE WHIZ WAGON. THE ONLY WAY AURON COULD FIND THEM IN THESE TUNNELS...
BETCHA DIDN'T T'INK DIS CRATE COULD TAKE A CORNER AT DAT SPEED AN' STAY ON DA TRACKS, HUH?
DAT TIN-PLATED SO'JER WON'T KNOW WHICH WAY WE WENT!
OH, YEAH? BETTER TELL HIM THAT!

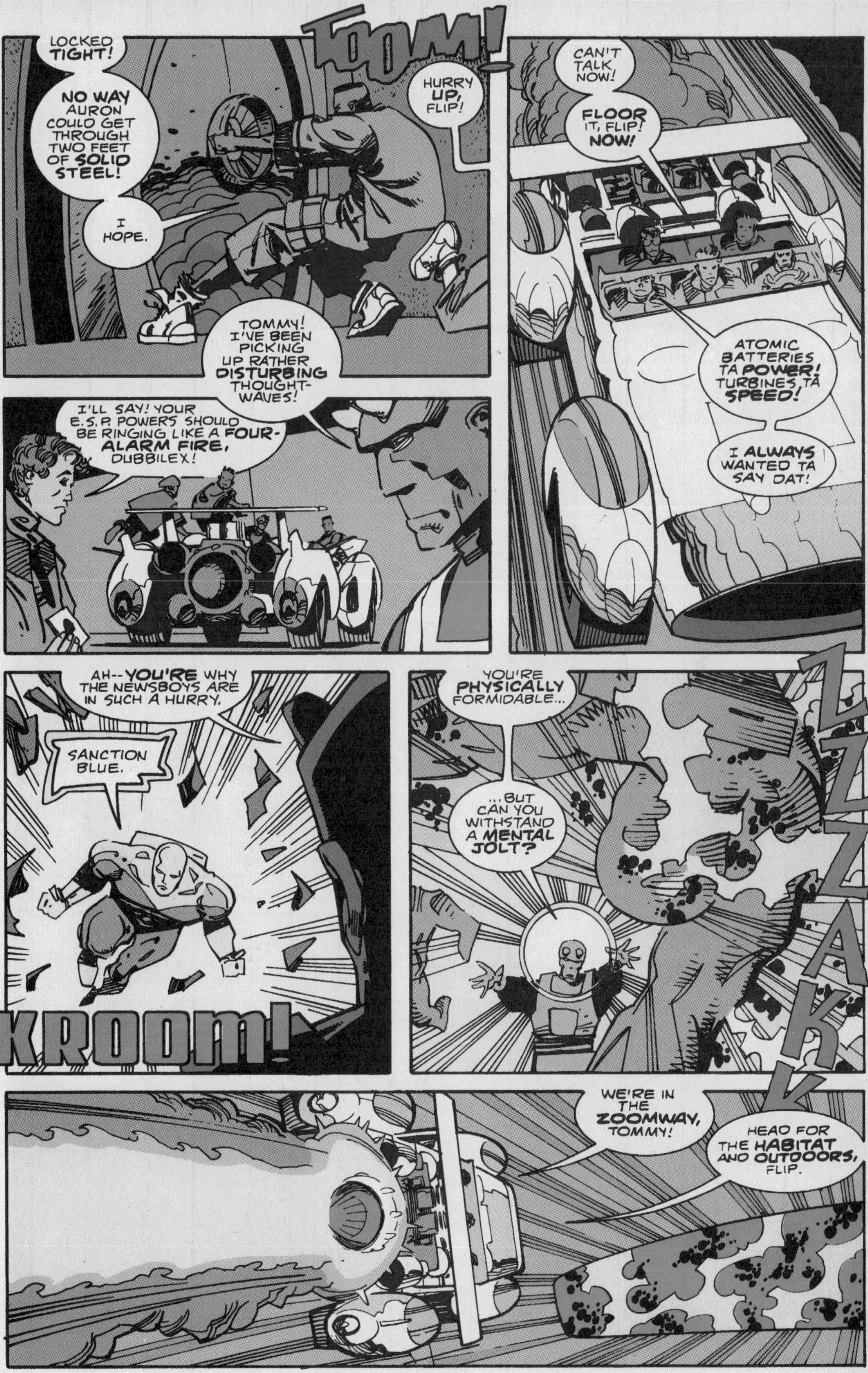
LOCKED TIGHT!
NO WAY AURON COULD GET THROUGH TWO FEET OF SOLID STEEL!
I HOPE.
FOOM!
HURRY UP, FLIP!
TOMMY! I'VE BEEN PICKING UP RATHER DISTURBING THOUGHT-WAVES!
I'LL SAY! YOUR E.S.P. POWERS SHOULD BE RINGING LIKE A FOUR-ALARM FIRE, DUBBILEX!
CAN'T TALK NOW!
FLOOR IT, FLIP! NOW!
ATOMIC BATTERIES TA POWER! TURBINES TA SPEED!
I ALWAYS WANTED TA SAY DAT!
AH--YOU'RE WHY THE NEWSBOYS ARE IN SUCH A HURRY.
SANCTION BLUE.
KROOM!
YOU'RE PHYSICALLY FORMIDABLE...
...BUT CAN YOU WITHSTAND A MENTAL JOLT?
ZZZZAKK
WE'RE IN THE ZOOMWAY, TOMMY!
HEAD FOR THE HABITAT AND OUTDOORS, FLIP.

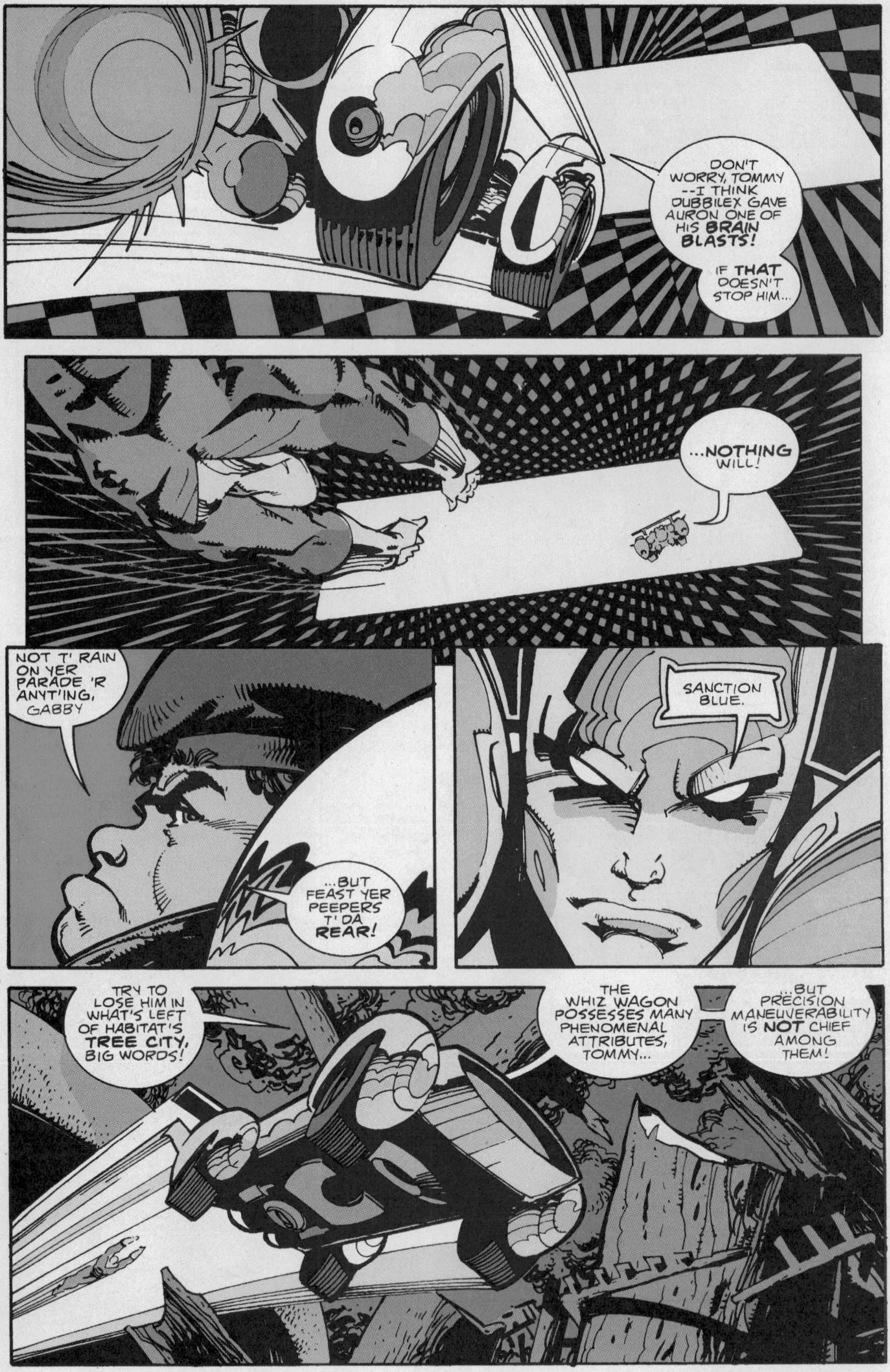
DON'T WORRY, TOMMY --I THINK DUBBILEX GAVE AURON ONE OF HIS BRAIN BLASTS!
IF THAT DOESN'T STOP HIM...
...NOTHING WILL!
NOT T' RAIN ON YER PARADE 'R ANYT'ING, GABBY
...BUT FEAST YER PEEPERS T' DA REAR!
SANCTION BLUE.
TRY TO LOSE HIM IN WHAT'S LEFT OF HABITAT'S TREE CITY, BIG WORDS!
THE WHIZ WAGON POSSESSES MANY PHENOMENAL ATTRIBUTES, TOMMY...
...BUT PRECISION MANEUVERABILITY IS NOT CHIEF AMONG THEM!

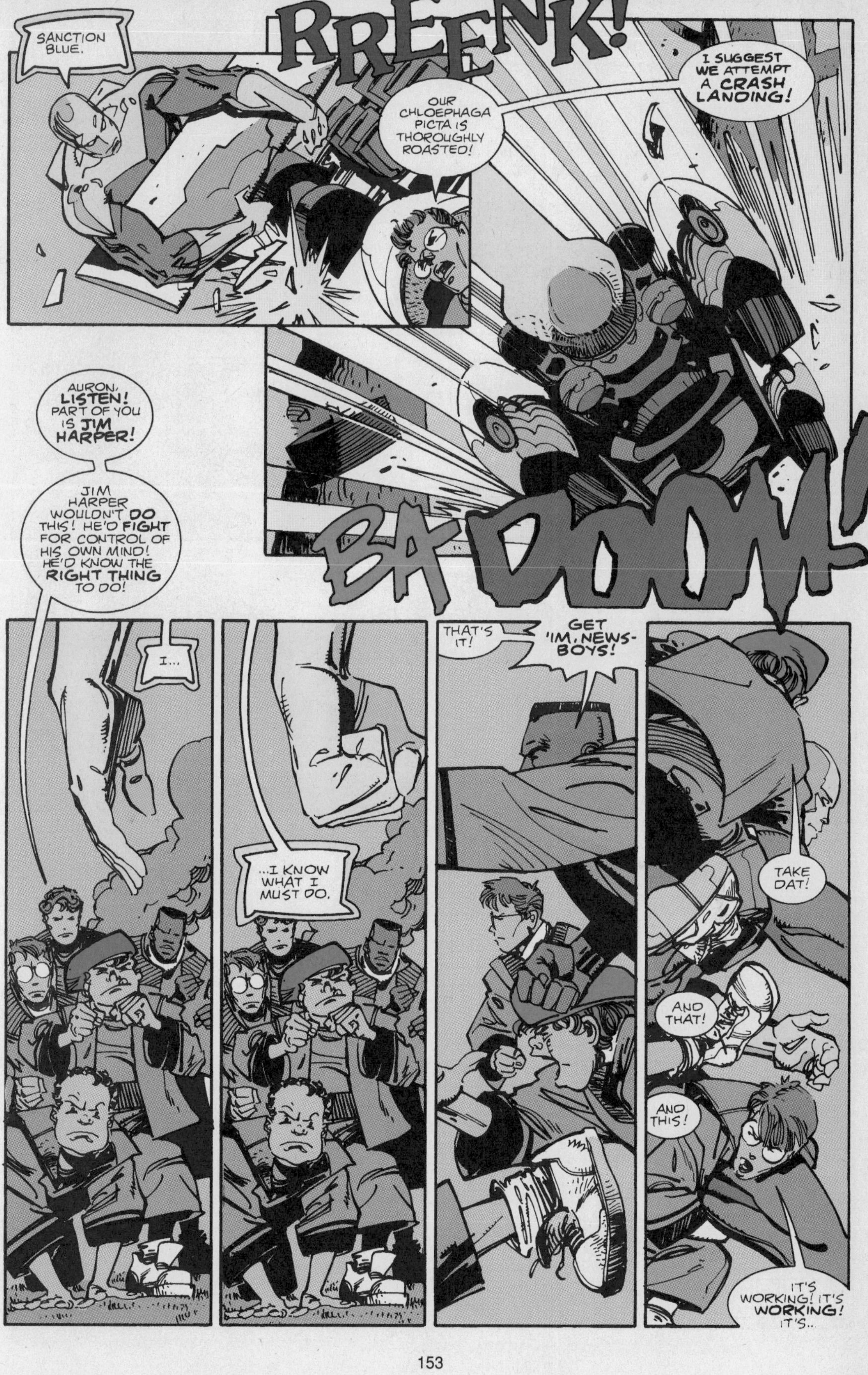
RREENK!
SANCTION BLUE.
OUR CHLOEPHAGA PICTA IS THOROUGHLY ROASTED!
I SUGGEST WE ATTEMPT A CRASH LANDING!
BA DOOM!
AURON, LISTEN! PART OF YOU IS JIM HARPER!
JIM HARPER WOULDN'T DO THIS! HE'D FIGHT FOR CONTROL OF HIS OWN MIND! HE'D KNOW THE RIGHT THING TO DO!
I...
...I KNOW WHAT I MUST DO.
THAT'S IT!
GET 'IM, NEWS-BOYS!
TAKE DAT!
AND THAT!
AND THIS!
IT'S WORKING! IT'S WORKING! IT'S..

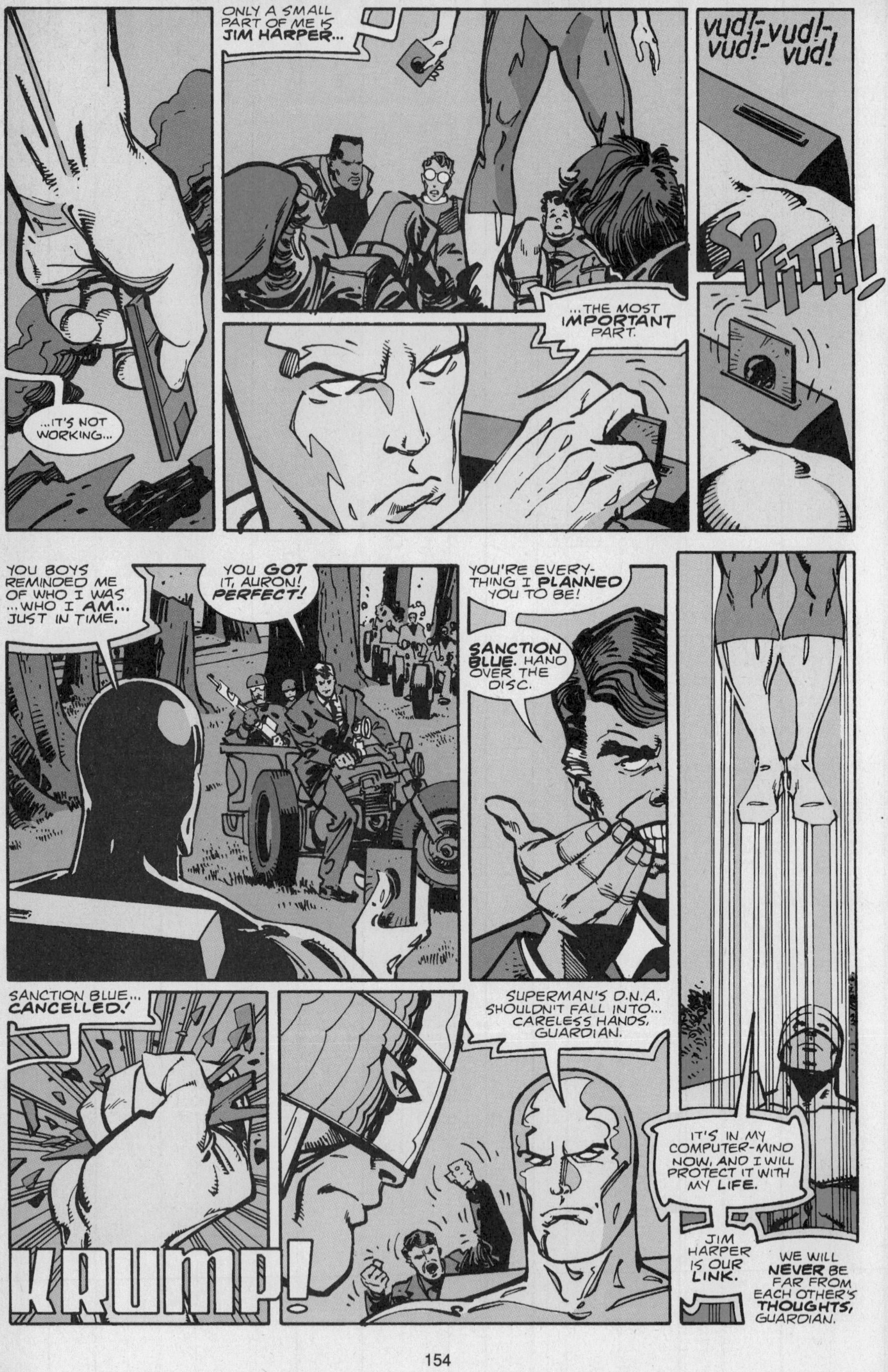
...IT'S NOT WORKING...
ONLY A SMALL PART OF ME IS **JIM HARPER**...
...THE MOST **IMPORTANT** PART.
vud!-vud!-vud!-vud!
SPFFTH!
YOU BOYS REMINDED ME OF WHO I WAS ...WHO I **AM**... JUST IN TIME.
YOU **GOT** IT, AURON! ***PERFECT!***
YOU'RE EVERY-THING I **PLANNED** YOU TO BE!
SANCTION BLUE. HAND OVER THE DISC.
SANCTION BLUE... ***CANCELLED!***
KRUMP!
SUPERMAN'S D.N.A. SHOULDN'T FALL INTO... CARELESS HANDS, GUARDIAN.
IT'S IN MY COMPUTER-MIND NOW, AND I WILL PROTECT IT WITH MY **LIFE**.
JIM HARPER IS OUR **LINK**.
WE WILL **NEVER** BE FAR FROM EACH OTHER'S ***THOUGHTS,*** GUARDIAN.

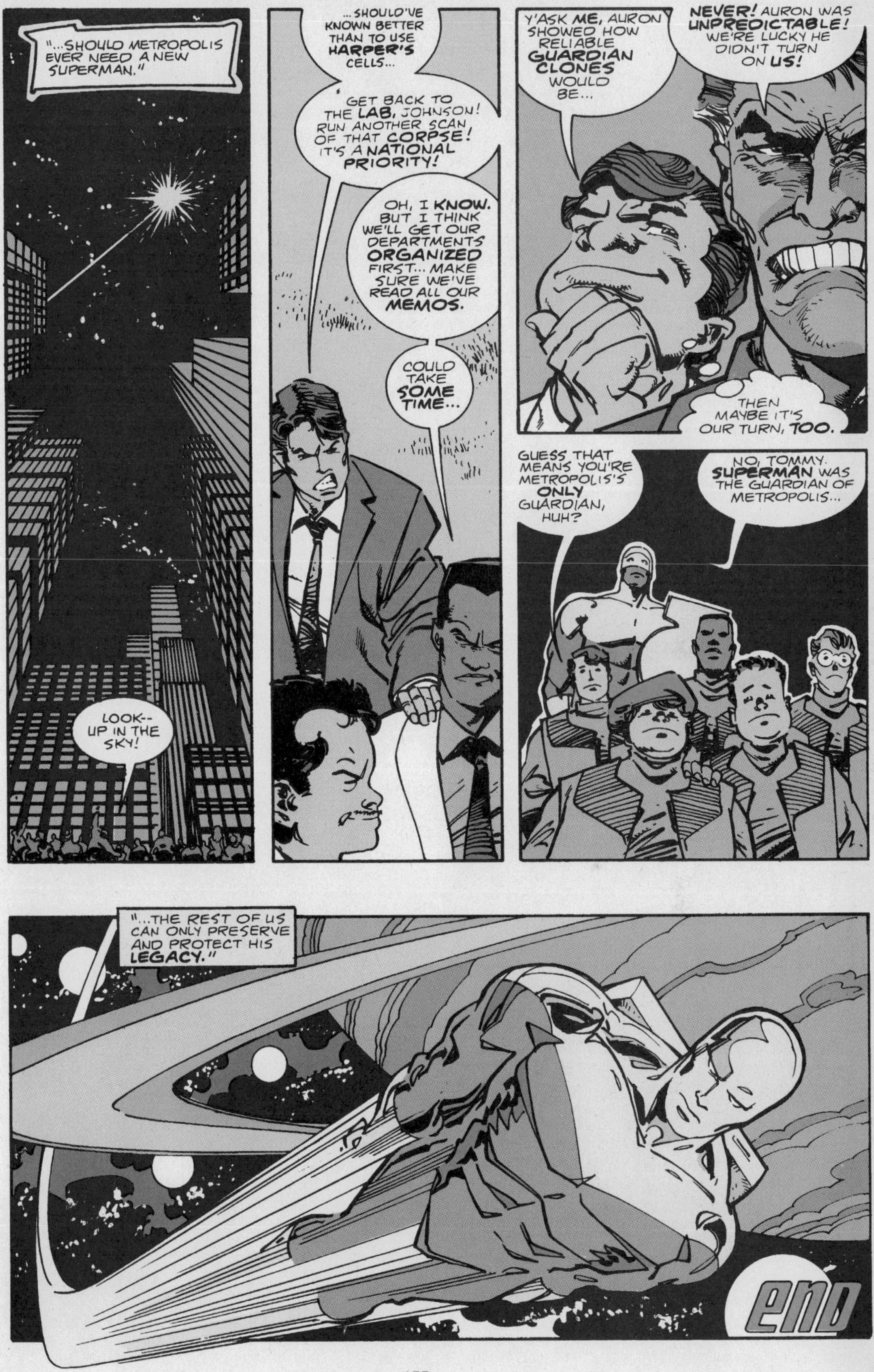
"...SHOULD METROPOLIS EVER NEED A NEW SUPERMAN."
LOOK-- UP IN THE SKY!
...SHOULD'VE KNOWN BETTER THAN TO USE HARPER'S CELLS...
GET BACK TO THE LAB, JOHNSON! RUN ANOTHER SCAN OF THAT CORPSE! IT'S A NATIONAL PRIORITY!
OH, I KNOW. BUT I THINK WE'LL GET OUR DEPARTMENTS ORGANIZED FIRST... MAKE SURE WE'VE READ ALL OUR MEMOS.
COULD TAKE SOME TIME...
Y'ASK ME, AURON SHOWED HOW RELIABLE GUARDIAN CLONES WOULD BE...
NEVER! AURON WAS UNPREDICTABLE! WE'RE LUCKY HE DIDN'T TURN ON US!
THEN MAYBE IT'S OUR TURN, TOO.
GUESS THAT MEANS YOU'RE METROPOLIS'S ONLY GUARDIAN, HUH?
NO, TOMMY. SUPERMAN WAS THE GUARDIAN OF METROPOLIS...
"...THE REST OF US CAN ONLY PRESERVE AND PROTECT HIS LEGACY."
end

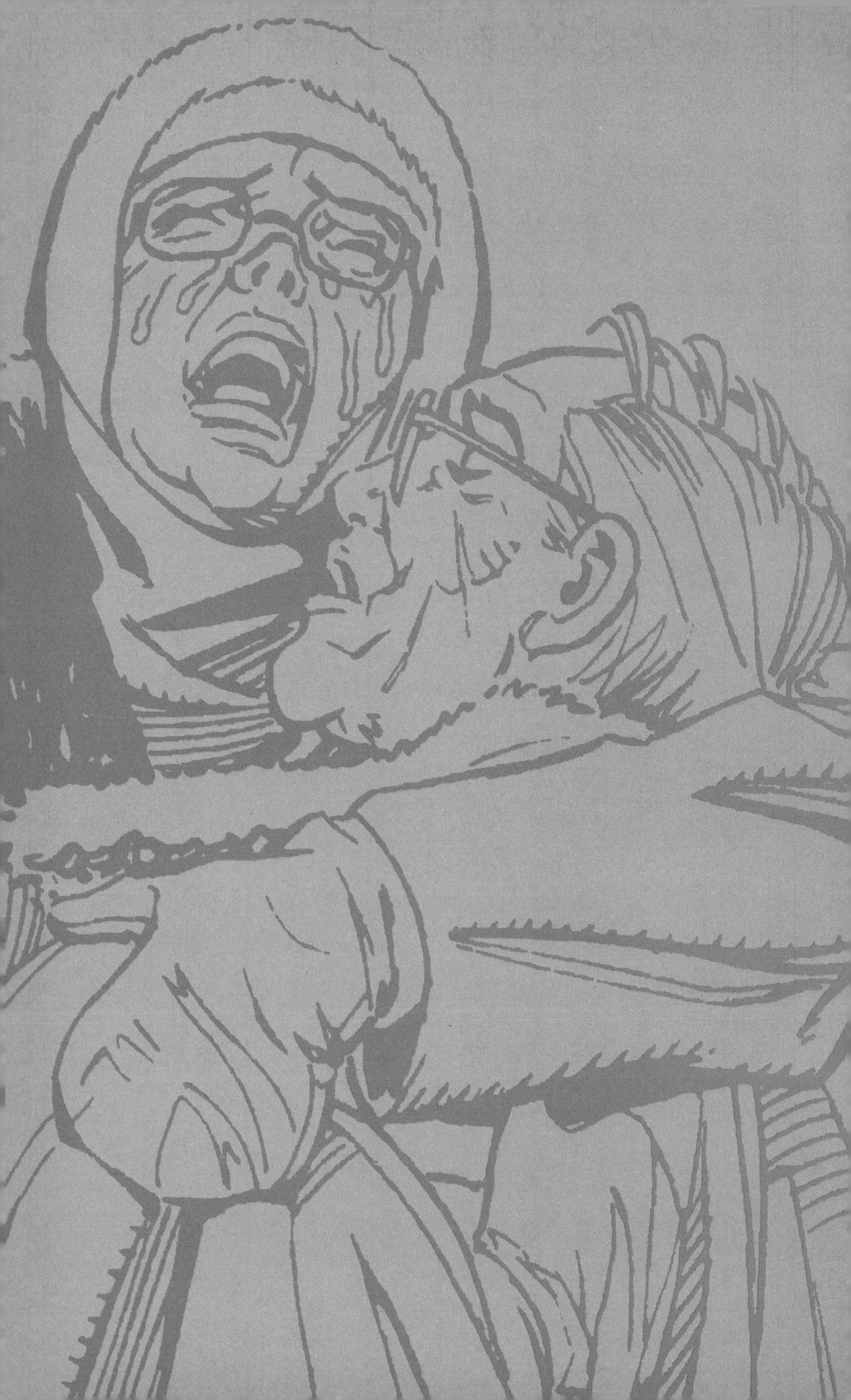

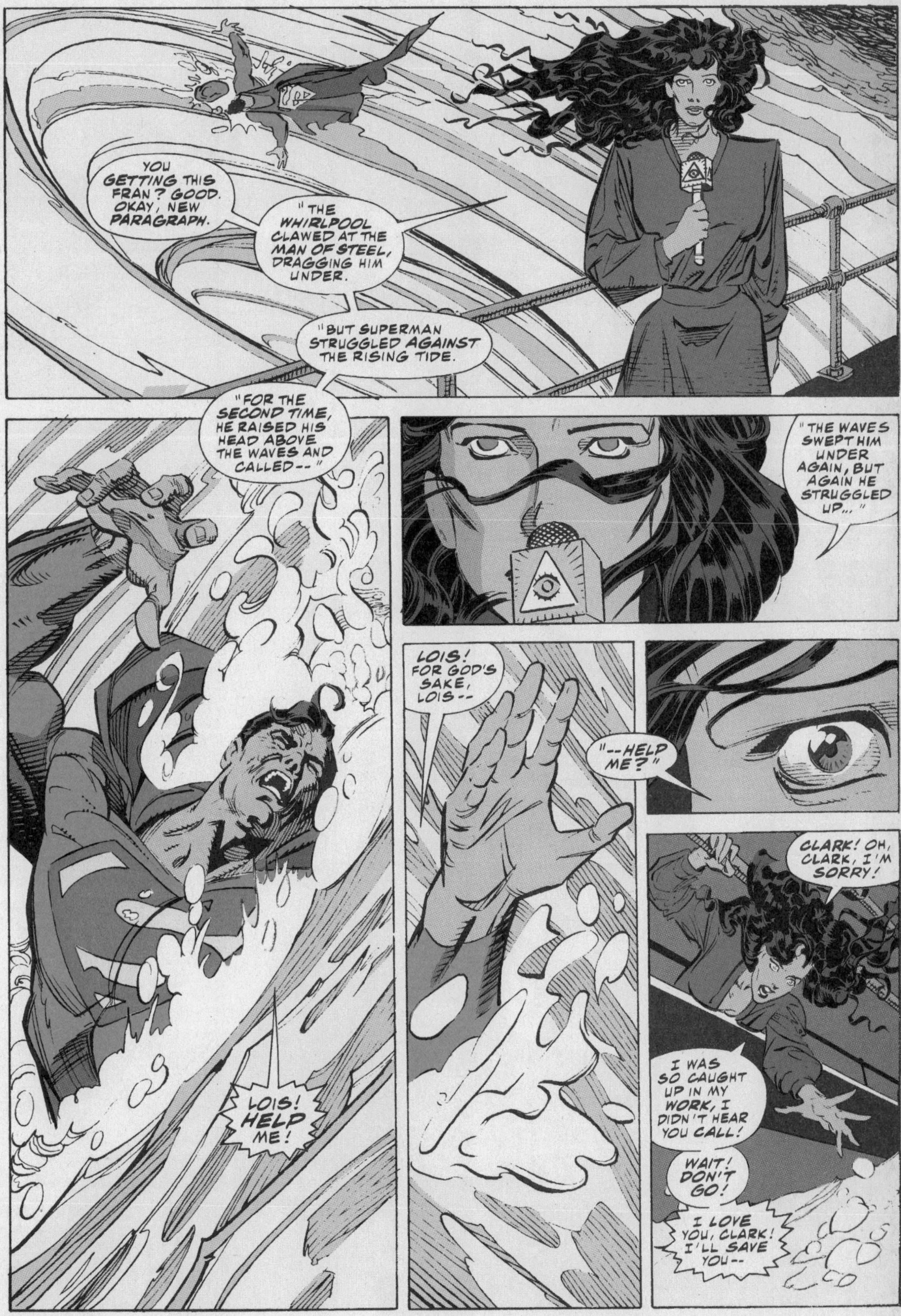
YOU GETTING THIS FRAN? GOOD. OKAY, NEW PARAGRAPH.
"THE WHIRLPOOL CLAWED AT THE MAN OF STEEL, DRAGGING HIM UNDER.
"BUT SUPERMAN STRUGGLED AGAINST THE RISING TIDE.
"FOR THE SECOND TIME, HE RAISED HIS HEAD ABOVE THE WAVES AND CALLED--"
LOIS! HELP ME!
"THE WAVES SWEPT HIM UNDER AGAIN, BUT AGAIN HE STRUGGLED UP..."
LOIS! FOR GOD'S SAKE, LOIS--
"--HELP ME?"
CLARK! OH, CLARK, I'M SORRY!
I WAS SO CAUGHT UP IN MY WORK, I DIDN'T HEAR YOU CALL!
WAIT! DON'T GO!
I LOVE YOU, CLARK! I'LL SAVE YOU--

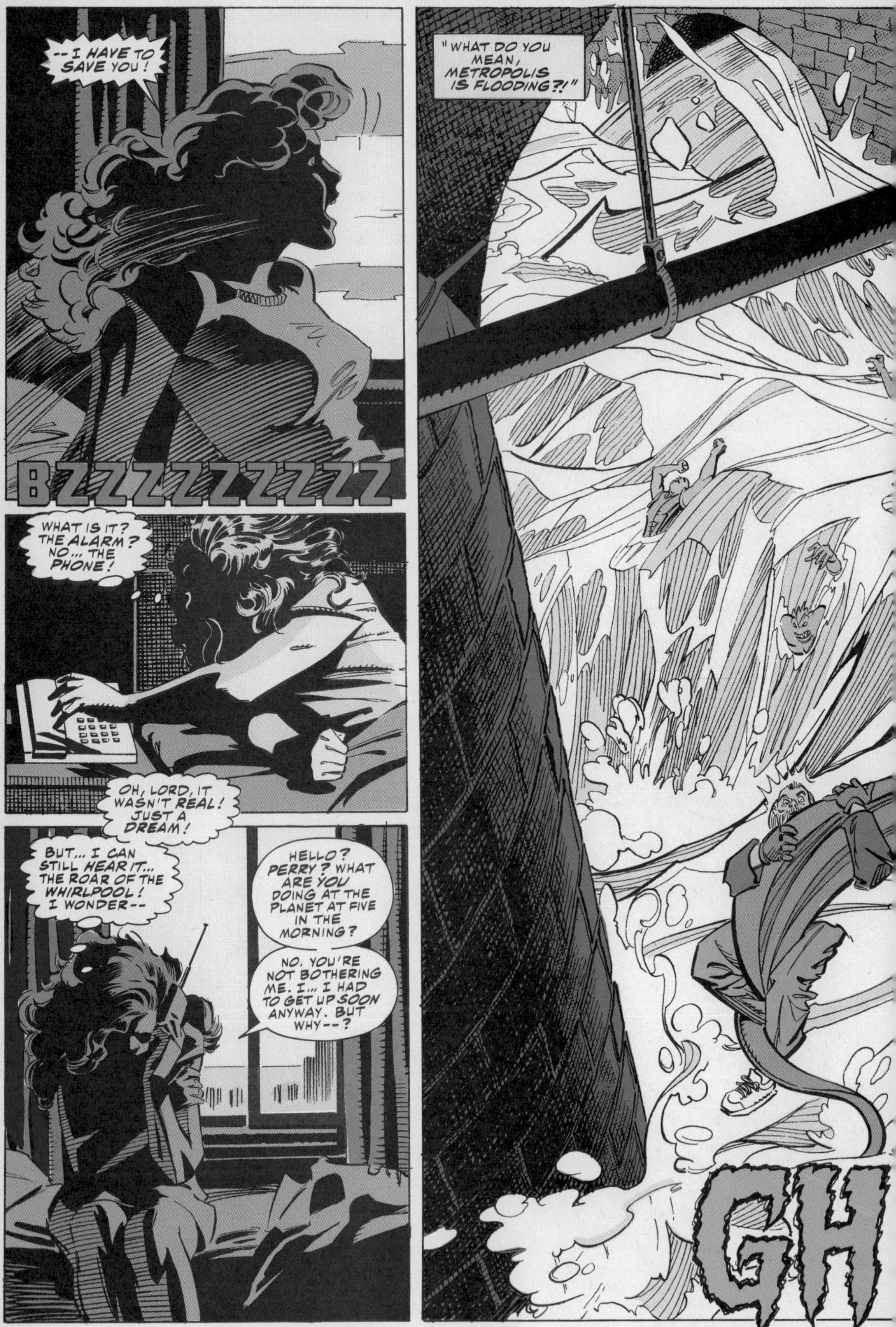
--I HAVE TO SAVE YOU!
BZZZZZZZZZZ
WHAT IS IT? THE ALARM? NO... THE PHONE!
OH, LORD, IT WASN'T REAL! JUST A DREAM!
BUT... I CAN STILL HEAR IT... THE ROAR OF THE WHIRLPOOL! I WONDER--
HELLO? PERRY? WHAT ARE YOU DOING AT THE PLANET AT FIVE IN THE MORNING?
NO. YOU'RE NOT BOTHERING ME. I... I HAD TO GET UP SOON ANYWAY. BUT WHY--?
"WHAT DO YOU MEAN, METROPOLIS IS FLOODING?!"
GH

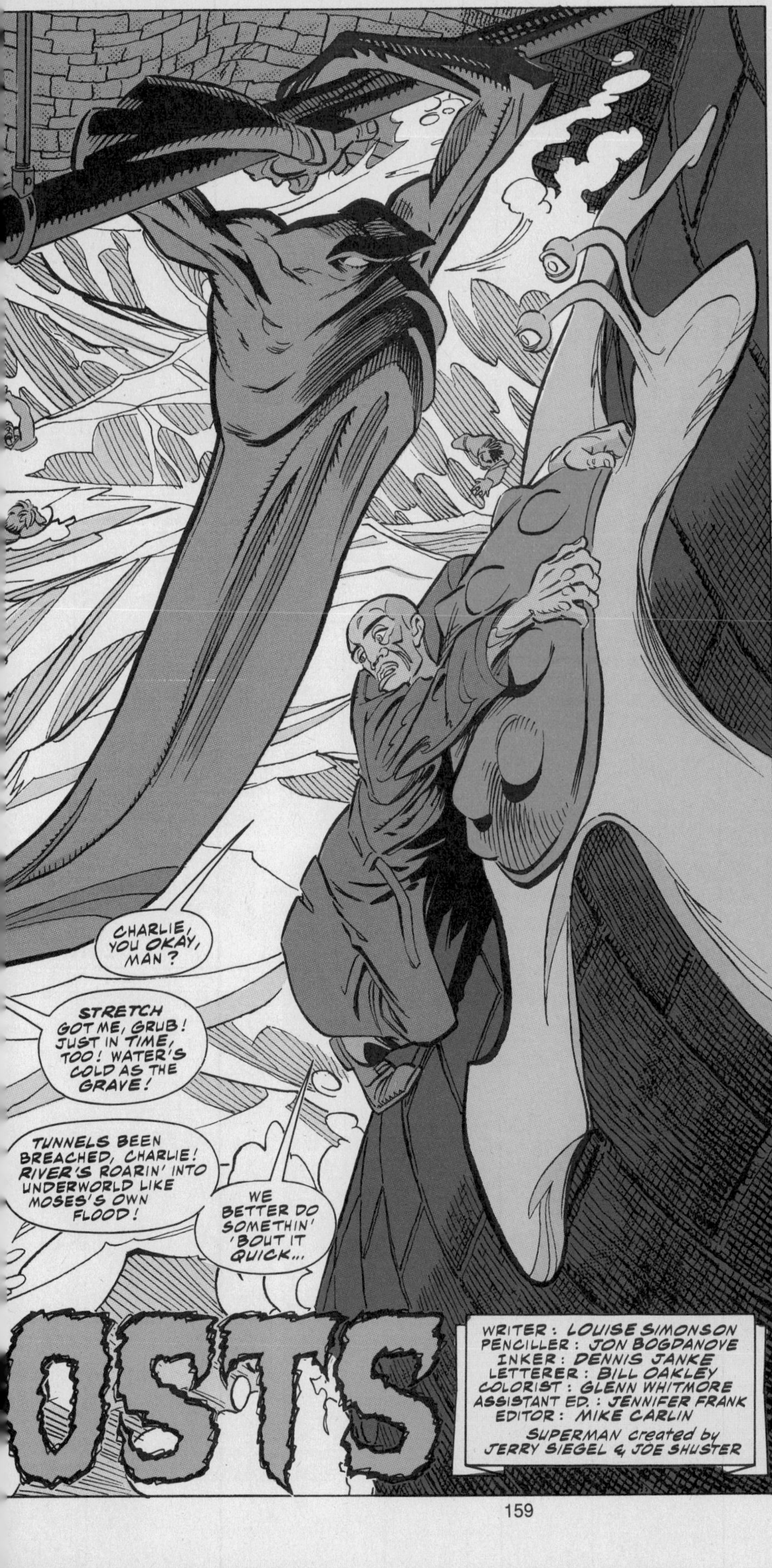
CHARLIE, YOU OKAY, MAN?
STRETCH GOT ME, GRUB! JUST IN TIME, TOO! WATER'S COLD AS THE GRAVE!
TUNNELS BEEN BREACHED, CHARLIE! RIVER'S ROARIN' INTO UNDERWORLD LIKE MOSES'S OWN FLOOD!
WE BETTER DO SOMETHIN' 'BOUT IT QUICK...
OSTS
WRITER: LOUISE SIMONSON
PENCILLER: JON BOGDANOVE
INKER: DENNIS JANKE
LETTERER: BILL OAKLEY
COLORIST: GLENN WHITMORE
ASSISTANT ED.: JENNIFER FRANK
EDITOR: MIKE CARLIN
SUPERMAN created by JERRY SIEGEL & JOE SHUSTER

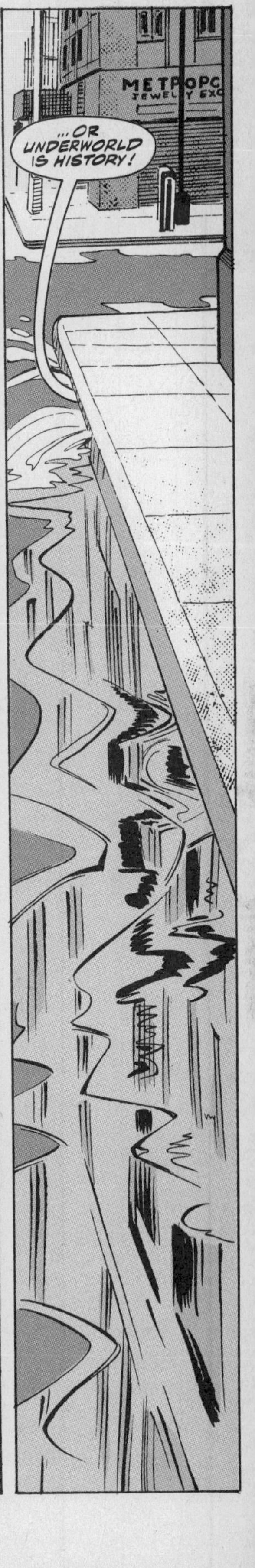
METROPO
JEWEL
...OR UNDERWORLD IS HISTORY!

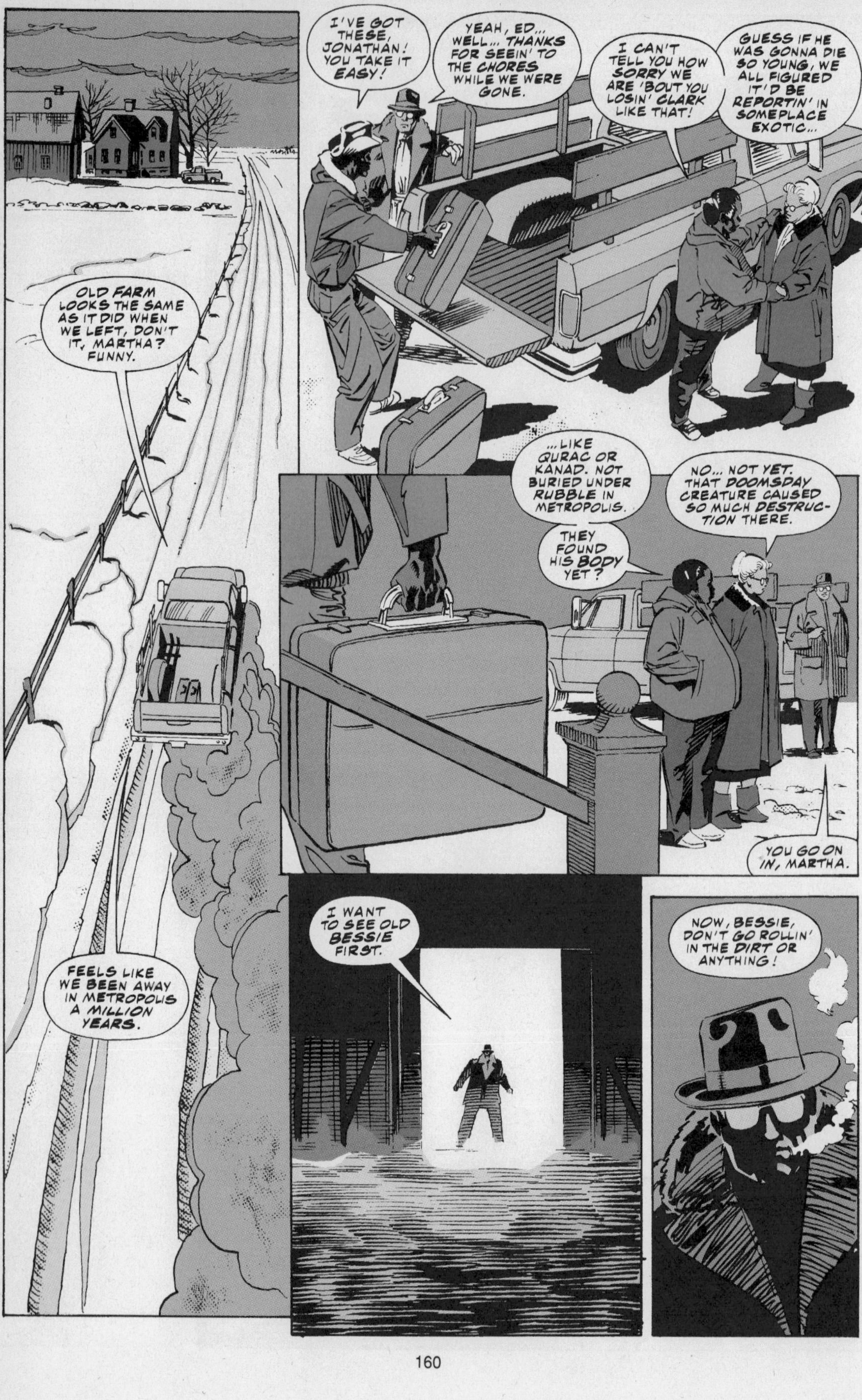
OLD FARM LOOKS THE SAME AS IT DID WHEN WE LEFT, DON'T IT, MARTHA? FUNNY.
FEELS LIKE WE BEEN AWAY IN METROPOLIS A MILLION YEARS.
I'VE GOT THESE, JONATHAN! YOU TAKE IT EASY!
YEAH, ED... WELL... THANKS FOR SEEIN' TO THE CHORES WHILE WE WERE GONE.
I CAN'T TELL YOU HOW SORRY WE ARE 'BOUT YOU LOSIN' CLARK LIKE THAT!
GUESS IF HE WAS GONNA DIE SO YOUNG, WE ALL FIGURED IT'D BE REPORTIN' IN SOMEPLACE EXOTIC...
...LIKE QURAC OR KANAD. NOT BURIED UNDER RUBBLE IN METROPOLIS.
THEY FOUND HIS BODY YET?
NO... NOT YET. THAT DOOMSDAY CREATURE CAUSED SO MUCH DESTRUCTION THERE.
YOU GO ON IN, MARTHA.
I WANT TO SEE OLD BESSIE FIRST.
NOW, BESSIE, DON'T GO ROLLIN' IN THE DIRT OR ANYTHING!

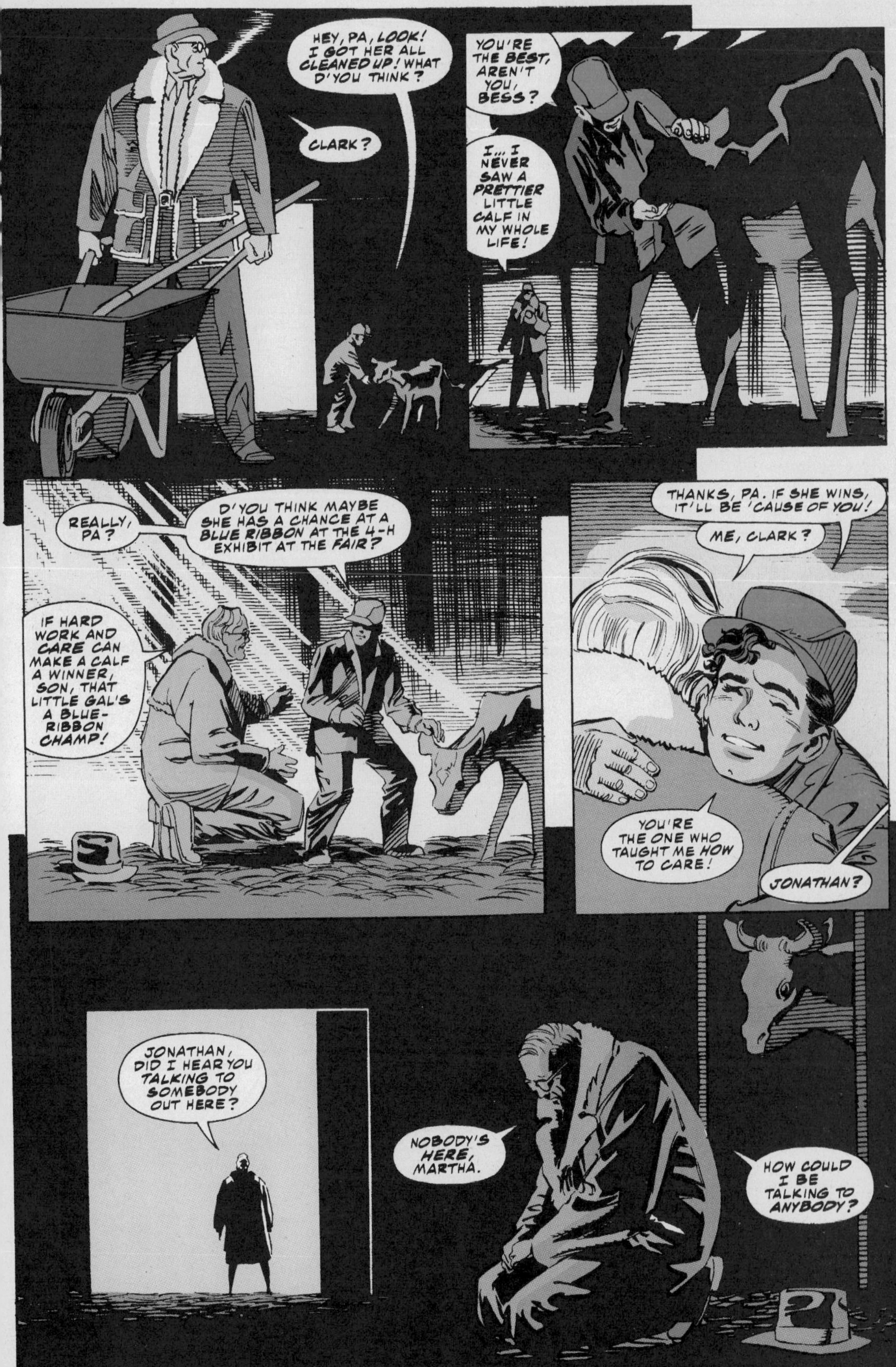
HEY, PA, LOOK! I GOT HER ALL CLEANED UP! WHAT D'YOU THINK?
CLARK?
YOU'RE THE BEST, AREN'T YOU, BESS?
I... I NEVER SAW A PRETTIER LITTLE CALF IN MY WHOLE LIFE!
REALLY, PA?
D'YOU THINK MAYBE SHE HAS A CHANCE AT A BLUE RIBBON AT THE 4-H EXHIBIT AT THE FAIR?
IF HARD WORK AND CARE CAN MAKE A CALF A WINNER, SON, THAT LITTLE GAL'S A BLUE-RIBBON CHAMP!
THANKS, PA. IF SHE WINS, IT'LL BE 'CAUSE OF YOU!
ME, CLARK?
YOU'RE THE ONE WHO TAUGHT ME HOW TO CARE!
JONATHAN?
JONATHAN, DID I HEAR YOU TALKING TO SOMEBODY OUT HERE?
NOBODY'S HERE, MARTHA.
HOW COULD I BE TALKING TO ANYBODY?

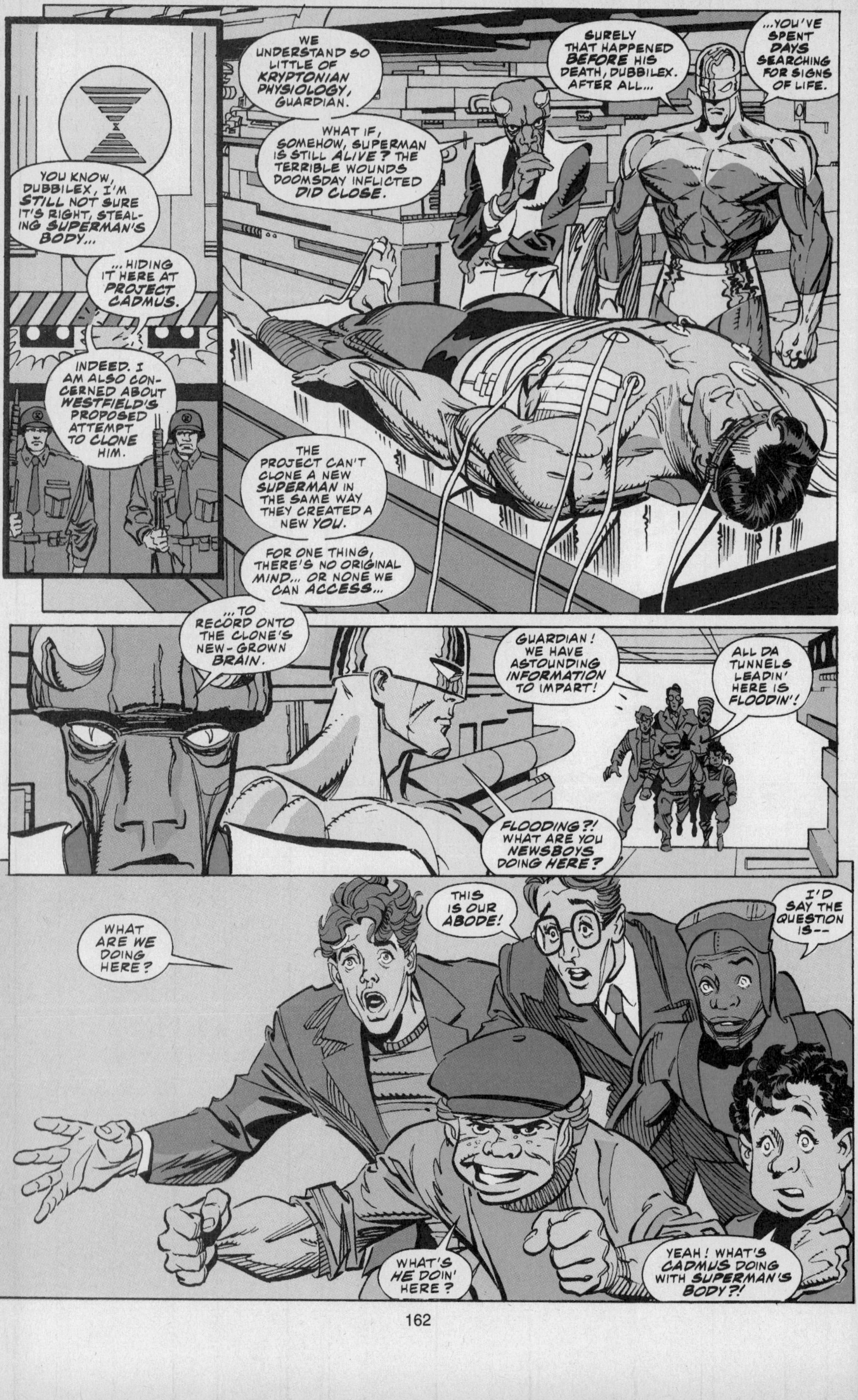
YOU KNOW, DUBBILEX, I'M STILL NOT SURE IT'S RIGHT, STEALING SUPERMAN'S BODY...
...HIDING IT HERE AT PROJECT CADMUS.
INDEED. I AM ALSO CONCERNED ABOUT WESTFIELD'S PROPOSED ATTEMPT TO CLONE HIM.
WE UNDERSTAND SO LITTLE OF KRYPTONIAN PHYSIOLOGY, GUARDIAN.
WHAT IF, SOMEHOW, SUPERMAN IS STILL ALIVE? THE TERRIBLE WOUNDS DOOMSDAY INFLICTED DID CLOSE.
SURELY THAT HAPPENED BEFORE HIS DEATH, DUBBILEX. AFTER ALL...
...YOU'VE SPENT DAYS SEARCHING FOR SIGNS OF LIFE.
THE PROJECT CAN'T CLONE A NEW SUPERMAN IN THE SAME WAY THEY CREATED A NEW YOU.
FOR ONE THING, THERE'S NO ORIGINAL MIND... OR NONE WE CAN ACCESS...
...TO RECORD ONTO THE CLONE'S NEW-GROWN BRAIN.
GUARDIAN! WE HAVE ASTOUNDING INFORMATION TO IMPART!
ALL DA TUNNELS LEADIN' HERE IS FLOODIN'!
FLOODING?! WHAT ARE YOU NEWSBOYS DOING HERE?
WHAT ARE WE DOING HERE?
THIS IS OUR ABODE!
I'D SAY THE QUESTION IS--
WHAT'S HE DOIN' HERE?
YEAH! WHAT'S CADMUS DOING WITH SUPERMAN'S BODY?!

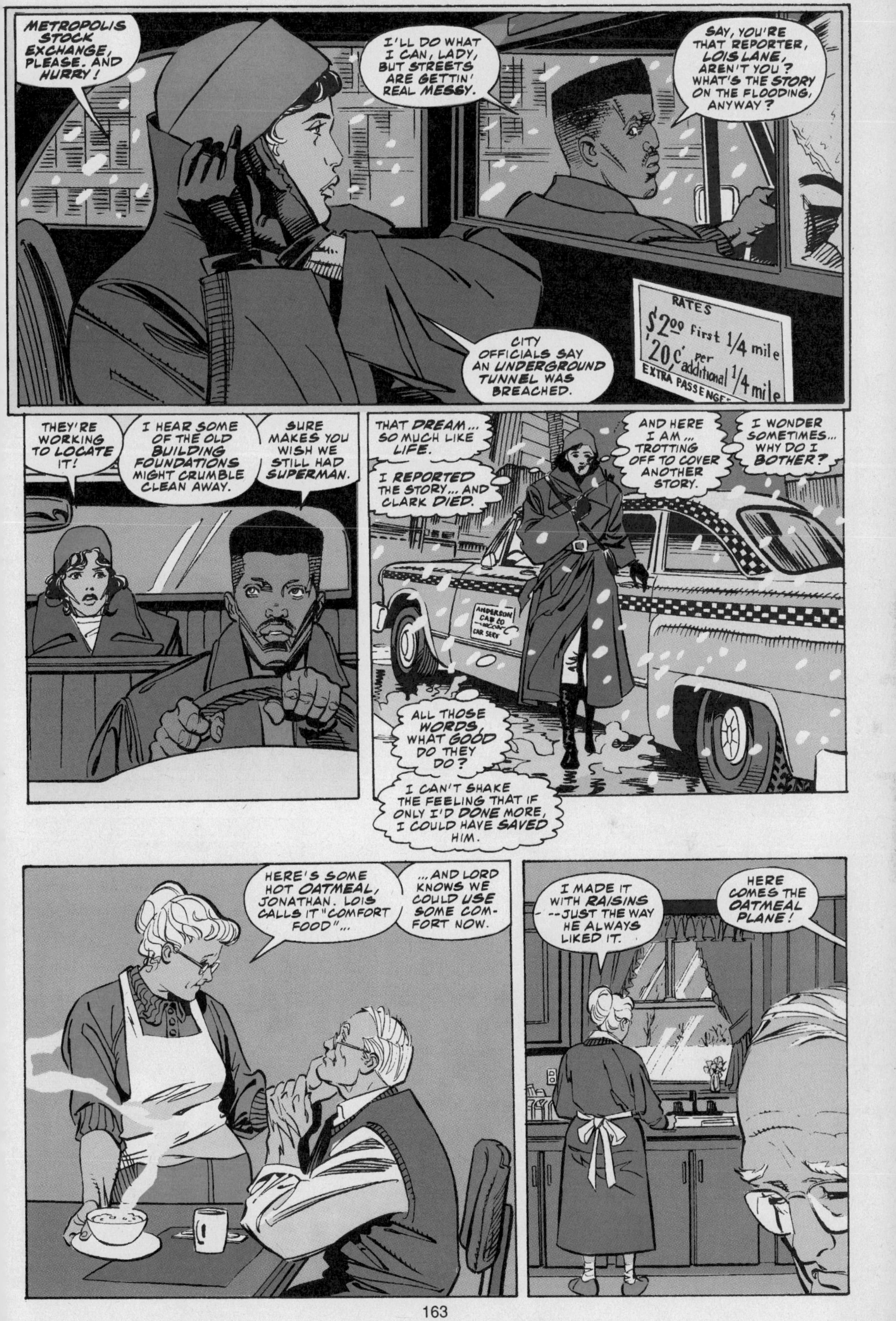
METROPOLIS STOCK EXCHANGE, PLEASE. AND HURRY!
I'LL DO WHAT I CAN, LADY, BUT STREETS ARE GETTIN' REAL MESSY.
SAY, YOU'RE THAT REPORTER, LOIS LANE, AREN'T YOU? WHAT'S THE STORY ON THE FLOODING, ANYWAY?
RATES
$2.00 First 1/4 mile
20¢ per additional 1/4 mile
EXTRA PASSENGE
CITY OFFICIALS SAY AN UNDERGROUND TUNNEL WAS BREACHED.
THEY'RE WORKING TO LOCATE IT!
I HEAR SOME OF THE OLD BUILDING FOUNDATIONS MIGHT CRUMBLE CLEAN AWAY.
SURE MAKES YOU WISH WE STILL HAD SUPERMAN.
THAT DREAM... SO MUCH LIKE LIFE.
I REPORTED THE STORY... AND CLARK DIED.
AND HERE I AM... TROTTING OFF TO COVER ANOTHER STORY.
I WONDER SOMETIMES... WHY DO I BOTHER?
ALL THOSE WORDS, WHAT GOOD DO THEY DO?
I CAN'T SHAKE THE FEELING THAT IF ONLY I'D DONE MORE, I COULD HAVE SAVED HIM.
HERE'S SOME HOT OATMEAL, JONATHAN. LOIS CALLS IT "COMFORT FOOD"...
...AND LORD KNOWS WE COULD USE SOME COMFORT NOW.
I MADE IT WITH RAISINS --JUST THE WAY HE ALWAYS LIKED IT.
HERE COMES THE OATMEAL PLANE!

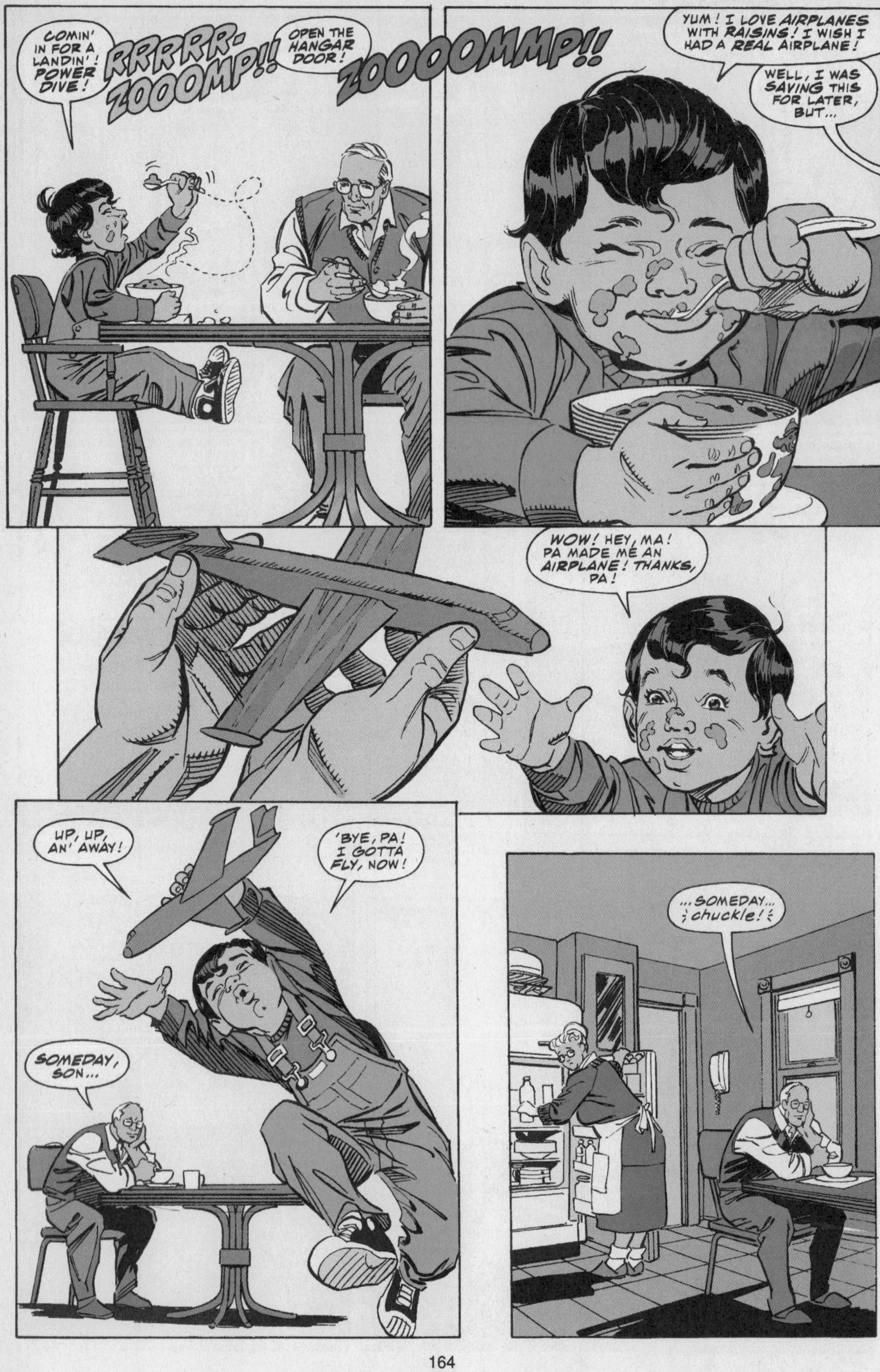
COMIN' IN FOR A LANDIN'! POWER DIVE!
RRRRR-ZOOOMP!!
OPEN THE HANGAR DOOR!
ZOOOOOMMMP!!
YUM! I LOVE AIRPLANES WITH RAISINS! I WISH I HAD A REAL AIRPLANE!
WELL, I WAS SAVING THIS FOR LATER, BUT...
WOW! HEY, MA! PA MADE ME AN AIRPLANE! THANKS, PA!
UP, UP, AN' AWAY!
'BYE, PA! I GOTTA FLY, NOW!
SOMEDAY, SON...
...SOMEDAY... ;chuckle!;

UP YA GO! SPONGE AN' *HOT HOUSE* GONNA DRY YOU OFF... THEN YOU HEAD ON INTO THE *HIGH TUNNELS.*

IF THEY GET TOO *CROWDED* THERE, TELL FOLKS TO HEAD UP INTO THE *BASEMENTS* AN' SUBWAY PLATFORMS.

WE *THINK* THIS IS AS HIGH AS THE WATER'S GOING, BUT IF IT STARTS TO *RISE* AGAIN...

...WE'LL BE SAFER ON THE *OUTSIDE* THAN HERE IN UNDERWORLD.

C'MON OUT, NEEP-NOSE! GET OVER THERE AND GET *WARM!*

SQUANK!

WHAT IS IT, *TELETYPE?*

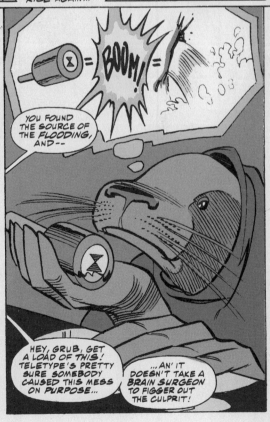

BOOM!

YOU FOUND THE SOURCE OF THE *FLOODING,* AND--

HEY, GRUB, GET A LOAD OF THIS! TELETYPE'S PRETTY SURE SOMEBODY *CAUSED* THIS MESS ON PURPOSE...

...AN' IT DOESN'T TAKE A *BRAIN SURGEON* TO FIGGER OUT THE CULPRIT!

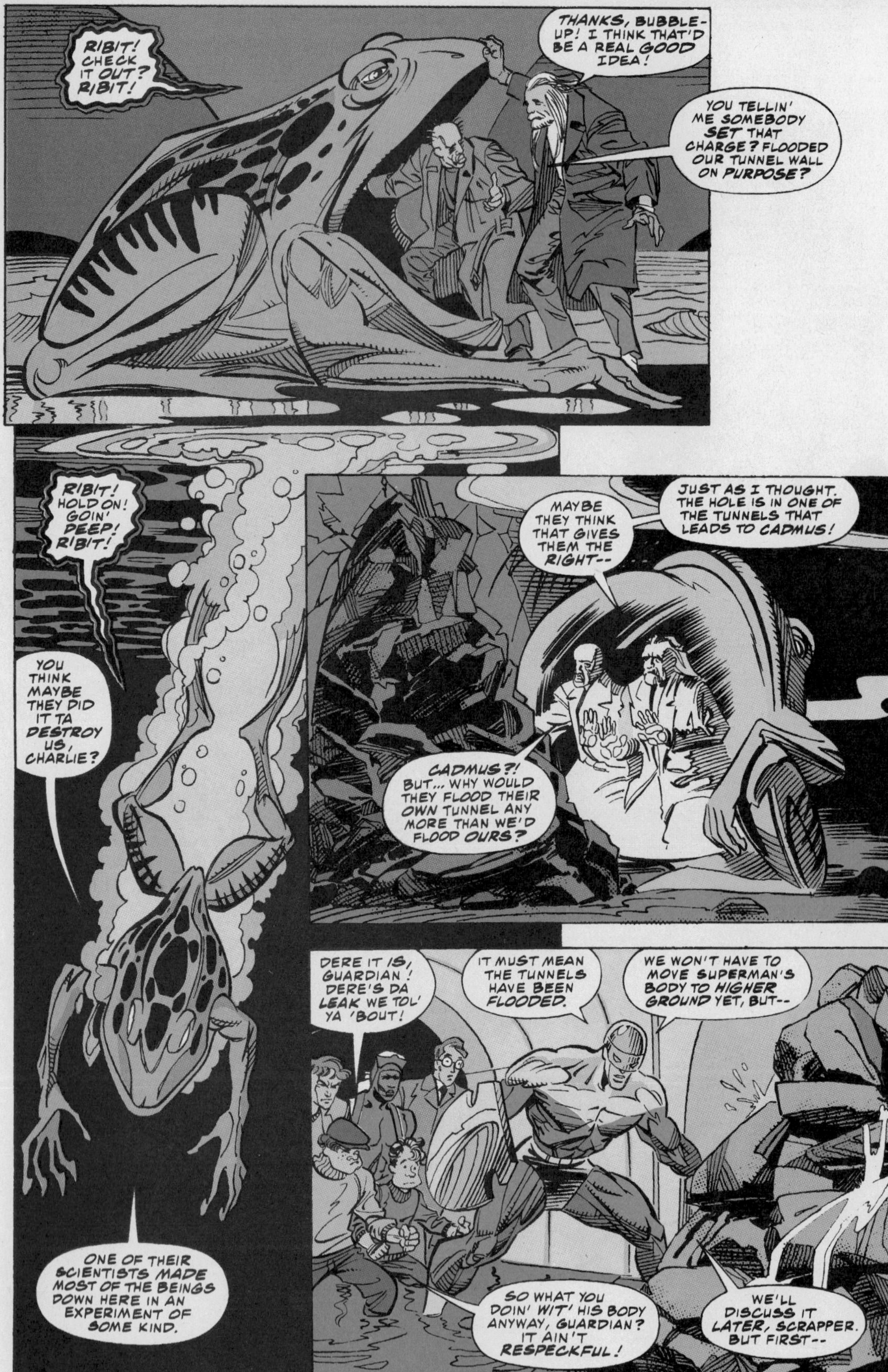
RIBIT! CHECK IT OUT? RIBIT!
THANKS, BUBBLE-UP! I THINK THAT'D BE A REAL GOOD IDEA!
YOU TELLIN' ME SOMEBODY SET THAT CHARGE? FLOODED OUR TUNNEL WALL ON PURPOSE?
RIBIT! HOLD ON! GOIN' DEEP! RIBIT!
YOU THINK MAYBE THEY DID IT TA DESTROY US, CHARLIE?
ONE OF THEIR SCIENTISTS MADE MOST OF THE BEINGS DOWN HERE IN AN EXPERIMENT OF SOME KIND.
MAYBE THEY THINK THAT GIVES THEM THE RIGHT--
JUST AS I THOUGHT. THE HOLE IS IN ONE OF THE TUNNELS THAT LEADS TO CADMUS!
CADMUS?! BUT... WHY WOULD THEY FLOOD THEIR OWN TUNNEL ANY MORE THAN WE'D FLOOD OURS?
DERE IT IS, GUARDIAN! DERE'S DA LEAK WE TOL' YA 'BOUT!
IT MUST MEAN THE TUNNELS HAVE BEEN FLOODED.
WE WON'T HAVE TO MOVE SUPERMAN'S BODY TO HIGHER GROUND YET, BUT--
SO WHAT YOU DOIN' WIT' HIS BODY ANYWAY, GUARDIAN? IT AIN'T RESPECKFUL!
WE'LL DISCUSS IT LATER, SCRAPPER. BUT FIRST--

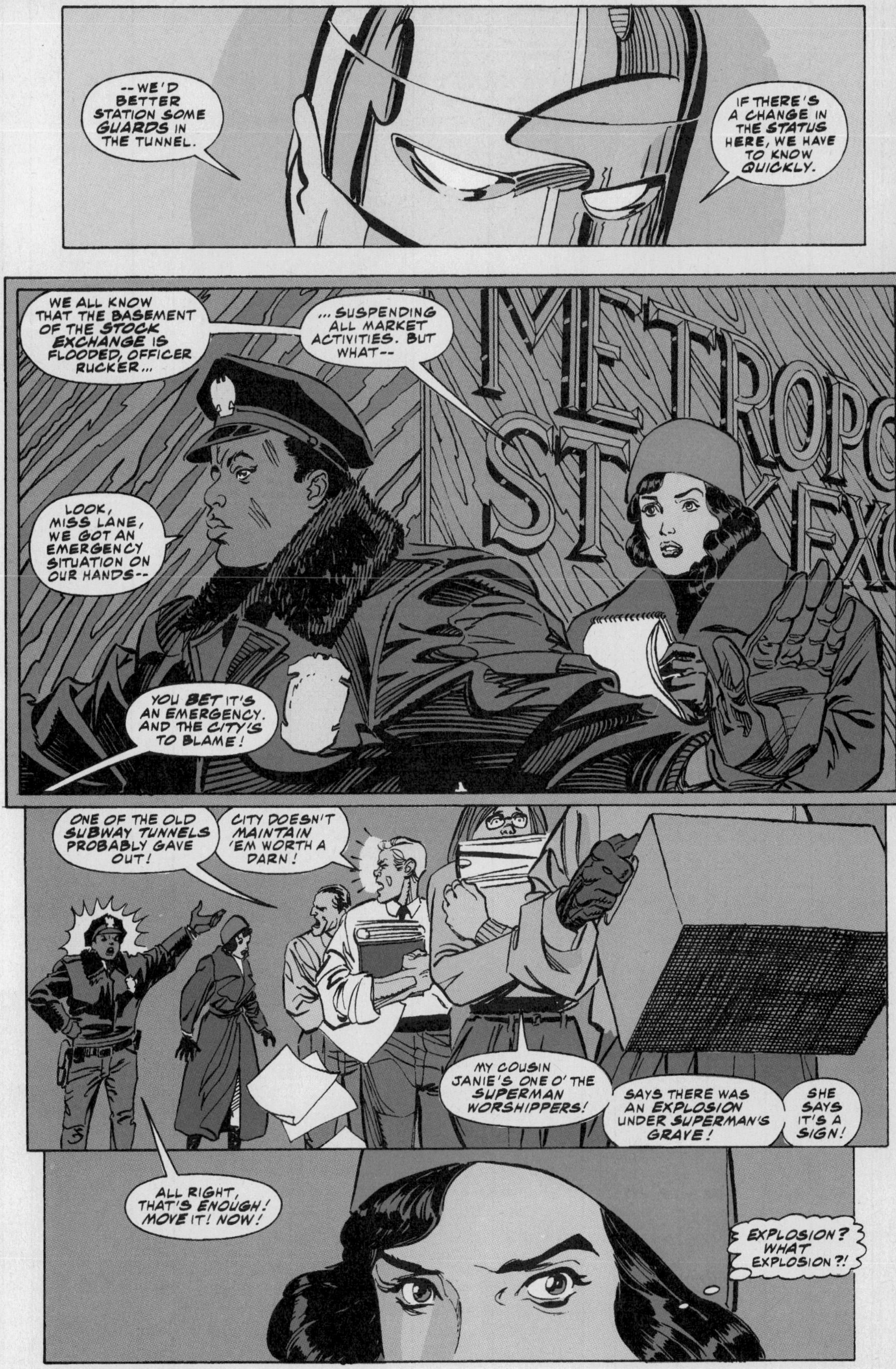
--WE'D BETTER STATION SOME GUARDS IN THE TUNNEL.
IF THERE'S A CHANGE IN THE STATUS HERE, WE HAVE TO KNOW QUICKLY.
WE ALL KNOW THAT THE BASEMENT OF THE STOCK EXCHANGE IS FLOODED, OFFICER RUCKER...
...SUSPENDING ALL MARKET ACTIVITIES. BUT WHAT--
METROPO
ST
EXC
LOOK, MISS LANE, WE GOT AN EMERGENCY SITUATION ON OUR HANDS--
YOU BET IT'S AN EMERGENCY. AND THE CITY'S TO BLAME!
ONE OF THE OLD SUBWAY TUNNELS PROBABLY GAVE OUT!
CITY DOESN'T MAINTAIN 'EM WORTH A DARN!
MY COUSIN JANIE'S ONE O' THE SUPERMAN WORSHIPPERS!
SAYS THERE WAS AN EXPLOSION UNDER SUPERMAN'S GRAVE!
SHE SAYS IT'S A SIGN!
ALL RIGHT, THAT'S ENOUGH! MOVE IT! NOW!
EXPLOSION? WHAT EXPLOSION?!

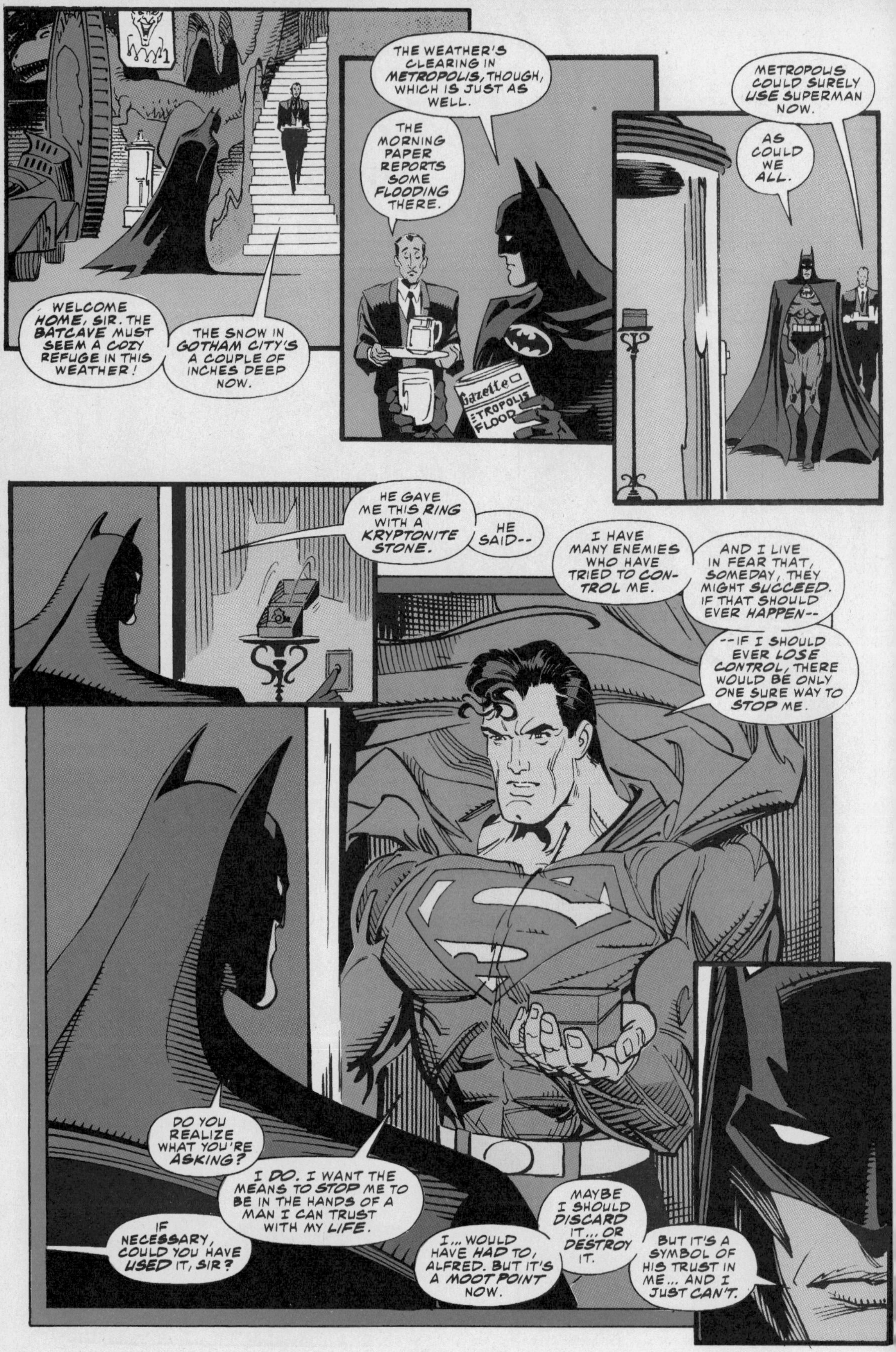

WELCOME HOME, SIR. THE BATCAVE MUST SEEM A COZY REFUGE IN THIS WEATHER!
THE SNOW IN GOTHAM CITY'S A COUPLE OF INCHES DEEP NOW.
THE WEATHER'S CLEARING IN METROPOLIS, THOUGH, WHICH IS JUST AS WELL.
THE MORNING PAPER REPORTS SOME FLOODING THERE.
Gazette
ETROPOLIS FLOOD
METROPOLIS COULD SURELY USE SUPERMAN NOW.
AS COULD WE ALL.
HE GAVE ME THIS RING WITH A KRYPTONITE STONE.
HE SAID--
I HAVE MANY ENEMIES WHO HAVE TRIED TO CONTROL ME.
AND I LIVE IN FEAR THAT, SOMEDAY, THEY MIGHT SUCCEED. IF THAT SHOULD EVER HAPPEN--
--IF I SHOULD EVER LOSE CONTROL, THERE WOULD BE ONLY ONE SURE WAY TO STOP ME.
DO YOU REALIZE WHAT YOU'RE ASKING?
I DO. I WANT THE MEANS TO STOP ME TO BE IN THE HANDS OF A MAN I CAN TRUST WITH MY LIFE.
IF NECESSARY, COULD YOU HAVE USED IT, SIR?
I... WOULD HAVE HAD TO, ALFRED. BUT IT'S A MOOT POINT NOW.
MAYBE I SHOULD DISCARD IT... OR DESTROY IT.
BUT IT'S A SYMBOL OF HIS TRUST IN ME... AND I JUST CAN'T.

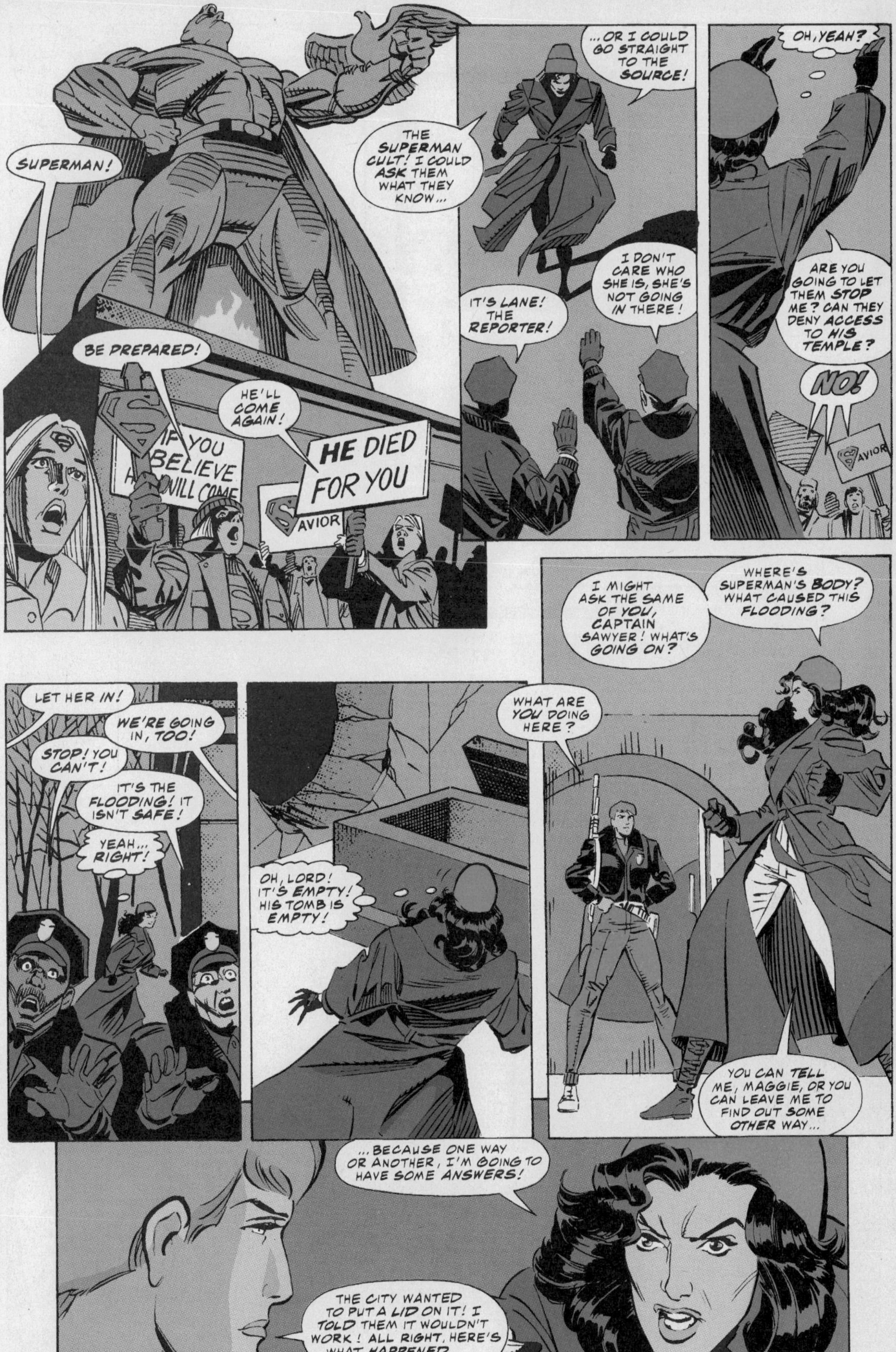
SUPERMAN!
BE PREPARED!
HE'LL COME AGAIN!
IF YOU BELIEVE ... WILL COME
HE DIED FOR YOU
SAVIOR
THE SUPERMAN CULT! I COULD ASK THEM WHAT THEY KNOW...
...OR I COULD GO STRAIGHT TO THE SOURCE!
IT'S LANE! THE REPORTER!
I DON'T CARE WHO SHE IS, SHE'S NOT GOING IN THERE!
OH, YEAH?
ARE YOU GOING TO LET THEM STOP ME? CAN THEY DENY ACCESS TO HIS TEMPLE?
NO!
SAVIOR
LET HER IN!
WE'RE GOING IN, TOO!
STOP! YOU CAN'T!
IT'S THE FLOODING! IT ISN'T SAFE!
YEAH... RIGHT!
OH, LORD! IT'S EMPTY! HIS TOMB IS EMPTY!
WHAT ARE YOU DOING HERE?
I MIGHT ASK THE SAME OF YOU, CAPTAIN SAWYER! WHAT'S GOING ON?
WHERE'S SUPERMAN'S BODY? WHAT CAUSED THIS FLOODING?
YOU CAN TELL ME, MAGGIE, OR YOU CAN LEAVE ME TO FIND OUT SOME OTHER WAY...
...BECAUSE ONE WAY OR ANOTHER, I'M GOING TO HAVE SOME ANSWERS!
THE CITY WANTED TO PUT A LID ON IT! I TOLD THEM IT WOULDN'T WORK! ALL RIGHT, HERE'S WHAT HAPPENED...

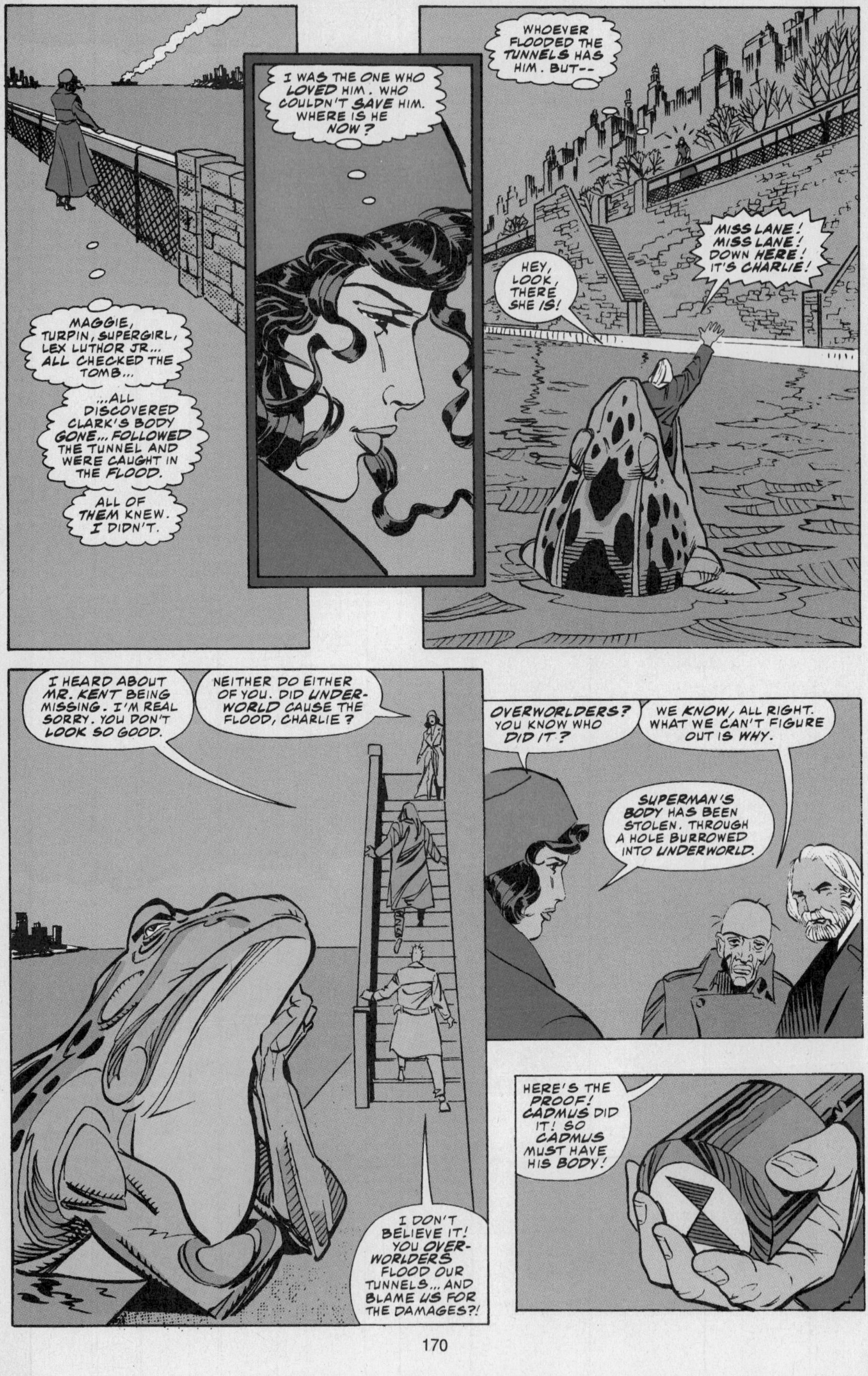
I WAS THE ONE WHO LOVED HIM. WHO COULDN'T SAVE HIM. WHERE IS HE NOW?
MAGGIE, TURPIN, SUPERGIRL, LEX LUTHOR JR... ALL CHECKED THE TOMB...
...ALL DISCOVERED CLARK'S BODY GONE... FOLLOWED THE TUNNEL AND WERE CAUGHT IN THE FLOOD.
ALL OF THEM KNEW. I DIDN'T.
WHOEVER FLOODED THE TUNNELS HAS HIM. BUT--
MISS LANE! MISS LANE! DOWN HERE! IT'S CHARLIE!
HEY, LOOK, THERE SHE IS!
I HEARD ABOUT MR. KENT BEING MISSING. I'M REAL SORRY. YOU DON'T LOOK SO GOOD.
NEITHER DO EITHER OF YOU. DID UNDERWORLD CAUSE THE FLOOD, CHARLIE?
I DON'T BELIEVE IT! YOU OVERWORLDERS FLOOD OUR TUNNELS... AND BLAME US FOR THE DAMAGES?!
OVERWORLDERS? YOU KNOW WHO DID IT?
WE KNOW, ALL RIGHT. WHAT WE CAN'T FIGURE OUT IS WHY.
SUPERMAN'S BODY HAS BEEN STOLEN. THROUGH A HOLE BURROWED INTO UNDERWORLD.
HERE'S THE PROOF! CADMUS DID IT! SO CADMUS MUST HAVE HIS BODY!

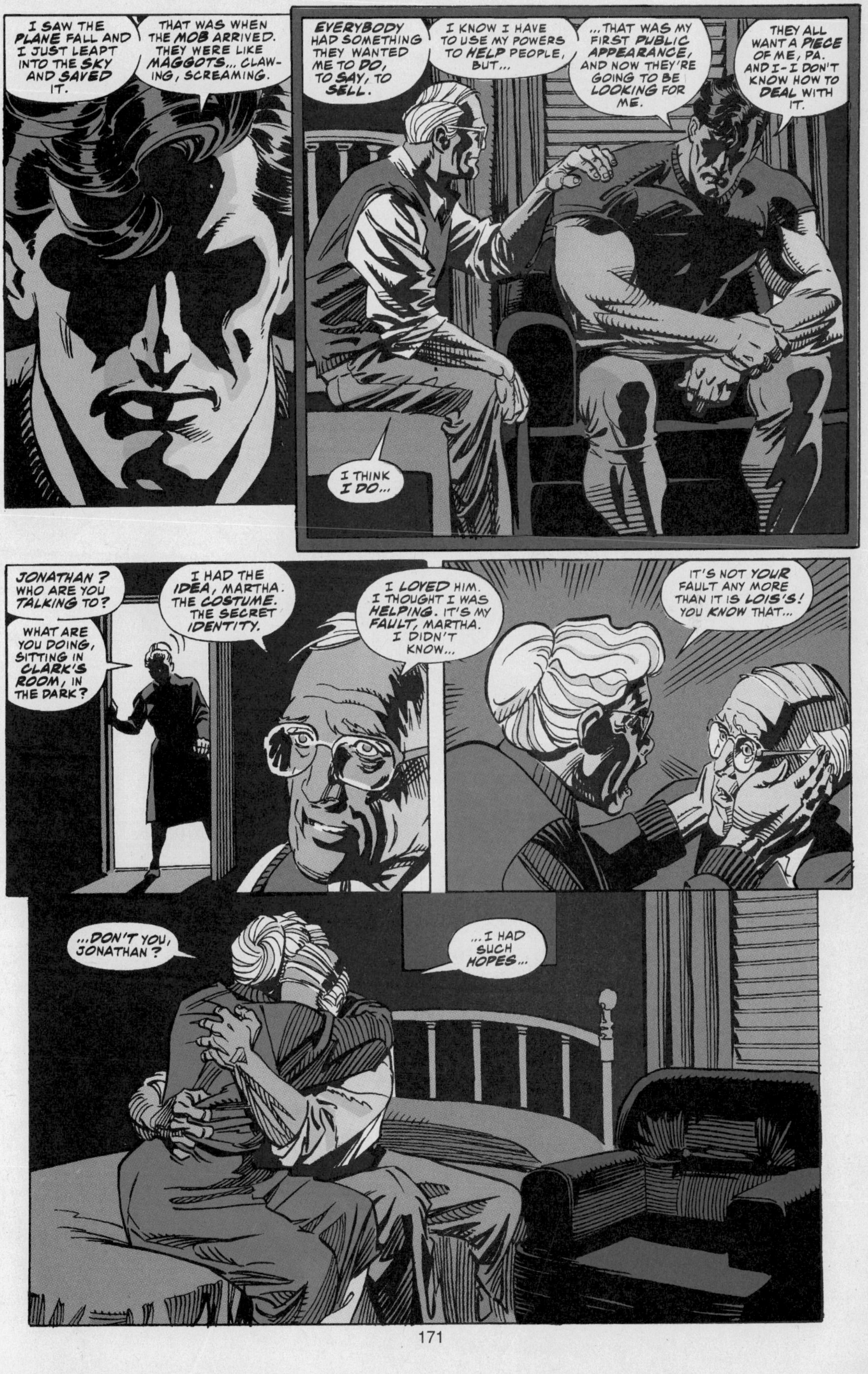
I SAW THE PLANE FALL AND I JUST LEAPT INTO THE SKY AND SAVED IT.
THAT WAS WHEN THE MOB ARRIVED. THEY WERE LIKE MAGGOTS... CLAW-ING, SCREAMING.
EVERYBODY HAD SOMETHING THEY WANTED ME TO DO, TO SAY, TO SELL.
I KNOW I HAVE TO USE MY POWERS TO HELP PEOPLE, BUT...
...THAT WAS MY FIRST PUBLIC APPEARANCE, AND NOW THEY'RE GOING TO BE LOOKING FOR ME.
THEY ALL WANT A PIECE OF ME, PA. AND I- I DON'T KNOW HOW TO DEAL WITH IT.
I THINK I DO...
JONATHAN? WHO ARE YOU TALKING TO?
WHAT ARE YOU DOING, SITTING IN CLARK'S ROOM, IN THE DARK?
I HAD THE IDEA, MARTHA. THE COSTUME. THE SECRET IDENTITY.
I LOVED HIM. I THOUGHT I WAS HELPING. IT'S MY FAULT, MARTHA. I DIDN'T KNOW...
IT'S NOT YOUR FAULT ANY MORE THAN IT IS LOIS'S! YOU KNOW THAT...
...DON'T YOU, JONATHAN?
...I HAD SUCH HOPES...

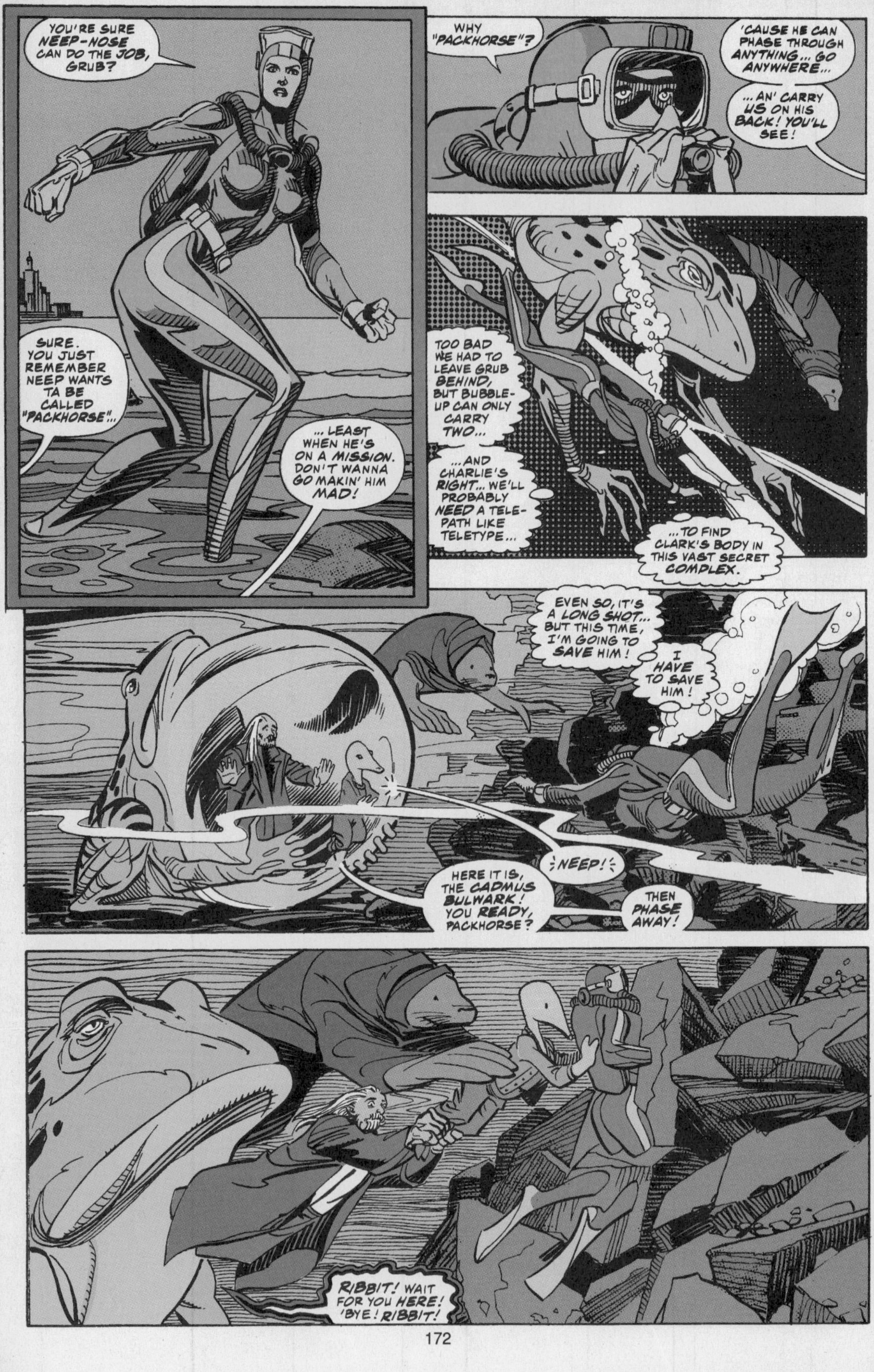
YOU'RE SURE NEEP-NOSE CAN DO THE JOB, GRUB?
SURE. YOU JUST REMEMBER NEEP WANTS TA BE CALLED "PACKHORSE"...
... LEAST WHEN HE'S ON A MISSION. DON'T WANNA GO MAKIN' HIM MAD!
WHY "PACKHORSE"?
'CAUSE HE CAN PHASE THROUGH ANYTHING... GO ANYWHERE...
... AN' CARRY US ON HIS BACK! YOU'LL SEE!
TOO BAD WE HAD TO LEAVE GRUB BEHIND, BUT BUBBLE-UP CAN ONLY CARRY TWO...
... AND CHARLIE'S RIGHT... WE'LL PROBABLY NEED A TELEPATH LIKE TELETYPE...
... TO FIND CLARK'S BODY IN THIS VAST SECRET COMPLEX.
EVEN SO, IT'S A LONG SHOT... BUT THIS TIME, I'M GOING TO SAVE HIM!
I HAVE TO SAVE HIM!
NEEP!
HERE IT IS, THE CADMUS BULWARK! YOU READY, PACKHORSE?
THEN PHASE AWAY!
RIBBIT! WAIT FOR YOU HERE! 'BYE! RIBBIT!

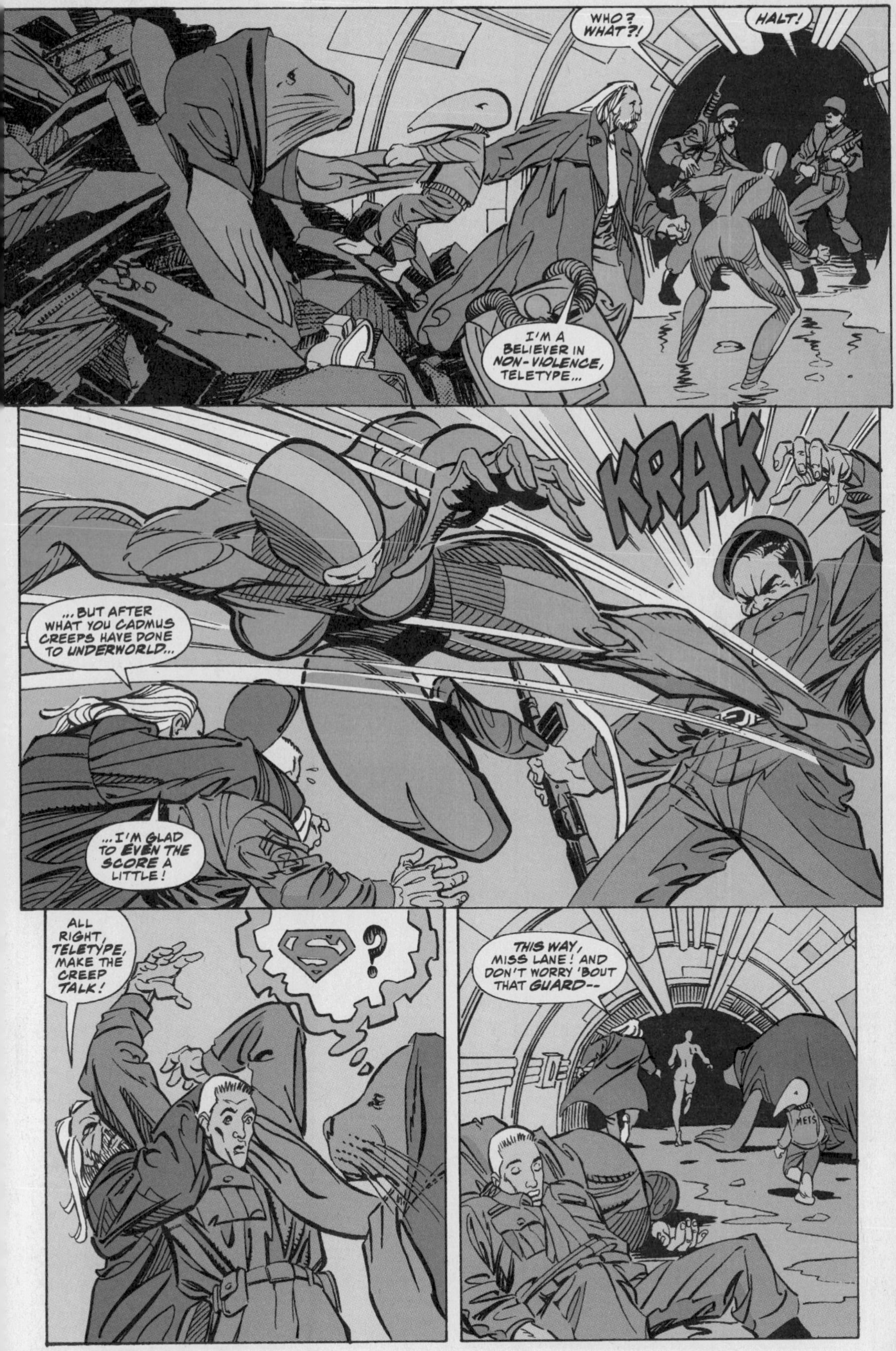
WHO? WHAT?!
HALT!
I'M A BELIEVER IN NON-VIOLENCE, TELETYPE...
KRAK
...BUT AFTER WHAT YOU CADMUS CREEPS HAVE DONE TO UNDERWORLD...
...I'M GLAD TO EVEN THE SCORE A LITTLE!
ALL RIGHT, TELETYPE, MAKE THE CREEP TALK!
?
THIS WAY, MISS LANE! AND DON'T WORRY 'BOUT THAT GUARD--

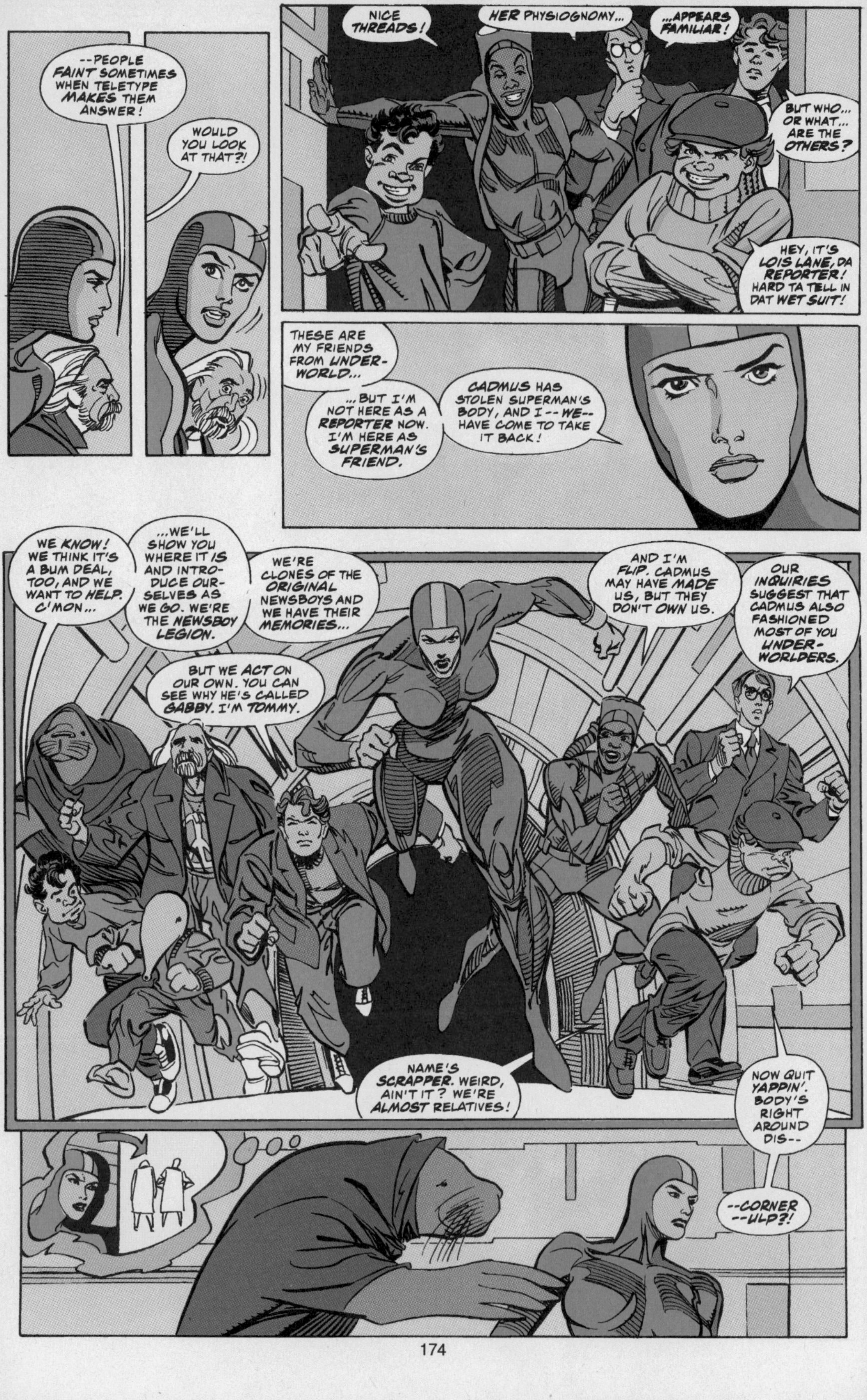
--PEOPLE FAINT SOMETIMES WHEN TELETYPE MAKES THEM ANSWER!
WOULD YOU LOOK AT THAT?!
NICE THREADS!
HER PHYSIOGNOMY...
...APPEARS FAMILIAR!
BUT WHO... OR WHAT... ARE THE OTHERS?
HEY, IT'S LOIS LANE, DA REPORTER! HARD TA TELL IN DAT WET SUIT!
THESE ARE MY FRIENDS FROM UNDER-WORLD...
...BUT I'M NOT HERE AS A REPORTER NOW. I'M HERE AS SUPERMAN'S FRIEND.
CADMUS HAS STOLEN SUPERMAN'S BODY, AND I--WE--HAVE COME TO TAKE IT BACK!
WE KNOW! WE THINK IT'S A BUM DEAL, TOO, AND WE WANT TO HELP. C'MON...
...WE'LL SHOW YOU WHERE IT IS AND INTRO-DUCE OUR-SELVES AS WE GO. WE'RE THE NEWSBOY LEGION.
WE'RE CLONES OF THE ORIGINAL NEWSBOYS AND WE HAVE THEIR MEMORIES...
BUT WE ACT ON OUR OWN. YOU CAN SEE WHY HE'S CALLED GABBY. I'M TOMMY.
AND I'M FLIP. CADMUS MAY HAVE MADE US, BUT THEY DON'T OWN US.
OUR INQUIRIES SUGGEST THAT CADMUS ALSO FASHIONED MOST OF YOU UNDER-WORLDERS.
NAME'S SCRAPPER. WEIRD, AIN'T IT? WE'RE ALMOST RELATIVES!
NOW QUIT YAPPIN'. BODY'S RIGHT AROUND DIS--
--CORNER --ULP?!

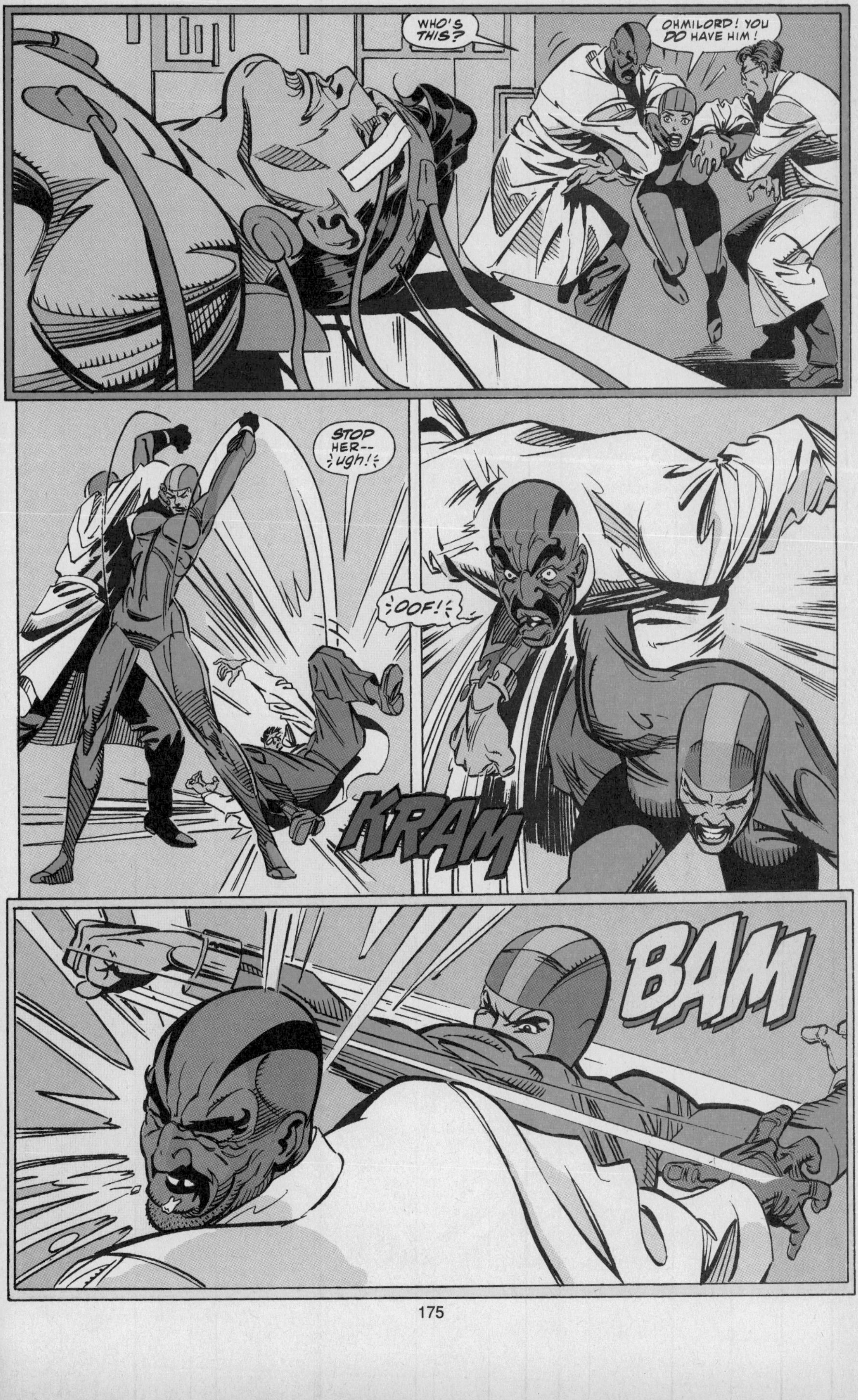
WHO'S THIS?
OHMILORD! YOU DO HAVE HIM!
STOP HER-- ugh!
OOF!
KRAM
BAM

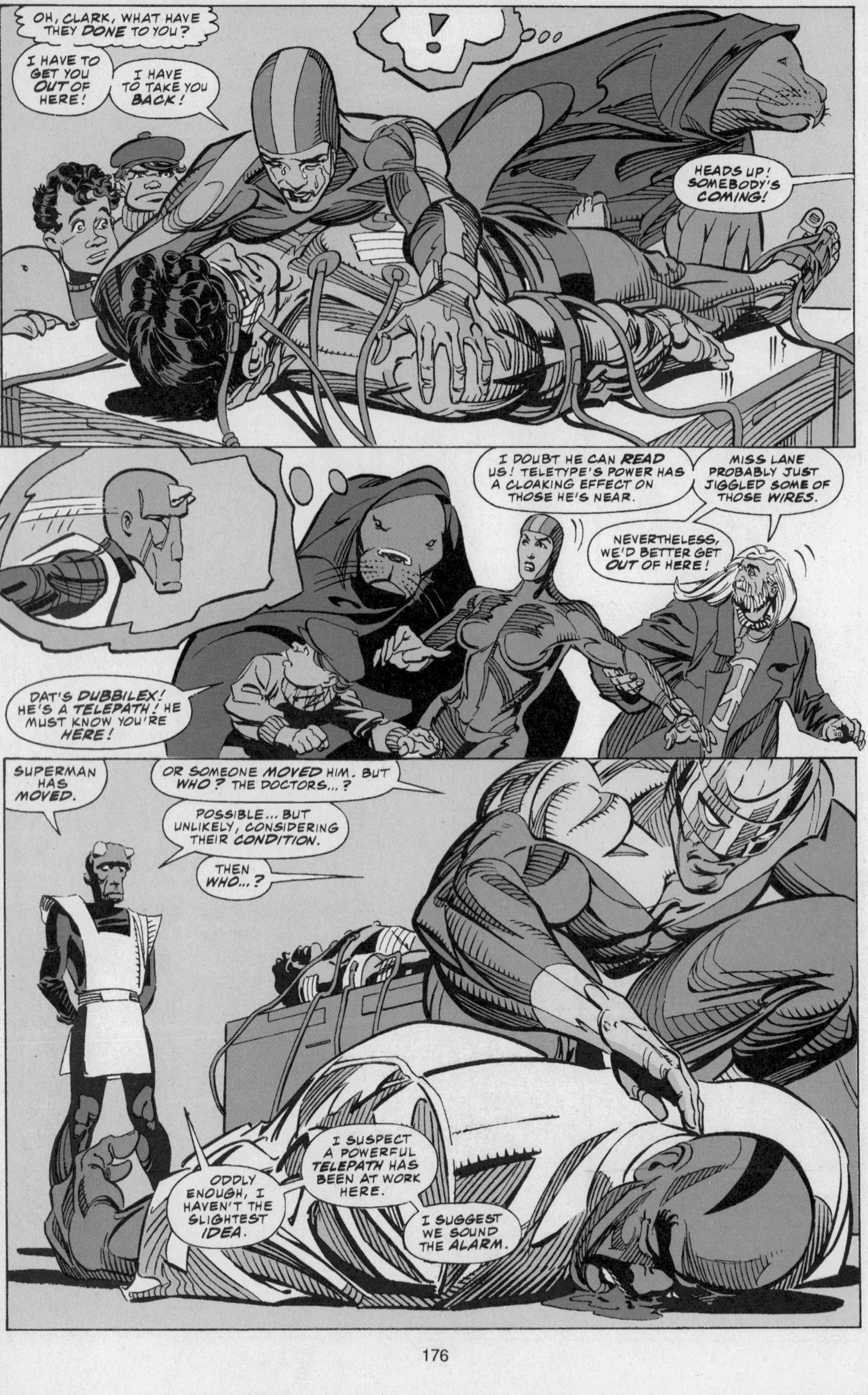
OH, CLARK, WHAT HAVE THEY DONE TO YOU?
I HAVE TO GET YOU OUT OF HERE!
I HAVE TO TAKE YOU BACK!
!
HEADS UP! SOMEBODY'S COMING!
DAT'S DUBBILEX! HE'S A TELEPATH! HE MUST KNOW YOU'RE HERE!
I DOUBT HE CAN READ US! TELETYPE'S POWER HAS A CLOAKING EFFECT ON THOSE HE'S NEAR.
MISS LANE PROBABLY JUST JIGGLED SOME OF THOSE WIRES.
NEVERTHELESS, WE'D BETTER GET OUT OF HERE!
SUPERMAN HAS MOVED.
OR SOMEONE MOVED HIM. BUT WHO? THE DOCTORS...?
POSSIBLE... BUT UNLIKELY, CONSIDERING THEIR CONDITION.
THEN WHO...?
ODDLY ENOUGH, I HAVEN'T THE SLIGHTEST IDEA.
I SUSPECT A POWERFUL TELEPATH HAS BEEN AT WORK HERE.
I SUGGEST WE SOUND THE ALARM.

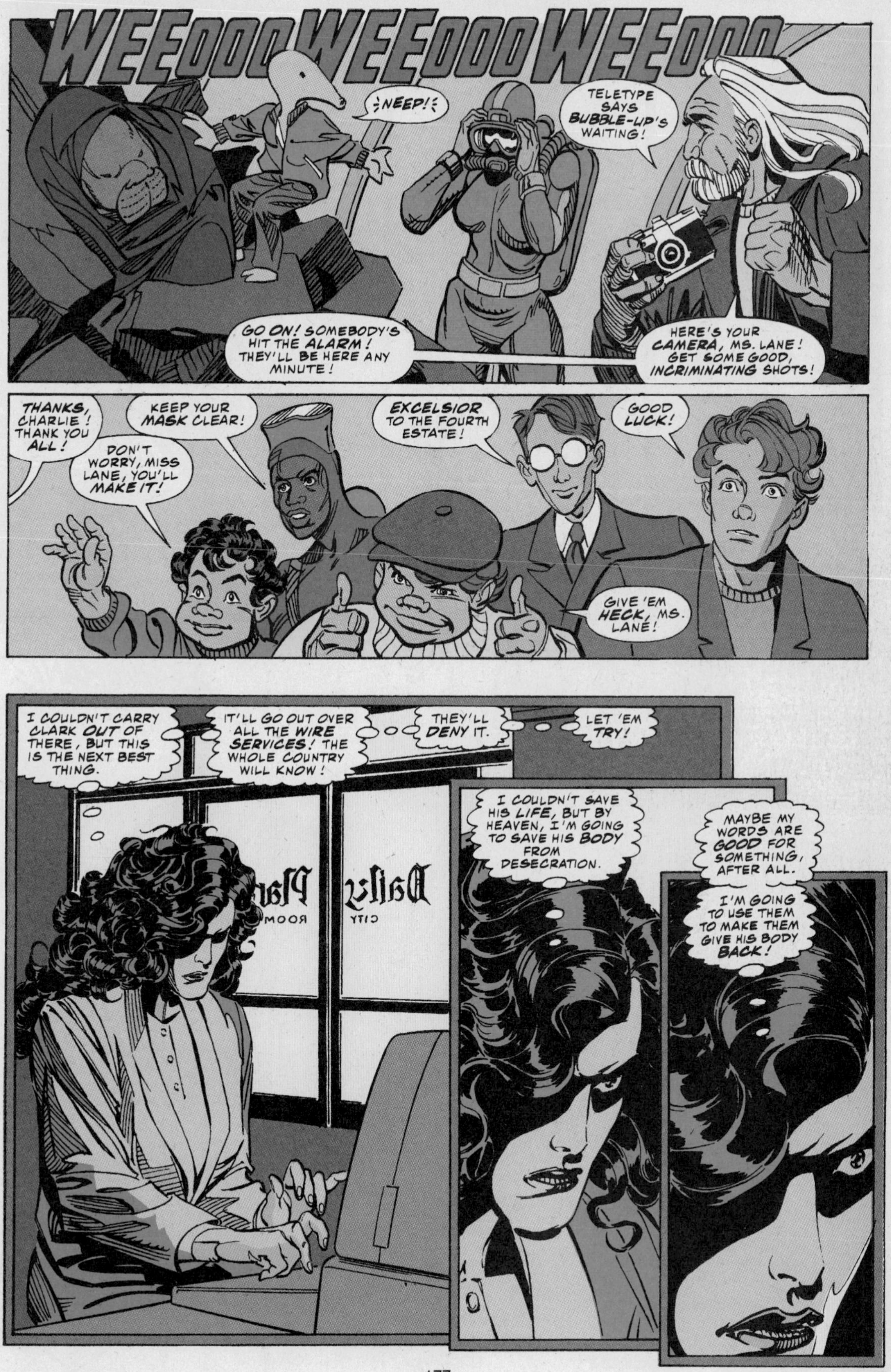
WEEOOOWEEOOOWEEOOO
NEEP!
TELETYPE SAYS BUBBLE-UP'S WAITING!
GO ON! SOMEBODY'S HIT THE ALARM! THEY'LL BE HERE ANY MINUTE!
HERE'S YOUR CAMERA, MS. LANE! GET SOME GOOD, INCRIMINATING SHOTS!
THANKS, CHARLIE! THANK YOU ALL!
KEEP YOUR MASK CLEAR!
DON'T WORRY, MISS LANE, YOU'LL MAKE IT!
EXCELSIOR TO THE FOURTH ESTATE!
GOOD LUCK!
GIVE 'EM HECK, MS. LANE!
I COULDN'T CARRY CLARK OUT OF THERE, BUT THIS IS THE NEXT BEST THING.
IT'LL GO OUT OVER ALL THE WIRE SERVICES! THE WHOLE COUNTRY WILL KNOW!
THEY'LL DENY IT.
LET 'EM TRY!
I COULDN'T SAVE HIS LIFE, BUT BY HEAVEN, I'M GOING TO SAVE HIS BODY FROM DESECRATION.
MAYBE MY WORDS ARE GOOD FOR SOMETHING, AFTER ALL.
I'M GOING TO USE THEM TO MAKE THEM GIVE HIS BODY BACK!

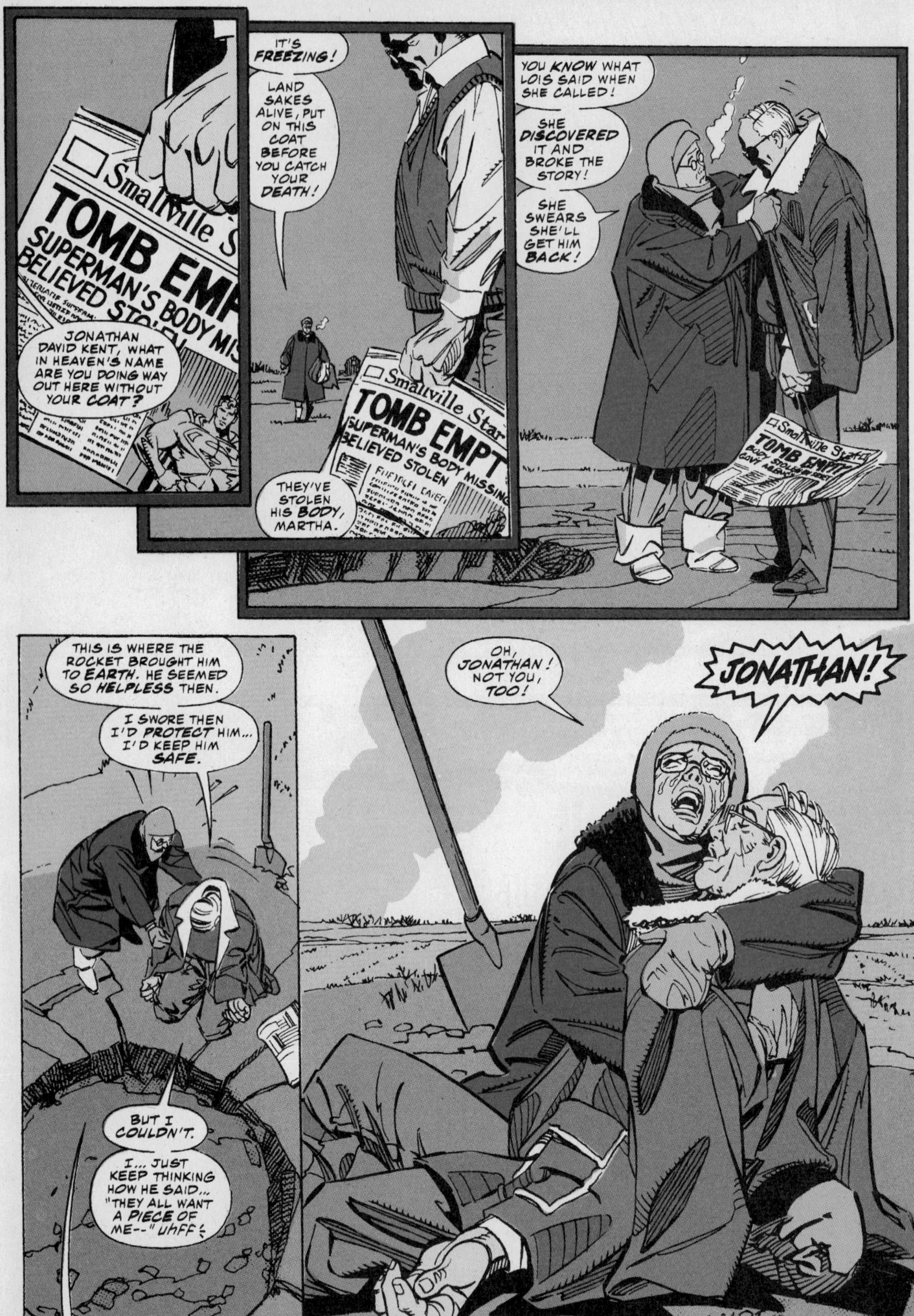
Smallville Star
TOMB EMPTY
SUPERMAN'S BODY MISSING
BELIEVED STOLEN
JONATHAN DAVID KENT, WHAT IN HEAVEN'S NAME ARE YOU DOING WAY OUT HERE WITHOUT YOUR COAT?
IT'S FREEZING!
LAND SAKES ALIVE, PUT ON THIS COAT BEFORE YOU CATCH YOUR DEATH!
THEY'VE STOLEN HIS BODY, MARTHA.
YOU KNOW WHAT LOIS SAID WHEN SHE CALLED!
SHE DISCOVERED IT AND BROKE THE STORY!
SHE SWEARS SHE'LL GET HIM BACK!
THIS IS WHERE THE ROCKET BROUGHT HIM TO EARTH. HE SEEMED SO HELPLESS THEN.
I SWORE THEN I'D PROTECT HIM... I'D KEEP HIM SAFE.
BUT I COULDN'T.
I... JUST KEEP THINKING HOW HE SAID... "THEY ALL WANT A PIECE OF ME--" UHFF!
JONATHAN ??!
OH, JONATHAN! NOT YOU, TOO!
JONATHAN!
END

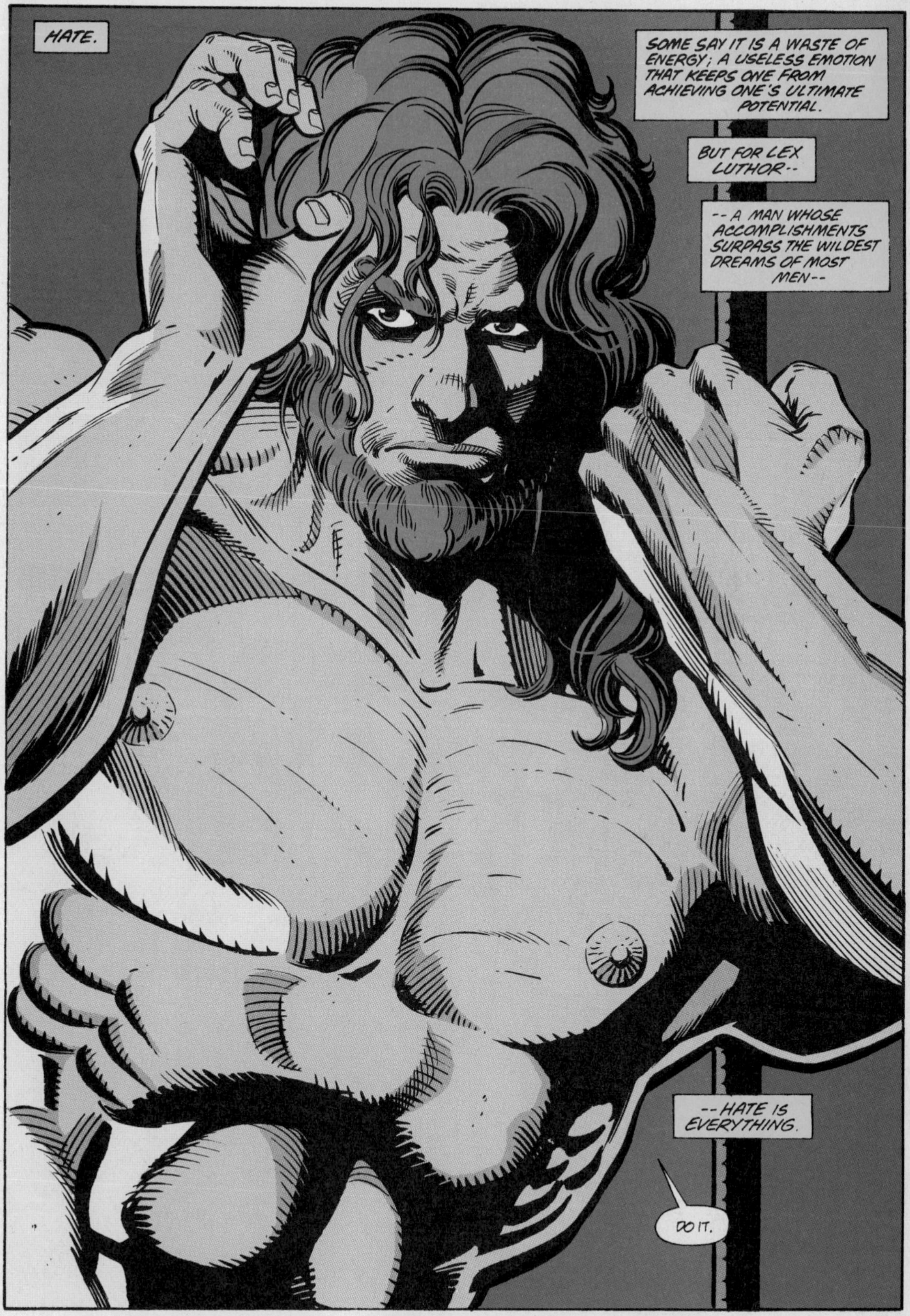
HATE.
SOME SAY IT IS A WASTE OF ENERGY; A USELESS EMOTION THAT KEEPS ONE FROM ACHIEVING ONE'S ULTIMATE POTENTIAL.
BUT FOR LEX LUTHOR--
--A MAN WHOSE ACCOMPLISHMENTS SURPASS THE WILDEST DREAMS OF MOST MEN--
--HATE IS EVERYTHING.
DO IT.

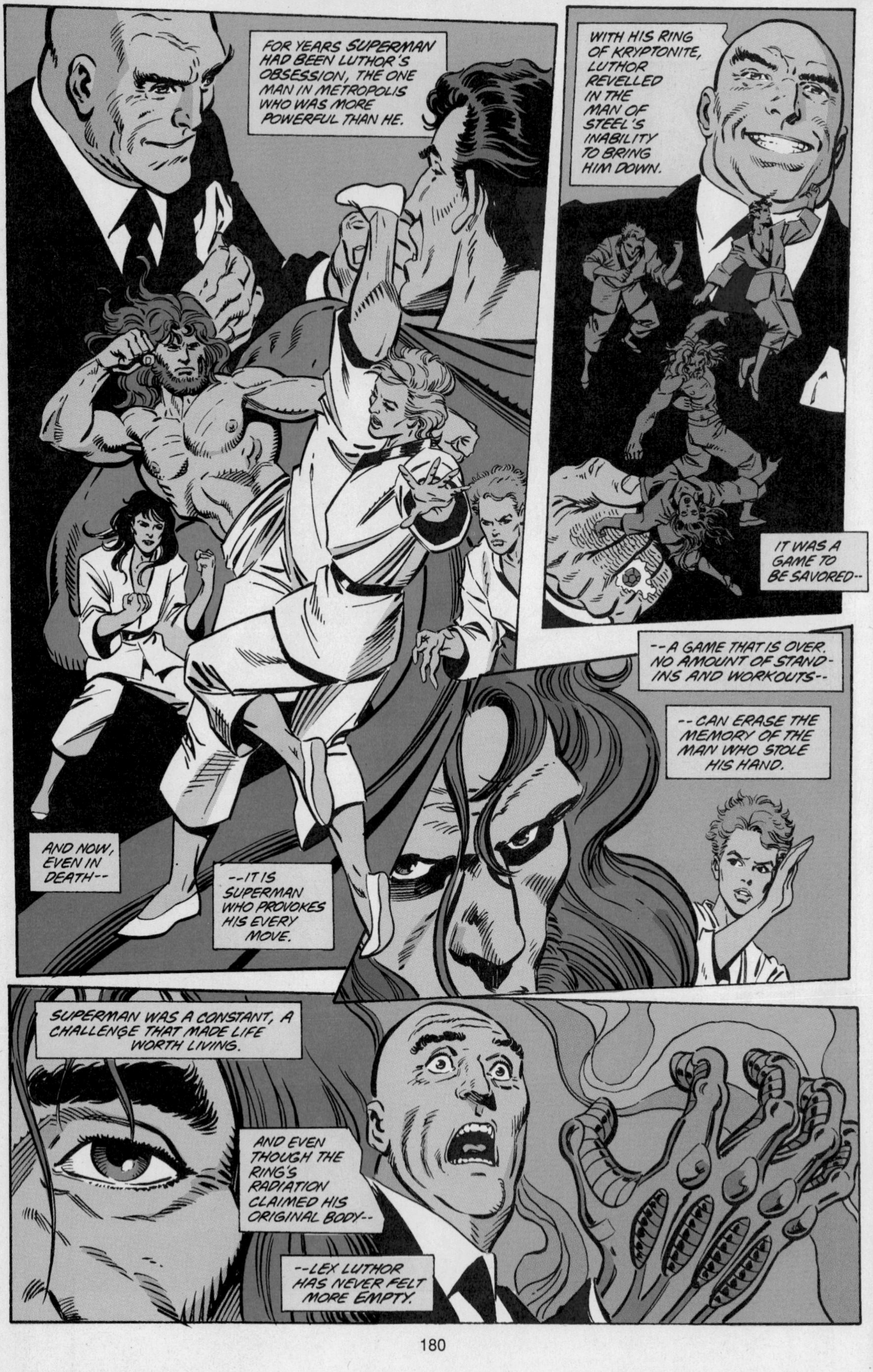
FOR YEARS SUPERMAN HAD BEEN LUTHOR'S OBSESSION, THE ONE MAN IN METROPOLIS WHO WAS MORE POWERFUL THAN HE.
WITH HIS RING OF KRYPTONITE, LUTHOR REVELLED IN THE MAN OF STEEL'S INABILITY TO BRING HIM DOWN.
IT WAS A GAME TO BE SAVORED--
AND NOW, EVEN IN DEATH--
--IT IS SUPERMAN WHO PROVOKES HIS EVERY MOVE.
--A GAME THAT IS OVER. NO AMOUNT OF STAND-INS AND WORKOUTS--
--CAN ERASE THE MEMORY OF THE MAN WHO STOLE HIS HAND.
SUPERMAN WAS A CONSTANT, A CHALLENGE THAT MADE LIFE WORTH LIVING.
AND EVEN THOUGH THE RING'S RADIATION CLAIMED HIS ORIGINAL BODY--
--LEX LUTHOR HAS NEVER FELT MORE EMPTY.

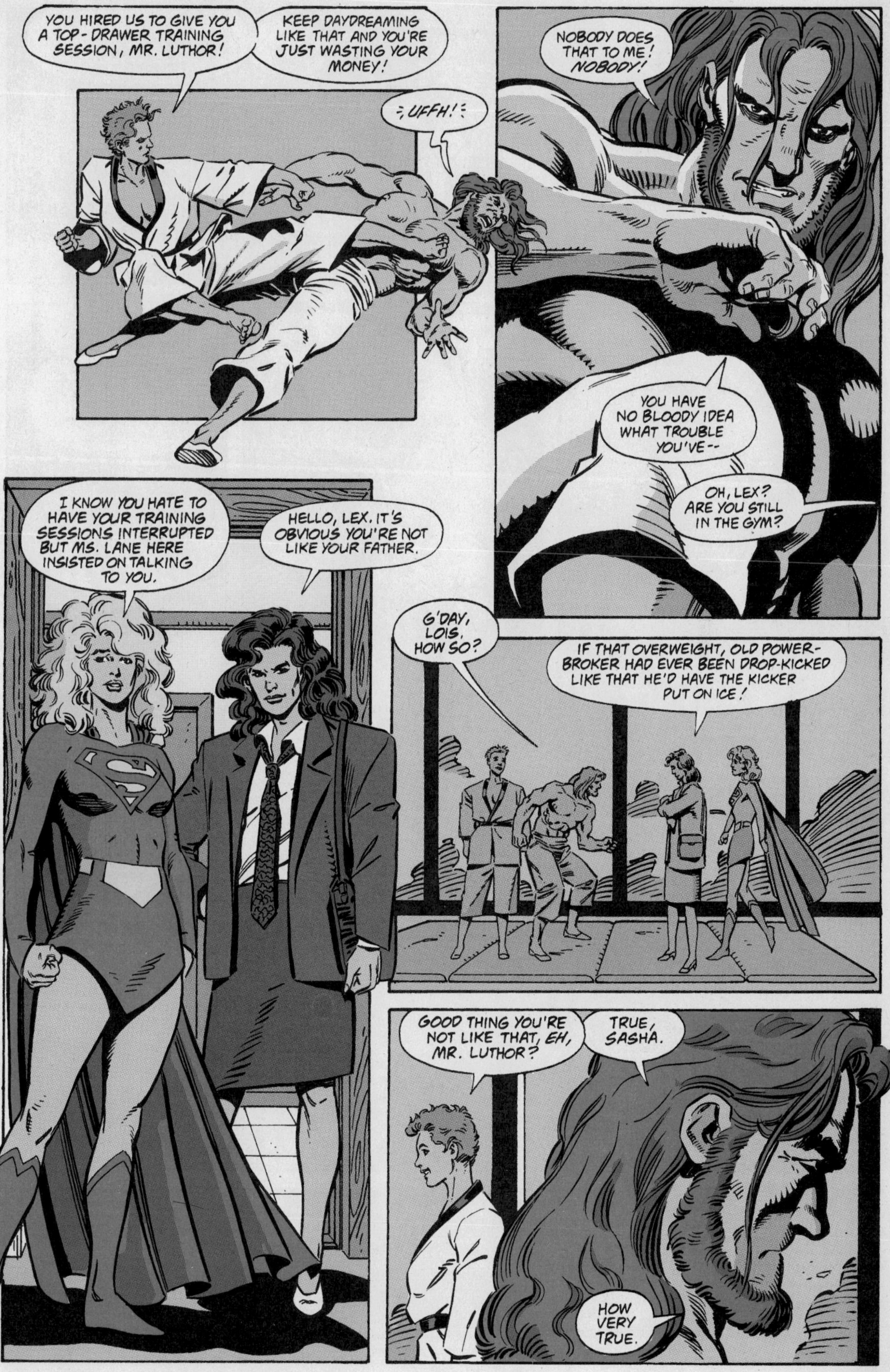
YOU HIRED US TO GIVE YOU A TOP-DRAWER TRAINING SESSION, MR. LUTHOR!
KEEP DAYDREAMING LIKE THAT AND YOU'RE JUST WASTING YOUR MONEY!
UFFH!
NOBODY DOES THAT TO ME! NOBODY!
YOU HAVE NO BLOODY IDEA WHAT TROUBLE YOU'VE--
OH, LEX? ARE YOU STILL IN THE GYM?
I KNOW YOU HATE TO HAVE YOUR TRAINING SESSIONS INTERRUPTED BUT MS. LANE HERE INSISTED ON TALKING TO YOU.
HELLO, LEX. IT'S OBVIOUS YOU'RE NOT LIKE YOUR FATHER.
G'DAY, LOIS. HOW SO?
IF THAT OVERWEIGHT, OLD POWER-BROKER HAD EVER BEEN DROP-KICKED LIKE THAT HE'D HAVE THE KICKER PUT ON ICE!
GOOD THING YOU'RE NOT LIKE THAT, EH, MR. LUTHOR?
TRUE, SASHA.
HOW VERY TRUE.

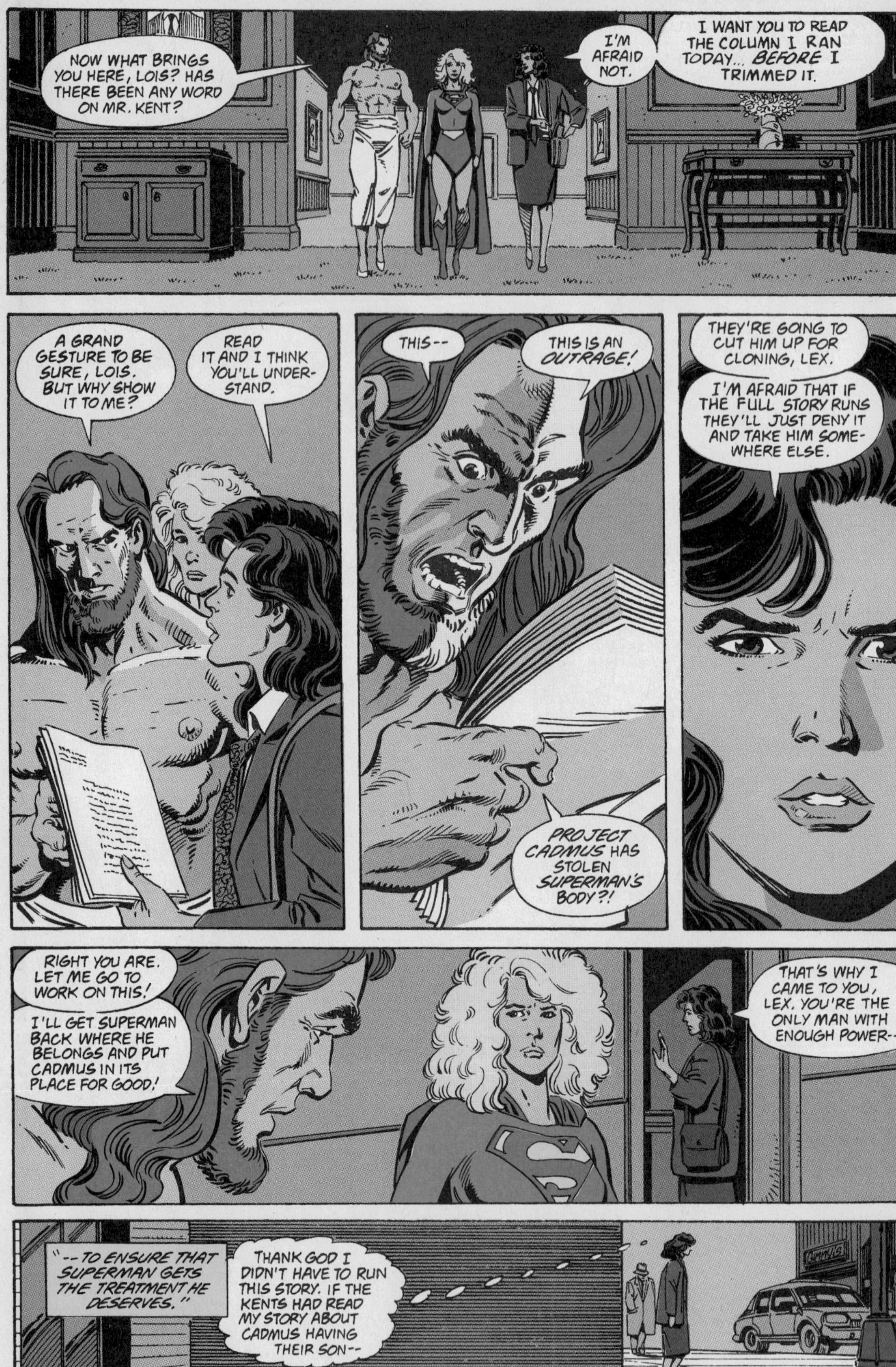
NOW WHAT BRINGS YOU HERE, LOIS? HAS THERE BEEN ANY WORD ON MR. KENT?
I'M AFRAID NOT.
I WANT YOU TO READ THE COLUMN I RAN TODAY... BEFORE I TRIMMED IT.
A GRAND GESTURE TO BE SURE, LOIS. BUT WHY SHOW IT TO ME?
READ IT AND I THINK YOU'LL UNDERSTAND.
THIS--
THIS IS AN OUTRAGE!
PROJECT CADMUS HAS STOLEN SUPERMAN'S BODY?!
THEY'RE GOING TO CUT HIM UP FOR CLONING, LEX.
I'M AFRAID THAT IF THE FULL STORY RUNS THEY'LL JUST DENY IT AND TAKE HIM SOMEWHERE ELSE.
RIGHT YOU ARE. LET ME GO TO WORK ON THIS!
I'LL GET SUPERMAN BACK WHERE HE BELONGS AND PUT CADMUS IN ITS PLACE FOR GOOD!
THAT'S WHY I CAME TO YOU, LEX. YOU'RE THE ONLY MAN WITH ENOUGH POWER--
"--TO ENSURE THAT SUPERMAN GETS THE TREATMENT HE DESERVES."
THANK GOD I DIDN'T HAVE TO RUN THIS STORY. IF THE KENTS HAD READ MY STORY ABOUT CADMUS HAVING THEIR SON--

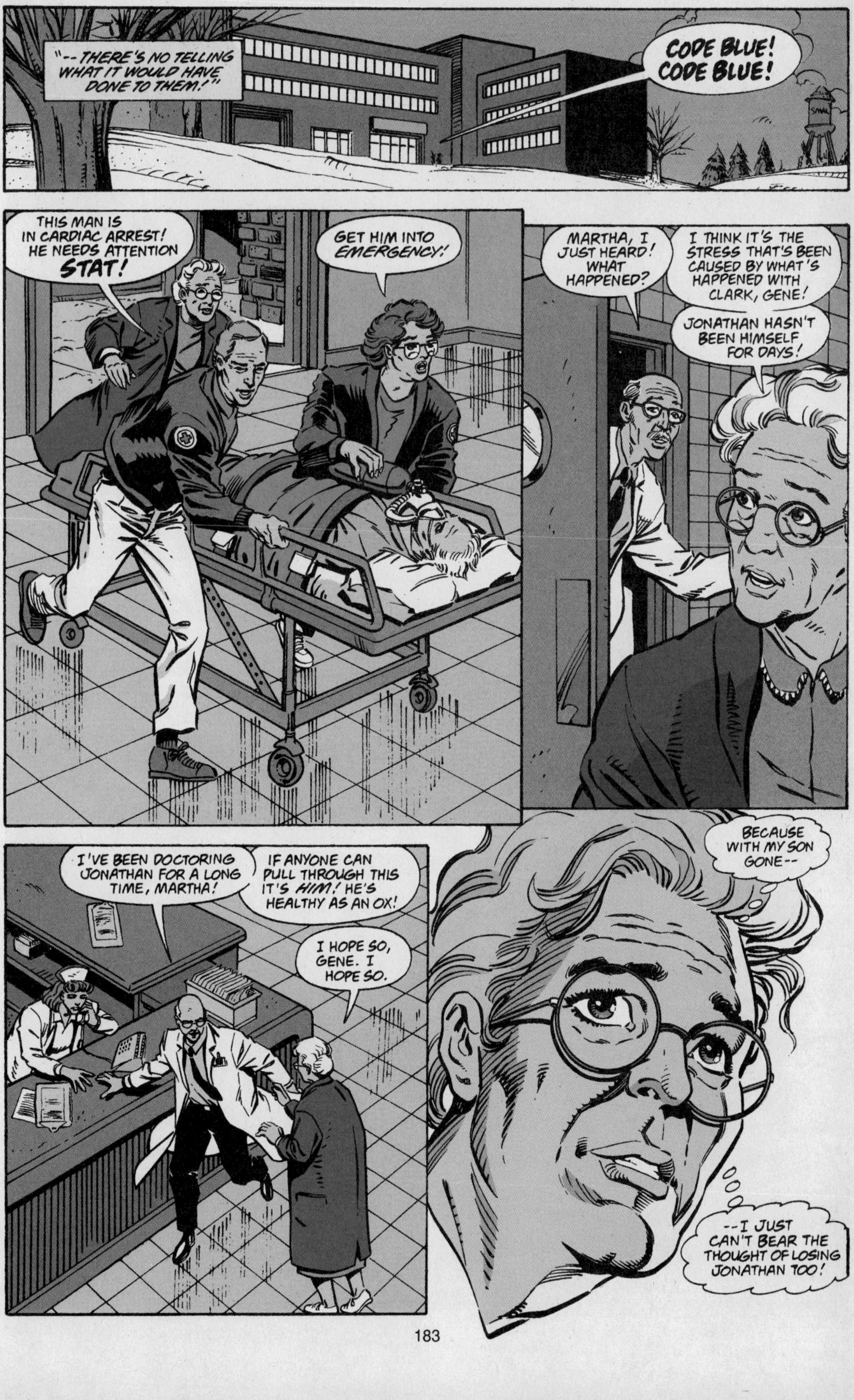
"--THERE'S NO TELLING WHAT IT WOULD HAVE DONE TO THEM!"
CODE BLUE! CODE BLUE!
THIS MAN IS IN CARDIAC ARREST! HE NEEDS ATTENTION STAT!
GET HIM INTO EMERGENCY!
MARTHA, I JUST HEARD! WHAT HAPPENED?
I THINK IT'S THE STRESS THAT'S BEEN CAUSED BY WHAT'S HAPPENED WITH CLARK, GENE!
JONATHAN HASN'T BEEN HIMSELF FOR DAYS!
I'VE BEEN DOCTORING JONATHAN FOR A LONG TIME, MARTHA!
IF ANYONE CAN PULL THROUGH THIS IT'S HIM! HE'S HEALTHY AS AN OX!
I HOPE SO, GENE. I HOPE SO.
BECAUSE WITH MY SON GONE--
--I JUST CAN'T BEAR THE THOUGHT OF LOSING JONATHAN TOO!

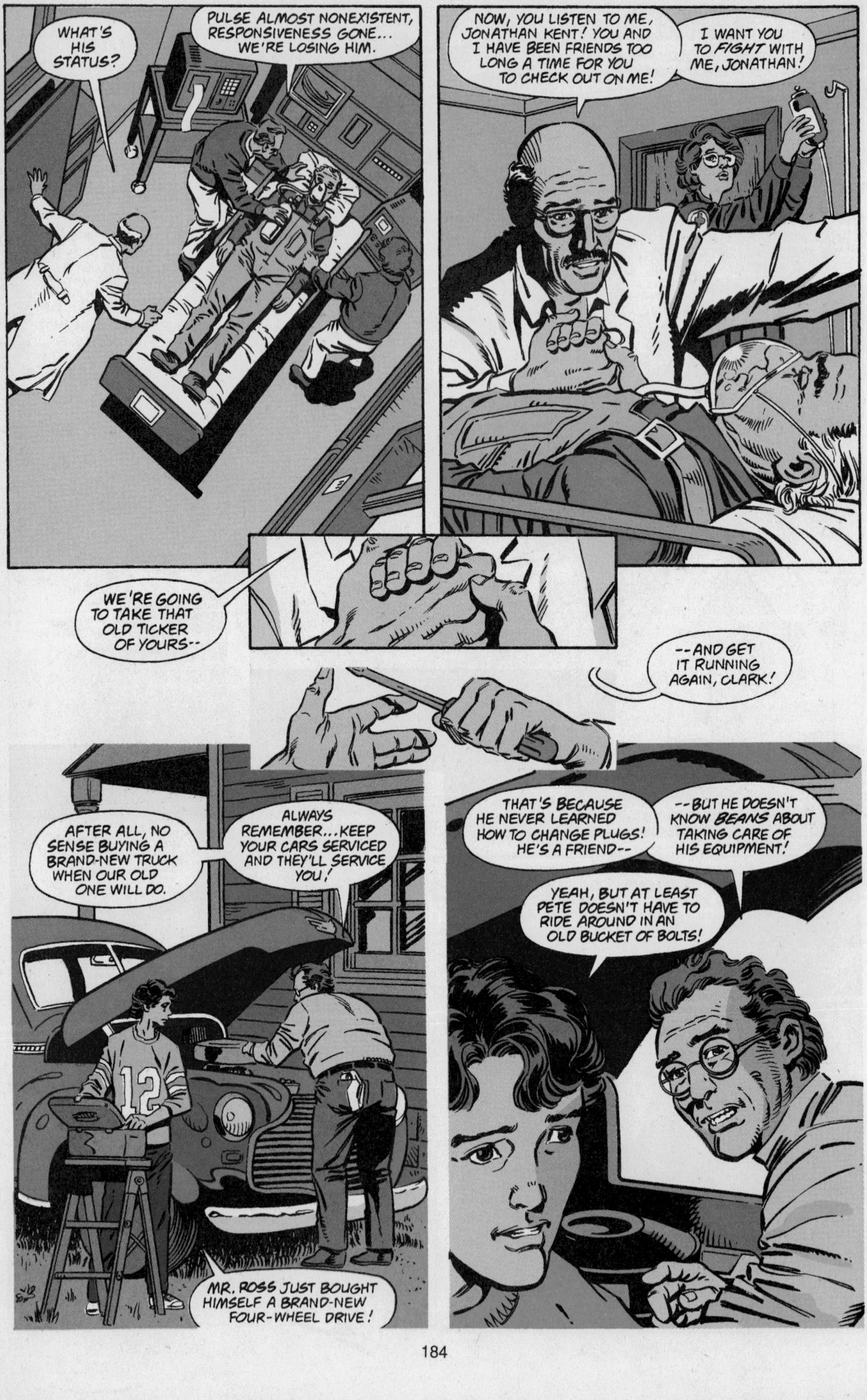
WHAT'S HIS STATUS?
PULSE ALMOST NONEXISTENT, RESPONSIVENESS GONE... WE'RE LOSING HIM.
NOW, YOU LISTEN TO ME, JONATHAN KENT! YOU AND I HAVE BEEN FRIENDS TOO LONG A TIME FOR YOU TO CHECK OUT ON ME!
I WANT YOU TO FIGHT WITH ME, JONATHAN!
WE'RE GOING TO TAKE THAT OLD TICKER OF YOURS--
--AND GET IT RUNNING AGAIN, CLARK!
AFTER ALL, NO SENSE BUYING A BRAND-NEW TRUCK WHEN OUR OLD ONE WILL DO.
ALWAYS REMEMBER... KEEP YOUR CARS SERVICED AND THEY'LL SERVICE YOU!
MR. ROSS JUST BOUGHT HIMSELF A BRAND-NEW FOUR-WHEEL DRIVE!
THAT'S BECAUSE HE NEVER LEARNED HOW TO CHANGE PLUGS! HE'S A FRIEND--
--BUT HE DOESN'T KNOW BEANS ABOUT TAKING CARE OF HIS EQUIPMENT!
YEAH, BUT AT LEAST PETE DOESN'T HAVE TO RIDE AROUND IN AN OLD BUCKET OF BOLTS!

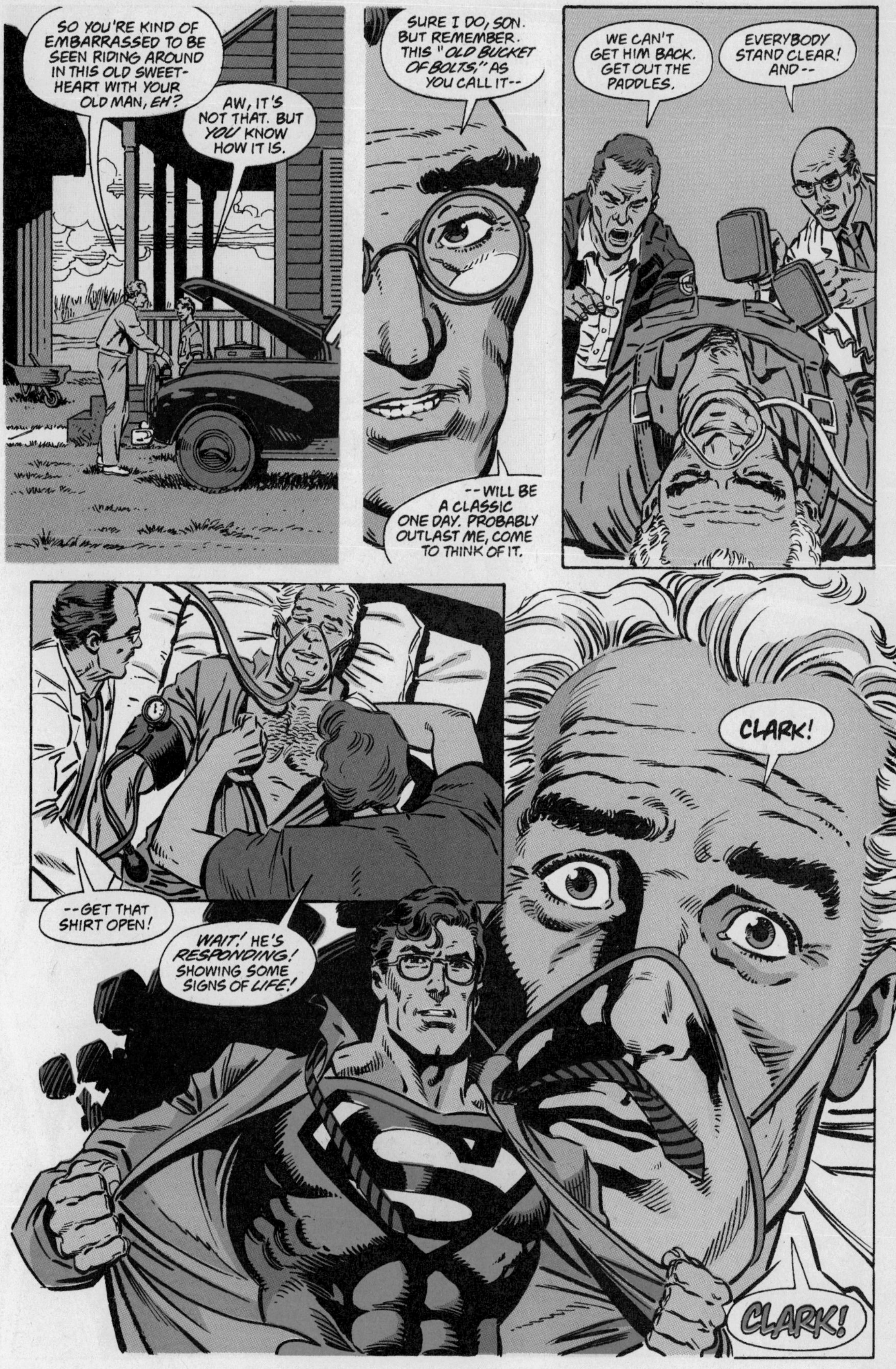
SO YOU'RE KIND OF EMBARRASSED TO BE SEEN RIDING AROUND IN THIS OLD SWEET-HEART WITH YOUR OLD MAN, EH?
AW, IT'S NOT THAT. BUT YOU KNOW HOW IT IS.
SURE I DO, SON. BUT REMEMBER. THIS "OLD BUCKET OF BOLTS," AS YOU CALL IT--
--WILL BE A CLASSIC ONE DAY. PROBABLY OUTLAST ME, COME TO THINK OF IT.
WE CAN'T GET HIM BACK. GET OUT THE PADDLES.
EVERYBODY STAND CLEAR! AND--
--GET THAT SHIRT OPEN!
WAIT! HE'S RESPONDING! SHOWING SOME SIGNS OF LIFE!
CLARK!
CLARK!

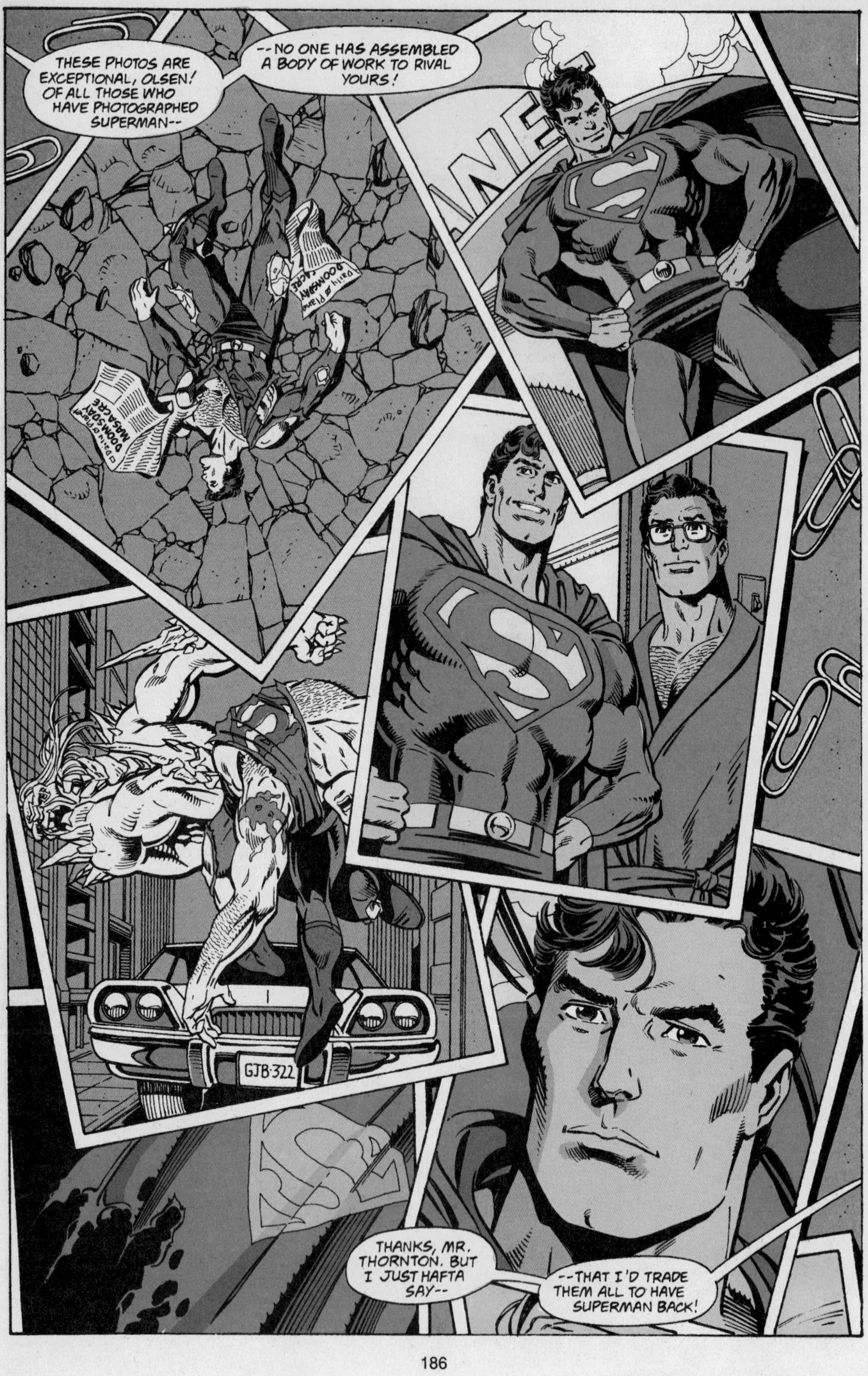
THESE PHOTOS ARE EXCEPTIONAL, OLSEN! OF ALL THOSE WHO HAVE PHOTOGRAPHED SUPERMAN--
--NO ONE HAS ASSEMBLED A BODY OF WORK TO RIVAL YOURS!
GJB-322
THANKS, MR. THORNTON. BUT I JUST HAFTA SAY--
--THAT I'D TRADE THEM ALL TO HAVE SUPERMAN BACK!

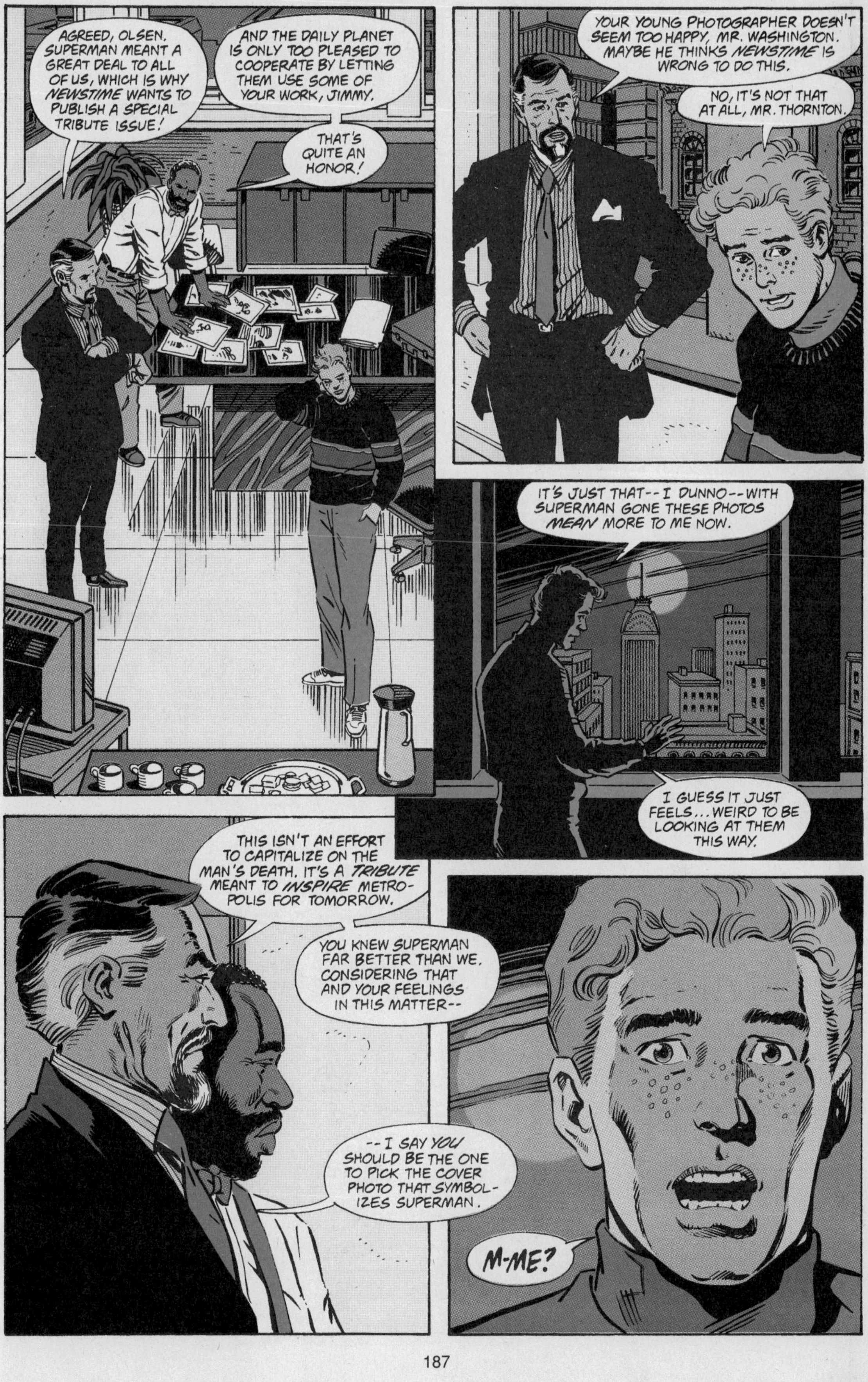
AGREED, OLSEN. SUPERMAN MEANT A GREAT DEAL TO ALL OF US, WHICH IS WHY NEWSTIME WANTS TO PUBLISH A SPECIAL TRIBUTE ISSUE!
AND THE DAILY PLANET IS ONLY TOO PLEASED TO COOPERATE BY LETTING THEM USE SOME OF YOUR WORK, JIMMY.
THAT'S QUITE AN HONOR!
YOUR YOUNG PHOTOGRAPHER DOESN'T SEEM TOO HAPPY, MR. WASHINGTON. MAYBE HE THINKS NEWSTIME IS WRONG TO DO THIS.
NO, IT'S NOT THAT AT ALL, MR. THORNTON.
IT'S JUST THAT-- I DUNNO-- WITH SUPERMAN GONE THESE PHOTOS MEAN MORE TO ME NOW.
I GUESS IT JUST FEELS... WEIRD TO BE LOOKING AT THEM THIS WAY.
THIS ISN'T AN EFFORT TO CAPITALIZE ON THE MAN'S DEATH. IT'S A TRIBUTE MEANT TO INSPIRE METROPOLIS FOR TOMORROW.
YOU KNEW SUPERMAN FAR BETTER THAN WE. CONSIDERING THAT AND YOUR FEELINGS IN THIS MATTER--
-- I SAY YOU SHOULD BE THE ONE TO PICK THE COVER PHOTO THAT SYMBOLIZES SUPERMAN.
M-ME?

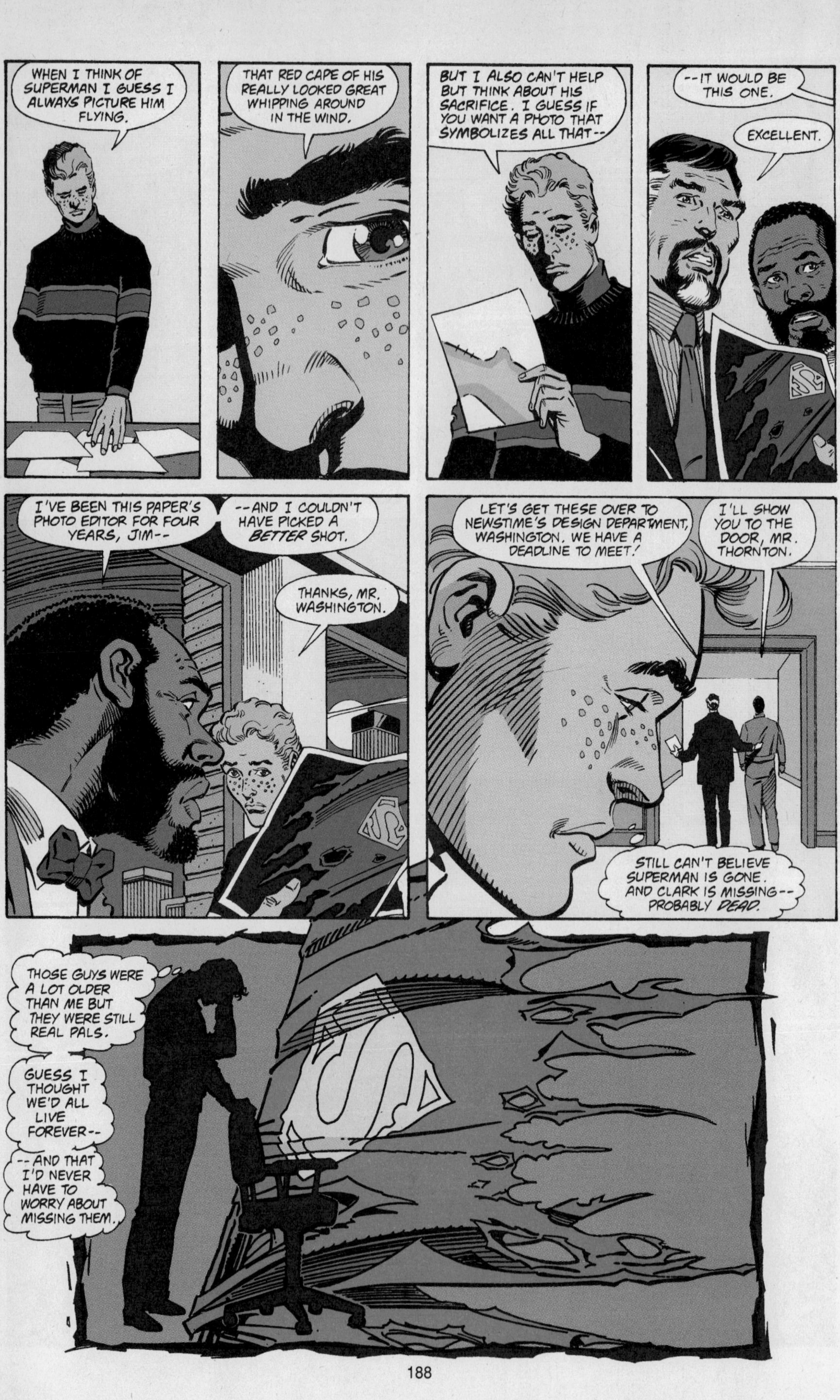
WHEN I THINK OF SUPERMAN I GUESS I ALWAYS PICTURE HIM FLYING.
THAT RED CAPE OF HIS REALLY LOOKED GREAT WHIPPING AROUND IN THE WIND.
BUT I ALSO CAN'T HELP BUT THINK ABOUT HIS SACRIFICE. I GUESS IF YOU WANT A PHOTO THAT SYMBOLIZES ALL THAT--
--IT WOULD BE THIS ONE.
EXCELLENT.
I'VE BEEN THIS PAPER'S PHOTO EDITOR FOR FOUR YEARS, JIM--
--AND I COULDN'T HAVE PICKED A BETTER SHOT.
THANKS, MR. WASHINGTON.
LET'S GET THESE OVER TO NEWSTIME'S DESIGN DEPARTMENT, WASHINGTON. WE HAVE A DEADLINE TO MEET.'
I'LL SHOW YOU TO THE DOOR, MR. THORNTON.
STILL CAN'T BELIEVE SUPERMAN IS GONE. AND CLARK IS MISSING--PROBABLY DEAD.
THOSE GUYS WERE A LOT OLDER THAN ME BUT THEY WERE STILL REAL PALS.
GUESS I THOUGHT WE'D ALL LIVE FOREVER--
--AND THAT I'D NEVER HAVE TO WORRY ABOUT MISSING THEM.

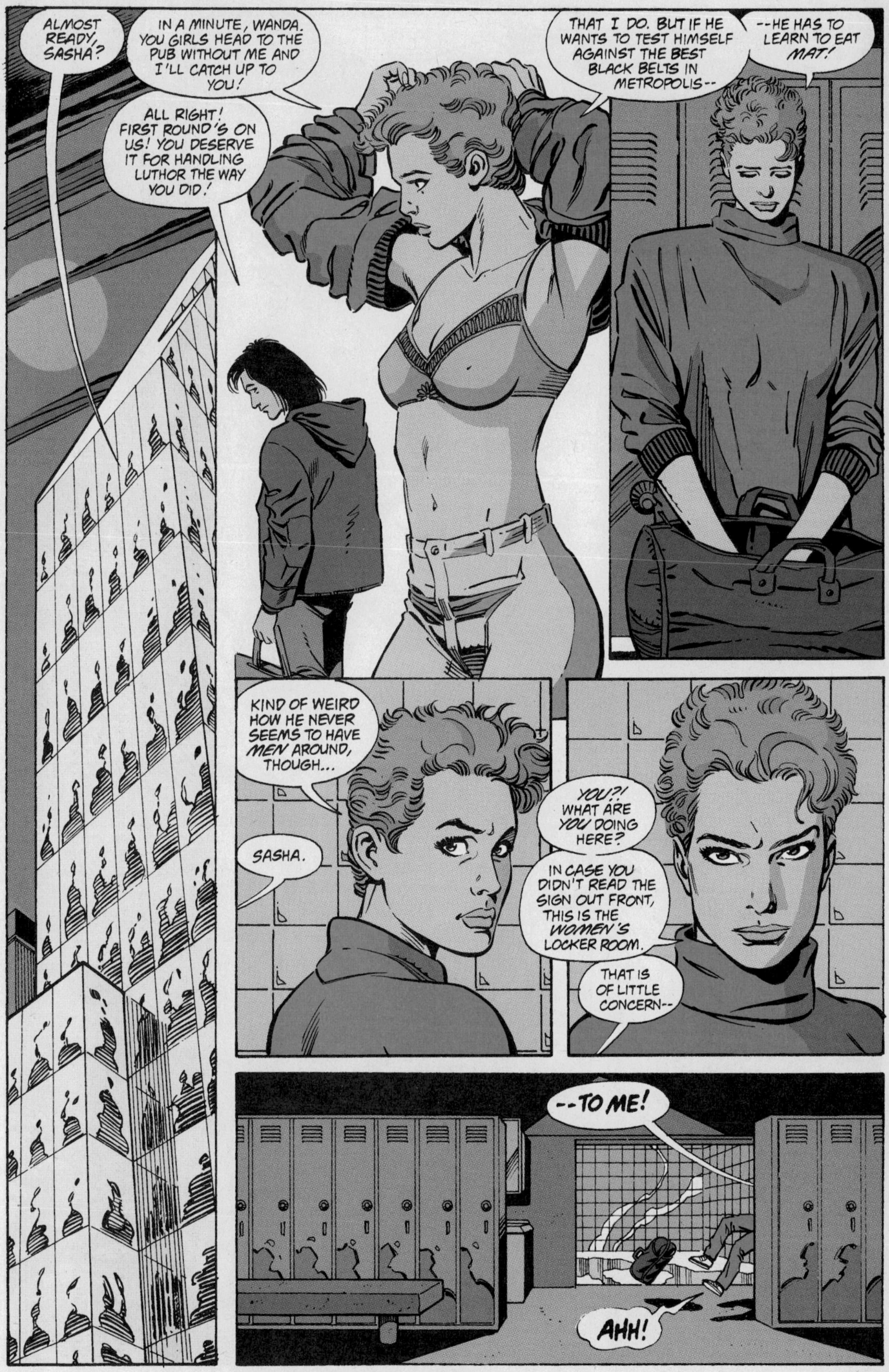
ALMOST READY, SASHA?
IN A MINUTE, WANDA. YOU GIRLS HEAD TO THE PUB WITHOUT ME AND I'LL CATCH UP TO YOU!
ALL RIGHT! FIRST ROUND'S ON US! YOU DESERVE IT FOR HANDLING LUTHOR THE WAY YOU DID!
THAT I DO. BUT IF HE WANTS TO TEST HIMSELF AGAINST THE BEST BLACK BELTS IN METROPOLIS--
--HE HAS TO LEARN TO EAT MAT!
KIND OF WEIRD HOW HE NEVER SEEMS TO HAVE MEN AROUND, THOUGH...
SASHA.
YOU?! WHAT ARE YOU DOING HERE?
IN CASE YOU DIDN'T READ THE SIGN OUT FRONT, THIS IS THE WOMEN'S LOCKER ROOM.
THAT IS OF LITTLE CONCERN--
--TO ME!
AHH!

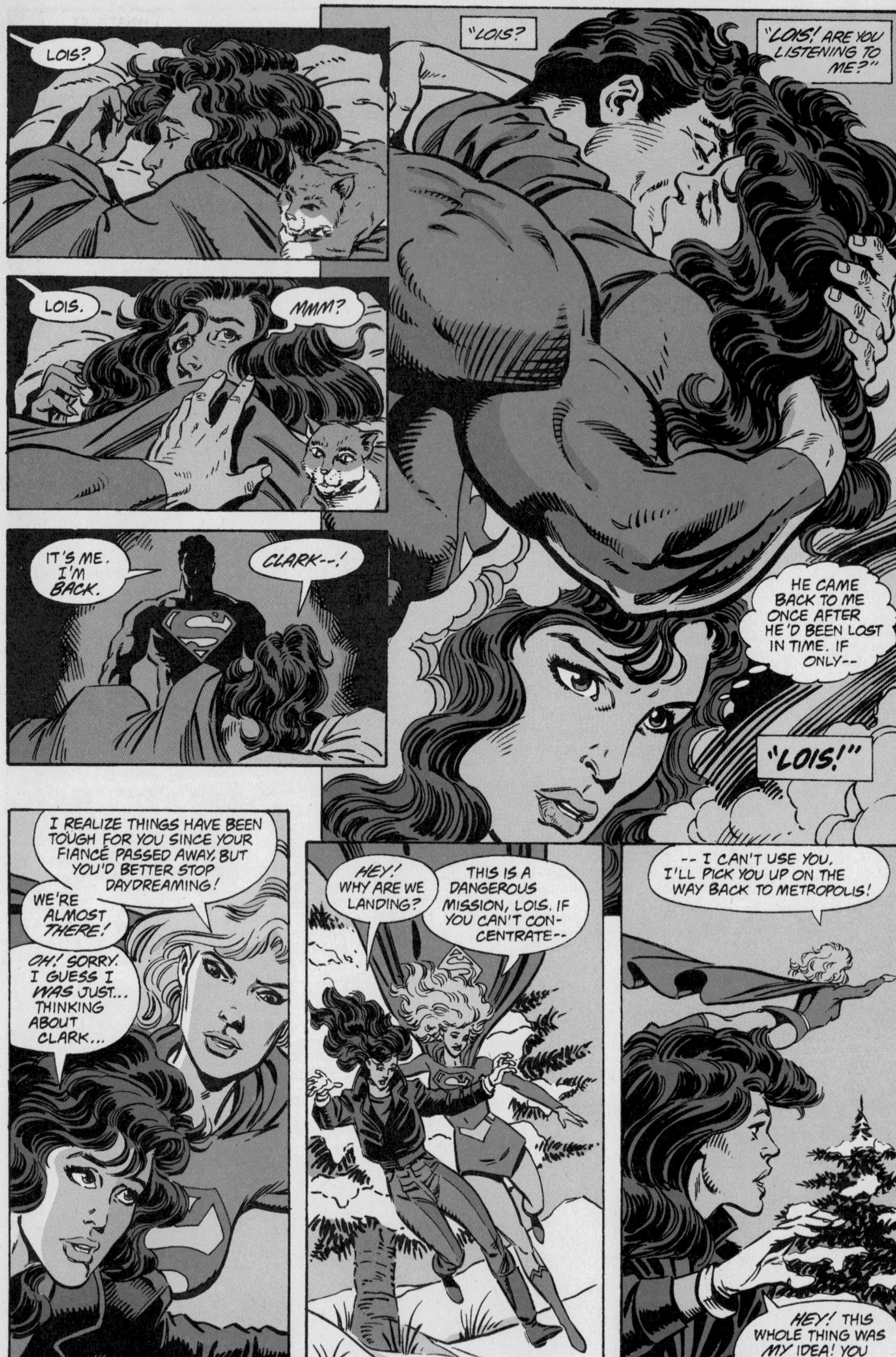
LOIS?
"LOIS?
"LOIS! ARE YOU LISTENING TO ME?"
LOIS.
MMM?
IT'S ME. I'M BACK.
CLARK--!
HE CAME BACK TO ME ONCE AFTER HE'D BEEN LOST IN TIME. IF ONLY--
"LOIS!"
I REALIZE THINGS HAVE BEEN TOUGH FOR YOU SINCE YOUR FIANCÉ PASSED AWAY, BUT YOU'D BETTER STOP DAYDREAMING!
WE'RE ALMOST THERE!
OH! SORRY. I GUESS I WAS JUST... THINKING ABOUT CLARK...
HEY! WHY ARE WE LANDING?
THIS IS A DANGEROUS MISSION, LOIS. IF YOU CAN'T CONCENTRATE--
-- I CAN'T USE YOU. I'LL PICK YOU UP ON THE WAY BACK TO METROPOLIS!
HEY! THIS WHOLE THING WAS MY IDEA! YOU CAN'T LEAVE ME HERE!

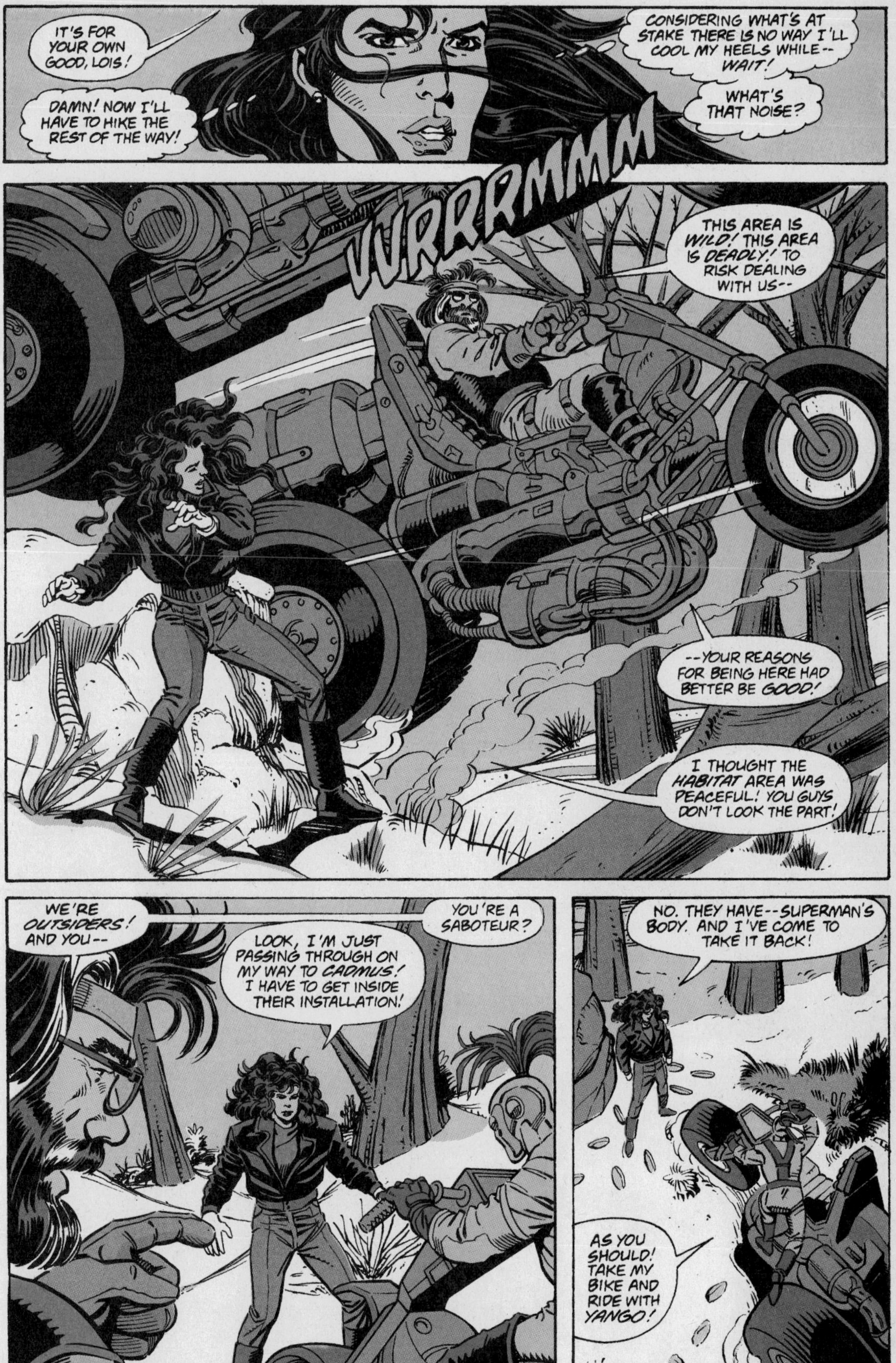
IT'S FOR YOUR OWN GOOD, LOIS!
DAMN! NOW I'LL HAVE TO HIKE THE REST OF THE WAY!
CONSIDERING WHAT'S AT STAKE THERE IS NO WAY I'LL COOL MY HEELS WHILE-- WAIT!
WHAT'S THAT NOISE?
VVRRRMMM
THIS AREA IS WILD! THIS AREA IS DEADLY! TO RISK DEALING WITH US--
--YOUR REASONS FOR BEING HERE HAD BETTER BE GOOD!
I THOUGHT THE HABITAT AREA WAS PEACEFUL! YOU GUYS DON'T LOOK THE PART!
WE'RE OUTSIDERS! AND YOU--
YOU'RE A SABOTEUR?
LOOK, I'M JUST PASSING THROUGH ON MY WAY TO CADMUS! I HAVE TO GET INSIDE THEIR INSTALLATION!
NO. THEY HAVE--SUPERMAN'S BODY. AND I'VE COME TO TAKE IT BACK!
AS YOU SHOULD! TAKE MY BIKE AND RIDE WITH YANGO!

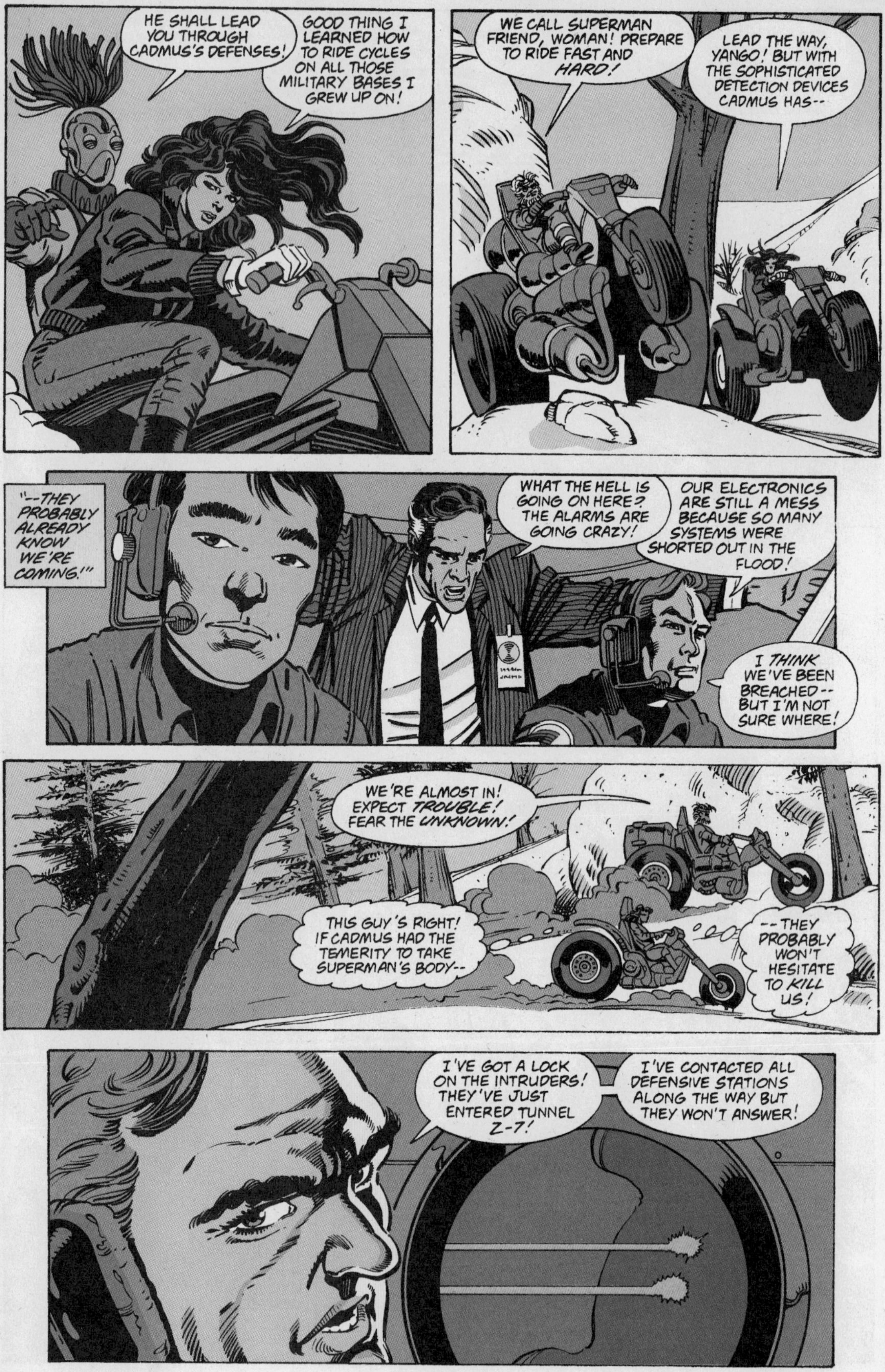
HE SHALL LEAD YOU THROUGH CADMUS'S DEFENSES!
GOOD THING I LEARNED HOW TO RIDE CYCLES ON ALL THOSE MILITARY BASES I GREW UP ON!
WE CALL SUPERMAN FRIEND, WOMAN! PREPARE TO RIDE FAST AND HARD!
LEAD THE WAY, YANGO! BUT WITH THE SOPHISTICATED DETECTION DEVICES CADMUS HAS--
"--THEY PROBABLY ALREADY KNOW WE'RE COMING!"
WHAT THE HELL IS GOING ON HERE? THE ALARMS ARE GOING CRAZY!
OUR ELECTRONICS ARE STILL A MESS BECAUSE SO MANY SYSTEMS WERE SHORTED OUT IN THE FLOOD!
I THINK WE'VE BEEN BREACHED--BUT I'M NOT SURE WHERE!
WE'RE ALMOST IN! EXPECT TROUBLE! FEAR THE UNKNOWN!
THIS GUY'S RIGHT! IF CADMUS HAD THE TEMERITY TO TAKE SUPERMAN'S BODY--
--THEY PROBABLY WON'T HESITATE TO KILL US!
I'VE GOT A LOCK ON THE INTRUDERS! THEY'VE JUST ENTERED TUNNEL Z-7!
I'VE CONTACTED ALL DEFENSIVE STATIONS ALONG THE WAY BUT THEY WON'T ANSWER!

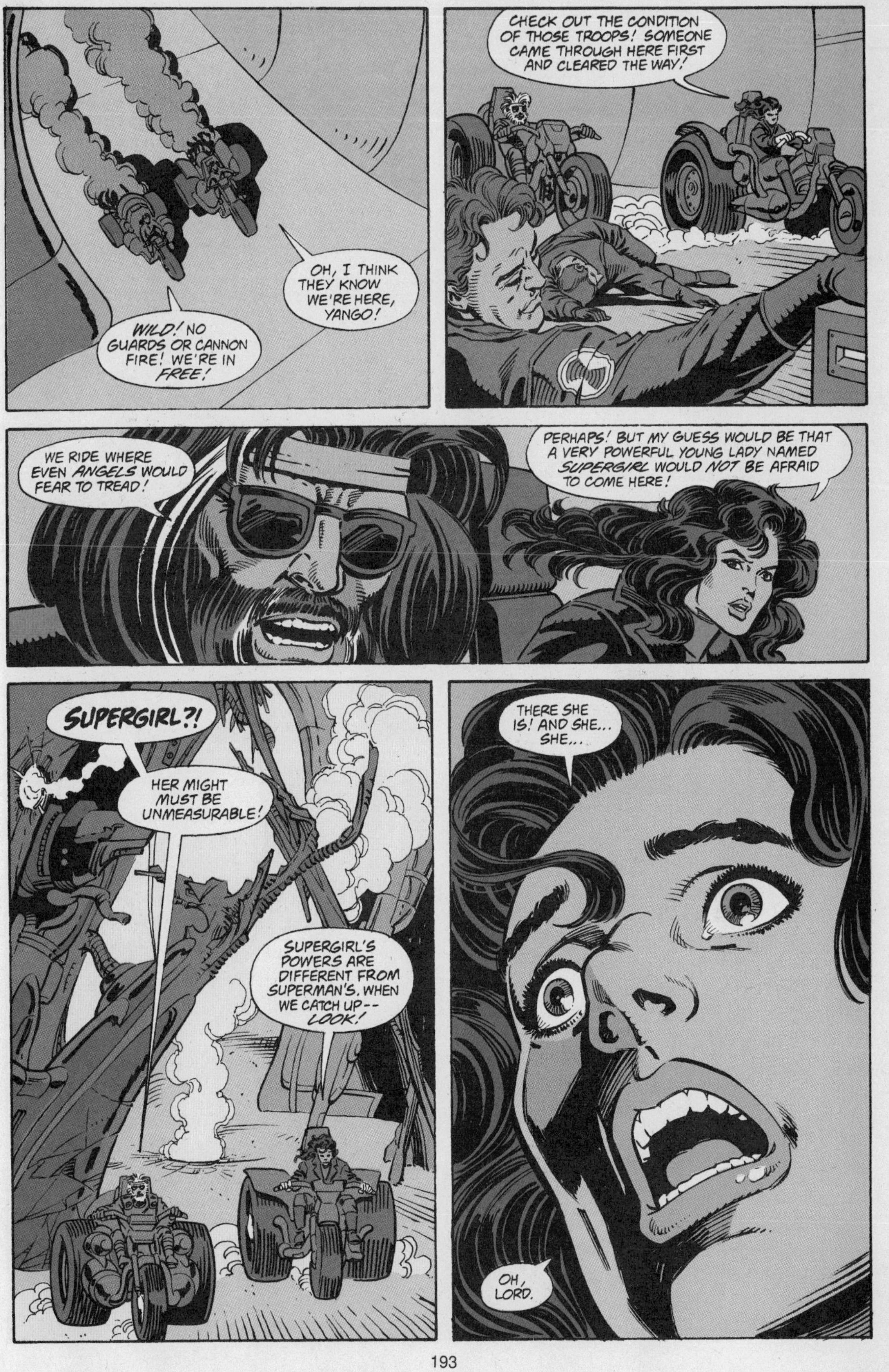

WILD! NO GUARDS OR CANNON FIRE! WE'RE IN FREE!
OH, I THINK THEY KNOW WE'RE HERE, YANGO!
CHECK OUT THE CONDITION OF THOSE TROOPS! SOMEONE CAME THROUGH HERE FIRST AND CLEARED THE WAY!
WE RIDE WHERE EVEN ANGELS WOULD FEAR TO TREAD!
PERHAPS! BUT MY GUESS WOULD BE THAT A VERY POWERFUL YOUNG LADY NAMED SUPERGIRL WOULD NOT BE AFRAID TO COME HERE!
SUPERGIRL?!
HER MIGHT MUST BE UNMEASURABLE!
SUPERGIRL'S POWERS ARE DIFFERENT FROM SUPERMAN'S. WHEN WE CATCH UP-- LOOK!
THERE SHE IS! AND SHE... SHE...
OH, LORD.

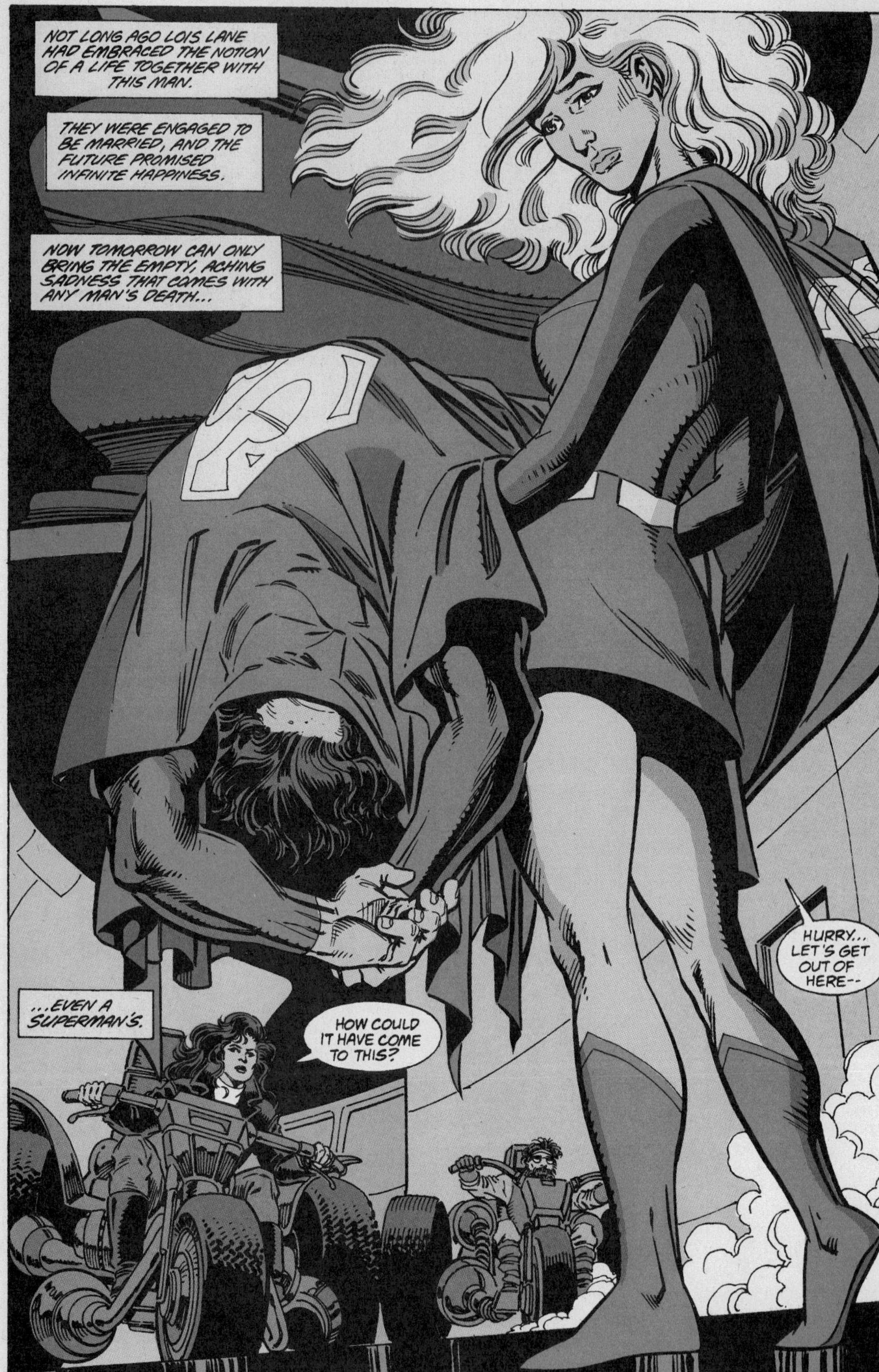
NOT LONG AGO LOIS LANE HAD EMBRACED THE NOTION OF A LIFE TOGETHER WITH THIS MAN.
THEY WERE ENGAGED TO BE MARRIED, AND THE FUTURE PROMISED INFINITE HAPPINESS.
NOW TOMORROW CAN ONLY BRING THE EMPTY, ACHING SADNESS THAT COMES WITH ANY MAN'S DEATH...
...EVEN A SUPERMAN'S.
HOW COULD IT HAVE COME TO THIS?
HURRY... LET'S GET OUT OF HERE--

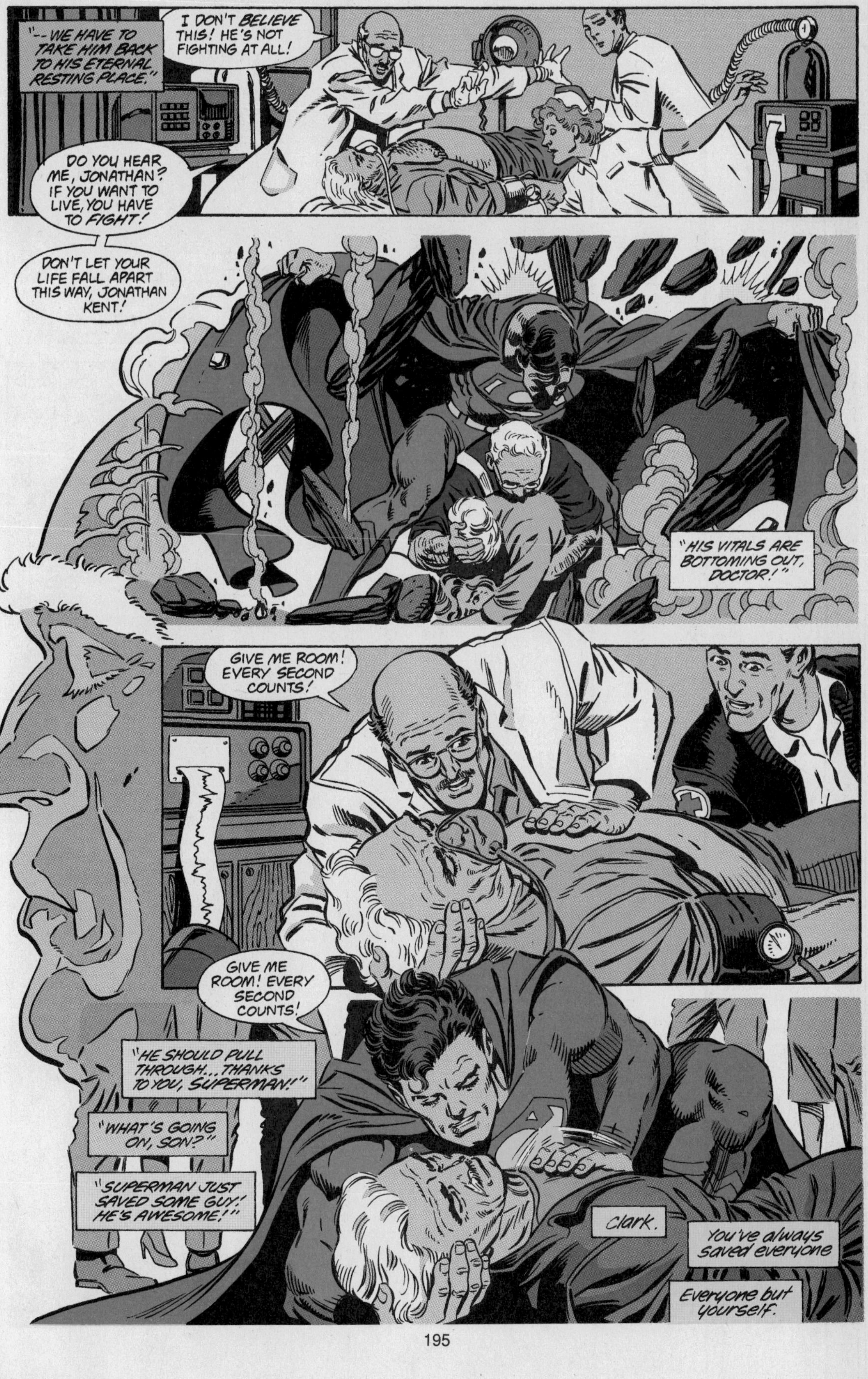
"-- WE HAVE TO TAKE HIM BACK TO HIS ETERNAL RESTING PLACE."
I DON'T BELIEVE THIS! HE'S NOT FIGHTING AT ALL!
DO YOU HEAR ME, JONATHAN? IF YOU WANT TO LIVE, YOU HAVE TO FIGHT!
DON'T LET YOUR LIFE FALL APART THIS WAY, JONATHAN KENT!
"HIS VITALS ARE BOTTOMING OUT, DOCTOR!"
GIVE ME ROOM! EVERY SECOND COUNTS!
GIVE ME ROOM! EVERY SECOND COUNTS!
"HE SHOULD PULL THROUGH... THANKS TO YOU, SUPERMAN!"
"WHAT'S GOING ON, SON?"
"SUPERMAN JUST SAVED SOME GUY! HE'S AWESOME!"
Clark.
You've always saved everyone
Everyone but yourself.

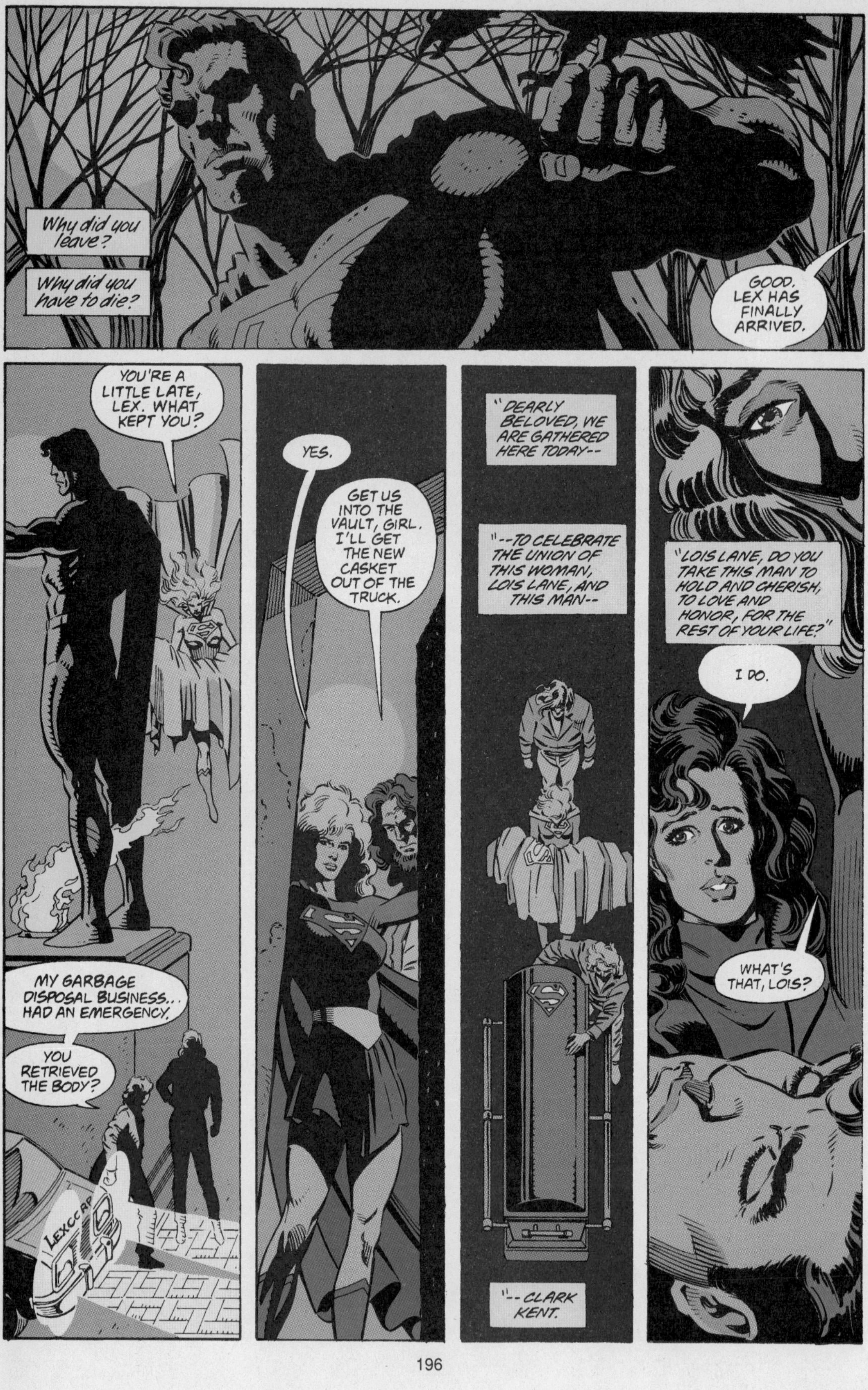
Why did you leave?
Why did you have to die?
GOOD. LEX HAS FINALLY ARRIVED.
YOU'RE A LITTLE LATE, LEX. WHAT KEPT YOU?
MY GARBAGE DISPOSAL BUSINESS... HAD AN EMERGENCY.
YOU RETRIEVED THE BODY?
LEXCORP
YES.
GET US INTO THE VAULT, GIRL. I'LL GET THE NEW CASKET OUT OF THE TRUCK.
"DEARLY BELOVED, WE ARE GATHERED HERE TODAY--
"--TO CELEBRATE THE UNION OF THIS WOMAN, LOIS LANE, AND THIS MAN--
"--CLARK KENT.
"LOIS LANE, DO YOU TAKE THIS MAN TO HOLD AND CHERISH, TO LOVE AND HONOR, FOR THE REST OF YOUR LIFE?"
I DO.
WHAT'S THAT, LOIS?

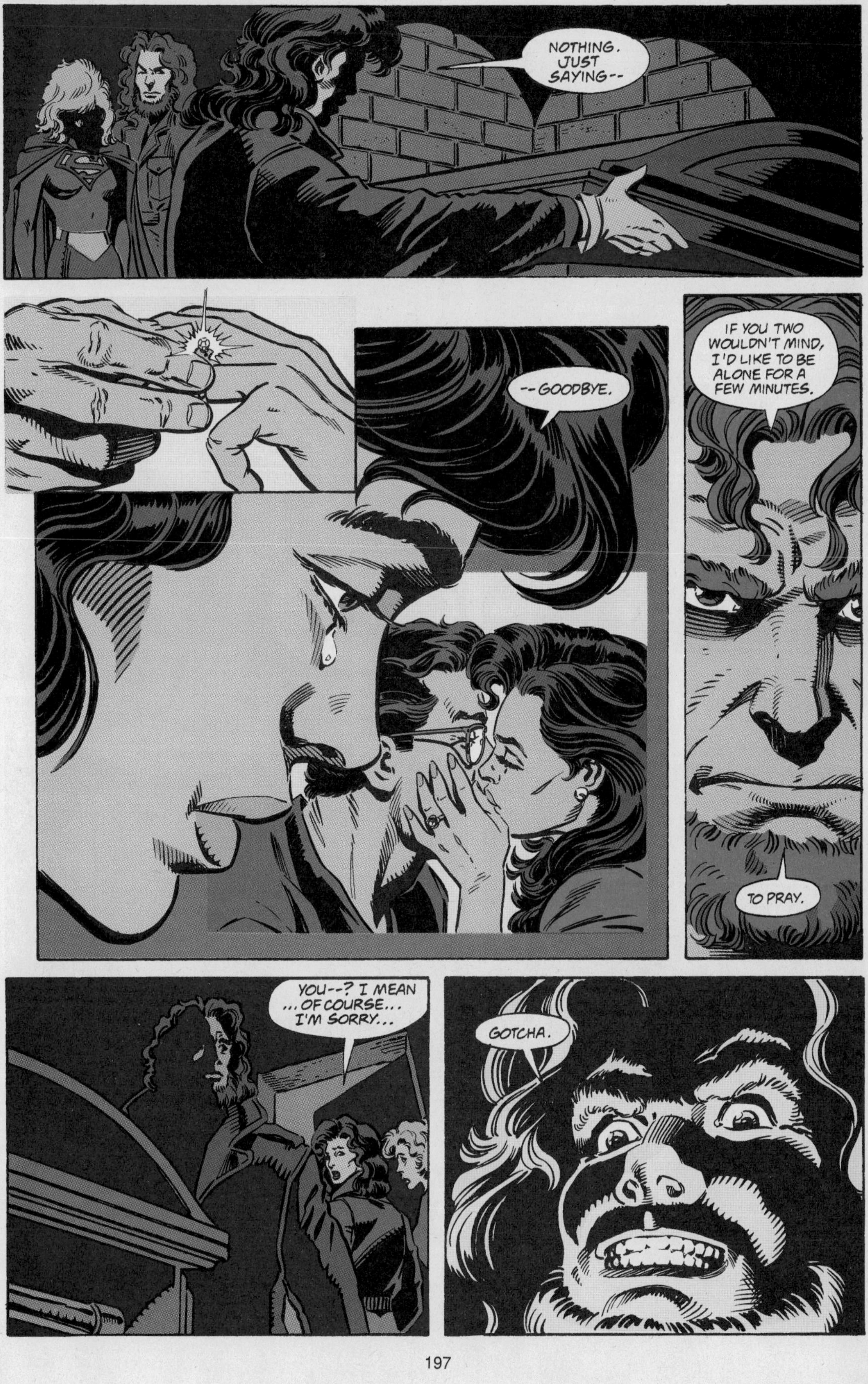
NOTHING. JUST SAYING--
--GOODBYE.
IF YOU TWO WOULDN'T MIND, I'D LIKE TO BE ALONE FOR A FEW MINUTES.
TO PRAY.
YOU--? I MEAN ...OF COURSE... I'M SORRY...
GOTCHA.

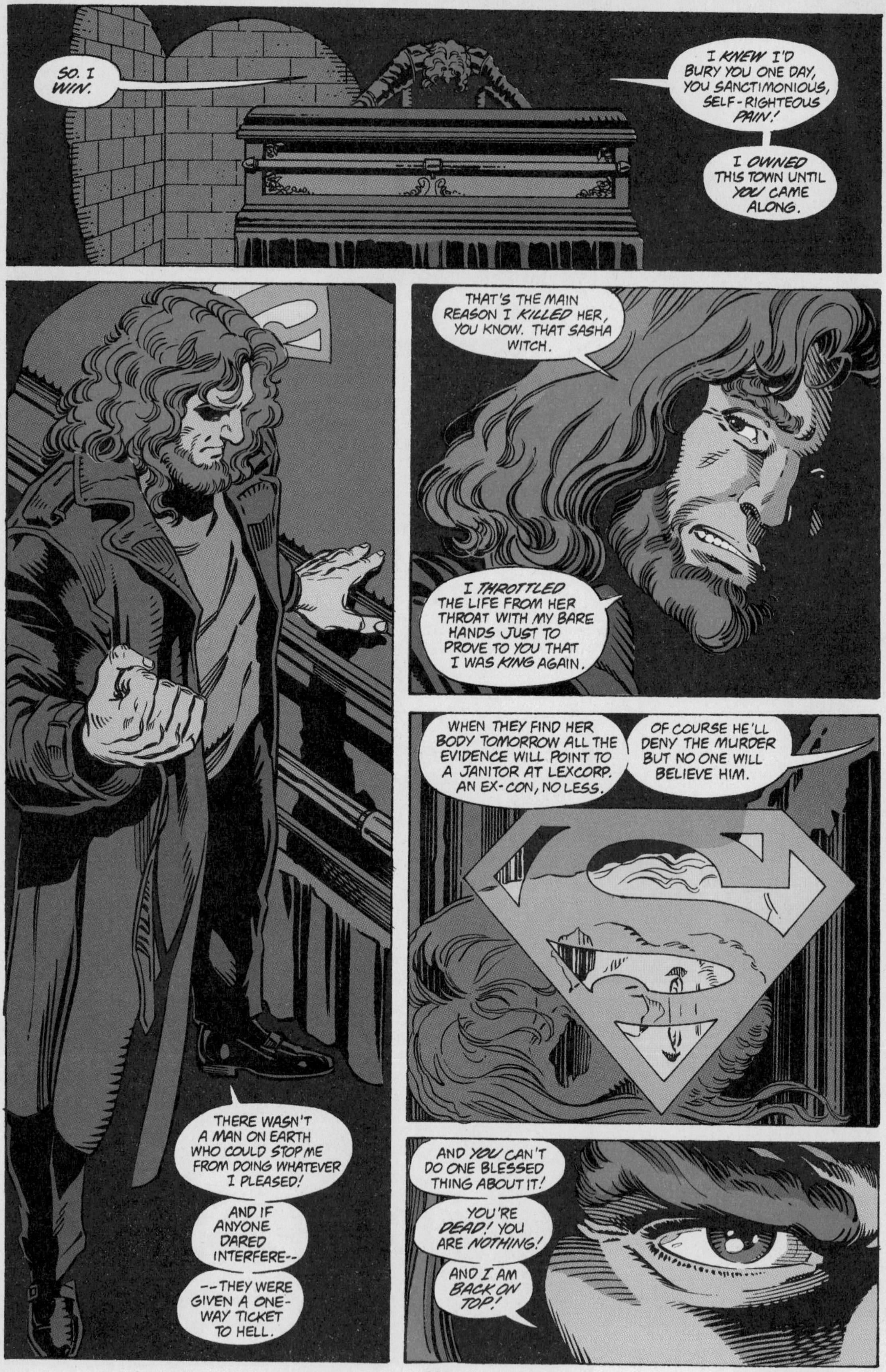
SO. I WIN.
I KNEW I'D BURY YOU ONE DAY, YOU SANCTIMONIOUS, SELF-RIGHTEOUS PAIN!
I OWNED THIS TOWN UNTIL YOU CAME ALONG.
THERE WASN'T A MAN ON EARTH WHO COULD STOP ME FROM DOING WHATEVER I PLEASED!
AND IF ANYONE DARED INTERFERE--
--THEY WERE GIVEN A ONE-WAY TICKET TO HELL.
THAT'S THE MAIN REASON I KILLED HER, YOU KNOW. THAT SASHA WITCH.
I THROTTLED THE LIFE FROM HER THROAT WITH MY BARE HANDS JUST TO PROVE TO YOU THAT I WAS KING AGAIN.
WHEN THEY FIND HER BODY TOMORROW ALL THE EVIDENCE WILL POINT TO A JANITOR AT LEXCORP. AN EX-CON, NO LESS.
OF COURSE HE'LL DENY THE MURDER BUT NO ONE WILL BELIEVE HIM.
AND YOU CAN'T DO ONE BLESSED THING ABOUT IT!
YOU'RE DEAD! YOU ARE NOTHING!
AND I AM BACK ON TOP!

METROPOLIS IS MINE AGAIN, SUPERMAN!
AND YOU ARE AN EMPTY, LIFELESS, WITHERING HUSK!
BREATHE, JONATHAN! BREATHE!
Clark!
Look out!
EEEEEEEEEE
DON'T LEAVE ME, JONATHAN! PLEASE!
IT'S ME, PA. DON'T BE AFRAID.
clark.
EEEEEEEEEEEEEEEEEEEEEEEEEE

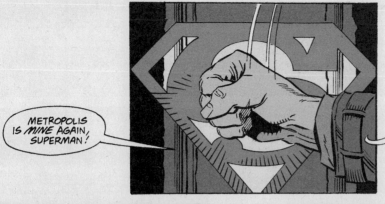

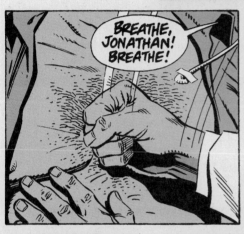

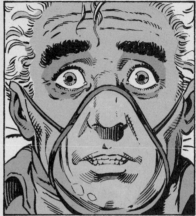

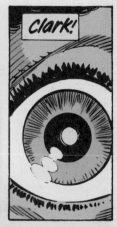

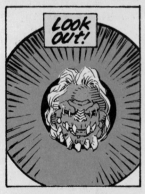

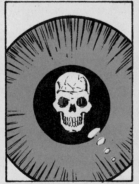

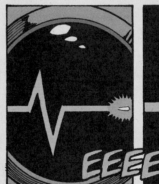

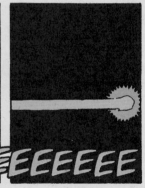

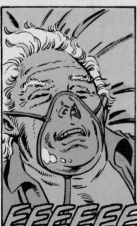

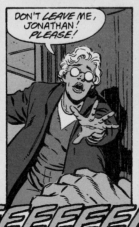

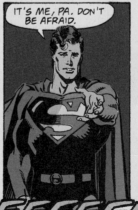

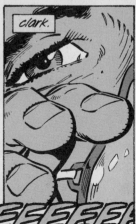

I'm coming, son.

EEEEEEEEEEEEEEEEEEEEEEE

OH, JONATHAN... NO...

EEEEEEEEEEEEEEEEEEEEEEEEE

EEEEEEEEEEEEEEEEEEEEEEE

EEEEEEEEEEEEEEEEEEEEEE

EEEEEEEEEEEEEEE

EEEEEEEEEEE

DON'T LEAVE ME ALONE...

The End

DAN JURGENS . BRETT BREEDING
words & layouts . *finishes*
JOHN COSTANZA . GLENN WHITMORE
letters . *colors*
JENNIFER FRANK . MIKE CARLIN
assistant edits . *edits*

SUPERMAN *Created by*
JERRY SIEGEL & JOE SHUSTER

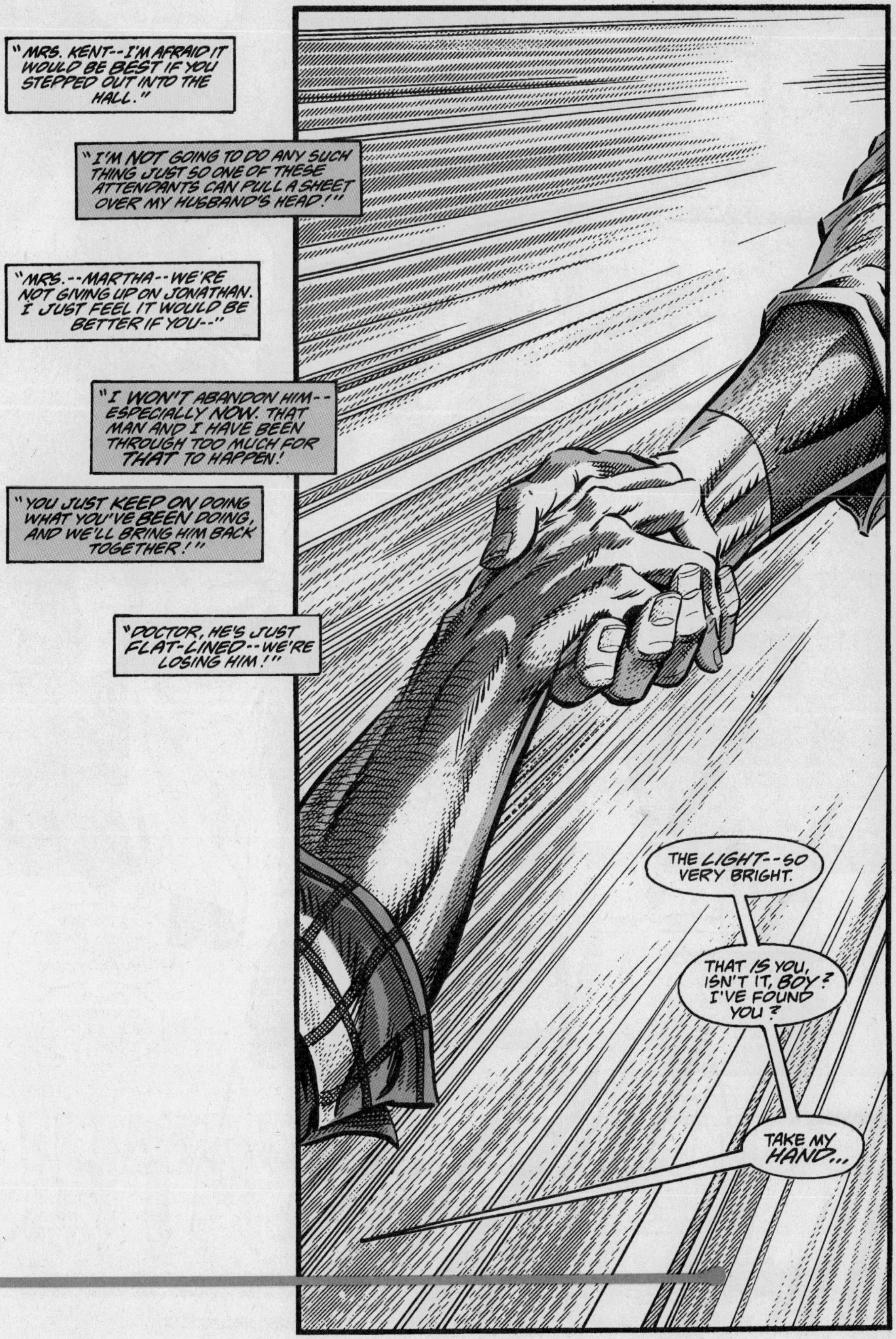
"MRS. KENT--I'M AFRAID IT WOULD BE BEST IF YOU STEPPED OUT INTO THE HALL."
"I'M NOT GOING TO DO ANY SUCH THING JUST SO ONE OF THESE ATTENDANTS CAN PULL A SHEET OVER MY HUSBAND'S HEAD!"
"MRS.--MARTHA--WE'RE NOT GIVING UP ON JONATHAN. I JUST FEEL IT WOULD BE BETTER IF YOU--"
"I WON'T ABANDON HIM--ESPECIALLY NOW. THAT MAN AND I HAVE BEEN THROUGH TOO MUCH FOR THAT TO HAPPEN!
"YOU JUST KEEP ON DOING WHAT YOU'VE BEEN DOING, AND WE'LL BRING HIM BACK TOGETHER!"
"DOCTOR, HE'S JUST FLAT-LINED--WE'RE LOSING HIM!"
THE LIGHT--SO VERY BRIGHT.
THAT IS YOU, ISN'T IT, BOY? I'VE FOUND YOU?
TAKE MY HAND...

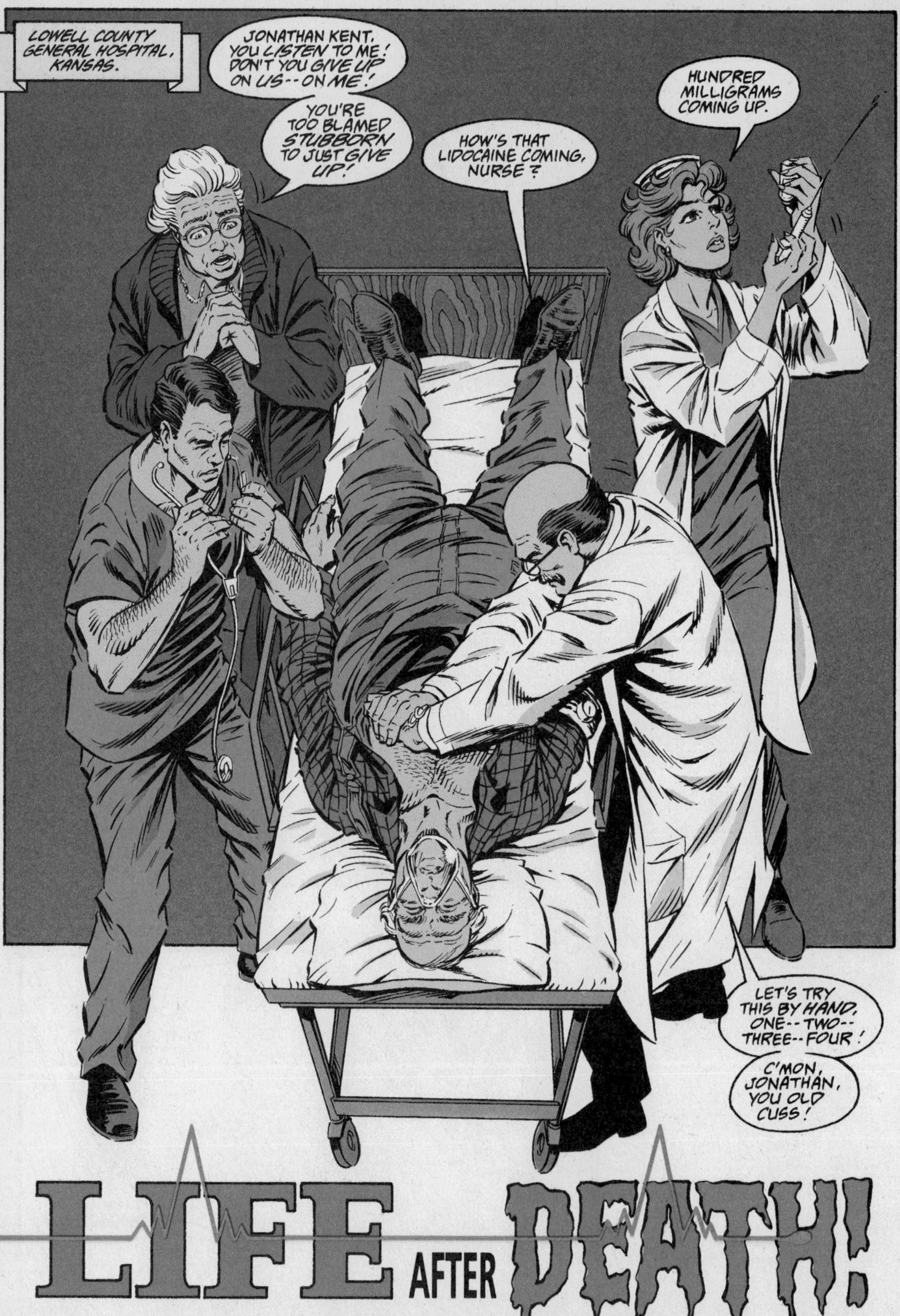
LOWELL COUNTY GENERAL HOSPITAL, KANSAS.
JONATHAN KENT, YOU LISTEN TO ME! DON'T YOU GIVE UP ON US--ON ME!
YOU'RE TOO BLAMED STUBBORN TO JUST GIVE UP!
HOW'S THAT LIDOCAINE COMING, NURSE?
HUNDRED MILLIGRAMS COMING UP.
LET'S TRY THIS BY HAND, ONE--TWO--THREE--FOUR!
C'MON, JONATHAN, YOU OLD CUSS!

LIFE AFTER DEATH!

TOM GRUMMETT-PENCILS * DOUG HAZLEWOOD-INKS & TONES * JERRY ORDWAY-STORY
ALBERT DEGUZMAN-LETTERER * GLENN WHITMORE-COLORIST * JENNIFER FRANK-ASSISTANT EDITOR
MIKE CARLIN-EDITOR
SUPERMAN Created by JERRY SIEGEL and JOE SHUSTER

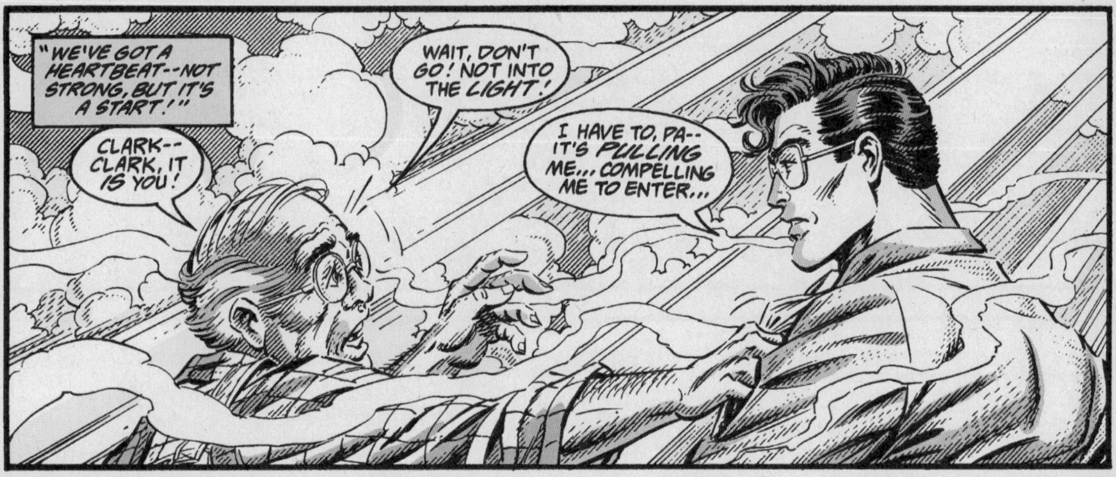
"WE'VE GOT A HEARTBEAT--NOT STRONG, BUT IT'S A START!"
CLARK--CLARK, IT IS YOU!
WAIT, DON'T GO! NOT INTO THE LIGHT!
I HAVE TO, PA--IT'S PULLING ME... COMPELLING ME TO ENTER...

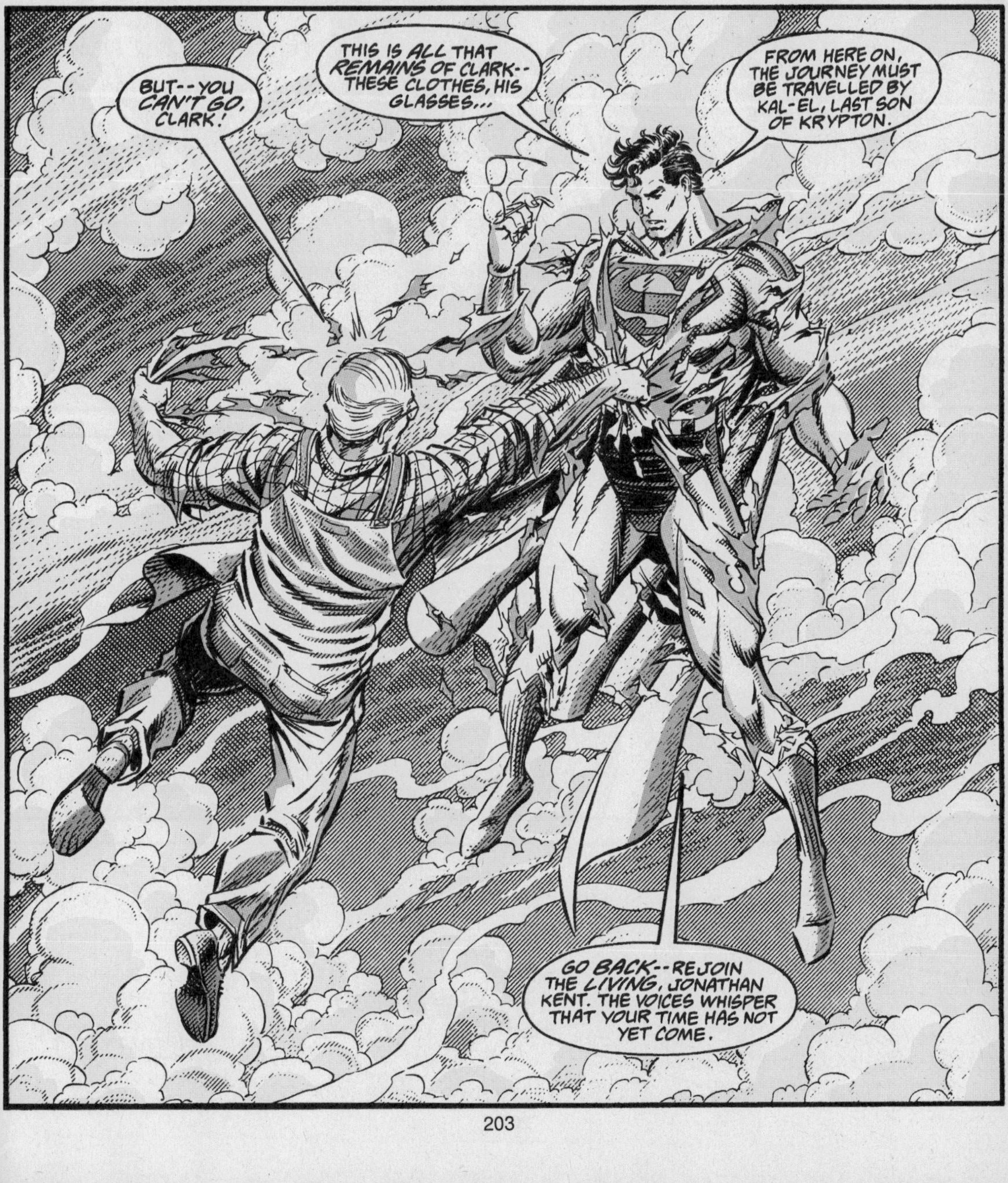
BUT--YOU CAN'T GO, CLARK!
THIS IS ALL THAT REMAINS OF CLARK--THESE CLOTHES, HIS GLASSES...
FROM HERE ON, THE JOURNEY MUST BE TRAVELLED BY KAL-EL, LAST SON OF KRYPTON.
GO BACK--REJOIN THE LIVING, JONATHAN KENT. THE VOICES WHISPER THAT YOUR TIME HAS NOT YET COME.

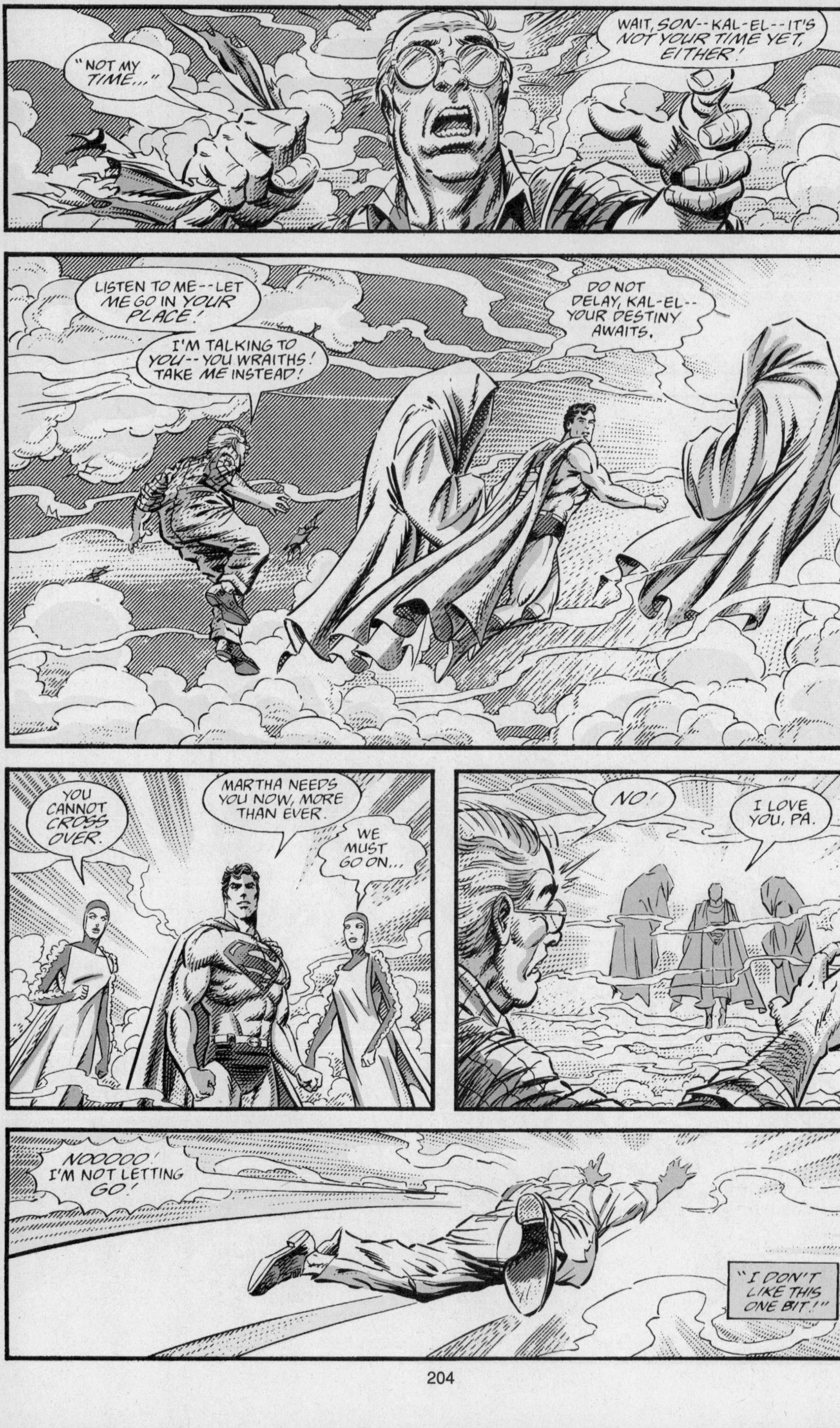
"NOT MY TIME..."
WAIT, SON--KAL-EL--IT'S NOT YOUR TIME YET, EITHER!
LISTEN TO ME--LET ME GO IN YOUR PLACE!
I'M TALKING TO YOU--YOU WRAITHS! TAKE ME INSTEAD!
DO NOT DELAY, KAL-EL--YOUR DESTINY AWAITS.
YOU CANNOT CROSS OVER.
MARTHA NEEDS YOU NOW, MORE THAN EVER.
WE MUST GO ON...
NO!
I LOVE YOU, PA.
NOOOOO! I'M NOT LETTING GO!
"I DON'T LIKE THIS ONE BIT!"

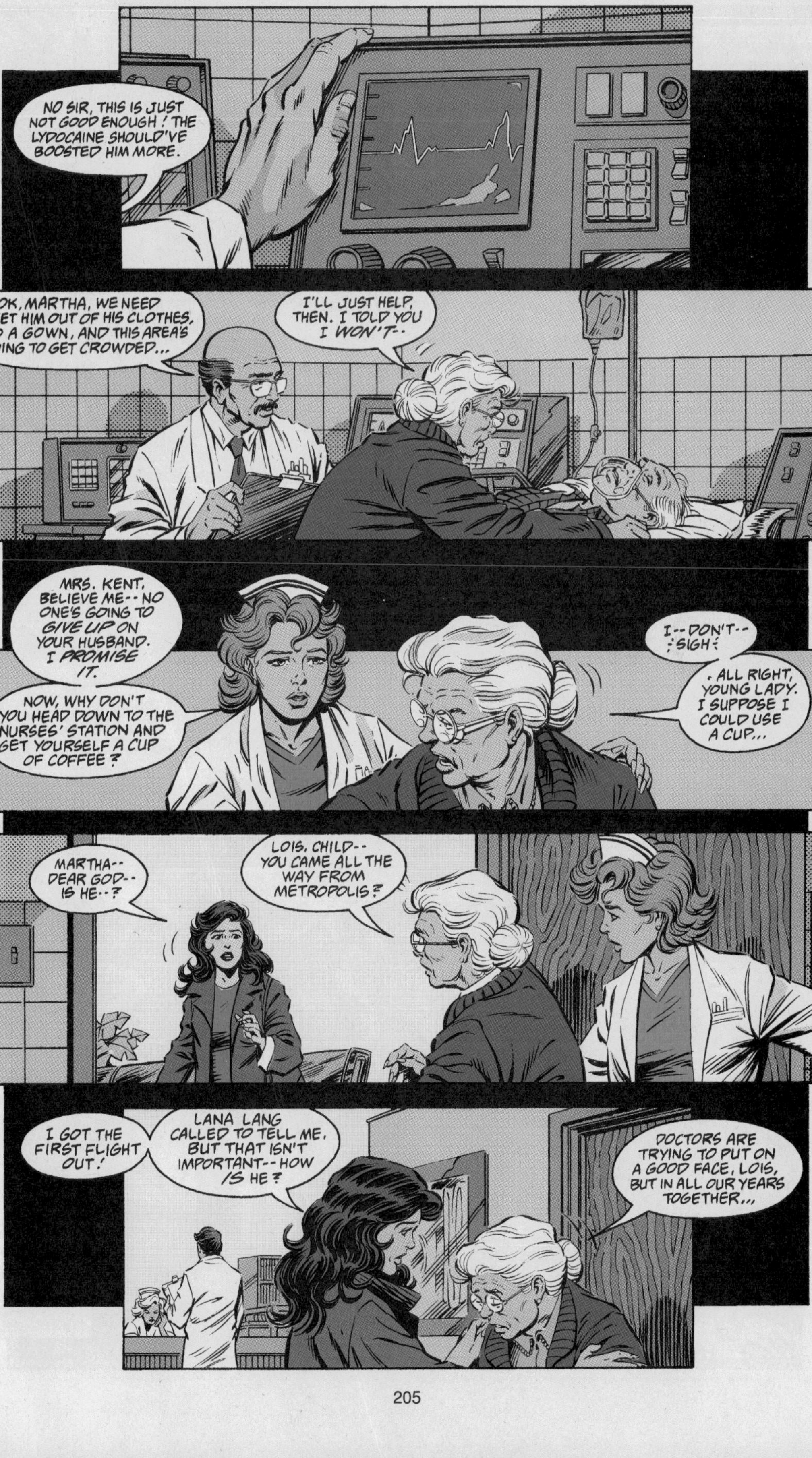
NO SIR, THIS IS JUST NOT GOOD ENOUGH! THE LYDOCAINE SHOULD'VE BOOSTED HIM MORE.
LOOK, MARTHA, WE NEED TO GET HIM OUT OF HIS CLOTHES, INTO A GOWN, AND THIS AREA'S GOING TO GET CROWDED...
I'LL JUST HELP, THEN. I TOLD YOU I WON'T--
MRS. KENT, BELIEVE ME-- NO ONE'S GOING TO GIVE UP ON YOUR HUSBAND. I PROMISE IT.
NOW, WHY DON'T YOU HEAD DOWN TO THE NURSES' STATION AND GET YOURSELF A CUP OF COFFEE?
I-- DON'T-- :SIGH:
. ALL RIGHT, YOUNG LADY. I SUPPOSE I COULD USE A CUP...
MARTHA-- DEAR GOD-- IS HE--?
LOIS, CHILD-- YOU CAME ALL THE WAY FROM METROPOLIS?
I GOT THE FIRST FLIGHT OUT!
LANA LANG CALLED TO TELL ME, BUT THAT ISN'T IMPORTANT-- HOW IS HE?
DOCTORS ARE TRYING TO PUT ON A GOOD FACE, LOIS, BUT IN ALL OUR YEARS TOGETHER...

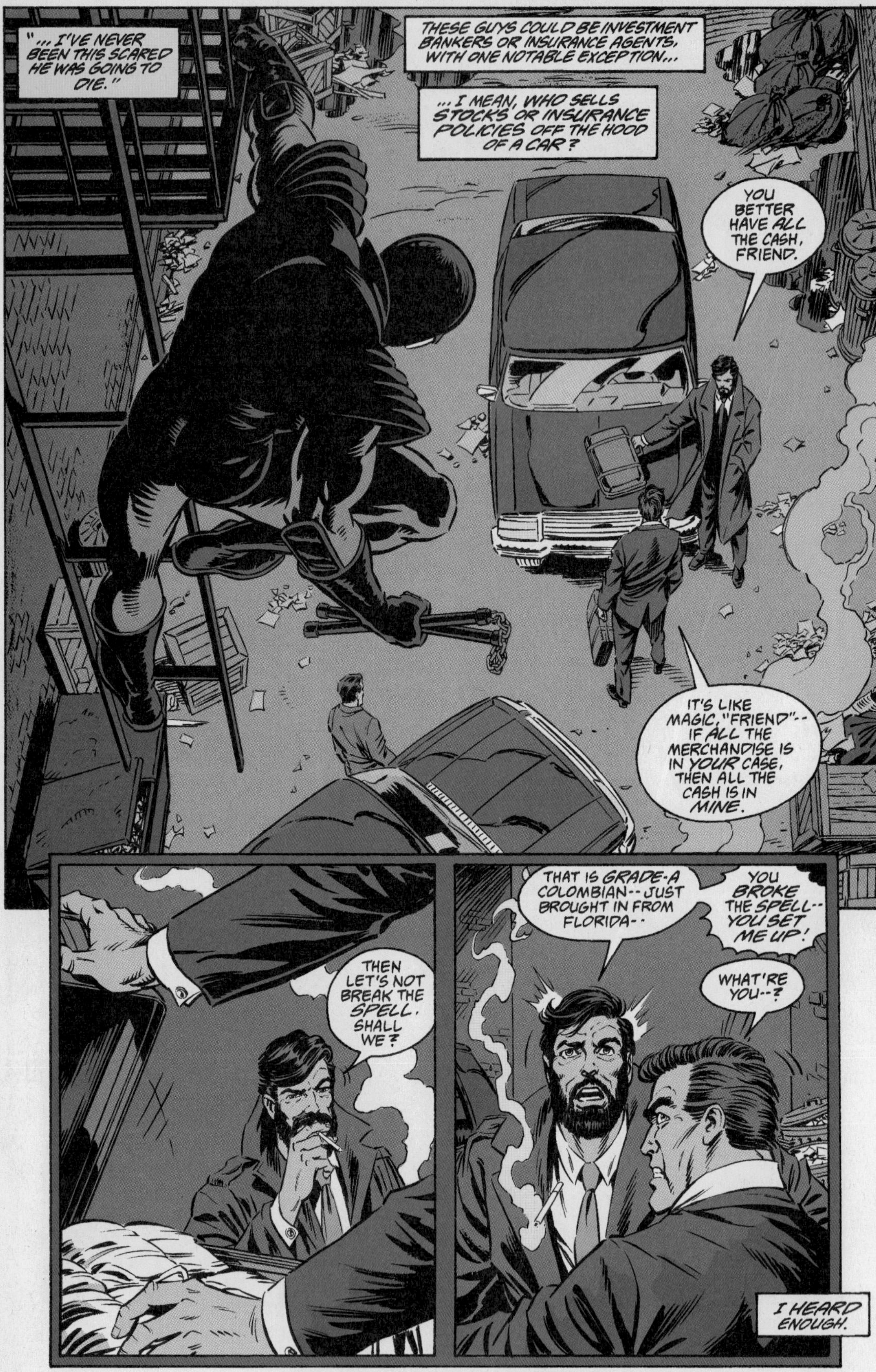
"...I'VE NEVER BEEN THIS SCARED HE WAS GOING TO DIE."
THESE GUYS COULD BE INVESTMENT BANKERS OR INSURANCE AGENTS, WITH ONE NOTABLE EXCEPTION...
...I MEAN, WHO SELLS STOCKS OR INSURANCE POLICIES OFF THE HOOD OF A CAR?
YOU BETTER HAVE ALL THE CASH, FRIEND.
IT'S LIKE MAGIC, "FRIEND"-- IF ALL THE MERCHANDISE IS IN YOUR CASE, THEN ALL THE CASH IS IN MINE.
THEN LET'S NOT BREAK THE SPELL, SHALL WE?
THAT IS GRADE-A COLOMBIAN-- JUST BROUGHT IN FROM FLORIDA--
YOU BROKE THE SPELL-- YOU SET ME UP!
WHAT'RE YOU--?
I HEARD ENOUGH.

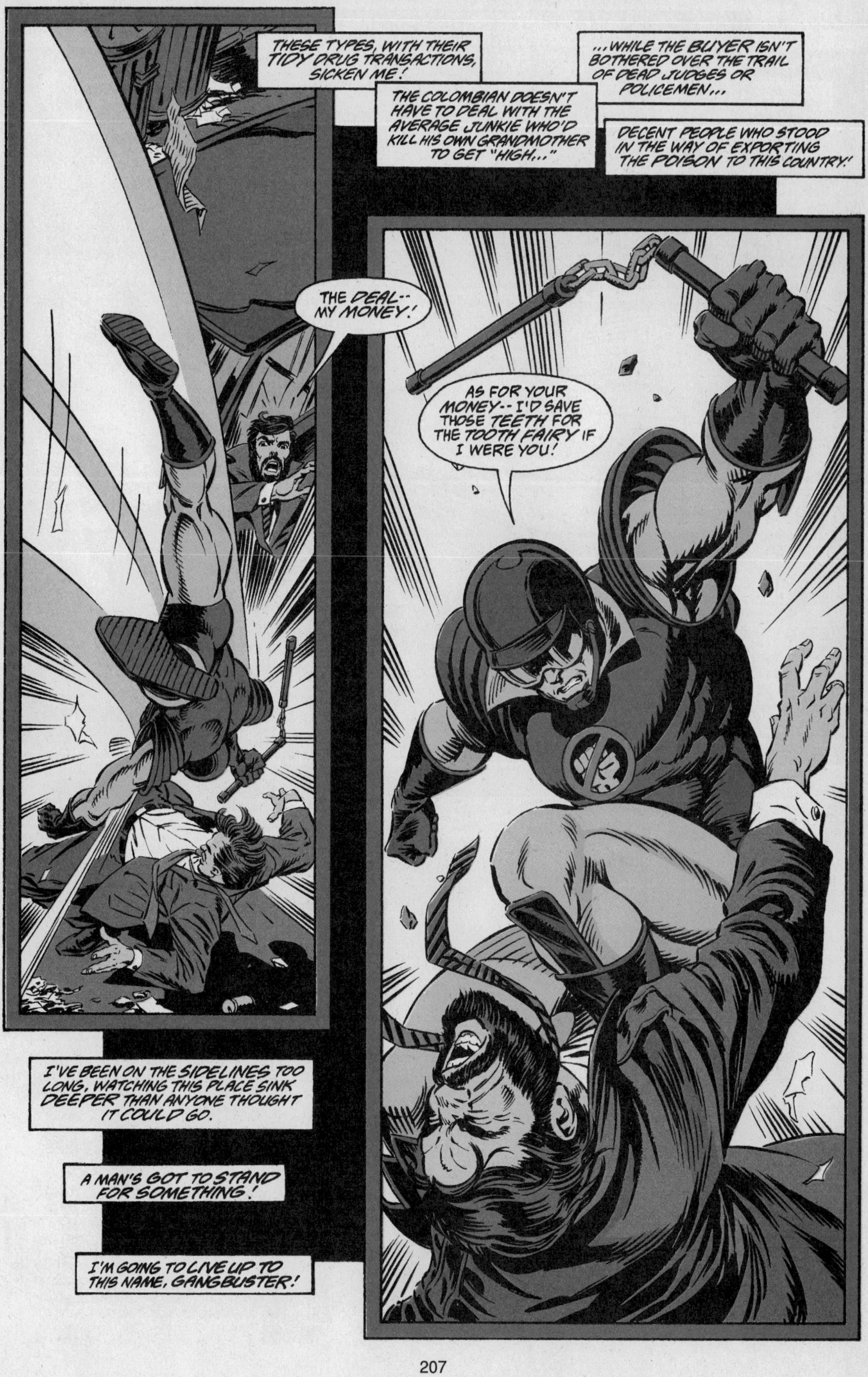
THESE TYPES, WITH THEIR TIDY DRUG TRANSACTIONS, SICKEN ME!
THE COLOMBIAN DOESN'T HAVE TO DEAL WITH THE AVERAGE JUNKIE WHO'D KILL HIS OWN GRANDMOTHER TO GET "HIGH..."
...WHILE THE BUYER ISN'T BOTHERED OVER THE TRAIL OF DEAD JUDGES OR POLICEMEN...
DECENT PEOPLE WHO STOOD IN THE WAY OF EXPORTING THE POISON TO THIS COUNTRY!
THE DEAL-- MY MONEY!
AS FOR YOUR MONEY-- I'D SAVE THOSE TEETH FOR THE TOOTH FAIRY IF I WERE YOU!
I'VE BEEN ON THE SIDELINES TOO LONG, WATCHING THIS PLACE SINK DEEPER THAN ANYONE THOUGHT IT COULD GO.
A MAN'S GOT TO STAND FOR SOMETHING!
I'M GOING TO LIVE UP TO THIS NAME, GANGBUSTER!

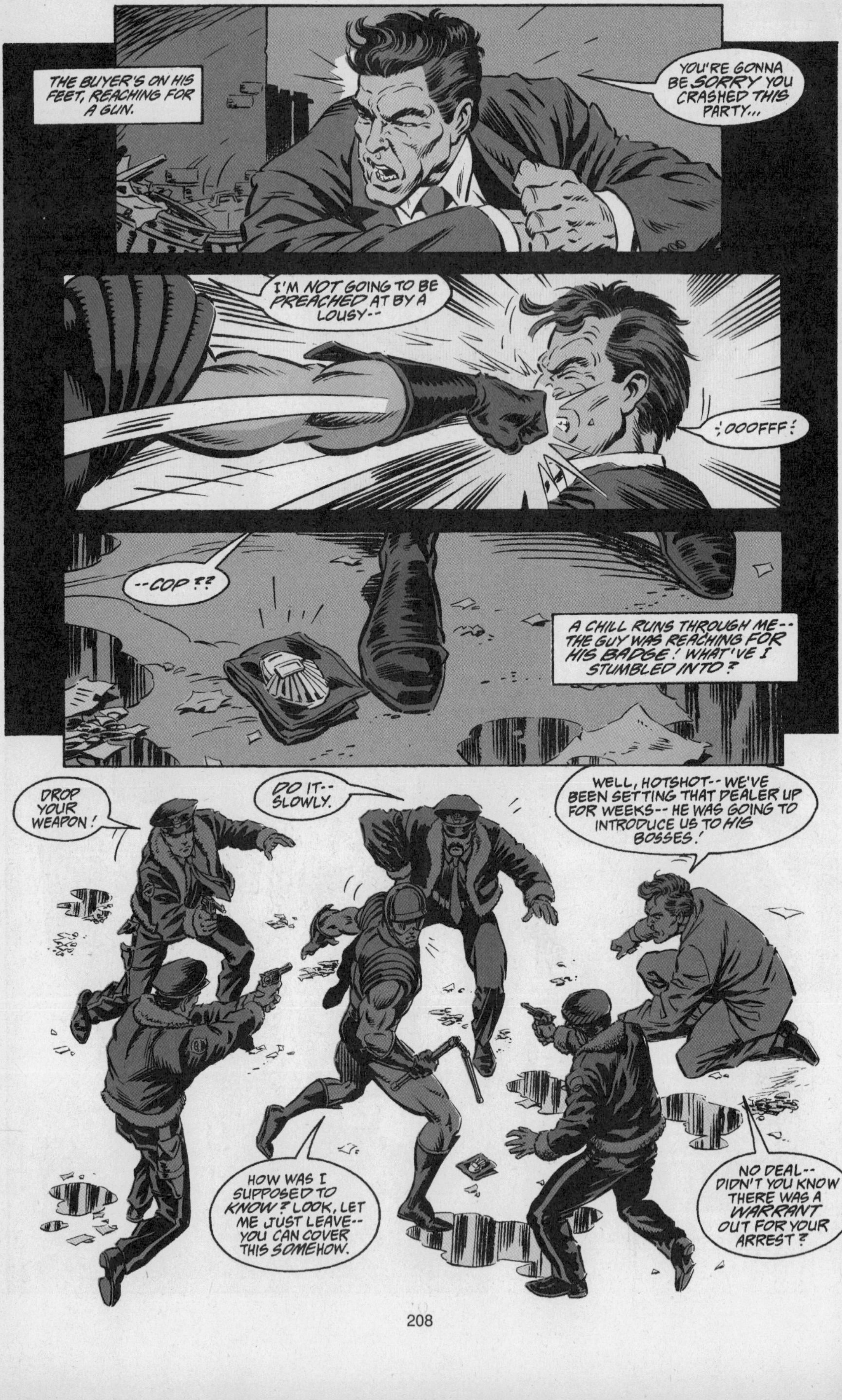

THE BUYER'S ON HIS FEET, REACHING FOR A GUN.
YOU'RE GONNA BE SORRY YOU CRASHED THIS PARTY...
I'M NOT GOING TO BE PREACHED AT BY A LOUSY--
OOOFFF
--COP ??
A CHILL RUNS THROUGH ME-- THE GUY WAS REACHING FOR HIS BADGE! WHAT'VE I STUMBLED INTO?
DROP YOUR WEAPON!
DO IT-- SLOWLY.
WELL, HOTSHOT-- WE'VE BEEN SETTING THAT DEALER UP FOR WEEKS-- HE WAS GOING TO INTRODUCE US TO HIS BOSSES!
HOW WAS I SUPPOSED TO KNOW? LOOK, LET ME JUST LEAVE-- YOU CAN COVER THIS SOMEHOW.
NO DEAL-- DIDN'T YOU KNOW THERE WAS A WARRANT OUT FOR YOUR ARREST?

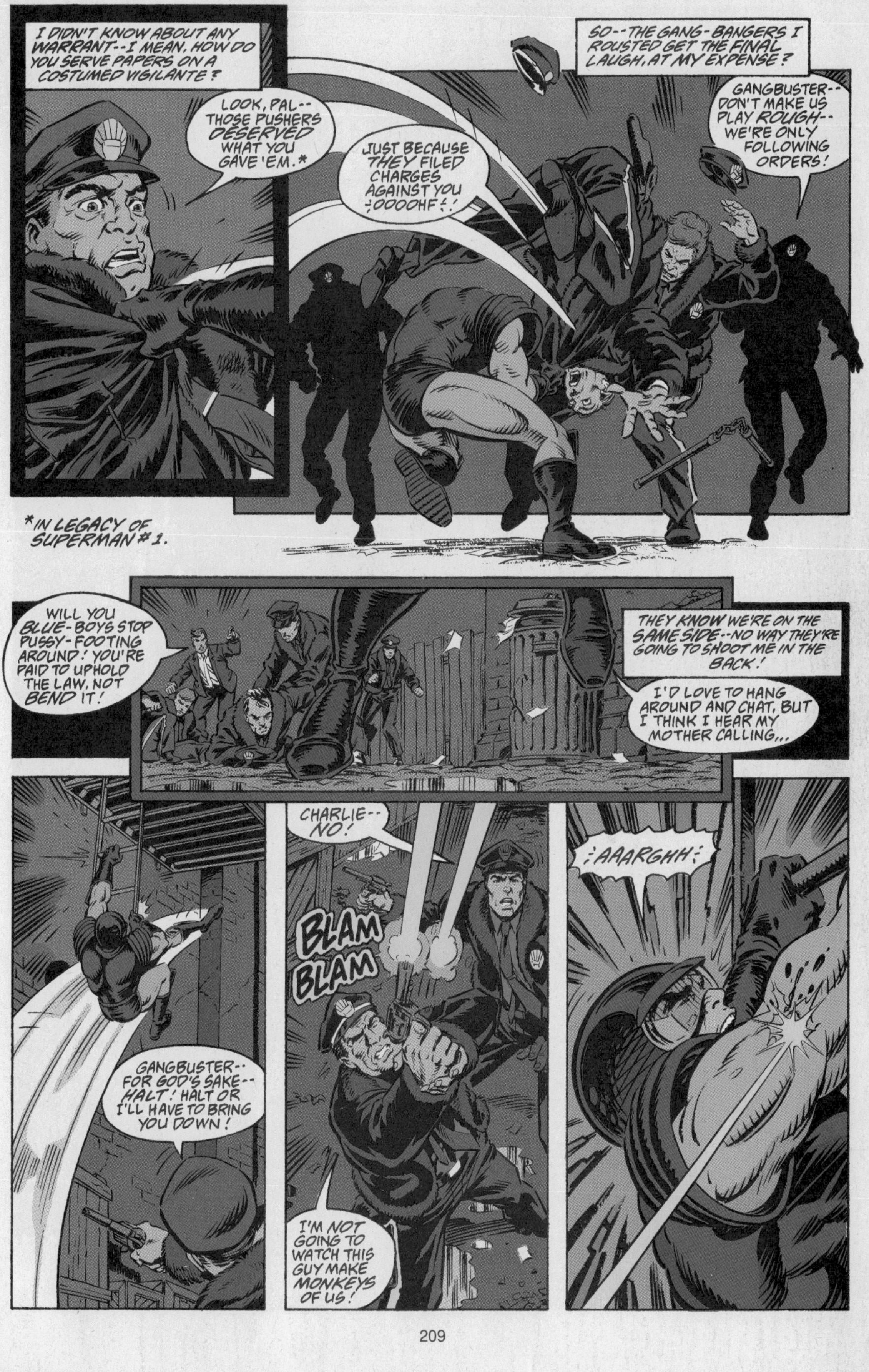
I DIDN'T KNOW ABOUT ANY WARRANT--I MEAN, HOW DO YOU SERVE PAPERS ON A COSTUMED VIGILANTE?
LOOK, PAL-- THOSE PUSHERS DESERVED WHAT YOU GAVE 'EM.*
JUST BECAUSE THEY FILED CHARGES AGAINST YOU ¡OOOOHF!!
SO--THE GANG-BANGERS I ROUSTED GET THE FINAL LAUGH, AT MY EXPENSE?
GANGBUSTER-- DON'T MAKE US PLAY ROUGH-- WE'RE ONLY FOLLOWING ORDERS!
*IN LEGACY OF SUPERMAN #1.
WILL YOU BLUE-BOYS STOP PUSSY-FOOTING AROUND! YOU'RE PAID TO UPHOLD THE LAW, NOT BEND IT!
THEY KNOW WE'RE ON THE SAME SIDE--NO WAY THEY'RE GOING TO SHOOT ME IN THE BACK!
I'D LOVE TO HANG AROUND AND CHAT, BUT I THINK I HEAR MY MOTHER CALLING...
GANGBUSTER-- FOR GOD'S SAKE-- HALT! HALT OR I'LL HAVE TO BRING YOU DOWN!
CHARLIE-- NO!
BLAM BLAM
I'M NOT GOING TO WATCH THIS GUY MAKE MONKEYS OF US!
¡AAARGHH!

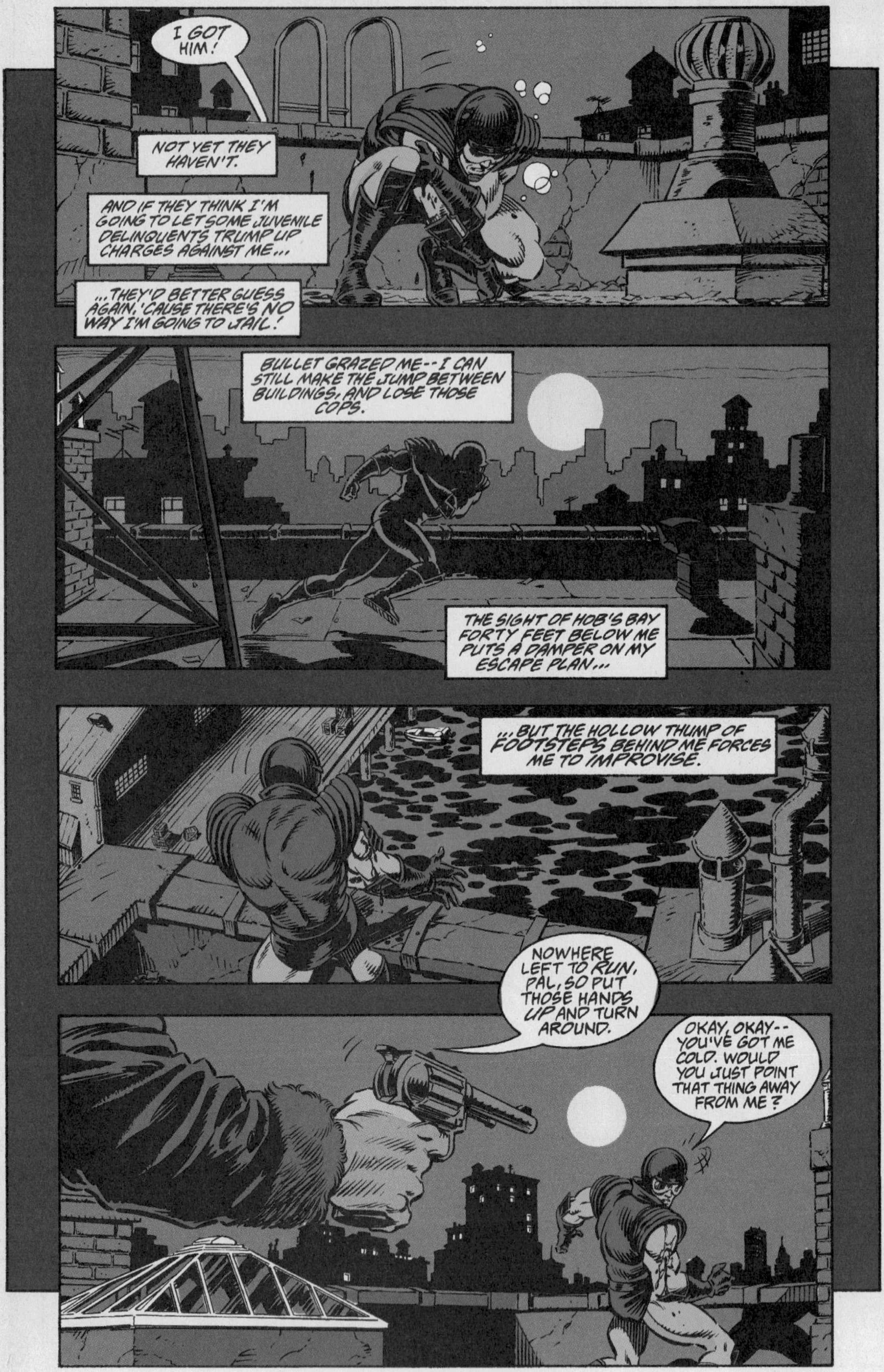
I GOT HIM!
NOT YET THEY HAVEN'T.
AND IF THEY THINK I'M GOING TO LET SOME JUVENILE DELINQUENTS TRUMP UP CHARGES AGAINST ME...
...THEY'D BETTER GUESS AGAIN. 'CAUSE THERE'S NO WAY I'M GOING TO JAIL!
BULLET GRAZED ME--I CAN STILL MAKE THE JUMP BETWEEN BUILDINGS, AND LOSE THOSE COPS.
THE SIGHT OF HOB'S BAY FORTY FEET BELOW ME PUTS A DAMPER ON MY ESCAPE PLAN...
...BUT THE HOLLOW THUMP OF FOOTSTEPS BEHIND ME FORCES ME TO IMPROVISE.
NOWHERE LEFT TO RUN, PAL, SO PUT THOSE HANDS UP AND TURN AROUND.
OKAY, OKAY--YOU'VE GOT ME COLD. WOULD YOU JUST POINT THAT THING AWAY FROM ME?

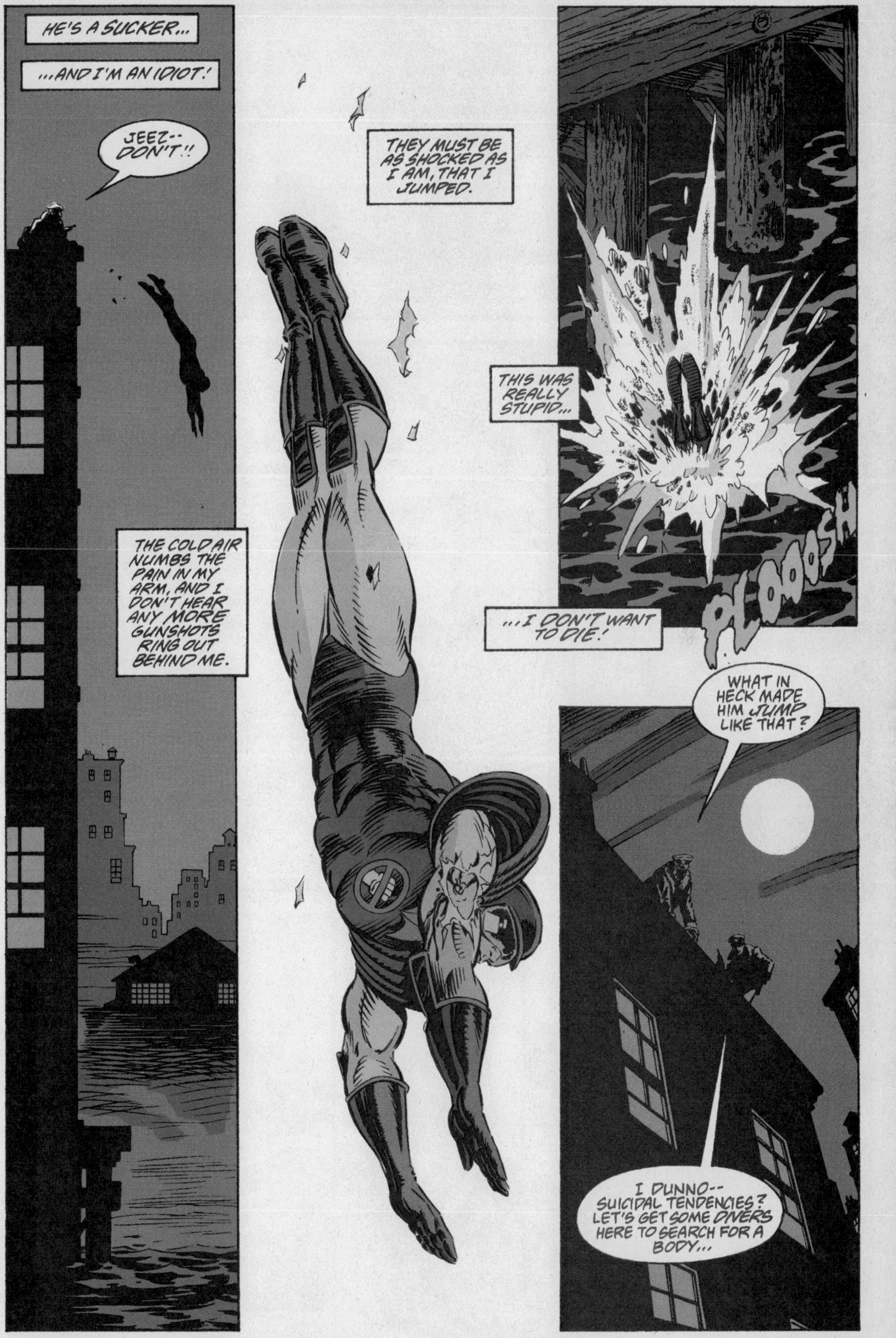
HE'S A SUCKER...
...AND I'M AN IDIOT!
JEEZ-- DON'T!!
THE COLD AIR NUMBS THE PAIN IN MY ARM, AND I DON'T HEAR ANY MORE GUNSHOTS RING OUT BEHIND ME.
THEY MUST BE AS SHOCKED AS I AM, THAT I JUMPED.
THIS WAS REALLY STUPID...
PLOOOOSH
...I DON'T WANT TO DIE!
WHAT IN HECK MADE HIM JUMP LIKE THAT?
I DUNNO-- SUICIDAL TENDENCIES? LET'S GET SOME DIVERS HERE TO SEARCH FOR A BODY...

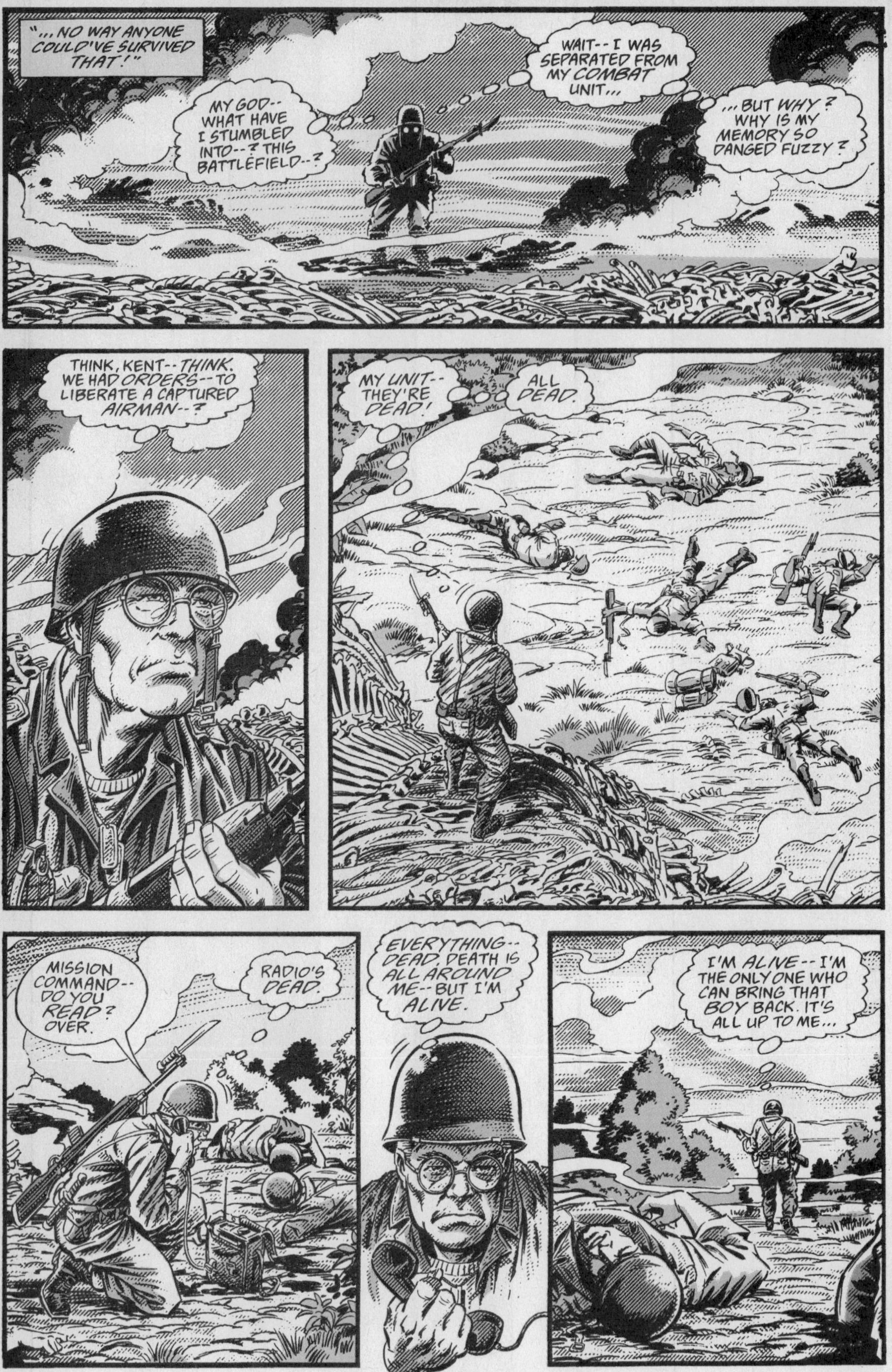
"...NO WAY ANYONE COULD'VE SURVIVED THAT!"
MY GOD-- WHAT HAVE I STUMBLED INTO--? THIS BATTLEFIELD--?
WAIT-- I WAS SEPARATED FROM MY COMBAT UNIT...
...BUT WHY? WHY IS MY MEMORY SO DANGED FUZZY?
THINK, KENT--THINK. WE HAD ORDERS--TO LIBERATE A CAPTURED AIRMAN--?
MY UNIT-- THEY'RE DEAD!
ALL DEAD.
MISSION COMMAND-- DO YOU READ? OVER.
RADIO'S DEAD.
EVERYTHING-- DEAD. DEATH IS ALL AROUND ME--BUT I'M ALIVE.
I'M ALIVE--I'M THE ONLY ONE WHO CAN BRING THAT BOY BACK. IT'S ALL UP TO ME...

... THERE'S JUST NO WAY WE CAN ABANDON ONE OF OUR *OWN*.

MORE DEATH. THEY'VE BEEN THROUGH THIS WAY.

GOD KNOWS WHY THEY BURNED OUT THESE POOR FARMERS -- NONE OF THEM IS ARMED.

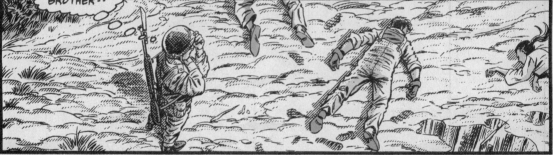

DARN SHAME. THAT ONE LOOKS TO BE THE SAME AGE AS MY BROTHER--

--HARRY! HARRY--?! WHAT IN HEAVEN'S NAME ARE YOU DOING IN KOREA?

JON? DON'T YOU REMEMBER? I FELL UNDER THE THRESHER MACHINE BACK ON PA'S FARM.

I'M *DEAD*, JONNY-- WE'RE ALL DEAD HERE.

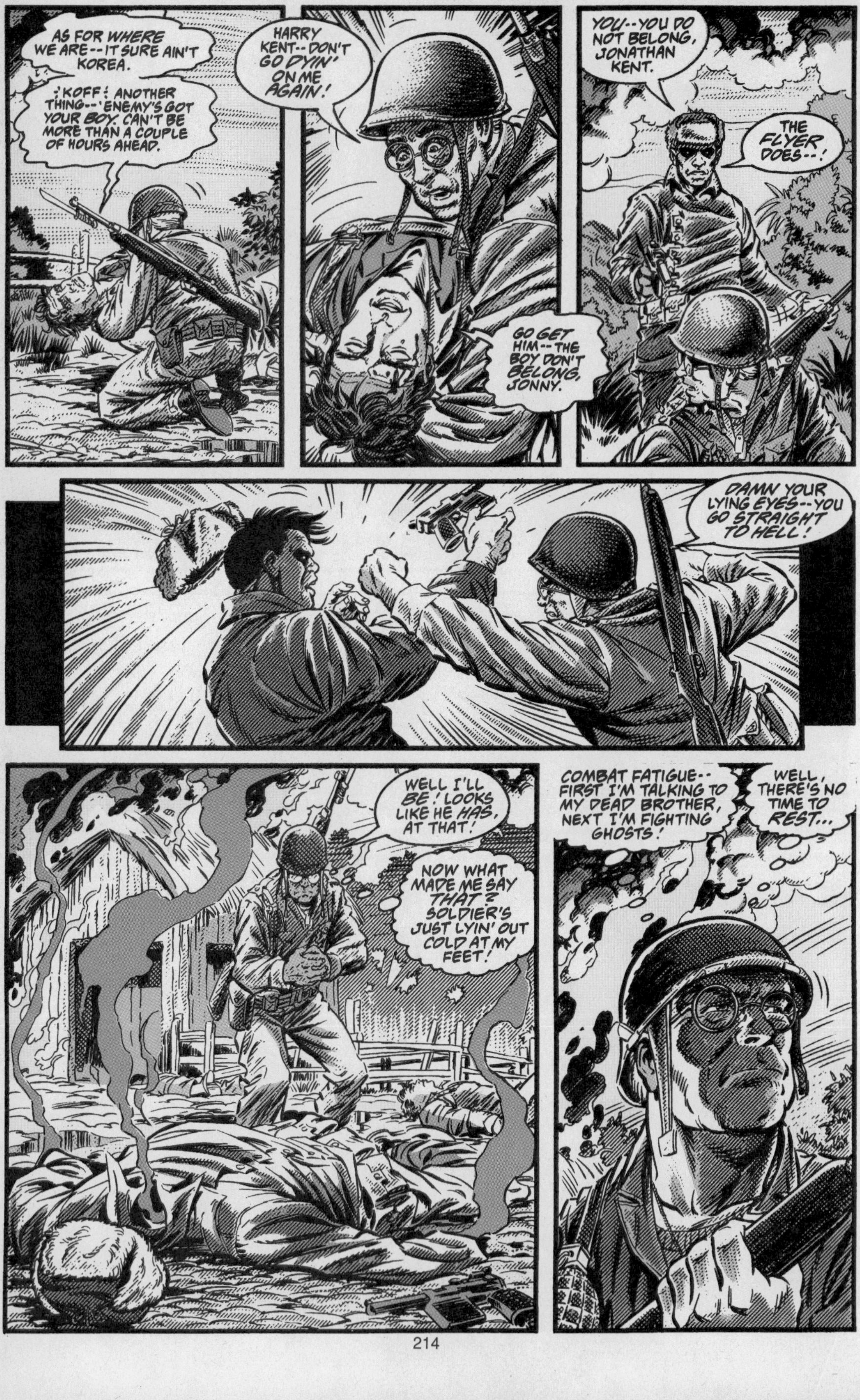
AS FOR WHERE WE ARE--IT SURE AIN'T KOREA.
:KOFF: ANOTHER THING--'ENEMY'S GOT YOUR BOY. CAN'T BE MORE THAN A COUPLE OF HOURS AHEAD.
HARRY KENT--DON'T GO DYIN' ON ME AGAIN!
YOU--YOU DO NOT BELONG, JONATHAN KENT.
THE FLYER DOES--!
GO GET HIM--THE BOY DON'T BELONG, JONNY.
DAMN YOUR LYING EYES--YOU GO STRAIGHT TO HELL!
WELL I'LL BE! LOOKS LIKE HE HAS, AT THAT!
NOW WHAT MADE ME SAY THAT? SOLDIER'S JUST LYIN' OUT COLD AT MY FEET!
COMBAT FATIGUE--FIRST I'M TALKING TO MY DEAD BROTHER, NEXT I'M FIGHTING GHOSTS!
WELL, THERE'S NO TIME TO REST...

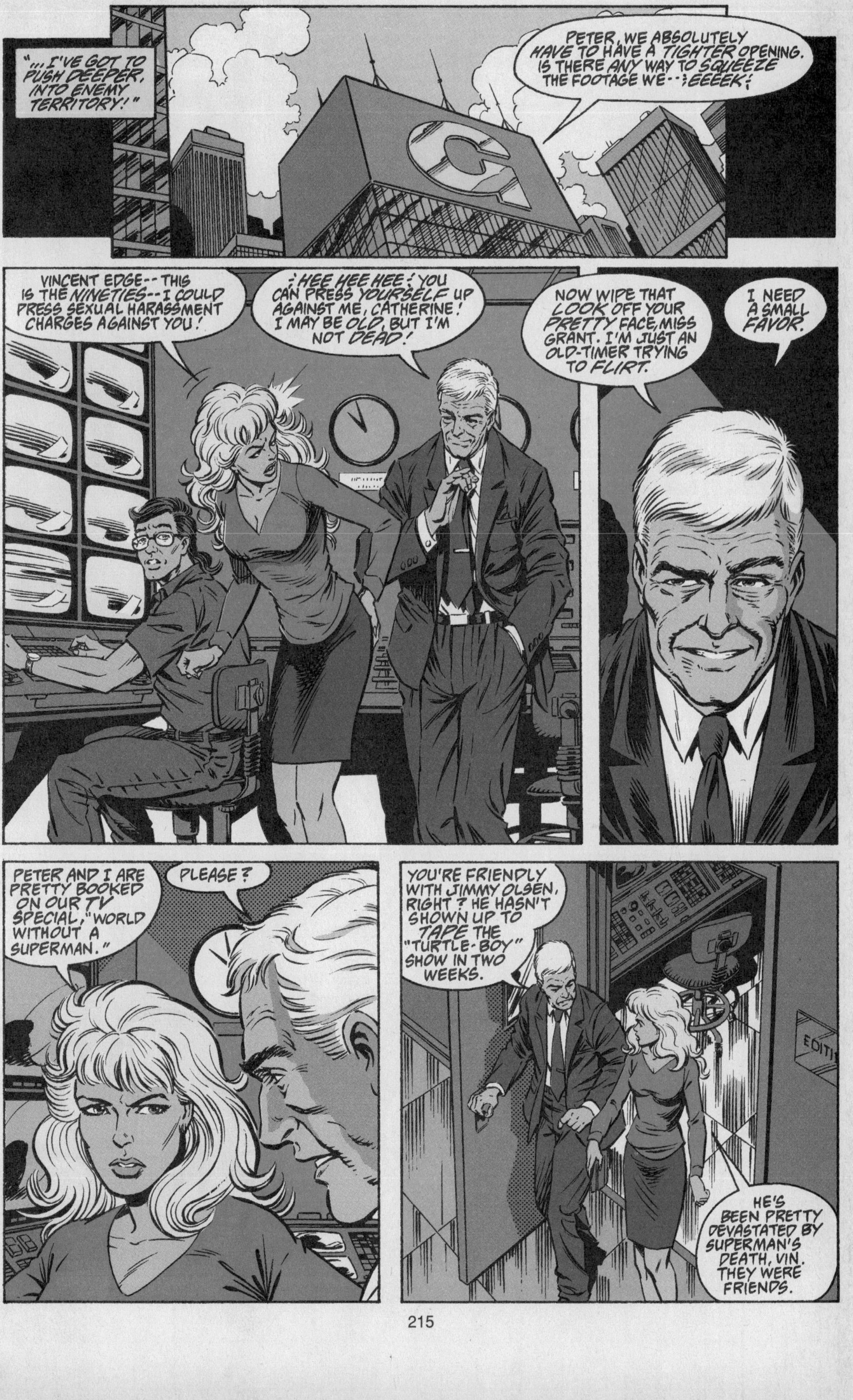
"...I'VE GOT TO PUSH DEEPER, INTO ENEMY TERRITORY!"
PETER, WE ABSOLUTELY HAVE TO HAVE A TIGHTER OPENING. IS THERE ANY WAY TO SQUEEZE THE FOOTAGE WE--EEEEK!
VINCENT EDGE-- THIS IS THE NINETIES--I COULD PRESS SEXUAL HARASSMENT CHARGES AGAINST YOU!
HEE HEE HEE! YOU CAN PRESS YOURSELF UP AGAINST ME, CATHERINE! I MAY BE OLD, BUT I'M NOT DEAD!
NOW WIPE THAT LOOK OFF YOUR PRETTY FACE, MISS GRANT. I'M JUST AN OLD-TIMER TRYING TO FLIRT.
I NEED A SMALL FAVOR.
PETER AND I ARE PRETTY BOOKED ON OUR TV SPECIAL, "WORLD WITHOUT A SUPERMAN."
PLEASE?
YOU'RE FRIENDLY WITH JIMMY OLSEN, RIGHT? HE HASN'T SHOWN UP TO TAPE THE "TURTLE-BOY" SHOW IN TWO WEEKS.
EDIT
HE'S BEEN PRETTY DEVASTATED BY SUPERMAN'S DEATH, VIN. THEY WERE FRIENDS.

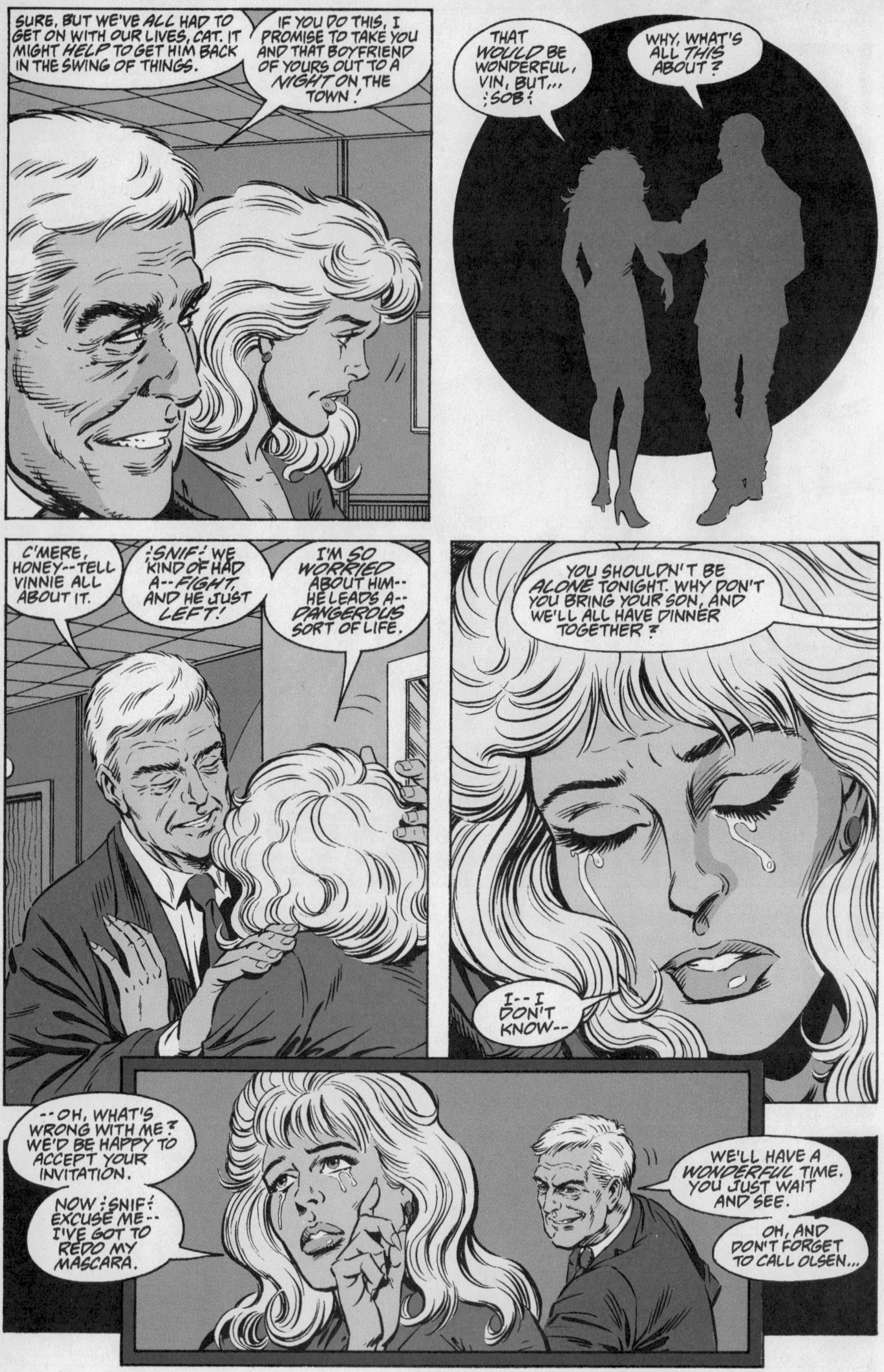
SURE, BUT WE'VE ALL HAD TO GET ON WITH OUR LIVES, CAT. IT MIGHT HELP TO GET HIM BACK IN THE SWING OF THINGS.
IF YOU DO THIS, I PROMISE TO TAKE YOU AND THAT BOYFRIEND OF YOURS OUT TO A NIGHT ON THE TOWN!
THAT WOULD BE WONDERFUL, VIN, BUT... :SOB:
WHY, WHAT'S ALL THIS ABOUT?
C'MERE, HONEY--TELL VINNIE ALL ABOUT IT.
:SNIF: WE KIND OF HAD A--FIGHT, AND HE JUST LEFT!
I'M SO WORRIED ABOUT HIM--HE LEADS A--DANGEROUS SORT OF LIFE.
YOU SHOULDN'T BE ALONE TONIGHT. WHY DON'T YOU BRING YOUR SON, AND WE'LL ALL HAVE DINNER TOGETHER?
I-- I DON'T KNOW--
--OH, WHAT'S WRONG WITH ME? WE'D BE HAPPY TO ACCEPT YOUR INVITATION.
NOW :SNIF: EXCUSE ME-- I'VE GOT TO REDO MY MASCARA.
WE'LL HAVE A WONDERFUL TIME. YOU JUST WAIT AND SEE.
OH, AND DON'T FORGET TO CALL OLSEN...

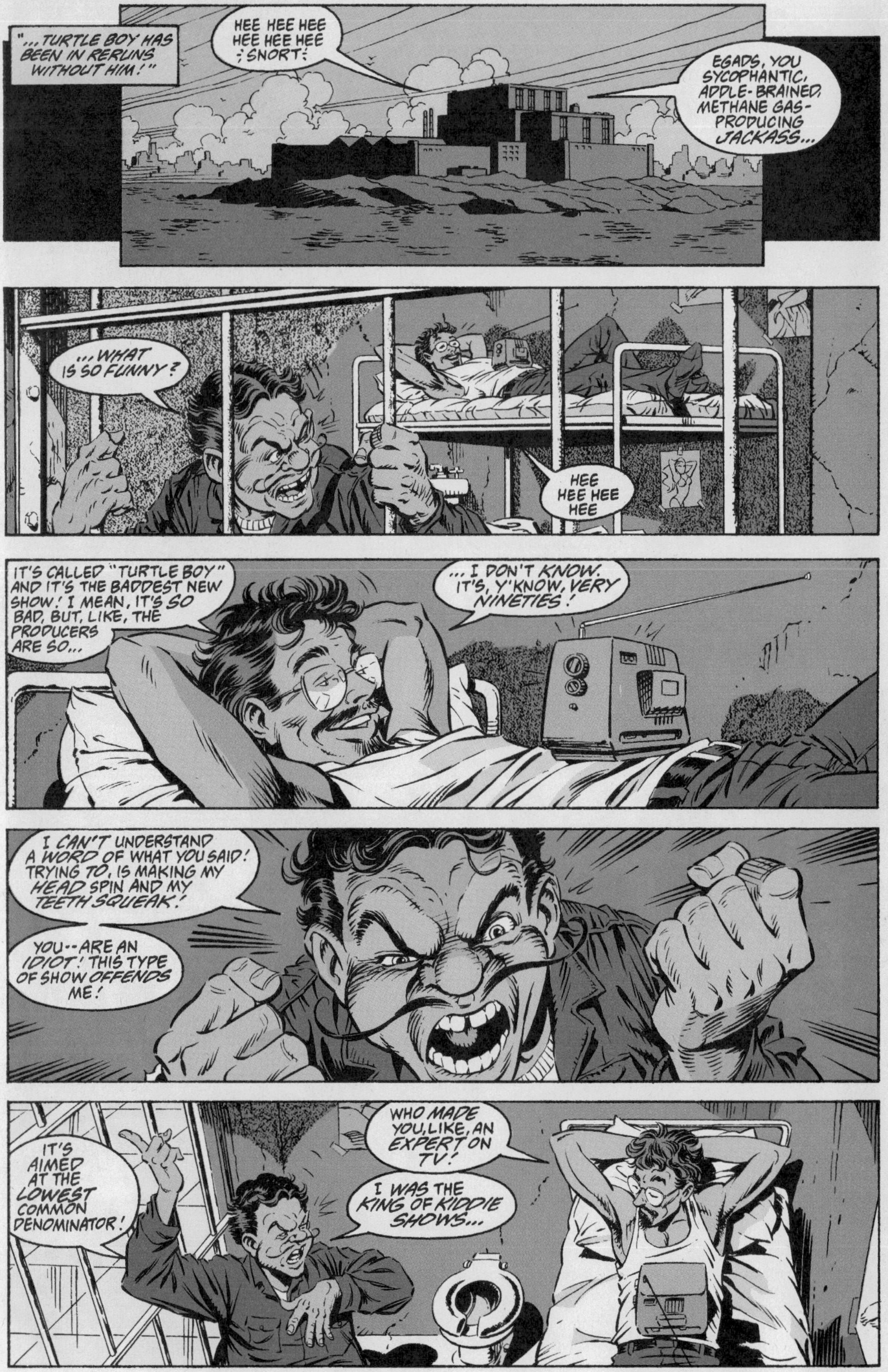
"...TURTLE BOY HAS BEEN IN RERUNS WITHOUT HIM!"
HEE HEE HEE HEE HEE HEE ⁏SNORT⁏
EGADS, YOU SYCOPHANTIC, ADDLE-BRAINED, METHANE GAS-PRODUCING JACKASS...
...WHAT IS SO FUNNY?
HEE HEE HEE HEE
IT'S CALLED "TURTLE BOY" AND IT'S THE BADDEST NEW SHOW! I MEAN, IT'S SO BAD, BUT, LIKE, THE PRODUCERS ARE SO...
...I DON'T KNOW. IT'S, Y'KNOW, VERY NINETIES!
I CAN'T UNDERSTAND A WORD OF WHAT YOU SAID! TRYING TO, IS MAKING MY HEAD SPIN AND MY TEETH SQUEAK!
YOU--ARE AN IDIOT! THIS TYPE OF SHOW OFFENDS ME!
IT'S AIMED AT THE LOWEST COMMON DENOMINATOR!
WHO MADE YOU, LIKE, AN EXPERT ON TV!
I WAS THE KING OF KIDDIE SHOWS...

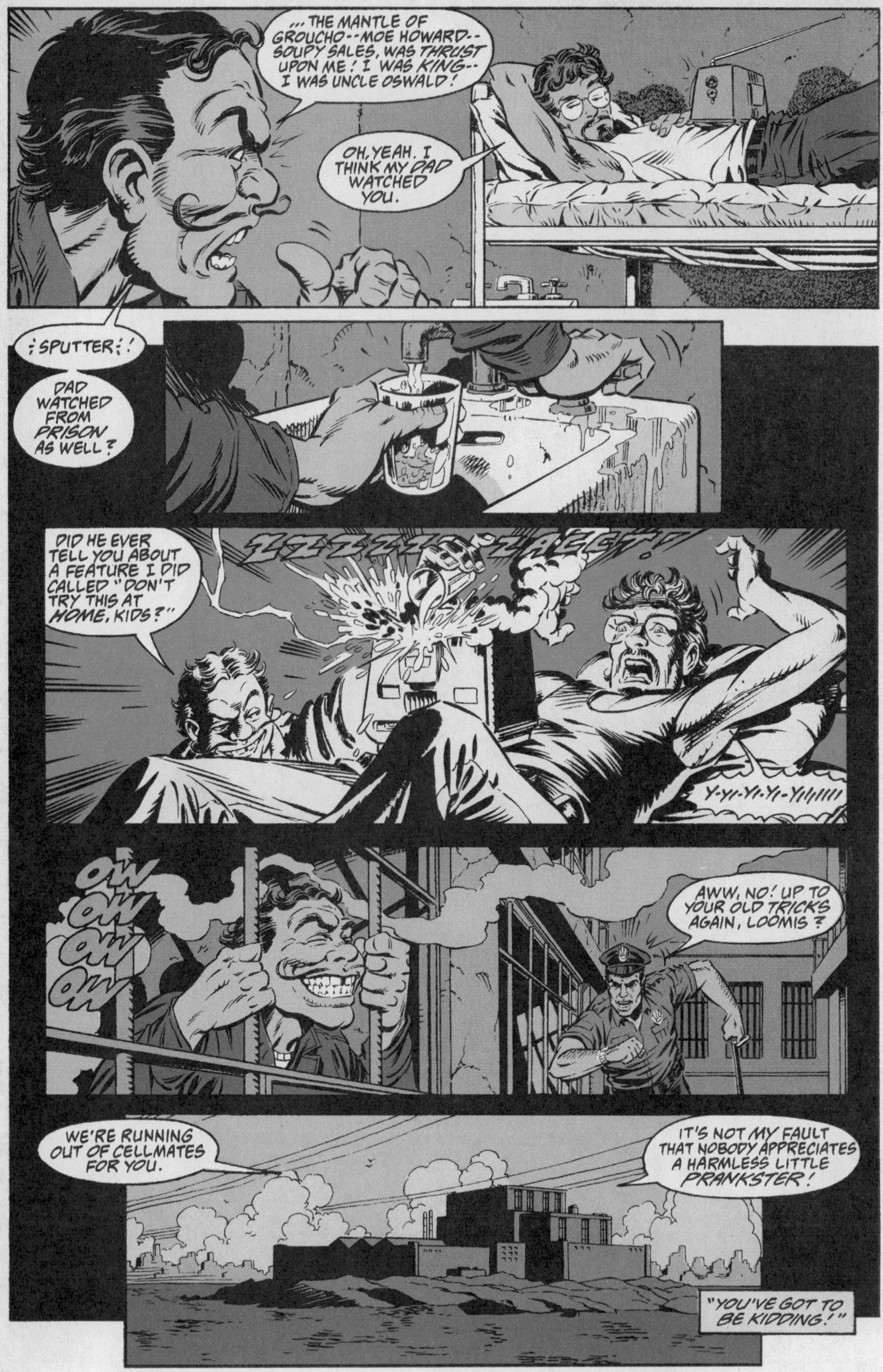
...THE MANTLE OF GROUCHO--MOE HOWARD--SOUPY SALES, WAS THRUST UPON ME! I WAS KING--I WAS UNCLE OSWALD!
OH, YEAH. I THINK MY DAD WATCHED YOU.
SPUTTER!
DAD WATCHED FROM PRISON AS WELL?
DID HE EVER TELL YOU ABOUT A FEATURE I DID CALLED "DON'T TRY THIS AT HOME, KIDS?"
Y-YI-YI-YI-YI!!!!
OW OW OW OW OW
AWW, NO! UP TO YOUR OLD TRICKS AGAIN, LOOMIS?
WE'RE RUNNING OUT OF CELLMATES FOR YOU.
IT'S NOT MY FAULT THAT NOBODY APPRECIATES A HARMLESS LITTLE PRANKSTER!
"YOU'VE GOT TO BE KIDDING!"

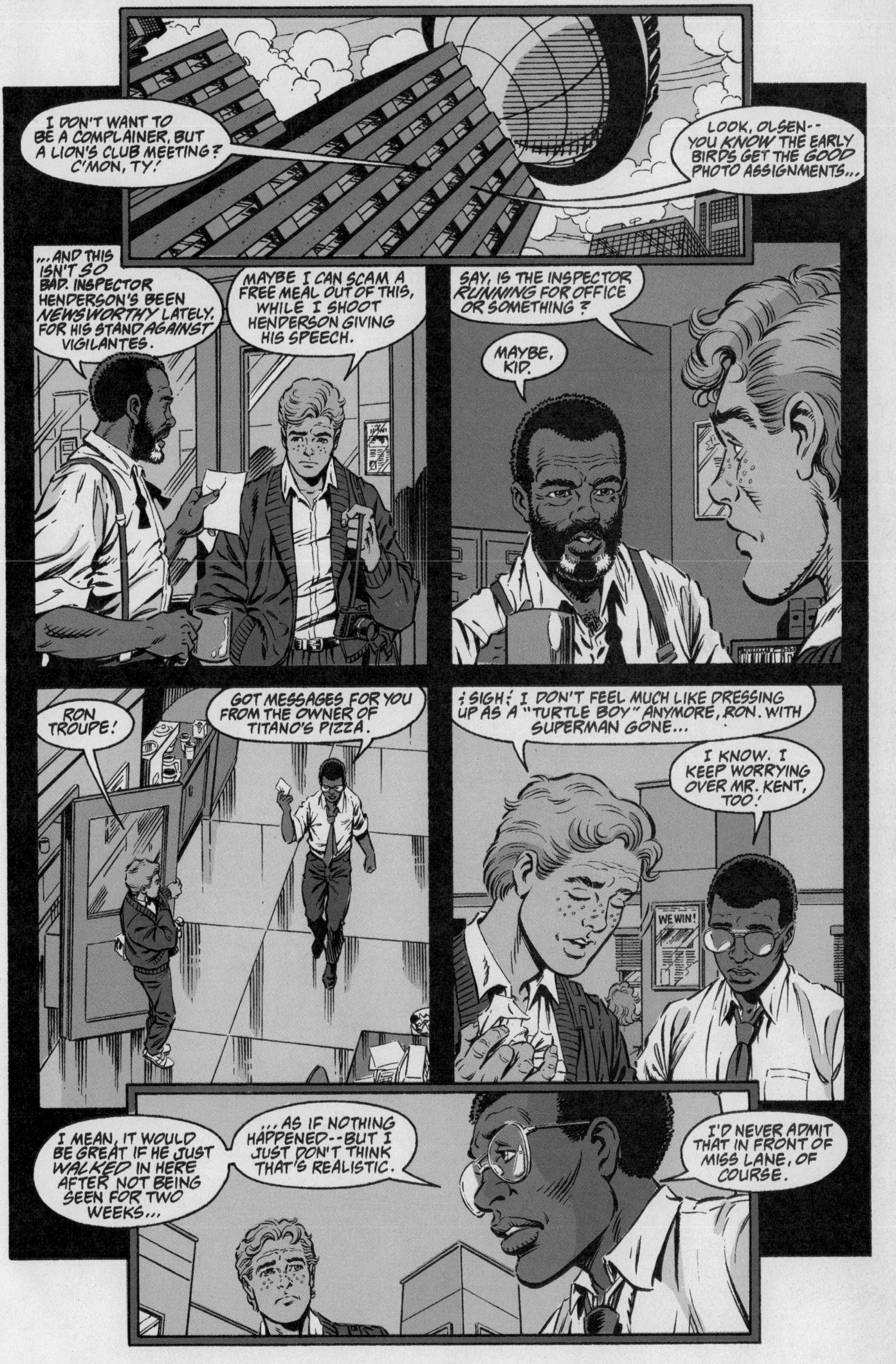

I DON'T WANT TO BE A COMPLAINER, BUT A LION'S CLUB MEETING? C'MON, TY!
LOOK, OLSEN-- YOU KNOW THE EARLY BIRDS GET THE GOOD PHOTO ASSIGNMENTS...
...AND THIS ISN'T SO BAD. INSPECTOR HENDERSON'S BEEN NEWSWORTHY LATELY. FOR HIS STAND AGAINST VIGILANTES.
MAYBE I CAN SCAM A FREE MEAL OUT OF THIS, WHILE I SHOOT HENDERSON GIVING HIS SPEECH.
SAY, IS THE INSPECTOR RUNNING FOR OFFICE OR SOMETHING?
MAYBE, KID.
RON TROUPE!
GOT MESSAGES FOR YOU FROM THE OWNER OF TITANO'S PIZZA.
:SIGH: I DON'T FEEL MUCH LIKE DRESSING UP AS A "TURTLE BOY" ANYMORE, RON. WITH SUPERMAN GONE...
I KNOW. I KEEP WORRYING OVER MR. KENT, TOO!
WE WIN!
I MEAN, IT WOULD BE GREAT IF HE JUST WALKED IN HERE AFTER NOT BEING SEEN FOR TWO WEEKS...
...AS IF NOTHING HAPPENED--BUT I JUST DON'T THINK THAT'S REALISTIC.
I'D NEVER ADMIT THAT IN FRONT OF MISS LANE, OF COURSE.

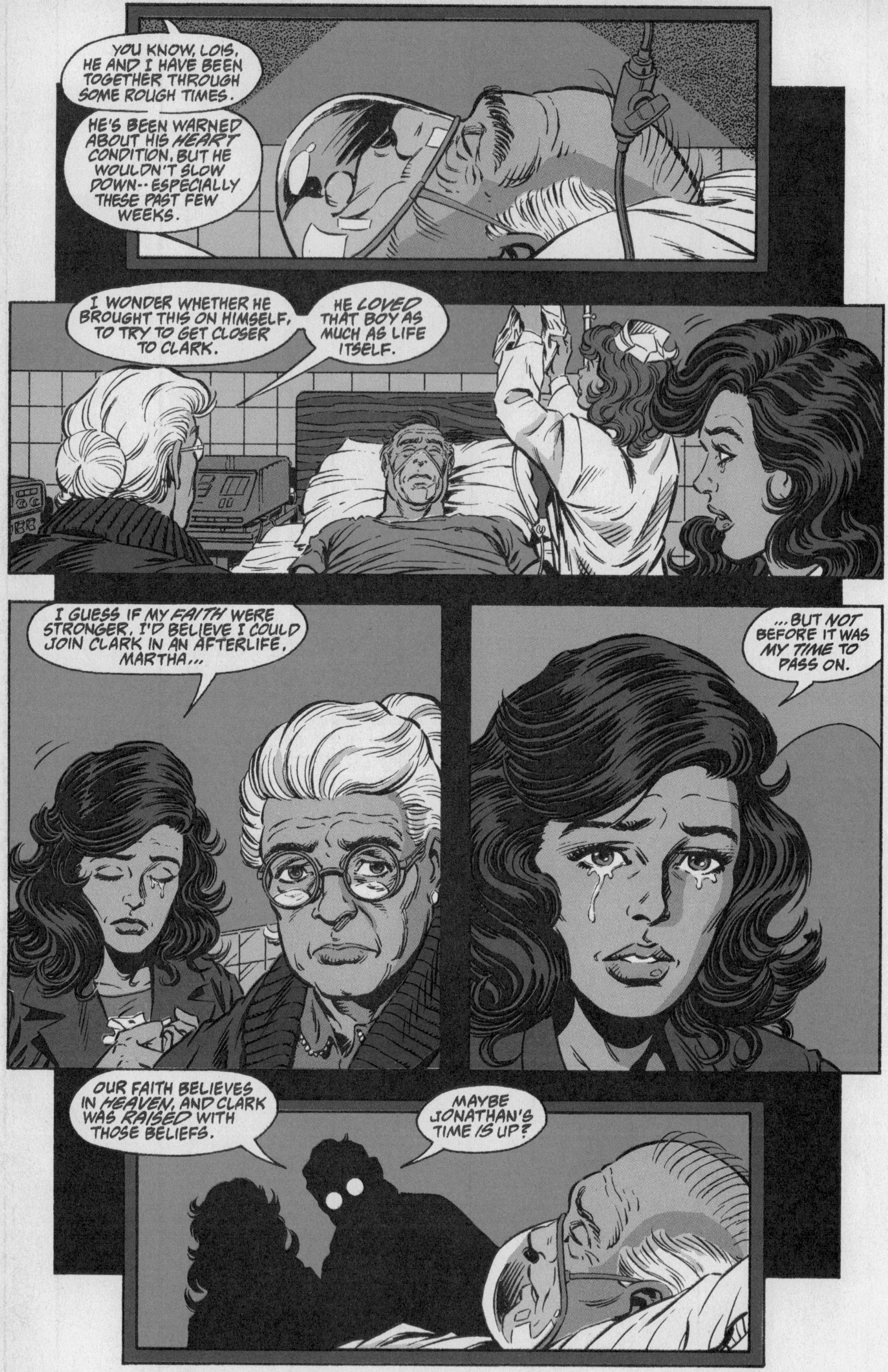
YOU KNOW, LOIS, HE AND I HAVE BEEN TOGETHER THROUGH SOME ROUGH TIMES.
HE'S BEEN WARNED ABOUT HIS HEART CONDITION, BUT HE WOULDN'T SLOW DOWN--ESPECIALLY THESE PAST FEW WEEKS.
I WONDER WHETHER HE BROUGHT THIS ON HIMSELF, TO TRY TO GET CLOSER TO CLARK.
HE LOVED THAT BOY AS MUCH AS LIFE ITSELF.
I GUESS IF MY FAITH WERE STRONGER, I'D BELIEVE I COULD JOIN CLARK IN AN AFTERLIFE, MARTHA...
...BUT NOT BEFORE IT WAS MY TIME TO PASS ON.
OUR FAITH BELIEVES IN HEAVEN, AND CLARK WAS RAISED WITH THOSE BELIEFS.
MAYBE JONATHAN'S TIME IS UP?

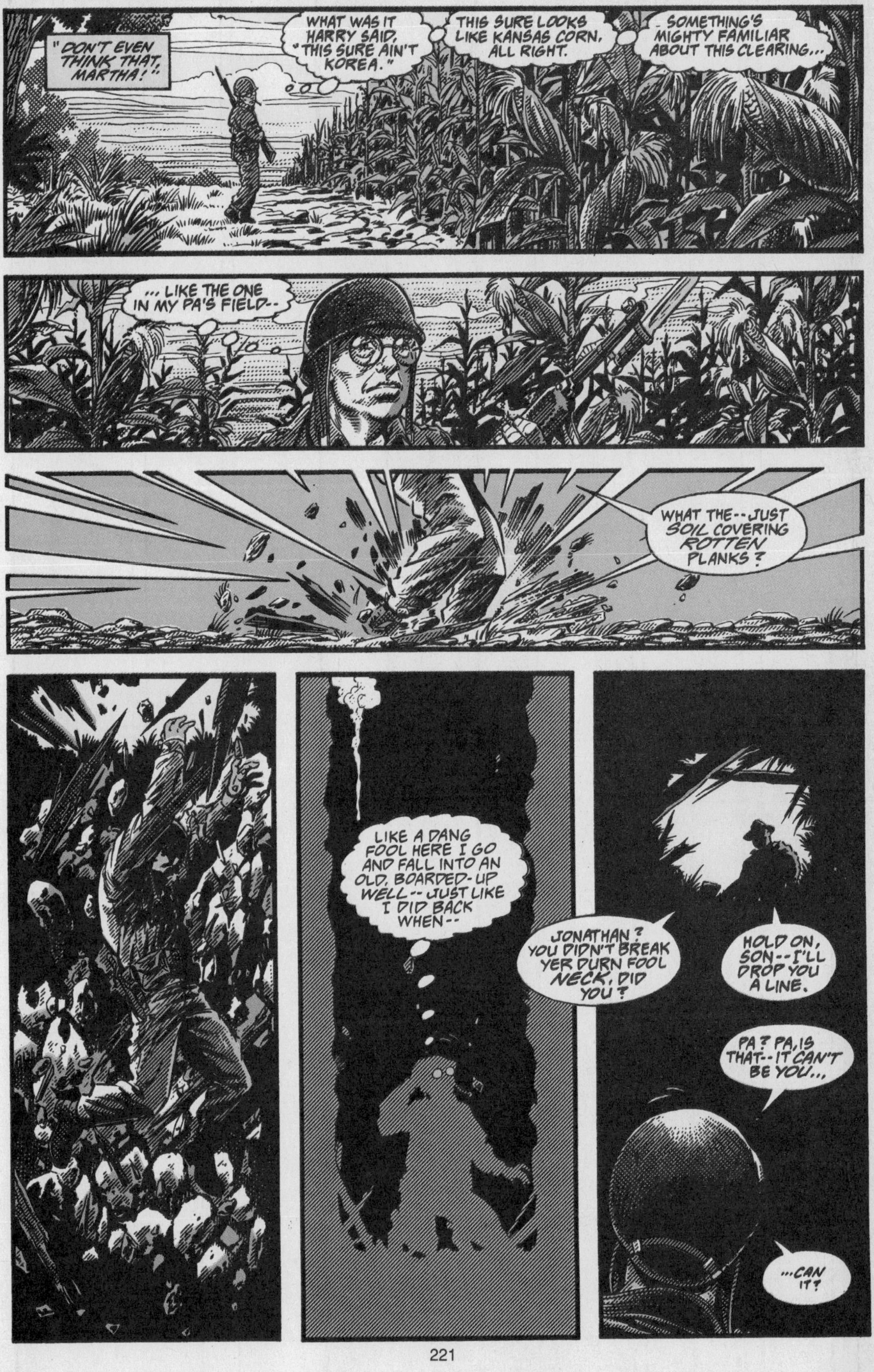
"DON'T EVEN THINK THAT, MARTHA!".
WHAT WAS IT HARRY SAID, "THIS SURE AIN'T KOREA."
THIS SURE LOOKS LIKE KANSAS CORN, ALL RIGHT.
- SOMETHING'S MIGHTY FAMILIAR ABOUT THIS CLEARING...
... LIKE THE ONE IN MY PA'S FIELD--
WHAT THE--JUST SOIL COVERING ROTTEN PLANKS?
LIKE A DANG FOOL HERE I GO AND FALL INTO AN OLD, BOARDED-UP WELL--JUST LIKE I DID BACK WHEN--
JONATHAN? YOU DIDN'T BREAK YER DURN FOOL NECK, DID YOU?
HOLD ON, SON--I'LL DROP YOU A LINE.
PA? PA, IS THAT--IT CAN'T BE YOU...
...CAN IT?

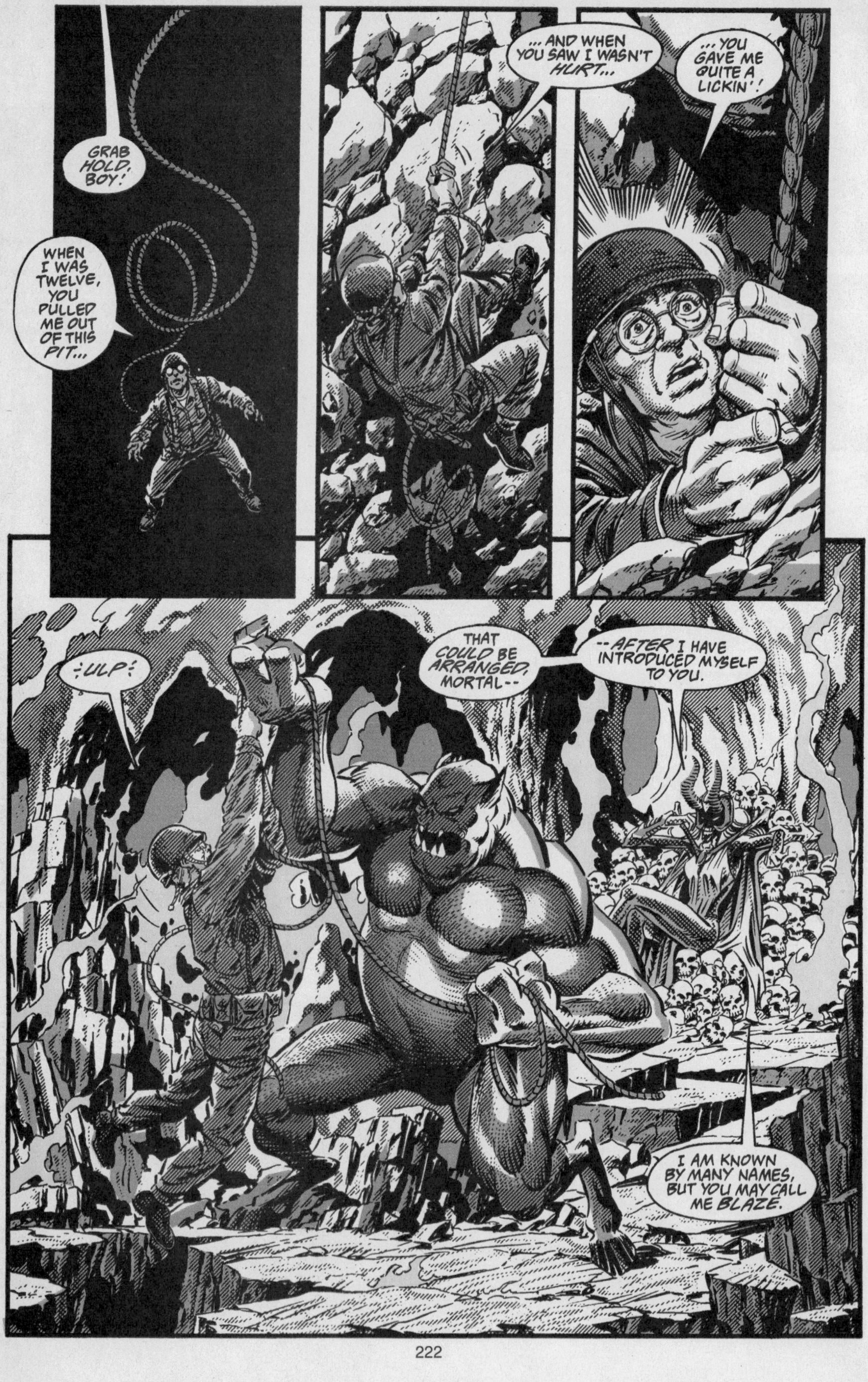
GRAB HOLD, BOY!
WHEN I WAS TWELVE, YOU PULLED ME OUT OF THIS PIT...
...AND WHEN YOU SAW I WASN'T HURT...
...YOU GAVE ME QUITE A LICKIN'!
-ULP-
THAT COULD BE ARRANGED, MORTAL--
--AFTER I HAVE INTRODUCED MYSELF TO YOU.
I AM KNOWN BY MANY NAMES, BUT YOU MAY CALL ME BLAZE.

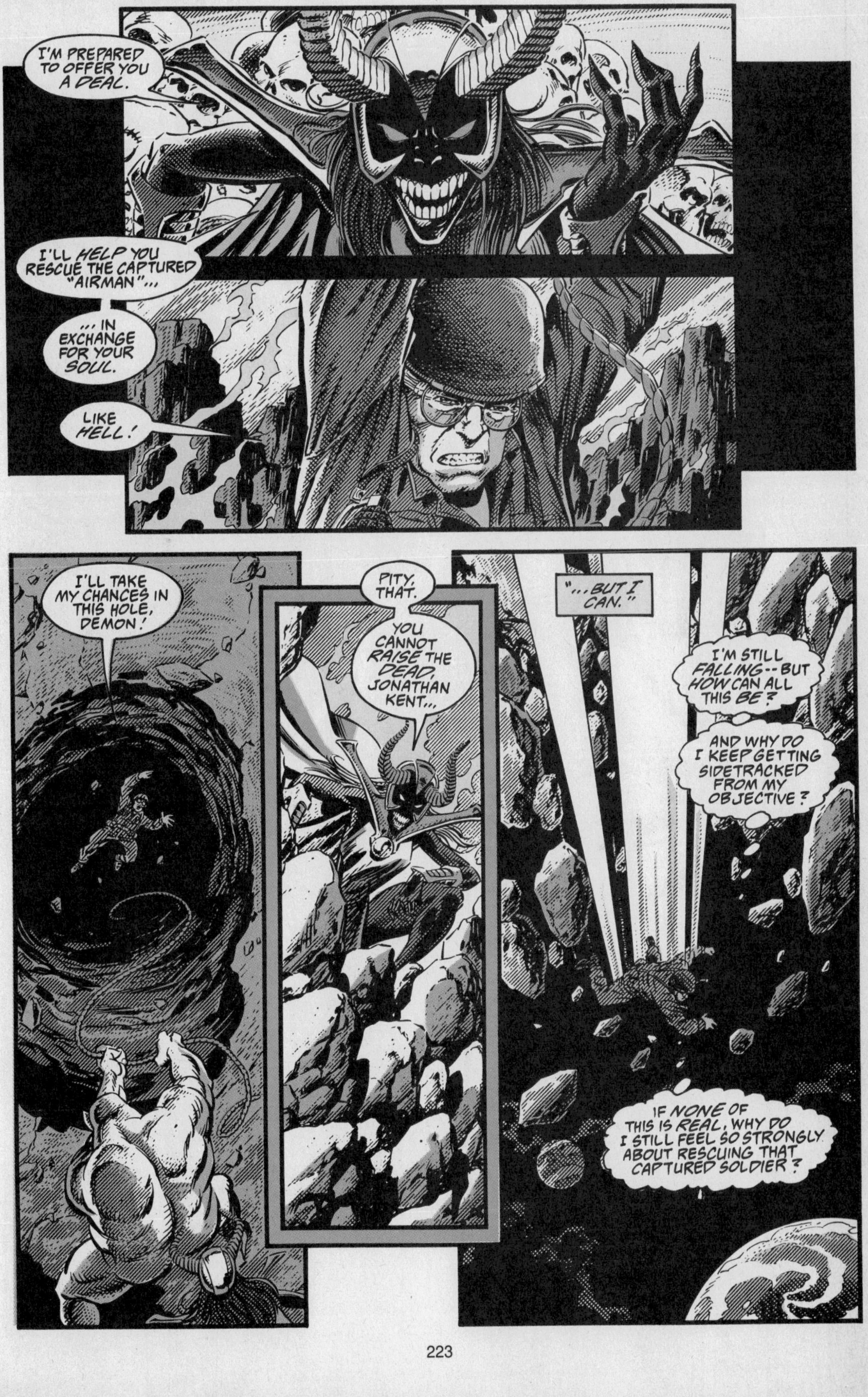
I'M PREPARED TO OFFER YOU A DEAL.
I'LL HELP YOU RESCUE THE CAPTURED "AIRMAN"...
... IN EXCHANGE FOR YOUR SOUL.
LIKE HELL!
I'LL TAKE MY CHANCES IN THIS HOLE, DEMON!
PITY, THAT.
YOU CANNOT RAISE THE DEAD, JONATHAN KENT...
"...BUT I CAN."
I'M STILL FALLING--BUT HOW CAN ALL THIS BE?
AND WHY DO I KEEP GETTING SIDETRACKED FROM MY OBJECTIVE?
IF NONE OF THIS IS REAL, WHY DO I STILL FEEL SO STRONGLY ABOUT RESCUING THAT CAPTURED SOLDIER?

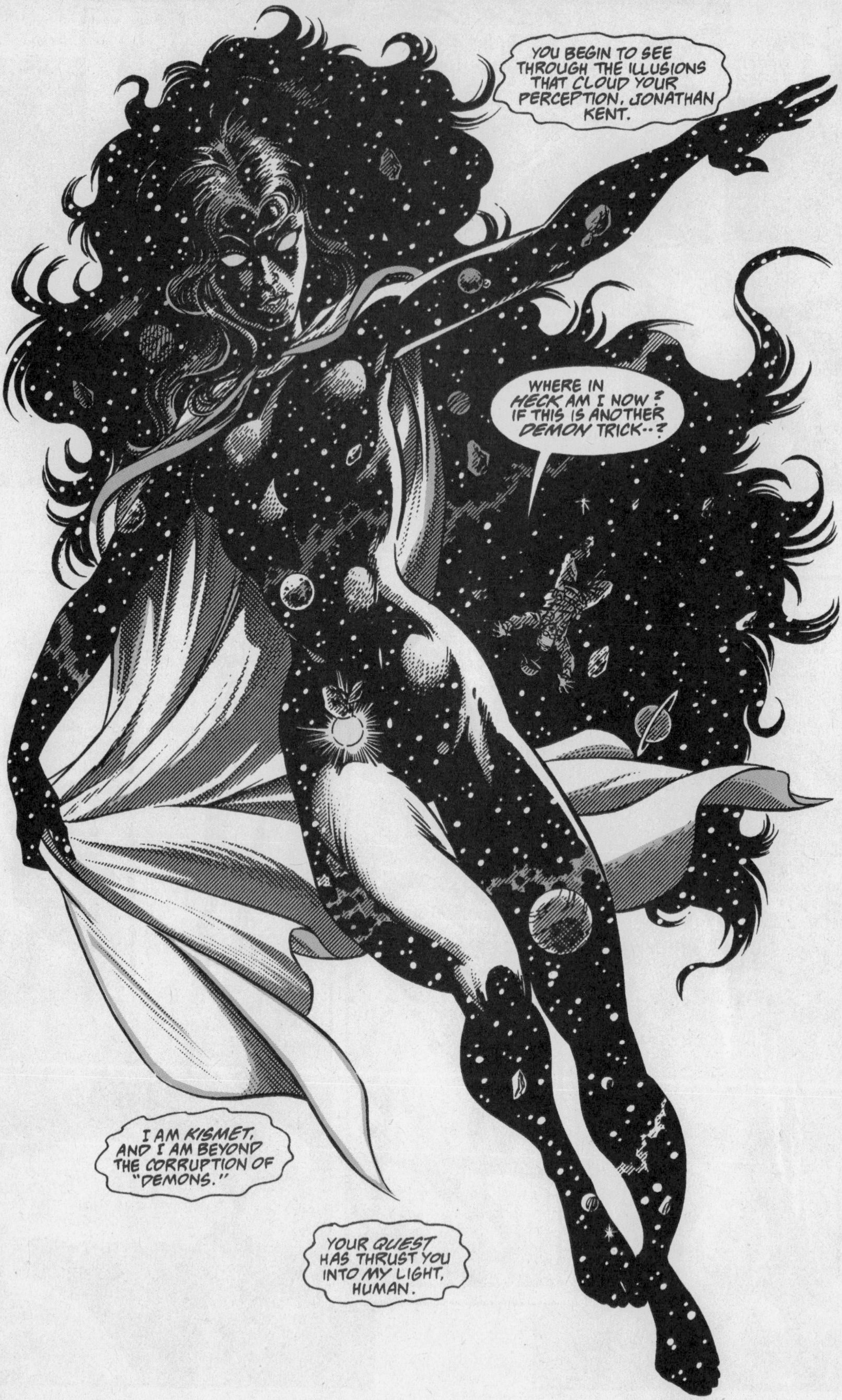
YOU BEGIN TO SEE THROUGH THE ILLUSIONS THAT CLOUD YOUR PERCEPTION, JONATHAN KENT.
WHERE IN HECK AM I NOW? IF THIS IS ANOTHER DEMON TRICK--?
I AM KISMET, AND I AM BEYOND THE CORRUPTION OF "DEMONS."
YOUR QUEST HAS THRUST YOU INTO MY LIGHT, HUMAN.

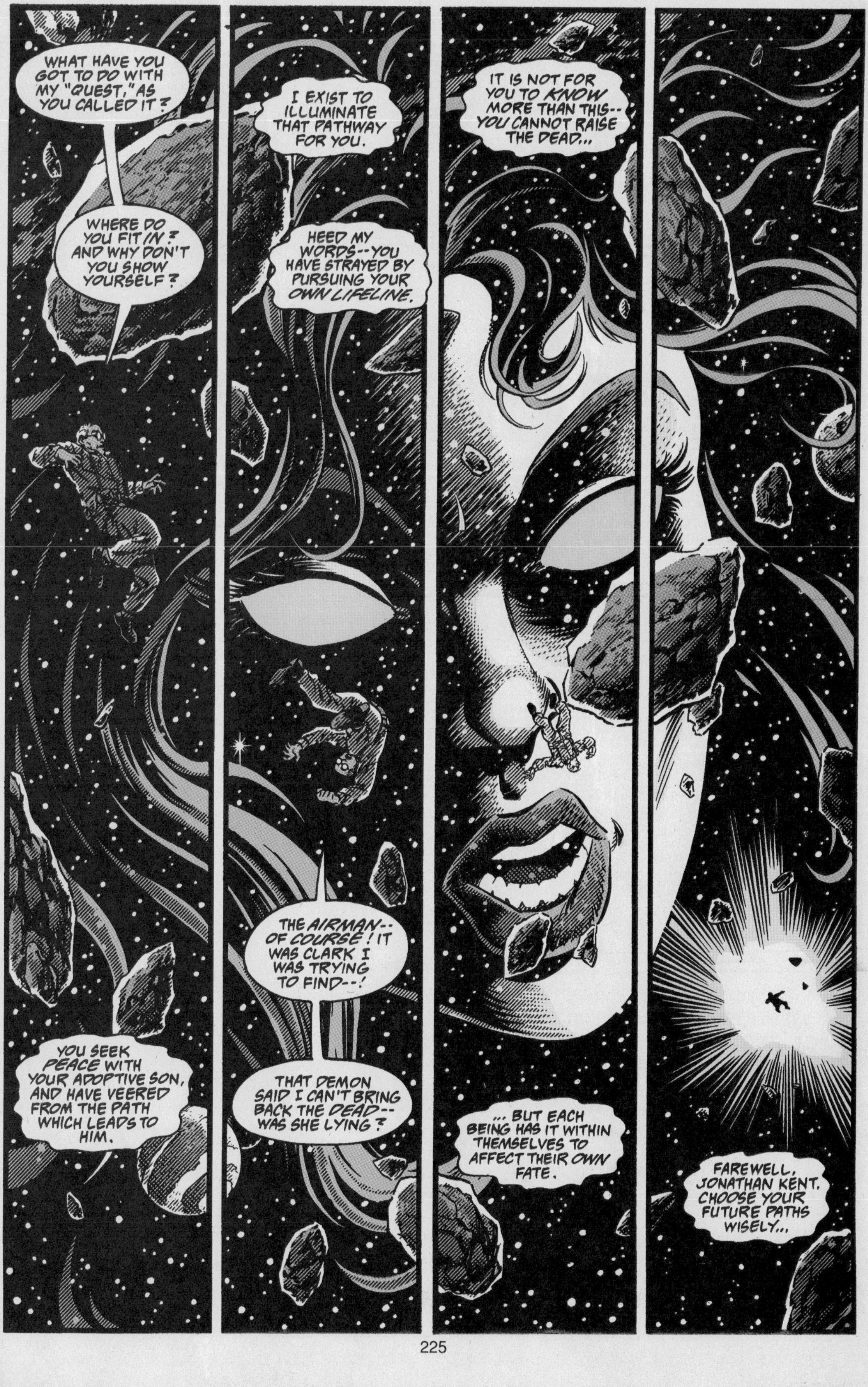
WHAT HAVE YOU GOT TO DO WITH MY "QUEST," AS YOU CALLED IT?
WHERE DO YOU FIT IN? AND WHY DON'T YOU SHOW YOURSELF?
YOU SEEK PEACE WITH YOUR ADOPTIVE SON, AND HAVE VEERED FROM THE PATH WHICH LEADS TO HIM.
I EXIST TO ILLUMINATE THAT PATHWAY FOR YOU.
HEED MY WORDS--YOU HAVE STRAYED BY PURSUING YOUR OWN LIFELINE.
THE AIRMAN--OF COURSE! IT WAS CLARK I WAS TRYING TO FIND--!
THAT DEMON SAID I CAN'T BRING BACK THE DEAD--WAS SHE LYING?
IT IS NOT FOR YOU TO KNOW MORE THAN THIS--YOU CANNOT RAISE THE DEAD...
... BUT EACH BEING HAS IT WITHIN THEMSELVES TO AFFECT THEIR OWN FATE.
FAREWELL, JONATHAN KENT. CHOOSE YOUR FUTURE PATHS WISELY...

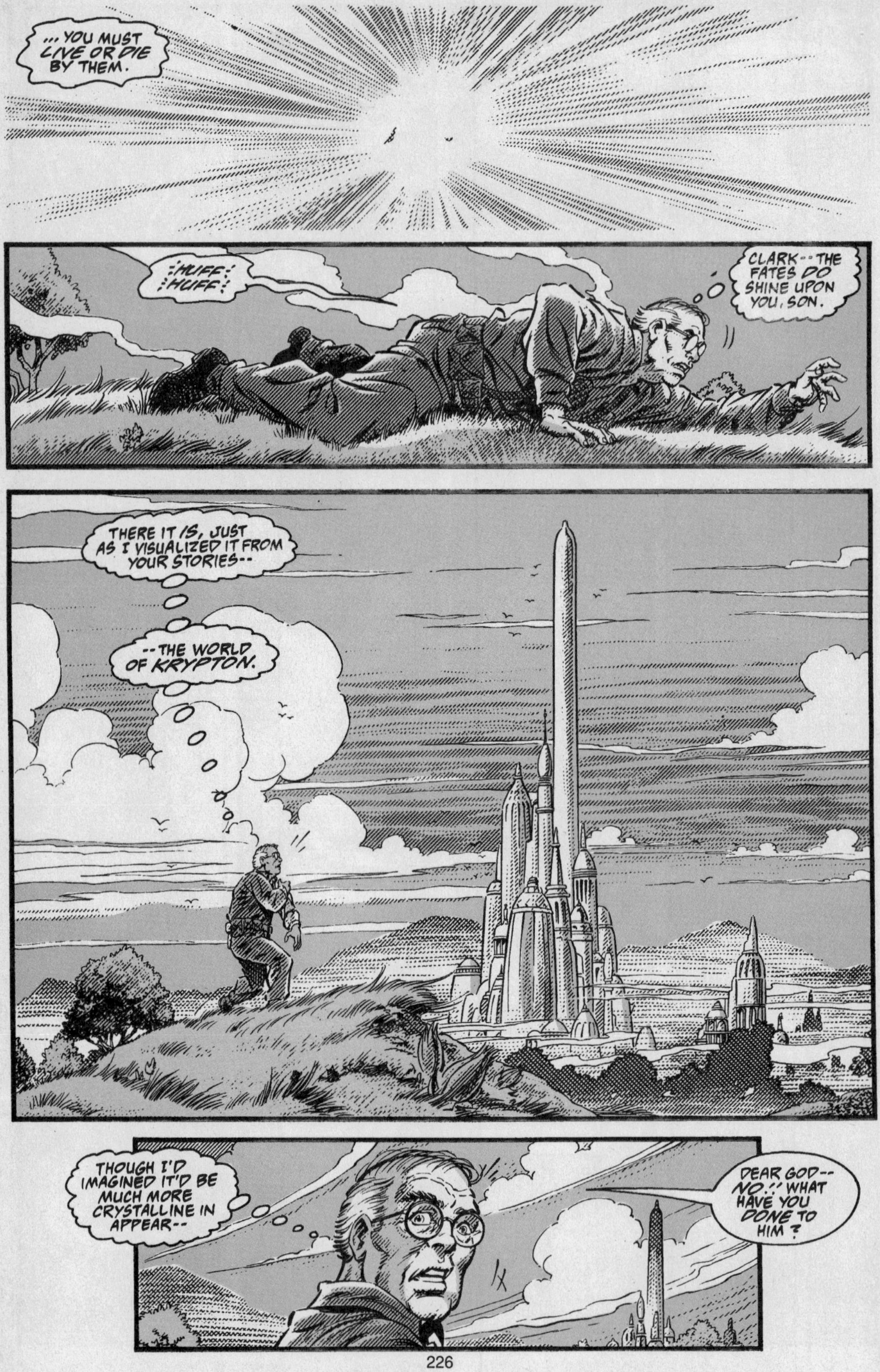
...YOU MUST LIVE OR DIE BY THEM.
HUFF HUFF
CLARK--THE FATES DO SHINE UPON YOU, SON.
THERE IT IS, JUST AS I VISUALIZED IT FROM YOUR STORIES--
--THE WORLD OF KRYPTON.
THOUGH I'D IMAGINED IT'D BE MUCH MORE CRYSTALLINE IN APPEAR--
DEAR GOD--NO!! WHAT HAVE YOU DONE TO HIM?

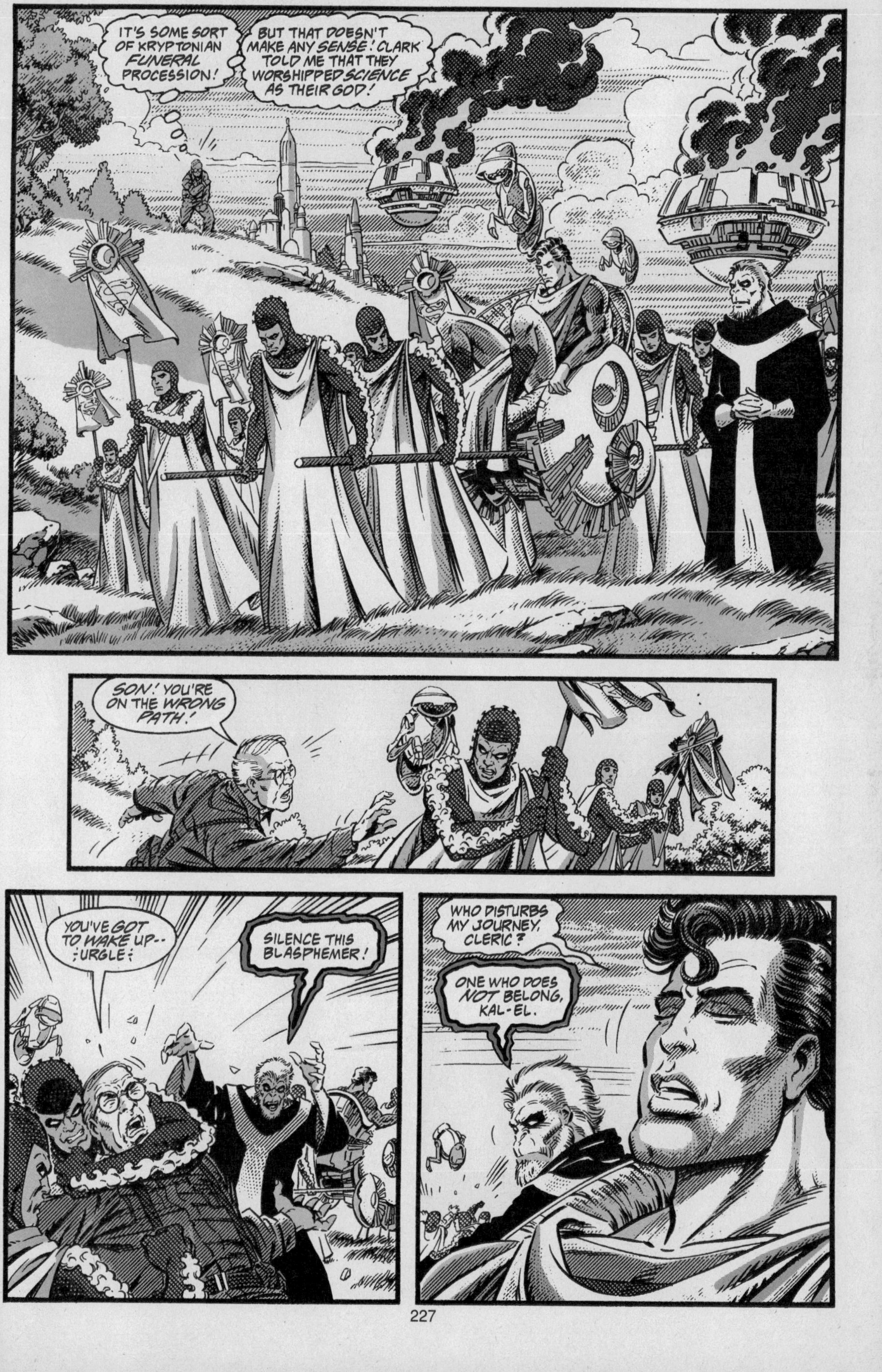
IT'S SOME SORT OF KRYPTONIAN FUNERAL PROCESSION!
BUT THAT DOESN'T MAKE ANY SENSE! CLARK TOLD ME THAT THEY WORSHIPPED SCIENCE AS THEIR GOD!
SON! YOU'RE ON THE WRONG PATH!
YOU'VE GOT TO WAKE UP-- ;URGLE;
SILENCE THIS BLASPHEMER!
WHO DISTURBS MY JOURNEY, CLERIC?
ONE WHO DOES NOT BELONG, KAL-EL.

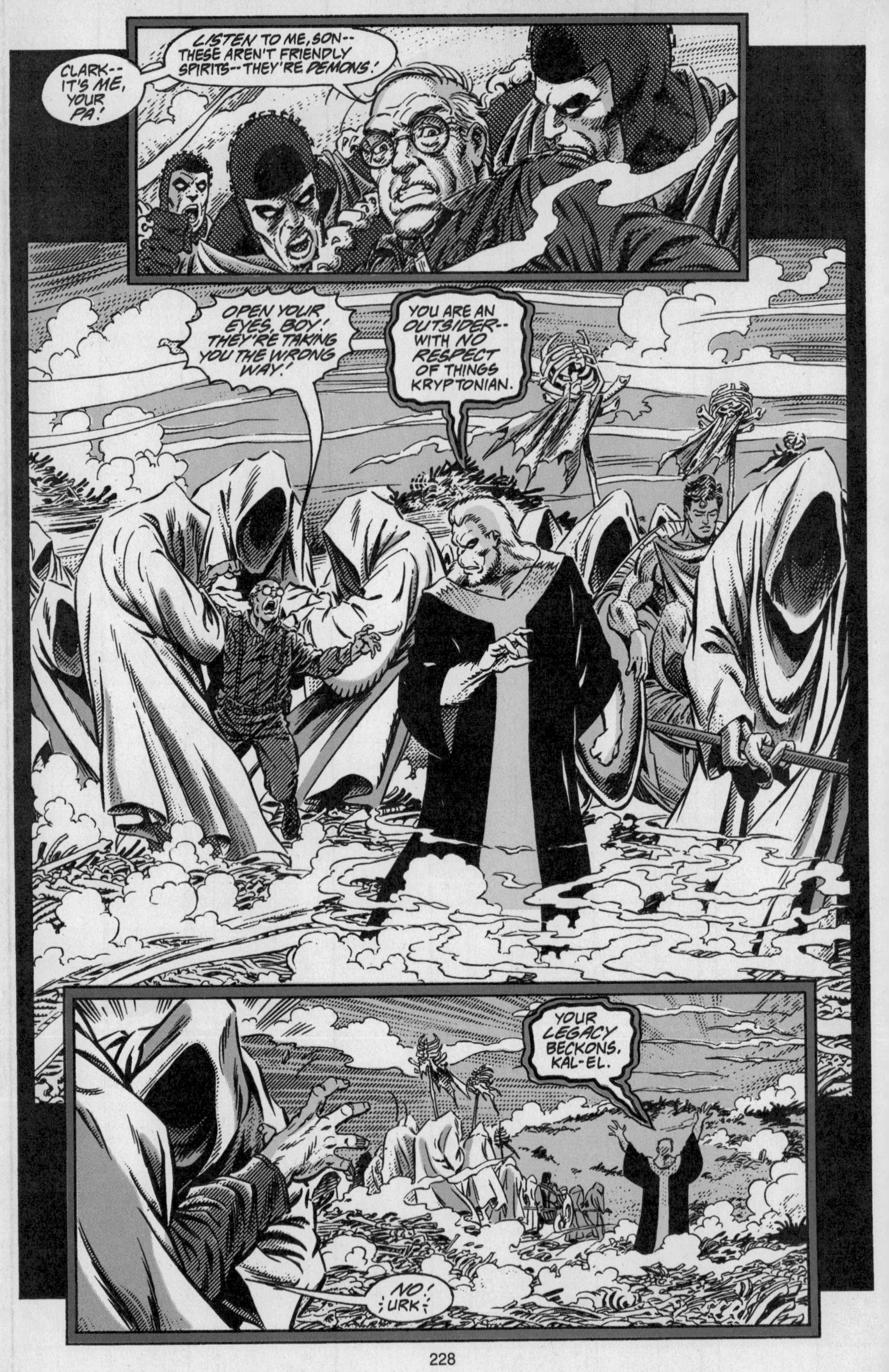
CLARK-- IT'S ME, YOUR PA!
LISTEN TO ME, SON-- THESE AREN'T FRIENDLY SPIRITS-- THEY'RE DEMONS!
OPEN YOUR EYES, BOY! THEY'RE TAKING YOU THE WRONG WAY!
YOU ARE AN OUTSIDER-- WITH NO RESPECT OF THINGS KRYPTONIAN.
YOUR LEGACY BECKONS, KAL-EL.
NO! URK!

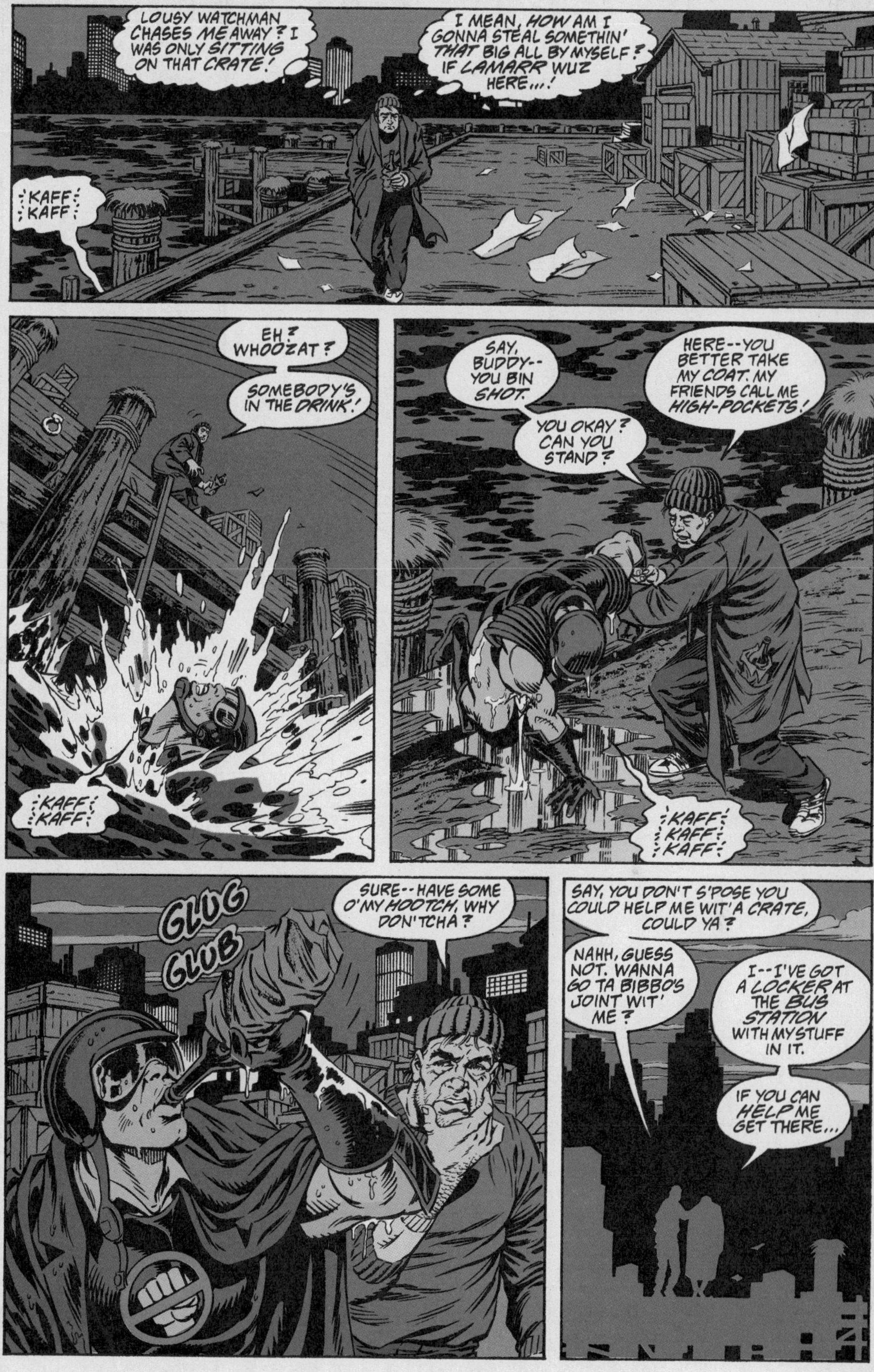
LOUSY WATCHMAN CHASES ME AWAY? I WAS ONLY SITTING ON THAT CRATE!
I MEAN, HOW AM I GONNA STEAL SOMETHIN' THAT BIG ALL BY MYSELF? IF LAMARR WUZ HERE...!
KAFF KAFF
EH? WHOOZAT?
SOMEBODY'S IN THE DRINK!
KAFF KAFF
SAY, BUDDY-- YOU BIN SHOT.
YOU OKAY? CAN YOU STAND?
HERE--YOU BETTER TAKE MY COAT. MY FRIENDS CALL ME HIGH-POCKETS!
KAFF KAFF KAFF
GLUG GLUB
SURE--HAVE SOME O' MY HOOTCH, WHY DON'TCHA?
SAY, YOU DON'T S'POSE YOU COULD HELP ME WIT' A CRATE, COULD YA?
NAHH, GUESS NOT. WANNA GO TA BIBBO'S JOINT WIT' ME?
I--I'VE GOT A LOCKER AT THE BUS STATION WITH MY STUFF IN IT.
IF YOU CAN HELP ME GET THERE...

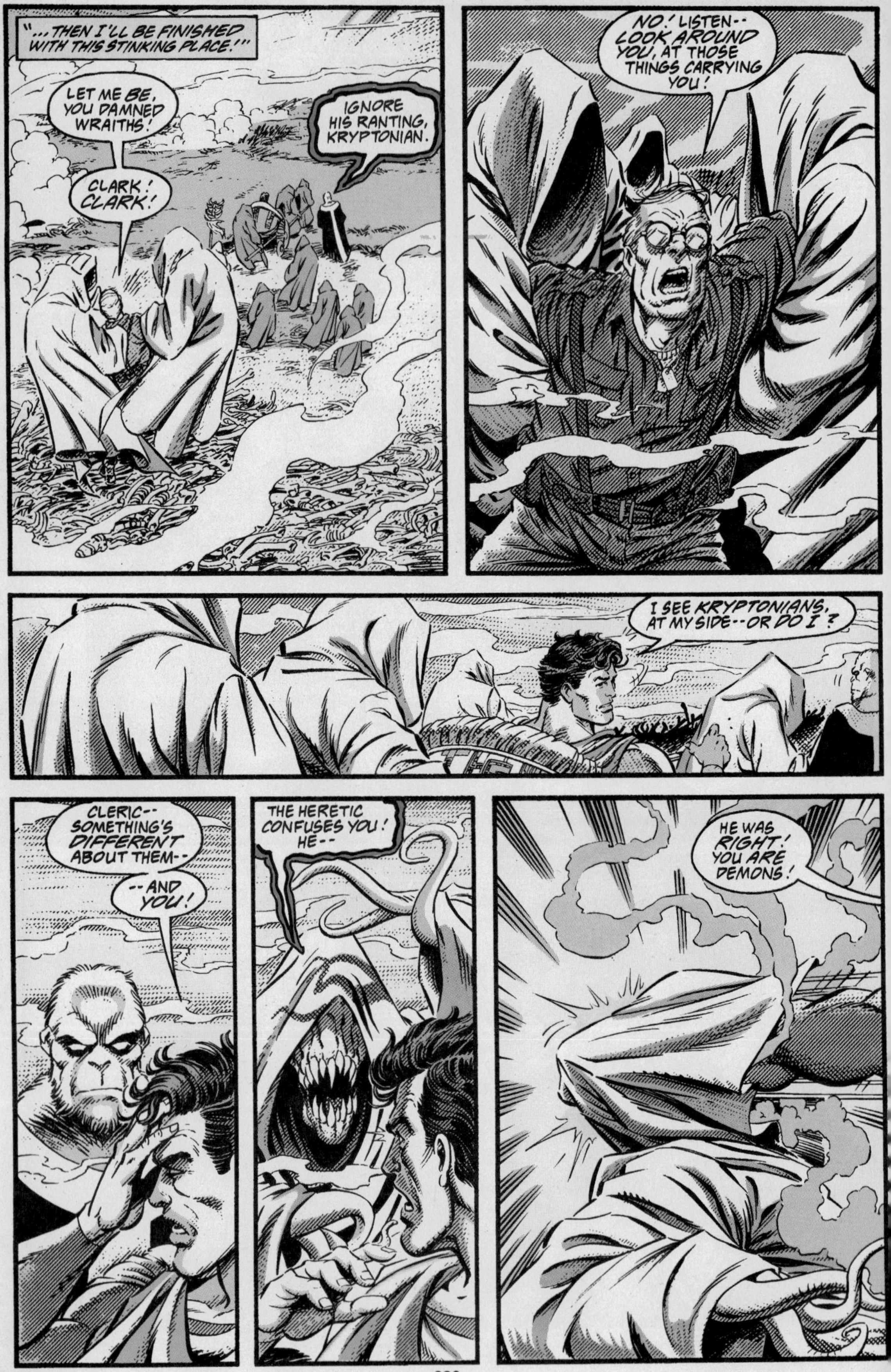
"...THEN I'LL BE FINISHED WITH THIS STINKING PLACE!"
LET ME BE, YOU DAMNED WRAITHS!
CLARK! CLARK!
IGNORE HIS RANTING, KRYPTONIAN.
NO! LISTEN-- LOOK AROUND YOU, AT THOSE THINGS CARRYING YOU!
I SEE KRYPTONIANS, AT MY SIDE--OR DO I?
CLERIC-- SOMETHING'S DIFFERENT ABOUT THEM--
--AND YOU!
THE HERETIC CONFUSES YOU! HE--
HE WAS RIGHT! YOU ARE DEMONS!

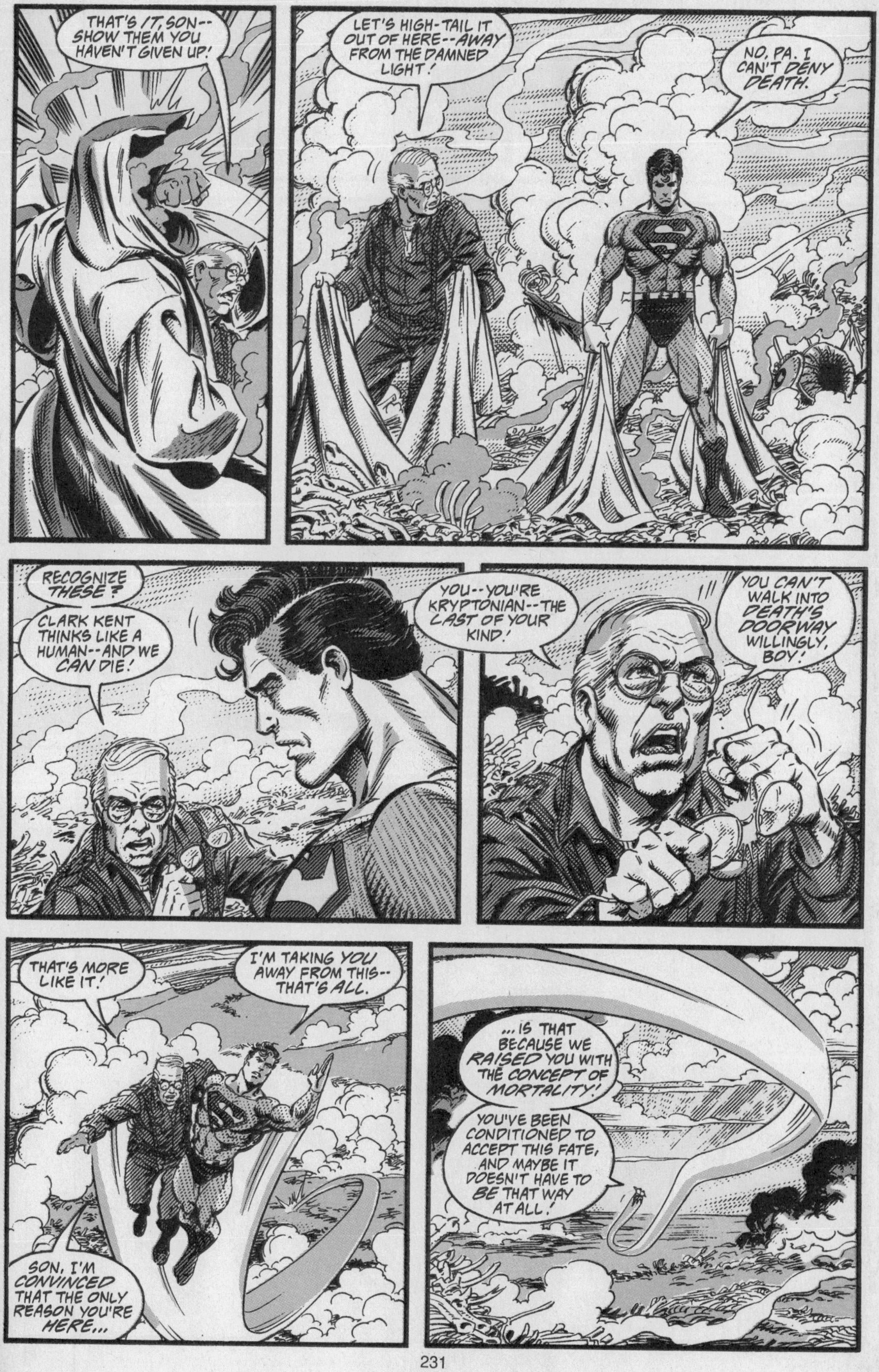

THAT'S IT, SON--SHOW THEM YOU HAVEN'T GIVEN UP!
LET'S HIGH-TAIL IT OUT OF HERE--AWAY FROM THE DAMNED LIGHT!
NO, PA. I CAN'T DENY DEATH.
RECOGNIZE THESE?
CLARK KENT THINKS LIKE A HUMAN--AND WE CAN DIE!
YOU--YOU'RE KRYPTONIAN--THE LAST OF YOUR KIND!
YOU CAN'T WALK INTO DEATH'S DOORWAY WILLINGLY, BOY!
THAT'S MORE LIKE IT!
I'M TAKING YOU AWAY FROM THIS--THAT'S ALL.
SON, I'M CONVINCED THAT THE ONLY REASON YOU'RE HERE...
...IS THAT BECAUSE WE RAISED YOU WITH THE CONCEPT OF MORTALITY!
YOU'VE BEEN CONDITIONED TO ACCEPT THIS FATE, AND MAYBE IT DOESN'T HAVE TO BE THAT WAY AT ALL!

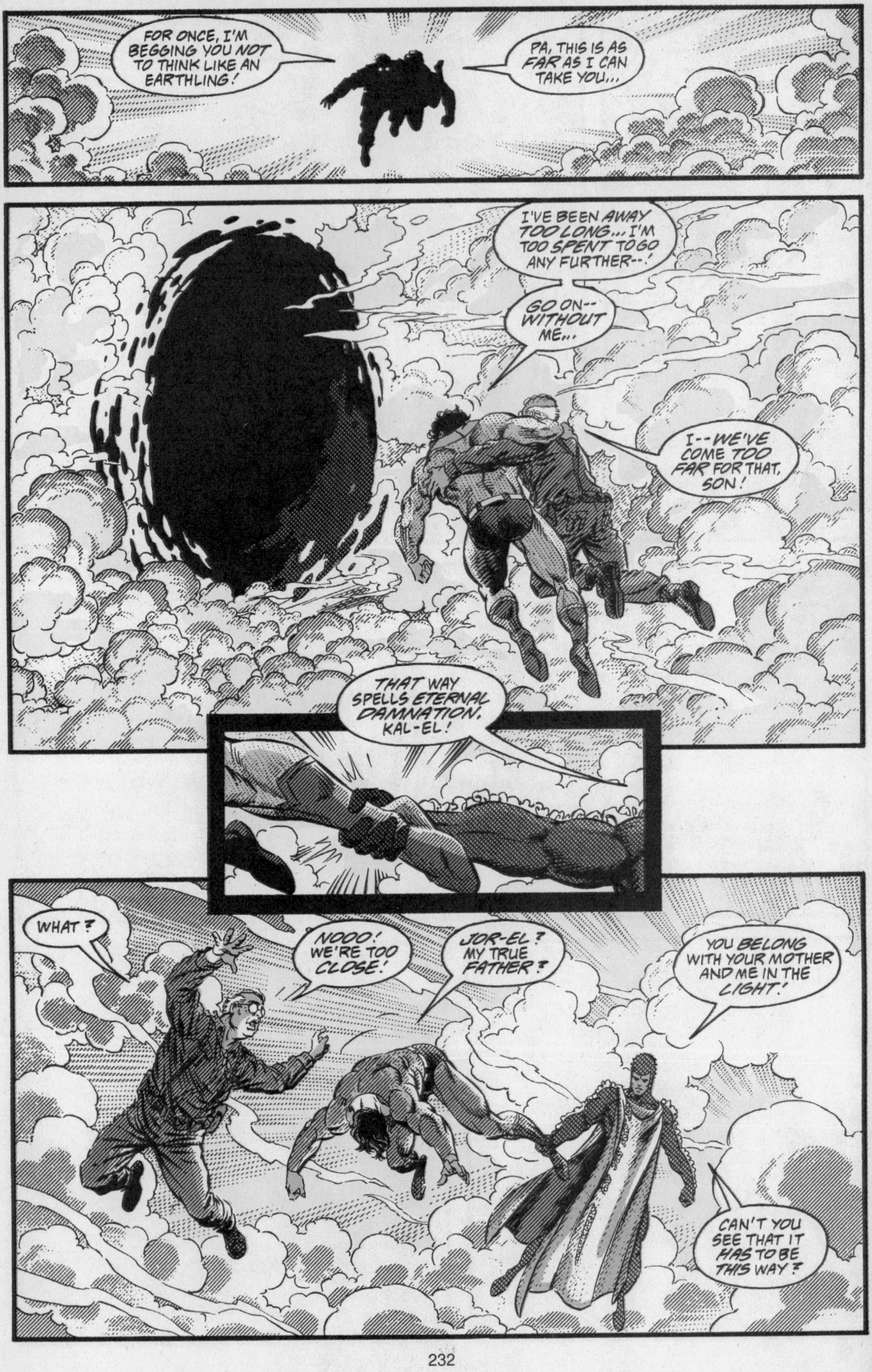
FOR ONCE, I'M BEGGING YOU NOT TO THINK LIKE AN EARTHLING!
PA, THIS IS AS FAR AS I CAN TAKE YOU...
I'VE BEEN AWAY TOO LONG... I'M TOO SPENT TO GO ANY FURTHER--!
GO ON-- WITHOUT ME...
I--WE'VE COME TOO FAR FOR THAT, SON!
THAT WAY SPELLS ETERNAL DAMNATION, KAL-EL!
WHAT?
NOOO! WE'RE TOO CLOSE!
JOR-EL? MY TRUE FATHER?
YOU BELONG WITH YOUR MOTHER AND ME IN THE LIGHT!
CAN'T YOU SEE THAT IT HAS TO BE THIS WAY?

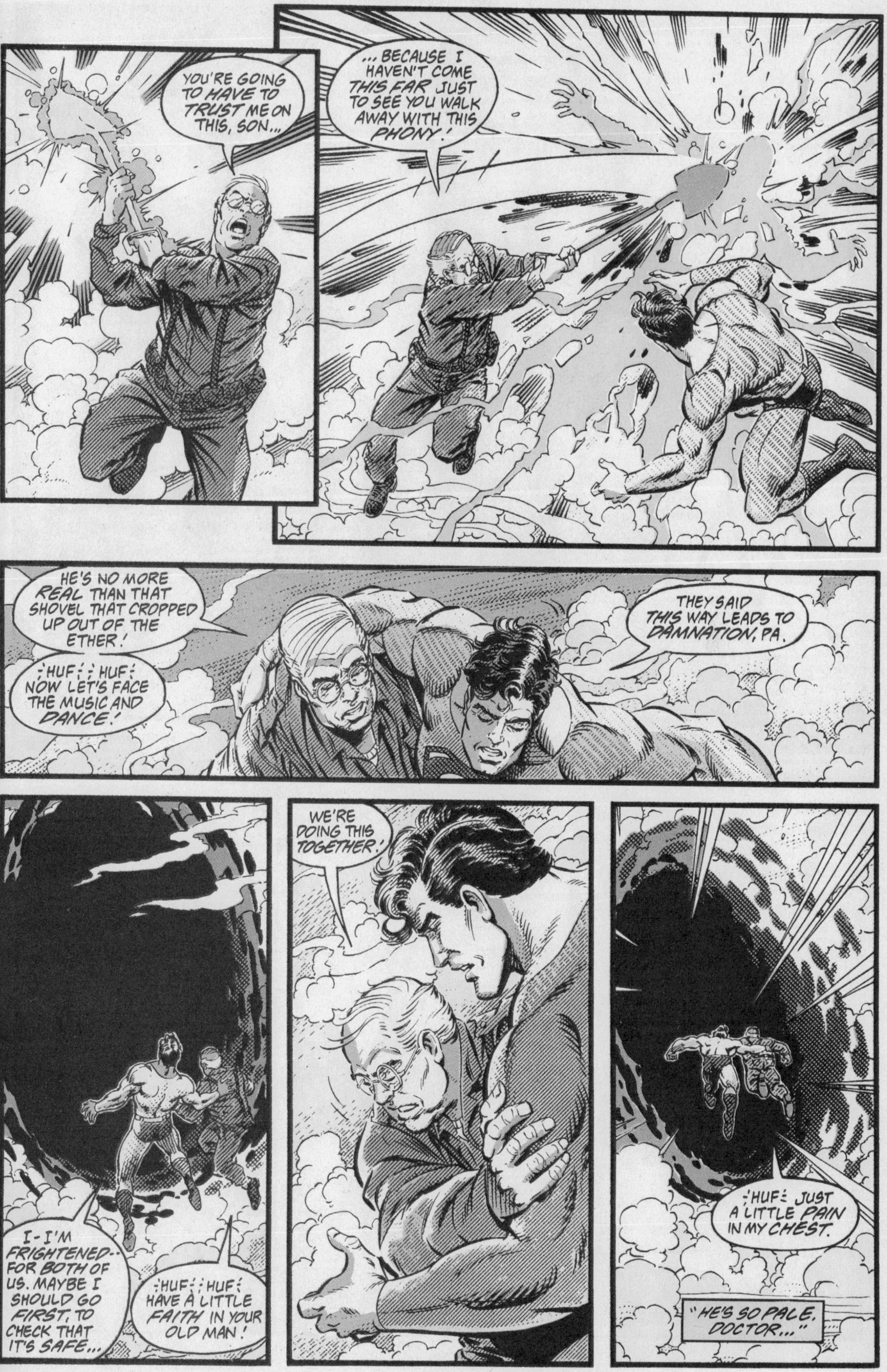
YOU'RE GOING TO HAVE TO TRUST ME ON THIS, SON...
...BECAUSE I HAVEN'T COME THIS FAR JUST TO SEE YOU WALK AWAY WITH THIS PHONY!
HE'S NO MORE REAL THAN THAT SHOVEL THAT CROPPED UP OUT OF THE ETHER!
HUF HUF NOW LET'S FACE THE MUSIC AND DANCE!
THEY SAID THIS WAY LEADS TO DAMNATION, PA.
I-I'M FRIGHTENED-- FOR BOTH OF US. MAYBE I SHOULD GO FIRST, TO CHECK THAT IT'S SAFE...
HUF HUF HAVE A LITTLE FAITH IN YOUR OLD MAN!
WE'RE DOING THIS TOGETHER!
HUF JUST A LITTLE PAIN IN MY CHEST.
"HE'S SO PALE, DOCTOR..."

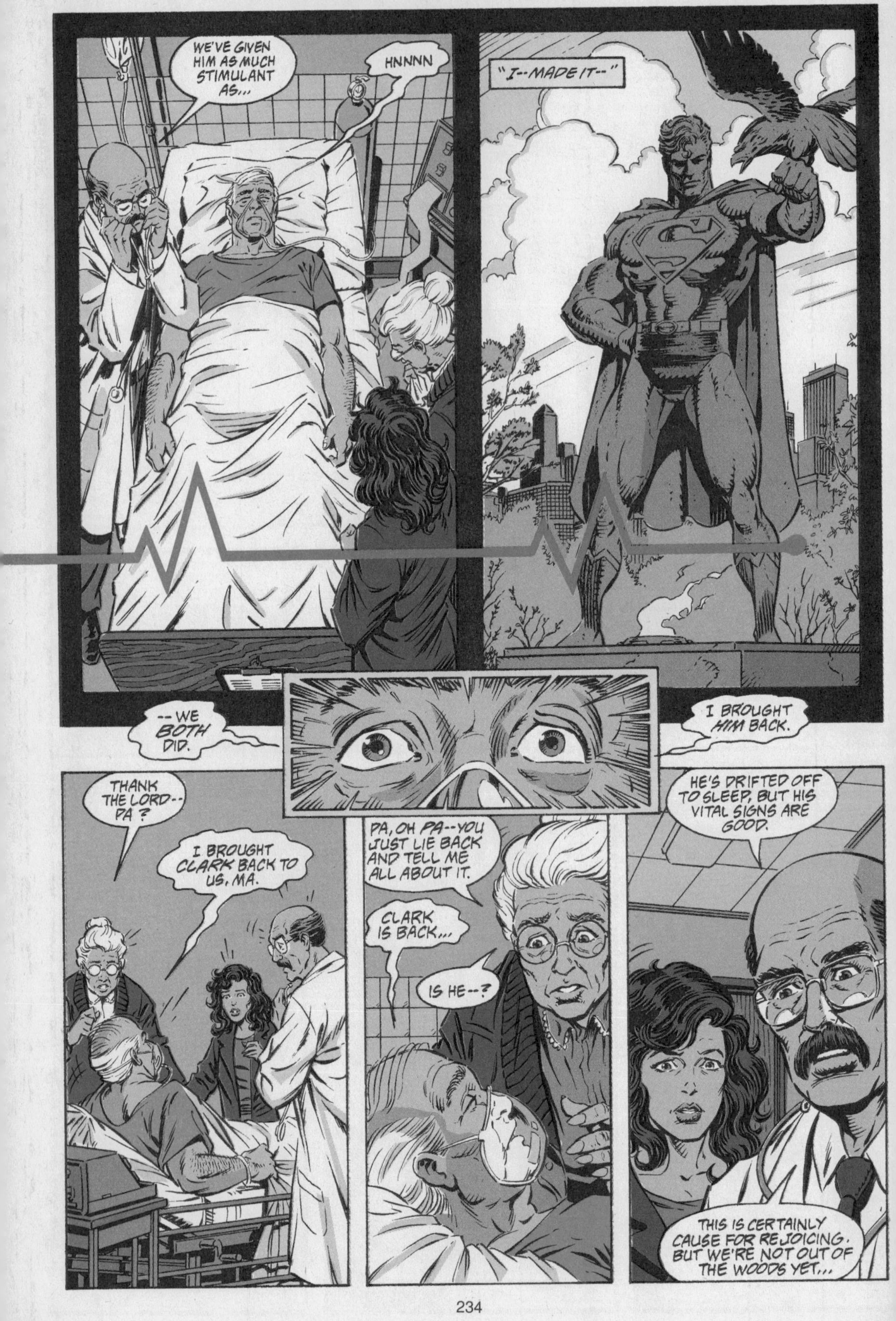
WE'VE GIVEN HIM AS MUCH STIMULANT AS...
HNNNN
"I--MADE IT--"
--WE BOTH DID.
I BROUGHT HIM BACK.
THANK THE LORD--PA?
I BROUGHT CLARK BACK TO US, MA.
PA, OH PA--YOU JUST LIE BACK AND TELL ME ALL ABOUT IT.
CLARK IS BACK...
IS HE--?
HE'S DRIFTED OFF TO SLEEP, BUT HIS VITAL SIGNS ARE GOOD.
THIS IS CERTAINLY CAUSE FOR REJOICING. BUT WE'RE NOT OUT OF THE WOODS YET...

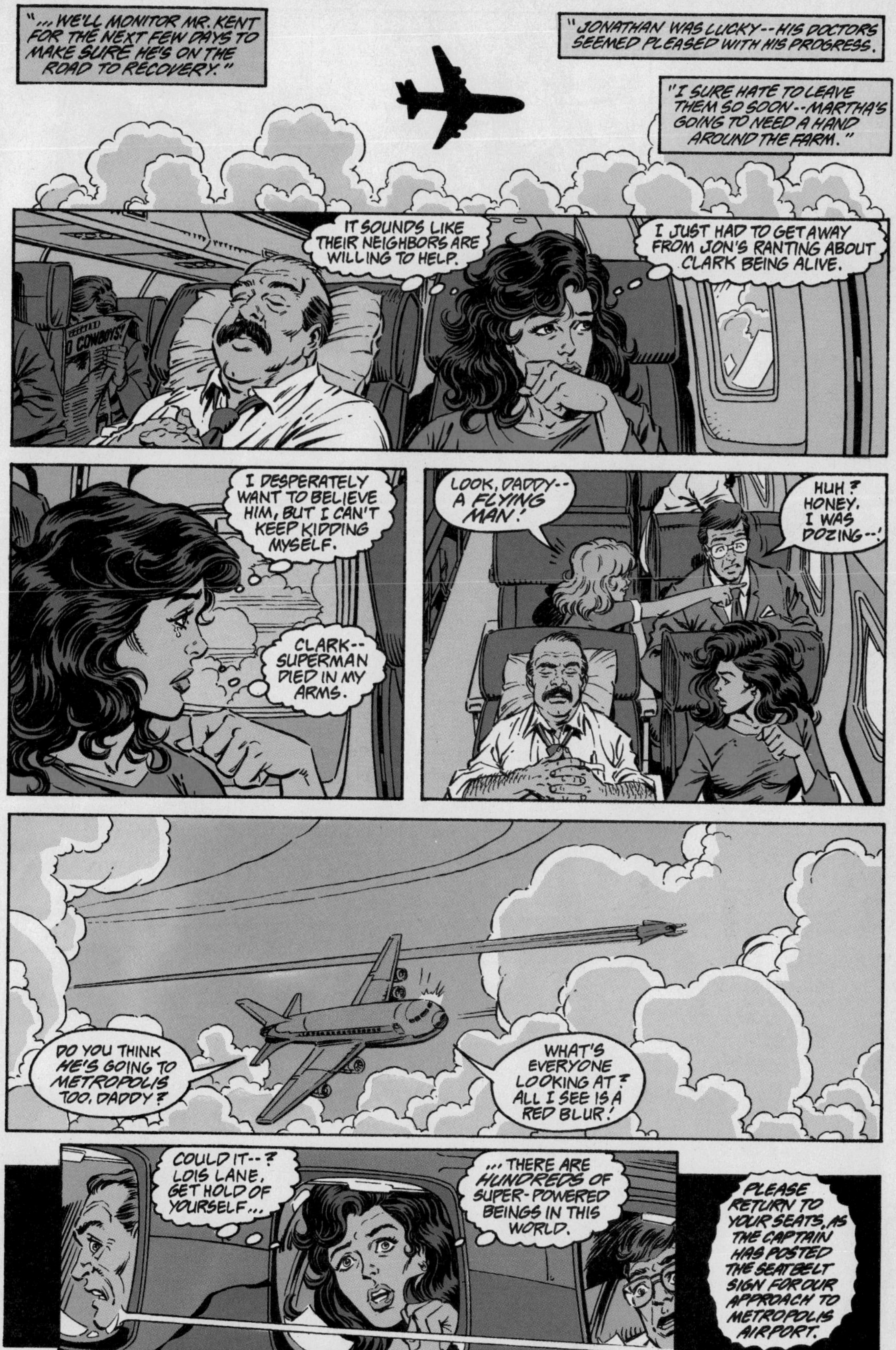
"...WE'LL MONITOR MR. KENT FOR THE NEXT FEW DAYS TO MAKE SURE HE'S ON THE ROAD TO RECOVERY."
"JONATHAN WAS LUCKY--HIS DOCTORS SEEMED PLEASED WITH HIS PROGRESS.
"I SURE HATE TO LEAVE THEM SO SOON--MARTHA'S GOING TO NEED A HAND AROUND THE FARM."
IT SOUNDS LIKE THEIR NEIGHBORS ARE WILLING TO HELP.
I JUST HAD TO GET AWAY FROM JON'S RANTING ABOUT CLARK BEING ALIVE.
I DESPERATELY WANT TO BELIEVE HIM, BUT I CAN'T KEEP KIDDING MYSELF.
CLARK--SUPERMAN DIED IN MY ARMS.
LOOK, DADDY--A FLYING MAN!
HUH? HONEY, I WAS DOZING--!
DO YOU THINK HE'S GOING TO METROPOLIS TOO, DADDY?
WHAT'S EVERYONE LOOKING AT? ALL I SEE IS A RED BLUR!
COULD IT--? LOIS LANE, GET HOLD OF YOURSELF...
...THERE ARE HUNDREDS OF SUPER-POWERED BEINGS IN THIS WORLD.
PLEASE RETURN TO YOUR SEATS, AS THE CAPTAIN HAS POSTED THE SEATBELT SIGN FOR OUR APPROACH TO METROPOLIS AIRPORT.

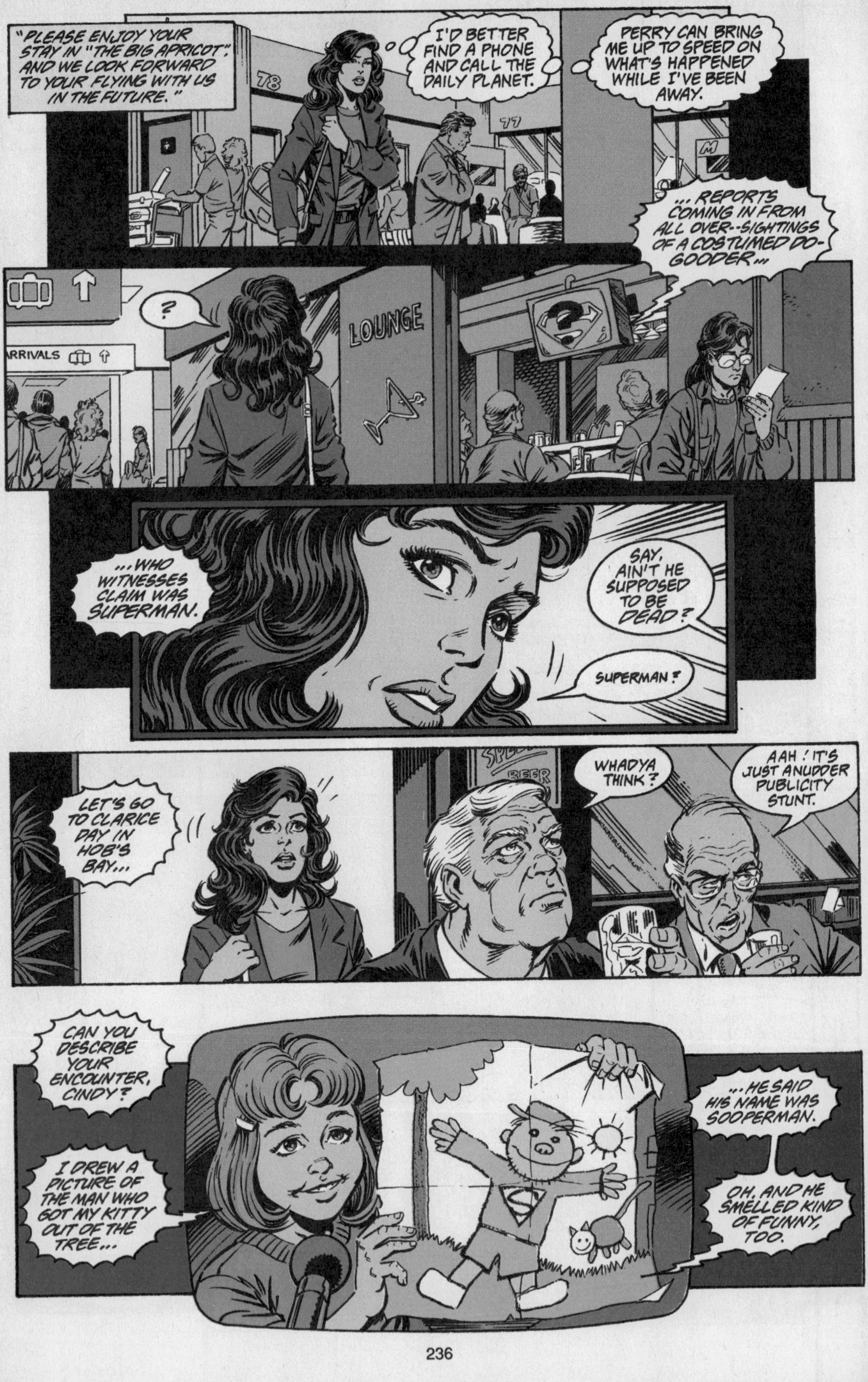
"PLEASE ENJOY YOUR STAY IN "THE BIG APRICOT". AND WE LOOK FORWARD TO YOUR FLYING WITH US IN THE FUTURE."
I'D BETTER FIND A PHONE AND CALL THE DAILY PLANET.
PERRY CAN BRING ME UP TO SPEED ON WHAT'S HAPPENED WHILE I'VE BEEN AWAY.
78
77
...REPORTS COMING IN FROM ALL OVER--SIGHTINGS OF A COSTUMED DO-GOODER...
?
ARRIVALS
LOUNGE
...WHO WITNESSES CLAIM WAS SUPERMAN.
SAY, AIN'T HE SUPPOSED TO BE DEAD?
SUPERMAN?
LET'S GO TO CLARICE DAY IN HOB'S BAY...
WHADYA THINK?
AAH! IT'S JUST ANUDDER PUBLICITY STUNT.
CAN YOU DESCRIBE YOUR ENCOUNTER, CINDY?
I DREW A PICTURE OF THE MAN WHO GOT MY KITTY OUT OF THE TREE...
...HE SAID HIS NAME WAS SOOPERMAN.
OH, AND HE SMELLED KIND OF FUNNY, TOO.

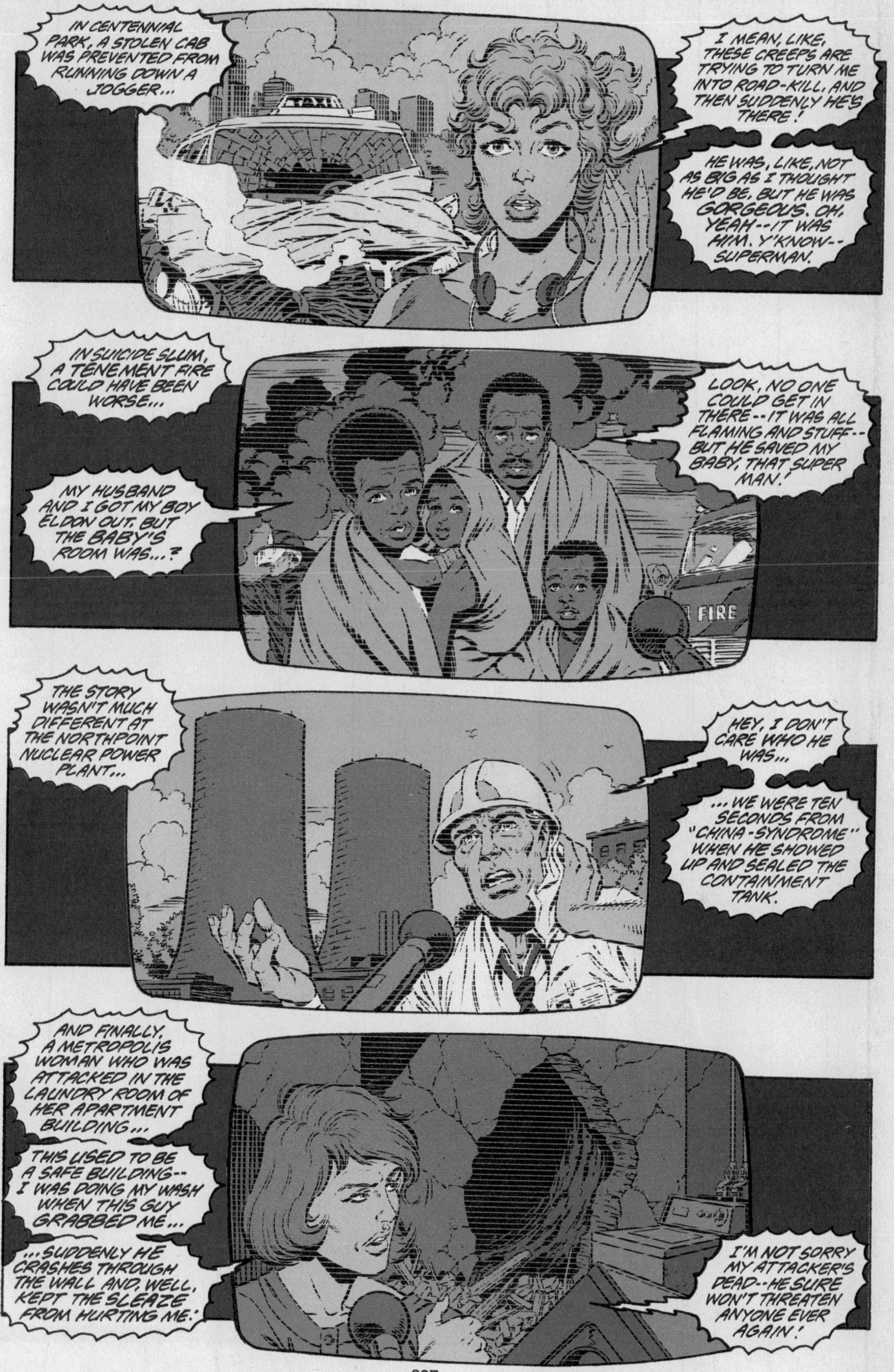
IN CENTENNIAL PARK, A STOLEN CAB WAS PREVENTED FROM RUNNING DOWN A JOGGER...
TAXI
I MEAN, LIKE, THESE CREEPS ARE TRYING TO TURN ME INTO ROAD-KILL, AND THEN SUDDENLY HE'S THERE!
HE WAS, LIKE, NOT AS BIG AS I THOUGHT HE'D BE. BUT HE WAS GORGEOUS. OH, YEAH--IT WAS HIM. Y'KNOW--SUPERMAN.
IN SUICIDE SLUM, A TENEMENT FIRE COULD HAVE BEEN WORSE...
MY HUSBAND AND I GOT MY BOY ELDON OUT. BUT THE BABY'S ROOM WAS...?
LOOK, NO ONE COULD GET IN THERE--IT WAS ALL FLAMING AND STUFF--BUT HE SAVED MY BABY, THAT SUPER MAN!
FIRE
THE STORY WASN'T MUCH DIFFERENT AT THE NORTHPOINT NUCLEAR POWER PLANT...
HEY, I DON'T CARE WHO HE WAS...
...WE WERE TEN SECONDS FROM "CHINA-SYNDROME" WHEN HE SHOWED UP AND SEALED THE CONTAINMENT TANK.
AND FINALLY, A METROPOLIS WOMAN WHO WAS ATTACKED IN THE LAUNDRY ROOM OF HER APARTMENT BUILDING...
THIS USED TO BE A SAFE BUILDING--I WAS DOING MY WASH WHEN THIS GUY GRABBED ME...
...SUDDENLY HE CRASHES THROUGH THE WALL AND, WELL, KEPT THE SLEAZE FROM HURTING ME!
I'M NOT SORRY MY ATTACKER'S DEAD--HE SURE WON'T THREATEN ANYONE EVER AGAIN!

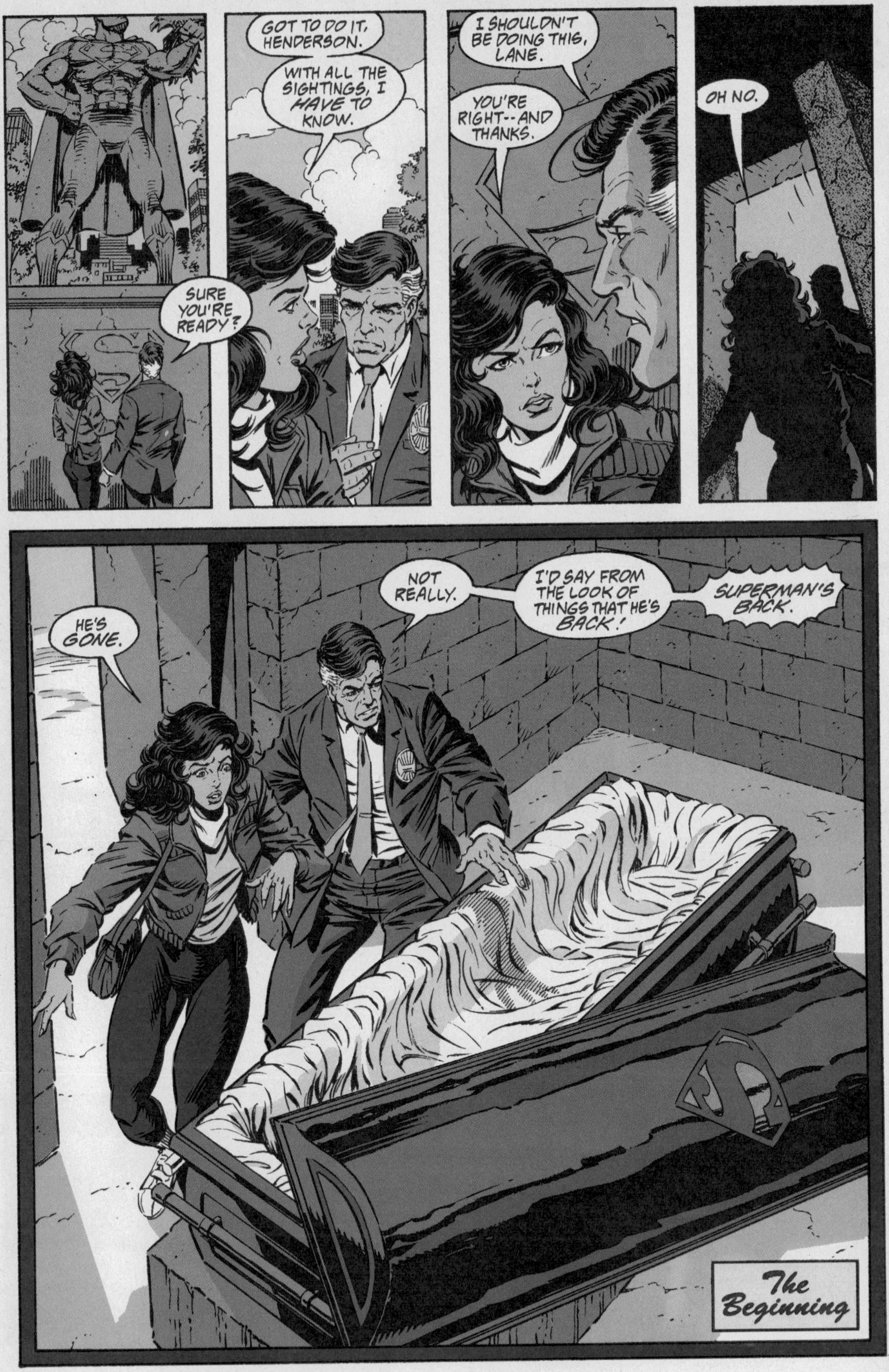
SURE YOU'RE READY?
GOT TO DO IT, HENDERSON.
WITH ALL THE SIGHTINGS, I HAVE TO KNOW.
I SHOULDN'T BE DOING THIS, LANE.
YOU'RE RIGHT--AND THANKS.
OH NO.
HE'S GONE.
NOT REALLY.
I'D SAY FROM THE LOOK OF THINGS THAT HE'S BACK!
SUPERMAN'S BACK.
The Beginning

"I had the idea,
Martha. The costume.
The secret identity.
I loved him. I thought
I was helping.
It's my fault, Martha.
I didn't know...
...I had such hopes."

JONATHAN KENT